Connect Communication

CONNECT to Personalized Learning

LearnSmart, McGraw-Hill's adaptive learning system, assesses students' knowledge of course content and maps out dynamic, personalized study plans that ground students in the fundamental concepts of communication. Available within **Connect Communication**, LearnSmart uses a series of adaptive questions to pinpoint the concepts students understand—and those they don't.

The result is a proven online tool that helps students learn faster, study more efficiently, and improve their performance. LearnSmart allows instructors to focus valuable class time on higher-level concepts, discussion, and student speeches.

Diagnostic questions adapt to individual students' needs, providing a personalized round-the-clock study program to help students succeed in the course.

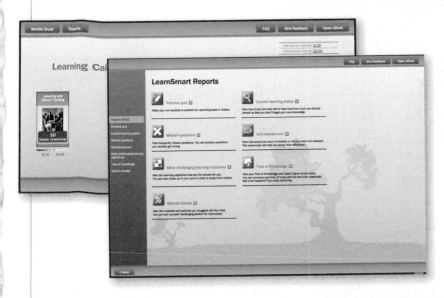

A personalized learning calendar shows each student her or his progress through the course. Reports help students take responsibility for their own learning.

CONNECT to Success

FIFTH EDITION

Human Communication

Judy C. Pearson
North Dakota State University

Paul E. Nelson
North Dakota State University

Scott Titsworth
Ohio University

Lynn Harter
Ohio University

McGraw Hill

Connect
Learn
Succeed™

HUMAN COMMUNICATION, FIFTH EDITION

Published by McGraw-Hill, a business unit of The McGraw-Hill Companies, Inc., 1221 Avenue of the Americas, New York, NY 10020. Copyright © 2013 by The McGraw-Hill Companies, Inc. All rights reserved. Printed in the United States of America. Previous editions © 2011, 2008, and 2006. No part of this publication may be reproduced or distributed in any form or by any means, or stored in a database or retrieval system, without the prior written consent of The McGraw-Hill Companies, Inc., including, but not limited to, in any network or other electronic storage or transmission, or broadcast for distance learning.

Some ancillaries, including electronic and print components, may not be available to customers outside the United States.

This book is printed on acid-free paper.

3 4 5 6 7 8 9 0 DOW/DOW 10 9 8 7 6 5 4

ISBN 978-0-07-803687-3
MHID 0-07-803687-9

Senior Vice President, Products & Markets: *Kurt L. Strand*
Vice President, General Manager, Products & Markets: *Michael Ryan*
Vice President, Content Production & Technology Services: *Kimberly Meriwether David*
Managing Director: *David Patterson*
Brand Manager: *Susan Gouijnstook*
Director of Development: *Rhona Robbin*
Senior Development Editor: *Kirstan Price*
Lead Digital Content Editor: *Scott Harris*
Marketing Manager: *Clare Cashen*

Content Project Manager: *Jodi Banowetz*
Senior Buyer: *Laura Fuller*
Designer: *Margarite Reynolds*
Interior Designer: *Amanda Kavanagh/Ark Design*
Cover Designer: *Irene Morris Design*
Cover Image: © *Adam Gregor / Fotolia*
Content Licensing Specialist: *Brenda Rolwes*
Photo Research: *Emily Tietz/Editorial Image, LLC*
Compositor: *Aptara®, Inc.*
Typeface: *10.5/12 Garamond Premier Pro*
Printer: *R. R. Donnelley*

All credits appearing on page or at the end of the book are considered to be an extension of the copyright page.

Library of Congress Cataloging-in-Publication Data

Human communication / Judy C. Pearson ... [et al.]. – 5th ed., [Rev. ed.]
    p. cm.
    Includes index.
    ISBN 978-0-07-803687-3 — ISBN 0-07-803687-9 (acid-free paper)
    1. Communication. I. Pearson, Judy C.
P90.H745 2013
302.2–dc23

2012020395

brief contents

contents

Chapter 3
Language and Meaning 46

Chapter 4
Nonverbal Communication 64

contents

Part 2   Communication Contexts

Chapter 7
Intercultural Communication 138

contents

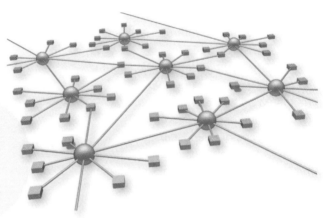

Part 3 Fundamentals of Public Speaking

Chapter 10
Topic Selection and Audience Analysis 212

contents

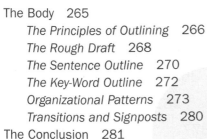

contents

preface

From the Authors

We've experienced a communication explosion in our lifetime, and people are linked to each other as they've never been before. We carry smartphones and are in constant contact with friends and relatives. Many of us tweet, IM, and blog; make and lose friends on Facebook; and Link-in with our colleagues. We may become anxious or irritable if we're unable to use some communication device even for a brief time.

But inside this communication explosion lie some persistent problems and challenges: couples break up, marital partners divorce, and friends come and go. Some people know how to express themselves, while others can only use their fists or a weapon. And all people in a democracy need to know how to communicate their ideas and evaluate the words and arguments of others. We've dedicated our professional lives to helping people become better communicators. *Human Communication* is our best effort to help students navigate in a digital world that in many ways has made communication faster but not necessarily better.

Our writing mantra, "Make It Smart, Keep It Real," reflects our goal of striking a practical balance between current scholarship and everyday application—to enlighten students about how communication works in personal relationships, interviews, work teams, and public speaking. As teachers, we know this is a time-challenged course, and we developed this focus to help instructors with their key course goals: to help students understand the foundations of communication as a discipline and to apply them outside the classroom.

For the fifth edition, we are excited to build on this focus through the integration of CONNECT into the *Human Communication* program. CONNECT makes managing assignments easier for instructors and learning and studying more motivating and efficient for students. CONNECT includes LearnSmart, a proven adaptive online learning program that guides students through personalized learning plans and frees up valuable class time for discussion and activities.

By sharing what we've learned from our years in the communication field and from working with thousands of students, we aim to make it smart and keep it real for them—to help prepare students to face all their communication challenges, now and in the future.

— *Judy Pearson*
— *Paul Nelson*
— *Scott Titsworth*
— *Lynn Harter*

preface

Make It Smart

Human Communication is built on a research-based approach to teaching introductory communication.

- **From the field of communication:** We reviewed communication journals and read hundreds of articles to ensure coverage of key findings from recent research.

- **From the experience of instructors:** We surveyed instructors teaching the basic course to identify the topics and skills that students find most challenging, and for the fifth edition, we crafted new and updated content and activities to target those challenges. See the inside front cover for more on the survey results.

- **From research into how students study and learn:** We integrated LearnSmart, McGraw-Hill's adaptive learning system, which helps students study more efficiently and effectively. LearnSmart intelligently pinpoints concepts students do not understand and maps out personalized study plans, improving student success and retention. It allows instructors to save valuable class time and customize classroom lectures and activities to meet their students' needs.

Keep It Real

Human Communication encourages students to think intelligently, actively, and critically about communication concepts and to apply them to everyday communication contexts.

- **Self-assessment and critical thinking:** Sizing Things Up self-assessment activities help students pinpoint their communication strengths and weaknesses, while critical thinking questions lead to a deeper and more systematic exploration of communication.

- **Real-world contexts and challenges:** New to the fifth edition, Social Media: Make It Matter boxes help raise awareness of how social media can impact communication, among the most challenging topics for students today to master; corresponding activities are located in Connect. Chapter-opening vignettes, new Keeping It Real sections, and Cultural Note boxes also examine everyday communication challenges.

social media make it matter

Listening on Facebook

Take a moment to scan your Facebook newsfeed. As you look through the status updates of your friends, how do you "listen to" those posts? Do certain things cause you to pay more attention? Social media challenge our listening habits in unique ways. Facebook newsfeeds and Twitter timelines do not easily filter important from unimportant messages—we often have more clutter to wade through. Learning to listen well to our friends in virtual spaces created by social media sites may require even greater attention than face-to-face conversations. If you wanted your friends to listen carefully to something you said on Twitter or Facebook, what would you do?

skill builder

Verbally Citing Sources

Making verbal citations is one of the most important skills you will learn in this course, and it will benefit you for years to come. Start by drafting possible ways to state your sources in written form. For each source you plan to use in your presentation, write down statements similar to those in table 11.5 that you could use when identifying your sources. You should not read aloud from these drafts during your presentation, but planning the wording ahead of time will help you state the information more effectively. When writing your drafts, take care to emphasize the credentials, expertise, and timeliness of the sources.

sizing things up

Individualism-Collectivism Scale

In this chapter you learned that people from different cultures, and even people from the same culture, can differ across several cultural dimensions. This scale helps you learn how you might compare with others on one such dimension—individualism and collectivism. Read each statement carefully and use the following scale to indicate how well the statement describes you. Place a 1 on the line in front of the number if the statement does not describe you, a 5 if the statement describes you well, or a 2–4 on the line if those items best describe you in that situation. A guide for interpreting your responses appears in the appendix at the end of the text (p. 348).

1 = Does not describe me at all
2 = Does not describe me very well
3 = Describes me somewhat
4 = Describes me well
5 = Describes me very well

1. I often "do my own thing."
2. The well-being of my co-workers is important to me.
3. One should live one's life independently.
4. If a co-worker got a prize, I would feel proud.
5. I like my privacy.
6. If a relative were in financial difficulty, I would help within my means.
7. I prefer to be direct and forthright when discussing with people.
8. It is important to maintain harmony with my group.
9. I am a unique individual.
10. I like sharing little things with my neighbors.
11. What happens to me is my own doing.
12. I feel good when I cooperate with others.
13. When I succeed, it is usually because of my abilities.
14. My happiness depends very much on the happiness of those around me.
15. I enjoy being unique and different from others in many ways.
16. To me, pleasure is spending time with others.

Source: Sengilis, T. M., Trandis, H. C., Bhawuk, P. S., & Geifand, M. J. (1995). Horizontal and vertical dimensions of individualism and collectivism: A theoretical and measurement refinement. *Cross-Cultural Research, 29*, 240–275. Reprinted by permission.

- **Communication skills:** Skill Builder activities appear throughout *Human Communication,* supported by a wealth of practical tips, sample speeches, and speech outlines.

preface

Connect Communication

Human Communication is available to instructors and students in print and eBook formats, as well as integrated within the Connect online assignment and assessment platform. Connect makes managing assignments easier for instructors—and makes learning and studying more motivating and efficient for students. The fully loaded Connect eBook allows students to review *Human Communication* anytime and anywhere. They can highlight, take notes, and quickly search for key terms and phrases.

Assignable and Assessable Activities
Instructors can deliver assignments and tests easily online, and students can practice skills related to key course challenges at their own pace and on their own schedule. Available activities include chapter quizzes, interactive and video activities, and situation analysis activities.

LearnSmart This adaptive diagnostic tool helps students take charge of their own learning. LearnSmart assists students in discovering what they do and don't know, while guiding them to experience and learn through exercises and readings. Interactive assessments measure and monitor students' knowledge levels, so the content is personalized to their needs. Individual study plans adapt based on each student's performance level in order to increase learning and retention. Dynamically generated reports document progress and areas for additional reinforcement.

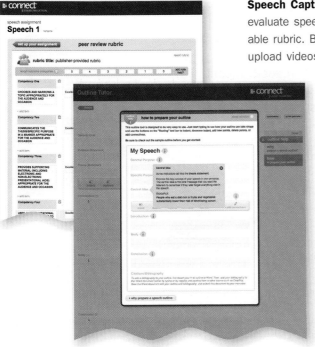

Speech Capture In Connect, instructors can evaluate speeches live, using a fully customizable rubric. Both instructors and students can upload videos for self-review or peer review.

Outline Tool With an enhanced user interface, this tool guides students systematically through the process of organizing and outlining their speeches. Instructors can customize part of the outline tool or turn it off if they don't want students to use it. This tool will help students improve their proficiency in one of the areas they find most challenging—outlining.

Topic Finder, EasyBib, and Survey Monkey
The Topic Finder helps students select a topic for speech assignments. Through Connect, students may also access EasyBib to automate the formatting of citations and bibliographies and Survey Monkey to create and manage audience-analysis questionnaires.

SpeechPrep App With SpeechPrep, students have a mobile tool they can use to build confidence in public speaking skills through practice and review. It is available through Google Play and the iTunes App Store.

preface

Chapter-by-Chapter Changes to the Fifth Edition: Highlights

New and updated material in the fifth edition reflects recent research findings and the results of the survey identifying the skills and topics students find most challenging.

Chapter 1: New sections on peer support, social media sites commonly used by students, and how communication skills can help in employment interviews

Chapter 2: Expanded coverage of first impressions, the impact of appearance, self-perception on Facebook, and symbolic interactionism in action

Chapter 3: Updated coverage of euphemisms, regionalisms, and the Ladder of Abstraction; new sections on paraphrasing and the impact of new media on language

Chapter 4: New sections on nonverbal communication in social media and the possible role of texting as "noise" in certain settings; updated coverage of the impact of physical attractiveness and the importance of nonverbal communication in medicine

Chapter 5: New coverage of multitasking, Toulmin's Layout of Argument as a tool for analyzing the statements of others, the ethical implications of "pretend listening," and how new technologies can impact effective listening; updated statistics and research on communication patterns and the importance of listening in professional life

Chapter 6: New and updated sections on developing relationships, social media sites relevant for interpersonal relationships, and guidelines for successful interpersonal communication

Chapter 7: New and updated sections on the value of silence, how to relate to the dominant culture, and cultural differences in nonverbal communication; new guidelines for "greeting, meeting, and eating" with people from different cultural backgrounds

Chapter 8: Enhanced discussion of group norms and roles, group culture, and group leadership; new and updated sections on Facebook groups, the prevalence of small groups in the workplace, and technologies that support group communication

Chapter 9: New and updated coverage of job trends, resources for leveraging previous knowledge and skills in new careers, fair hiring practices, the use of social networks to create and expand personal job-search networks, and the impact of aggressive communication in the workplace; enhanced coverage of e-résumés, professional portfolios, and strategies for addressing interview questions

Chapter 10: New section on researching the audience; enhanced discussions of direct and indirect inferences, adapting topics to specific audiences, and using the Internet for topic research

Chapter 11: Enhanced discussion of strategies for using Web searches and heuristics to find high-quality sources and for analyzing and establishing source credibility; new section on whether Wikipedia should be used as a source in a presentation

Chapter 12: Enhanced discussion of strategies for gaining and maintaining audience attention and for creating an introduction that fulfills the five functions; new examples in the sections on outlines, reference lists, and introductions and conclusions

Chapter 13: Updated sections on extemporaneous delivery, vocal aspects of delivery, eye contact, and the advantages and disadvantages of different types of visual aids; new coverage of using social media to obtain peer feedback, creating effective presentation slides (PowerPoint, Keynote, Prezi), and avoiding common mistakes in delivering business presentations

Chapter 14: New suggested speech topics and sample student speeches

Chapter 15: New and updated sections on revealing purpose, choosing and evaluating evidence, persuading through visualization, and using persuasion in everyday life; new student examples

Appendix: New appendix includes guides for scoring and interpreting the results of Sizing Things Up activities.

preface

Teaching and Learning with *Human Communication*

Online Learning Center
(www.mhhe.com/pearson5e)

The Online Learning Center for *Human Communication* includes comprehensive teaching resources:

- Instructor's Manual, with teaching strategies, activities, and resources
- Test Bank
- PowerPoint presentations

McGraw-Hill Create
(www.mcgrawhillcreate.com)

Design your own ideal course materials with McGraw-Hill's Create™. Rearrange or omit chapters, combine material from other sources, and upload your syllabus or any other content you have written to make the perfect resource for your students. Search thousands of leading McGraw-Hill textbooks to find the best content for your students; then arrange it to fit your teaching style. You can even personalize your book's appearance by selecting the cover and adding your name, school, and course information. When you order a Create book, you receive a complimentary review copy. Get a printed copy in three to five business days or an electronic copy (e-Comp) via e-mail in about an hour. Register today at www.mcgrawhillcreate.com, and craft your course resources to match the way you teach.

CourseSmart
(www.coursesmart.com)

CourseSmart offers thousands of the most commonly adopted textbooks across hundreds of courses from a wide variety of higher education publishers. It is the only place for faculty to review and compare the full text of a book online, providing immediate access without the environmental impact of requesting a printed exam copy. At CourseSmart, students can save up to 50 percent off the cost of a printed book, reduce their impact on the environment, and gain access to powerful Web tools for learning, including full text search, notes and highlighting, and e-mail tools for sharing notes among classmates. Visit coursesmart.com to learn more or to purchase registration codes for this exciting product.

Tegrity Campus
(http://tegritycampus.mhhe.com)

Tegrity is a service that makes class time available around the clock. It automatically captures every lecture in a searchable format for students to review when they study and complete assignments. With a simple one-click start-and-stop process, you capture all computer screens and corresponding audio. Students replay any part of any class with easy-to-use browser-based viewing on a PC or Mac. With Tegrity Campus, students quickly recall key moments by using Tegrity Campus's unique search feature, which lets them efficiently find what they need, when they need it, across an entire semester of class recordings. Help turn all your students' study time into learning moments immediately supported by your lecture. To learn more about Tegrity, watch a two-minute Flash demo at http://tegritycampus.mhhe.com.

McGraw-Hill Campus™

McGraw-Hill Campus is a new one-stop teaching and learning experience available to users of any learning management system. This institutional service allows faculty and students to enjoy single sign-on (SSO) access to all McGraw-Hill Higher Education materials, including the award-winning McGraw-Hill Connect® platform, from directly within the institution's website. McGraw-Hill Campus provides faculty with instant access to all McGraw-Hill Higher Education teaching materials (e.g., eTextbooks, test banks, PowerPoint slides, animations, and learning objects), allowing them to browse, search, and use any instructor ancillary content in our vast library at no additional cost to instructors or students. Students enjoy SSO access to a variety of free (e.g., quizzes, flash cards, narrated presentations) and subscription-based (e.g., McGraw-Hill Connect) products. With this program enabled, faculty and students will never need to create another account to access McGraw-Hill products and services.

acknowledgments

The authors are grateful to colleagues across the country who reviewed the book, contributed to the digital tools, recommended improvements, and shared information about their courses. Because of their detailed and insightful comments, a much better fifth edition emerged for the benefit of our adopters and their students. A warm thank you to each of you!

Text Reviewers

Gwen Dooley
Jackson State University
Amber Finn
Texas Christian University
Chris Goble
Monmouth College
Angela Johansson
Kishwaukee College
Katherine Lehman-Meyer
St. Mary's University
Amy Lenoce
Naugatuck Valley Community College
Yvette Lujan
Miami Dade College, InterAmerican Campus
Daniel McRoberts
Northcentral Technical College
Greg Ormson
Northcentral Technical College
Thomas Ruddick
Edison Community College
Shari Santoriello
Suffolk County Community College, Eastern
Patricia Smith
Northcentral Technical College
Susan Smith
Broward College, South Campus
Adam Vellone
Miami Dade College, Homestead Campus

Connect and LearnSmart Contributors

Jocelyn DeGroot Brown
Southern Illinois University, Edwardsville
Leah Bryant
DePaul University
Brady Carey
Mt. Hood Community College

Tim Chandler
Hardin-Simmons University
Denise Sperruzza
St. Louis Community College
Charlene Widener
Hutchinson Community College

Feature and Connect Plan Reviewers

Lawrence Albert
Morehead State University
Theresa Albury
Miami Dade College, Wolfson Campus
Brady Carey
Mt. Hood Community College
Nader Chaaban
Montgomery College, Rockville
Diane Egdorf
Des Moines Area Community College
Philip Lane
Miami Dade College, Wolfson Campus
Kara Laskowski
Shippensburg University of Pennsylvania
Linda Long
North Lake College
Xin-An Lu
Shippensburg University of Pennsylvania
Kay Mueller
Des Moines Area Community College
Renee Strom
St. Cloud State University
Anestine Theophile-LaFond
Montgomery College, Rockville

Survey Participants

Rebekah Pointer Adderley
Tarrant County College
Dr. Amy M. Atchley
Baton Rouge Community College

Joseph Bailey
Hardin-Simmons University
Erin Begnaud
South Louisiana Community College
Tonya D. Bell
Labette Community College
Christy Burns
Jacksonville State University
Brady Carey
Mt. Hood Community College
Tim Chandler
Hardin-Simmons University
Gena Christopher
Jacksonville State University
Kevin Ells
Louisiana State University, Alexandria
Diana Elrod-Sarnecki
Des Moines Area Community College
Jill Evans
Kettering College
John B. French
Cape Cod Community College
Chris Goble
Monmouth College
Mike Harsh
Hagerstown Community College
Daniel Hildenbrandt
Owensboro Community and Technical College
Sandy Humphries
South Louisiana Community College
Nancy A. Hutchinson
Lipscomb University
Khalil Islam-Zwart
Eastern Washington University
Tonya Blivens Kariuki
Tarrant County College
Carolyn Kershaw
Charter Oak State College
Erica Lamm
Northern Virginia Community College
Philip Lane
Miami Dade College, Wolfson Campus
Amy K. Lenoce
Naugatuck Valley Community College

Darren L. Linvill
Clemson University
Matthew Malloy
Caldwell Community College and Technical Institute
Jennifer Millspaugh
Richland College
Robert Mott
York College of Pennsylvania
Lois B. Nemetz
Louisiana State University, Eunice
Steve "Butch" Owens
Navarro College
Trudi Peterson
Monmouth College
Paul E. Potter
Hardin-Simmons University
Danna Prather
Suffolk County Community College
Rebecca Putt
Charter Oak State College
Gary D. Reeves
Baton Rouge Community College
Maryanna Richardson
Forsyth Technical Community College
Rosemary Robertson-Smith
Louisiana State University, Eunice
Shari Santoriello
Suffolk County Community College, Eastern
Jesse Schroeder
Northwestern Oklahoma State University
Don Simmons
Asbury University
Patricia Spence
Richland College
Kari Stouffer
University of Texas, Dallas
Charlene Strickland
Hardin-Simmons University
Karol L. Walchak
Alpena Community College

introduction to
human communication

When you have read and thought about this chapter, you will be able to:

1. State reasons why the study of communication is essential.

2. Define communication.

3. Name the components of communication.

4. Explain some principles of communication.

5. Explain how the contexts of communication differ from each other.

6. Define communication competence, ethics, and the social scientific method.

In this chapter you will learn about the importance of communication in your everyday life. You will find that communication is the foundation on which you build your personal, social, and professional life. You will also learn about communication on a deeper level, including the terms, processes, and contexts of communication.

Communication allows you to improve your life in many ways. Reyna Reynolds, unlike many of her high school friends, has enrolled in a technical school. She has been criticized by others who say that she could not get into a traditional school, that anyone can get into a school focused on careers, and that she will never get a job when she has completed her degree. However, Reyna has an older brother who received a traditional college education and is now unemployed. His degree is in business with a minor in finance. He told her that he talked with well over 20 possible employers, including those in retail and investment banking. He was even willing to sell hedge funds.

Reyna has a passion for technology. She loves working with computers, software, and hardware. She is eager to learn about every new development, regardless of the platform. Because she worked long hours during high school, she had more spendable income than her peers. As a result, she was the first one among her friends to try the latest cell phones, and she had a Twitter account before others knew what "tweet" meant.

Reyna knows that she will need to work while attending school, but she is living in a new town and does not have former employers or old friends to help her find a job. She does have a plan, though, and it includes taking two communication courses. She is enrolling in human communication this semester, and she is going to take business communication next semester. She had a friend in high school who told her how important communication courses are for getting and keeping a job.

Reyna really wants to work as a work-study student on campus in the computer lab. She thinks she might be able to get another part-time job in a local software firm, performing basic tasks. What would you recommend to help Reyna get the job? How can she compete with others who want these jobs? How should she dress for the interviews; what should she prepare? How can she learn about the work settings in the two different places? Should she show that she knows the jargon associated with technology? What will be most persuasive to a potential employer?

Reyna is enrolled in this class to learn the answers to many of these questions. She believes that communication skills may make the difference between being employed and being unemployed. On page 23, we'll take another look at Reyna's situation.

How would you rate your own communication skills? What are your strengths and weaknesses as a communicator? This chapter will help you recognize the importance of communication in your life.

The Study of Communication Is Essential

Studying communication is essential for you. Communication is central to your life. Effective communication can help you solve problems in your professional life and improve relationships in your personal life.[1] Communication experts believe that poor communication is at the root of many problems and that effective communication is one solution to these problems.

Communication has consequences. Understanding the theory, research, and application of communication will make a significant difference in your life and in the lives of people around the world.[2] The world changed on September 11, 2001, and people became

■ Effective communication can strengthen interpersonal relationships.

far more aware of the importance of communication principles—particularly, intercultural communication principles. Communication principles and practices can resolve disputes among nations, as well as among friends and family. Effective communication may not solve all the world's problems, but better communication practices can help us solve or avoid many problems.

Communication is everywhere. You cannot avoid communication, and you will engage in communication nearly every minute of every day of your life. Communication plays a major role in nearly every aspect of your life.

Regardless of your interests and goals, the ability to communicate effectively will enhance and enrich your life. But learning *how* to communicate is just as important as learning *about* communication. Studying communication comprehensively offers at least seven advantages:

1. *Studying communication can improve the way you see yourself.* Communication is "vital to the development of the whole person."[3] As we will see in chapter 2, most of our self-knowledge comes from the communicative experience. As we engage in thought (*intra*personal communication) and in interactions with significant other people (*inter*personal communication), we learn about ourselves. People who are naive about the communication process and the development of self-awareness, self-concept, and self-efficacy may not see themselves accurately or may be unaware of their own self-development. Knowing how communication affects self-perception can lead to greater awareness and appreciation of the self.

Learning communication skills can improve the way you see yourself in a second way. As you learn how to communicate effectively in a variety of situations—from interpersonal relationships to public speeches—your self-confidence will increase. In a study based on the responses from 344 students at a large public university, students who completed a communication course perceived their communication competence to be greater in the classroom, at work, and in social settings. Most dramatic were their perceived improvements in feeling confident about themselves, feeling comfortable with others' perceptions of them, reasoning with people, and using language appropriately.[4] In short, your success in interacting with other people in social situations and your achievements in professional settings will lead to more positive feelings about yourself.

2. *Studying communication can improve the way others see you.* In chapter 2 we will discuss self-presentation, identity management, and locus of control. You will learn that you can control your own behavior to a considerable extent, which will lead to positive outcomes with others. You will find that your interactions can be smoother and that you can achieve your goals more easily as you manage the impression you make on others.

You can improve the way others see you a second way. Generally, people like communicating with others who can communicate well. Compare your interactions with someone who stumbles over words, falls silent, interrupts, and uses inappropriate language to express thoughts to your interactions with someone who has a good vocabulary, listens when you speak, reveals appropriate personal information, and smoothly exchanges talk turns with you. Which person do you prefer? Most of us prefer competent communicators. As you become increasingly competent, you will find that others seek you out for conversations, assistance, and advice.

3. *Studying communication can increase what you know about human relationships.* The field of communication includes learning about how people relate to each other and about what type of communication is appropriate for a given situation. Most people value human relationships and find great comfort in friendships, family relationships, and community relationships. Within these relationships we learn about trust, intimacy, and reciprocity.

Human relationships are vital to each of us. Human babies thrive when they are touched and when they hear sounds; similarly, adults who engage in human relationships appear to be more successful and satisfied than do those who are isolated. Human relationships serve a variety of functions. They provide us with affection (receiving and providing warmth and friendliness), inclusion (experiencing feelings that we belong and providing others with messages that they belong), pleasure (sharing happiness and fun), escape (providing diversion), and control (managing our lives and influencing others).[5]

We learn about the complexity of human relationships as we study communication. We learn, first, that other people in relationships are vastly different from each other. We learn that they may be receptive or dismissive toward us. We learn that they may behave as if they were superior or inferior to us. We learn that they might be approachable or highly formal. People are clearly not interchangeable with each other.

We also learn that our interactions with others may be helpful or harmful. Communicators can share personal information that builds trust and rapport. The same personal information can be used outside the relationship to humiliate or shame the other person. Whereas some relationships enhance social support, others are riddled with deception and conflict. Interactions are not neutral.

We learn that people coconstruct the reality of the relationship. Families, for example, love to tell stories of experiences they have had when on vacation, when moving across the country, or when some particularly positive or negative event occurred. Indeed, they often take turns "telling the story." Couples, too, create and tell stories of their lives. Couples' stories may be positive as the couple emphasizes their feelings of belongingness and their identity as a couple. On the other end of the spectrum, stories may be highly negative as people deceive others with information that allows them to cover up criminal acts, such as drug use, child abuse, or murder.

Human relationships are complex. As you study communication, you will clarify the variables involved in relationships—the people, the verbal and nonverbal cues provided, the effect of time, the nature of the relationship, and the goals of the participants. You will be far better equipped to engage in relationships with an understanding of the communication process.

People who have communication skills also experience greater relational satisfaction.[6] If you receive training in communication skills, you are more likely to report greater relationship satisfaction than are those who do not receive such training.[7] The link between communication skills and life satisfaction is strong. The connection holds true in health contexts,[8] including situations in which family members are experiencing life-threatening illnesses.[9]

4. *Studying communication can teach you important life skills.* Studying communication involves learning important skills that everyone will use at some point in his or her life, such as critical thinking, problem solving, decision making, conflict resolution, team building, media literacy, and public speaking. Allen, Berkowitz, Hunt, and Louden analyzed dozens of studies and concluded that "communication instruction improves the critical thinking ability of the participants."[10] Our visual literacy is improved as we understand the technical and artistic aspects of the visual communication medium.[11]

■ Studying communication improves critical thinking skills and can help people achieve success in college and on the job.

Studying communication early in your college career can enhance your success throughout college. Consider the centrality of oral communication to all of your college classes. You regularly are called on to answer questions in class, to provide reports, to offer explanations, and to make presentations. In addition, both your oral and written work depend on your ability to think critically and creatively, to solve problems, and to make decisions. Most likely, you will be engaged in group projects in which skills such as team building and conflict resolution will be central. The same skills will be essential throughout your life.

5. *Studying communication can help you exercise your constitutionally guaranteed freedom of speech.* Few nations have a bill of rights that invites people to convey their opinions and ideas, yet freedom of speech is essential to a democratic form of government. Being a practicing citizen in a democratic society means knowing about current issues and being able to speak about them in conversations, in speeches, and through the mass media; it also involves being able to critically examine messages from others.

Our understanding of communication shapes our political lives. Mass communication and communication technology have sharply altered the political process. Today many more people have the opportunity to receive information than ever before. Through the mass media, people in remote locations are as well informed as those in large urban centers. The public agenda is largely set through the media. Pressing problems are given immediate attention. Blumer notes, "At a time when so many forces—volatility, apathy, skepticism, a sense of powerlessness, and intensified group hostility—appear to be undermining political stability, media organizations have become pivotal to the conduct of human affairs."[12]

Whereas some people may feel more enfranchised by the common denominator of the media, others feel more alienated as they become increasingly passive in the process. Face-to-face town meetings were the focus of democratic decision making in times past, but today people receive answers to questions, solutions to problems, and decisions about important matters from the media. Many feel powerless and anonymous.

In the wake of the terrorist attacks of September 11, 2001, U.S. citizens began to rediscover and recognize the value of a democratic form of government. At the same time, they recognized how vulnerable they were to people who did not endorse basic democratic principles. They also learned that terrorist dictators could use the media as easily as could those who came from more reasonable and more democratic ideologies.

The study and understanding of communication processes is profoundly political. Hart opines that "those who teach public address and media studies teach that social power can be shifted and public visions exalted if people learn to think well and speak well."[13] Paraphrasing the ancient Greek rhetorician Isocrates, Hart notes, "To become eloquent is to activate one's humanity, to apply the imagination, and to solve the practical problems of human living."[14] Freedom goes to the articulate.

You have the opportunity to be a fully functioning member of a democratic society. You also have the challenge of understanding the media and other information technologies. Studying communication will help you learn how to speak effectively, analyze arguments, synthesize large quantities of information, and critically consume information from a variety of sources. The future of our society depends on such mastery.

6. *Studying communication can help you succeed professionally.* A look at the job postings in any newspaper will give you an immediate understanding of the importance of improving your knowledge and practice of communication. The employment section of a newspaper or Internet posting has entries like these:

    ■ "We need a results-oriented, seasoned professional who is a good communicator and innovator" reads one posting for a marketing manager.

    ■ Another posting, this one for a marketing analyst, reads "You should be creative, inquisitive, and a good communicator both in writing and orally."

    ■ A posting for a training specialist calls for "excellent presentation, verbal, and written communication skills, with ability to interact with all levels within organization."

As a person educated in communication, you will be able to gain a more desirable job.[15] You may believe that some professions are enhanced by communication skills but that many are not. Professionals in fields such as accounting, auditing, banking, counseling, engineering, industrial hygiene, information science, public relations, and sales have all written about the importance of oral communication skills.[16] More recently, professionals in the computer industry,[17] genetics and science,[18] farming and ranching,[19] education,[20] and the health field[21] have stressed the importance of communication skills to potential employees. The variety of these careers suggests that communication skills are important across the board.

Communication skills are crucial in your first contact with a prospective employer. By studying communication, you can enhance your interviewing skills. Further, human resource interviewers note that oral communication skills, in general, significantly affect hiring decisions.[22] One survey showed that human resource managers identified effective speaking and listening as the most important factors in hiring people.[23]

Employers view your written and oral communication competencies and your ability to listen and analyze messages as essential job

sizing things up

Learn More About Yourself as a Communicator

Throughout the book you will learn about a variety of communication skills, theories, and concepts. When scholars do research on these topics, they must find a way to assess or measure specific things, which they typically call *variables*. For instance, researchers might use a survey to measure how effective people are at communicating in personal relationships. The "Sizing Things Up" feature allows you to learn about your own communication skills and attitudes using similar tools. After completing surveys in each chapter, you can compare your results with those of other students, or simply use your results as a starting point for understanding your own potential strengths. The surveys are useful only as very rough guesses about some of your tendencies. You should not interpret your personal results as definitive or stable over time.

skills.[24] Similarly, college graduates perceive communication coursework as essential.[25] In short, communication competence is important.

Communication skills are important not only at the beginning of your career but throughout the work life span. Dauphinais observes that communication skills can increase upward mobility in one's career.[26] Business executives note the importance of communication competence.[27] Finally, communication skills are among the top priorities for entrepreneurs.

What communication skills are employers seeking? Clearly, listening skills are one of the most important components of communication,[28] and you will learn about listening in chapter 5. Speaking clearly, succinctly, and persuasively is crucial to many jobs, including those in sales,[29] and we cover these topics in chapters 3, 13, and 15. An ability to work in teams or groups is vital,[30] and you will learn about this in chapter 9. Employers are also seeking interpersonal skills,[31] which we will consider in chapter 6. Public speaking skills, covered in chapters 11–15, are important in most professions because of the requirement that employees give talks and presentations.[32] Finally, employers seek employees with strong written communication skills.[33] You will have an opportunity to improve your writing skills as you prepare outlines and manuscripts for public speeches, which we also cover in chapters 11–15.

7. *Studying communication can help you navigate an increasingly diverse world.* As you stroll through a mall, deposit money in a bank, go to a movie, or work at your job, odds are that about one in every five people you come into contact with will speak English as a second language. According to the 2007 American Community Survey, conducted by the U.S. Census Bureau, nearly 20% of respondents speak a language other than English in their home. The increasingly diverse population of the United States means that multilingual communication encounters are, for most of us, the norm rather than the exception. Learning how to communicate in today's world, whether English is your first language or not, requires an understanding of communication and culture and how those two concepts are related.

As you develop an understanding of basic communication concepts and learn how to apply those concepts in everyday interactions, you will be better equipped to bridge language and cultural barriers. As you progress through this book, you will learn a number of specific skills that promote effective interpersonal relationships, teamwork, and online communication. Most chapters include advice on how you can adapt specific skills during interactions with people whose first language is not English.

Communication: The Process of Using Messages to Generate Meaning

Now that you have considered why learning about communication is important, you need to know exactly what the term means. Over the years, scholars have created hundreds of definitions of communication. How they define the term can limit or expand the study of the subject. In this text, the definition is simple and broad—simple enough to allow understanding and broad enough to include many contexts.

Communication comes from the Latin word *communicare,* which means "to make common" or "to share." The root definition is consistent with our definition of communication. In this book, **communication** is defined as the process of using messages to generate meaning. Communication is considered a **process** because it is an activity, an exchange, or a set of behaviors—not an unchanging product. Communication is not an object you can hold in your hand; it is an activity in which you participate. David Berlo, a pioneer in the field

communication
The process of using messages to generate meaning.

process
An activity, an exchange, or a set of behaviors that occurs over time.

■ Understanding emerges from shared experience.

meaning
The understanding of the message.

of communication, probably provided the clearest statement about communication as a process:

> If we accept the concept of process, we view events and relationships as dynamic, ongoing, ever changing, continuous. When we label something as a process, we also mean that it does not have a beginning, an end, a fixed sequence of events. It is not static, at rest. It is moving. The ingredients within a process interact; each affects all the others.[34]

What is an example of how process works in everyday communication? Picture three students meeting on the sidewalk between classes and exchanging a few sentences. This "snapshot" does not begin and end with the students' first words and last sentence. Since they all stopped to chat with each other, you might assume that their relationship began before this encounter. Since they all seem to have a common understanding of what is being said, you might assume that they share experiences that similarly shape their perceptions. You also might assume that this brief encounter does not end when the students go their ways, but rather that they think about their conversation later in the day or that it leads to another meeting later in the week. In other words, a snapshot cannot capture all that occurs during communication, a process that starts before the words begin and ends long after the words end.

Messages include verbal and nonverbal symbols, signs, and behaviors. When you smile at another person, you are sending a message. When a radio announcer chooses language to emphasize the seriousness of a recent event, she is creating a message. The public speaker might spend days choosing just the right words and considering his bodily movements, gestures, and facial expression.

People hope to generate common meanings through the messages they provide. **Meaning** is the understanding of the message. You know that all of the messages you generate are not shared by others with whom you try to communicate. You try to flirt with someone you meet in class, but the other person seems oblivious to your subtle nonverbal signals. College professors are generally very knowledgeable about a subject matter, but they vary greatly in their ability to convey shared meanings.

Understanding the meaning of another person's message does not occur unless the two communicators can elicit common meanings for words, phrases, and nonverbal codes. When you use language, meaning facilitates an appropriate response that indicates that the message was understood. For example, suppose you ask a friend for a sheet of paper. She says nothing and gives you one sheet of paper. You and your friend share the same meaning of the message exchanged. But a message can be interpreted in more than one way, especially if the people involved have little shared experience. In such a case, a more accurate understanding of the intended meaning can be discerned by *negotiating*, that is, by asking questions.

Components of Communication

In this section you will learn how communication in action really works. The components of communication are people, messages, channels, feedback, codes, encoding and decoding, and noise.

PEOPLE

People are involved in the human communication process in two roles—as both the sources and the receivers of messages. A **source** initiates a message, and a **receiver** is the intended target of the message. Individuals do not perform these two roles independently, however; instead, they are the sources and the receivers of messages simultaneously and continually.

People do not respond uniformly to all messages, nor do they always provide the same messages in exactly the same way. Individual characteristics, including race, sex, age, culture, values, and attitudes, affect the ways people send and receive messages. (Throughout this text you will find discussions about the ways in which culture and sex affect communication.)

skill builder

Understanding Others

Although you may believe that you accurately interpret the meaning others are trying to convey, you probably do not always do so. On at least six different occasions in the next week, ask a person with whom you are communicating whether you can paraphrase the meaning of his or her message. Write down how well you did in each of these instances. How can you improve your understanding of others' messages?

source
A message initiator.

receiver
A message target.

message
The verbal or nonverbal form of the idea, thought, or feeling that one person (the source) wishes to communicate to another person or a group of people (the receivers).

THE MESSAGE

The **message** is the verbal and nonverbal form of the idea, thought, or feeling that one person (the source) wishes to communicate to another person or a group of people (the receivers). The message is the content of the interaction. The message includes the symbols (words and phrases) you use to communicate your ideas, as well as your facial expressions, bodily movements, gestures, physical contact, and tone of voice, as well as other nonverbal codes. The message may be relatively brief and easy to understand or long and complex. Some experts believe that real communication stems only from messages that are intentional, those that have a purpose. However, since intent is sometimes difficult to prove in a communication situation, the authors of this text believe that real communication can occur through either intentional or unintentional messages.

THE CHANNEL

The **channel** is the means by which a message moves from the source to the receiver of the message. A message moves from one place to another, from one person to another, by traveling through a medium, or channel. Airwaves, sound waves, copper wires, glass fibers, and cable are all communication channels. Airwaves and cable are two of the various channels through which you receive television messages. Radio messages move through sound waves. Computer images (and sound, if there is any) travel through light waves, and sometimes both light and sound waves. In person-to-person communication, you send your messages through a channel of sound waves and light waves that enable receivers to see and hear you.

channel
The means by which a message moves from the source to the receiver of the message.

FEEDBACK

Feedback is the receiver's verbal and nonverbal response to the source's message. Ideally, you respond to another person's messages by providing feedback, so that the source knows the message was received as intended. Feedback is part of any communication situation. Even no response, or silence, is feedback, as are restless behavior and quizzical looks from students in a classroom. Suppose you are looking for a restroom in an unfamiliar building. You ask a person quickly passing by, "Excuse me, can you tell me . . . ," but the person keeps on going without acknowledging you. In this case, the intended receiver did not respond, yet even the lack of a response provides you with some feedback. You may think that perhaps the receiver did not hear you, was in too much of a hurry to stop, did not speak English, or was just being insulting.

feedback
The receiver's verbal and nonverbal response to the source's message.

cultural **note**

What's in a Name?

U.S. parents name their children after relatives, entertainers, famous people, and biblical figures. Many Spanish-speaking males are named after Jesus, and thousands of Muslim males are named after Mohammed. In China, too, names have meanings that can influence how a person feels about him- or herself. Wen Shu Lee, a professor originally from Taiwan, published an article about the names of women in China.[35] She claims that naming practices often reflect gender- and class-based oppression. The name Zhao Di, for example, "commands a daughter to bring to the family a younger brother, while 'expelling' more younger sisters." The name reflects a higher value placed on male children. Does your name influence what you think of yourself? Does your name affect how, when, and with whom you communicate? What's in a name?

CODE

A computer carries messages via binary code on cable, wire, or fiber; similarly, you converse with others by using a code called "language." A **code** is a systematic arrangement of symbols used to create meanings in the mind of another person or persons. Words, phrases, and sentences become "symbols" used to evoke images, thoughts, and ideas in the mind of others. If someone yells "Stop" as you approach the street, the word *stop* has become a symbol that you are likely to interpret as a warning of danger.

Verbal and nonverbal codes are the two types of code used in communication. **Verbal codes** consist of symbols and their grammatical arrangement. All languages are codes. **Nonverbal codes** consist of all symbols that are not words, including bodily movements, the use of space and time, clothing and other adornments, and sounds other than words. *Nonverbal* codes should not be confused with *nonoral* codes. All nonoral codes, such as bodily movement, are nonverbal codes. However, nonverbal codes also include oral codes, such as pitch, duration, rate of speech, and sounds like "eh" and "ah."

ENCODING AND DECODING

If communication involves the use of codes, the process of communicating can be viewed as one of encoding and decoding. **Encoding** is the process of translating an idea or a thought into a code. **Decoding** is the process of assigning meaning to that idea or thought. For instance, suppose you are interested in purchasing a new car. You are trying to describe a compact model to your father, who wants to help you with your purchase. You might be visualizing the car with the black interior, sporty design, and red exterior that belongs to your best friend. Putting this vision into words, you tell your father you are interested in a car that is "small and well designed." You encode your perceptions of a particular car into words that describe the model. Your father, on hearing this, decodes your words and develops his own mental image. But his love of larger cars affects this process, and as a result, he envisions a big sedan. As you can see, misunderstanding often occurs because of the limitations of language and the inadequacy of descriptions. Nonetheless, encoding and decoding are essential in sharing your thoughts, ideas, and feelings with others.

NOISE

In the communication process, **noise** is any interference in the encoding and decoding processes that reduces the clarity of a message. Noise can be physical, such as loud sounds; distracting sights, such as a piece of food between someone's front teeth; or an unusual behavior, such as someone standing too close for comfort. Noise can be mental, psychological, or semantic, such as daydreams about a loved one, worry about the bills, pain from a tooth, or uncertainty about what the other person's words mean. Noise can be anything that interferes with receiving, interpreting, or providing feedback about a message.

Communication Principles

A definition of communication may be insufficient to clarify the nature of communication. To explain communication in more detail, we consider here some principles that guide our understanding of communication.

code
A systematic arrangement of symbols used to create meanings in the mind of another person or persons.

verbal codes
Symbols and their grammatical arrangement, such as languages.

nonverbal codes
All symbols that are not words, including bodily movements, the use of space and time, clothing and adornments, and sounds other than words.

encoding
The process of translating an idea or a thought into a code.

decoding
The process of assigning meaning to the idea or thought in a code.

noise
Any interference in the encoding and decoding processes that reduces message clarity.

COMMUNICATION BEGINS WITH THE SELF

How you see yourself can make a great difference in how you communicate. Carl Rogers[36] wrote, "Every individual exists in a continually changing world of experience of which he [or she] is the center." For instance, when people are treated as though they are inferior, or intelligent, or gifted, or unattractive, they will often begin acting accordingly. Many communication scholars and social scientists believe that people are products of how others treat them and of the messages others send them.

As persons, our understanding of the world is limited by our experiences with it. Shotter suggests that we cannot understand communication through external, abstract, and systematic processes. Instead, he describes communication as a "ceaseless flow of speech-entwined, dialogically structured, social activity."[37] In other words, communication is participatory; we are actively involved and relationally responsive in our use of communication. Shotter would contrast his perspective of a participatory-holistic view of communication with one that is abstract and systematic.

To contrast these two perspectives, let us consider an example. Suppose you have a roommate who is from another country. The roommate's religion, belief system, and daily habits challenge your perspective of communication, derived from interacting primarily with people in the United States who hold Western and Christian values. To the extent that you each try to impose your own preconceptions on the communication you share, you may be dissatisfied and experience conflict. By preimposing "rules" of communication derived from your earlier experiences in two distinctive cultures, you are bound to fail in this new relationship. If you are able to move beyond such a view and allow your perception of your communication to become a product of your interactions, you may be able to communicate in interesting and effective ways.

Every day, we experience the centrality of ourselves in communication. As a participant in communication, you are limited by your own view of every situation. A student, for instance, may describe a conflict with an instructor as unfair treatment: "I know my instructor doesn't like the fact that I don't agree with his opinions, and that's why he gave me such a poor grade in that class." The instructor might counter, "That student doesn't understand all the factors that go into a final grade." Each person may believe that he or she is correct and that the other person's view is wrong. As you study communication, you will learn ways to better manage such conflict.

sizing things up

Evaluate Your Own Communication Skills

We communicate in a variety of contexts. To improve your skill as a communicator, you should assess your own communication skills in each of the general communication contexts, so that you can identify your strengths and areas for growth. Read each of the following questions carefully, and respond using the following scale:

1 = Strongly disagree
2 = Disagree
3 = Neither agree nor disagree
4 = Agree
5 = Strongly agree

1. I can use communication to solve conflicts with friends.
2. I am able to express my ideas clearly when working in a group.
3. I am comfortable when giving public speeches.
4. I can use the Internet to locate highly reputable information.
5. Other people tell me that I am a good speaker.
6. My friends tell me that I am a good listener.
7. Others listen to my opinions in group meetings.
8. People rely on me to find information on the Web.
9. I am good at delivering speeches.
10. I can effectively lead groups to discuss problems.
11. I make friends easily.
12. I am skilled at using computers to communicate with others (e.g., using Skype, IM, chat rooms, and other communication tools).

Note: This list has no "right" or "wrong" answers. It simply provides an overview of your communication skills at the beginning of the course. You might want to complete the survey again at the end of the course to determine whether your scores have changed. A guide for interpreting your responses appears in the appendix at the end of the text (p. 348).

COMMUNICATION INVOLVES OTHERS

George Herbert Mead said that the self originates in communication.[38] Through verbal and nonverbal symbols, a child learns to accept roles in response to the expectations of others. For example, Dominique Moceanu, a successful Olympic gymnast, was influenced quite early in life by what others wanted her to be. Both her parents had been gymnasts, and apparently her father told her for years that her destiny was to be a world-class gymnast.[39] Most likely, she had an inherent ability to be a good one, but she may not have become a medal-winning gymnast without the early messages she received from her parents and trainers. Like Moceanu, you establish self-image, the sort of person you believe you are, by the ways others categorize you. Positive, negative, and neutral messages that you receive from others all play a role in determining who you are.

You may be aware of how important your peers are to your academic career. Students report that peers provide support for a variety of reasons: they allow you to vent about teachers and classes; provide you with information about assignments, classes, and other academic matters; offer positive statements that build your self-esteem and sense of worth; and make statements that motivate you to attend class, to do your homework, and to generally succeed at your work.[40] Other people are essential to how you feel about yourself during college and throughout your life.

dialogue
The act of taking part in a conversation, discussion, or negotiation.

Communication itself is probably best understood as a dialogic process. A **dialogue** is simply the act of taking part in a conversation, discussion, or negotiation. When we describe and explain our communicative exchanges with others, we are doing so from a perspective of self and from a perspective derived from interacting with others. Our understanding of communication occurs not in a vacuum but in light of our interactions with other people.[41]

In a more obvious way, communication involves others in the sense that a competent communicator considers the other person's needs and expectations when selecting messages to share. The competent communicator understands that a large number of messages can be shared at any time, but sensitivity and responsiveness to the other communicators are essential. In short, communication begins with the self, as defined largely by others, and involves others, as defined largely by the self.

■ Understanding can emerge from dialogue.

COMMUNICATION HAS BOTH A CONTENT AND A RELATIONAL DIMENSION

All messages have both a content and a relational dimension. Messages provide substance and suggest a relationship among communicators. Another way to think about this distinction is that the content of the message describes the behavior that is expected, whereas the relational message suggests how it should be interpreted. For example, if I say, "Sit down," the content of the brief message is a request for you to be seated. Relationally, I am suggesting that I have the authority to tell you to be seated. Consider the difference between "Sit down!" and "Would you care to be seated?" Whereas the content is essentially the same, the relational aspect seems far different. Generally, the content of the message is less ambiguous than is the relational message.

COMMUNICATION IS COMPLICATED

Communication, some believe, is a simple matter of passing information from one source to another person. In a sense, communication defined in this way would occur whenever you accessed information on the Web. However, you know that even in this most basic case communication does not necessarily occur. For example, if you access a website written in a language you do not understand, no communication occurs. If the material is highly complex, you might not understand its message. Similarly, you might be able to repeat what someone else says to you, but with absolutely no understanding of the intent, or the content, of the message.

   Communication is far more than simple information transmission. Communication involves choices about the multiple aspects of the message: the verbal, nonverbal, and behavioral aspects; the choices surrounding the transmission channels used; the characteristics of the speaker; the relationship between the speaker and the audience; the characteristics of the audience; and the situation in which the communication occurs. A change in any one of these variables affects the entire communication process.

COMMUNICATION QUANTITY DOES NOT INCREASE COMMUNICATION QUALITY

You might believe that a textbook on communication would stake claims on the importance of increased communication. You may have heard counselors or therapists say: "What we need is more communication." However, greater amounts of communication do not necessarily lead to more harmony or more accurate and shared meanings. Sometimes people disagree, and the more they talk, the more they learn that they are in conflict. Other times people have very poor listening or empathy skills and misunderstand vast quantities of information. Communication, defined simply as verbiage, does not necessarily lead to positive outcomes.

COMMUNICATION IS INEVITABLE

Although communication is complicated and more communication is not necessarily better communication, communication occurs almost every minute of your life. If you are not communicating with yourself (thinking, planning, reacting to the world around you), you are observing others and drawing inferences from their behavior. Even if others did not intend messages for you, you gather observations and draw specific conclusions. A person yawns, and you believe that he is bored with your message. A second person looks away, and you conclude that she is not listening to you. A third person smiles (perhaps because of a memory of a joke he heard recently), and you believe that he is attracted to you. We are continually gleaning meanings from others' behaviors, and we are constantly behaving in ways that have communicative value for them.

COMMUNICATION CANNOT BE REVERSED

Have you ever insulted someone accidentally? You may have tried to explain that you did not intend to insult anybody, said you were sorry for your statement, or made a joke out of your misstatement. Nonetheless, your comment lingers both in the mind of the other person and in your own mind. As you understand the irreversibility of communication, you may become more careful in your conversations with others, and you may take more time preparing public presentations. You cannot go back in time and erase your messages to others.

COMMUNICATION CANNOT BE REPEATED

Have you ever had an incredible evening with someone and remarked, "Let's do this again," but when you tried to re-create the ambience, the conversation, and the setting, nothing seemed right? Your second experience with a similar setting and person yielded far different results. Just as you cannot repeat an experience, you cannot repeat communication.

What Are Communication Contexts?

context
A set of circumstances or a situation.

Communication occurs in a **context**—a set of circumstances or a situation. Communication occurs between two friends, among five business acquaintances in a small-group setting, and between a lecturer and an audience that fills an auditorium. At many colleges and universities, the communication courses are arranged by context: interpersonal communication, interviewing, small-group communication, public speaking, and mass communication. The number of people involved in communication affects the kind of communication that occurs. You may communicate with yourself, with another person, or with many others. The differences among these situations affect your choices of the most appropriate verbal and nonverbal codes.

INTRAPERSONAL COMMUNICATION

intrapersonal communication
The process of using messages to generate meaning within the self.

Intrapersonal communication is the process of using messages to generate meaning within the self. Intrapersonal communication is the communication that occurs within your own mind. For example, suppose you and the person you've been dating for two years share the same attitude toward education and your futures. Although no one in either of your families has gone to college, you have lofty aspirations. Not only do you plan on graduating from college, but you are both planning on going on to get advanced degrees that will allow you to run your own business. But one day your partner informs you that he or she is dropping out of school to get a job to help support his or her parents, who are unemployed. The changing economy allows no other alternative. This alters everything in the future you envision. When you begin to share your feelings with your partner, he or she becomes angry and says your attitude is just another example of your inflexibility. You tell your partner that you cannot discuss the issue now and that you need to think things over for a while. You leave, thinking about what has just happened and what the future holds for the two of you. You are engaged in intrapersonal communication.

Intrapersonal communication occurs, as this example suggests, when you evaluate or examine the interaction that occurs between yourself and others, but it is not limited to such situations. This form of communication occurs before and during other forms of communication as well. For instance, you might argue with yourself during a conversation in which someone asks you to do something you do not really want to do: before you accept or decline, you mull over the alternatives in your mind.

Intrapersonal communication also includes such activities as solving problems internally, resolving internal conflict, planning for the future, and evaluating yourself and your relationships with others. Intrapersonal communication—the basis for all other communication—involves only the self.

Each one of us is continually engaged in intrapersonal communication. Although you might become more easily absorbed in talking to yourself when you are alone (while walking to class, driving to work, or taking a shower, for instance), you are likely to be involved in this form of communication in crowded circumstances as well (such as during a lecture, at a party, or with friends). Think about the last time you looked at yourself in a mirror. What were your thoughts? Although intrapersonal communication is almost continuous, people seldom focus on this form of communication.

Indeed, not all communication experts believe that intrapersonal communication should be examined within communication studies. The naysayers argue that communication requires two or more receivers of a message, and since there are no receivers in intrapersonal communication, no communication actually occurs. They reason that intrapersonal communication should be studied in a discipline such as psychology or neurology—a field in which experts study the mind or the brain. Nonetheless, intrapersonal communication is recognized by most scholars within the discipline as one context of communication for you to know and understand.

■ Intrapersonal communication occurs in our reflections.

INTERPERSONAL COMMUNICATION

When you move from intrapersonal to interpersonal communication, you move from communication that occurs within your own mind to communication that involves one or more other persons. **Interpersonal communication** is the process of using messages to generate meaning between at least two people in a situation that allows mutual opportunities for both speaking and listening. Like intrapersonal communication, interpersonal communication occurs for a variety of reasons: to solve problems, to resolve conflicts, to share information, to improve perceptions of oneself, or to fulfill social needs, such as the need to belong or to be loved. Through our interpersonal communication, we are able to establish relationships with others that include friendships and romantic relationships.

Dyadic and small-group communication are two subsets of interpersonal communication. **Dyadic communication** is simply two-person communication, such as interviews with an employer or a teacher; talks with a parent, spouse, or child; and interactions among strangers, acquaintances, and friends. **Small-group communication** is the process of using messages to generate meaning in a small group of people.[42] Small-group communication occurs in families, work groups, support groups, religious groups, and study groups. Communication experts agree that two people are a dyad and that more than two people are a small group if they have a common purpose, goal, or mission. However, disagreement emerges about the maximum number of participants in a small group. Technology also poses questions for communication scholars to debate: for instance, does a small group have to meet face-to-face? That teleconferences can involve small-group communication is

interpersonal communication
The process of using messages to generate meaning between at least two people in a situation that allows mutual opportunities for both speaking and listening.

dyadic communication
Two-person communication.

small-group communication
The process of using messages to generate meaning in a small group of people.

social media
make it matter

The Internet and Communication Models

Individually or in groups, consider and develop answers to these questions about technology and communication models:

1. How has the Internet—with social networking sites as well as informational websites—altered the way individuals communicate with each other? Consider the sites you use, such as Facebook, Plaxo, Xing, or Kickstarter. Do you have a blog? Have you sent photos to others on Flickr? Have you made presentations using Prezi or video clips from YouTube? Have you communicated with friends, family, or a potential employer on Skype? Do you tweet or text?

2. What is lost and what is gained when a human transaction is mediated by a computer?

public communication
The process of using messages to generate meaning; in a situation in which a single source transmits a message to a number of receivers.

mass communication
The process of using messages to generate meaning; in a mediated system, between a source and a large number of unseen receivers.

media convergence
The way that broadcasting, publishing, and digital communication are congregating.

uncontroversial, but what about discussions in chat rooms on the Internet? Small-group communication is discussed in greater detail later in this text.

PUBLIC COMMUNICATION

Public communication is the process of using messages to generate meanings in a situation in which a single source transmits a message to a number of receivers, who give nonverbal and sometimes question-and-answer feedback. In public communication, the source adapts the message to the audience in an attempt to achieve maximum understanding. Sometimes virtually everyone in the audience understands the speaker's message; other times many people fail to understand.

Public communication, or public speaking, is recognized by its formality, structure, and planning. You probably are frequently a receiver of public communication in classes, at convocations, and at religious services. Occasionally, you also may be a source: when you speak in a group, when you try to convince other voters of the merits of a particular candidate for office, or when you introduce a guest speaker to an audience. Public communication most often informs or persuades, but it can also entertain, introduce, announce, welcome, or pay tribute.

MASS COMMUNICATION

Mass communication is the process of using messages to generate meanings in a mediated system, between a source and a large number of unseen receivers. Mass communication always has a transmission system (mediator) between the sender and the receiver. When you watch your favorite TV show, the signals are going from a broadcast studio to a satellite or cable system and then from that system to your TV set: the mediator is the channel, the method of distribution. This type of communication is called "mass" because the message goes to newspaper and magazine readers, TV viewers, and radio listeners. Mass communication is often taught in a college or university department of mass communication, radio and television, or journalism.

People who study mass communication may be interested in the processes by which communication is transmitted, and therefore they study the diffusion of information. Alternatively, they may be interested in the effects of media on people and study persuasion or how public opinion is created and altered. Mass communication has become of increasing interest today because of the expanded opportunities for communication on the Internet. Today many students are interested in **media convergence,** or the way that broadcasting, publishing, and digital communication are now congregating and in some instances becoming one.

COMPUTER-MEDIATED COMMUNICATION

Computer-mediated communication (CMC) includes human communication and information shared through communication networks. CMC requires digital literacy, which is the ability to find, evaluate, and use information that is available via computer. The e-mail messages, discussion group threads, newsgroup notes, instant messages, text messages, and tweets serve as the message, whereas humans continue to serve as the sources or receivers of those messages. In the same way that media convergence has become an important avenue of study in mass communication, technological convergence has piqued the interest of scholars and practitioners alike. **Technological convergence** focuses on the way that technological systems, including voice, data, and video, now share modes of communication and they are changing to perform similar tasks. Consider the variety of electronic devices you use today and what you might have used five years ago to gain some understanding of how quickly these changes are occurring.

> **technological convergence**
> The way that technological systems are changing to perform similar tasks.

How is CMC unique as a communication context? Messages can be sent and received asynchronously (at different times). People can prestructure messages to which they give a great deal of thought, or they can quickly dash off a message with no thought at all. CMC occurs over a single channel, although people have cleverly added emoticons (which we will define and discuss in chapter 4) to lend another dimension to CMC. CMC may allow equality among people as demographic features and social status are removed. But CMC can also encourage racism, sexism, and other biases by the nature of the messages that are created and provided to literally millions of people.

The various communication contexts can be determined by several factors: the number of people involved, the level of formality or intimacy, the opportunities for feedback, the need for restructuring messages, and the degree of stability of the roles of speaker and listener. Table 1.1 compares the contexts on the basis of these factors.

What Are the Goals of Communication Study?

You learned the importance of studying communication at the beginning of this chapter. You will derive many benefits: you can improve the way you see yourself and the ways others see you; you can increase what you know about human relationships; you can learn important life skills; you can better exercise your constitutionally guaranteed freedom of speech; and you can increase your chances of succeeding professionally. How will you achieve these outcomes? To the extent that you become a more effective and ethical communicator, you will enhance the likelihood of these positive results.

UNDERSTANDING COMMUNICATION COMPETENCE

Communication competence is simply the ability to effectively exchange meaning through a common system of symbols or behavior. As you will learn in this book, communication competence is not necessarily easy to achieve. Communication competence can be difficult because your goals and others' goals may be discrepant. Similarly, you and those with whom you communicate may have a different understanding of your relationship. Cultural differences may cause you to view the world and other people differently. Indeed, different perspectives about communication may themselves create problems in your interactions with others. As you read this text, you will learn about the multiple variables involved in communication, and you will become more competent in your communication.

> **communication competence**
> The ability to effectively exchange meaning through a common system of symbols, signs, or behavior.

You need to recognize now that, although communication competence is the goal, the complexity of communication should encourage you to be a student of communication over your lifetime. In this course you will begin to learn the terminology and the multiple variables comprised in communication. Although you will not emerge from the course as totally effective, you should see significant changes in your communication abilities. The professional public speaker or comedian, the glib TV reporter, and the highly satisfied spouse in a long-term marriage make communication look easy. However, as you will learn, their skills are complex and interwoven with multiple layers of understanding.

Table 1.1 Differences Among Communication Contexts

Contexts	Intrapersonal Communication	Interpersonal Communication		Public Communication	Mass Communication	Computer-Mediated Communication
		Dyadic Communication	Small-Group Communication			
Number of People	1	2	Usually 3 to 10; may be more	Usually more than 10	Usually thousands	2 to billions
Degree of Formality or Intimacy	Most intimate	Generally intimate; interview is formal	Intimate or formal	Generally formal	Generally formal	Intimate or formal
Opportunities for Feedback	Complete feedback	A great deal of feedback	Less than in intrapersonal communication but more than in public communication	Less than in small-group communication but more than in mass communication	Usually more	None to a great deal
Need for Prestructuring Messages	None	Some	Some	A great deal	Almost totally scripted	None to totally scripted
Degree of Stability of the Roles of Speaker and Listener	Highly unstable; the individual as both speaker and listener	Unstable; speaker and listener alternate	Unstable; speakers and listeners alternate	Highly stable; one speaker with many listeners	Highly stable; on-air speakers, invisible listeners	Unstable to highly stable

UNDERSTANDING ETHICAL COMMUNICATION

The second goal in studying communication lies in its ethical dimension. **Ethics** may be defined as a set of moral principles or values. Ethical standards may vary from one discipline to another, just as they differ from one culture to another. The standards within the communication discipline are derived from Western conceptions of communication, democratic decision making, and the ideologies of people in the communication discipline.

ethics
A set of moral principles or values.

Within the communication discipline, the National Communication Association (NCA) has created a set of ethics guidelines. The NCA Credo that lists these is provided inside the back cover of this book. You may wish to read these guidelines for communication behavior and consider the extent to which they are true in your life. As you listen to politicians, activists, and people with opposing views, consider how these ethical principles are violated.

Communication professionals believe that people should be open, honest, and reasonable. They affirm the First Amendment to the Constitution of the United States of America, which guarantees freedom of speech. They agree that respect for other people and their messages is essential. They acknowledge the need for access to information and to people. Finally, they view responsible behavior as important.

■ Ethical communication is critical for the development of relationships and communities.

Consider how you can learn to be an effective and ethical communicator. One example is provided by Wheaton College students in Massachusetts, who got a boost in their service-learning projects. A local bank provided a grant that allowed the students to gain some minor financing as they worked at an emergency shelter for women, a food distribution outlet, and a national program that promotes early literacy. Can you think of a local project in which you could involve your fellow students as a way to both serve others and improve your communication skills through engaging with others?

UNDERSTANDING THE SOCIAL SCIENTIFIC METHOD

In this book, you will read about a number of social scientific studies. You might wonder how social scientific studies are different from common sense. For example, you will read about how physical attractiveness is defined and the effects of physical attractiveness on a variety of other factors. You might think to yourself that you have a different perspective on these matters. How are the results of these studies different from an opinion? Your opinion is a belief or a feeling about phenomena, whereas a fact is based on direct evidence, actual experience, or observation.

Social scientists learn about social phenomena in the disciplines of communication, sociology, psychology, criminal justice, and other fields by applying the scientific method. The scientific method entails several steps. First, researchers identify and formulate questions about which they are curious. Second, they design and plan a study in which they can gather evidence or observe behavior. Third, they sample a group of people from whom they can generalize their findings. These people may complete surveys, they may be asked to complete a task, or they may be observed. Using statistical methods, or other ways to measure and summarize, the social scientists process and analyze the data. Finally, they interpret the data, draw inferences from it, and write research reports, which they send to other scientists, who judge the reports' importance and trustworthiness. If this group of peers judges the work to add new knowledge in the discipline, the researchers publish it in an academic journal. All the studies cited in this book have gone through this process and have been published.

Contemporary Jobs in Communication

What can you do with a communication degree? The communication field covers many subdisciplines, including public relations, advertising, business communication, journalism, corporate training, health communication, and marketing. Some students combine their communication courses with courses in health to work in health communication careers; others combine communication with political science to serve as a legislative assistant or political analyst; still others take business courses to prepare themselves to be a corporate recruiter, training specialist, or sales representative. The following are some of the contemporary jobs of recent communication graduates:

Title	Organization
PR professional	Major hospital
Audio editor	Production firm
Teacher	High school
Advance person	Political campaign
Web designer	City government
Administrative assistant	Bank
Tour guide	Travel firm
Community affairs liaison	Medium-sized city
Auto service manager	Regional auto service agency
Nurse	Large hospital
Legal assistant	Medium-sized law firm
Mobile device consultant	National business consulting company
Event planner	Medium-sized city
Flight attendant	Major airline
Government lobbyist	Small midwestern state
Salesperson	Insurance company

Although new graduates are likely to find jobs in a variety of entry-level positions, individuals with communication degrees frequently find that advancement comes fairly quickly. Some communication graduates take advantage of graduate school, professional school, or other further education. Others apply themselves and find advancement within organizations in which they began their employment, or they are willing to move from organization to organization to progress in their careers. These are some positions of communication graduates who received their undergraduate degrees 10 years ago or more:

Title	Organization
Fundraiser	International women's organization
Minister	Medium-sized church
Human resource generalist	Large advertising company
Political talk show host	Large-market television station
Professor	College or university
Health administrator	Regional health agency
News anchor	Major network news channel
Weather reporter	Mid-sized city
Film critic	Major city newspaper
Health educator	Major city hospital
Sales manager	Multi-location PR firm
College recruiter	Large state university
President	Advertising agency
Copywriter	Major academic press

keeping it real

The Employment Interview

Although this chapter introduces you only to the content of the course, you have already learned that communication is important in your personal and professional life. You know that communication is far more complicated than many people understand. You also know that you can learn to become a more competent communicator. You will build on this knowledge as you continue your study of communication.

Like Reyna Reynolds, whom we met at the beginning of the chapter, you might find that you will need part-time or full-time work while attending college. What advice do the experts offer for achieving that goal?[43] First, be proactive. Investigate every lead. Look at online sites, such as www.ajb.dni.us (America's Job Bank), www.careeronestop.org, www.monster.com, or www.wantedtech.com. Talk with friends and family for possible leads, and do not hesitate to speak with recruitment agencies.

If you are fortunate to get an interview, you can be sure that the employer will ask you to talk about yourself. Plan and practice your answer. Try to anticipate the kinds of information an employer may want to know, and include it in your answer. You can save the potential employer and yourself a great deal of time by foreseeing possible questions and answering them before they are asked.

At the same time, you should not belabor the interview. Be sensitive to cues that suggest that the interview time is concluded. End the time with the interviewer positively. You might consider a short statement about what you could bring to the job and how the organization could benefit by hiring you.

What should you avoid doing in an employment interview? The website www .quintcareers.com lists the following, among other items:

- Offering a poor handshake
- Talking too much
- Talking negatively about current or past employers
- Showing up late or too early
- Falling back on vocal pauses and verbal fillers, such as "umm," "you know," and "like"
- Making too little or too much eye contact

Chapter Review & Study Guide

Summary

In this chapter you learned the following:

1. Communication is essential because
   - Understanding communication can improve the way people view themselves and the way others view them.
   - People learn more about human relationships as they study communication and learn important life skills.
   - Studying communication can help people exercise their constitutionally guaranteed freedom of speech.
   - An understanding of communication can help people succeed professionally.

2. Communication is the process of using messages to exchange meaning.

3. The components of communication are people, messages, channels, feedback, codes, encoding and decoding, and noise.

4. Among the principles of communication are that
   - Communication begins with the self and involves others.
   - Communication has both a content and a relational dimension.

- Communication is complicated.
- An increased quantity of communication does not necessarily increase the quality of communication.
- Communication is inevitable, irreversible, and unrepeatable.

5. Communication occurs in intrapersonal, interpersonal, public, mass, and computer-mediated contexts. The number of people involved, the degree of formality or intimacy, the opportunities for feedback, the need for prestructuring messages, and the degree of stability of the roles of speaker and listener all vary with the communication context.

6. Communication competence is the ability to effectively exchange meaning through a common system of symbols, signs, or behavior. Within the communication discipline, the National Communication Association (NCA) has created a set of ethics guidelines. Social scientists learn about social phenomena in the disciplines of communication, sociology, psychology, criminal justice, and other fields by applying the scientific method.

Key Terms

Channel
Code
Communication
Communication competence
Context
Decoding
Dialogue
Dyadic communication
Encoding

Ethics
Feedback
Interpersonal communication
Intrapersonal communication
Mass communication
Meaning
Media convergence
Message
Noise

Nonverbal codes
Process
Public communication
Receiver
Small-group communication
Source
Technological convergence
Verbal codes

Study Questions

connect For further review, go to the LearnSmart study module for this chapter.

1. Communication is considered a process of using messages to generate meaning because it is
   a. an activity or exchange instead of an unchanging product.
   b. a tangible object.
   c. something with a beginning, a middle, and an end.
   d. static.

2. Understanding another person's messages does not occur unless
   a. the speaker uses nonverbal messages.
   b. common meanings for words, phrases, and nonverbal codes are elicited.
   c. the listener asks questions.
   d. both parties use verbal and nonverbal symbols.

3. The process of translating an idea or a thought into a code is known as
   a. communicating.
   b. decoding.
   c. encoding.
   d. deciphering.

4. Which communication principle considers variables such as verbal, nonverbal, and behavioral aspects; the channel used; and audience characteristics?
   a. Communication has a content and a relational dimension.
   b. Communication begins with the self.
   c. Communication involves others.
   d. Communication is complicated.

5. Intrapersonal communication is communication _____, and interpersonal communication is communication _____.
   a. between two or more people; within the self
   b. between two or more people; with a large number of people
   c. within the self; between two or more people
   d. within the self; within a small group of people

6. A main difference between public communication and mass communication is that
   a. mass communication is unstable.
   b. public communication is mediated by television.
   c. public communication allows for feedback from the listeners.
   d. mass communication is generally informal and public communication is formal.

7. Which of the following is defined as the ability to effectively exchange meaning through a common system of symbols, signs, or behavior?
   a. dyadic communication
   b. communication competence
   c. message
   d. feedback

8. Ethical standards within the communication discipline have been created by the

    a. National Communication Association.
    b. American Communication Association.
    c. Communication Administration.
    d. Public Speaking Administration.

9. Studying communication is essential because it can

    a. allow you to find a job very easily.
    b. enhance your chances of selling questionable products to unknowing customers.
    c. allow you to multiply the number of friends you have on social networks.
    d. improve the way you see yourself and the way others see you.

10. When you respond to a speaker with a verbal or non-verbal cue, you are

    a. giving feedback.
    b. not communicating.
    c. providing noise.
    d. using a metaphor.

Answers:

1. (a); 2. (b); 3. (c); 4. (d); 5. (c); 6. (c); 7. (b); 8. (a); 9. (d); 10. (a)

Critical Thinking

1. In the beginning of the chapter, six advantages to studying communication are discussed. Explain how these benefits apply to you in your chosen area of study.

2. Think of your own computer use. How do you use computer-mediated communication (CMC) in your daily life (that is, for school, personal use, or work)? Do you use one kind of CMC more than another?

perception, self,
and communication

When you have read and thought about this chapter, you will be able to:

1. Describe what perception is.

2. Explain some of the reasons why differences occur in perception.

3. Describe how selection, organization, and interpretation occur during perception and how they affect the way you see yourself and others in communication situations.

4. Differentiate among figure and ground, proximity, closure, and similarity in communication examples.

5. Identify errors you might make when you perceive others that affect your communication with them.

6. Understand how your view of yourself influences to whom you speak and how you speak to others.

7. Define *identity management*, which is how you present yourself to others in communication.

This chapter introduces you to the role of perception and the role of the self in communication. The chapter explains what perception is and why differences in perception occur. Next we explore our perceptions of others and the role of the self in communication.

How do other people's perceptions of you affect communication? Read these words from a student who knows:

My name is William Mason Turner; I stand six feet six inches tall and weigh three hundred pounds. I am African American with long dreadlocks that go down my back. I have eight tattoos. Typically a very energetic, outgoing individual, I tend to talk about other people because they always seem to stare at me. I have come to realize that people stare at me a lot because I could very well be the biggest person they have ever seen. My physical characteristics tend to affect my communication with others a lot more than one might think. Just the other day I was having a conversation with one of my closer friends, and she told me a story about the year before, when we first met. She said to me, "Last year in the dining center I wasn't paying attention and I accidentally bumped into you. I have never been more scared in my life." It is not the first time I have heard someone tell me that I am a scary-looking or intimidating individual. Most of the people that come up to me and talk to me without knowing me are usually outgoing individuals themselves, because everyone else thinks I am scary or unapproachable. It is almost like I am a monster! My size affects my communication ability more than any other physical characteristic I have.

Mr. Turner nailed it! The way others see us affects their communication with us. The way others see us also affects how or even whether we will communicate with them. That is why this chapter focuses on the role of perception in communication.

What Is Perception?

In this chapter we focus on perception, the self, and communication. Differences in perception affect the way we understand events, others, and ourselves. Consequently, perception affects the way we view ourselves and the way we present ourselves. In turn, perception influences our experiences, our assessment of others, and our communication with them. The way you sense the world—the way you see, hear, smell, touch, and taste—is subjective, uniquely your own. Nobody else sees the world the way you do, and nobody experiences events exactly as you do.

The uniqueness of human experience is based largely on differences in **perception**—using the senses to process information about the external environment. Since our perceptions are unique, communication between and among people becomes complicated.

At one time, experts tended to see perception as passive. Passive perception means that, like video recorders, people are simply recorders of stimuli. Today perception is considered to be more active. **Active perception** means that your mind selects, organizes, and interprets what you sense, so each person is a different video camera, and each person aims the camera at different things. Each person's lens is different; each person sees different colors; and each person's audio picks up different sounds. Perception is subjective because you interpret what you sense; you make it your own, and you add to and subtract from what you see, hear, smell, and touch. **Subjective perception** is your uniquely constructed meaning attributed to sensed stimuli.

Consider how much your inner state affects your perceptions. If you have a bad headache, the pain probably will affect the way you treat your children, the way you respond to

perception
the process of using the senses to acquire information about the surrounding environment or situation.

active perception
Perception in which your mind selects, organizes, and interprets that which you sense.

subjective perception
Your uniquely constructed meaning attributed to sensed stimuli.

the workers at the shop, and even the way you see yourself in the mirror. One woman expressed the problem like this: "I need to work on disguising my mood because when I act indifferent toward what people are saying, they may think I'm silent because I do not like them as a person or I disagree with what they are saying. However, this is usually never the case. I am just not in the mood for having a conversation." Consider also how complicated communication becomes when you know that everyone has his or her own view, uniquely developed and varying according to what is happening both outside and inside the mind. Perception is a factor that complicates communication.

How do you see the world around you? Perhaps comparing the way your mind works to the way a computer works will help you answer this. Think of your conscious experiences as the images that appear on your notebook. Think of what you sense with your eyes, nose, tongue, ears, and fingertips as that which is read off your thumb drive. The picture you see on the screen is not the same as the bits on the disk; instead, an image is generated from the bits to create something you can see. "What we perceive in the world around us is not a direct and faithful representation of that world itself, but rather a 'computer enhanced' version based upon very limited data from that world," according to Wright.[1]

Why Do Differences in Perception Occur?

Perception is subjective, active, and creative. Differences in perception may be the result of physiological factors, people's past experiences and roles, and their present feelings and circumstances.

PHYSIOLOGICAL FACTORS

You are not physiologically identical to anyone else. People differ from each other in sex, height, weight, body type, and senses. You may be tall or short, have poor eyesight, or have impaired hearing; you may be particularly sensitive to smells; or your body temperature may be colder than those of the rest of your family. Student William Turner at the beginning of this chapter told about how his large size and ethnicity affected his everyday communication. Similarly, hair color, height, and attractiveness greatly affect the way you feel about yourself and the way others treat you. One female student said, "All my life I have had very blonde hair, and because of my hair color, people often take one look at me and think of the stereotypical blonde girl—someone with no brains or common sense."[2]

Sex is another physiological factor that may lead to perceptual differences. One student explained the problem like this: "I am a younger white female. I do believe that because I am younger, white, and a female people tend to talk to me as though I am not capable of doing certain tasks. When older gentlemen or even older ladies speak to me, I do think they talk down to me because I do look younger, and to them I am just a young college student."[3] Some authors have suggested that hemispheric differences in the cerebral cortex of the brain are sex-linked. These differences account for females' language facility and fine hand control and for males' spatial and mathematical abilities, as well as males' increased likelihood of dyslexia, stuttering, delayed speech, autism, and hyperactivity.[4] Regardless of these findings, experts have found no conclusive evidence establishing an anatomical difference between the brain structures of human females and males.

Differences in perception also may arise from temporary conditions. A headache, fatigue, or a pulled muscle can cause you to perceive a critical comment when a friendly one is being offered. You may not see a stop sign if your thoughts are on texting or tweeting.

You could be using cold medicine or painkillers that make you tired or irritable. Other physiological needs, such as hunger and thirst, may also affect your perceptive skills. Once you are aware of all the conditions that can affect your perceptions, you might be amazed that we can communicate with each other at all.

PAST EXPERIENCES AND ROLES

perceptual constancy
The idea that your past experiences lead you to see the world in a way that is difficult to change; your initial perceptions persist.

Just as your size, sex, and senses can affect your perceptions, so can your past experiences and your various roles. The concept that best explains the influence of your past experiences on your perceptions is **perceptual constancy**—the idea that your past experiences lead you to see the world in a way that is difficult to change; your initial perceptions persist. "A perceptual characteristic that affects my communication with others," said a male student, "is that I am very well-mannered. I am an only child, and my parents raised me very strictly to always treat others with respect, and put them before yourself. I also attended a Catholic elementary, middle, and high school where the golden rule of 'treat your neighbor as yourself' was always endorsed and upheld."[5] What happened to you in the past influences your current perceptions. A bad experience in a given situation may cause you to avoid that situation in the future. Your experiences affect how you respond to professors, police, and politicians.

role
The part you play in various social contexts.

Roles also influence perceptions. A **role** is the part you play in various social contexts. Jason observed that being "the boss" was effective at work, but not in his student role. "When I worked as a manager for a retail store, my assertiveness and confidence were viewed in a positive light. Many of my subordinates saw these characteristics [as] typical for a leader in my position. If I treated my fellow classmates with the same level of assertiveness that I did at work, I would come across as 'cocky' or 'full of it,' and my communication would be affected negatively."[6]

■ Differences in perception that are created by cultural differences can be overcome in our interaction with others.

You may be a single parent, a shift manager, an auto mechanic, or some other role. Your roles affect your communication: to whom you talk, how you talk to them, what language you use, and how you respond to feedback. A good example of how perceptual constancy and role are related is parents' treatment of their children. Even after some people become adults, their parents treat them as they did when they were growing up. Roles also tend to change with context: in your parents' home you are a son or daughter; in your own home you may be a roommate or a mother or father; in the classroom you are a student; and at work you may be a welder, a fry cook, or a retail associate.

PRESENT FEELINGS AND CIRCUMSTANCES

How you feel at the moment affects your perceptions and alters your communication. Your child kept you up all night, so you are tired and stressed. Your friend's "How are you?" releases a torrent of whiny complaints that are not your usual response. A headache, great news about your mother's health, a brief fight this evening before class—all these life experiences influence with whom and how you communicate.

Now that you know why differences in perception occur, how can you apply this information to your communication skills? Imagine you are talking to a classmate about an assignment. She looks away from you and does not respond to your attempts at conversation, but she does ask an occasional question. Why is she acting distant and disinterested? She might be catching a cold and is uncomfortable talking. Or maybe she has had the experience of helping other classmates with their work with no gratitude on their part. Finally, she might feel that she should not be telling you what to do on the assignment. It turns out she is hungry, so she is just trying to get away from you so she could go eat! Present circumstances and internal states influence your communication with others.

What Occurs in Perception?

You engage in three separate activities during perception: selection, organization, and interpretation. You are likely unaware of these processes because they occur quickly and all at once. Nonetheless, each plays a discrete role in perception. In turn, our perceptions affect our communication.

SELECTION

No one perceives all the stimuli in his or her environment. Through selection, you neglect some stimuli and focus on others. For example, when you commute to school, you are bombarded with sights, sounds, smells, and other sensations. You don't remember every car you saw on the road, nor do you focus on every person you pass on the sidewalk. Instead, you choose to pay attention to some things while ignoring many others. At school you probably scan students passing by, so that you can select out any friends or classmates who deserve a nod, wave, or other greeting. While awake, you are always actively engaged in selecting which stimuli to which you will respond—or not.

selective exposure
The tendency to expose yourself to information that reinforces, rather than contradicts, your beliefs or opinions.

You also select the messages to which you attend. You may tune out one of your teachers while you listen to the hard rainfall outside the classroom window. You might not listen to your roommate nagging you about cleaning the kitchen but listen to every word of praise from your boss. You hear and see thousands of ads, but you choose to respond to very few.

selective attention
The tendency, when you expose yourself to information and ideas, to focus on certain cues and ignore others.

Four types of selectivity are selective exposure, selective attention, selective perception, and selective retention. In **selective exposure** you expose yourself to information that reinforces, rather than contradicts, your beliefs or opinions.[7] In other words, conservative Republicans are more likely than liberal Democrats to listen to Rush Limbaugh on the radio, watch Fox TV, and read editorials by George Will. Liberal Democrats, on the other hand, are more likely to watch Chris Matthews, Rachel Maddow, and Jon Stewart. Selective exposure has the value of protecting our positions and the downside of protecting our prejudices.

■ Perception is affected by our choice of which messages to attend to and which to ignore.

In **selective attention,** even when you do expose yourself to information and ideas, you focus on certain cues and ignore others. In class, you might notice the new outfit your friend is wearing but not the earring worn by the man three seats in front of you. At a buffet table, you might be drawn to familiar foods while avoiding anything unfamiliar. In an elevator, you may notice the conversation between the two other passengers but not the music that's being piped in overhead.

social media
make it matter

Managing Perceptions with a Facebook Profile

Social media invite us to manage perceptions by posting only what we want others to see or read. Your Facebook page can portray you as a party animal, a social butterfly, a top athlete, a beauty queen, or a serious student. Analyze your own profile to uncover how you manipulate the way others see you by selectively sharing your information. If class time permits, share your analysis with a classmate or the class.

selective perception
The tendency to see, hear, and believe only what you want to see, hear, and believe.

selective retention
The tendency to remember better the things that reinforce your beliefs than those that oppose them.

In communication, you do not treat all sounds, words, phrases, and sentences equally. You almost always respond to your name or a command, such as "Come here!" If you do not like swearing, you might respond very negatively to other people's foul language. In classes you don't like, you drag through the course without learning much at all, whereas in your favorite class you are highly attentive. Selective attention is in full-time operation during your waking hours, and your use of this aspect of perception affects your communication in many ways.

After you expose yourself to a message and pay attention to it, you see that message through your own special lens. **Selective perception** is the tendency to see, hear, and believe only what you want to see, hear, and believe.[8] Suppose someone accused your trustworthy, law-abiding friend of 20 years of stealing; would you believe that person? You may not listen to the accusations, or even look at the evidence, because you believe it simply is not possible that your friend would ever do such a thing.

We see one example of selective perception in the way teachers observe signs of confusion or frustration from students. A study exploring how different types of teachers respond to the unique needs of people who speak English as a second language (ESL) found that some are more adept than others at perceiving nonverbal signals of confusion from ESL students.[9] Teachers who tend to use more interaction and dialogue in their classroom are quick to observe nonverbal behaviors signaling a lack of understanding; in contrast, teachers who rely more on lecture tend to miss such signals. These findings illustrate how selective perception, perhaps driven by past experiences and roles, can cause some teachers to selectively perceive and react to such nonverbal signs while others do not. Although these findings point to the need for all teachers to be more observant of students' nonverbal behaviors, they may also suggest that ESL students need to be more active in telling teachers when they have difficulty understanding specific terms or ideas.

Finally, you selectively remember some things while selectively forgetting others. **Selective retention** is the tendency to remember better the things that reinforce your beliefs than those that oppose them[10] Even a loving mother may have put you on "time out" now and then, but your dominant impression of her as positive gets reinforced by your selectively remembering happy family holidays, vacations, and graduation. Often any negative events are suppressed, unless they were unusually traumatic.

How does selective retention function in your everyday communication? You unexpectedly meet someone on the street with whom you went to school some years ago. You immediately remember the person—as a bully who picked on you. Do you greet him or head in the other direction without a word? If you do speak, what do you say? Your selective retention of this person's past deeds greatly influences your choice.

You remember traumatic events and experiences that you found exciting or threatening. You remember when someone was unfairly critical of you, and when someone of importance praised your work. You might repress the pain of giving birth but remember the baby with fondness. You size up people every day. Based on your experience with them—your selective retention—you treat them with respect, talk with them, or avoid them. Such is the power of your selective retention. Next you will learn how organization functions in perceptions and affects communication.

ORGANIZATION

You organize what your senses tell you about your surroundings. **Organization** in perception is the grouping of stimuli into meaningful units or wholes. You organize stimuli in a number of ways, through figure and ground, closure, proximity, and similarity.

Figure and Ground

One organization method is to distinguish between figure and ground. **Figure** is the focal point of your attention, and **ground** is the background against which your focused attention occurs. When looking at figure 2.1, some people might perceive a vase or a candlestick, whereas others perceive twins facing each other. People who see a vase identify the center of the drawing as the figure and the area on the right and left as the ground (background). Conversely, people who see twins facing each other identify the center as the ground and the area on the right and left as the figure.

How do figure and ground work in communication encounters? In your verbal and nonverbal exchanges, you perform a similar feat of focusing on some parts (figure) and distancing yourself from others (ground). When you hear your name in a noisy room, your name becomes figure and the remaining noise becomes ground; on a posted list of which applicants should return for an interview, your name is figure and everyone else's name becomes ground.

Here's another example. During a job evaluation your manager may talk about your weaknesses and strengths, but the so-called weaknesses may make you so angry that you don't even remember the strengths. The messages about weaknesses are figure, and the ones about strengths are ground. Because of who and what you are and because of your unique perceptual processes, your attention focuses and fades, and you choose the figure or ground of what you see, hear, smell, touch, and taste.

Closure

Another way of organizing stimuli is through **closure,** the tendency to fill in missing information to complete an otherwise incomplete figure or statement. If someone were to show you figure 2.2 and ask you what you see, you might say it is a picture of a cat. But as you can see, the figure is incomplete. You see a cat only if you are willing to fill in the blank areas.

organization
The grouping of stimuli into meaningful units or wholes.

figure
The focal point of your attention.

ground
The background against which your focused attention occurs.

closure
The tendency to fill in missing information in order to complete an otherwise incomplete figure or statement.

Figure 2.1 (left)
An example of figure and ground: a vase or twins?

Figure 2.2 (right)
An example of closure: ink blobs or a cat?

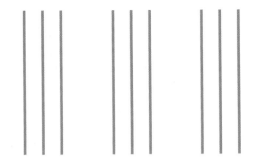

> ### Figure **2.3**
>
> An example of proximity: three groups of lines or nine separate lines?

Another example of closure happens with text. Can you read these lines?

I cdnuolt blveiee that I cluod aulacity uesdnatnrd waht I was rdanieg. The phaonmneal pweor of the hmuan mnid! It deson't matter in what oredr the ltteers in a wrod are; the olny iprmoatnt tihng is that the frist and lsat ltteer be in the rghit pclae.[11]

The reason you can read these words in spite of the crazy spelling is your mind's ability to achieve closure.

Closure functions in your communication interactions. You see two people standing face-to-face and gazing deeply into each other's eyes, and you "fill in" your inference that they are lovers. A public speaker says, "We need to preserve our neighborhoods," and you assume she is against the proposed low-income housing. Visual closure might involve completing the circle or seeing the cat, but mental closure means filling in the meaning of what you hear and observe.

Proximity

proximity
The principle that objects physically close to each other will be perceived as a unit or group.

You also organize stimuli on the basis of their proximity. According to the principle of **proximity,** people or objects that are close to each other in time or space are seen as meaningfully related. This principle is at work in figure 2.3. You are most likely to perceive three groups of three lines, rather than nine separate lines.

Proximity works verbally and nonverbally in communication. Nonverbal examples include thinking that the person standing next to the cash register is the cashier and that the two people entering the room at the same time are together. And here is a verbal example: your boss announces that, due to an economic downturn, she is forced to lay off 25 employees. Fifteen minutes later, she calls you into her office. The proximity of the messages leads you to believe that you will be laid off.

Similarity

similarity
The principle that elements are grouped together because they share attributes, such as size, color, or shape.

Similarity is probably one of the simplest means of organizing stimuli. On the basis of the principle of **similarity,** elements are grouped together because they resemble each other in size, color, shape, or other attributes. The saying "Birds of a feather flock together" can hold true as well for human groups, who are often organized by ethnicity, religion, politics, or their interest in bowling, golfing, or NASCA racing. In figure 2.4, you probably perceive circles and squares, rather than a group of geometric shapes, because of the principle of similarity.

How does similarity work in our relationships and our interactions? Generally, we seek mates, friends, and work partners based on similarity. We choose to interact with those who are similar, on some dimension, to ourselves. Because our perceptions are egocentric, we choose to communicate with those we believe are similar to us. In other words, our friends tend to represent some part of ourselves.[12] We reject, or certainly are less interested in interacting with people who are highly different from the way we see ourselves. The TV

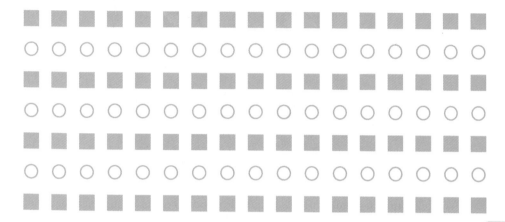

Figure 2.4

An example of similarity: squares and circles or a group of geometric shapes?

show *The Big Bang Theory* illustrates the concept nicely: Sheldon, Howard, and Raj hang out together because of their high IQs and their interest in physics and engineering.

To understand the relationship between the organization of stimuli and communication, think about a classroom setting. When you enter the room, your tendency is to organize the stimuli, or people there, into specific groups. Your primary focus is on acquaintances and friends—the *figure*—rather than on the strangers, who function as the *ground*. You talk to friends sitting near the doorway as you enter, due to their *proximity*. You then seat yourself near a group of students you perceive as having interests identical to yours, thus illustrating *similarity*. Finally, you see your instructor arrive with another professor of communication; they are laughing, smiling, and conversing enthusiastically. *Closure* is a result of your assumption that they have a social relationship outside the classroom.

INTERPRETATION

The third activity you engage in during perception is interpretation, the assignment of meaning to stimuli. **Interpretive perception,** then, is a blend of internal states and external stimuli. The more ambiguous the stimuli, the more room for interpretation. The basis for the well-known inkblot test lies in the principle of interpretation of stimuli. Figure 2.5 shows three inkblots that a psychologist might ask you to interpret. The ambiguity of the figures is typical.

interpretive perception Perception that involves a blend of internal states and external stimuli.

Figure 2.5

An example of interpretation: the inkblot.

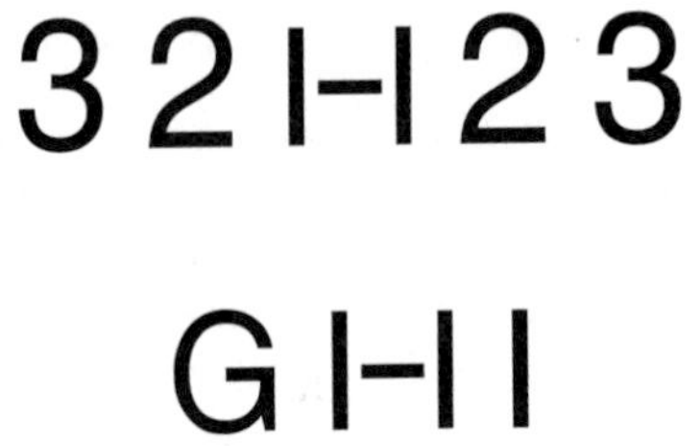

3 2 1-1 2 3

G 1-1 1

Figure 2.6

An example of the usefulness of context in the interpretation of stimuli.

When interpreting stimuli, people frequently rely on the context in which the stimuli are perceived, or they compare the stimuli to other stimuli (figure 2.6). Sometimes context helps, but other times it can create confusion in interpretation.

You can become so accustomed to seeing people, places, and situations in a certain way that your senses do not pick up on the obvious. Many people who read the following sentence will overlook the problem with it:

The cop saw the man standing on the the street corner.

We achieve closure on the sentence and interpret its meaning without being conscious of the details, so we overlook the repeated *the*. Context provides cues for how an action, an object, or a situation is to be interpreted or perceived. Not seeing the double *the* in the sentence would be no problem for a reader trying to comprehend meaning, but a proof-reader's job would be in jeopardy if such an error were missed often.

How does interpretation work in our interactions with others? Imagine that you are working in a group in one of your classes. One member of the group always comes prepared and seems to dominate the group interaction and to dictate the direction the project is taking. Another member of the group frequently misses agreed-upon group meeting times, arrives late when he does come, and is never prepared. How do you interpret the behavior of these two people?

Suppose you are more like the first group member than the second. You might feel that the first person is challenging your leadership in the group. On the other hand, you consider the enormous contributions she makes by bringing a great deal of research and planning each time. You dismiss the second person as lazy and unmotivated and as a poor student. You are worried that he will bring the group grade down.

Now suppose you are more like the second group member than the first. You miss meetings, arrive late, and do virtually nothing to prepare. You might interpret the first person's behavior as showing off, but, at the same time, you are glad she is going to lead the group to a good grade. You see the second person as laid-back and fun. In fact, you decide you would like to hang out with him. Thus, our own behavior can lead us to make very different interpretations.

What Errors Do We Make in Our Perceptions?

Once we understand the active nature of perception and recognize that people hold unique perceptions as a consequence, we can see that we might make errors when we perceive other people. Although many types of errors exist, we discuss only two of the most common errors here, stereotyping and relying on first impressions. Detailed discussions of the many types of errors are an exercise for psychology classes or upper-level communication classes.

STEREOTYPING

Stereotyping occurs when we offer a hasty generalization about a group based on a judgment about an individual from that group. How does stereotyping work? First we categorize other people into groups based on a variety of criteria—age, sex, race, sexual orientation, occupation, region of the country, or physical abilities. Next we infer that everyone within that group has the same characteristics. For instance, we might conclude that all lesbians are masculine, that people on the East Coast are fast-talking, or that older people are conservative. The trouble with stereotyping is that we practically insist that our stereotypes are correct through selective attention (we see what we want to see) and selective retention (we selectively sift through our past for memories that reinforce our stereotypes).

Our expectations and interpretations of the behavior of others are then guided by these perceptions. When we observe people from other groups, we exaggerate, or overestimate, how frequently they engage in the stereotypic behaviors we believe they engage in. We ignore, or underestimate, how frequently they engage in the behaviors that we do not believe they engage in. Although some stereotypes are positive (such as Asians and Indians are brilliant at math, engineering, and science), most are negative and harmful.

Unfortunately, our stereotypes of people from different groups are often negative.[13] Men might hold some negative views of women. White Americans might incorrectly believe that African Americans are not as qualified for higher education as they are. If you are able-bodied, you might not empathize with someone in a wheelchair. Hughes and Baldwin found that these negative stereotypes created different communication patterns when white and black individuals, for example, interacted. They suggest that "macrolevel interpretations between interracial speakers may be problematic."[14]

Our explanations for the expected and unexpected behaviors of people are frequently in error, as we assume situational reasons for unexpected outcomes and personal reasons for expected outcomes. For example, if we believe that teenagers are foolhardy and high risk takers, we explain the behavior of a careful and conservative teenager by concluding that this is her "public behavior" and that she actually behaves differently in private.

Finally, we differentiate ourselves from people whom we stereotype. A woman who has some African American heritage but does not identify with that heritage might view other black people as possessing qualities that are different from her own. A man who has only a little Hispanic background but is proud of this heritage may see people who are not Hispanic as boring and too cautious.

Stereotypes can lead to prejudices. **Prejudice** refers to an unfavorable predisposition about an individual because of his or her membership in a stereotyped group. Although prejudice can be positive or negative, most often it reflects a harmful or hostile attitude about a person based on his or her membership in a particular social or ethnic group. Throughout history and around the world, people have held negative stereotypes, and they have been prejudiced against others. But such perceptual problems can stand in the way of fruitful communication among people who are different from each other.

Prejudice interferes with our accurate perceptions of others, and it can lead to discrimination. For example, women might not be hired for particular jobs because of prejudice against them. People may be disallowed housing because of their religious beliefs. People may fear others because of their racial or ethnic background. The color of people's skin, the texture of their hair, the shape and size of their facial features, and their clothing are sometimes used to identify an **out-group,** that is, a group marginalized by the dominant culture.

FIRST IMPRESSIONS

Each of us seeks to form a **first impression** of others—an initial opinion about people upon meeting that person. Frequently, these first impressions are based on other people's appearance

stereotyping
A hasty generalization about a group based on a judgment about an individual from that group.

prejudice
An unfavorable predisposition about an individual because of his membership in a stereotyped group.

out-group
a group of people excluded from another group with higher status; a group marginalized by the dominant culture

first impression
An initial opinion about people upon meeting them.

First impressions are quick, powerful, and sometimes inaccurate.

perceptual checking
A process of describing, interpreting, and verifying that helps us understand another person and his or her message more accurately.

and may form in as little as 3 seconds.[15] The nonverbal cues they offer are particularly powerful. We notice clothing, height and weight, physical attractiveness, and interaction skills. From these nonverbal cues we make a snap judgment.

As we form our first impressions of others, we also compare the new person with ourselves. According to Sterling, we make certain comparisons and draw certain conclusions in business settings.[16] For example, if others appear to be of a business or social level comparable to our own, we decide they are worthy of further interaction. If they appear to be of a higher level, we admire them and cultivate them as a valuable contact. If they appear to be of lower status, we tolerate them but keep them at arm's length.

Our first impressions are powerful, and sometimes they lead to errors in our assessment of others. Imagine a businessperson who has traveled all day and arrives late for a meeting. Her flight was delayed, her luggage was lost en route, and she is disheveled and harried. New business acquaintances might dismiss her simply on the grounds of her appearance.

First impressions can be affected by specific situations or circumstances that the other person is experiencing, making our initial assessment inaccurate. Just the same, we tend to cling to these impressions in future interactions. Rather than altering our opinion, we filter out new information that disputes our original appraisal. According to Ambady and Skowronski in their book *First Impressions,* "a positive first impression may be easily reversed by information to the contrary, but a negative first impression may persist even in the face of contradictory information."[17]

Our perceptions of others rest on a subjective, active, and creative perceptual process. Our perceptions of others are unique, and we perceive individuals in multiple ways through multiple interactions. We can more fairly appraise others and their behavior by understanding common attribution and perceptual errors and the extent to which we are engaged in them.

Another important skill is **perceptual checking,** a process of describing, interpreting, and verifying that helps you understand another person and his or her message more accurately. Perceptual checking has three steps. First, you describe to the other person the behavior—including the verbal and nonverbal cues—that you observed. Second, you suggest plausible interpretations. Third, you seek verification through clarification, explanation, or amplification.

For example, imagine that you are assigned a group research project in one of your classes. Another member of the group asks you to produce all your primary sources for the project. You presented this source material weeks ago. You respond by saying, "I understand that you want me to give you my primary sources" (describe the behavior or the message). "I have a feeling that you do not trust me" (first interpretation). "Or maybe you just want to create the bibliography for the whole group" (second interpretation). "Can you explain why you want my primary sources" (request for clarification).

Perceptual checking may be even more important in our personal or romantic relationships. Suppose a casual friend provides you with a very romantic birthday present. You begin by describing the behavior: "The gift you gave me was very romantic." You then suggest alternative interpretations: "Perhaps you want to change the nature of our relationship" (first interpretation). "Maybe this gift was for someone else" (second interpretation). "Maybe you don't view the gift as romantic" (third interpretation). Or you can just ask for clarification at the outset by inquiring: "Can you tell me what you intended?"

In perceptual checking, you must suggest interpretations that do not cause the other person to be defensive. In the first instance, imagine that you offered as one explanation

"Maybe you want my primary sources so you can claim that you did all the research." The other person is most likely to become defensive. In the second instance, you could have offered "Maybe you don't realize that I don't want a romantic relationship with you." Most likely, embarrassment and a loss of face would follow.

Another example occurred in Falls Church, Virginia, at a medical clinic where patients from Central America did not keep their appointments. The healthcare workers had to do some follow-up to learn about the cultural differences. They needed to describe

skill builder

Check Your Perceptions

With a partner in class, name a physical feature of yourself that you think affects your communication with others, such as height, weight, skin color, age, hairstyle, clothing, jewelry, scars, or tattoos. First say how you think this feature affects your communication with others. Next let the other person says how he or she perceives this feature. Then switch roles and repeat. You are checking each other's perceptions about a feature that affects your communication.

the behavior of keeping appointments, suggest an interpretation, but then allow the patients to explain the practice. Perceptual checks were also necessary when physicians learned that they could not look directly at a Hmong man and that breast self-exam programs for Muslim women needed to be conducted before regular hours, so that no men were on the property. Women from other countries report being surprised by the directness and invasiveness of male physicians' questions and sometimes do not answer these questions truthfully or fully.[18] The healthcare workers must continue to do perceptual checks to ensure that the women are receiving the best medical care possible.

Who Are You?

Discussing perception naturally leads us to look at self-perception. How you perceive yourself plays a central role in communication, regardless of whether the communication is on Facebook, in a text message, or on your smartphone. An early step in considering yourself a communicator is to think about who you are.

HOW YOU BECAME WHO YOU ARE

What you know about yourself includes your past, present, and future. Your past goes all the way back to how you were reared or how your family taught you to think, believe, and behave. You began as a spontaneous creature who cried when hungry or frustrated, lashed out when angry, and giggled and beamed when happy. Over time, adults took away some of your spontaneity until you behaved as a little adult—you ate at mealtimes, held your anger in check, laughed when appropriate, and cried little if at all. Your emotions, as well as your physical responses, were altered to make you responsible for your own behavior.

The personal identity that you have developed influences your perceptions of others.[19] If you see yourself as a shy person who keeps to yourself and does not invite social exchange with others, then you are likely to perceive others as unwelcome or possibly even threatening. Your self-perception will have a profound effect on your communication with others because you dislike interacting with other people. You are not, however, stuck with whatever self-perception you have at the moment.

Personal identities can be changed, and people can improve their behavior as a result. For example, some low-income and minority teens who had low academic attainment were taught strategies that allowed them to develop a "new academic possible self." These students then achieved higher grades, scored higher on standardized tests, and showed greater academic initiative. At the same time, their levels of depression, absenteeism, and in-school misbehavior declined.[20]

How can personal identity research be applied to communication? When a speaker creates a message that points up shared values with listeners, then the listeners perceive a personal identity match and are more likely to be persuaded by the message. Other factors may interfere with this cause–effect relationship, however. For example, if the shared values are unexpected because of someone's political party membership or other social group affiliations, the message may be rejected and the persuasive attempt may fail.[21]

Your awareness of who you are develops in your communication with yourself, that is, your intrapersonal communication as defined in Chapter 1. Shedletsky writes that intrapersonal communication includes "our perceptions, memories, experiences, feelings, interpretations, inferences, evaluations, attitudes, opinions, ideas, strategies, images, and states of consciousness."[22] Intrapersonal communication can be viewed as talking to ourselves; it is also synonymous with thinking. Intrapersonal communication appears to be the most common context of communication, the foundation for the other contexts.

Your awareness of who you are also develops in your communication with others. Once you mastered language, **symbolic interactionism**—the process of development of the self through the messages and feedback received from others[23]—shaped you in ways that made you what you are today. You may have been punished for acting up in class, rewarded for athletic skill, or ignored for saying too little. The result is the person you see in the mirror today.

To explore who you are, you may be assigned a speech of self-introduction. This speech may be the first one you deliver in class. Since you know more about yourself than does anyone else in the classroom, you will probably feel very little anxiety about this assignment. Of course, you will want to provide some basic information about yourself—your name, where you are from, and your current major in college.

But consider some of the more remarkable and memorable information you can share. Instead of beginning your brief talk with basic information, consider providing some information that is provocative and that will gain the attention of your audience. For example, one student began, "How many people do you know who fly an airplane and have also jumped out of one?" Another speaker stated, "I've been in 40 of the 50 states." A third noted, "I have never lived anyplace but in this city." These three students found some aspect about themselves to be unique. In one case, the student was adventuresome and a risk taker; the second student had enjoyed a great deal of travel with his family; and the third realized that her stability allowed her to nurture her roots.

The speech of self-introduction will allow you to draw on the information in this chapter and it will give you a relatively stress-free way to begin giving talks in this class. Here are some tips for being effective in your self-introduction:

1. Be honest and don't exaggerate. You might be tempted to invent information about yourself or to make some of your experiences more extreme than they actually were. This idea is not a good one because it destroys your credibility. Your fellow students will not believe information you provide in later speeches.

symbolic interactionism The process in which the self develops through the messages and feedback received from others.

sizing things up

What Messages Shaped You?

Answer the following questions about yourself to test for the influence of symbolic interactionism.

1. What messages did you receive that urged you to seek education beyond high school? From whom did you receive them?
2. What messages did you receive about what you should study in your education beyond high school? From whom did you receive them?
3. What messages did you receive about how you are supposed to relate to men? To women? From whom did you receive them?
4. What messages did you receive about your religious beliefs, if any? From whom did you receive them?
5. What messages did you receive about your political beliefs, if any? From whom did you receive them?

This exercise has no right answers, but the lesson you can learn is that others throughout our lives communicate with us about how we are supposed to think and behave. We are shaped by the many messages we receive from parents, teachers, friends, and others.

2. Make sure the information you provide makes a point. To conclude your talk, you should provide an answer to the "so what?" question. Why did you choose to share the information you did? Was the point of your skydiving about goal setting and goal achievement? Was it part of a group that allowed team building? Why did you choose to skydive?

3. Be creative in your language when you tell the story of who you are. Carefully selected language encourages audience interest. Using comparisons with other known information might be helpful. For example, if you are telling the class about how safe airline travel is, you could note, "Many people are afraid of spiders, but in the United States the only dangerous species are the widows and the recluse spiders. People also have an unreasonable fear of piloting a plane, but your risk of dying in a plane crash is only 1 in 11 million."

4. Do not provide detail that is unnecessary in telling the story. Some speakers go off on tangents and get off the topic. Others offer every element of their experiences: "Then after we took Interstate 29 South, we chose state highway 34 East, which becomes highway 32 in the next state."

5. If you can, gather information from people who are close to you. Can they provide a useful quote or additional information from their point of view that helps tell the story? Sometimes another person's point of view adds spice to the story.

6. Finally, you want to conclude with a memorable statement that parallels the introduction to your presentation. If you begin with the statement "I am not a registered voter," you might want to end it with "I am going to register now because I live in Florida, the state that determines presidential elections."

LEARNING MORE ABOUT YOURSELF

Perhaps you now understand why the ancients said, "Know thyself." They, like people today, believed that self-awareness is a discovery worth making. Accurate self-awareness tells you which choices are open to you and which ones are not. If you hate chemistry, you should not become a physician or pharmacist. If you like to write and are good at it, you may have a future as a writer. If you are skillful at athletics, perhaps you can take advantage of that talent with scholarships, varsity sports, and even professional sports. What you have learned about yourself in the past, and what you learn about yourself today, will affect your future.

In the here-and-now, you should be aware of what kind of person you are. Are you timid, shy, and unassertive? Are you healthy, vigorous, and energetic? Do you welcome change, adventure, and risk? Do you see yourself as capable, unstoppable, and hard-driving? The answers to these and many other questions are the key to your self-awareness. As Will Schutz notes, "Given a complete knowledge of myself, I can determine my life; lacking that mastery, I am controlled in ways that are often undesirable, unproductive, worrisome, and confusing."[24]

Joseph O'Connor was a high school junior when he spent two weeks in the Sierra Nevada mountain range of northeastern California—a challenge that changed his level of self-awareness. Rain poured, hail pelted, and the beauty of dawn at 13,000 feet entranced him. Writing about his self-awareness in an article titled "A View from Mount Ritter: Two Weeks in the Sierras Changed My Attitude Toward Life and What It Takes to Succeed," O'Connor states:

> The wonder of all I'd experienced made me think seriously about what comes next. "Life after high school," I said to myself. "Uh-oh." What had I been doing the last three years? I was so caught up in defying the advice of my parents and teachers to study and play by the rules that I hadn't considered the effects my actions would have on me.[25]

New experiences may lead to increased self-knowledge.

O'Connor's experience changed his self-awareness, and he went from being a D student to one who made the honor roll.

You don't have to go to the mountains to come to a new awareness of yourself. If you want to learn more about yourself, you can take several steps to achieve that goal. If you want to learn more about your physical self, you should get an annual physical examination. You can also talk to your relatives about the causes of death of older people in your family. What health ailments do your parents and grandparents face? Are these problems inherited?

If you want to learn more about your personality and how others perceive you, you can talk with your spouse or partner, friends, co-workers, bosses, and even your children if you are a parent. Consider other features of your life that will suggest how you are perceived. Do people seek you out as a relational partner? Do others ask you to participate in social events? Do friends ask you for advice? Also consider the number of friends you have.

What kind of worker are you? Do you like to work alone or with others? What kinds of jobs have you held? Have you been given increasing amounts of responsibility in those jobs, or have you frequently lost jobs? Do your grades indicate that you are motivated and disciplined or that you are not living up to your potential? Do others seek you out to partner with them on work or school projects?

Are you skillful in communication? Do you enjoy public speaking and receive invitations to talk to others at work or in the community? Can you listen to others uncritically and empathize with them? Are you adept at problem solving or conflict resolution? Are you an effective and adaptive leader? Are you apprehensive about communication? Are you argumentative? You can learn about your communication skills or deficits through a number of research methods. For example, the last three concepts can be found on the Web by typing "Leader Effectiveness and Adaptability," "Personal Report of Communication Apprehension," and "Argumentativeness Scale," respectively, into a search engine. Many valid and reliable instruments measuring communication constructs can be found online, in communication journals, and in resource books.

How Do You Present Yourself?

In this chapter we have shown the relationship among perception, self-perception, and communication. Communication and perception influence each other. Communication is largely responsible for our self-perceptions. Communication can also be used to change the perceptions that others have of us. We attempt to influence others' perceptions of ourselves through self-presentation.

In our daily interactions we present ourselves to people, both consciously and unconsciously. Self-presentation can be defined as the way we portray ourselves to others. Generally, our self-presentation is consistent with an ideal self-image, allows us to enact an appropriate role, influences others' view of us, permits us to define the situation in our terms, and/or influences the progress of an interaction.

identity management
The control (or lack of control) of the communication of information through a performance.

Erving Goffman first described the process of self-presentation.[26] Goffman adopted the symbolic interactionist perspective mentioned earlier. He described everyday interactions through a dramaturgical, or theater arts, viewpoint. His theory embraces individual identity, group relationships, the context (the situation), and the interactive meaning of information. Individuals are viewed as "actors," and interaction is seen as a "performance" shaped by the context and constructed to provide others with "impressions" consistent with the desired goals of the actor. **Identity management** is thus defined as the control (or lack of control) of the communication of information through a performance. Through identity management, people try to present an idealized version of themselves to reach desired ends.

You may believe that you do not engage in identity management. However, a number of research studies illustrate that people act differently when they are being viewed than when they are not. For example, people speaking on a telephone who are expressing empathy or shared emotions do not engage in facial responsiveness, whereas people expressing the same sentiments in face-to-face encounters do.[27] Investigations in this area suggest that people generally do engage in identity management in their face-to-face interactions.

In the next two chapters, you will learn more about verbal and nonverbal communication. Your understanding of these symbolic means of communicating will be enhanced by your understanding of identity management. Wiggins, Wiggins, and Vander Zanden suggest that three essential types of communication are used to manage impressions: manner, appearance, and setting.[28] Manner includes both verbal and nonverbal codes. Your manner might be seen as brusque, silly, businesslike, immature, friendly, warm, or gracious. Your appearance may suggest a role you are playing (administrative assistant), a value you hold (concern for the environment), your personality (easygoing), or your view of the communication setting (unimportant). The setting includes your immediate environment (the space in which you communicate) as well as other public displays of who you are (the kind of home in which you live, the type of automobile you drive).

cultural note

Differences in Memory

The dominant culture in the United States places the self in the spotlight, whereas most Asian cultures, such as the Chinese, emphasize the group over the individual. Notice that people in the United States write their given (first) name followed by the family name, whereas the Chinese start with the family name followed by their given name. For the Chinese, the group (family) comes before the self. These differences in emphasis extend even to the way people remember.

Research by Qi Wang and her associates shows that American adults and preschool children recall their personal memories differently than do indigenous Chinese. Since our self-concept is dependent on our self-awareness, these cultural differences are important.

"Americans often report lengthy, specific, emotionally elaborate memories that focus on the self as a central character," says Wang. "Chinese tend to give brief accounts of general routine events that center on collective activities and are often emotionally neutral. These individual-focused vs. group-oriented styles characterize the mainstream values in American and Chinese cultures, respectively."

Source: Han, J. J., Leichtman, M. D., & Wang, Q. (1998). Autobiographical memory in Korean, Chinese, and American children. *Developmental Psychology, 34*(4): 701–713.

sizing things up

Self-Esteem Scale

Below is a list of statements dealing with your general feelings about yourself. Read each statement carefully and respond by using the following scale:

1 = Strongly agree
2 = Agree
3 = Disagree
4 = Strongly disagree

1. On the whole, I am satisfied with myself.
2. At times I think that I am no good at all.
3. I feel that I have a number of good qualities.
4. I am able to do things as well as most other people.
5. I feel I do not have much to be proud of.
6. I certainly feel useless at times.
7. I feel that I am a person of worth, at least the equal of others.
8. I wish I could have more respect for myself.
9. All in all, I am inclined to feel that I am a failure.
10. I take a positive attitude toward myself.

This exercise has no right or wrong answers; instead, the answers will tell you something about how you feel about yourself. A guide for interpreting your responses appears in the appendix at the end of the text (p. 348).

Source: Rosenberg, M. (1989). *Society and adolescent self-image* (rev. ed.). Middletown, CT: Wesleyan University Press.

keeping it real

Perception and Communication

Think back to William Turner's comments, which appeared at the beginning of the chapter. How aware are you of the impression you make on people? What types of first impressions do you form of others? Try the following:

■ Think of an example similar to the description by Mr. Turner's friend—a situation in which a first impression you formed turned out to be very inaccurate. Consider why you formed the inaccurate first impression. What types of attribution and perceptual errors were involved? What can you do to avoid those types of errors in the future?

■ Think of an event that recently occurred in your life in which your perception of what happened might have been quite different from the perception of others. Evaluate the reasons why the perception differences occurred.

This chapter invited you to know and understand the link between perception and communication. You have learned now that everything from how you look to how you think can affect your communication with others—on whether you communicate, with whom you communicate, and how you communicate. As part of your growing communication skills, you have to take seriously how you look, dress, and present yourself to others. You have learned the power of perception in communication.

Chapter Review & Study Guide

Summary

In this chapter, you learned the following:

1. Perception is our use of our senses to gather information about the environment or the situation we are in.

2. Differences occur in perception for many reasons, including psychological factors, past experiences, and our present feelings and circumstances.

3. Through selection, we neglect some stimuli in our environment and focus on others. Organization in perception is the grouping of stimuli into meaningful units or wholes. Interpretation is the way we assign meaning to stimuli.

4. Some ways in which we organize stimuli are figure and ground, closure, proximity, and similarity. Figure and ground refers to our focusing on some parts of an experience

(figure) and distancing ourselves from others (ground). Closure is the tendency to fill in missing information. Proximity encourages us to perceive objects close in space or time as meaningfully related, and similarity is the basis on which we group elements that resemble each other in size, color, or shape.

5. Perceptual errors that affect communication include stereotyping and reliance on first impressions.

6. The way you see yourself affects how and to whom you communicate, regardless of the medium.

7. Identity management is a way for you to influence how others perceive you, usually as an idealized version of yourself.

Key Terms

Active perception
Closure
Figure
First impression
Ground
Identity management
Interpretive perception
Organization

Out-group
Perception
Perceptual checking
Perceptual constancy
Prejudice
Proximity
Role
Selective attention

Selective exposure
Selective perception
Selective retention
Similarity
Stereotyping
Subjective perception
Symbolic interactionism

Study Questions

connect For further review, go to the LearnSmart study module for this chapter.

1. Which of the following may be the result of physiological factors, past experiences and roles, and present conditions?

   a. selection
   b. similarity
   c. self-serving bias
   d. differences in perception

2. By neglecting some stimuli and focusing on other stimuli, you are engaging in which process of perception?

   a. organization
   b. selection
   c. classification
   d. interpretation

3. _____ is an organizational method whereby missing information is filled in to create the appearance of a complete unit, and _____ is another organizational technique whereby elements are grouped based on their similarities in size, color, and shape.

   a. Closure; similarity
   b. Proximity; figure and ground
   c. Similarity; proximity
   d. Closure; proximity

4. The more ambiguous the stimuli,

   a. the less room for confusion.
   b. the more room for interpretation.
   c. the less room for interpretation.
   d. the less you rely on context.

5. Perceptual constancy results because of

   a. physiological factors.
   b. past experiences and roles.
   c. figure and ground.
   d. people's present feelings and circumstances.

6. A system of shared beliefs, values, customs, and behaviors is known as a

   a. person
   b. communicator
   c. role
   d. culture

7. Selection occurs in perception in all of the following ways *except*

   a. attention.
   b. exposure.
   c. distraction.
   d. retention.

8. Which of the following is a perceptual error frequently made by people?

   a. believing stereotypes about people who are different from themselves
   b. believing other people are courageous, whereas they, themselves, are cowardly
   c. believing that others are considerably older than themselves
   d. believing that uneducated people are happier than educated people

9. When people seek to present an ideal version of themselves, they are engaging in

   a. identity management.
   b. active perception.
   c. attribution.
   d. selection.

10. First impressions

    a. generally take weeks or more to develop.
    b. are based on people's sense of humor, their personality, and their religion.
    c. are frequently based on other people's appearance.
    d. are generally accurate and therefore are lasting impressions.

Answers:

1. (d); 2. (b); 3. (a); 4. (b); 5. (b); 6. (d); 7. (c); 8. (a); 9. (a); 10. (c)

Critical Thinking

1. Singer states that people's perceptions are largely learned because what people see, hear, taste, touch, and smell is conditioned by their culture. What parts of your culture are key factors in how you perceive events in day-to-day life?

2. The text discusses how people form impressions of who they are and how communication affects self-perceptions. How do you see yourself? How is this affected by your past, present, and projected future? How do you see yourself differently now than you did when you were younger? How have conversations you have had with friends, coworkers, or other people at college altered the way you see yourself?

language
and meaning

When you have read and thought about this chapter, you will be able to:

1. Define language and understand how it works.

2. Learn the common errors people make in speaking.

3. Avoid those common errors.

This chapter is about the importance of language and how language functions in communication. In this chapter you will learn about the world of language, including the definition of language and its many characteristics. You will learn how you can use language more effectively in your day-to-day interactions with others. Finally, we provide specific suggestions for improving your verbal skills.

Sally Navaro could text or tweet with the best of them, but you don't have to be good with words to do that. Now she was expected to make a make a presentation to a group at work. She was one of several employees being considered for a promotion because she was so good at her job. At least one manager from the head office was going to be listening to her presentation.

Sally had grown up in a family in which speaking perfect English was not expected.

In fact, most of the friends she grew up with were pretty careless about the way they spoke. But as a college student seeking a promotion in the job that was paying for her classes, Sally needed to speak like a college-educated person. She especially needed to impress that manager who was going to decide who would be promoted. Sally could only dream about how much the increase in pay was going to mean to her.

Have you ever found yourself in a situation similar to Sally's? What would you suggest for her? At the end of the chapter, we'll take another look at Sally's situation and consider how she might learn and practice speaking to meet the expectations of managers at her workplace.

This chapter provides the kind of advice you need when you are required to do your very best at speaking to others who have higher expectations for how you use language. When speaking, you don't have a spell checker to tell you when you say something incorrectly, but often you do have time to plan what you are going to say. Learn here about common errors and problems with language and some ways to solve them, so you will do well (not "good") on any presentation that really counts.

Your spouse, your friends, or your supervisor will not tell you that you do not use language correctly, but they probably will notice, and they may judge you negatively without ever telling you. That is why this chapter is dedicated to helping you to know and understand your language and to find and remedy common errors.

We will begin by learning what language is and how words function in your speech. By the end of the chapter you also will have learned about language errors and how to correct them.

What Is Language?

language
A collection of symbols, letters, or words with arbitrary meanings that are governed by rules and used to communicate.

decode
The process of assigning meaning to others' words in order to translate them into thoughts of your own.

Language is a collection of symbols, letters, or words with arbitrary meanings that are governed by rules and used to communicate. Language consists of words or symbols that represent things without being those things. The word *automobile* is a symbol for a vehicle that runs on gasoline, but the symbol is not the vehicle itself. When you listen to others' verbal communication, you **decode,** or assign meaning to, their words to translate them into thoughts of your own. Because language is an imperfect means of transmission, the thoughts expressed by one person never exactly match what is decoded by another. So, lesson one about language is that it is an imperfect process that often requires corrections.

Verbal communication is essential in practically everything we do, from doing well at work to relating to friends and relatives. Both writing and speaking rely on the use of language. Verbal communication represents one of the two major codes of communication;

the other is nonverbal communication, which we will discuss in the next chapter. In chapter 4 we will consider the similarities and differences between these two codes.

Our definition tells you that language consists of words or symbols, has rules, and is arbitrary, but the definition does not reveal some of the other important characteristics of language. Language is also abstract, is intertwined with culture, and organizes and classifies reality. In this section we take a closer look at each of these characteristics.

LANGUAGE HAS RULES

Language has multiple rules. Three sets of rules are relevant to our discussion: semantic rules, syntactic rules, and pragmatic rules. **Semantics** is the study of the way humans use language to evoke meaning in others. Semantics focuses on individual words and their meaning. Semanticists—people who study semantics—are interested in how language and its meaning change over time.

Whereas semantics focuses on the definition of specific words, **syntax** is the way in which words are arranged to form phrases and sentences. For example, in the English language the subject is usually placed before the verb, and the object after the verb. Other languages have different rules of syntax, including reading from right to left. You **encode** by translating your thoughts into words. Syntax changes the meaning of the same set of words. For example, the declarative statement "I am going tomorrow" uses syntax to signal that someone is leaving the next day. If you change the word arrangement to "Am I going tomorrow?" the statement becomes a question and acquires a different meaning.

Pragmatics is the study of language as it is used in a social context, including its effect on the communicators. Messages are variable, depending on the situation. Ambiguous messages, such as "How are you?" "What's new?" and "You're looking good," have different meanings, depending on the context. For example, many people use such phrases as **phatic communication**—communication that is used to establish a mood of sociability rather than to communicate information or ideas. Indeed, they would be surprised if someone offered serious or thoughtful answers to such questions or statements. On the other hand, if you are visiting your grandmother who has been ill, your questions about how she is feeling are sincere and designed to elicit information. Similarly, you might genuinely be complimenting another person's new haircut, tattoo, or tongue bolt when you tell him he is looking good. Pragmatic rules help us interpret meaning in specific contexts.

LANGUAGE AND CULTURE ARE INTERTWINED

Although we will talk about the role of intercultural communication in a later chapter, it is important to note the relationship between language and culture here. **Culture** may be defined as all of the socially transmitted behavior patterns, beliefs, attitudes, and values of a particular period, class, community, or population. We often think of the culture of a country (Greek culture), institution (the culture of higher education), organization (the Facebook culture), or group of people (the Hispanic culture). Culture and language are thus related as the transmission of culture occurs through language.

The relationship between culture and language is not as simple as it might first appear, however. Let us take the example of women and men and communication. Several years ago, books and articles were written on the differences between women and men in their communicative practices. As this research further developed, *gender* was expanded to refer to a complex social construct rather than simple biological sex. Some authors argued that gender was just as important as social class in understanding variations in communication.[1]

semantics
The study of the way humans use language to evoke meaning in others.

syntax
The way in which words are arranged to form phrases and sentences.

encode
The process of translating your thoughts into words.

pragmatics
The study of language as it is used in a social context, including its effect on the communicators.

phatic communication
Communication that is used to establish a mood of sociability rather than to communicate information or ideas.

culture
The socially transmitted behavior patterns, beliefs, attitudes, and values of a particular period, class, community, or population.

Language and culture are related in a second way. Culture creates a lens through which we perceive the world and create shared meaning. Language thus develops in response to the needs of the culture or to the perceptions of the world. Edward Sapir and Benjamin Lee Whorf were among the first to discuss the relationship between language and perception. The **Sapir-Whorf hypothesis,** as their theory has become known, states that our perception of reality is determined by our thought processes, our thought processes are limited by our language, and therefore that language shapes our reality.[2] Language is the principal way that we learn about ourselves, others, and our culture.[3]

Sapir-Whorf hypothesis
A theory that our perception of reality is determined by our thought processes, our thought processes are limited by our language, and therefore that language shapes our reality.

The Sapir-Whorf hypothesis has been illustrated in multiple cultures.[4] The Hopi language serves as an early example. The Hopi people do not distinguish between nouns and verbs. In many languages, nouns are given names that suggest that they remain static over time. For example, we assume that words such as *professor, physician, lamp,* and *computer* refer to people or objects that are relatively unchanging. Verbs are action words that suggest change. When we use words such as *heard, rehearsed, spoke,* and *ran,* we assume alterations and movement. The Hopi, by avoiding the distinction between nouns and verbs, thus refer to people and objects in the world as always changing.

Other examples come from the terms we use for various colors. For instance, the color spectrum allows us to understand colors as blending into each other and allowing an infinite number of colors, but leading scientists agree on only seven component colors of white light: red, orange, yellow, green, blue, indigo, and violet.

People who use color in their work (artists, designers) probably use many more color terms than do those for whom color is not so important (firefighters, police officers). The first group might readily describe persimmon, puce, lavender, and fuchsia, whereas the second group limits their vocabulary (and thus their perceptions) to orange, red, purple, and pink.

People who speak different languages also have different color terms than those who speak English. The color blue is familiar to most English speakers—both in their vocabulary and as a recognized color. English speakers use the word *blue* to refer to shades ranging from cyan to sky to navy to midnight blue. In Vietnamese and in Korean, a single word refers to blue or green. Japanese people use the word *ao* to refer to blue, but the color they are referencing is (for English speakers) green. Finally, Russian speakers do not have a single word for the range of colors that English speakers denote as blue; instead, they have one word for light blue and another for dark blue.

Waquet and Howe wrote an enlightening treatise on this topic. In *Latin: A Symbol's Empire,* they trace the domination of Latin in the civic and religious worlds of Europe.[5] Latin's influence on the entire world followed as scholars, educational institutions, and the Roman Catholic Church adopted Latin as their official language. Like any other language, Latin affects perception and the development of culture. The domination of the language has surely shaped the cultures of many Western countries.

The Sapir-Whorf hypothesis, although complex, is not universally accepted by people who study language. For example, critics point out that Inuits may have a large number of words for snow because of their view of snow or because they actually have more varieties of snow in their world. Artists may have more color terms, and printers more words for different fonts, simply because of their work and environment. Thus, the critics note, thought and language may not be intimately related, but experience and language are. Our need to describe our environment and the items within it cause us to create language to do so.

LANGUAGE ORGANIZES AND CLASSIFIES REALITY

Because you cannot account for all the individual things in the world when you speak, you lump them into groups; thus, all four-legged pieces of furniture with seats and backs are called "chairs." Following is an example of how you might use classification when trying to identify someone in a crowd:

"See that guy over there?"

"Which one?"

"The tall one."

"The one with short brown hair?"

"No, the heavy one with shoulder-length hair and glasses."

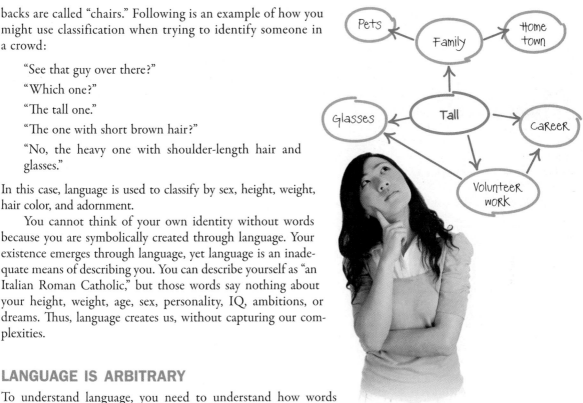

In this case, language is used to classify by sex, height, weight, hair color, and adornment.

You cannot think of your own identity without words because you are symbolically created through language. Your existence emerges through language, yet language is an inadequate means of describing you. You can describe yourself as "an Italian Roman Catholic," but those words say nothing about your height, weight, age, sex, personality, IQ, ambitions, or dreams. Thus, language creates us, without capturing our complexities.

LANGUAGE IS ARBITRARY

To understand language, you need to understand how words engender meaning. Words are arbitrary: They have no inherent meanings; they have only the meanings people give them. For example, in the English language, a person who has suffered from a difficult past experience is known as a "victim." When many people use a word to represent an object or idea, the word is included in the dictionary. The agreed-upon meaning or dictionary meaning is called the **denotative meaning.** Including a word in the dictionary, however, neither keeps its meaning from changing nor tells you the **connotative meaning**—an individualized or personalized meaning that may be emotionally laden. Connotative meanings are meanings others have come to hold because of personal or individual experience. For example, the word *love* holds vastly different meanings for people because of their unique experiences with that concept.

To understand connotative meaning further, consider the language that relational couples create. In a romantic relationship you may have pet names for each other, special terms for activities in which you participate, and unique ways to communicate private thoughts in public settings. Bruess and Pearson showed that married couples are most likely to create such terms early in their relationships and that the creation of such terms is associated with relational satisfaction.[6]

Language is symbolic. The words we choose are arbitrary and based on an agreed-upon connection between them and the object or idea that we are referencing. Language varies based on a variety of features of the communicators, including their relational history. When two people hold different arbitrary symbols for a concept or object, they share messages, but not meanings.

Language and its meaning are personal. Each person talks, listens, and thinks in a unique language (and sometimes several), which contains slight variations of its agreed-upon meanings and which may change each minute. Your personal language varies slightly from the agreed-upon meanings. It is shaped by your culture, country, neighborhood, job,

■ Words can have both denotative and connotative meanings.

denotative meaning
The agreed-upon meaning or dictionary meaning of a word.

connotative meaning
An individualized or personalized meaning of a word, which may be emotionally laden.

cultural note

The Importance of Context: The Gullah Mystery

White people in coastal South Carolina thought the black people in their area spoke a very strange kind of English until a linguist unlocked a 200-year-old mystery. The linguist discovered, through ancient records of slave dealers, that the Gullahs—the black people of lowland, coastal Carolina—had originally come from Sierra Leone in West Africa. The reason the Gullahs' language persisted for so long when other tribal languages disappeared in the United States was that the Gullahs proved highly resistant to malaria, a disease that drove the slave owners inland and left the Gullahs in relative isolation.

Source: *Family Across the Sea*, a public television documentary produced by Educational Television of South Carolina.

personality, education, family, friends, recreation, sex, experiences, age, and other factors. The uniqueness of each individual's language provides valuable information as people attempt to achieve common, shared meaning. But because language is so personal, it can also present some difficulties in communication.

The meanings of words also vary when someone uses the same words in different contexts and situations. For example, *glasses* might mean "drinking glasses" if you are in a housewares store but most likely means "eyeglasses" if you are at the optometrist's office. Semanticists say that meaning emerges from context. But in the case of language, context is more than just the situation in which the communication occurs: context includes the communicators' histories, relationships, thoughts, and feelings.

LANGUAGE IS ABSTRACT

Words are abstractions, or simplifications of what they stand for. Words stand for ideas and things, but they are not the same as those ideas and things. People who study meaning say "the word is not the thing." Semanticist S. I. Hayakawa introduced the "ladder of abstraction," which illustrates that words fall somewhere on a continuum from concrete to abstract.[7] Figure 3.1 shows an example of a ladder of abstraction for a dog named Bentley. The words used to describe him become increasingly abstract as you go up the ladder.

Language to Avoid When Speaking

Next we look closely at language to avoid, including grammatical errors and the use of clichés, slang, euphemisms, profanity, jargon, regionalisms, and sexist, racist, heterosexist, and ageist language.

GRAMMATICAL ERRORS

Oral communication, in some situations, does not require the same attention to grammar as does written communication. For example, to hear people say, "Can I go with?" and "We're not sure which restaurant we're going to" are common, but neither of these sentences is desirable in written communication. "May I go with you?" and "We're not sure to which restaurant we're going" are correct but sound stilted because of the informal nature of these hypothetical utterances. Although we are often corrected for making grammatical errors in our writing, we are rarely corrected for speaking incorrectly. On the other hand, some grammatical errors are more obvious than others—for example, "I told him I ain't going to do it" or "Could you pass them there peanuts?" Communicators who make such errors may find that others form negative opinions about them. Grammatical errors are thus particularly problematic in more formal situations or when another person is assessing your competence. When you are in a classroom, a job interview, or a new relationship, grammatical errors may result in a negative outcome.

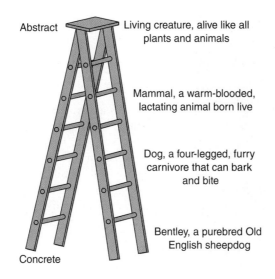

Abstract — Living creature, alive like all plants and animals

Mammal, a warm-blooded, lactating animal born live

Dog, a four-legged, furry carnivore that can bark and bite

Bentley, a purebred Old English sheepdog

Concrete

Figure 3.1

The ladder of abstraction.

Source: Adapted from Hayakawa, S. I. (1978). *Language in thought and action*. Orlando, FL: Harcourt Brace Jovanovich.

Let's tackle a few of the most common grammatical errors in speaking *and* the correct way to say the same thing. These five come from Karen Bond's "Most Annoying Grammar Mistakes in English."

"He don't care about me anymore" should be "He doesn't care about me anymore."

The grocer's "Ten Items or Less" is incorrect because anything countable uses *fewer;* so "Ten Items or Fewer" is correct, as is "You should eat less meat" (not countable).

"I never would of thought he would act like that" should be "I never would have thought he would act like that."

"I'm not speaking to nobody in this class" should be "I'm not speaking to anybody in this class."

"I should have went to school yesterday" should be "I should have gone to school yesterday."[8]

We will look next at words that are a bit too casual for formal presentations but that can slip into your speech if you are not careful, because you may be accustomed to using them every day.

SLANG

Slang is informal, casual street language used among equals with words unsuitable for more formal contexts. In other words, you certainly do use slang among friends out on the street, but such language may be very inappropriate in front of a more formal audience. From www.ManyThings.org come these examples of American slang:

"OK, so don't *get bent*" is slang for "OK, so don't get angry."

"He was *decked* in a bar fight" is slang for "He was knocked down hard in a bar fight."

"Don't *make waves* at the office if you want a promotion" is slang for "Don't cause trouble at the office if you want a promotion."

"Two *big guns* showed up from the head office" is slang for "Two important bosses came from the main office."[9]

slang
Informal, casual street language used among equals with words unsuitable for more formal contexts.

Slang is frequently used in informal situations.

cliché
An expression that has lost originality and force through overuse.

If you want to see hundreds more examples of slang, just type the word *slang* into an online search engine.

CLICHÉS

A **cliché** is an expression that has lost originality and force through overuse. Common clichés include "No pain, no gain," "Beauty is only skin deep," "One for all and all for one," and "No use crying over spilled milk." So many clichés exist that avoiding them would be impossible in your day-to-day conversations, and doing so is unnecessary. Clichés can be a shorthand way to express a common thought. But clichés may be unclear to individuals who are unfamiliar with the underlying idea, and they are usually ineffective in expressing ideas in fresh ways.

The following are a few examples of common American clichés. We provide them here not because we want you to use them, but because we want you to think of more original ways to express your ideas.

all in a day's work

airing dirty laundry

ace in the hole

all's fair in love and war

all thumbs

ants in his pants

at the drop of a hat

as snug as a bug in a rug

barking up the wrong tree

Go to ClicheSite.com for 2,100 more examples of clichés in U.S. English.

EUPHEMISMS

euphemism
A more polite, pleasant expression used instead of a socially unacceptable form.

Like clichés, euphemisms can confuse people who are unfamiliar with their meaning. A **euphemism** is a socially acceptable synonym used to avoid using language that would be offensive in a formal setting. Rothwell observes that euphemisms enter the language to "camouflage the naked truth."[10] Most people use euphemisms in their everyday language. Euphemisms are frequently substituted for short, abrupt words, the names of physical functions, or the terms for some unpleasant social situations. Although euphemisms are frequently considered more polite than the words for which they are substituted, they distort reality. For example, you might hear people say "powder my nose," "see a man about a dog," "visit the little girls' room," or "go to the bathroom" instead of "urinate" or "defecate."

Other examples from military, government, business, and sports contexts include

Military: "Friendly fire" means "killed by your own soldiers" (decidedly unfriendly)

Government: "undocumented worker" means "illegal alien" (worker can be deported)

Business: "preowned" means "used" (and possibly a "junker," a wrecked car)

Sports: "negative yardage" means "thrown for a loss" (an embarrassing reversal)[11]

Euphemisms are not necessarily to be avoided. Although they can disguise the meaning a person is attempting to convey, they can also substitute for rude or obnoxious commentary. Euphemisms, especially unique euphemisms, can add interest to a conversation. They can also reinforce relational closeness as friends and colleagues regularly use similar euphemisms.

PROFANITY

The word *profane* comes from a Latin word meaning "outside the temple." Thus, **profanity** is language that is disrespectful of things sacred or downright vulgar or abusive. That is why many so-called swear words have a religious origin: *God, Jesus, hell,* and *damn* are examples. Other forms of profanity refer to forbidden acts: "Son of a _____" or "Mother _____." Certainly, some people participate in groups in which profanity is common, as it is with the young people on *Jersey Shore*. But when you are speaking to people outside your "group"—especially in professional interviews, work teams, or public-speaking situations—the use of profanity can offend. Profanity, like slang, may provide a vehicle for establishing group norms or developing relational closeness in some settings, but it can also make you immediately lose credibility in other situations.

profanity
Language that is disrespectful of things sacred.

JARGON

Jargon is the language particular to a specific profession, work group, or culture and not meant to be understood by outsiders. In most workplaces the technical support people are famous for their use of words that others do not understand. The *Hacker Dictionary,* available at catb.org/jargon/, reveals the "etiquette" of jargon use by computer experts: "One should use just enough jargon to communication precisely and identify oneself as a member of the culture; overuse of jargon or a breathless, excessively gun-ho attitude is considered tacky and the mark of a loser." In other words, try not to sound like Dr. Sheldon Cooper, the physics Ph.D. on *The Big Bang Theory,* who confuses Penny in every conversation because he apparently cannot talk without using jargon.

jargon
Language particular to a specific profession, work group, or culture and not meant to be understood by outsiders.

If you would like to see hundreds of examples of computer jargon, just go online to www.jonstorm.com/glossary/, where you will find the beginning of a four-part work dedicated to explaining computer jargon.

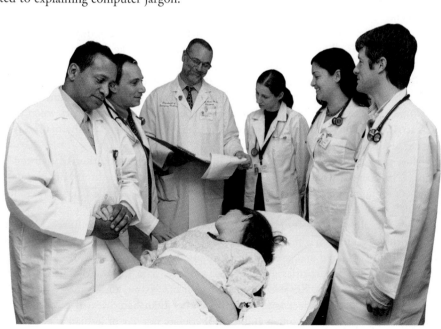

■ Although medical jargon may obstruct communication with patients, nonverbal cues can provide comfort.

You should also consider jargon that you use on the job and how you would translate that jargon to an audience of listeners who were unfamiliar with your work. Very likely, everyone in your class uses some jargon that is unfamiliar to others in the class, but in a communication course the idea is to know how to relate, define, and explain so that your audience learns what you are talking about.

REGIONALISMS

regionalisms
Words and phrases specific to a particular region or part of the country.

Regionalisms are words and phrases specific to a particular region or part of the country. The word *coke* in Texas has the same meaning as *soda* in New York and *pop* in Indiana. When people from different parts of the country try to talk with each other, clarity can break down. Some of us move with frequency from one region of the country to another; others tend to stay in one area. You may believe that you will never leave your home state but find that you are transferred for a new job. Careful listening, which is almost always a good idea, is especially important when you move to a new region. You can fairly easily identify and learn to use language that is particular to a location. Regionalisms encourage group membership for those who use them.

Perhaps the easiest way to illustrate regionalisms is to show the many ways in which people in different areas of the United States refer to those submarine sandwiches that become *hoagies* in Philadelphia, *po' boys* in New Orleans, *grinders* in Boston, *torpedoes* in Los Angeles, *wedgies* in Rhode Island, and *heros* in New York City.[12] Listen before you order your food or drink when you change locations, because your language can mark you as an outsider.

SEXIST, RACIST, HETEROSEXIST, AND AGEIST LANGUAGE

sexist language
Language that excludes individuals on the basis of gender.

racist language
Language that insults a group because of its skin color or ethnicity.

heterosexist language
Language that implies that everyone is heterosexual.

ageist language
Language that denigrates people for being young or old.

Language can communicate prejudice and even silence some members of marginalized groups while privileging other groups.[13] **Sexist language** is language that excludes individuals on the basis of gender; **racist language** is language that insults a group because of its skin color or ethnicity; **heterosexist language** is language that implies that everyone is heterosexual; and **ageist language** is language that denigrates people for being young or old. Whereas some of the other unique language choices have both positive and negative features, language that is sexist, racist, heterosexist, or ageist tends to have only negative consequences.

Avoid generalizations and stereotypes—beliefs based on previously formed opinions and attitudes—that all members of a group are more or less alike. Your language can unintentionally suggest gender, as when you say, "A professor needs to read incessantly to keep up with his field," which hints that professors are men. Say instead, "Professors need to read incessantly to keep up with their field." Also avoid gender-specific compound words, such as *chairman* and *salesman*. Finally, avoid gender-specific occupational titles when the gender is irrelevant. For example, instead of "Our clergyman is a great fisherman," say "Our pastor is a great angler."

Most people have a good idea of what racist language is. Rather than using racist language, call people what they want to be called. White people should not decide what black people should be called, and straight people should not decide what gay and lesbian individuals should be called.

Homosexuality has always existed, in our culture and in other cultures. However, in many cultures language has masked that reality. An increasing number of gay and lesbian individuals have declared or shared their sexual orientation in recent years. Among the gay, lesbian, and bisexual celebrities are Drew Barrymore, Sara Bernhard, Ellen DeGeneres, Barney Frank, Elton John, Rosie O'Donnell,[14] Cynthia Nixon, and Wanda Sykes.[15] At the same time, many people reject any orientation other than heterosexual in their language choices and their pairing of women and men. If you are not gay or lesbian and do not have close friends who have this orientation, you may not be sensitive to your language that privileges heterosexuality. Consider using terms such as *partner, companion,* and *friend* instead of *husband, girlfriend,* and *spouse.*

Today many people in their sixties, seventies, and even eighties continue to have active lives, many of which include paid labor or service obligations. The workforce, partly because of the economy and partly because of the health of older people, is becoming more age-diverse.

Clearly, ageist language is outdated. Ageist language in the workplace negatively affects worker productivity and corporate profitability.[16] In interpersonal communication, ageism is evident in language that infantilizes older persons and diminishes people's concepts of themselves as vigorous and vital. Examples of this practice include when a person's name is used in the diminutive, such as "Johnny" instead of "John," or "Annie" instead of "Ann." Inappropriate terms of affection also mark ageism: "honey," "poor dear," and "good boy." Finally, terms such as "Grandma," and "Gramps" for older people to whom you are not related signals a bias based on age.[17]

descriptiveness
The practice of describing observed behavior or phenomena instead of offering personal reactions or judgments.

How Can Language Skills Be Improved?

To recognize that the names for different kinds of language are not mutually exclusive is important; that is, a particular expression can fit in more than one category. Can you see how the brief sentence "How's it going?" can be a cliché and perhaps even a regionalism? Nonetheless, these categories provide a vocabulary you can use to describe the language you hear every day.

You can make specific changes in your language usage that will help you become a more effective communicator. The changes include being descriptive by checking your perceptions, paraphrasing, using operational definitions, and defining your terms. Another change is to be concrete in your use of language by using dating and indexing. Still another change is to use figurative language to get your listener to visualize what you are describing. Finally, you can change your use of language by understanding and practicing the difference between observation and inference.

USE DESCRIPTIVENESS

Descriptiveness is the practice of describing observed behavior or phenomena instead of offering personal reactions or judgments. You can be descriptive in different ways: by checking your perceptions, paraphrasing, using operational definitions, and defining terms.

skill builder

Test Your Ability to Recognize Weaknesses in Language

To determine how well you understand the uses of language discussed in this section, complete the following quiz. Which of the following represent clichés, euphemisms, slang, jargon, regionalisms, or sexist, racist, heterosexist, or ageist language?

1. "Flake off!"
2. "She's a shrunken old Granny."
3. "She's a cute chick."
4. "Don't add insult to injury."
5. "We are engaged in ethnic cleansing."
6. "I haven't seen you in a coon's age."
7. "Who is the reporting authority?"
8. "Old Johnny is on death watch."
9. To a woman: "Who's your boyfriend?"
10. "How much spam do you receive every day?"
11. "Better late than never."
12. "No time for a thorough cleaning, so I will just clat over the floor."
13. "I can really burn rubber."
14. "The employer is engaged in right-sizing."

Answers:
1. Slang; 2. Ageism; 3. Sexist/heterosexist language; 4. Cliché; 5. Euphemism; 6. Regionalism; 7. Jargon; 8. Ageism; 9. Sexist/heterosexist language; 10. Jargon; 11. Cliché; 12. Regionalism; 13. Slang; 14. Euphemism

skill **builder**

Check Your Perceptions

One of the most common ways you can be descriptive is through simple checks on your perception. To communicate effectively with another person, you and the other person need to have a common understanding of an event that has occurred or a common definition of a particular phenomenon. You can check with another person to determine whether his or her perception is the same as yours. For example, if a room feels too hot to you, you might ask, "Isn't it hot in here?" After a particularly difficult week, you might ask, "It's been a long week, hasn't it?" Or after an exam, you might ask, "Wasn't that test difficult?" Many disagreements occur because people do not stop to make these simple checks on their perception.

Paraphrase

Paraphrasing can also help you improve your use of descriptive language. **Paraphrasing** is

paraphrasing
Restating another person's message by rephrasing the content or intent of the message.

restating another person's message by rephrasing the content or intent of the message. Paraphrasing is not simply repeating exactly what you heard. Paraphrasing allows the other person—the original speaker—to make corrections, in case you misinterpreted what he or she said. The original speaker must actively listen to your paraphrase to determine whether you understood both the *content* and the *intent* of what he or she said.

You may be well practiced at paraphrasing while instant messaging or tweeting, because these forms force you to paraphrase longer messages into very brief ones. But the important element about paraphrasing in general is not so much being brief as capturing the intended meaning of the other person's message. Thus, a paraphrase really requires a response about whether it was reasonably accurate. Even a simple statement such as "Do you want to celebrate tonight by going out to eat?" invites a paraphrase like "Do you mean you want to celebrate by eating tonight at an expensive restaurant?"—to which the original speaker says, "I do want to celebrate, and I do want to go out tonight, but not necessarily to an expensive restaurant." Through statements, paraphrases, and responses to another's paraphrase, the pair increasingly arrive at the intent and content of the original statement about going out to eat tonight.

Use Operational Definitions

operational definition
A definition that identifies something by revealing how it works, how it is made, or what it consists of.

Another kind of descriptiveness involves using **operational definitions**—that is, definitions that identify something by revealing how it works, how it is made, or what it consists of. Suppose a professor's syllabus states that students will be allowed an excused absence for illness. A student spends a sleepless night studying for an exam in another course, misses class, and claims an excused absence because of illness. The student explains that she was too tired to come to class, and the professor explains that illness is surgery, injury, vomiting, diarrhea, or a very bad headache. This operational definition of illness does not please the student, but it does clarify what the professor means by "illness." In other examples, a cake can be operationally defined by a recipe, and a job by its description. Even abstractions become understandable when they are operationalized. Saying that someone is "romantic" does not reveal much, compared with saying that someone gave you flowers, invited you out for lunch, and took you to an event.

Define Your Terms

Confusion can also arise when you use unusual terms or use words in a special way. If you suspect someone might misunderstand your terminology, you must define the term. In such an instance, you need to be careful not to offend the other person; simply offer a definition that clarifies the term. Similarly, you need to ask others for definitions when they use words in new or unusual ways.

Many terms that we see every day are not necessarily well understood. One student gave a presentation on the difference between "4-wheel drive" and "all-wheel drive," terms that we see on the back of most SUVs without knowing the difference. By defining the two terms, the student helped his audience to know terms they see often without understanding.

■ Define potentially confusing terms to help accurately convey your meaning.

Use Figures of Speech

You may wish to consider figures of speech in your attempts to be increasingly descriptive. Although figures of speech may lead to confusion in some instances, they can also clarify meaning. For example, a woman in her seventies learned that she had a heart problem, and her physician described the blockage in her heart valve by specifying the number of millimeters the valve was open. The woman was distressed because she did not have a frame of reference for the measurement. A nurse who overheard the conversation explained, "The valve should be the size of a water hose, but your valve has an opening that is smaller than a drinking straw." The comparison was one the woman could understand.

BE CONCRETE

A person who uses **concrete language** uses words and statements that are specific rather than abstract or vague. "You have interrupted me three times when I have begun to talk. I feel as though you do not consider my point of view as important as yours" is concrete. In contrast, "You should consider my viewpoint, too," is vague.

concrete language Words and statements that are specific rather than abstract or vague.

Earlier in the chapter, semanticists were briefly mentioned. Count Alfred Korzybski started the field of general semantics with the noble purpose of improving human behavior through the careful use of language.[18] The general semanticists' contribution includes the use of more precise, concrete language to facilitate the transmission and reception of symbols as accurately as possible. They encourage practices that make language more certain to engender shared meanings. Two such practices are dating and indexing.

sizing things up

Role Category Questionnaire

This chapter taught you how language can be used to create hierarchy and classification. To illustrate this function of language, this survey asks you to describe two people, one of whom you really like and one you really do not like. For each person, you should use sentences to describe the person's personality, mannerisms, behaviors, and other general characteristics; you should not be concerned with appearance and other physical characteristics.

Describe a person you really like:
Describe a person you really dislike:

This exercise has no right or wrong answers, but you can learn. If language shapes reality, then what meaning do you attribute to the number of sentences that were inspired by each person? See the appendix (p. 348) for more on interpreting your responses.

Source: Adapted from Crockett, W. H. (1965). Cognitive complexity and impression formation. In B. A. Maher (Ed.), *Progress in experimental personality research* (Vol. 2, pp. 47–90). New York: Academic.

dating
Specifying when you made an observation, since everything changes over time.

frozen evaluation
An assessment of a concept that does not change over time.

indexing
Identifying the uniqueness of objects, events, and people.

Dating

Dating is specifying when you made an observation, which is necessary because everything changes over time. Often, you view objects, people, or situations as remaining the same. You form a judgment or view of a person, an idea, or a phenomenon and maintain that view, even though the person, idea, or phenomenon may have changed. Dating is the opposite of **frozen evaluation,** in which you do not allow your assessment to change over time. An example of a frozen evaluation is always seeing someone as a bully because he or she once was. When using dating, instead of saying that something is always or universally a certain way, you state *when* you made your judgment and clarify that your perception was based on that experience.

For example, if you took a course with a particular instructor two years ago, any judgment you make about the course and the instructor must be qualified as to time. You may tell someone, "English 101 with Professor Jones is a breeze," but that judgment may no longer be true. Or suppose you went out with someone a year ago, and now your friend is thinking about going out with him. You might say that he is quiet and withdrawn, but that may no longer be accurate: time has passed, the situation is different, and the person you knew may have changed. You can prevent communication problems by saying "English 101 with Professor Jones was a breeze for me when I took it during the spring of 2002" or "Joe seemed quiet and withdrawn when I dated him last year, but I haven't seen him since."

Indexing

Indexing is identifying the uniqueness of objects, events, and people. Indexing simply means recognizing the differences among the various members of a group. Stereotyping, which was defined earlier in the chapter, is the opposite of indexing. People often assume that the characteristics of one member of a group apply to all members of a group. For example, you might assume that, because you have a good communication instructor, all instructors in the department are exceptional, but that may not be the case. Indexing can help you avoid such generalizations. You could say, "I have a great communication instructor. What is yours like?" Or instead of saying "Hondas get good gas mileage—I know, I own one," which is a generalization about all Hondas based on only one, try "I have a Honda that uses very little gas. How does your Honda do on gas mileage?" And rather than "Firstborn children are more responsible than their younger brothers or sisters," try using indexing: "My older brother is far more responsible than I. Is the same true of your older brother?"

DIFFERENTIATE BETWEEN OBSERVATIONS AND INFERENCES

Another way to improve language skills is to discern between observations and inferences. Observations are descriptions of what is sensed; inferences are conclusions drawn from observations. For example, during the day you make observations as to where objects in a room are placed. However, at night, when you walk through the room, although you cannot see where the objects are placed, you conclude that they are still where they were during the day, and you are able to walk through the room without bumping into anything. You have no problem with this kind of simple exchange of an inference for an observation—unless someone has moved the furniture or placed a new object in the room, or unless your memory is inaccurate. Even simple inferences can be wrong. Many shins have been bruised because someone relied on inference rather than observation.

If you speak English as a second language, you know that language skills take time and effort to develop. Although much work still needs to be done to better understand how to help non-native speakers build their language skills, the National Teachers of English as a Second Language (www. tesol.org) provides this advice:

cultural note

Inferences and Observations Among U.S. Students in Denmark

The differences between observations and inferences become even more clouded when two cultures meet. For example, U.S. students studying in Denmark concluded that Danish students were not very friendly. Their inference was based on their experiences attending parties that included both Danish and U.S. undergrads. The Danes tended to arrive in groups and spend the bulk of the evening conversing with those particular groups of friends. The U.S. students were accustomed to moving among several groups and talking with many of the people present. The Danish students were amiable, but they expressed their friendliness differently than the U.S. students. The U.S. students, in this instance, confused their observation of the Danish students with an inference about their feelings toward others.

1. *Keep language functional.* Rather than initially learning a second language through vocabulary lists and formal rules of grammar, you should try to learn how to use language in conversation. By learning the functional rules of language, you will develop skills more quickly.

2. *Be aware of language nuances.* As you learn the English language, recognize that how it functions differs, depending on whom you are talking to and in what context. As with your native language, the English language has many nuances. As you pay attention to slight variations in how English is used, your skills in English will accumulate rapidly. Being flexible, observant, and patient is important as you learn about these differences.

3. *Recognize that language learning is long-term.* Native speakers begin learning language from infancy, so it should be no surprise that non-native speakers need time to develop skills. Many non-native speakers may take five to seven years to attain proficiency with English. You can try to speed your learning by engaging in consistent, meaningful interactions with native speakers.

4. *Develop language processes interdependently.* Old views of language acquisition assumed that language learning was linear—that you learned first to listen, then to speak, and finally to read in a second language. Newer views suggest that these processes happen at the same time. Thus, to develop your skills more quickly, you should engage in all of these activities consistently.

5. *Use your own language to help.* Your intuitive understanding of your native tongue can assist you in learning English. For example, your native language has some differences between spoken and written language. Using those differences as a guide, can you discover similar differences in English? By comparing and contrasting your language with English, you will more quickly develop an automatic understanding of how to use English appropriately in different situations.

keeping it real

Speaking English Correctly

This chapter began with Sally struggling with a situation in which she had to make a presentation to fellow workers and a visiting manager who was going to decide whether she was the one who should be promoted with higher pay. What can you do to prepare yourself to speak correctly?

1. Try active listening to others who speak English correctly. As a student you listen to teachers every day who are college-educated and who strive to speak correctly. You don't have to sound like a college professor, but you do have the opportunity to learn correct grammar and usage from one.

2. Try to avoid common errors, such as those listed in this chapter. Enlist the help of anyone around you who can help improve your language skills. Even some supervisors and bosses would be impressed if you asked them to tell you when you make errors in language because you are trying to improve.

3. Try to avoid language that offends. This chapter provided a useful list of mistakes that are easy to make but also relatively easy to avoid: sexist, racist, heterosexist, and ageist language.

Chapter Review & Study Guide

Summary

In this chapter, you learned the following:

1. Language is a collection of symbols, letters, and words with arbitrary meanings that are governed by rules and are used to communicate. It is arbitrary, organizes and classifies reality, is abstract, and shapes perceptions.

2. People sometimes use language poorly, which can present a barrier to communication. Examples include

    - Grammatical errors
    - Slang
    - Clichés
    - Euphemisms
    - Profanity
    - Jargon
    - Regionalisms
    - Sexist, racist, heterosexist, and ageist language

3. You can change and improve your use of language by

    - Being more descriptive
    - Being more concrete
    - Using figurative language
    - Differentiating between observations and inferences

Key Terms

Ageist language
Cliché
Concrete language
Connotative meaning
Culture
Dating
Decode
Denotative meaning
Descriptiveness
Encode

Euphemism
Frozen evaluation
Heterosexist language
Indexing
Jargon
Language
Operational definition
Paraphrasing
Phatic communication
Pragmatics

Profanity
Racist language
Regionalisms
Sapir-Whorf hypothesis
Semantics
Sexist language
Slang
Syntax

Study Questions

1. Which of the following is *not* a characteristic of language?
   a. classifies reality
   b. organizes reality
   c. is arbitrary
   d. is concrete

2. Because messages can vary depending on the situation, to examine the context of the communication is important. This concept is called
   a. syntax.
   b. pragmatics.
   c. semantics.
   d. encoding.

3. Which statement reflects the relationship between language and culture?
   a. Language does not progress in response to the needs of the culture, but culture does progress in response to language.
   b. Language is a minor way that we learn about our culture.
   c. Culture creates a lens through which we perceive the world and create shared meaning.
   d. Language and culture are not related.

4. When doctors communicate with technical language, they are using
   a. profanity.
   b. euphemisms.
   c. clichés.
   d. jargon.

5. One way to improve language skills is to restate the content of the other person's message, a process called
   a. defining your terms.
   b. paraphrasing.
   c. using concrete language.
   d. indexing.

6. A word's dictionary definition is its _____ meaning, and an individualized or personalized definition is its _____ meaning.
   a. denotative; connotative
   b. denotative; abstract
   c. connotative; denotative
   d. concrete; connotative

7. Communication may be hindered in all the following cases *except* when
   a. we use improper grammar.
   b. we use descriptive language.
   c. we use clichés.
   d. we use sexist language.

8. Dating is important because
   a. you tend to view objects, people, or situations as remaining the same.
   b. situations change little or not at all over time.
   c. you are saying that something is always static, or universally staying a certain way.
   d. you clarify a perception based on a particular experience in a specific context.

9. Which of the following terms refers to disrespectful language?
   a. profanity
   b. jargon
   c. clichés
   d. regionalisms

10. When you describe observed behavior instead of offering personal reactions, you are
    a. drawing inferences.
    b. being concrete.
    c. using descriptiveness.
    d. being judgmental.

Answers:

1. (d); 2. (b); 3. (c); 4. (d); 5. (b); 6. (a); 7. (b); 8. (d); 9. (a); 10. (c)

connect For further review, go to the LearnSmart study module for this chapter.

Critical Thinking

1. Think hard about some things for which we have no words. If we have no words for something, can we still think about that thing?

2. The Whorf-Sapir hypothesis says that our language shapes our reality. One fact about language is that we have many more negative words to describe women than to describe men. What does that fact say about how English-speaking people in the United States think about women?

nonverbal communication

When you have read and thought about this chapter, you will be able to:

1. Define nonverbal communication.

2. Describe how verbal and nonverbal codes work in conjunction.

3. Identify two problems people have in interpreting nonverbal codes.

4. Define and identify nonverbal codes.

5. Recognize the types of bodily movement in nonverbal communication.

6. Describe the role of physical attraction in communication.

7. State the factors that determine the amount of personal space you use.

8. Understand how objects are used in nonverbal communication.

9. Utilize strategies for improving your nonverbal communication.

This chapter focuses on the role of nonverbal codes in communication. The chapter first looks at the problems that can occur in interpreting nonverbal codes. Next, some of the major nonverbal codes are identified and defined, including bodily movement and facial expression, bodily appearance, space, time, touching, and vocal cues. The chapter concludes with a discussion of some solutions to the problems you might encounter in interpreting nonverbal codes.

Nonverbal communication is often overlooked, yet many of our first impressions of others and the first impressions we provide to others occur nonverbally. Amrit Rao is an international student from the Indian subcontinent. He has moved to the United States just three days before classes are to begin. He has been very observant of others, and he notices that people use different nonverbal ways of greeting each other, that they stand at a different distance from each other than people do in his home country, and that they certainly wear different clothing. He wants to make a good first impression on the first day of class and yet he is uncertain about what to do. Should he behave as he would in India or should he try to adopt American behaviors? He does not feel comfortable with some of the casual and abbreviated clothing he sees on others. He is hoping to learn more about appropriate behavior in his communication course.

What would you recommend for Amrit Rao? At the end of the chapter, we'll revisit Amrit and how he used nonverbal communication to make a good first impression.

As a beginning communication student, you might be unaware of the subtle, but important, nature of nonverbal communication. You may have grown up in a large city or a small town but you find that, in college, people do not necessarily act the same as they did in your place of origin. If you are seeking employment near your college, you may find that you must make different choices about the way you treat time, how much you touch others, and how you dress. In this chapter you will begin to understand the role of nonverbal communication and how to become a more competent communicator by improving your nonverbal communication.

What Is Nonverbal Communication?

This chapter focuses on nonverbal communication and the relationship between nonverbal and verbal communication. The chapter should help you make sense of the most frequently seen nonverbal codes, as well as provide you with some suggestions for improving your nonverbal communication. Let us begin with a definition of nonverbal communication and a brief discussion on its significance.

Nonverbal communication is the process of using wordless messages to generate meaning. Nonverbal communication includes nonword vocalizations, such as inflection, and nonword sounds, such as "ah" and "hmm." Communication is complex. We cannot quantify the relative contribution of nonverbal communication to verbal communication,[1] but nonverbal communication often provides much more meaning than people realize. Indeed, when we are not certain about another person's feelings or our feeling about him or her, we may rely far more on nonverbal cues and less on the words that are used.[2] You know the importance of nonverbal communication in your own life. Imagine how difficult communication would be if you could not see the people with whom you are communicating, hear their voices, or sense their presence. Actually, this is what occurs when you send e-mail or instant messages or chat with others online. As electronic forms of communication have become more prevalent, people have found creative ways to communicate feeling and emotions. Emoticons are sequences of characters composed in two-dimensional written formats for the purpose of

nonverbal communication
The process of using wordless messages to generate meaning.

expressing emotions. The most common example of the emoticon is the "smiley," or "smiley face." Emoticons are a form of nonverbal communication, and they illustrate the importance of this means of communication, no matter the context.

How Are Verbal and Nonverbal Communication Related?

In chapter 3 we examined verbal communication and verbal codes. Both verbal and nonverbal communication are essential for effective interactions with others. How are the two related? In a recent study, the roles of verbal and nonverbal elements were examined to determine which was most important in a persuasive message. The results showed that the content (verbal portion of the speech) was most important in determining the effect of the speech. Emphasis and gestures, however, added to some aspects of the presentation and caused the speech to be viewed as lively and powerful.[3] In other words, both the verbal and the nonverbal elements of the speech were important.

Nonverbal communication works in conjunction with the words that we utter in six ways: to repeat, to emphasize, to complement, to contradict, to substitute, and to regulate. Let us consider each of these briefly.

Repeating occurs when the same message is sent verbally and nonverbally. For example, you frown at a PowerPoint presentation while you ask the speaker what he means. Or you direct a passing motorist by pointing at the next street corner and explaining where she should turn.

Emphasizing is the use of nonverbal cues to strengthen your message. Hugging a friend and telling him that you really care about him is a stronger statement than using either words or bodily movement alone.

Complementing is different from repeating in that it goes beyond duplication of the message in two channels. It is also not a substitution of one channel for the other. The verbal and nonverbal codes add meaning to each other and expand the meaning of either message alone. Your tone of voice, your gestures, and your bodily movement can all indicate your feeling, which goes beyond your verbal message.

Contradicting occurs when your verbal and nonverbal messages conflict. Often this occurs accidentally. If you have ever been angry at a teacher or parent, you may have stated verbally that you were fine—but your bodily movements, facial expression, and use of space may have "leaked" your actual feelings. Contradiction occurs intentionally in humor and sarcasm. Your words provide one message, but your nonverbal delivery tells how you really feel.

Substituting occurs when nonverbal codes are used instead of verbal codes. You roll your eyes, you stick out

repeating
The same message is sent both verbally and nonverbally.

emphasizing
The use of nonverbal cues to strengthen verbal messages.

complementing
Using nonverbal and verbal codes to add meaning to each other and to expand the meaning of either message alone.

contradicting
Verbal and nonverbal messages conflict.

substituting
Nonverbal codes are used instead of verbal codes.

social media make it matter

Emoticons

Emoticons are important tools when you are trying to convey your feelings to another person electronically. Without vocal inflections, facial expression, and bodily movement, your emotions are difficult to interpret. Emoticons can be helpful in avoiding misunderstanding. No absolute, standard definitions exist for individual emoticons, but many people have common understandings for a variety of these symbols. Generally, emoticons are made to resemble a face. Four examples are provided here. You can easily find additional examples online by using a search engine and the key word *emoticons*.

You should be aware that these symbols should be reserved for communication with friends and family. They should not be used in business correspondence or when seeking employment. Be cautious in using them with professors unless they invite humor and this sort of informal interaction.

:-) Happiness or humor

:-I Indifference

:-Q Confusion

:-O Surprise

your tongue, you gesture thumbs down, or you shrug. In most cases your intended message is fairly clear.

Regulating occurs when nonverbal codes are used to monitor and control interactions with others. For example, you look away when someone else is trying to talk and you are not finished with your thought. You walk away from someone who has hurt your feelings or made you angry. You shake your head and encourage another person to continue talking. Although verbal and nonverbal codes often work in concert, they also exhibit differences, which we will consider next.

Why Are Nonverbal Codes Difficult to Interpret?

Nonverbal communication is responsible for much of the misunderstanding that occurs during communication. Just as people have difficulty interpreting verbal symbols, so do they struggle to interpret nonverbal codes. The ambiguity of nonverbal communication occurs for two reasons: people use the same code to communicate a variety of meanings, and they use a variety of codes to communicate the same meaning.

ONE CODE COMMUNICATES A VARIETY OF MEANINGS

The ambiguity of nonverbal codes occurs in part because one code may communicate several different meanings. For example, the nonverbal code of raising your right hand may mean that you are taking an oath, you are demonstrating for a cause, you are indicating to an instructor that you would like to answer a question, a physician is examining your right side, or you want a taxi to stop for you. Also consider how you may stand close to someone because of a feeling of affection, because the room is crowded, or because you have difficulty hearing.

Although people in laboratory experiments have demonstrated some success in decoding nonverbal behavior accurately,[4] in actual situations receivers of nonverbal cues can only guess about the meaning of the cue.[5] Several lay authors have been successful in selling books suggesting that observers can learn to easily and accurately distinguish meaning from specific nonverbal cues. Unfortunately, these authors have not been able to demonstrate any significant improvement among their readers. Single cues can be interpreted in multiple ways.

A VARIETY OF CODES COMMUNICATE THE SAME MEANING

Nonverbal communication is not a science; any number of codes may be used to communicate the same meaning. One example is the many nonverbal ways by which adults communicate love or affection. You may sit or stand more closely to someone you love. You might speak more softly, use a certain vocal intonation, or alter how quickly you speak when you communicate with someone with whom you are affectionate. Or perhaps you choose to dress differently when you are going to be in the company of someone you love.

Cultural differences are especially relevant when we consider that multiple cues may be used to express a similar message. How do you show respect to a speaker in a public-speaking situation? In some cultures listeners show respect when they avert their eyes; in other cultures listeners show respect

skill **builder**

Nonverbal Self-Appraisal

You can improve your own nonverbal communication by first becoming aware of how you communicate. Using one of the multiple video technologies, record yourself when you are engaged in a conversation, group discussion, or public speech. Watch the recording with classmates, and take note of your facial expressions, gestures, posture, and other nonverbal features. How might you improve your nonverbal communication?

and attention by looking directly at the speaker. You may believe that showing your emotions is an important first step in resolving conflict, whereas a classmate may feel that emotional responses interfere with conflict resolution.

What Are Nonverbal Codes?

Nonverbal codes are codes of communication consisting of symbols that are not words, including nonword vocalizations. Bodily movement, facial expression, physical attraction, the use of space, the use of time, touch, vocal cues, and clothing and other artifacts are all nonverbal codes. Let us consider these systematic arrangements of symbols that have been given arbitrary meaning and are used in communication.

BODILY MOVEMENT AND FACIAL EXPRESSION

The study of bodily movements, including posture, gestures, and facial expressions, is called **kinesics,** a word derived from the Greek word *kinesis,* meaning "movement." Some popular books purport to teach you how to "read" nonverbal communication, so that you will know, for example, who is sexually aroused, who is just kidding, and whom you should avoid. Nonverbal communication, however, is more complicated than that. Interpreting the meaning of nonverbal communication is partly a matter of assessing the other person's unique behavior and considering the context. You don't just "read" another person's body language; instead, you observe, analyze, and interpret before you decide the probable meaning.

Assessing another person's unique behavior means that you need to know how that person usually acts. A quiet person might be unflappable even in an emergency situation. A person who never smiles may not be unhappy, and someone who acts happy might not actually be happy. You need to know how the person expresses emotions before you can interpret what his or her nonverbal communication means.

To look more deeply into interpreting nonverbal communication, let us consider the work of some experts on the subject: Albert Mehrabian, Paul Ekman, and Wallace Friesen.

Mehrabian studied nonverbal communication by examining the concepts of liking, status, and responsiveness among the participants in communication situations.[6]

- We express *liking* by forward leaning, a direct body orientation (such as standing face-to-face), close proximity, increased touching, relaxed posture, open arms and body, positive facial expression, and direct eye contact. Liking is essential in communication. For example, people who work for supervisors who engage in these kinds of behaviors tend to have higher self-reported satisfaction than do people who work for managers who do not use these behaviors.[7] Indeed, babies as young as two to five days of age prefer faces that offer a direct gaze rather than those that look to one side.[8]

- *Status,* especially high status, is communicated nonverbally by bigger gestures, relaxed posture, and less eye contact. Male bosses sometimes put their feet up on their desks when talking to subordinates, but subordinates rarely act that way when talking to their boss.

- *Responsiveness* is exhibited by movement toward the other person, by spontaneous gestures, by shifts in posture and position, and by facial expressiveness. In other words, the face and body provide positive feedback to the other person.

◼ You must know a person in order to interpret his or her nonverbal communication.

nonverbal codes
Codes of communication consisting of symbols that are not words, including nonword vocalizations.

kinesics
The study of bodily movements, including posture, gestures, and facial expressions.

cultural note

Greetings

Chinese, Japanese, and Koreans bow, and Thais bow their heads while holding their hands in a prayer-like position. The bumi putra, or Muslim Malaysians, have a greeting of their own: they shake hands as Westerners do, but they follow up by touching their heart with their right hand to indicate that they are greeting you "from the heart."

Ekman categorized movement on the basis of its functions, origins, and meanings.[9] The categories include emblems, illustrators, affect displays, regulators, and adaptors.

emblems
Nonverbal movements that substitute for words and phrases.

■ **Emblems** are nonverbal movements that substitute for words and phrases. Examples of emblems are a beckoning first finger to mean "come here," an open hand held up to mean "stop," and a forefinger and thumb forming a circle to mean "OK." Be wary of emblems; they may mean something else in another culture.

illustrators
Nonverbal movements that accompany or reinforce verbal messages.

■ **Illustrators** are nonverbal movements that accompany or reinforce verbal messages. Examples of illustrators are nodding your head when you say yes, shaking your head when you say no, stroking your stomach when you say you are hungry, and shaking your fist in the air when you say, "Get out of here." These nonverbal cues tend to be more universal than many in the other four categories of movement.

affect displays
Nonverbal movements of the face and body used to show emotion.

■ **Affect displays** are nonverbal movements of the face and body used to show emotion. Watch people's behavior when their favorite team wins a game, listen to the door slam when an angry person leaves the room, and watch men make threatening moves when they are very upset with each other but don't really want to fight.

regulators
Nonverbal movements that control the flow or pace of communication.

■ **Regulators** are nonverbal movements that control the flow or pace of communication. Examples of regulators are starting to move away when you want the conversation to stop, gazing at the floor or looking away when you are not interested, and yawning and glancing at your watch when you are bored. Turn-taking in conversations is generally managed with gestures, gaze, and touch. However, turn-taking regulators vary from one culture to another.[10]

adaptors
Nonverbal movements that you might perform fully in private but only partially in public.

■ **Adaptors** are nonverbal movements that you might perform fully in private but only partially in public. For example, you might rub your nose in public, but you would probably never pick it.

Finally, Ekman and Friesen determined that a person's facial expressions provide information to others about how he or she feels.[11] Consider the smile. Findings are overwhelming that a person who smiles is rated more positively than a person who uses a neutral facial expression. Indeed, you are more likely to be offered a job if you smile.[12]

Perhaps a more provocative finding is that people are more likely to attend to faces that are angry or threatening than they are to neutral facial expressions. When adults were presented with multiple faces, including some that appeared threatening, they were more likely to attend to the angry faces than they were to others. Recently, it was shown that children have the same bias, and they observed angry and frightened faces more rapidly than they did happy or sad faces.[13] This response to threatening stimuli may have evolved as a protective means to help people avoid danger.

What is the effect of showing disagreement with a negative facial expression and head shaking, compared to using a neutral facial expression? In a study investigating opponents who stood behind a political speaker and displayed neutral facial expression, occasional negative facial expression, constant negative expression, or both negative and positive expression, surprising results were found. When either negative or negative and positive expressions were used, respondents viewed the speaker as less credible, less appropriate, and less skillful in debate.[14] In other words, some positive facial expressions did not lessen the negative response toward the speaker.

Research on bodily movement today includes considerations of how our body and mind work together. Although we have known for some time that bodily movement has some basis in the brain and in our neurological functioning, a new focus combining these areas has shown promise. Choreographers, neuroscientists, and psychologists have joined together to study body and mind. This kind of collaboration between dancers and scientists may allow new discoveries that were not possible when people from these areas worked independently.[15] The future is bright for additional creative discoveries.

Facial expressions are important in conveying information to others and in learning what others are feeling. Bodily movement and orientation add to that information by suggesting how intense the feeling might be. When you are able to observe and interpret both facial expression and bodily movement, you gain a fuller understanding of the other person's message.

PHYSICAL ATTRACTION

Beauty, it has been noted, is in the eye of the beholder. However, some research has suggested that particular characteristics—bright eyes, symmetrical features, and thin or medium build—are generally associated with physical attraction.[16] Moreover, such characteristics may not be limited to our culture but may be universal.[17]

Physical attractiveness affects many aspects of our lives. Generally, people who are physically attractive are privileged over those who are not physically attractive. This bias is stronger for women than for men.[18] In other words, in our culture it is more important that women are physically attractive than are men.

Physical attractiveness has been studied over the life course. Jaeger's comprehensive study found that taller men have higher earnings than do shorter men, that attractive women who are not overweight have higher socioeconomic status late in their careers, and that both women and men who are attractive are more likely to be married at younger ages.[19]

The influence of physical appearance begins when we are young. By age four, children are treated differently based on their physical appearance by their daycare teachers.[20] When children misbehave, their behavior is viewed as an isolated, momentary aberration if they are physically attractive but as evidence of a chronic tendency to be bad if they are unattractive. These patterns continue throughout childhood and adolescence.[21]

Physical attractiveness generally leads to more social success in adulthood. Women who are attractive report a larger number of dates in college. Attractiveness may be affected by skin tone and hair color. Swami, Furnham, and Joshi found that men clearly prefer brunettes over blondes, and they slightly prefer women who have light skin tones.[22] Both women and men who are attractive are seen as more sociable and sensitive.[23]

Do people change their view of mate preferences over time? Eastwick and Finkel found that men ideally desire a physically attractive mate whereas women ideally desire a mate who has strong earning prospects.[24] In real-life potential partners, women and men did not evidence these preferences or differences. Stereotypes may exist in abstract thinking about potential mates, but they do not appear to be realized in actual behavior.

The "matching hypothesis" suggests that women and men seek others who are of similar attractiveness. Lee, Loewenstein, Ariely, Hong, and Young demonstrated this consistent finding, although they did find that men were more oblivious to their own physical attractiveness in selecting a woman to date, whereas women were keenly aware of their "physical attraction quotient."[25] They also asked whether less attractive people delude themselves when they are dating less attractive people with the sense that they are more attractive than others view them. They found that this is not the case. People have a fairly objective sense of their own, and their partner's, attractiveness.

Similarly, people who are obese are less likely to have physically attractive partners than are people of normal weight. Body type is not the only factor in mate selection; obese people are seen as more attractive if they have a good education, good grooming, and more

■ Physical attractiveness is an important nonverbal attribute, but the media may distort realistic views of physical attractiveness.

proxemics
The study of the human use of space and distance.

attractive personalities. Nonetheless, similarity in body type remains the strongest predictor in mate selection among these qualities.[26]

Physical attractiveness affects both credibility and one's ability to persuade others. Attractive people receive higher initial credibility ratings than do those who are viewed as unattractive.[27] Women have more success in persuading the opposite sex when they are attractive than men have in persuading the opposite sex when they are attractive, but attractive women find that this effect dissipates as they grow older.[28] When two attractive women interact, they compete dynamically for status, which suggests that they feel they have more social status or interactional power as a result of their physical beauty.[29]

Mediated communication affects the importance of physical attractiveness in another way. Today many people get to know each other online. As a result, attractiveness may now be based on words and messages rather than on physical traits. People who are not perfect specimens have the opportunity to flirt and to charm. And physically attractive people can be deemed desirable on the basis of other characteristics, including their intellect and their interests. Clearly, online relationships will change the nature of physical attraction in the future.[30]

SPACE

Anthropologist Edward T. Hall introduced the concept of **proxemics**—the study of the human use of space and distance—in his book *The Hidden Dimension*.[31] This researcher and others, such as Werner,[32] have demonstrated the role space plays in human communication. Two concepts considered essential to the study of the use of space are territoriality and personal space.

■ *Territoriality* refers to your need to establish and maintain certain spaces as your own. In a shared dormitory room, the items on the common desk area mark the territory. For example, you might place your notebook, pens and pencils, and PDA on the right side of the desk and your roommate might place books, a cell phone, and a laptop on the left side. While the desk is shared, you are each claiming part of the area. On a cafeteria table the placement of the plate, glass, napkin, and eating utensils marks the territory. In a neighborhood it might be fences, hedges, trees, or rocks that mark the territory. All are nonverbal indicators that signal ownership.

■ *Personal space* is the personal "bubble" that moves around with you. It is the distance you maintain between yourself and others, the amount of space you claim as your own. Large people usually claim more space because of their size, and men often take more space than women. For example, in a lecture hall, observe who claims the armrests as part of their personal bubbles.

Hall was the first to define the four distances people regularly use while they communicate.[33] His categories have been helpful in understanding the communicative behavior that might occur when two people are a particular distance from each other. Beginning with the closest contact and the least personal space, and moving to the greatest distance, Hall's categories are intimate distance, personal distance, social distance, and public distance.

■ *Intimate distance* extends from you outward to 18 inches, and it is used by people who are relationally close to you. Used more often in private than in public, this intimate distance is employed to show affection, to give comfort, and to protect. Burgoon noted that the use of intimate distance usually elicits a positive response because individuals tend to stand and sit close to people to whom they are attracted.[34]

■ *Personal distance* ranges from 18 inches to 4 feet, and it is the distance used by most Americans for conversation and other nonintimate exchanges.

■ *Social distance* ranges from 4 to 12 feet, and it is used most often to carry out business in the workplace, especially in formal, less personal situations. The higher the status of one person, the greater the distance.

■ *Public distance* exceeds 12 feet and is used most often in public speaking in such settings as lecture halls; churches, mosques, and synagogues; courtrooms; and convention halls. Professors often stand at this distance while lecturing.

Distance, then, is a nonverbal means of communicating everything from the size of your personal bubble to your relationship with the person to whom you are speaking or listening. A great deal of research has been done on proxemics.[35] Virtual environments allow researchers to study the human use of space in relatively unobtrusive ways.[36] Sex, size, and similarity seem to be among the important determiners of personal space.

Gender affects the amount of space people are given and the space in which they choose to communicate.[37] Men tend to take more space because they are often larger than women.[38] Women take less space, and children take and are given the least space. Women exhibit less discomfort with small space and tend to interact at closer range.[39] Perhaps because women are so often given little space, they come to expect it. Also, women and children in our society seem to desire more relational closeness than do men.

Your relationship to other people is related to your use of space. You stand closer to friends and farther from enemies. You stand farther from strangers, authority figures, high-status people, physically challenged people, and people from racial groups different from your own. You stand closer to people you perceive as similar or unthreatening because closeness communicates trust.

The physical setting also can alter the use of space. People tend to stand closer together in large rooms and farther apart in small rooms.[40] In addition, physical obstacles and furniture arrangements can affect the use of personal space.

The cultural background of the people communicating also must be considered in the evaluation of personal space.[41] Hall was among the first to recognize the importance of cultural background when he was training American service personnel for service overseas. He wrote:

> Americans overseas were confronted with a variety of difficulties because of cultural differences in the handling of space. People stood "too close" during conversations, and when the Americans backed away to a comfortable conversational distance, this was taken to mean that Americans were cold, aloof, withdrawn, and disinterested in the people of the country. USA housewives muttered about "waste-space" in houses in the Middle East. In England, Americans who were used to neighborliness were hurt when they discovered that their neighbors were no more accessible or friendly than other people, and in Latin America, exsuburbanites, accustomed to unfenced yards, found that the high walls there made them feel "shut out." Even in Germany, where so many of my countrymen felt at home, radically different patterns in the use of space led to unexpected tensions.[42]

Cultural background can result in great differences in the use of space and in people's interpretation of such use. As our world continues to shrink, more people will be working in multinational corporations, regularly traveling to different countries and interacting with others from a variety of backgrounds. Sensitivity to space use in different cultures and quick, appropriate responses to those variations are imperative.

skill builder

chronemics

Also called temporal communication; the way people organize and use time and the messages that are created because of their organization and use of it.

tactile communication

The use of touch in communication.

TIME

Temporal communication, or **chronemics,** is the way that people organize and use time and the messages that are created because of their organization and use of it. Time can be examined on a macro level. How do you perceive the past, future, and present? Some people value the past and collect photographs and souvenirs to remind themselves of times gone by. They emphasize how things have been. Others live in the future and are always chasing dreams or planning future events. They may be more eager when planning a vacation or party than they are when the event arrives. Still others live in the present and savor the current time. They try to live each day to its fullest and neither lament the past nor show concern for the future.

One distinction that has been drawn that helps us understand how individuals view and use time differently is the contrast between monochronic and polychronic people. *Monochronic* people view time as very serious and they complete one task at a time. Often their jobs are more important to them than anything else—perhaps even including their families. Monochronic people view privacy as important. They tend to work independently, and they rarely borrow or lend money or other items. They may appear to be secluded or even isolated. Although we cannot generalize to all people, we may view particular countries as generally monochronic. They include the United States, Canada, Germany, and Switzerland. In contrast, *polychronic* people work on several tasks at a time. Time is important, but it is not revered. Interpersonal relationships are more important to them than their work. Polychronic individuals tend to be highly engaged with others. Again, without generalizing to all people, countries such as Egypt, Saudia Arabia, Mexico, and the Philippines tend to include people who are polychronic.

Time is viewed dissimilarly in different cultures.[43] In the United States, two recent applications of the use of time—one in electronic communication and one in the workplace—have been studied. The first is the effect of relatively slow or quick responses to e-mail. Earlier research suggested that delayed e-mail messages could cause perceptions of decreased closeness. More recently, though, it appears that several factors interact to produce feelings of increased closeness or more distance. In addition to reply rate are biological sex and emotional empathy. People who demonstrate concern for the other person may offset feelings of detachment that a delayed e-mail message could ordinarily signal.

The second study looked at how several features of time affected worker job satisfaction and worker satisfaction with their communication. The researchers learned that the highest job satisfaction occurred among people who viewed their work as more punctual and oriented toward the future. When workers experienced delayed time, they were least satisfied with their interactions.[44]

TOUCHING

Tactile communication is the use of touch in communication. Because touch always involves invasion of another person's personal space, it commands attention. It can be welcome, as when a crying child is held by a parent, or unwelcome, as in sexual harassment. Our need for and appreciation of tactile communication start early in life.[45] Schutz observed:

> The unconscious parental feelings communicated through touch or lack of touch can lead to feelings of confusion and conflict in a child. Sometimes a "modern"

Touch commands attention and is essential to many rituals.

parent will say all the right things but not want to touch the child very much. The child's confusion comes from the inconsistency of levels: if they really approve of me so much like they say they do, why don't they touch me?[46]

Insufficient touching can lead to health disorders, such as allergies and eczema, speech problems, and even death. Researchers have found that untouched babies and small children can grow increasingly ill and die.[47]

For adults, touch is a powerful means of communication.[48] Usually, touch is perceived as positive, pleasurable, and reinforcing. The association of touch with the warmth and caring that began in infancy carries over into adulthood. People who are comfortable with touch are more likely to be satisfied with their past and current lives. They are self-confident, assertive, socially acceptable, and active in confronting problems. Think about how you use nonverbal communication. Are you comfortable touching and being touched? Do you frequently hug others or shake hands with others?

Touch is part of many important rituals. In baptism the practice can range from as little as a touch on the head during the ceremony to as much as a total immersion in water. Prayers in some churches are said with the pastor's hand touching the person being prayed for. In some fundamentalist Christian churches, the healer might accompany the touch with a mighty shove, right into the hands of two catchers. Physician Bernie Siegel wrote the following in his book on mind–body communication:

> I'd like to see some teaching time devoted to the healing power of touch—a subject that only 12 of 169 medical schools in the English-speaking world deal with at all . . . despite the fact that touch is one of the most basic forms of communication between people. . . . We need to teach medical students how to touch people.[49]

Siegel's appeal did not go unheard. A number of medical schools are now training their students to decode patients' nonverbal cues and to provide nonverbal communication, including touch, to their patients.[50] The results of the training is mixed, however; as students' awareness of nonverbal communication increases, their actual performance does not.[51] Religion and medicine are just two professions in which touch is important for ceremonial and curative purposes.

Touch varies by gender.[52] The findings relating touch with gender indicate the following:

- Women value touch more than men do.[53]
- Women are touched more than men, beginning when they are six-month-old girls.[54]
- Women touch female children more often than they touch male children.[55]
- Men and their sons touch each other the least.[56]
- Female students are touched more often and in more places than are male students.[57]
- Males touch others more often than females touch others.[58]
- Males may use touch to indicate power or dominance.[59]

On the last point, to observe who can touch whom among people in the workplace is interesting. Although fear of being accused of sexual harassment has eliminated a great deal of touch except for handshaking, the general nonverbal principle is that the higher-status individual gets to initiate touch, but touch is not reciprocal: the president might pat you on the back for a job well done, but in our society you don't pat back.

Further, both co-culture, such as gender, discussed above, and culture determine the frequency and kind of nonverbal communication. People from different countries handle nonverbal communication differently—even something as simple as touch.[60] Sidney Jourard determined the rates of touch per hour among adults from various cultures.[61] In a coffee shop, adults in San Juan, Puerto Rico, touched 180 times per hour, whereas those in Paris, France, touched about 110 times per hour, followed by those in Gainesville, Florida, who touched about 2 times per hour, and those in London, England, who touched only once per hour.

Touch sends such a powerful message that it has to be handled with responsibility. Touch may be welcomed by some in work or clinical settings, but it is equally likely that touch is undesirable or annoying. Certainly, touch can be misunderstood in such settings.[62] When the right to touch is abused, it can result in a breach of trust, anxiety, and hostility. When touch is used to communicate concern, caring, and affection, it is welcome, desired, and appreciated.

VOCAL CUES

Nonverbal communication includes some sounds, as long as they are not words. We call them **paralinguistic features**—the nonword sounds and nonword characteristics of language, such as pitch, volume, rate, and quality. The prefix *para* means "alongside" or "parallel to," so *paralinguistic* means "alongside the words or language."

The paralinguistic feature examined here is **vocal cues**—all of the oral aspects of sound except words themselves. Vocal cues include

- **Pitch:** the highness or lowness of your voice
- **Rate:** how rapidly or slowly you speak
- **Inflection:** the variety or changes in pitch
- **Volume:** the loudness or softness of your voice

paralinguistic features
The nonword sounds and nonword characteristics of language, such as pitch, volume, rate, and quality.

vocal cues
All of the oral aspects of sound except words themselves.

pitch
The highness or lowness of the speaker's voice.

rate
The pace of your speech.

inflection
The variety or changes in pitch.

volume
The loudness or softness of the voice.

- **Quality:** the unique resonance of your voice, such as huskiness, nasality, raspiness, or whininess

- **Nonword sounds:** "mmh," "huh," "ahh," and the like, as well as pauses or the absence of sound used for effect in speaking

- **Pronunciation:** whether or not you say a word correctly

- **Articulation:** whether or not your mouth, tongue, and teeth coordinate to make a word understandable to others (such as a lisp)

- **Enunciation:** whether or not you combine pronunciation and articulation to produce a word with clarity and distinction so that it can be understood; a person who mumbles has an enunciation problem

- **Silence:** the lack of sound

These vocal cues are important because they are linked in our mind with a speaker's physical characteristics, emotional state, personality characteristics, gender characteristics, and even credibility. For example, when you talk to strangers on the telephone, you form an impression of how they look and how their personality might be described. In addition, vocal cues, alone, have a persuasive effect for people when they are as young as 12 months.[63]

According to Kramer, vocal cues frequently convey information about the speaker's characteristics, such as age, height, appearance, and body type.[64] For example, people often associate a high-pitched voice with someone who is female, younger, and/or smaller. You may visualize someone who uses a loud voice as being big or someone who speaks quickly as being nervous. People who tend to speak slowly and deliberately may be perceived as being high-status individuals or as having high credibility.

A number of studies have related emotional states to specific vocal cues. Joy and hate appear to be the most accurately communicated emotions, whereas shame and love are among the most difficult to communicate accurately.[65] Joy and hate appear to be conveyed by fewer vocal cues, and this makes them less difficult to interpret than emotions such as shame and love, which are conveyed by complex sets of vocal cues. "Active" feelings, such as joy and hate, are associated with a loud voice, a high pitch, and a rapid rate. Conversely, "passive" feelings, which include affection and sadness, are communicated with a soft voice, a low pitch, and a relatively slow rate.[66]

Personality characteristics also have been related to vocal cues. Dominance, social adjustment, and sociability have been clearly correlated with specific vocal cues.[67] Irony, on the other hand, cannot be determined on the basis of vocal cues alone.[68]

Although the personality characteristics attributed to individuals displaying particular vocal cues have not been shown to accurately portray the person, as determined by standardized personality tests, our impressions affect our interactions. In other words, although you may perceive loud-voiced, high-pitched, fast-speaking individuals as dominant, they might not be measured as dominant by a personality inventory. Nonetheless, in your interactions with such people, you may become increasingly submissive because of your perception that they are dominant. In addition, these people may begin to become more dominant because they are treated as though they have this personality characteristic.

Vocal cues can help a public speaker establish credibility with an audience and can clarify the message. Pitch and inflection can be used to make the speech sound aesthetically pleasing, to accomplish subtle changes in meaning, and to tell an audience whether you are asking a question or making a statement, being sincere or sarcastic, or being doubtful or assertive. A rapid speaking rate may indicate you are confident about speaking in public or that you are

quality
The unique resonance of the voice, such as huskiness, nasality, raspiness, or whininess.

nonword sounds
Sounds like "mmh," "huh," and "ahh," as well as the pauses or the absence of sounds used for effect.

pronunciation
Saying a word correctly or incorrectly.

articulation
Coordinating one's mouth, tongue, and teeth to make words understandable to others.

enunciation
Combining pronunciation and articulation to produce a word with clarity and distinction.

silence
The lack of sound.

cultural note

Nod Your Head "No"?!

You will meet people from other cultures in your classes, and you may well travel to other countries. The number of students from other countries who are enrolling in U.S. colleges and universities increases each year. In academic year 2008–2009, the most recent year for which data are available, 671,616 international students were enrolled in U.S. institutions.

Many U.S. students travel to other countries through organizations such as the Peace Corps. Elizabeth (Vernon) Kelley joined the Peace Corps after serving as a journalist for five years. She explained that she was tired of sitting in front of a computer and wanted to do something to help others, and she wanted to see more of the world. She served in Bulgaria from 2003 to 2005. Those who travel to other countries experience the same concerns about nonverbal communication that Amrit Rao had in moving from India to the United States.

Kelley describes an interaction in a restaurant when she was trying to order a beverage. First she asked for coffee and the waitress shook her head from side to side. Kelley then tried, "Tea?" The response from the waitress was the same. Finally, she asked for cola, but the waitress again shook her head from side to side. What Kelley did not know is that a sideways shake of the head means "yes" in Bulgaria, not "no" as it does in the United States.

Even after learning this, Kelley did not do much better. Part of her assignment in Bulgaria was classroom teaching. When her students answered a question correctly, she nodded positively, but then the students immediately tried to change their answers. They believed her nod meant they had given the wrong answer.

Source: Fischer, K. (2009, November 16). Number of foreign students in U.S. hit a new high last year. *Chronicle of Higher Education* (http://chronicle.com/article/Number-of-Foreign-Students-/49142/).

nervously attempting to conclude your speech. Variations in volume can be used to add emphasis or to create suspense. Enunciation is especially important in public speaking because of the increased size of the audience and the fewer opportunities for direct feedback. Pauses can be used in a public speech to create dramatic effect and to arouse audience interest. Vocalized pauses—"ah," "uh-huh," "um," and so on—are not desirable in public speaking and may distract the audience.

Silence is a complex behavior steeped in contradictions. To be sure, silence is far better than vocalized pauses in public speaking. Too, silence may signal respect and empathy when another person is speaking or disclosing personal information. One observer notes: "Sometimes silence is best. Words are curious things, at best approximations. And every human being is a separate language.... [Sometimes] silence is best."[69] On the other hand, silence may signal the dark side of communication. People in power, in dominant cultures, or in positions of authority may silence others. Those with whom they come in contact may be marginalized or embarrassed and feel that they must remain silent because of sexism, racism, taboo, incidents of violence or abuse, shame, or a hostile environment.[70]

CLOTHING AND OTHER ARTIFACTS

objectics
Also called object language; the study of the human use of clothing and other artifacts as nonverbal codes.

artifacts
Ornaments or adornments you display that hold communicative potential.

Objectics, or object language, is the study of the human use of clothing and other artifacts as nonverbal codes. **Artifacts** are ornaments or adornments you display that hold communicative potential, including jewelry, hairstyles, cosmetics, automobiles, canes, watches, shoes, portfolios, hats, glasses, tattoos, body piercings, and even the fillings in teeth. Your clothing and other adornments communicate your age, gender, status, role, socioeconomic class, group memberships, personality, and relation to the opposite sex. Dresses are seldom worn by men, low-cut gowns are not the choice of shy women, bright colors are avoided by reticent people, and the most recent Paris fashions are seldom seen in the small towns of America.

These cues also indicate the time in history, the time of day, the climate, and one's culture.[71] Clothing and artifacts provide physical and psychological protection, and they are used to spur sexual attraction and to indicate self-concept. Your clothing and artifacts clarify the sort of person you believe you are.[72] They permit personal expression,[73] and they satisfy your need for creative self-expression.[74]

Many studies have established a relationship between an individual's clothing and artifacts and his or her characteristics. Conforming to current styles is correlated with an individual's desire to be accepted and liked.[75] In addition, individuals feel that clothing is important in forming first impressions.[76]

Perhaps of more importance are the studies that consider the relationship between clothing and an observer's perception of that person. In an early study, clothing was shown to affect others' impressions of status and personality traits.[77] People also seem to base their acceptance of others on their clothing and artifacts. In another early study, women who were asked to describe the most popular women they knew cited clothing as the most important characteristic.[78]

Clothing also communicates authority and people's roles. Physicians have historically worn a white coat to indicate their role. For many people the white coat signified healing and better health. As the white coat has begun to be phased out, however, the physician's ability to persuade patients to follow advice may have declined as well. Thus, physicians may need to learn alternative symbolic means of persuasion.[79]

Renewed interest in clothing as it relates to religion and identity has occurred in the last decade. Since 9/11, Americans have become increasingly aware of Muslim people and all facets of their lives. The dress of the Muslim woman. which tends to be modest and consist of loose and fairly heavy materials, is distinctive. Some Muslim women cover their entire body, including their face and/or hands, whereas others wear a simple Hijab on their head, with long sleeves and long skirts. Others modify this look with head scarves and Western-style clothing. Muslim women in Saudi Arabia are among the most conservatively dressed, with dark colors and bodies totally covered by abayas and chadors, whereas Muslim women in Malaysia wear bright colors, jewelry, makeup, and scarves in place of the traditional head pieces, and they may sport long skirts with slits up the side.

Indian people are well represented in universities, technology fields, and medicine in the United States. Some women from India who are Hindu may wear dhotis and saris, at least for formal occasions. Although the skirts are long, frequently the middle area of the body can be glimpsed in these outfits. And because a number of Mormons have been actively engaged in politics, including running for the U.S. presidency, their unique clothing has been discussed.

Christian crosses have been banned in most public elementary schools in the United States and Europe.[80] The cross has become associated with gangs, and the reasoning is that, by prohibiting the cross, schools might curtail gang behavior. In some schools, religious symbols of other major religions are allowed, whereas some schools have banned all religious symbols. Needless to say, parents and school boards have been vocal in their debates over such prohibitions.

Another area of controversy centers on children, particularly toddlers, who are active in beauty pageants. Parents of pageant children contend that their children's sexy costumes are only costumes and that they have no effect on the child's body image or development. At the same time, they believe that participating in pageants leads to poise and self-assurance. The television program *Toddlers & Tiaras* on the TLC network has exploited children's participation in pageants. Expensive clothing, shoes, and other adornments; painful treatments, including the waxing of eyebrows; "flippers," which are

■ What do you conclude about this person based on the artifacts?

social media
make it matter

Unstated Rules of Social Networks

Think about the number and variety of social networks you use. You might believe that social networking includes only verbal communication, but a great number of nonverbal decisions are implicit. As you browse social networks, consider the goal of each. Is it a place that provides you with potential dating partners? Does the network center on professional or academic interests? Choose networks that meet your needs.

You should also understand the unstated communication rules for the site. Do people use humor, sarcasm, and double meanings? The culture of the site may be best understood by the timing of responses and the paralanguage, emblems, or other symbols being used. What kind of photos are included? How much is revealed, and how much information is kept private? What are the expectations of others on the network? What is the average age of users, what is their background, and what goals do you believe they have? Nonverbal communication plays a significant role in understanding social networks.

whitened fake teeth that are snapped into place; and padding to enhance chests and rear ends have led to a great deal of criticism.[81]

Body modifications are a type of artifact. They include tattoos and piercing, which have been popular in recent years. Although they can be removed, the procedures may be both costly and time intensive. What do tattoos signal to others? Most people probably choose to adorn themselves with tattoos and piercings because they believe it adds to their overall attractiveness. A recent study, however, showed some different findings. Men with tattoos were viewed as more dominant than nontattooed men, and women with tattoos were seen as less healthy than women without tattoos. These findings hold implications for a biological signaling effect of tattoos.[82]

What Are Some Ways to Improve Nonverbal Communication?

Sensitivity to nonverbal cues is highly variable among people.[83] You can improve your understanding of nonverbal communication, though, by being sensitive to context, audience, and feedback.

The *context* includes the physical setting, the occasion, and the situation. In conversation, your vocal cues are rarely a problem unless you stutter, stammer, lisp, or suffer from some speech pathology. Paralinguistic features loom large in importance in small-group communication, in which you have to adapt to the distance and to a variety of receivers. These features are perhaps most important in public speaking because you have to adjust volume and rate, you have to enunciate more clearly, and you have to introduce more vocal variety to keep the audience's attention. The strategic use of pauses and silence is also more apparent in public speaking than it is in an interpersonal context in conversations or small-group discussion.

The occasion and physical setting also affect the potential meaning of a nonverbal cue. For example, when would it be appropriate for you to wear a cap over unwashed, uncombed hair and when would it be interpreted as inappropriate? The distance at which you communicate may be different based on the setting and the occasion: you may stand farther away from people in formal situations when space allows but closer to family members or to strangers in an elevator.

The *audience* makes a difference in your nonverbal communication, so you have to adapt. When speaking to children, you must use a simple vocabulary and careful enunciation, articulation, and pronunciation. With an older audience or with younger audiences whose hearing has been impaired by too much loud music, you must adapt your volume. Generally, children and older people in both interpersonal and public-speaking situations appreciate slower speech. Also, adaptation to an audience may determine your choice of clothing, hairstyle, and jewelry. For instance, a shaved head, a facial piercing, and a shirt open to the navel will not go over well in a job interview unless you are trying for a job as an entertainer.

Your attention to giving *feedback* can be very important in helping others interpret your nonverbal cues that might otherwise distract your listeners. For example, some pregnant women avoid questions and distraction by wearing a shirt that says, "I'm not fat, I'm pregnant"; such feedback prevents listeners from wondering instead of listening. Similarly, your listeners' own descriptive feedback—giving quizzical looks, staring, or nodding off—can signal you to talk louder, introduce variety, restate your points, or clarify your message.

If your conversational partner or audience does not provide you with feedback, what can you do? Practice asking questions and checking on the perceptions of others with whom you communicate. Silence has many meanings, and you sometimes must take great effort to interpret the lack of feedback in a communicative setting. You can also consider your past experience with particular individuals or a similar audience. Do they ever provide feedback? Under what circumstances are they expressive? How can you become more accurate in your interpretation of their feedback?

Although this chapter only introduces you to nonverbal communication, you know that your success in college and in the workplace is dependent on your sensitivity to nonverbal cues and your ability to alter familiar nonverbal cues, given the context and the situation. The following are some suggestions offered by professors and employers:

sizing things up

Berkeley Nonverbal Expressiveness Questionnaire

In this chapter you learned that your nonverbal communication is used to express meaning generally and emotion in particular. Each statement below describes ways in which you express your emotions through nonverbal communication. Respond to each statement using the following scale. A guide for interpreting your responses appears in the appendix at the end of the text (p. 348).

1 = Strongly disagree
2
3
4 = Neutral
5
6
7 = Strongly agree

1. Whenever I feel positive emotions, people can easily see exactly what I am feeling.
2. I sometimes cry during sad movies.
3. People often do not know what I am feeling.
4. I laugh out loud when someone tells me a joke that I think is funny.
5. It is difficult for me to hide my fear.
6. When I'm happy, my feelings show.
7. My body reacts very strongly to emotional situations.
8. I've learned it is better to suppress my anger than to show it.
9. No matter how nervous or upset I am, I tend to keep a calm exterior.
10. I am an emotionally expressive person.
11. I have strong emotions.
12. I am sometimes unable to hide my feelings, even though I would like to.
13. Whenever I feel negative emotions, people can easily see exactly what I am feeling.
14. There have been times when I have not been able to stop crying even though I tried to stop.
15. I experience my emotions very strongly.
16. What I'm feeling is written all over my face.

Source: Copyright © 1997 by the American Psychological Association. Reproduced with permission. Gross, J. J., & John, O. P. (1997). Revealing feelings: Facets of emotional expressivity in self-reports, peer ratings, and behavior. *Journal of Personality and Social Psychology, 72,* 435–448.

1. Establish eye contact and demonstrate interest through bodily movement and the use of space. Both professors and employers observe that students and new workers appear to be tied to their handheld devices. How much time do you spend on Facebook, Twitter, and YouTube? Do you plan on "media-free" time while in class, while studying, and while at work? In a recent study, professors attempted to curtail the use of text messaging in class by using positive facial expression, standing closer to

cultural note

Understanding Differences in Nonverbal Communication

As you will learn in chapter 7, a variety of characteristics can be used to identify distinctions among cultures—many of which include nonverbal differences in how we use gestures, space, touch, and even time. If you come from a country other than the United States, the amount of nonverbal adaptation you will need to undertake depends on how similar your culture is to U.S. culture. Although many nonverbal characteristics will likely be similar—the use of facial expression to convey emotion, for instance—there are also likely to be several differences. Understanding those differences can help you avoid misperceiving others and potentially avoid creating misperceptions yourself. Key considerations include the following:

- *Americans tend to expect consistent uses of space.* In normal conversations, U.S. speakers tend to stay in Hall's personal distance zone. Standing closer can violate expectations and cause discomfort and unease; standing farther apart can be perceived as unfriendly. Unless you are very close to another person, touching is generally considered a violation of space rather than a signal of warmth, particularly among adults.

- *A greater emphasis is placed on verbal messages.* Although most communication is still done nonverbally during interactions, U.S. speakers tend to be verbally explicit in terms of describing feelings, opinions, and thoughts. A non-native speaker may need to be more explicit and should not assume that such explicitness is rude—such directness is simply a cultural characteristic.

- *U.S. uses of emblems are often for less formal messages.* Commonly used emblems range from obscene gestures to specific emblems representing athletic teams. Unlike emblems in other cultures, very few U.S. emblems signify status or respect.

- *Eye contact is expected.* In nearly every communication situation, consistent eye contact is viewed positively as a signal of confidence, warmth, and attentiveness. Even in situations in which there are strong power differences, such as the communication between a supervisor and an employee, eye contact is desirable; a lack of consistent eye contact can cause you to be viewed as untrustworthy or noncredible.

- *For vocal characteristics, bigger tends to be better.* Listeners tend to react positively to speakers who have strong volume, good vocal variety, and forceful projection and articulation.

As a general principle, U.S. speakers tend to be expressive with most nonverbal behaviors, though such expressiveness is typically not found with respect to space and touch. You will notice many other cultural characteristics of U.S. nonverbal behavior as you gain more experience observing native speakers. You may integrate some of those differences into your own communication repertoire; others you may dismiss. Being observant and asking native speakers about their use of various nonverbal behaviors, as well as their expectations for how others use those behaviors, will help non-native speakers develop their own skills more quickly.

the students, using a relaxed stance, and speaking in an animated manner, but these behaviors did not discourage the use of handheld devices.[84] If your professors cannot influence your behavior, consider what you might do to show interest and to avoid being distracted.

2. Recognize that others may use time differently than you do. It is always important to attend class and to be on time. Your professor probably offers office hours. Take advantage of meeting with him or her during these scheduled times, rather than waiting until the last minute and then demanding an emergency meeting or having an electronic "meltdown."

3. Manage your time just as your professors and employers do. Find time to do your homework, to study for exams, to write papers, and to meet with your study groups. Similarly, go to work on time or earlier, stay until your shift or time is completed, and do your job while you are at work.

4. Manage your time in your interactions with others. Allow others to share their experiences, and be willing to exchange talk time. Do you tend to interrupt or overlap your professors or employers? Allow other people a full hearing.

5. Be aware that most professors and most employers are not interested in a personal relationship. Do not engage in romantic behaviors with either one. Touching, using intimate physical space, requiring time alone after hours, and engaging in other behaviors are generally inappropriate.

6. Dress appropriately for school and for work. Students have

assumed very relaxed standards for classroom attire. If your college allows revealing casual clothes, you may be able to dress similarly. However, you will want to consider dressing more conservatively for your job. Some work sites do not even allow jeans.

7. Avoid using back-channel nonverbal communication to suggest that you disagree with the professor or employer. If you have a question or honest disagreement, express it clearly and explicitly. Most people appreciate hearing about differences in opinions, but they do not value sneers or being mocked.

keeping it real

Understanding Cultural Differences in Nonverbal Communication

Amrit Rao has learned a great deal about nonverbal communication. He knows that we reduce our uncertainty about others through our interactions with them. What strategies did he employ? On the first day of class, he behaved cautiously and adopted those U.S. customs with which he felt comfortable. He went to class early, he was positive and smiled a lot, he did not invade others' physical space, he used some gestures, he tried to be at ease and confident, and he avoided wearing clothing unique to his culture. Happily, the other students were welcoming and interested in his background. They asked him to give a talk on the customs and traditions of his people. They told him that they would like to see his native dress, as well. Amrit even made Shahi Tukri for the class when he gave his presentation; surprisingly, his classmates thought it tasted like French toast.

Chapter Review & Study Guide

Summary

In this chapter, you learned the following:

1. Nonverbal communication is defined as the process of using wordless messages to generate meaning.

2. Verbal and nonverbal codes work in conjunction with each other in six ways: to repeat, to emphasize, to complement, to contradict, to substitute, and to regulate.

3. People often have difficulty interpreting nonverbal codes because

   - They use the same code to communicate a variety of meanings.

   - They use a variety of codes to communicate the same meaning.

4. Nonverbal codes consist of nonword symbols, such as the following:

   - Bodily movements and facial expression include posture, gestures, and other bodily movements and facial expressions, known as kinesics.

   - Bodily appearance includes how physically attractive one is.

   - Proxemics is the study of the human use of space and distance.

   - Temporal communication, or chronemics, is the way people organize and use time and the messages that are created because of their organization and use of it.

   - Tactile communication is the use of touch in communication.

   - Paralinguistic features include the nonword sounds and nonword characteristics of language, such as pitch, volume, rate, and quality.

   - Objectics, or object language, is the study of the human use of clothing and other artifacts as nonverbal codes.

5. The types of bodily movement are posture, gestures, and facial expression.

6. Physical attraction affects how other people treat us, how socially successful we are, with whom we have a relationship, how credible we are, and how persuasive we are.

7. Personal space is affected by one's size and one's biological sex.

8. Objects are used in communication to indicate one's age, gender, status, role, socioeconomic class, group memberships, personality, and relationship to the opposite sex.

9. You can solve some of the difficulties in interpreting nonverbal codes if you

- Consider all the variables in each communication situation.
- Consider all the available verbal and nonverbal codes.
- Use descriptive feedback to minimize misunderstandings.

Key Terms

Adaptors	Inflection	Rate
Affect displays	Kinesics	Regulating
Articulation	Nonverbal codes	Regulators
Artifacts	Nonverbal communication	Repeating
Chronemics	Nonword sounds	Silence
Complementing	Objectics	Substituting
Contradicting	Paralinguistic features	Tactile communication
Emblems	Pitch	Vocal cues
Emphasizing	Pronunciation	Volume
Enunciation	Proxemics	
Illustrators	Quality	

Study Questions

connect
For further review, go to the LearnSmart study module for this chapter.

1. What is included in nonverbal communication?
   a. only vocalized cues
   b. only nonvocalized cues
   c. nonword vocalizations as well as nonvocalized cues
   d. vocalized words

2. Nonverbal codes work together with vocalized words to
   a. generalize and broaden.
   b. analyze and synthesize.
   c. confuse and distinguish.
   d. contradict and substitute.

3. One of the difficulties of interpreting nonverbal codes is
   a. one code may communicate several different meanings.
   b. no two nonverbal codes communicate the same meaning.
   c. each nonverbal cue has only one perceived meaning.
   d. observers can easily distinguish meaning from specific nonverbal cues.

4. Bodily movement, facial expression, the use of time, and vocal cues, among other actions, are examples of
   a. kinesics.
   b. complementation.
   c. nonverbal codes.
   d. adaptors.

5. When interpreting nonverbal communication, it is important to consider
   a. context.
   b. only observed behavior.
   c. gut instinct.
   d. "reading" people.

6. Pointing to your wrist while asking for the time is an example of a(n)
   a. adaptor.
   b. illustrator.
   c. regulator.
   d. emblem.

7. Compared with those who are unattractive, physically attractive people
   a. tend to be snobbish.
   b. never learn how to work well with others.
   c. are more likely to wait until they are older to marry.
   d. are treated differently as children.

8. With regard to chronemics, Americans of high status
   a. are granted the opportunity of arriving late.
   b. are always on time.
   c. work on several tasks at a time.
   d. view privacy as important.

9. In relation to gender and tactile communication, which of the following is true?
   a. Females and their daughters touch each other the least.
   b. Men value touch more than women do.
   c. Women are touched more than men.
   d. Females touch others more often than males touch others.

10. Which of the following provide physical and psychological protection, permit personal expression, and communicate age, gender, socioeconomic class, and personality?
   a. vocal cues
   b. affect displays
   c. illustrators
   d. artifacts

Answers:

1. (c); 2. (d); 3. (a); 4. (c); 5. (a); 6. (b); 7. (d); 8. (a); 9. (c); 10. (b)

Critical Thinking

1. Think back to chapter 2, on perception. Which nonverbal cues have you demonstrated that led others to make errors in perception? Which nonverbal cues have others demonstrated that led you to make errors in your perception? Why do you think these particular cues resulted in misinterpretation or confusion?

2. When you are at the library or other public place, note how people "mark their territory." Do they use their backpack or purse, books, or nothing at all? Also observe the size of people's personal space. Does one gender have a smaller space than the other? Does age make a difference? In what situations does that distance decrease?

listening
and critical thinking

When you have read and thought about this chapter, you will be able to:

1. Discuss three reasons why listening is important in our lives.

2. Define and describe various types of listening as a process.

3. Analyze how noise, perceptions, and your own characteristics can influence the listening process.

4. Use critical thinking, nonverbal, and verbal strategies to become a better listener.

5. Adapt strategies for effective listening to specific situations, including the workplace, the classroom, and mediated environments.

6. Engage in ethical listening behaviors.

Listening is our most frequently used but least studied communication skill. In this chapter you will learn about the listening process, some factors that can inhibit effective listening, different types of listening, and strategies for becoming a more effective listener. Our hope is that you will learn that listening, like any other communication behavior, is a skill that must be developed through forethought and practice.

Walk into any classroom and you will likely see a variety of screens open. At the front of the room, the teacher may have a projection screen showing a slideshow or other visual supplement to the lecture. As you scan across the room you will no doubt see students with smartphones, iPads, laptops, netbooks, e-readers, and other devices open. The sheer array of computing power available in just one small classroom today could rival that found on space capsules only a few decades ago! Does all this classroom computing capability help?

Rachel, a recent high school graduate attending a school of art and design, thinks so. While her art history teacher lectures, Rachel is able to stay tapped into her favorite blogs about fashion, she can connect with her friends on Facebook, and she can even tweet things that pop into her mind. Rachel is not unlike many college students today—she is an active member of the digital social world and uses her smartphone to stay connected. Few minutes go by without her handling her phone to do something online.

While in class one day, Rachel was posting a status update to Facebook when her professor asked her a question. After several moments of silence, Rachel realized she had been called on; with an embarrassed apology, she caught on to the teacher's question and offered a quick answer. She did not intend to be disrespectful, but her use of technology definitely impeded her ability to listen.

Rachel's story is a common one. The dizzying availability of mobile digital media forces our attention in many directions, which often disrupts our fundamental ability to listen to those around us. As you will learn, multitasking is one of many barriers to effective listening—an unanticipated lesson that Rachel learned in class.

How do you think Rachel could improve her listening habits? Is putting her phone away the only thing she needs to do? At the end of the chapter, we'll take another look at Rachel's situation and consider how she might become a more effective listener.

How would you rate yourself as a listener? Listening is an important skill that takes careful practice and commitment. In this chapter you'll learn ways to identify your own strengths and weaknesses as a listener and to improve your listening skills in your relationships with others, in the workplace, and in the classroom.

The Importance of Listening in Our Lives

Listening is one of our most common communication activities. According to a 2009 study, typical college students spend roughly 51% of their time listening to others or using mass media.[1] As shown in figure 5.1, the largest portion of our time communicating, approximately 24%, is spent listening to others in face-to-face settings. Given how important listening is to our work as communicators, learning to listen well is critical.

As you can imagine from the amount of time we spend listening to others, listening helps us accomplish important things. Listening helps us build and maintain relationships and can even help us determine whether the person we are talking to is being deceitful. How do we learn to be better listeners in our interpersonal relationships? A study reported by Andrew Ledbetter and Paul Schrodt found that listening skills and

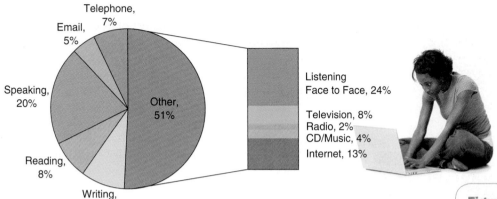

Figure 5.1

Proportions of time spent by college students in communication activities. Source: Janusic, L. A., & Wolvin, A. D. (2009). 24 hours in a day: A listening update to the time studies. *The International Journal of Listening, 23,* 104–120.

behaviors are influenced by family communication patterns we experience early in life. As they noted, "when families create an environment where family members are encouraged to openly discuss a variety of topics, children may be more likely to learn how to process complex and ambiguous information without anxiety."[2]

Listening is also recognized as an essential skill for business success.[3] Because of effective listening, we are able to improve workplace relationships and be more productive.[4] Richard Schulze, the founder of Best Buy, stressed in a keynote speech to other chief executive officers that listening to customers is critical to business success in an increasingly competitive global marketplace.[5] He noted that, because customer interests rapidly evolve, failing to listen guarantees failure. Corporations and small businesses alike are developing robust tools to listen. A recent article in *AdWeek* described tools used by various types of organizations to track what is trending on Twitter for various types of audiences.[6] For example, a service called TrendingTarget follows Twitter feeds for over 2,000 mothers to determine what they are interested in at the moment. Consumers of this service might learn that moms are interested in "#GNO" (Girls Night Out) or certain types of recipes for locally grown foods. By listening to what certain audience demographics stress on social media sites, such as Twitter or Facebook, businesses can better target products to consumers. Listening is even more strongly linked to successful communication within highly technical fields, such as medicine, in which doctors' improved listening skills are associated with reduced numbers of malpractice claims from patients.[7]

What Is Listening?

John Dewey, a twentieth-century educational and social philosopher, observed in his book *The Public and Its Problems* that true democracy happens when we take time to listen to the people around us—our friends and family, our neighbors, and the people in our community.[8] Dewey's observation seems intuitive; however, how often have you "faked" listening? Your friend may tell you about something that happened to him or her, but you only "half listened," or you listened to a neighbor talk about a community event but quickly forgot about it. In fact, good listening is hard and takes sustained effort. Learning to be an effective listener starts with understanding what the listening process involves, then trying to improve how you enact that process.

The first step in learning about listening is to understand the distinction between hearing and listening. **Hearing** is simply the act of receiving sound. Although much of this

hearing
The act of receiving sound.

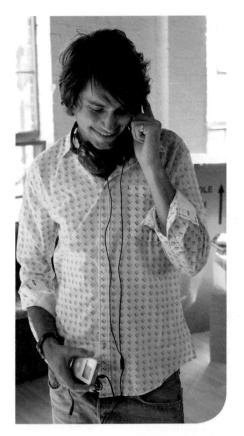

Listening for enjoyment is an easy way to relax.

chapter is devoted to listening rather than hearing, there are important things to learn about the physical act of hearing. First, your listening behaviors now will influence your hearing later in life.[9] In fact, many audiologists warn that young adults and even children should be careful when listening to music using headphones or earbuds. When using lower-quality earbuds that do not block external noise, people have a tendency to increase the volume to levels that can cause long-term damage to their hearing. Even without hearing loss stemming from loud noise, some people have other physical problems with their hearing. Tinnitus is a condition that results in a constant "ringing" in the ears. The American Tinnitus Association (www.ata.org) estimates that over 50 million Americans experience tinnitus to some degree—the condition can be caused by many factors, ranging from allergies to certain types of benign tumors. Thus, we should not assume that everyone can hear equally well, even those in your group of friends.

Hearing is not the same as listening. **Listening,** as defined by the International Listening Association, is "the active process of receiving, constructing meaning from, and responding to spoken and/or nonverbal messages. It involves the ability to retain information, as well as to react empathically and/or appreciatively to spoken and/or nonverbal messages."[10] **Active listening** is "involved listening with a purpose."[11] Active listening includes (1) listening carefully by using all available senses, (2) paraphrasing what we hear both mentally and verbally, (3) checking your understanding to ensure accuracy, and (4) providing feedback. Feedback consists of the listener's verbal and nonverbal responses to the speaker and the speaker's message.

Active listening can occur in different forms, including empathetic listening and critical listening:

- **Empathic listening** is attempting to understand the other person. You engage in empathic listening by using both mindfulness, which is being "fully engaged in the moment,"[12] and empathy, which is the ability to perceive another person's worldview as if it were your own.

- In **critical listening** you challenge the speaker's message by evaluating its accuracy, meaningfulness, and utility. Critical listening and critical thinking go hand in hand: you cannot listen critically if you do not think critically. Skills in critical listening are especially important because we are constantly bombarded with commercials, telemarketing calls, and other persuasive messages.

Not all listening is active listening. **Listening for enjoyment** occurs in situations that are relaxing, fun, or emotionally stimulating. Whether you are listening to your favorite band or television show, or to your friend telling a story, you continue listening because you enjoy it. Besides aiding relaxation, listening to enjoyable music can even reduce pain for hospital patients.[13]

The Process of Listening

The process of listening is summarized in figure 5.2. As the illustration shows, we receive stimuli (such as music, words, or sounds) in the ear, where the smallest bones in the body translate the vibrations into sensations registered by the brain. The brain focuses on the sensations and gives them meaning. Your brain might, for example,

listening
The active process of receiving, constructing meaning from, and responding to spoken and/or nonverbal messages. It involves the ability to retain information, as well as to react empathically and/or appreciatively to spoken and/or nonverbal messages.

active listening
Involved listening with a purpose.

empathic listening
Listening with a purpose and attempting to understand the other person.

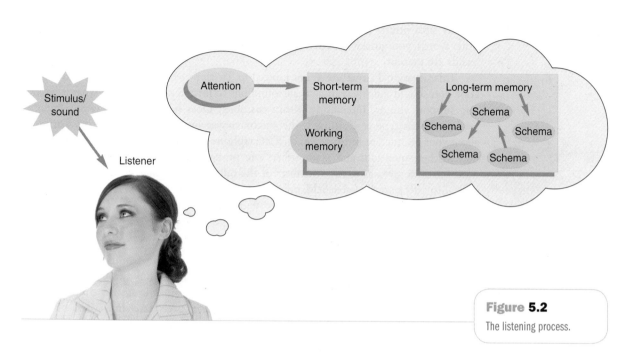

Figure 5.2

The listening process.

recognize the first few bars of a favorite song, the voice of a favorite artist, or the sound of a police siren. On hearing these sounds, you immediately know what they mean. Your interpreted message is then stored in your memory for immediate use or future recall.[14]

As we discuss later, people create many obstacles to effective listening. Not all obstacles, however, are the fault of lazy, unethical, or ineffective listeners. Because listening is a process, natural barriers present themselves at various stages. In the following sections, these natural barriers are explained for each major step in the listening process: attention, working memory, short-term memory, and long-term memory.

ATTENTION

Anyone who has been a student has heard the command "Pay attention!" What exactly are teachers expecting when they say this? Paying attention means controlling your selective and automatic attention.[15] **Selective attention** is the sustained focus we give to things that are important. Your favorite music, conversation with your friend, statements made by your date over dinner, and your professor at the front of the class are things that draw our selective attention. Selective attention is a form of selective perception, which you learned about in chapter 2. In contrast, **automatic attention** is the instinctive focus we give to important things we experience in our surroundings. A siren, a loud noise, your name shouted from across the room, or a new person walking into the room can capture your automatic attention. In any listening situation we must manage our selective attention to keep it from being overwhelmed by our automatic attention. In essence, in saying "Pay attention," your teacher is asking you to ignore your automatic attention and focus your selective attention. In practicing your attention skills, you should not assume that selective attention means paying attention to only one thing. Studies exploring how people use social media and the Internet suggest that we actually learn to quickly scan our surroundings and assess the importance of several items of interest as they relate to one another.[16] Think about the timeline in a Twitter feed. Obviously, you would not open Twitter and focus on only one tweet; rather, you would

critical listening
Listening that challenges the speaker's message by evaluating its accuracy, meaningfulness, and utility.

listening for enjoyment
Situations involving relaxing, fun, or emotionally stimulating information.

selective attention
The sustained focus we give to stimuli we deem important.

automatic attention
The instinctive focus we give to stimuli signaling a change in our surroundings, stimuli that we deem important, or stimuli that we perceive to signal danger.

quickly scan hours worth of tweets from those you follow to see what is trending. In other words, you quickly give selective attention to each tweet and then determine what trends are present.

This situational awareness is not limited to Twitter or Facebook. In any listening situation you should quickly scan your surroundings to form a perspective on what is happening. Suppose you are interacting with a customer. Does he or she have family members present? What type of clothing is the customer wearing? Does he or she have printouts about your product, or information on a smartphone screen? Quickly giving selective attention to these questions and many others can probably help you listen more carefully to what the customer has to say. Members of the military know that situational awareness is critical to safety on the battlefield, on the sea, or in the air. Those skills are equally important when dealing with others in less threatening situations.

WORKING MEMORY

working memory
The part of our consciousness that interprets and assigns meaning to stimuli we pay attention to.

Once we have paid selective attention to relevant sounds and stimuli, our brain must initially process and make sense of those stimuli. **Working memory** is where we interpret and assign meaning to things we hear. Our working memory looks for shortcuts when processing information. Rather than trying to interpret each letter in a word, our working memory quickly recognizes the pattern of letters and assigns meaning. Likewise, when we hear the sounds of a word, our working memory recognizes the pattern of sounds rather than trying to process each sound separately. On a larger scale, our working memory can recognize patterns of words. For instance, when you hear over a store intercom "MOD line 1," you might interpret that pattern to mean that the manager on duty should pick up line 1.

Working memory uses patterns of words or other symbols stored in long-term memory to apply these shortcuts for assigning meaning. Not surprisingly, research has found that when children have difficulty with language development they have less efficient working memory.[17] That is, when children do not learn language skills and develop strong vocabularies, their working memory must work harder to decipher new information. Of course, the opposite is also true. Helping children develop strong language skills early in life will likely help them become better listeners later.

SHORT-TERM MEMORY

short-term memory
A temporary storage place for information.

Once interpreted in working memory, information is sent to either short-term or long-term memory. **Short-term memory** is a temporary storage place for information. All of us use short-term memory to retain thoughts needed for immediate use. You might think of short-term memory as being similar to a Post-it note. You will use the information on the note for a quick reference but will soon discard it or decide to write it down in a more secure location.

We constantly use short-term memory, but it is the least efficient of our memory resources. Classic studies in the field of psychology have documented that short-term memory is limited in both the quantity of information stored and the length of time information is retained.[18] In terms of quantity, short-term memory is limited to 7 ± 2 bits of information. A bit of information is any organized unit of information, including sounds, letters, words, sentences, or something less concrete, such as ideas, depending on the ability of working memory to recognize patterns. If your short-term memory becomes overloaded (for average people, more than 9 bits of information), you begin to forget. Short-term memory is also limited to about 20 seconds in duration unless some strategy, such as rehearsal, is used. If you quickly scan and rehearse a definition from your textbook in preparation for a quiz, you will likely remember it. However, if something breaks your concentration and you stop rehearsing the definition, the words will likely be lost. Unfortunately, many listeners rely too much on short-term memory during the listening process. Researchers in the field of communication have found that individuals recall only 50% of a message immediately after listening to it, and only 25% after a short delay.[19] Relying on our short-term memory is not a substitute for trying to encode information into long-term memory.

LONG-TERM MEMORY

Information processed in working memory can also be stored in long-term memory for later recall. Similarly, information temporarily stored in short-term memory can be deemed important and subsequently stored in long-term memory. If short-term memory is the Post-it note in the listening process, long-term memory is the supercomputer. **Long-term memory** is our permanent storage place for information, including but not limited to past experiences; language; values; knowledge; images of people; memories of sights, sounds, and smells; and even fantasies. Unlike short-term memory, long-term memory has no known limitations in the quantity or duration of stored information.

Being startled can break your concentration and cause you to forget what is in short-term memory.

long-term memory
Our permanent storage place for information, including but not limited to past experiences; language; values; knowledge; images of people; memories of sights, sounds, and smells; and even fantasies.

schema
Organizational "filing systems" for thoughts held in long-term memory.

Explanations of how long-term memory works are only speculative; however, researchers hypothesize that our thoughts are organized according to **schema,** which are organizational "filing systems" for thoughts held in long-term memory. We might think of schema as an interconnected web of information. Our ability to remember information in long-term memory is dependent on finding connections to the correct schema containing the particular memory, thought, idea, or image we are trying to recall.

In theory, people with normally functioning brains never lose information stored in long-term memory. How is it, then, that we often forget things we listen to? When we try to access information in long-term memory, we access schema holding needed information through the use of stimulus cues, which can be words, images, or even smells and tastes. If the cue we receive does not give us enough information to access the corresponding schema, we may be unable to recall the information. Consider, for example, a situation in which you see a person who looks familiar. In this case you recognize the person (a visual cue); however, that stimulus does not provide you with enough information to recall who it is. If you hear the person's voice or if he or she mentions a previous encounter with you, you may then have enough information to activate the correct schema and recall specific details about that person.

Long-term memory plays a key role in the listening process. As we receive sounds, our working memory looks for patterns based on schema contained in our long-term memory. Thus, our ability to use language, to recognize concepts, and to interpret meaning is based on the schema we accumulate over a lifetime. If we encounter new information that does not relate to preexisting schema, our working memory instructs our long-term memory to create new schema to hold the information. The arrows in figure 5.2 depict this working relationship between schema and working memory.

Barriers to Listening

Although you might agree that listening is important, you may not be properly prepared for effective listening. A survey conducted by a corporate training and development firm noted that 80% of the corporate executives taking part in the survey rated listening as the most important skill in the workforce. Unfortunately, nearly 30% of the same executives

Table 5.1 Barriers to Listening

Type of Barrier	Explanation and Example
Noise	
Physical distractions	All the stimuli in the environment that keep you from focusing on the message. Example: loud music playing at a party
Mental distractions	The wandering of the mind when it is supposed to be focusing on something. Example: thinking about a lunch date while listening to a teacher
Multitasking	Trying to do two or more tasks simultaneously. Example: talking on the phone while reading Facebook updates
Factual distractions	Focusing so intently on details that you miss the main point. Example: listening to all the details of a conversation but forgetting the main idea
Semantic distractions	Overresponding to an emotion-laden word or concept. Example: not listening to a teacher when she mentions "Marxist theory"
Perception of Others	
Status	Devoting attention based on the social standing, rank, or perceived value of another. Example: not listening to a freshman in a group activity
Stereotypes	Treating individuals as if they were the same as others in a given category. Example: assuming all older people have similar opinions
Sights and sounds	Letting appearances or voice qualities affect your listening. Example: not listening to a person with a screechy voice
Yourself	
Egocentrism	Excessive self-focus, or seeing yourself as the central concern in every conversation. Example: redirecting conversations to your own problems
Defensiveness	Acting threatened and feeling as though you must defend what you have said or done. Example: assuming others' comments are veiled criticisms of you
Experiential superiority	Looking down on others as if their experience with life were not as good as yours. Example: not listening to those with less experience
Personal bias	Letting your own predispositions, or strongly held beliefs, interfere with your ability to interpret information correctly. Example: assuming that people are generally truthful (or deceitful)
Pseudolistening	Pretending to listen but letting your mind or attention wander to something else. Example: daydreaming while your professor is lecturing

said that listening was the most lacking communication skill among their employees.[20] In the section explaining the connection between listening and thinking, we discussed several natural impediments to listening. In this section we explain barriers we create for ourselves in the listening process. Table 5.1 identifies noise, perceptions of others, and yourself as potential listening barriers.

The barriers listed in table 5.1 are common, but as our cultural listening habits change, these barriers evolve and new ones are added. A conference sponsored by the International

Commission on Biological Effects of Noise noted that the proliferation of noise created by humans—everything from cars and airplanes to iPods and videogames—is starting to cause fatal accidents for adults and poorer achievement in children just because of the sheer number of audible distractions.[21] Likewise, Lenore Skenazy, writing in *Advertising Age*, complained that smartphones and other personal communication devices might be diminishing ongoing practice with face-to-face communication skills, such as listening.[22] Other studies show that listening to loud, fast music significantly diminishes our ability to comprehend things we read or hear.[23] In sum, these barriers point to one conclusion: our listening practices are more complicated because more and more things draw our attention.

Modern technology, including smartphones, laptops, the Internet, and tablet computers, can pose challenges for good listening. Do you remember the story about Rachel at the beginning of this chapter? How often have you texted or checked Facebook while in class? If you are in a large class, you have probably even seen people carry on telephone conversations! When we multitask by trying to listen to someone while texting, tweeting, or just playing on the Internet, we are likely diminishing our ability to function well as a listener. Recall that short-term memory is limited. When we multitask we place greater strain on our short-term and working memory, which can impede all other aspects of our ability to process information. For instance, assume you are listening to a training podcast for your job and you decide to answer a text from your partner. Each time you stop listening to the podcast to read/answer a text, you lose mental momentum on your listening and have to restart. Scholars who study multitasking conclude that completing the primary task, such as listening to a podcast, takes longer and likely is done with less success because of the interruptions.[24] Of all the barriers to listening, you have most control over this one: in important listening situations, minimize distractions and avoid multitasking!

Obviously, there are many challenges to effective listening, not the least of which is faking being a good listener, which we might do for various reasons. Some scholars argue that "pretend listening" is "a perfectly useful, and sometimes indispensable, feature of the pragmatics of ordinary communication."[25] In some situations we may need to be polite and act like we are listening, even though we really don't want to. We might portray the act of listening to avoid hurting another's feelings, we may pretend to listen in an effort to get others to model our behavior, or we may act like we are listening because we know others expect us to do so in a given situation. These scholars argue that there are definite risks in poor listening; however, they also point out that expecting or assuming that everyone can be a perfect listener in every circumstance is unrealistic. Although they do not conclude that we should become better at fake listening, they do suggest that we recognize the realities facing people with whom we communicate, because they may not listen with 100% effort all the time.

■ Men and women tend to enact different behaviors when listening.

Gender Differences in Listening

Have you ever had a conversation with a person of the opposite sex and thought afterwards that he or she just did not listen well? If so, you are not alone. Debra Tannen, a linguistics professor and acclaimed author of the book *You Just Don't Understand: Women and Men in Conversation*, suggests that men and women have

Table 5.2 Listening Differences Between Men and Women

	Women	Men
Purpose for Listening	Listen to understand the other person's emotions and to find common interests	Listen in order to take action and solve problems
Listening Preferences	Like complex information that requires careful evaluation	Like short, concise, unambiguous, and error-free communication
Listening Awareness	Are highly perceptive to how well the other person understands	Often fail to recognize when others do not understand
Nonverbal Listening Behaviors	Tend to be attentive and to have sustained eye contact with the other person	Tend to be less attentive and to use glances to monitor reactions; use eye contact to indicate liking
Interruptive Behaviors	Interrupt less often, with interruptions usually signaling agreement and support	Interrupt more often, with interruptions often used to switch topics

Sources: Tannen, D. (2001). *You just don't understand: Women and men in conversation.* New York: Harper-Collins. Watson, K., Lazarus, C. J., & Todd, T. (1999). First-year medical students' listener preferences: A longitudinal study. *International Journal of Listening, 13,* 1–11. Weisfeld, C. C., & Stack, M. A. (2002). When I look into your eyes. *Psychology, Evolution and Gender, 4,* 125–147.

very distinct communication styles, which influence everything from how they use vocal inflections to how they listen. For example, Tannen suggests that men tend to be more instrumental or task-oriented when communicating, whereas women tend to be more relationally oriented.[26] Although there are many similarities between men and women, table 5.2 lists some of the more commonly observed differences relevant to listening.

How Can You Become a Better Listener?

So far in this chapter, we have emphasized the importance of listening while pointing out both natural and self-taught barriers to effective listening. Faced with this knowledge, you might wonder how any of us can hope to become effective listeners. After all, the potential barriers are many. Fortunately, each of us can take several steps to overcome these barriers to good listening. In this section we highlight how you can become a better listener by listening critically and using verbal and nonverbal communication effectively.

LISTEN AND THINK CRITICALLY

critical thinking
Analyzing the speaker, the situation, and the speaker's ideas to make critical judgments about the message being presented.

As mentioned earlier in the chapter, critical listening and critical thinking go hand in hand: you cannot listen critically without also thinking critically. We have already noted that critical listening is a form of active listening in which you carefully analyze the accuracy, meaningfulness, and utility of a speaker's message. Similarly, **critical thinking** involves analyzing the speaker, the situation, and the speaker's ideas to make critical judgments about the message being presented. Although we discuss critical thinking in terms of its relationship to critical listening, you also use critical thinking when reading, watching television, or analyzing the ingredients of a tasty meal.

One way to think critically is to analyze the communication situation. As mentioned at the beginning of the chapter, situational awareness means that you reflect carefully on the space around you and consider how aspects of that space should influence how you listen. Are there characteristics of the situation that tip you off that the information will be important? If your supervisor organized a staff meeting, would you pay more attention if she came in with a somber look on her face after a long meeting with the department manager? The communication context will provide cues about the situation and suggest key things to remain aware of while listening.

A second skill in critical listening is to analyze the credibility of the speaker. **Source credibility** is the extent to which you perceive the speaker as competent and trustworthy. If you wanted to know what procedures were required to study in Europe for a semester, who would give you the best information? Would you be more likely to trust your roommate, who heard about foreign exchange programs during freshman orientation; your adviser, who had an exchange student a few years back; or the director of international programs on your campus? If your car ran poorly, would you trust your neighbor's advice or that of an auto mechanic? The choice seems obvious in these situations. When assessing the credibility of a speaker, you should determine the credibility of the person in relation to his or her qualifications, experience, and potential biases or ulterior motives for taking a certain position.

One way of analyzing the credibility of speakers is to determine whether they are reporting something they have seen or experienced personally, or something they have heard from someone else. Also important is whether they are providing factual accounts or opinions. The following questions can guide your preliminary analysis of source credibility.

1. *Is the person presenting observations or inferences?* Observations are descriptions of things that can be seen, heard, tasted, smelled, or felt. Inferences are conclusions drawn from observations. You might observe that a number of people who are homeless live in your community. Based on that observation, you might infer that your community does not have enough affordable housing.

sizing things up

Barriers to Listening

The following are several statements describing how you might react to specific listening situations. Read each statement carefully and indicate how strongly you agree or disagree by using the following scale:

1 = Strongly disagree

2 = Disagree

3 = Neither agree nor disagree

4 = Agree

5 = Strongly agree

When listening to others I often . . .

1. Assume that their viewpoint will be similar to those of other people like them.
2. Respect others' opinions, even when they have less experience than I have.
3. Think about other things while the person is talking.
4. Get distracted by their physical appearance.
5. Pay close attention but have trouble remembering their main ideas.
6. Feel threatened or that the person is attacking me or my beliefs.
7. Get put off by terms or phrases used by others.
8. Pay less attention to people who are not important.
9. Pay less attention if what they are saying does not pertain to me.

There are no right or wrong answers to these statements. A guide for scoring your responses appears in the appendix at the end of the text (p. 348).

source credibility
The extent to which the speaker is perceived as competent to make the claims he or she is making.

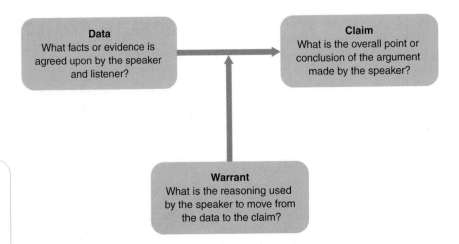

Figure 5.3

Stephen Toulmin's concepts of data, claim, and warrant. Source: Toulmin, S. E. (1958). *The uses of argument.* New York: Cambridge University Press.

first-person observation
An observation based on something you personally have sensed.

second-person observation
A report of what another person observed.

2. *If presenting observations, are they first-person or second-person?* A **first-person observation** is based on something that was personally sensed; a **second-person observation** is a report of what another person observed. First-person observations are typically more accurate, because they are direct accounts rather than inferences drawn from others' accounts.

Although a careful analysis of these questions will help you develop initial perceptions about a person's credibility, your analysis should not end there. The speaker's sincerity, trustworthiness, passion, and use of evidence and reasoning are among many factors that you might take into account to refine your assessment of the person's credibility.

After you have analyzed the situation and formed initial impressions about the person's credibility, a final step in critical thinking is to analyze the arguments the person is making. One of the simplest ways of analyzing an argument is to use Stephen Toulmin's concepts of data, claim, and warrant.[27] As shown in figure 5.3, Toulmin provides a way of diagramming how the components of an argument fit together. Starting on the right, a claim is the overall point or conclusion of the argument. Every argument begins with data, which consist of factual or agreed-upon evidence. Based on the evidence, a speaker uses a warrant to develop a logical connection, or bridge, between the agreed-upon data and the claim. If any of these elements are missing, the argument has no foundation.

We see examples of Toulmin's argument layout in nearly every persuasive speech. When Apple launched the iPad, Chairperson Steve Jobs developed arguments for why consumers should purchase the device. He started with agreed-upon data that consumers want easy-to-use mobile computing devices that help them accomplish daily tasks with ease. This was easy to establish, given the success of the iPhone and other mobile computing devices. Second, Jobs established the warrant that the iPad accomplishes this objective. His reasoning was based on a series of examples, in which he demonstrated various things the iPad can do. Finally, he concluded with the claim that people should purchase the iPad because of how it helps them accomplish common tasks. You can use the questions posed in figure 5.3 to dissect arguments presented by the speaker. Not only will you think more critically about what you are hearing, but you will also likely identify key questions you can ask of the speaker.

USE NONVERBAL COMMUNICATION EFFECTIVELY

Although you demonstrate active listening through verbal skills, the majority of your active listening ability is shown through nonverbal communication. The following nonverbal skills are essential to your ability to demonstrate active listening. As you listen to another person, have a friend observe you to determine if you are practicing these skills.

1. *Demonstrate bodily responsiveness.* Use movement and gestures to show your awareness of the speaker's message. Shaking your head in disbelief, checking the measurements of an object by indicating the size with your hands, and moving toward a person who is disclosing negative information are appropriate bodily responses.

2. *Lean forward.* By leaning toward the speaker, you demonstrate interest in the speaker. A forward lean suggests responsiveness as well as interest. In addition, leaning places you in a physical state of readiness to listen to the speaker.

3. *Use direct body orientation.* Do not angle yourself away from the speaker; instead, sit or stand so that you are directly facing him or her. A parallel body position allows the greatest possibility for observing and listening to the speaker's verbal and nonverbal messages. When you stand or sit at an angle to the speaker, you may be creating the impression that you are attempting to get away or that you are moving away from the speaker. An angled position also blocks your vision and allows you to be distracted by other stimuli in the environment.

4. *Maintain relaxed but alert posture.* Your posture should not be tense or "proper," but neither should it be so relaxed that you appear to be resting. Slouching suggests unresponsiveness; a tense body position suggests nervousness or discomfort; and a relaxed position accompanied by crossed arms and legs, a backward lean in a chair, and a confident facial expression suggests arrogance. Your posture should suggest to others that you are interested and that you are comfortable talking with them.

5. *Establish an open body position.* Sit or stand with your body open to the other person. Crossing your arms or legs may be more comfortable, but that posture frequently suggests that you are closed off psychologically as well as physically. In order to maximize your nonverbal message to the other person that you are "open" to him or her, you should sit or stand without crossing your arms or legs.

6. *Use positive, responsive facial expressions and head movement.* Your face and head will be the speaker's primary focus. The speaker will be observing you, and your facial expressions and head movement will be the key. You can demonstrate your interest by nodding your head to show interest or agreement. You can use positive and responsive facial expressions, such as smiling and raising your eyebrows.

7. *Establish direct eye contact.* The speaker will be watching your eyes for interest. One of the first signs of a lack of interest is the tendency to be distracted by other stimuli in the environment. For example, an instructor who continually glances out the door of her office, a roommate who sneaks peeks at the television program that is on, or a business executive who regularly looks at his watch is, while appearing to listen, indicating lack of interest. Try to focus on and direct your gaze at the

skill builder

Using TED to Practice Critical Thinking

Critical thinking is one of the most important listening skills you can develop while in college. Being a good critical listener is critical to all aspects of your adult life. You can practice suggestions for critical thinking discussed in this chapter by watching a TED video on a topic of interest to you (www.Ted.com, or use the free mobile TED app). While watching the video, analyze the speaker's credibility and attempt to dissect the arguments presented by the speaker using Toulmin's layout of argument.

speaker. When you begin to look around the room, you may find any number of other stimuli to distract your attention from the speaker and the message.

8. *Sit or stand close to the speaker.* Establishing close proximity to the speaker has two benefits. First, you put yourself in a position that allows you to hear the other person and that minimizes distracting noises, sights, and other stimuli. Second, you demonstrate your concern or your positive feelings for the speaker. You probably do not stand or sit close to people you do not like or respect, or with whom you do not have common experiences. Close physical proximity enables active listening.

9. *Be vocally responsive.* Change your pitch, rate, inflection, and volume as you respond to the speaker. Making appropriate changes and choices shows that you are actually listening, in contrast to responding in a standard, patterned manner that suggests you are only appearing to listen. The stereotypic picture of a husband and wife at the breakfast table, with the husband, hidden behind a newspaper, responding "yes, yes, yes" in a monotone while the wife tells him that their son has shaved his head, she is running off with the mail carrier, and the house is on fire provides a familiar example of the appearance of listening while one is actually oblivious to the speaker's message.

10. *Provide supportive utterances.* Sometimes you can demonstrate more concern through nonverbal sounds, such as "mmm," "mmm-hmm," and "uh-huh" than you can by stating "Yes, I understand." You can easily provide supportive utterances while others are talking or when they pause. You are suggesting to them that you are listening but do not want to interrupt with a verbalization of your own at this particular time. Such sounds encourage the speaker to continue without interruption.

USE VERBAL COMMUNICATION EFFECTIVELY

The notion of the verbal components of listening may seem strange to you. You may reason that, if you are engaged in listening, you cannot also be speaking. However, transactional communication assumes that you are simultaneously a sender and a receiver. That is, you can make verbal responses even as you are deeply involved in listening. To measure your current competence in this area, consider the skills you regularly practice:

■ Close proximity, and even touching, can show that you are listening with empathy.

1. *Invite additional comments.* Suggest that the speaker add more details or give additional information. Phrases such as "Go on," "What else?" "How did you feel about that?" and "Did anything else occur?" encourage the speaker to continue to share ideas and information.

2. *Ask questions.* One method of inviting the speaker to continue is to ask direct questions, requesting more in-depth details, definitions, or clarification.

3. *Identify areas of agreement or common experience.* Briefly relate similar past experiences, or briefly explain a similar point of view that you hold. Sharing ideas, attitudes, values, and beliefs is the basis of communication. In addition, such comments demonstrate your understanding.

4. *Vary verbal responses.* Use a variety of responses, such as "Yes," "I see," "Go on," and "Right," instead of relying on one standard, unaltered response, such as "Yes," "Yes," "Yes."

5. *Provide clear verbal responses.* Use specific and concrete words and phrases in your feedback to the speaker. Misunderstandings can occur if you do not provide easily understood responses.

6. *Use descriptive, non-evaluative responses.* Better to say "Your statistics are from an organization that is biased against gun control" (descriptive) than to say "Your speech was a bunch of lies" (evaluative). Trivializing or joking about serious disclosures suggests a negative evaluation of the speaker. Similarly, derogatory remarks are seen as offensive. Acting superior to the speaker by stating that you believe you have a more advanced understanding suggests an evaluative tone.

7. *Provide affirmative and affirming statements.* Comments such as "Yes," "I see," "I understand," and "I know" provide affirmation. Offering praise and specific positive statements demonstrates concern.

8. *Avoid complete silence.* The lack of any response suggests that you are not listening to the speaker. The "silent treatment" induced by sleepiness or lack of interest may result in defensiveness or anger on the part of the speaker. Appropriate verbal feedback demonstrates your active listening.

9. *Allow the other person the opportunity of a complete hearing.* When you discuss common feelings or experiences, avoid dominating the conversation. Allow the other person to go into depth and detail; give him or her the option of changing the topic under discussion; and let him or her talk without being interrupted.

CHECK YOUR UNDERSTANDING

When we listen to others, we are actually engaging in a specialized form of the perception process you read about in chapter 2. Because listening is a specialized form of perceiving, you should engage in perception checking to ensure that your perceptions match what the speaker intends. In the context of listening, rather than calling this perception checking, we might refer to it as checking your understanding. You can check your understanding by practicing these skills:

■ Use questions to check your understanding of what someone is saying.

1. *Ask questions for clarification.* Before testing your understanding of the speaker's message, make sure you have a clear idea of what he is saying. Begin by asking questions to gain more information. For specific factual information you may use closed questions (such as "yes/no" questions), and for more general information you may ask open-ended questions (questions pertaining to what, when, where, how, and why). Once you have gained sufficient information, you can ask the speaker to check your understanding against what he intended.

2. *Paraphrase the speaker's message.* Using "I statements," attempt to paraphrase what you think the speaker was saying, so that she can determine whether your understanding matches what she intended.

3. *Paraphrase the speaker's intent.* Using "I statements," attempt to paraphrase what you interpret as the intent or motivation of the speaker. After hearing your assumptions about his intent, the speaker may talk with you more to refine your understanding.

4. *Identify areas of confusion.* If there are specific aspects of the message that you are still confused about, mention those to the speaker while you are expressing your initial understanding of the message.

5. *Invite clarification and correction.* Asking the speaker to correct your interpretation of the message will invite additional explanation. The ensuing dialogue will help you and the speaker share meaning more effectively.

6. *Go back to the beginning.* As necessary, return to the first step in this process to check your new understanding of the speaker's message, intent, and so on. Good listening is a process without clear beginning and ending points, so you should check your understanding at each stage in the process.

Effective Listening in Different Situations

Most listening skills will serve you well in every communication situation. Listening critically, mastering nonverbal cues, and checking your understanding always aid your understanding. In the following sections are some additional suggestions for listening in the workplace, in the classroom, to the media, and in a second language.

LISTENING IN THE WORKPLACE

As our nation has shifted from an industrial-based economy to an information-based economy, effective listening has become recognized as an essential skill for workers. Statistics from the U.S. Bureau of Labor Statistics show that by 2014 just under 80% of the workforce in the United States will be employed in service-oriented industries, such as education, healthcare, retail sales, and state and local government.[28] These jobs all have one thing in common—they require employee–customer interaction in which listening skills translate into revenue.

Bob Gunn, president of a consulting firm with many Fortune 500 companies among its clients, notes the importance of empathic listening in professional situations:

> Feelings are to the quality of hearing as our sense of smell is to the enjoyment of a great meal or our sense of touch is to the expression of love. You are listening deeply when you become "lost in the words" and find yourself experiencing deep feelings of joy, gratitude, surprise, curiosity, warmth, closeness, wonder, beauty, or appreciation. You are hearing at a more profound level. The stronger the feeling, the more profound the understanding. And the more profound the understanding, the clearer the subsequent course of action.[29]

Gunn's point is that effective listeners must understand not only what their customers are saying but also what they are feeling. Those who do this effectively are able to build stronger relationships with customers and clients.

LISTENING IN THE CLASSROOM

Take a moment to think about how often, as a student, you find yourself listening to a lecture. If you were to estimate how much of your time is spent listening to lectures, how much would it be? If you said "a lot," you would not be alone. Researchers have estimated that college students spend at least 10 hours per week attending lectures.[30] If you take a typical 15 credit/hour load, that 10 hours per week translates into about 80% of your time in class being spent listening to lectures.[31] The prominence of listening in students' lives led Vinson and Johnson to coin the term **lecture listening**—the ability to listen to, mentally process, and recall lecture information.[32]

lecture listening
The ability to listen to, mentally process, and recall lecture information.

What constitutes effective lecture listening? Although a variety of answers have been offered, educational researcher Michael Gilbert provides the following general suggestions:

1. *Find areas of interest in what you are listening to.* Constantly look for how you can use the information.

2. *Remain open.* Avoid the temptation to focus only on the lecturer's delivery; withhold evaluative judgments until the lecturer has finished; recognize your emotional triggers and avoid letting them distract you.

3. *Work at listening.* Capitalize on your mind's ability to think faster than the lecturer can talk. Mentally summarize and review what has been said, mentally organize information, and find connections to what you already know or are currently learning.

4. *Avoid letting distractions distract.* Monitor your attention and recognize when it is waning. If you are becoming distracted, refocus your attention on the lecturer.

5. *Listen for and note main ideas.* Focus on the central themes of what is being presented, and make notes about those themes. Effective notes outlining the main ideas of a lecture can, in some cases, be more useful than pages of notes containing unorganized details.[33]

In addition to Gilbert's suggestions, communication researcher Dan O'Hair and colleagues recommend that you practice flexibility in listening.[34] By practicing your listening skills while watching information-packed documentaries or while attending public presentations on campus, you will not only become a more effective lecture listener but also will learn valuable information!

A final lecture listening strategy, one that is essential, is to take effective notes. Research has found that effective note taking during lectures can increase scores on exams by more than 20%—a difference between receiving a C and receiving an A.[35] Unfortunately, students typically do not record enough notes during a lecture. Research generally shows that less than 40% of the information in a lecture makes it into students' notes. In short, most students are unable to capitalize on the benefits of note taking simply because their notes are incomplete.

Now that you understand why note taking is so important, how can you become a more effective note taker? Most universities have study skills centers, where you can find information on different note-taking formats. Although the exact format for note taking might vary from one person to another, the objective is the same. In your notes your goal should be to record both the outline of the lecture—called organizational points—and the details supporting those points. The most effective way to ensure that you record all of these points is to listen for **lecture cues**—verbal or nonverbal signals that stress points or indicate transitions between ideas during a lecture. Table 5.3 summarizes various types of lecture cues commonly used by teachers. While taking notes, you should listen and watch for these types of cues.

Research has examined the importance of cues for students.[36] A group of students were taught about organizational cues and were asked to listen for those cues and take notes during a videotaped lecture. Students in another group were not informed about organizational cues but viewed and took notes during the same lecture. The students who were taught about organizational cues recorded four times the number of organizational points and twice the number of details in their notes. These students were able to capitalize on their note-taking effectiveness; they received the equivalent of an A on a quiz about the lecture. Their counterparts, who were unaware of and did not listen for organizational cues, received the equivalent of a C. This research looked at the effects of teaching students

lecture cues
Verbal or nonverbal signals that stress points or indicate transitions between ideas during a lecture.

Table 5.3 Common Lecture Cues Teachers Use

Type of Cue	Example	Main Uses
Written Outlines	Outline of lecture on transparency or PowerPoint slide	Indicate main and subordinate ideas
Words/phrases	Term written on the chalkboard	Stress important terms and accompanying definitions
Verbal importance cues	"Now, *and this will be on the exam next week*, we will explore . . ."	Stress important concepts deemed essential for recall/understanding
Semantic cues	"Here is an *example* [*definition, explanation, conclusion, implication,* or *illustration*] of uncertainty reduction theory in action . . ."	Signal common types of details that make up the lecture content
Organizational cues	"The *third thing* I want to discuss today is . . ."	Orally provide indications of main and subordinate points in a lecture
Nonverbal cues	Holding up two fingers when saying "I will discuss two concepts today . . ."	Can serve any of the functions of nonverbal behaviors discussed in the chapter on nonverbal communication

about organizational cues only. Imagine what could have happened if these students had been taught about all types of lecture cues! Fortunately, you are now equipped with this information.

LISTENING TO MEDIA

Think about how much time you spend watching television; listening to the radio; reading magazines, newspapers, or books; reading and writing e-mail; chatting online; or just surfing the Web. Many of us might avoid that thought because it might frighten us. The Centers for Disease Control and Prevention (CDC) has reported statistics showing that, on a typical day, children who are at least two years old spend over two hours per day watching television.[37] If other forms of media consumption, such as playing video games or using the Internet, were factored into these statistics, the number would be much higher. These statistics show that our saturation with mediated messages begins at an early age. Also, the CDC warns that such ubiquitous use of the media might be linked to important health issues, such as childhood obesity.

Given the quantity of mediated communication to which we are exposed each day, we must become critical consumers of such information. Think how much money you would spend if you "bought in" to every commercial you saw, or think of how much time it would take for you to read every e-mail message you get (including "junk" e-mail). Simply put, good listening behaviors are essential because mediated communication is so prevalent.

One way to be an effective listener in a mediated culture is to have information literacy. **Information literacy** is defined by the American Library Association in the following way: "To be information literate an individual must recognize when information is needed and have the ability to locate, evaluate and use effectively the information needed."[38] According to this definition, information-literate individuals are able to think critically, know when and how to find more information, and know how to evaluate information.

Mediated communication is not limited to advertising and television. In 2011 it was estimated that 35% of the world population uses the Internet regularly.[39] How do people

information literacy
The ability to recognize when information is needed and to locate, evaluate, and effectively use the information needed.

use the Internet? The Nielsen Social Media Report found that four of four active Internet users visit social networking sites, such as Facebook or Linkedin, and blogs covering topics of interest.[40] These findings suggest that much of what we listen to and consume comes from online sources. In fact, most college-age students get most of their news from online sources rather than more traditional print, broadcast, and cable outlets. Moreover, much of our communication with others flows through digital channels, such as e-mail, text messages, and social media posts.

■ Many of us spend over two hours per day listening to the media.

Digital communication tools on the Internet or mobile devices require different approaches to being an effective listener/consumer of communication. The principal problem with digital communication—whether you are using e-mail or text messages—is that nonverbal communication is difficult. Recall that nonverbal communication provides significant clues about another person's emotions and feelings. Without the ability to see and hear the other person, how can you tell what that person is really thinking? When communicating using digital tools, you may perceive messages in ways not intended. For instance, you may interpret a short message to be angry or abrupt when, in fact, the person was texting while doing something else. When using other tools, such as Twitter or Facebook, remember that our tweets and posts are often full of subtexts and hidden meanings. Take care to check your understanding of messages and intentions when consuming personal messages from others.

LISTENING IN A SECOND LANGUAGE

Many of the suggestions provided in this chapter are common for both native and English as a second language (ESL) speakers. However, if you are a non-native speaker, some understanding of how to further develop your listening skills can speed your progress as an effective listener. Research suggests that second-language listening development requires two skills: vocabulary comprehension and metacognitive awareness.[41] Vocabulary comprehension is more than just memorizing lists of terms. Rather, vocabulary is strengthened by recognizing the sounds of words and associating those sounds with their meaning. Being immersed in a new culture will assist you in developing such connections, particularly if you seek out and engage in sustained conversations with others. You can also use television and other media to broaden your listening experiences and assist you in vocabulary development.

In addition to developing your vocabulary, you should also try to develop your metacognitive skills. Metacognition is your ability to use "mental strategies" to assist in quickly determining the meaning of words. Learning to decipher words by drawing inferences on their meaning from the context and other words around them is one such strategy. Another example of metacognition is drawing parallels between English vocabulary and your native vocabulary. Through such strategies you will make quicker inferences about what new terms

social media
make it matter

Listening on Facebook

Take a moment to scan your Facebook newsfeed. As you look through the status updates of your friends, how do you "listen to" those posts? Do certain things cause you to pay more attention? Social media challenge our listening habits in unique ways. Facebook newsfeeds and Twitter timelines do not easily filter important from unimportant messages—we often have more clutter to wade through. Learning to listen well to our friends in virtual spaces created by social media sites may require even greater attention than face-to-face conversations. If you wanted your friends to listen carefully to something you said on Twitter or Facebook, what would you do?

cultural note

Differences in Active Listening

The way individuals actively listen can vary from culture to culture. College students in Finland, for example, listen carefully and take notes but do not respond overtly while being addressed by the professor. In fact, they remain quite expressionless. In some Native American tribes and some Hispanic groups, people avert their eyes when listening, but in groups such as northern whites and blacks, people tend to maintain eye contact while actively listening. How would you describe the norms of listening in your culture, community, or school?

mean and will be able to listen more efficiently.

Even if ESL students do not enact formal listening strategies, such as vocabulary comprehension and meta-cognitive awareness, research has discovered that simply talking with others is an effective strategy for promoting listening skills. The results of one experiment explored whether ESL students listened to news reports more effectively after receiving training on how to use various listening strategies.[42] That experiment found that there were no significant differences between ESL students receiving training and those receiving no training. The researcher speculated that, in the group not receiving training, students talked among themselves prior to the listening exercises, which equipped them with effective informal strategies. The lesson learned from this study is this: recognizing that you are in a difficult listening situation and talking with others about how to listen more effectively may be just as effective as undergoing formal listening training for some students.

Of course, if you have difficulty listening because the other person is speaking rapidly or using words you have not heard, you should feel comfortable telling the person. Adaptation to language differences is the responsibility of everyone involved in a communication situation, and you should not take on the entire challenge of trying to make the interaction succeed.

How Can You Be an Ethical Listener?

Although effective listening requires you to adapt your verbal, nonverbal, and perception-checking skills to specific situations, such as the workplace, the classroom, and mediated environments, you must also take care to enact ethical listening behaviors. To be an ethical listener, you should practice the following behaviors:

1. *Recognize the sources of your own conversational habits.* Your family, school, and other life experiences have allowed you to develop certain habits, which in some situations could be strengths and in others could represent areas for improvement. Recognizing those habits will allow you to more fully adapt to those with whom you are communicating.

2. *Monitor your communication to recognize when you are engaging in poor listening behaviors.* Perhaps the most important step in becoming an ethical listener is recognizing that you must work hard to be a good listener—a step that begins with an awareness of what you are doing in the situation.

3. *Apply general ethical principles to how you respond.* Planning your responses so that you are respectful to others is an example of how your personal ethics can influence your listening behaviors.

4. *Adapt to others.* Recognize that other people also have unique communication styles and that you might need to adapt your listening behaviors, so that you can fully understand what they are trying to say.[43]

keeping it real

Listening Well in a Techno-World

You have already learned about several verbal and nonverbal strategies for becoming a more effective listener. Returning to the story about Rachel at the beginning of the chapter, how could she use some of these skills to improve her listening? Here are some suggestions that she (and you) could use:

1. Limit your distractions by avoiding the use of your phone or other devices except for activities pertinent to the situation in which you are participating.

2. Monitor your nonverbal behaviors to determine whether you are giving appropriate feedback to the speaker.

3. Follow the speaker's message by taking notes.

4. Write down questions that you can pose to the speaker. Even if you do not end up asking them, thinking about those questions will help keep you engaged.

5. Summarize what the person said, and check to make sure you understand correctly.

Using these suggestions, you will be able to listen more effectively when interacting with teachers, friends, customers, and clients. As you practice these and other skills discussed in this chapter, you will become a better listener in all aspects of your life!

Chapter Review & Study Guide

Summary

In this chapter, you learned the following:

1. Listening is an important skill because it is one of our most common communication activities, it helps us build and maintain relationships, and it is essential for success in most professional situations.

2. Listening is a process that includes different types of behaviors.

   - Hearing is the physical act of receiving a sound. We hear all of the noises around us. Listening is the active process of receiving, paying attention to, assigning meaning to, and responding to sounds. Listening is an active process, whereas hearing is reflexive.

   - Listening is generally divided into active, empathic, critical, and enjoyment listening. Active listening, which is listening with a purpose, includes both empathic and critical listening. Empathic listening occurs when you are attempting to understand another person. Critical listening requires evaluating a speaker's message for accuracy, meaningfulness, and usefulness. We also listen to things, such as music, for enjoyment purposes.

3. A variety of internal and external barriers prevent many of us from being effective listeners.

   - One barrier is noise, which includes both physical and internal distractions.

   - Physical distractions are any audible noises in the communication environment.

   - Internal distractions can include mental, factual, or semantic distractions.

   - Perceptions of others and your own behaviors can also become barriers to effective listening.

4. Developing your critical thinking, nonverbal, and verbal skills will help you become a more effective listener.

   - Critical thinking involves the careful analysis of both the communication situation and the speaker's message. To analyze the message, you should evaluate the arguments and supporting material presented by the speaker and whether or not the speaker is credible.

- Being nonverbally responsive, using positive facial expressions, making direct eye contact, and providing positive vocal utterances are effective nonverbal strategies.

- Asking questions, inviting additional comments, using descriptive responses, and providing affirming statements are all examples of effective verbal strategies.

5. Effective listening in the workplace, classroom, and mediated environment requires you to adapt the nonverbal, verbal, and critical thinking skills discussed in the chapter.

6. Ethical listening means that you should recognize and monitor your own communication style, apply general ethical principles to your responses, and adapt your communication style to others.

Key Terms

Active listening
Automatic attention
Critical listening
Critical thinking
Empathic listening
First-person observation
Hearing

Information literacy
Lecture cues
Lecture listening
Listening
Listening for enjoyment
Long-term memory
Schema

Second-person observation
Selective attention
Short-term memory
Source credibility
Working memory

Study Questions

1. Hearing is a _____ process, and listening is a _____ process.

   a. mental; physical
   b. mental; psychological
   c. physical; mental
   d. physical; physical

2. Which of the following statements is true?

   a. Personal and business relationships are not affected by listening.
   b. When communicating, college students spend over half their lives listening.
   c. Listening constitutes only a small fraction of our communication activities.
   d. Listening does not contribute to recognizing deceit.

3. After your brain has sorted sound waves by importance, it processes the material in a part of your consciousness termed

   a. working memory.
   b. selective attention.
   c. long-term recall.
   d. short-term memory.

4. When you are listening and attempting to understand the other person's worldview, what type of listening are you utilizing?

   a. active
   b. empathic
   c. critical
   d. for enjoyment

5. If you are thinking about what happened last weekend at college while listening to your mother on the phone, you are exhibiting what type of barrier to listening?

   a. stereotypes
   b. egocentrism
   c. personal bias
   d. mental distraction

6. Which gender tends to listen in order to solve problems, is less attentive to nonverbal cues, and interrupts to switch topics?

   a. men
   b. women
   c. both genders
   d. neither gender

7. Critical thinking

   a. focuses solely on the details instead of the main point.
   b. ignores the context in which communication is occurring.
   c. is important when making judgments about the message being presented.
   d. is only associated with listening.

8. Asking questions to clarify information, paraphrasing messages, and identifying confusing areas are examples of

   a. barriers to listening.
   b. listening for enjoyment.
   c. techniques for checking your understanding of a message.
   d. information literacy.

connect

For further review, go to the LearnSmart study module for this chapter.

9. Suggestions for lecture listening include

   a. focusing on the lecturer's delivery and avoiding summarizing and reviewing the information.
   b. letting your attention stray in order to think creatively, listening for details, and ignoring lecture cues.
   c. avoiding taking notes, so that you can focus on the lecture and the message delivery.
   d. finding areas of interest to you, avoiding distractions, and listening for main ideas.

10. The ability to locate, evaluate, and effectively use information is an important trait known as

    a. critical thinking.
    b. information literacy.
    c. hearing.
    d. selective attention.

Answers:

1. (c); 2. (b); 3. (a); 4. (b); 5. (d); 6. (a); 7. (c); 8. (c); 9. (d); 10. (b)

Critical Thinking

1. Identify and define some barriers to listening that you have been aware of in your own experiences. Were you able to overcome the barriers?

2. Which of the verbal and nonverbal communication skills do you make use of in your conversations? Which of them do others use when conversing with you? Are there any that you like or dislike more than others in either situation?

interpersonal communication

When you have read and thought about this chapter, you will be able to:

1. Define interpersonal communication.

2. Define interpersonal relationships.

3. Explain the importance of interpersonal relationships and the qualities of healthy and unhealthy relationships.

4. Describe how self-disclosure affects relationships.

5. Describe friendships and how they have changed.

6. Explain the importance of cross-cultural relationships.

7. Name and explain the three stages in interpersonal relationships.

8. Name three essential interpersonal communication behaviors.

Interpersonal relationships can be complicated and require a lot of work. This chapter highlights some of the basic elements of interpersonal relationships and interpersonal communication. You will learn why people start, maintain, and end relationships. You will also study essential skills such as self-disclosing, using affectionate and supportive communication, influencing others, and developing a unique relationship.

Both students and professors believe that improving interpersonal communication skills is a top priority for college students. Sometimes the problems that students experience are not expected. Ashley, for example, is a well-adjusted first-year college student. However, she wrote,

One problem I faced coming to college was not so much making my own adjustment, but helping a friend adjust. I came to school with a few people from my high school, and although I didn't room with any of them, my friend Kate lives right down the hall from me. She and her boyfriend broke up right before she came to college and her two best friends went to other Minnesota schools. She misses the way high school was structured; she misses her house and our home town and just being somewhere that she feels comfortable and connected. As a result, she hasn't really put a lot of effort into making new friends here.

This has made it hard for me because, while she's my friend and I enjoy hanging out with her, I feel like she is always around me. Instead of making her own friends she's just tagged along with mine, so she isn't particularly close to any of them. I want to be there for her when she's upset, but she's upset a lot and that burden falls on me. Coming to college has brought along with it a lot of responsibilities I hadn't expected.

Major changes in interpersonal relationships and new challenges in interpersonal communication are things many college students face. What would you suggest for Ashley and Kate? What can Ashley do to improve her situation? What about Kate? At the end of the chapter, we'll come back to Ashley and consider what steps she might take to address her communication challenge with Kate.

How do you rate your own skills at interpersonal relationships and communication? Do you disclose information about yourself to others? How do you handle conflict? In this chapter, you'll learn more about improving your communication in interpersonal relationships.

What is a friend? With whom do you share a sexual relationship? These questions were not so difficult to answer in the past, but today they have become complicated with social networking sites, such as MySpace and Facebook, and with a new phenomenon known as "friends with benefits." In the past, a friend was a person with whom we had face-to-face conversations and with whom we shared details of our life. Sexual partners may have been restricted to one person, or to a relatively small number of people, with whom we had first established a loving and trusting relationship and whom, perhaps, we intended to marry or be committed to over our lifetime.

Today our definitions have shifted. People may count dozens, or even hundreds, of others as their "friends." College students may experience a sexual relationship with someone they consider to be a friend but with whom they have no long-term commitment. One advantage of these new relationships is the ease with which they can be begun or ended. The disadvantage is that they may be shallow or unfulfilling.

Scholars are fascinated by these new developments. They see them as raising some important issues about the definitions of interpersonal relationships and interpersonal communication. For what reasons do people form their online relationships? How do they know whom they can trust to have a sexual relationship with? How do people interact when a relationship is exclusively online rather than in face-to-face settings? What is their relationship with a friend with whom they have had a sexual relationship after the sex is gone?

Can people manage to move between online and offline friendships? Can they move into and out of sexual relationships with friends?

These questions are part of the fabric of our society today. In this chapter you will learn about interpersonal communication that cuts across more traditional relationships, as well as these developing relational forms. We will discover why we have interpersonal relationships, how we communicate within them, and how relationships are maintained and enriched.

The Nature of Communication in Interpersonal Relationships

What role do interpersonal relationships play in your life? Are all your relationships positive, or do some have negative aspects? How do you characterize your own style of interpersonal communication?

WHAT IS INTERPERSONAL COMMUNICATION?

In chapter 1 we defined interpersonal communication by the context, or the situation. In other words, interpersonal communication is the process of using messages to generate meaning between at least two people in a situation that allows mutual opportunities for both speaking and listening. Defined in this manner, interpersonal communication includes our interactions with strangers, with salespeople, and with waiters, as well as with our close friends, our lovers, and our family members. This definition is very broad.

We can also think of interpersonal communication as communication that occurs within interpersonal relationships.[1] This idea suggests that interpersonal communication can be limited to those situations in which we have knowledge of the personal characteristics, qualities, or behaviors of the other person. Indeed, Miller and Steinberg assert that, when we make guesses about the outcomes of conversations based on sociological or cultural information, we are communicating in a noninterpersonal way. When we make predictions based on more discriminating information about the other specific person, we are communicating interpersonally. When we communicate with others on the basis of general social interaction rules, such as engaging in turn taking, making pleasantries, and discussing nonpersonal matters, we are engaging in impersonal, or nonpersonal, communication. When we communicate with others based on some knowledge of their uniqueness as individuals and a shared history, we are communicating interpersonally.

None of our interpersonal relationships are quite like any of our other interpersonal relationships. A friendship you might have had in high school is not the same as your new friendships in college. Your relationship to your mother is not the same as your relationship to your father. Even if you have several intimate relationships with people, you will find that none of them is quite like the others. On the one hand, our interpersonal relationships are mundane; on the other, they can also be the "sites for spiritual practice and mystical experience."[2]

Nonetheless, we have accumulated a great deal of knowledge about how to communicate more successfully in our interpersonal relationships.[3] This chapter will explore that knowledge. We will consider those abilities that are essential in developing and developed relationships. But first, let us consider why we engage in interpersonal relationships.

WHAT ARE INTERPERSONAL RELATIONSHIPS?

On the simplest level, relationships are associations or connections. Interpersonal relationships, however, are far more complex. **Interpersonal relationships** may be defined as associations between at least two people who are interdependent, who use some consistent

interpersonal relationships
Associations between at least two people who are interdependent, who use some consistent patterns of interaction, and who have interacted for an extended period of time.

skill **builder**

Describing Your Relationships

In his book *Relational Communication,* William Wilmot discusses various metaphors we have for relationships. For instance, relationships can be described as work, in that two people must negotiate and engage in a process of give-and-take; as a journey, in that people progress along a path as they move through a relationship; and as a game, in that romance and perhaps friendship are viewed as play and competition. Consider how you would describe your relationships in figurative language. Are they safe places, dangerous territory, a rough ride, or a surprising adventure? Your descriptions can help you learn more about your relationships.

Source: Wilmot, W. W. (1995). *Relational communication.* New York: McGraw-Hill.

patterns of interaction, and who have interacted for an extended period of time. Consider the various elements of this definition in more detail:

- *Interpersonal relationships include two or more people.* Often, interpersonal relationships consist of just two people—a dating couple, a single parent and a child, a married couple, two close friends, or two co-workers. Interpersonal relationships can also include more than two people—a family unit, a group of friends, or a social group.

- *Interpersonal relationships involve people who are interdependent. Interdependence* refers to people's being mutually dependent on each other and having an impact on each other. Friendship easily illustrates this concept. Your best friend, for example, may be dependent on you for acceptance and guidance, whereas you might require support and admiration. When individuals are independent of each other, or when dependence occurs only in one direction, we do not define the resulting association as an interpersonal relationship.

- *Individuals in interpersonal relationships use some consistent patterns of interaction.* These patterns may include behaviors generally understood across a variety of situations, as well as behaviors unique to the relationship. For example, a husband may always greet his wife with a kiss. This kiss is generally understood as a sign of warmth and affection. On the other hand, the husband may have unique nicknames for his wife that are not understood outside the relationship.

- *Individuals in interpersonal relationships generally have interacted for some time.* When you nod and smile at someone as you leave the classroom, when you meet a girlfriend's siblings for the first time, or when you place an order at a fast-food counter, you do not have an interpersonal relationship. Although participants use interpersonal communication to accomplish these activities, one-time interactions do not constitute interpersonal relationships. We should note, however, that interpersonal relationships might last for varying lengths of time—some are relatively short but others continue for a lifetime.

THE IMPORTANCE OF INTERPERSONAL RELATIONSHIPS

According to William Schutz, we have three basic interpersonal needs that are satisfied through interaction with others:

1. The need for inclusion, or becoming involved with others
2. The need for affection, or holding fond or tender feelings toward another person
3. The need for control, or having the ability to influence others, our environment, and ourselves[4]

Although we may be able to fulfill some of our physical, safety, and security needs through interactions with relative strangers, we can fulfill the other needs only through our interpersonal relationships.

The interdependent nature of interpersonal relationships suggests that people mutually satisfy their needs in this type of association. Interdependence suggests that one person is

dependent on another to have some need fulfilled and that the other person (or persons) is dependent on the first to have the same or other needs fulfilled. For example, a child who is dependent on a parent may satisfy that parent's need for control. The parent, in turn, may supply the child's need for affection in hugging, kissing, or listening to the child.

Complementary relationships—those in which each person supplies something the other person or persons lack—provide good examples of the manner in which we have our needs fulfilled in interpersonal relationships. A romantic involvement between a popular male and an intelligent female is an example of a complementary relationship, since the woman may find herself involved in the social events she desires and the man may find himself increasingly successful in his classes. Another example is a friendship between an introverted individual and an extroverted one. The introvert may teach her friend to be more self-reflective or to listen to others more carefully, whereas the extrovert might, in exchange, encourage her to be more outspoken or assertive.

Our needs also may be fulfilled in **symmetrical relationships**—those in which the participants mirror each other or are highly similar. A relationship between two intelligent

complementary relationships
Relationships in which each person supplies something the other person or persons lack.

symmetrical relationships
Relationships in which participants mirror each other or are highly similar.

individuals may reflect their need for intellectual stimulation. Two people of similar ancestry might marry in part to preserve their heritage.

Conflict is inevitable and normal in interpersonal relationships; indeed, conflict can be constructive and creative. Conflict can be healthy when it is used to resolve differences and to "clear the air." On the other hand, it can also be dysfunctional. You or your friend might have grown up in a family in which sequences of conflict were ever present, and the only way you know how to have a conversation is by fighting. Or you might have had parents who never discussed differences, and the only way you know to manage conflict is to walk away or not talk about what bothers you.

Conflict is dysfunctional when you avoid talking about problems, withdraw, or become sullen. Conflict is also dysfunctional when you take any criticism or suggestions as a personal attack. Do you fight fairly or do you attack the other person rather than raising the issue that is at stake? If you feel out of control when you are engaged in an argument with a family member, you may experience conflict as dysfunctional. Finally, conflict can be dysfunctional when you store up many complaints and then attack your roommate with all of them.

If you have experienced conflict as dysfunctional, you can begin to experience it more positively when you follow some straightforward guidelines. First, you need to remain calm. You should also express your feelings in words rather than in actions such as breaking objects, driving recklessly, or using alcohol. Try to be specific about what is bothering you. Rather than bringing up multiple grievances of the past, try to deal with only one issue at a time. Consider your language and avoid words such as *never* and *always* in describing the problem—particularly when it is about your roommate's actions. Do not exaggerate or invent additional problems that are not central to the discussion. Finally, you may find that it is important to establish some ground rules that both you and your partner adopt.

sizing things up

Interpersonal Motives

We enter into interpersonal relationships for a variety of reasons. Below you will read several statements that describe possible reasons for joining interpersonal relationships. Indicate how likely you are to enter into an interpersonal relationship for each reason using the following scale:

1 = Never
2 = Unlikely
3 = Likely
4 = Frequently

I enter into interpersonal relationships . . .

1. Because I can have influence over others.
2. So that I can share emotions with others.
3. To feel part of a group.
4. To be involved in things with other people.
5. To gain affection from others.
6. To bring control to my life.
7. So that I can have more influence over my surroundings.
8. Because I need to know that people like me.
9. Because I want to be included in different activities.

A guide for interpreting your responses appears in the appendix at the end of the text (p. 348).

THE DARK SIDE OF INTERPERSONAL RELATIONSHIPS

Conflict is only one aspect of interpersonal relationships that seems to represent a "dark side" to these most personal affiliations. Although your interpersonal relationships are generally pleasurable and positive, you might also have experienced painful and negative liaisons. Spitzberg and Cupach have provided the most comprehensive treatment of the shadowy side of relationships.[5] What are some of the qualities of negative relationships? Obsession that includes fatal attraction and jealousy certainly creates negative outcomes. Similarly, misunderstanding, gossip, conflict, and codependency can lead to harmful results. Abuse, which includes sexual, physical, mental, and emotional abuse, is truly harmful to individuals and destroys relationships.

In addition, some of the qualities we associate with healthy relationships—self-disclosure, affectionate communication, mutual influence, and the development of a unique relationship—can all become extreme and therefore unhealthy. Effective communication, as you have been learning, is very challenging, and interpersonal communication may be the most challenging context of all. This chapter focuses primarily on positive interpersonal relationships and how to improve them.

SELF-DISCLOSURE IN THE DEVELOPMENT OF INTERPERSONAL RELATIONSHIPS

One change that occurs as relationships become deeper and closer is an increasing intentional revealing of personal information. **Self-disclosure** is the process of making intentional disclosures about yourself that others would be unlikely to know and that generally constitute private, sensitive, or confidential information. Pearce and Sharp distinguish among self-disclosure, confession, and revelation.[6] They define self-disclosure as voluntary, confession as forced or coerced information, and revelation as unintentional or inadvertent communication.

Jourard suggests that self-disclosure makes us "transparent" to others, that disclosure helps others to see us as a distinctive human being.[7] Self-disclosure goes beyond self-description. More specifically, your position on abortion, your close relationship with your grandfather, your sexual history, your deepest fears, your proudest moments, and your problems with drugs or alcohol are considered self-disclosure by most definitions. Self-disclosure is not always negative, but it is generally private information.

Why Is Self-Disclosure Important?

Self-disclosure is important for three reasons. First, it allows us to develop a greater understanding of ourselves. Consider the Johari window depicted in figure 6.1. Joseph Luft and Harrington Ingham created this diagram to depict four kinds of information about a person. The open area (I) includes information that is known to you and to other people, such as your approximate height and weight, and information you freely disclose, such as your hometown, major, or age. The blind area (II) consists of information known to others but unknown to you, such as your personality characteristics that

Successful interpersonal relationships are based on effective communication.

self-disclosure
The process of making intentional revelations about yourself that others would be unlikely to know and that generally constitute private, sensitive, or confidential information.

Figure **6.1**

Johari window.

Source: Luft, J. (1984). *Group Processes: An Introduction to Group Dynamics.* NY: Mayfield Publishing Company. Copyright 1984, 1970, and 1969 by Joseph Luft. © The McGraw-Hill Companies, Inc. Used by permission.

	Known to self	Not known to self
Known to others	I Open area	II Blind area
Not known to others	III Hidden area	IV Unknown area

others perceive but you do not recognize or acknowledge. The hidden area (III) includes information that you know about yourself but others do not. Any information that is hidden and that you do not self-disclose lies here. Finally, the unknown area (IV) comprises information that is unknown to you *and* to others. For instance, neither you nor others know when you will pass on (assuming that you have not been diagnosed with a terminal disease).

The quadrants of the Johari window can expand or contract in size. It can also have a different shape, with different family members, friends, or acquaintances. For example, you might have a very large open area when you are considering the relationship between you and your closest friend. On the other hand, the hidden area may be very large when you consider the relationship between you and your classmates. As the size of one of the quadrants changes, so do the sizes of all the others.

Self-disclosure allows you to develop a more positive attitude about yourself and others, as well as more meaningful relationships. Have you ever experienced a problem or faced a difficult situation? Most of us have, and we know that sharing our fears or telling others about our anguish provides comfort. For example, imagine that you committed a traffic violation and were caught. You might feel very guilty for having done the wrong thing, for having to pay a large fine, and for risking the loss of your driver's license. If you can find the courage to talk about your feelings to a friend, you might find that you are not alone, that almost everyone receives a traffic fine at one time or another. Similarly, if you have recently experienced the loss of a family member, you may find that talking about your feelings and sharing your grief will lead to positive growth for you. Hastings found that self-disclosure is a powerful form of communication in grieving and in healing a fractured identity.[8]

Through self-disclosure, relationships grow in depth and meaning. Partners in romantic relationships, for example, report greater feelings of security when self-disclosure between them is intentional and honest.[9] When you self-disclose more to others, they will most likely disclose more to you. On the other hand, the inability to self-disclose can result in the end of a relationship. Without the opportunity for self-disclosure and active listening, relationships appear to be doomed to shallowness, superficiality, and termination.

At the same time, self-disclosure can be used inappropriately. Have you ever sat on an airplane next to a stranger who revealed highly personal information to you? Have you ever dated someone who insisted on sharing private information too early in the relationship? In the next section we will consider some of the findings about self-disclosure that may provide guidelines for your self-disclosing behavior.

What Factors Affect Appropriate Self-Disclosure?

Disclosure generally increases as relational intimacy increases. We do not provide our life story to people we have just met. Instead, in the developing relationship, we gradually reveal an increasing amount of information. We might begin with positive information that is not highly intimate and then begin to share more personal information as we learn to trust the other person. In this way our disclosure tends to be incremental, to increase over time.

Disclosure tends to be reciprocal. This conclusion is related to the previous one. When people offer us information about themselves, we tend to return the behavior in kind. Indeed, when people reciprocate self-disclosure, we tend to view them positively; when they do not, we tend to view them as incompetent. Dindia, Fitzpatrick, and Kenny studied dyadic interaction between women and men and strangers and spouses. They concluded that, in conversations, the disclosure of highly intimate feelings was reciprocal.[10]

Reciprocal disclosure generally does not occur in families. Although parents have an expectation of self-disclosure from their children and adolescents, they do not perceive a need to reciprocate. A variety of factors affect adolescents' disclosures to their parents. Adolescents do not generally feel the need to disclose to their parents, and they are even more reluctant to disclose if their behavior is not sanctioned by their parents).[11] Grandparents may become the target of self-disclosures, since they are sometimes seen as more empathetic and positive.[12]

Negative disclosure is directly related to the intimacy of the relationship; however, positive disclosure does not necessarily increase as the relationship becomes more intimate. What does this mean? As we become closer to another person, we are more likely to reveal negative information about ourselves. Positive information, on the other hand, flows through conversations from the earliest developmental stages throughout the lifetime of the relationship. Hence, negative information increases over time, but positive disclosure does not necessarily increase.

Disclosure may be avoided for a variety of reasons. Self-disclosure does not flow freely on all topics. Indeed, relational partners may avoid self-disclosure for reasons of self-protection, relationship protection, partner unresponsiveness, and social appropriateness. As Afifi and Guerrero observe, "Some things are better left unsaid."[13] At the same time, topics that are taboo under some conditions may be appropriate later, when conditions change.[14]

People do not always avoid self-disclosure for noble reasons. College students who were in close relationships were asked whether they disclosed their sexual histories before engaging in sex. Although nearly all the students surveyed felt they were knowledgeable about safe sex, over 40% did not realize that revealing one's sexual history is a safe-sex practice. One-third of those who were sexually active had not disclosed their sexual history to at least one partner prior to becoming sexually involved. And at least one-fifth of the sexually active students purposefully misrepresented their sexual history to their sex partners.[15]

Disclosure varies across cultures. Self-disclosure is not uniformly valued or disvalued around the world. For example, Chinese professionals view interpersonal communication differently in Chinese organizations and in American businesses. They view Chinese interactions to be characterized by blunt assertiveness, smooth amiability, and surface humility. They view American workplaces as composed of sophisticated kindness, manipulative "stroking," and casual spontaneity.[16] Koreans and Americans avoid making requests of others for different reasons. Koreans are concerned with avoiding negative evaluation from the hearer and avoiding hurting the other person's feelings, whereas Americans are more concerned with clarity.[17] These differences most likely transfer to differences in disclosures as well.

Relational satisfaction and disclosure are curvilinearly related. Satisfaction is lowest with no disclosure and with excessive disclosure; it is highest when self-disclosure is provided at moderate levels. Consider your own personal relationships. Does this conclusion appear to be accurate?

skill builder

Guidelines for Self-Disclosure

Try the following strategies for appropriate self-disclosure in interpersonal relationships.

1. Gradually increase disclosure as your relationship develops.
2. Reveal information to others as they reveal information to you.
3. Do not disclose negative information until your relationship is established.
4. Do not disclose information that will cause you personal harm.
5. Be sensitive to cultural differences in your self-disclosure.
6. Be aware of non-dominant cultural differences in self-disclosure.
7. Be willing to self-disclose in interpersonal relationships.

Friendship

Friendship contributes to our well-being. People who have harmonious sibling relationships and same-gender friends report the highest levels of well-being.[18] Wereas we celebrate romantic relationships, we do not similarly honor friendships. Rawlins notes that we ought to have a "friendship day," because our friendships are at least as important as our romantic relationships.[19]

THE VALUE OF FRIENDSHIPS

What does friendship mean? Friendships can be based on shared activities or on the level of information we exchange with others. Young adolescents report that their friendships are based on shared activities, whereas for emerging adults they are based on self-disclosure.[20] The communication of private information appears to gain in importance as people mature. Most people identify both family and nonfamily members as friends.

Friendships also change over time. As people age, family members become more salient as friends.[21] For many older men, their only friend is their wife,[22] although the same is not true for older women. Do friendships actually improve over time? Although we cannot be sure, we do know that people *perceive* that they do.[23] Perhaps people come to better understand the importance of friendship as they mature.

The quality of friendships is affected by psychological predispositions, such as attachment styles. People who are securely attached to others have lower levels of conflict with their friends and are able to rise above problems in their friendships. People who are avoidant, or not attached, experience higher levels of conflict and lower levels of companionship.[24]

Rawlins provides a six-stage model of how friendships develop.[25] The first stage, role-limited interaction, includes an encounter in which individuals are polite and careful with their disclosures. Second, friendly relations occur when the two people determine that they have mutual interests or other common ground. Third, moving toward friendship allows them to introduce a personal topic or to set up times to get together. Fourth, in nascent friendship they think of themselves as friends and begin to establish their own private ways of interacting. Fifth, the friends feel established in each other's lives, in what is termed a stabilized friendship. Finally, friendships may move to a waning stage, when the relationship diminishes. Not all friendships reach this sixth stage.

Friendships are maintained differently, depending on the intent of the relational partners. Rawlins notes that issues of romantic attraction must be negotiated early in a relationship.[26] Guerrero and Chavez studied friends who both wanted the relationship to become romantic (mutual romance), friends neither of whom wanted the friendship to become romantic (platonic), and friends of whom one desired romance but felt that the partner did not (desiring or rejecting romance).[27] People in the mutual romance situation generally reported the most relationship maintenance behavior. Those in the platonic or the rejecting-romance situation had fewer routine contacts and activities, were more likely to talk about other romantic situations, and were less flirtatious. People in the desiring-romance and mutual-romance situations reported the most relationship talk. Clearly, friendships are dynamic and may lead to romantic relationships.

Partners behave differently in their communication with friends and romantic partners. For example, the scope of the "chilling effect," or the suppression of grievances, depends on whether you see the other person as a friend or a romantic partner. One study used binge drinking as the topic to determine whether friends or romantic partners would confront the other person. The researchers found that college students would not talk with their friends about their excessive drinking, but they would to their romantic partners. In other words, the chilling effect on this topic affected only friendships.[28]

Friendships are not necessarily defined the same way in all cultures. People in collectivist cultures tend to have more intimate but fewer friendships. As people have more contact with others cultures, however, these patterns are showing signs of change. For example, Indonesian people, traditionally from a collectivisitic culture, now display extensive social contacts.[29]

A new development, made possible by mediated communication, is friendships on the Internet. However, these friendships are perceived as less close and less supportive than are friendships that originate with face-to-face contact. Internet friends are also less likely to be engaged in joint activities.[30]

NEW TYPES OF FRIENDSHIPS

Social networking sites, such as Facebook, MySpace, Tagged, Twitter, hi5, and LinkedIn, have made new kinds of friendships possible by allowing people to communicate with each other online. Who uses these sites? According to Anderson Analytics, "Facebook users tend to be old, white and rich." This research firm notes that MySpace users are young, Twitterers generally have a part-time job, and LinkedIn networkers own more gadgets than others and like to exercise (www.readwriteweb.com).

Facebook claims over 800 million active users, more than half of whom log on during any given day. More than 350 million active users access Facebook through a mobile device. Although we might believe Facebook is distinctly American, more than 75% of current users are outside the United States and use more than seventy languages on the site. Finally, the average Facebook user has 130 Facebook friends.[31] (www.facebook.com).

Twitter was created in March 2006 and boasted 200 million users in 2011. Like Facebook, Twitter is an online social network, but it allows only text-based posts, and these "tweets" are limited to 140 characters. Twitter's use multiplies when prominent events occur. For example, during Beyoncé's performance at the MTV Video Music Awards, when she announced she was pregnant, tweets reached 8,868 per second, and when Osama Bin Laden was killed, Twitter recorded 5,000 tweets per second.[32] However, the greatest spike to date occurred at the passing of Apple's founder Steve Jobs, when 10,000 tweets per second were exchanged.[33]

Why do people choose to have online friends? Although extraversion and openness to new experiences have some predictive power in identifying people who are likely to use social networking, no clear personality factors distinguish social networkers from others.[34] Perhaps people are motivated to form online friends because they have a sense of safety and security—they do not need to meet the other person in a face-to-face setting. Others might perceive that online friendships are more exciting than day-to-day relationships. Finally, some people might be attracted to social networking sites because they can create a more idealized self—someone who is more attractive and has a different personality than they actually have.

Although people may have dozens of online friends, they rarely have large numbers of friends with benefits. Friends with benefits (FWB) are those who are not romantically involved but who have agreed to have a sexual relationship. Although studies vary regarding the percentage of college students who engage in such relationships, the most conservative study suggested that over half (51%) of college students are or have been in an FWB relationship.[35] One study found that women are more interested in having a friend, whereas men are more interested in the benefits of such a relationship.[36]

■ Social networking sites provide opportunities for new kinds of interpersonal relationships.

How do FWB relationships conclude? Bisson and Levine found that about 36% of the couples quit having sex but remained friends; 28% stayed friends and remained sexually active; 26% claimed that they were no longer either friends or lovers; and about 10% of the couples had a relationship that became completely romantic.[37] Generally, FWB do not talk at all about romance or the possibility of falling in love, but it is important for people who wish to engage in this kind of relationship to set clear rules and boundaries. They also need to be clear with their friend about their goals with the relationship. Finally, they need to choose their partner wisely: someone they trust, someone they enjoy being with, and someone who is looking for a similar experience.

CROSS-CULTURAL RELATIONSHIPS

Because our culture is increasingly diverse, the likelihood that you will be part of a cross-cultural friendship, or even romantic relationship, is far greater now than ever before. In many respects, cross-cultural relationships work like any other type of relationship—we enter into them for many of the same reasons; the processes of self-disclosure work the same; we even initiate and maintain them using many of the same skills.

One difference is that we may feel more tentative in initiating a dialogue with a person from another culture. Perhaps we are afraid of language barriers or of accidentally saying something wrong. In other situations, such as when two people are assigned to a residence hall room as roommates, the relationship may be forced upon them. In either case, one approach to establishing a relationship is to view it as a cooperative learning opportunity in which both participants work together to achieve a mutually shared understanding while learning about each other's culture.[38] In approaching the relationship in this way, try to do the following:

1. *Have meaningful personal interaction.* If you feel uncomfortable in the initial stages of interaction, you may be tempted to stick to very safe topics of conversation. Try to talk about some more personal and meaningful topics as well. For instance, what are the similarities and differences between your families? What religions do you practice? What are your hometowns like? What work experiences have you had? By talking about more personal topics like these, you will begin to learn about each other and start the self-disclosure cycle.

2. *Maintain equal status.* Research shows that, when one person assumes a role of "leader" or "teacher," the relationship will have more trouble developing. Both members of the relationship should recognize that each has something unique to offer in terms of knowledge, creativity, openness, listening, and so on. Remembering to keep the new relationship focused on interpersonal closeness rather than task concerns can help prevent a perception of inequality in the early stages of the relationship.

3. *Find ways to build interdependence.* Any relationship will be stronger if both individuals bring something to it. If each can find ways to help the other, interdependence will form, and the bond of the relationship will grow stronger.

4. *Respect individual differences.* People from different cultures are like anyone else. Some are shy, whereas others are outgoing; some are very cerebral, and others are very practical; some like romantic comedies, whereas others like action shows. Such differences and even disagreements over them do not mean you cannot make a cross-cultural relationship work; it may simply mean that you don't like certain personality characteristics. Just as with friends from your own culture, you occasionally have to overlook minor disagreements in light of the many areas of agreement.

The Stages in Interpersonal Relationships

Communication and relationship development are symbiotic; that is, communication affects the growth of relationships, and the growth of relationships affects communicative behavior.[39]

DEVELOPING RELATIONSHIPS

Relational development does not occur overnight, although many couples in long-term relationships recall falling in love "at first sight." College students outline a general pattern for the developing relationship. After they meet, they exchange names, majors, and hometowns. They might begin using social media and text each other from time to time. This early investigative stage lasts a fairly short time and allows the couple to determine whether they have anything in common.

> **relational development**
> The initial stage in a relationship that moves a couple from meeting to mating.

If the couple finds they are compatible, they may begin meeting face-to-face and go to parties, movies, dinners, and other social events together. They meet each other's friends and eventually engage in intimacy. Because intimacy is an emotional step in a relationship, couples may assess the cost as well as the benefits of becoming intimate with someone to whom they are not committed.[40] As a result of differences in opinion about the desirability of intimacy or the meaningfulness of it, the first fight might ensue shortly after intimacy has occurred. Too, partners are sometimes not equally astute at understanding the nonverbal and verbal cues that lead to intimacy, and one may be baffled while the other is keenly aware of the likelihood of engaging in a sexual relationship.[41] Assuming the fight has cleared the air and not ended the relationship, they next meet each other's family. At this point, the two become exclusive. They are no longer interested in dating others, or "playing the field." They develop mutual concerns, shared jokes, and a bit of a common history.

About this time they express their affection verbally, as one or both disclose, "I love you." Additional shared experiences, such as working on projects or traveling together, might occur next. The two develop rituals to manage both work and play. They might have a common language that allows them to communicate with each other without strangers understanding. They share each other's friends and perhaps eliminate other relationships.

Commitment is the final stage of relational development. Some couples exchange a promise ring or other pieces of jewelry next, to suggest to others that they are now a couple. They begin to spend increasing amounts of time at each other's apartment or room, and one member might suggest moving in together. A proposal of marriage may follow or precede this suggestion. The two may determine whether they can provide steady and dependable care for another live being by buying plants together or getting a pet. Some couples remain at this point for years whereas others marry, or marry and have children. Couples who do not choose to marry may host a public event that tells others of the bond they share.

MAINTAINING RELATIONSHIPS

Once individuals have bonded in a relationship, they enter a stage of **relational maintenance,** in which they begin establishing strategies for keeping the relationship together. Wilmot suggests that relationships stabilize when the partners reach a basic level of agreement about what they want from the relationship.[42] This can occur at any level of intimacy, and even "stabilized" relationships have internal movement.

> **relational maintenance**
> The stage in a relationship after a couple has bonded and in which they engage in the process of keeping the relationship together.

The relational maintenance stage is not like a plateau. Instead, people become more intimate or closer at some periods and more distant and less close at other times, usually describing a jagged rather than a straight line. Maintained relationships are in motion and healthy relationships are always changing. A relationship that is static is probably dead, or dying.

Table 6.1 Baxter's Dialectic Tensions

Integration	Separation
"Let's move in together."	"When we get married, I plan on keeping my maiden name and continuing in my career."
Stability	**Change**
"I'm glad we've never moved."	"I'm feeling restless. I think it is time to plan a vacation!"
Expression	**Privacy**
"I did absolutely the dumbest thing last night. Let me tell you."	"I would rather not explain how I spent the weekend."

dialectic
The tension that exists between two conflicting or interacting forces, elements, or ideas.

contradictions
In dialectic theory, the idea that each person in a relationship might have two opposing desires for maintaining the relationship.

Baxter and her colleagues, as well as other researchers, have developed and demonstrated the importance of dialectic theory in interpersonal relationships.[43] **Dialectic** refers to the tension that exists between two conflicting or interacting forces, elements, or ideas. When dialectic theory is applied to interpersonal relationships, we acknowledge that relationships often incorporate contradictions or contrasts within them and that relationships are always in process. By **contradictions,** we mean that each person might have two opposing desires for maintaining the relationship—you want to be with your partner, but you also have a need for space and time away from him or her. *Process* means that relationships are always changing. Thus, relational maintenance cannot be depicted as a flat line but, rather, one that has peaks and valleys.

What are some of the primary dialectics that Baxter identifies? Three emerged in the early work. The dialectic of *integration/separation* suggests the tension between wanting to be separate entities and wanting to be integrated with another person. The dialectic of *stability/change* suggests the tension between wanting events, conversations, and behavior to be the same and desiring change. The dialectic of *expression/privacy* suggests the tension between wanting to self-disclose and be completely open and wanting to be private and closed. Table 6.1 summarizes Baxter's primary dialectics.

The use of media has multiple effects on relationships and may play a greater role than we suspect. For example, people who consume a great deal of television and play video games frequently use fewer relational maintenance strategies than those who are modest or moderate media users. In one study, this difference was particularly strong for those who showed high dependence on video games, perhaps due to the competition games provide for relational development and maintenance time.[44]

On the other hand, college students regularly use texting and instant messaging to connect with others who are in both long-distance and geographically close relationships with them. With family and friends, students tend to use self-disclosure (directly discussing the nature of their relationship), positive comments (being cheerful and upbeat), and discussions of social networks (attempting to involve them in a variety of activities) in their messages. When interacting with romantic partners, they also use assurances that include stressing commitment and love.[45]

WHEN RELATIONSHIPS DETERIORATE

Although all relationships go through a period of development, and many go through the maintenance stage, some deteriorate. **Relational deterioration** may occur because of the pressures of external events, because of differences that develop within the couple, or because of relationships with other people. Couples may first observe that they are spending increasing amounts of time away from each other and they prefer this time of separation.

The couple may begin to physically, emotionally, and communicatively pull away from each other. Perhaps they do not attend public events together. They might decide to sleep in separate rooms or separate beds. They no longer appear to be a couple to each other or to others.

The parties may begin to look for others with whom to share their thoughts and feelings. They might find spending time with each other to be boring, stifling, and awkward. If they have children, they may attend the children's events but arrive and leave in separate vehicles. They may arrange events so that they do not have to be alone together.

Next, the couple avoids spending any time at all together. One person may move out. One might reschedule activities so he or she is gone when the other awakens or comes home sufficiently late that the other partner is already sleeping. Communication may actually increase at this point, but it is marked with anger and negative intent.

Finally, the couple takes legal action to end their relationship, if it has been legally sanctioned. They might engage in outright hostility and dissociation. They may divide their common property, returning jewelry and other sentimental gifts to the partner and shedding any symbols of their relationship. Common friends are now divided between the two. One member of the couple may assert him- or herself by taking a new job at a great geographic distance. The relationship is clearly over.

Not all relationships go through these stages, particularly deterioration or termination. People experience movement as they reconnect after periods of little intimacy. They may question their relationship but not move to dissolve it. Sometimes couples move back to the dating stage as they renew their love, perhaps after the children have left home or after retirement.

Communication skills can also alter the trajectory of a relationship. In relationships that are dysfunctional or deteriorating, communication can help heal or remedy problems. In new relationships it can stimulate relational development and growth. Communication skills thus allow us to subscribe to realistic hope in our relationships.

Finally, individuals do not move through each of these stages with everyone they meet. Research has shown that people base decisions to develop relationships on such factors as physical attractiveness,

social media make it matter

Using Flickr to Enhance Interpersonal Relationships

Flickr allows you an alternative to Facebook to share photos and experiences that might enhance your relationships with friends and family members. You can organize your photos, find your friends and family members on Flickr, add notes to the photos, and write comments on photos you receive from others. You can also add maps and put photos on them. (Consider showing someone where you lived, where you vacationed, or the location of a favorite restaurant.) You might use Flickr for a smaller audience than you reach on Facebook. What are some reasons for doing so?

relational deterioration
The stage in a relationship in which the prior bond disintegrates.

■ Relational deterioration is marked by differentiating behavior.

personal charisma, and communication behaviors.[46] In general, we are more likely to attempt to develop relationships with people who are attractive, emotionally expressive, extroverted, and spontaneous. In the next section we will consider some of the theories that suggest why we select some people with whom to relate and why we neglect, or even reject, other people.

Motivations for Initiating, Maintaining, and Terminating Relationships

Most relationships go through definable stages of development, maintenance, and deterioration.

MOTIVATIONS FOR INITIATING RELATIONSHIPS

How do you determine which people you will select to be your friends, lovers, or family members? Why do you cultivate relationships with them? How does communication figure into the equation?

First, **proximity**—the location, distance, or range between persons and things—is obvious but important. You are probably not going to have relationships with people from places you have never been. You are most likely to find others where you spend most of your time. For this reason a roommate or co-worker can easily become a friend.[47] People who attend the same religious services, belong to the same social clubs, or are members of the same gang are most likely to become friends. People who share a major or a dormitory, cafeteria, car pool, or part of the seating chart in a class are also likely candidates. To underline the power of proximity, consider that changes in location (high school to college and college to job) often change relationship patterns.

Second, from all the people we see, we select the ones we find high in **attractiveness**, which includes physical attractiveness, how desirable a person is to work with, and how much "social value" the person has for others.[48] In other words, a person who is desirable to work with, in whom others also show interest, and who physically looks good to us is attractive.[49] Attractiveness is not universal, however; it varies from culture to culture[50] and person to person. Because of perceptual differences, you will not be looking for the same person as everyone else.

Responsiveness describes the reason we tend to select our friends and loved ones from people who demonstrate positive interest in us. Few people are more attractive than those who actively listen to us, think our jokes are funny, find our vulnerabilities endearing, and see our faults as amusing. In short, we practically never select our friends from among those who dislike us.

Similarity, the idea that our friends and loved ones are usually people who like or dislike the same things we do, is another feature of attractiveness. Whatever we consider most important is the similarity we seek, so some friends or people in loving relationships are bound by their interests, others by their ideology, and still others by their mutual likes and dislikes. A hard-core environmentalist is unlikely to be close personal friends with a property developer, whereas the developer is likely to select friends from people in the same business, country club, and suburb. Thousands of people find their friends in the same circle where they work: clerical workers with clerical workers, managers with managers, and bosses with bosses. Similarity is a powerful source of attraction.

Complementarity is the idea that we sometimes bond with people whose strengths are our weaknesses. Whereas you may be slightly shy, your friend may be assertive. In situations that call for assertiveness, she may play that role for you. A math-loving engineer may find friendship with a people-loving communication major, who takes care of the

---

proximity
The location, distance, or range between persons and things.

attractiveness
A concept that includes physical attractiveness, how desirable a person is to work with, and how much "social value" the person has for others.

responsiveness
The idea that we tend to select our friends and loved ones from people who demonstrate positive interest in us.

similarity
The idea that our friends and loved ones are usually people who like or dislike the same things we do.

complementarity
The idea that we sometimes bond with people whose strengths are our weaknesses.

■ We select friends from among people who are responsive to us.

engineer's social life while the engineer helps his friend with math courses. Complementarity seems to occur in fiscal matters, too. Those who spend more than they should ("spendthrifts") tend to marry those who spend less than is ideal ("tightwads"). However, these marriages result in a great deal of conflict over fiscal matters, and the couples report diminished marital happiness.[51] At the same time, having a friend or spouse who is too much like us may also have negative effects on the relationship.

MOTIVATIONS FOR MAINTAINING RELATIONSHIPS

After you have gotten to know someone, why do you continue to relate to him or her? You may begin to relate to dozens of people, but you do not continue friendships, family relationships, or love relationships with everyone with whom you start a relationship. Let us consider some of the motivators that encourage continuing a relationship.

Although we initially develop a relationship on the basis of such factors as attractiveness and personal charisma, we maintain relationships for different reasons. Maintained relationships invite certain levels of predictability, or certainty.[52] Indeed, we attempt to create strategies that will provide us with additional personal information about our relational partners.[53] We are also less concerned with partners' expressive traits (such as being extroverted and spontaneous) and more concerned with their ability to focus on us through empathic, caring, and concerned involvement.[54] Indeed, as relationships are maintained, partners not only become more empathic but also begin to mirror each other's behavior.

Gender and Cultural Differences

Motivations for maintaining relationships are not simple. Many differences between women and men affect maintenance behaviors. For example, women use more maintenance strategies than do men.[55] People with different ethnicities express different primary needs in their interpersonal relationships. According to Collier, "Latinos emphasized relational support, Asian Americans emphasized a caring, positive exchange of ideas, African Americans emphasized respect and acceptance, and Anglo Americans emphasized recognizing the needs of the individual."[56] People from different generations view intergenerational communication differently.[57] In addition, people display different levels of nonverbal involvement and intimacy with their romantic partners.[58]

Satisfying Relationships

Couples can achieve satisfying and long-term relationships, however. Pearson looked at couples who had been happily married for more than 40 years. She found that many of these marriages were characterized by stubbornness ("This marriage will succeed no matter what"), distortion ("She is the most beautiful woman in the world"), unconditional acceptance (regardless of faults), and the continuous push and pull of autonomy or independence versus unity or interdependence.[59] Maintaining positive, satisfying relationships is not easy, but the people who are the most satisfied with their relationships are probably those who have worked hardest at maintaining them. Communicatively, people in long-term and satisfied relationships are distinctive from those in short-term or unhappy relationships. Sillars, Shellen, McIntosh, and Pomegranate found that people in long-term and satisfied relationships are more likely to use joint rather than individual identity pronouns ("we" and "us" rather than "I" or "me").[60]

MOTIVATIONS FOR TERMINATING RELATIONSHIPS

Although our goal may be to maintain satisfying relationships, this outcome is not always possible. Relationships do not last. About half of all marriages end in divorce, and in second and third marriages the failure rate is even higher. Why do interpersonal relationships end? What factors encourage people to seek the conclusion, rather than the continuation, of a relationship? We consider a few of those factors here.

hurtful messages
Messages that create emotional pain or upset.

Hurtful messages create emotional pain or upset. They fall into ten categories of behavior: accusation, evaluation, directive, advise, express desire, inform, question, threat, joke, and lie.[61] Among the most common are accusations (that imply or state fault or offense), evaluation (describe value, worth, or quality), and inform (those that disclose feelings that involve the partner).

Hurtful messages occur in most relationships, even those in which couples are very satisfied. They do not always end in disruption of the relationship, but they can if they become a pattern or are so intense that one partner cannot forget them. Why do some hurtful messages create significant relational problems, whereas others do not? Duck and Pond suggest that the relational history, the closeness of the couple, and their satisfaction with the relationship all affect how they perceive and respond to their own interaction.[62]

Vangelisti and Crumley determined that people respond in one of three ways: active verbal responses (for example, attacking the other, defending oneself, or asking for an explanation), acquiescent responses (for example, apologizing or crying), and invulnerable responses (for instance, laughing or ignoring the message).[63] People who felt extremely hurt were more likely to use acquiescing responses. Those who were less hurt used invulnerability more than did those who felt extremely hurt. The researchers also found that people expressed more satisfaction with the relationship when verbal responses were used.

deceptive communication
The practice of deliberately making somebody believe things that are not true.

Deceptive communication—the practice of deliberately making somebody believe things that are untrue—can also lead to relational dissatisfaction and termination. All relational partners probably engage in some level of deception from time to time. The "little white lie," the nonrevelation of the "whole truth," and the omission of some details are commonplace. However, deliberate and regular deception can lead to the destruction of trust and the end of the relationship.

People may tell familiar lies (stories that are manufactured and that they tell again and again) or unfamiliar lies (untruths that are constructed on the spot). They vary the length of their pauses, their eye gaze, and the amount of smiling and laughing in which they engage, depending on whether they are telling familiar or unfamiliar lies. Observers, however, cannot detect these alterations.[64] In short, we do not seem to be very able to accurately identify deceptive behaviors.

Aggressiveness occurs when people stand up for their rights at the expense of others and care about their own needs but no one else's. Aggressiveness might help you get your way a few times, but ultimately others will avoid you and let their resentment show. People who engage in aggressive behavior may do so because they have a negative self-concept or because they have learned this pattern of behavior growing up. Martin and Anderson show that both sons and daughters have patterns of verbal aggression that are similar to their mother's.[65]

Aggressiveness is not the same as argumentativeness. **Argumentativeness,** defined as the quality or state of being argumentative, is synonymous with being contentious or combative. People who are argumentative are not verbally aggressive.[66] Indeed, argumentative people may value argument as a normal social communicative activity. Argumentation varies across the life span.[67] Argumentativeness patterns are shown to be similar between mothers and their children.[68]

Defensiveness occurs when a person feels attacked. Jack Gibb suggests that trust is essential to healthy relationships.[69] But trust must be established between individuals and not be based on their roles, positions, or status. In other words, people should come to relationships without all the trappings of the roles they play. Reducing defensiveness is essential to building trust.

Gibb distinguished between behaviors that encourage defensiveness and those that reduce defensiveness. He identified evaluation, control, neutrality, superiority, certainty, and strategy as promoting defensive behaviors in others:

- *Evaluation* occurs when an individual makes a judgment about another person or his or her behavior.
- *Control* suggests that the speaker does not allow the second person to join in the discussion of how a problem should be solved.
- *Neutrality* means that the originator of the message does not show concern for the second person.
- *Superiority* occurs when the first person treats the second as a person of lower status.
- *Certainty* denotes a lack of openness to alternative ideas.
- *Strategy* refers to the employment of manipulative and premeditative behavior.

Gibb then categorized the following behaviors as reducing defensiveness: description, problem orientation, empathy, equality, provisionalism, and spontaneity. People who

aggressiveness
The assertion of one's rights at the expense of others and care about one's own needs but no one else's.

argumentativeness
The quality or state of being argumentative; synonymous with contentiousness or combativeness.

defensiveness
Occurs when a person feels attacked.

skill **builder**

Reducing Defensiveness

Rewrite the following statements in a way that would decrease defensiveness. Use the categories generated by Gibb. For example, you would replace evaluation with description.

1. "What's wrong with you, anyway?"
2. "Who's responsible for the mess in the library?"
3. "I don't really care what you do."
4. "We're not leaving here until I say we're leaving."
5. "We don't need to meet. I know how to solve the problem."
6. "I don't need your help."

Table 6.2   Jack Gibb's Contribution to Reducing Defensiveness

Create Defensiveness	Reduce Defensiveness
Evaluation	Description
Control	Problem orientation
Neutrality	Empathy
Superiority	Equality
Certainty	Provisionalism
Strategy	Spontaneity

use *description* report their observations rather than offering evaluative comments. People with a *problem orientation* do not act as though they have the solution but are eager to discuss multiple ideas. *Empathy* implies concern for others, as shown through careful listening for both the content and the intent of the other's message. *Equality* means that the communicator demonstrates that he or she is neither superior nor inferior to the second person. *Provisionalism* suggests that the communicator does not communicate certainty or a total conviction but is open to other ideas. *Spontaneity* implies naturalness and a lack of premeditation.

Gibb suggests that people replace those behaviors that create defensiveness with those that reduce it. Table 6.2 depicts the paired concepts. For example, rather than telling someone he is late for a meeting and you do not appreciate waiting, you might note the time he arrived and inquire empathically about his circumstances. Rather than being indifferent toward others and nonverbally suggesting you are superior, inquire about them and express your multiple similarities.

Essential Interpersonal Communication Behaviors

In interpersonal communication you need to be aware of factors such as perception, to have a good self-concept, to provide clear verbal and nonverbal cues to others, and to listen and empathize as others provide messages to you. In an interpersonal relationship you also show affection and support, influence others, and develop the unique nature of the relationship. In this section we consider three interpersonal communication areas: affectionate communication; influence, which includes compliance-gaining and interpersonal dominance; and the development of the distinctive relationship.

USING AFFECTIONATE AND SUPPORTIVE COMMUNICATION

Affection, the holding of fond or tender feelings toward another person, is essential in interpersonal relationships. You express your affectionate feelings for others in a variety of ways, often nonverbally as you touch, hug, kiss, or caress the person. You also use verbal statements of affection, such as "I care about you," "I really like being with you," or "I love you."

Affectionate communication can be risk-laden, and a number of variables affect its appropriateness, such as your own and the other person's sex, the kind of relationship you have (platonic or romantic), the privacy and emotional intensity of the situation, and your predispositions.[70] Telling another person you love him or her may hold significantly different meanings, depending on any of these factors.

Although the expression of affection is generally positive, if the receiver of the message does not reciprocate, the sender may be embarrassed or feel that he or she has lost face. Floyd and Burgoon found that, indeed, expressions of liking do not always result in positive relational outcomes.[71] In general, when people have particular expectations about communicative behavior and they are not met, they might rethink their relationship or they might change their behavior.[72]

Supportive communication is also important in interpersonal communication. Support includes giving advice, expressing concern, and offering assistance and can vary as a result of the receiver's age[73] and the support provider's goals.[74] In times of distress, comforting messages, such as suggesting a diversion, offering assistance, and expressing optimism, encourage people to feel less upset. At the same time, the recipients of such messages may also feel demeaned. The distressed person is most likely to feel less upset when the comforting message is offered by a close friend rather than an acquaintance.[75] Comfort, then, is viewed as most positive in close interpersonal relationships rather than in more distant ones.

INFLUENCING OTHERS

Influence is the power to affect other people's thinking or actions. It has been studied widely in the context of interpersonal communication. One body of research has focused on compliance-gaining and compliance-resisting. **Compliance-gaining** is a person's attempts to influence a target "to perform some desired behavior that the target otherwise might not perform."[76] It occurs frequently in interpersonal communication. We ask a friend for advice, we ask a parent for financial assistance, or we encourage a relational partner to feel more committed. Children become more skillful at identifying situational and personal cues in possible compliance-gaining as they develop, with girls showing more sensitivity than boys.[77]

Compliance-resisting occurs when targets of influence messages refuse to comply with requests. Targets often offer reasons for their refusal.[78] People who are more sensitive to others and who are more adaptive are more likely to engage in further attempts to influence.[79] Indeed, they may address some anticipated obstacles in their original request, and they may adapt later attempts by offering counterarguments.

For example, if you are asking a friend to let you borrow his car, you might consider some of the reasons he might refuse. He might state that he needs his car at the same time, that the last time you borrowed his car you returned it with no gas, or that the only time he ever hears from you is when you want something from him. In your initial message you might suggest to him that you believe you have been neglecting him, that you want to spend some time together, and that you have not been as considerate as you could be with him. When he suggests that he needs his car at the same time that you do, you might offer to use his car at a different time.

DEVELOPING A UNIQUE RELATIONSHIP

Interpersonal relationships are defined by their uniqueness. In a sense, relational couples create a "culture of two."[80] They may have unique names for each other and shared experiences that others do not have with them, and they may develop distinctive patterns of interaction. Bruess and Pearson found that couples who created **personal idioms**— or unique forms of expression and language understood only by them—expressed high

compliance-gaining
Attempts made by a source of messages to influence a target "to perform some desired behavior that the target otherwise might not perform."

compliance-resisting
The refusal of targets of influence messages to comply with requests.

personal idioms
Unique forms of expression and language understood only by individual couples.

skill **builder**

rituals
Formalized patterns of actions or words followed regularly.

relational satisfaction.[81] Did your parents have a unique name for you that no one else used? Do you have a way of referring to an event with an intimate that no one else understands? Do you have a way of expressing a thought, idea, or need to a friend that no one else can decipher? All these are personal idioms.

Through playful interaction and the creation of **rituals**—formalized patterns of actions or words followed regularly—couples create a shared culture. Rituals may become so routine that we do not realize that they are part of the fabric of a relationship. However, if a relational partner does not enact them, uneasiness often follows. For example, can you recall a time when your partner failed to call you, say "I love you," bring you flowers or a gift, or enact another regular behavior? Although the importance of the ritual might never have been verbalized, you probably felt hurt or neglected.

Bruess and Pearson suggest that the following rituals are important characteristics of long-term interpersonal relationships:

- *Couple-time rituals*—for example, exercising together or having dinner together every Saturday night
- *Idiosyncratic/symbolic rituals*—for example, calling each other by a special name or celebrating the anniversary of their first date
- *Daily routines and tasks*—for example, if living together, one partner always preparing the evening meal and the other always cleaning up afterward
- *Intimacy rituals*—for example, giving each other a massage or, when apart, talking on the telephone before going to bed
- *Communication rituals*—for example, saying "I love you" before they go to sleep
- *Patterns, habits, and mannerisms*—for example, meeting her need to be complimented when going out for a fancy evening and meeting his need to be reassured before family events
- *Spiritual rituals*—for example, attending services together or doing yoga together in the evening[82]

The Possibilities for Improvement

Can you improve your communication in interpersonal relationships? Most individuals feel it's possible. Are such changes easy? Generally, they are not. You should not expect that an introductory course in communication will solve all your relational problems. Self-help books that promise instant success will probably result only in disillusionment. Courses on assertiveness training, relaxation techniques, and marital satisfaction provide only part of the answer. Improving relationships is a lifelong process that nobody perfects but that many people can pursue for their own benefit.

BARGAINING

Often we engage in bargaining in our interpersonal relationships. **Bargaining** occurs when two or more parties attempt to reach an agreement on what each should give and receive in a transaction between them. Bargains may be explicit and formal, such as the kinds of agreements you reach with others to share tasks, to attend a particular event, or to behave in a specified way. Bargains may also be implicit and informal. For example, in exchange for receiving a compliment from your boyfriend every day, you might agree not to relate embarrassing stories about him. You may not even be aware of some of the unstated agreements you have with others with whom you communicate.

■ Couple-time rituals help maintain long-term interpersonal relationships.

bargaining
The process in which two or more parties attempt to reach an agreement on what each should give and receive in a transaction between them.

A study on interpersonal bargaining identified three essential features of a bargaining situation:

1. All parties perceive the possibility of reaching an agreement in which each party would be better off, or no worse off, than if no agreement were reached.

2. All parties perceive more than one such agreement that could be reached.

3. Each party perceives the others as having conflicting preferences or opposed interests.[83]

What are some examples of bargaining situations? You may want to go out with friends when your spouse would prefer a quiet evening at home. One person could use the word *forever* to mean a few days or weeks, whereas another assumes the word refers to a much longer period of time. In each of these instances, the disagreement can be resolved through bargaining.

Thibaut and Kelley underlined the importance of bargaining in interpersonal communication:

> Whatever the gratifications achieved in dyads, however lofty or fine the motives satisfied may be, the relationship may be viewed as a trading or bargaining one. The basic assumption running throughout our analysis is that every individual voluntarily enters and stays in any relationship only as long as it is adequately satisfactory in terms of rewards and costs.[84]

LEARNING COMMUNICATION SKILLS

If you wish to improve your communication in your interpersonal relationships, you must commit yourself to learning a variety of communication skills. You must understand the importance of perceptual differences among people, the role of self-concept in communication, the nature of verbal language, and the role of nonverbal communication. You must be willing to share yourself through self-disclosure, and you must be willing to attempt to understand other people through careful and conscientious listening. In addition, you must recognize that, even when you thoroughly understand these concepts and are able to implement them in your behavior, your interactions with others may not be successful. Communication is dependent on the interaction between two communicators, and one person cannot guarantee its success. Others may have conflicting goals, have different perspectives, or communicate incompetently.

Learning individual communication concepts and specific communication skills is essential to effective interaction. You also need to understand the impact of these skills. For example, you do not communicate at home the way you do in the classroom. Self-disclosure, which is especially appropriate and important within the family context, may be out of place in the classroom. Preparation and planning are important in an interview, but they may be seen as manipulative in a conversation between partners.

Is it possible to learn interpersonal communication skills while serving your community? Students at Brigham Young University in Hawaii did just that. On Make a Difference Day, they renovated and beautified Kahuku High School, a project filmed as a documentary for BYUTV. They also coached students in preparing for the Special Olympics and worked with patients in the Kahuku Hospital Social Work Department. Each of these activities contributed to the community and provided opportunities for the students to enhance their interpersonal communication skills. You can use the Internet to search for similar opportunities near your school and community.

MAINTAINING BEHAVIORAL FLEXIBILITY

behavioral flexibility
The ability to alter behavior to adapt to new situations and to relate in new ways when necessary.

In addition to applying your understanding of communication concepts, skills, and settings, you can enhance your interactions by using **behavioral flexibility**—the ability to alter behavior to adapt to new situations and to relate in new ways when necessary. Behavioral flexibility allows you to relax when you are with friends or to be your formal self while interviewing for a job. The key to behavioral flexibility may be self-monitoring, always being conscious of the effect of your words on the specific audience in a particular context.

Behavioral flexibility is especially important in interpersonal communication because relationships between people are in constant flux. For example, the family structure has gone through sharp changes in recent years, the United States has an increasingly older population, and changes in the labor force also require new skills and ways of interacting with others. People travel more often and move more frequently. Millions of people cohabit. As a result of these types of changes, people may interact differently today.

What kinds of changes can you expect in your own life that will affect your relationships with others? You may change your job ten or more times and move your place of residence even more frequently. You may marry at least once and have one child or more. You will experience loss of family members through death and the dissolution of relationships. When your life appears to be most stable and calm, unexpected changes will occur.

How can behavioral flexibility assist you through life's changes? A flexible person is confident about sharing messages with others, understands the messages others provide, self-discloses when appropriate, and at the same time demonstrates good listening skills. Flexibility lets us show concern for a child who needs assistance, be assertive on the job, yield when another person needs to exercise control, and be independent when called upon to stand alone. A flexible person is not dogmatic or narrow-minded. In short, flexibility means drawing on a large repertory of communication behaviors as appropriate to the situation.

Changes are not always negative. In fact, many are positive. For instance, when you graduate from college, the changes that occur are generally perceived as positive. When you enter into new relationships, you generally feel better about your life.

But even positive change can be stressful. Gail Sheehy, author of *Passages: Predictable Crises of Adult Life*, wrote:

> We must be willing to change chairs if we want to grow. There is no permanent compatibility between a chair and a person. And there is no one right chair. What is right at one stage may be restricting at another or too soft.[85]

keeping it real

Improving Interpersonal Communication Skills

Hannah, a sophomore, listened to Ashley's tale of her friend from high school. Her response was philosophical:

College students face many obstacles in their first year. Difficult classes, lots of freedom, and the pressure to commit to a major can complicate a college experience, but the most crucial experiences have to do with interpersonal relationships. The right roommate, group of friends, and significant other can make or break a college experience.

Hannah, who had taken a course in interpersonal communication, urged Ashley to slowly cut her ties with her high school friend.

Interpersonal relationships are complicated in high school. In college, they are even more difficult to maintain and keep healthy. Some students struggle enormously with social issues in college, but others adapt to their surroundings with ease. Choosing the right relationships and learning to deal with difficult issues are all part of growing up and learning more about communication.

What do experts identify as key strategies for improving interpersonal communication? Here is some advice that can help both Ashley and her friend:

1. Listen first. Communication is a two-way process; getting your message across depends on understanding the other person.

2. Be interested in the people with whom you are communicating. Remember, people are more attracted to those who are interested in them and will pay more attention to what they are saying.

3. Be relaxed. Bad body language, such as hunched shoulders, fidgeting, toe-tapping or hair-twiddling, gives the game away.

4. Smile and use eye contact. It's the most positive signal you can give.

5. Ask questions. It's a great way to show people that you are really interested in them.

6. If the other person has a different point of view than yours, find out more about why he or she thinks that way. The more you understand the reasons behind the person's thinking, the more you can understand his or her point of view or can help the person better understand your point of view.

7. Be assertive—try to value the other person's input as much as your own. Don't be pushy but don't be a pushover. Try for the right balance.

8. When you are speaking, try to be enthusiastic when appropriate. Use both your voice and body language to demonstrate interest.

9. Do not immediately try to latch onto something someone has just said, as in "Oh, yes, that happened to me," and then immediately tell your story. Make sure you ask enough questions of the other person first and be careful when or if you give your story, so as not to sound like it's a competition.

10. Learn from your interactions. If you had a really good conversation with someone, try to determine why it went well and remember the key points for next time. If it didn't go so well, again try and learn something from it.[86]

Chapter Review & Study Guide

Summary

In this chapter, you learned the following:

1. Interpersonal communication is the process of using messages to generate meaning between at least two people in a situation that allows mutual opportunities for both speaking and listening.

2. Interpersonal relationships provide one context in which people communicate with each other. Interpersonal relationships are associations between at least two people who are interdependent, who use some consistent patterns of interaction, and who have interacted for a period of time. Interpersonal relationships are established for a variety of reasons.

3. Interpersonal relationships are important because they allow us to fulfill our needs for inclusion, affection, and control. Most interpersonal relationships are positive,

but they also may have a dark side, which could include obsessions, jealousy, misunderstanding, gossip, conflict, codependency, and abuse.

4. Self-disclosure is fundamental to relationships.

5. Friendships are important, but they have changed over time largely due to social media.

6. Cross-cultural relationships are increasingly common.

7. Most relationships go through definable stages of development, maintenance, and deterioration.

8. Interpersonal communication includes affectionate and supportive communication, influence behaviors, and behaviors that allow people to develop unique relationships.

Key Terms

Aggressiveness
Argumentativeness
Attractiveness
Bargaining
Behavioral flexibility
Complementarity
Complementary relationships
Compliance-gaining
Compliance-resisting

Contradictions
Deceptive communication
Defensiveness
Dialectic
Hurtful messages
Interpersonal relationships
Personal idioms
Proximity
Relational deterioration

Relational development
Relational maintenance
Responsiveness
Rituals
Self-disclosure
Similarity
Symmetrical relationships

Study Questions

1. Which is *not* an element of an interpersonal relationship?

    a. It includes at least two people.
    b. It involves people who are interdependent.
    c. Its patterns of interaction are inconsistent.
    d. Individuals in an interpersonal relationship have interacted for some time.

2. Interpersonal relationships are important because

    a. they fulfill our needs for inclusion, affection, and control.
    b. physical, safety, and security needs cannot be met elsewhere.
    c. dependence is vital.
    d. we need to interact with people having similar interests.

3. An extrovert being friends with an introvert demonstrates which type of relationship?

    a. symmetrical   c. negotiated
    b. complementary   d. no relationship

4. Obsession, jealousy, gossip, and mental abuse are examples of

    a. healthy interpersonal communication.
    b. most marital relationships.
    c. possible negative qualities of some interpersonal relationships.
    d. positive problem-solving techniques and skills to develop.

5. Which of the following statements regarding friendship is true?

    a. Friendships remain unchanged over time.
    b. All friendships are maintained identically, regardless of relational partners' intent.
    c. The quality of friendship is affected by other psychological predispositions.
    d. For many older women, their only friend is their husband.

connect
For further review, go to the LearnSmart study module for this chapter.

6. If two people in a relationship start to merge their social circles and purchase items together, they are exhibiting actions in the
   a. relational development stage.
   b. relational maintenance stage.
   c. relational deterioration stage.
   d. relational dialectic stage.

7. We may begin a relationship with someone based on how desirable that person is to work with in the classroom. This type of motivation is called
   a. responsiveness.
   b. similarity.
   c. complementarity.
   d. attractiveness.

8. A motivation for terminating a relationship by deliberately making somebody believe untrue things is labeled
   a. deceptive communication.
   b. aggressiveness.
   c. argumentativeness.
   d. defensiveness.

9. Your childhood nickname and the pet name your significant other calls you are examples of
   a. compliance-gaining.
   b. personal idioms.
   c. rituals.
   d. contradictions.

10. Which of the following is very important in interpersonal communication, given that relationships between people are constantly changing?
    a. bargaining
    b. self-concept
    c. behavioral flexibility
    d. dialectic tensions

Answers:
1. (c); 2. (a); 3. (b); 4. (c); 5. (c); 6. (a); 7. (d); 8. (a); 9. (b); 10. (c)

Critical Thinking

1. Consider a friendship you have or had. Explain that friendship in terms of the interpersonal relationship stages. Give examples that describe each stage.

2. How have you maintained your relationships with various people over time? If you have come close to terminating a relationship, how was it regained? Using terminology from the text, what was the reason for the near-termination?

chapter 7

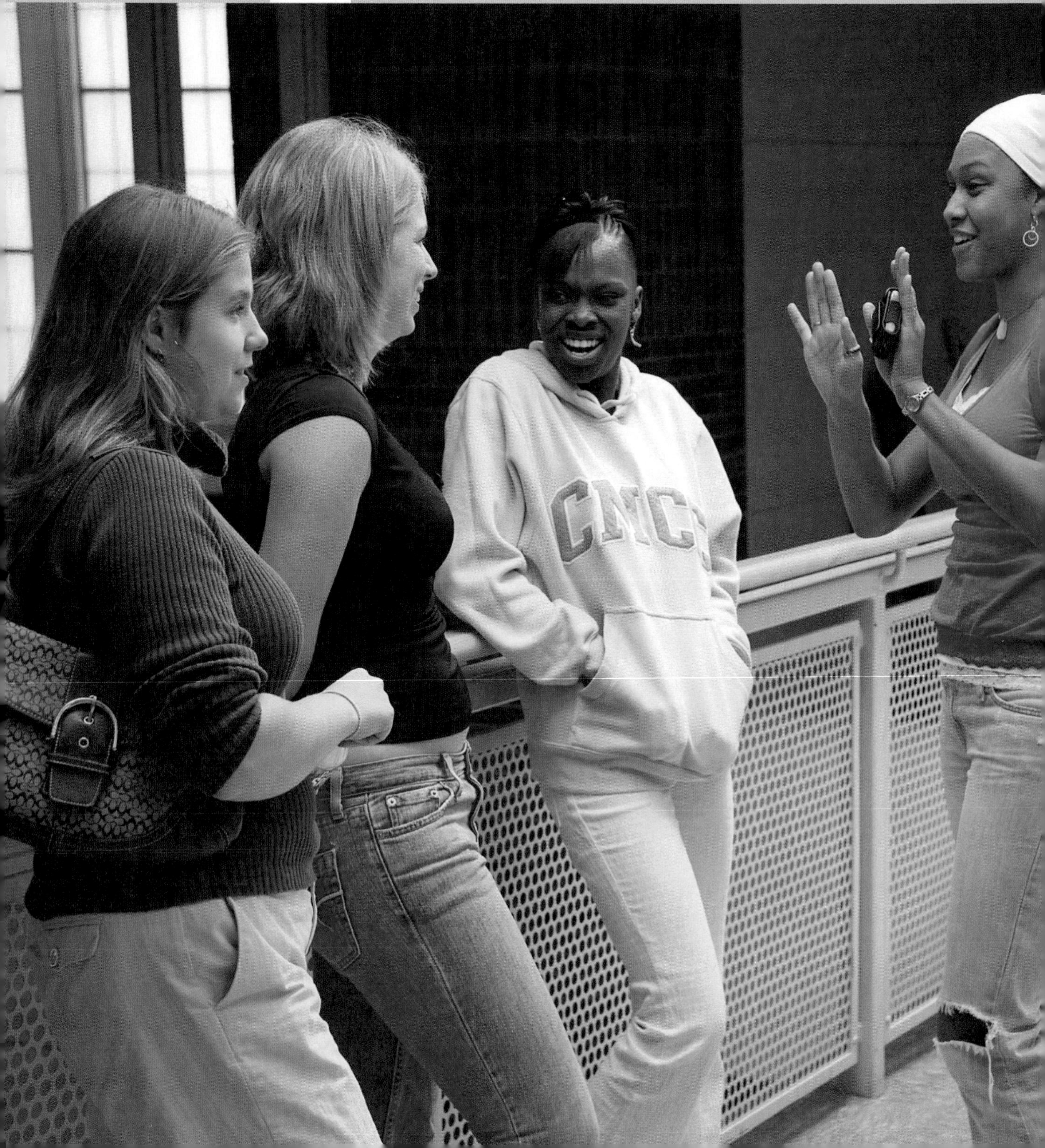

intercultural communication

When you have read and thought about this chapter, you will be able to:

1. Explain why the study of intercultural communication is important for you.

2. Distinguish between dominant and non-dominant cultures.

3. State the characteristics of various cultures, such as individualism, certainty, and time.

4. Practice some strategies for improving intercultural communication.

This chapter introduces you to intercultural communication. Being an effective communicator means interacting positively with people from various racial, ethnic, and cultural backgrounds. The chapter stresses the importance of communicating effectively in an ever-changing world. It reveals strategies used by ethnic groups and marginalized people to interact with dominant cultures, identifies broad characteristics of several cultures, and provides strategies for improving intercultural communication. When you have completed this chapter, you should know more about people outside your own group, and you should feel more confident about communicating successfully with others.

The lecture hall held around 100 students, all white except for a couple of African American athletes and a few international students. Near the front in the middle was a small woman whose appearance looked Native American but whose name—Vasquez—sounded Spanish. Was she a Mexican in this lecture hall full of white students? Here is Linda Vasquez's story:

I came to the Upper Midwest from California. When I first arrived, many individuals would ask if I were Native American. Maybe they figured that my features somehow looked like a Native American person's or perhaps it was because many Native Americans live in the Midwest. I told them that I wasn't Native American. Then they would see my last name, Vasquez, and ask me if I were Mexican. This still happens when I meet new people on campus. Most people consider Mexicans to be the same as Hispanics, but they're not. My mother is actually from Guatemala and my dad from El Salvador, countries both in Central America. When I tell people this, they usually ask, "Isn't that the same thing?"

So I have to explain to them that it's not. We may look the same, but that doesn't mean we are the same. For example, many Caucasian students' heritage comes from Europe, but many white people come from somewhere else. All white people are not European.

I'm Hispanic: an American with Latin heritage. And although my great-grandmother was born in Mexico, most of my family traditions come from Guatemala and El Salvador. These traditions may be similar to Mexican ones, but some are different. One thing that's different is the food. Many of the dishes in Guatemala and El Salvador are less spicy than the ones in Mexico. Another difference is the language. Mexico, Guatemala, and El Salvador all speak Spanish, but many of the words are different and can have different meanings. One example is the Spanish word *huevon*. This word translated into English means "to be lazy." In El Salvador it also is used to mean lazy, but in Guatemala it is considered to have sexual innuendo. Guatemalans get offended by this word, so instead they use the word *aragan,* which also means a lazy person.

Although I do have a lot of traditions from my parents' countries, many of my values and traditions are American. I can connect with both cultures and still feel in place.

Can you relate to Linda's situation? How do you approach communication with people from a cultural background different from your own? What would you recommend for others? We'll revisit Linda's situation at the end of the chapter.

Linda Vasquez's situation is increasingly common as the United States continues to attract people from other cultures. College-educated Americans are expected to know at least the basics of how to communicate with visitors, immigrants, and refugees from other cultures.

For centuries the United States looked to the United Kingdom and Western Europe as its main cultural and economic interest. But today the BRIC countries—Brazil, Russia, India, and China—are rapidly gaining power and influence. Because their economies are booming, many Americans will be interacting with their counterparts in those countries. U.S. college and universities have been and still are a magnet for international students.

How well can you actually talk to and learn from students at your own college who are immigrants, refugees, and international students? Do you know some of the basics of how to greet, meet, and eat with people from cultures besides your own? Can you understand the different ways that people from other cultures think and behave: their way of meeting and marrying; their religious beliefs; their family, tribe, or clan relationships; and their means of establishing trust in each other for personal or business reasons?

When you have finished studying this chapter, you will know much more about how to understand and communicate with people from other cultures.

Why Is the Study of Intercultural Communication Important?

Martin and Nakayama define **intercultural communication** as "the interaction between people from different cultural backgrounds."[1] Not long ago, intercultural communication involved only missionaries, jet-setting business executives, foreign correspondents, and political figures. Now, however, developments in technology and shifts in demographics have created a world in which intercultural communication is common. More people are exposed to different global cultures through vacation travel, transnational jobs, international conflicts, military and humanitarian service, and the presence of immigrants, refugees, and new citizens in the United States.

intercultural communication The exchange of information between individuals who are unalike culturally.

More people are also exposed to groups that operate outside the dominant culture: ethnic groups, neighborhood gangs, partisan political groups, and gay and lesbian societies. You may work and live every day with people different from yourself. Or you might only occasionally encounter unfamiliar groups. But today chances are excellent that you will need to know the basics of intercultural communication presented in this chapter. The first reason, then, that you should study intercultural communication is that communication with people from other cultures is increasingly common.

A second reason to study intercultural communication is economic. Today we sell our corn, wheat, and cars in Asia; we buy coffee from Colombia, bananas from Costa Rica, and oil from Africa, the Middle East, and South America. Our clothing comes from China and Panama, our shoes are made in Mexico, and our cars may have been assembled in Germany, Hungary, or Canada. Business that was previously domestic is now global. You will likely find yourself working with people from many different cultures because of our global economy.

A third reason to study intercultural communication is our curiosity about others. We are curious about people who don't look like us, sound like us, or live like us. We wonder why one woman always wears a long dress and veil, why someone would prefer polkas to rap, why a man wears a turban, and why some people do not eat pork or beef. We are curious about arranged marriages, rituals such as funerals and weddings, and sports such as sumo wrestling, kick boxing, and cricket. We express disbelief that fanatics in an otherwise peace-loving religion promise heaven to suicidal followers as a reward for murdering people. We do not understand religious fanatics and paramilitary groups in our own country who stockpile weapons to attack our own government. Intercultural communication includes better understanding of cultural friends and enemies.

The dominant culture of the United States values talk. So as a first step in learning how very different other cultures can be, let us consider how some cultures value silence over talk. Confucianism has a strong influence in China and some other Asian nations, but Confucius had a low opinion of eloquence, which is reflected in the preference of many East Asians for silence over talkativeness, as indicated in the box "The Value of Silence."

cultural note

The Value of Silence

One of the more striking differences among cultures is the value of silence. The dominant European American culture in the United States practically fears silence; people perceive silence as unintended and even embarrassing. But many East Asian cultures, such as the Japanese; autonomous cultures in the United States, such as the Amish; and Native American cultures, such as the Western Apache of Arizona see silence as an important way to know and understand another person through intuition and quietly figuring out the other person. Here are some sayings that illustrate the idea:

- It is what people say that gets them in trouble. (Japan)
- A loud voice shows an empty head. (Finland)
- To be always talking is against nature. (Taoist saying)
- One who speaks does not know. (Taoist saying)
- The cat that does not mew catches rats. (Japan)

Compared with some other cultures in the world, the dominant culture in North America consists of a bunch of chatterboxes who may or may not know what they are talking about. In any case, most European Americans do not use or respect silence as a means of communicating.

Source: Kim, Min-Sun. (2002). Non-Western perspectives on human communication: Implications for theory and practice. Thousand Oaks, CA: Sage, pp. 135, 137.

A fourth reason to study intercultural communication is the convergence of technologies. Urban youth around the world are armed with smartphones that can show a street fight in Libya on YouTube and CNN before the battle is over. New technologies have transformed interpersonal and face-to-face communication and have made possible instant communication across the world.

A fifth reason to study intercultural communication is the influx of foreign-born immigrants, aliens, and refugees who have changed the face of the United States. In metropolitan Washington, DC, your waiter is from Colombia, South America; your cab driver is from Ethiopia; the porter is from the Sudan; the dry cleaner is from Korea; and the barber is a Vietnamese woman. The story is similar for Miami, Los Angeles, New York City, Detroit, and Chicago. If not a melting pot, the United States is now (and always was) an exotic salad, with many cultures contributing to its overall flavor. You can communicate better with people from other cultures if you know something about theirs.

What Are Cultures?

You have just learned that intercultural communication is the exchange of information between people of different cultures, but you may be uncertain about the definitions of a culture. A **culture** is a unique combination of rituals (such as greeting and parting), religious beliefs, ways of thinking (such as how the earth was created), and ways of behaving (such as women can marry at 14 years of age in Iran) that unify a group of people. Often we perceive cultural differences (see chapter 2, on perception) as emerging from nation-states (France, the Czech Republic), religious groups (Muslims, Buddhists, Amish), tribal groups (Kurds, Ibos, Potawatomi Nation), or even people united by a cause (Palestinians, the Taliban, al-Qaeda).

culture
A unique combination of rituals, religious beliefs, ways of thinking, and ways of behaving that unify a group of people.

A **dominant culture** is determined by who has the power and influence in a group. For example, in the United States the dominant culture is white, male, able-bodied, straight, married, and employed.

White men dominate in politics: according to the congressional website, the U.S. Senate has 17 women among its 100 members, and the U.S. House of Representatives has 73 women among its 435 members.[2] In big business, men hold 82% of the positions on corporate boards, with both women and minorities losing ground in recent years. Among Fortune 500 companies, only 12 have women as their chief executive officer.[3]

dominant culture
Determined by who has the power and influence in a group; in the United States the dominant culture is white, male, able-bodied, straight, married, and employed.

If you have persistent bodily or mental deficiencies, you are no longer in the dominant culture, as indicated by the fact that you receive federal protection in the job market. Live openly as gay and you will discover that straightness is so dominant that in most states you cannot marry or have the legal rights of married people. The military remains white and male dominated (80%).[4] Higher education is still the bastion of white male professors, and most pastors and ministers, all imams, and all Roman Catholic cardinals, bishops, and priests are males.

To connect the issue of the dominant culture to communication, consider the burgeoning number of under- and unemployed. Lose your job and you find out quickly that the United States is a capitalist culture that strongly favors workers and casts the unemployed into a situation where they are devoid of power or influence. In fact, you end up in a dependent situation where you have to get unemployment, food stamps, and the like from government agencies. In the dominant U.S. culture, individual identity is tightly tied to occupation. When strangers meet, one of the first questions they ask each other is "What do you do?"

In Korea and some of the other Pacific Rim countries, the exchange between strangers is quite different. First, Korea is a country of 100 clans, so your name, whether it be Kim, Min, or Choi, tells the other person something of your lineage. But the first question people ask is not about what you do for a living. Instead, Koreans want to know whom you know in common. In other words, Koreans value human relationships, the linkage with others, over occupation.

A **non-dominant culture** exists within a larger, dominant culture but differs from the dominant culture in some significant characteristic. For instance, an Afghani who comes to the United States moves from a dominant culture (an Afghani in Afghanistan) to a non-dominant culture (an Afghani in the United States). An able-bodied, wealthy white male could move from the dominant culture to a non-dominant culture if he became disabled in an automobile accident. Non-dominant cultures are based on varied criteria: females because they are not equal to men in pay, power, or prestige; poor people because they are united in powerlessness; and gays and lesbians because they lack rights and privileges. An individual can belong to many non-dominant cultures. A U.S. adolescent female immigrant from Panama who is a Roman Catholic earning minimum wage belongs to at least five non-dominant cultures, but no one would say she is of the dominant U.S. culture.

Next we are going to explore some methods used by non-dominant cultures to communicate with dominant cultures. Consider a gay male working in an office with a dominant culture of straight men and women. What choices does he have in relating to other workers? The next section explains the goals of assimilation, accommodation, and separation.

non-dominant culture
This term includes people of color, women, gays/lesbians/bisexuals, people with disabilities, the lower/working class, the unemployed, the underemployed, the bankrupt, the young, and the elderly.

THE GOALS OF NON-DOMINANT CULTURAL COMMUNICATION

Some of the earlier studies of non-dominant cultures focused on how little influence women had, even when they were part of workforce teams. Kramarae, for instance, called women a "muted group" because their ideas were undervalued, underestimated, and sometimes unheard.[5] Like the "transparent man" in the musical *Chicago*—a person whom nobody noticed, addressed, or remembered—women were muted when their presence and voices were unheard or unheralded.

Non-dominant cultures are often called "marginalized groups" because they live on the edges of the dominant culture; in other words, they exist on the margins. Who are the marginalized groups? Orbe calls them "non-dominant groups" and categorizes them as "people of color, women, gays/lesbians/bisexuals, people with disabilities, lower/working class, and the young and the elderly."[6] To these groups we could now add others: people who are bankrupt, who have lost their jobs, who are unemployed or underemployed, or who have lost their homes due to the economic downturn.

■ Cultural identity is maintained by distinctive clothing and other adornments.

Who are the likely members of the dominant culture? Orbe quotes Folb's list of the dominant as male, European American, heterosexual, able-bodied, youthful, middle/upper class, and/or Christian groups.[7] Others dominant in our culture are the college-educated, people in the professions, business owners, homeowners, married couples, and people paid by the month instead of by the hour.

Usually, marginalized, non-dominant groups seek three possible goals to relate to dominant groups: assimilation, accommodation, or separation. The **assimilation goal** means that the marginalized group attempts to fit in with the dominant group. They wear suits; you wear a suit. They don't have body piercing or visible tattoos; you forgo the ear, lip, and eyebrow rings and body art. They talk sports; you learn the names of the teams and players.

The **accommodation goal** means that the marginalized group manages to keep its identity while striving for positive relationships with the dominant culture. For example, a woman takes her lesbian partner to the company picnic, makes no secret of the relationship at work, but does not discuss her lesbianism with her heterosexual colleagues. A fundamentalist Christian woman always wears long dresses and never cuts her hair or wears makeup, but she respects the right of co-workers to have their own religious beliefs without interference from her.

A **separation goal** is achieved when the marginalized group relates as exclusively as possible with its own group and as little as possible with the dominant group. A number of very conservative religious groups, such as Hasidic Jews, the Amish, and Black Muslims, are examples. But marginalized individuals can live separate lives in the midst of the dominant culture by relentlessly focusing on work, studiously avoiding any but the most necessary interactions, and never socializing outside work with any colleagues.

The separation goal can be carried to an extreme with an aggressive attitude about the non-dominant group's identity. Some skinheads are openly racist, some black and Hispanic groups are openly antiwhite, and some paramilitary groups are openly antigovernment. Queer Nation blatantly forces straight people to recognize the existence of gayness by outing prominent individuals. Such strategies are aggressive and confrontational and signal that the group does not want to be "transparent."

skill builder

Relating to the Dominant Culture

If you are an able-bodied, white, Christian, straight male, you can skip this exercise about how non-dominant cultures relate to you. If you are physically or mentally challenged, non-white, non-Christian, gay or lesbian, a woman, or a member of any other marginalized group, this exercise is for you.

The question is "As a member of a non-dominant culture facing a member of the dominant culture, how would you feel and how would you act in the following situations?" Select a couple of situations for discussion in or outside class. Each can create an awkward communication situation that requires some thoughtful planning for the person from a non-dominant culture.

- Exchanging an item for money at a pawn shop; the clerk is an older white man.

- Seeking to meet an attractive person from the dominant culture at a party full of them.

- Asking a well-dressed white man for a small loan at a credit union or bank.

- Meeting your lover's dominant-culture parents at their home in a suburban gated community.

- Buying a used car from a white man whose pickup sports a Confederate flag.

- Buying a small pistol in a state that allows you to carry a concealed weapon.

- Being stopped by the highway patrol when you are quite sure you have broken no laws.

What Are Some Intercultural Communication Problems?

Intercultural communication is subject to all the problems that can hamper effective interpersonal communication. Intercultural relationships are especially hindered by many of the perceptual distortions discussed in chapter 2, "Perception, Self, and Communication." How we select, organize, and interpret visual and message cues is even more important between cultures than among friends. Attribution and perceptual errors are more likely to occur between persons with many differences. Several additional problems may occur during intercultural interactions. Becoming aware of these issues can help you avoid them or reduce their effects. Keep in mind that, although the barriers identified here can be problematic, they do not occur in every exchange.

ETHNOCENTRISM

The largest problem that occurs during intercultural communication is that people bring the prejudices of their culture to the interaction. **Ethnocentrism** is the belief that your own group or culture is superior to all other groups or cultures. You are ethnocentric if you see and judge the rest of the world only from your own culture's perspective. Some common examples include thinking that everyone should speak English, that people in the United States should not have to learn languages other than English, that the U.S. culture is better than Mexico's, and that the Asian custom of bowing is odd.[8] Each of us operates from an ethnocentric perspective, but problems arise when we interpret and evaluate other cultures negatively compared with our own. Generally, a lack of interaction with another culture fosters high levels of ethnocentrism and encourages the notion of cultural superiority. Ethnocentrism makes others feel defensive.

In ethnocentrism you use your own culture as the measure that others are expected to meet; **cultural relativism** is the belief that another culture should be judged by its own context rather than measured against your culture. Saying that the Asian custom of bowing is odd overlooks the long history of bowing to one another as a sign of respect. To communicate effectively with people from different cultures, you need to accept people whose values and norms may be different from your own. An effective communicator avoids ethnocentrism and embraces cultural relativism. In the box "Cultural Relativism in Gestures Around the Globe," you will find some examples of behaviors that make sense only in the context of another culture.

STEREOTYPING

Ethnocentrism is not the only perceptual trap you can fall into in intercultural communication. Equally dangerous is the tendency to stereotype people in cultural groups. Rogers

assimilation goal
The marginalized group attempts to fit in with the dominant group.

accommodation goal
The marginalized group manages to keep its identity while striving for positive relationships with the dominant culture.

separation goal
The marginalized group relates as exclusively as possible with its own group and as little as possible with the dominant group.

ethnocentrism
The belief that your own group or culture is superior to other groups or cultures.

cultural relativism
The belief that another culture should be judged by its own context rather than measured against your culture.

cultural note

Cultural Relativism in Gestures Around the Globe

As you consider the ideas of cultural relativism, look at this list of nonverbal behaviors from around the world. Each of these behaviors needs to be judged not in comparison with what people do in the United States but in terms of its meaningfulness in another culture.

- *China:* Chinese always use both hands when passing food, a gift, or a business card.
- *Italy:* The U.S. indication of one (the index finger) means two in Italy.
- *Thailand:* Do not linger in the doorsill where Thais believe a spirit lives.
- *Greece and Turkey:* A small upward nod that means "yes" in the United States is the way to say "no."
- *Brazil:* The OK sign in the United States (circle made with thumb and forefinger) is obscene.
- *Japan:* Laughter in certain situations signals embarrassment, not amusement.
- *Kenya:* Pointing with the index finger is regarded as very insulting.

Source: Mancini, M. (2003). *Selling destinations: Geography for the travel professional.* Clifton Park, NY: Thompson/Delmar Learning.

■ What stereotypes come to mind when you see this image?

stereotype
A generalization about some group of people that oversimplifies their culture.

and Steinfatt define a **stereotype** as "a generalization about some group of people that oversimplifies their culture."[9] The stereotype of a gay male is an effeminate fellow, but gay people are just as likely to be truckers, physicians, and athletes. Similarly, Jews are both wealthy and poor, Asians are both gifted at math and not, and some black Americans are great athletes but some are not.

Why do people stereotype? Bruno observes, "The tribal drum beats in all societies, warning members of the tribe against the dangers of the others, those who are not members of the tribe, even those who are different within a society. The drum's messages result in different tribal behavior, from religious warfare in Northern Ireland and the Middle East, ethnic cleansing in Yugoslavia and Rwanda, to Neo-Nazi racial purification in Germany and America."[10] Bruno notes that prejudice may be bold or subtle and can even occur among physicians against the disabled people they treat.

Allport originally observed that people are more likely to stereotype individuals and groups with whom they have little contact.[11] For example, you might have a whole set of beliefs about Middle Eastern Muslim women, many of whom cover their body and face and walk well behind their husband. You may not realize that one of your neighbors is actually Muslim but does not follow some of the strict traditions of her religion.

Sometimes stereotyping occurs because people have had a negative or positive experience with a person from another culture. In one investigation, people stereotyped African Americans after only one observation of a negative behavior. In another, simply hearing about an alleged crime was sufficient to stereotype African Americans.[12] Clearly, people are willing to stereotype with very little evidence.

How do people feel about receiving either negative or positive comments that reflect on their social group rather than on them as individuals? In general, people respond adversely to negative comments that are about them either as an individual or as a member of a social group. They also respond negatively if the comment is positive, but reflects a stereotype. Participants in this study reported that even positive stereotypes caused increased anger and a desire to avoid or attack the speaker.[13]

What can an individual do who feels that another is stereotyping him or her? A study that tested the effectiveness of confrontation found that the following strategy helps. Although confrontations elicited negative emotions and evaluations toward the person doing the confronting, they also resulted in fewer stereotypic comments from the initial speaker. This change in behavior may be due to the negative self-directed affect that was felt by the stereotyping speaker.[14]

PREJUDICE

prejudice
A negative attitude toward a group of people just because they are who they are.

Whereas ethnocentrism is thinking your culture is better than others and stereotyping is acting as if all members of a group were alike, **prejudice** is a negative attitude toward a group of people just because they are who they are. Often the groups on the receiving end of prejudice are marginalized groups—people in poverty, people of color, people who speak a language other than English, and gay men and lesbian women. People who are accustomed to being on the receiving end of prejudice can become highly aware of that prejudice. One study showed that African Americans could identify previously identified prejudiced people in only 20 seconds, a much higher degree of accuracy than measured in whites.[15]

Sometimes the group experiencing the prejudice is actually larger than the group that exhibits it. For example, many countries, including the United States, show prejudice against women (lower pay, the glass ceiling) even though they are a majority. Woman experience sexist incidents—demeaning and degrading comments and sexual objectification—much more than men, and they suffer depression, anger, and lower self-esteem because of such incidents.[16] In still other countries, people who are a numerical minority control the fates and show prejudice toward a group that is larger but weaker. Some of the countries that deposed their leaders in the Arab Spring of 2011 were led by rulers from minority groups in their own country.

Prejudice is often based on ignorance. That is, the dominant culture chooses not to know much about the target of its prejudice, or the dominant group sees the objects of their prejudice as being in the place they belong. Women and African Americans have made some headway against prejudice, but "mistakes" indicate that prejudices persist: the man—not a woman—must be the manager or owner, the African American man by the luxury car must be someone's driver, and that Mexican must be a day laborer. How many African American married couples have you seen with their adopted white child? Education may be the best route to reducing prejudice, so one of the goals of this textbook is to help educated

cultural note

Meeting, Greeting, and Eating

- U.S. citizens and Europeans shake hands in greeting, whereas an even larger number of Chinese, Taiwanese, and Japanese bow when meeting.

- Chinese and other Pacific Rim countries exchange small, nicely wrapped presents between hosts/hostesses and guests, especially in formal visits.

- Men and women in Russia, Italy, and France give each other a cheek-to-cheek hug and even a bit of a kiss when greeting.

- Citizens of Pacific Rim countries exchange business cards on meeting by using both hands as if handing off a delicate gift. They look at and even comment on the card.

- The Chinese and other Asians eat with chopsticks, whereas many countries influenced by the British eat with the fork in the left hand and the knife in the right hand. North Americans hold the fork in the right hand.

- Muslim men in Malaysia and in some other countries touch their heart after shaking hands as if to say their greeting is "from the heart."

- Whereas many North Americans have alcoholic drinks before a big meal, millions of Muslims in the world shun alcohol at any time.

- Jews eat kosher food that has been blessed by a rabbi; Muslim people eat Hallal, foods prepared by custom by a butcher who faces east and says the name of Allah while draining the animal's blood. Neither Jews nor Muslims eat pork.

- Whereas North Americans are famous for their "fast foods," much of the rest of the world takes time to eat, to savor the food, and to enjoy conversations with others.

people overcome ethnocentrism, stereotyping, and prejudice. That will not occur, however, if you protect your prejudices against any outside interference.

What Are Some Characteristics of Different Cultures?

Accepting that your own culture is not superior to another person's culture is one way to improve intercultural communication. Another way is by understanding some of the values and norms of other cultures. For example, suppose you are an American teaching in Japan. Your students' first assignment is to give a speech before the class. After you give them the assignment, they automatically form groups, and each group selects a spokesperson to give the speech. In the United States, students would be unlikely to turn a public-speaking assignment into a small-group activity unless specifically directed to do so. If you don't know anything about the norms and customs of the Japanese culture, you might be totally baffled by your students' behavior. Before launching into some broad characteristics of international cultures, review the box "Meeting, Greeting, and Eating."

In the next section you will learn about three characteristics of cultures: individualistic versus collectivist cultures, uncertainty-accepting versus uncertainty-rejecting cultures, and

On-time versus Sometime cultures. Keep in mind that the characteristics discussed here are general tendencies. They are not always true of a culture, and they are not true of everyone in a culture.

INDIVIDUALISTIC VERSUS COLLECTIVIST CULTURES

Much of what is known about individualistic and collectivist cultures comes from a study by Hofstede that involved more than 100,000 managers from forty countries.[17] Although neither China nor Africa was included, the study is a classic in its comprehensiveness.

individualistic cultures Cultures that value individual freedom, choice, uniqueness, and independence.

Individualistic cultures value individual freedom, choice, uniqueness, and independence. These cultures place "I" before "we" and value competition over cooperation, private property over public or state-owned property, personal behavior over group behavior, and individual opinion over what anyone else might think. In an individualistic society, people are likely to leave the family home or the geographic area in which they were raised to pursue their dreams; their loyalty to an organization has qualifications; they move from job to job; and they may leave churches that no longer meet their needs. Loyalty to other people has limits: individualistic cultures have high rates of divorce and illegitimacy. According to the Hofstede study, the top-ranking individualistic cultures are the United States, Australia, Great Britain, Canada, and the Netherlands.[18] Table 7.1 charts the broad cultural characteristics including individualistic cultures; we discuss its other comparisons next.

Table 7.1 Summary of Cultural Characteristics

Individualistic Cultures Tend to:	Collectivist Cultures Tend to:
Value individual freedom; place "I" before "we."	Value the group over the individual; place "we" before "I."
Value independence.	Value commitment to family, tribe, and clan.
Value directness and clarity.	Value cooperation over competition.
Examples: United States, Australia, Great Britain	*Examples:* Venezuela, Pakistan, Taiwan, Thailand
Uncertainty-Accepting Cultures Tend to:	**Uncertainty-Rejecting Cultures Tend to:**
Be willing to take risks.	Be threatened by ideas and people from outside.
Avoid rules, seek flexibility, and reject hierarchy.	Establish formal rules for behavior; prefer stability, hierarchy, and structure.
Value individual opinion, general principles, and common sense	Embrace written rules, regulation, and rituals.
Examples: United States, Great Britain, Denmark	*Examples:* Japan, France, Spain, Greece, Argentina
On-Time Cultures Tend to:	**Sometime Cultures Tend to:**
Compartmentalize time.	Factor in time as one element of a larger context.
Say that they can waste or save time.	Value social relationships and time considerations together.
Separate work and social time, task and relational time.	Orchestrate family and social responsibilities and task dimensions.
Examples: North America, Northern Europe	*Examples:* Latin America, Middle East, Asia, France, Africa

Source: Adapted from Dodd, Carley. (1998). *Dynamics of intercultural communication.* New York: McGraw-Hill. © 1998 The McGraw-Hill Companies, Inc. Used by permission.

Collectivist cultures, on the other hand, value the group over the individual. These cultures place "we" before "I" and value commitment to family, tribe, and clan; their people tend to be loyal to spouse, employer, community, and country. Collectivist cultures value cooperation over competition, and group-defined social norms and duties over personal opinions.[19] An ancient Confucian saying captures the spirit of collectivist cultures: "If one wants to establish himself, he should help others to establish themselves first." The highest-ranking collectivist cultures in Hofstede's study were Venezuela, Pakistan, Peru, Taiwan, and Thailand,[20] to which we can easily add China and Japan.

skill builder

Interpret the Meaning of Common Sayings

Carefully examine the following sayings, and by yourself or with classmates determine whether they reflect a collectivist or an individualistic culture:

1. When spider webs unite, they can tie up a lion.
2. God helps those who help themselves.
3. The squeaky wheel gets the grease.
4. The ill-mannered child finds a father wherever he goes.

Answers:

1. An Ethiopian proverb, collectivist. 2. An American saying, individualistic. 3. An American saying. 4. An African saying, collectivist.

Source: Samovar, L. A., Porter, R. E., & Stefani, L. A. (1998). *Communication between cultures* (3rd ed.). Belmont, CA: Wadsworth.

UNCERTAINTY-ACCEPTING VERSUS UNCERTAINTY-REJECTING CULTURES

Uncertainty-accepting cultures tolerate ambiguity, uncertainty, and diversity. Some of these cultures already have a mixture of ethnic groups, religions, and races. They are more likely to accept political refugees, immigrants, and new citizens from other places. They are less likely to have a rule for everything and more likely to tolerate general principles. Uncertainty-accepting cultures include the United States, Great Britain, Denmark, Sweden, Singapore, Hong Kong, Ireland, and India.[21] Interestingly, Singapore is a city-state that is more tolerant of uncertainty and diversity but has many rules, including one prohibiting chewing gum. This oddity should serve as a reminder that these characteristics are generalizations and therefore are not found consistently in every culture.

Uncertainty-rejecting cultures have difficulty with ambiguity, uncertainty, and diversity. These cultures are more likely to have lots of rules, more likely to want to know exactly how to behave, and more likely to reject outsiders, such as immigrants, refugees, and migrants who look and act differently than them. Among the most common uncertainty-rejecting cultures are Japan, France, Spain, Greece, Portugal, Belgium, Peru, Chile, Russia, China, and Argentina.[22]

This uncertainty-rejection can lead to communication problems. For example, an increasing number of Asian people now reside in the United States. Teachers who are conferring with Asian parents may find that their communicative style is different from that of European Americans with whom they meet. Lee and Manning report that Asian parents do not start talking immediately in a

collectivist cultures
Cultures that value the group over the individual.

uncertainty-accepting cultures
Cultures that tolerate ambiguity, uncertainty, and diversity.

uncertainty-rejecting cultures
Cultures that have difficulty with ambiguity, uncertainty, and diversity.

social media make it matter

Blogs

As of February 2011 the Internet hosted about 156 million public blog sites; by now, you can find more. Blogs are often maintained by individuals, and their content (text, audio, and video) is usually updated frequently. Blog sites can get you in contact with individuals in other countries, most of whom are eager to communicate.

You can connect with blog sites in other countries with ease. Just do a search for Blogs in China (though many are routinely shut down by the government), Blogs in India, Blogs in South Africa, or just about any other country in the world. You can get the inside story about what is happening to the people in these places by reading what they post.

teacher–parent conference.[23] Instead, they rely on the teacher's tone of voice, gestures, facial expressions, posture, walk, and treatment of time and space to learn about how the teacher feels about their child. The nonverbal cues help the Asian parents reduce their uncertainty.

ON-TIME VERSUS SOMETIME CULTURES

The last intercultural characteristic we will consider here is time concepts for differentiating among cultures of the world. **On-time** cultures compartmentalize time to meet personal needs, to separate task and social dimensions, and to point to the future.[24] On-time is dominant in Canada, the United States, and Northern Europe.

On-time
The time schedule that compartmentalizes time to meet personal needs, separates task and social dimensions, and points to the future.

These cultures see time as something that can be controlled, wasted, or saved. Americans might schedule times to work out, to keep appointments, to go to meetings, and to take the family to a fast-food restaurant. Time is segmented, dedicated to work or social experiences (but usually not both), and plotted toward future events and activities. Within this scheme, getting to any appointment on time is given considerable importance.

If you travel to other parts of the world, including most countries in Latin America and the Middle East, you will probably experience being an On-time person in a **Sometime** world. You may feel psychologically stressed, as others always seem to be late. On the other hand, you may note that Sometime people focus only on you when they are conversing with you. They are not distracted by schedules or other commitments. For some behaviors in other cultures that go beyond the treatment of time, look at the box "Cultural Differences in Nonverbal Communication," where you will find some cultural differences in nonverbal behavior around the world.

Sometime
The time schedule that views time as "contextually based and relationally oriented."

cultural note

Cultural Differences in Nonverbal Communication

Did you know that

- Women in many parts of the world, including most Asian and Scandinavian countries, cover their mouths when they laugh or giggle.

- In Malaysia and other countries in South Asia, you do not raise your arm and hand above shoulder level even when you hail a cab (no flashing of the armpit).

- Australians consider it rude to put your hands on your lap during a meal.

- In Iran and much of the Middle East, people do not exhibit signs of affection in public.

- In the Middle East and parts of Africa, adult males may hold hands as a sign of friendship.

- In Turkey having your hand in your pocket when conversing is regarded as rude.

- In Pakistan you eat only with the right hand, because the left hand is regarded as unclean.

Source: Some of these items are from observations during the authors' travels, whereas others are from Axtell, Roger (1998). *The do's and taboos of body language around the world.* New York: John Wiley.

Sometime cultures view time as "contextually based and relationally oriented."[25] For Sometime cultures, time is not saved or wasted; instead, it is only one factor in a much larger and more complicated context. Why halt a conversation with an old friend to hurry off to an appointment on a relatively unimportant issue?

Relationships in some contexts trump time considerations. Sometime cultures orchestrate their relational and task obligations with the fluid movements of jazz, whereas On-time cultures treat life like a march in which people strive mainly to stay on schedule, be efficient, and value tasks over relationships. Typical Sometime cultures are found in Latin America, the Middle East, Asia, France, Africa, and Greece. The United States is predominantly an On-time culture because of the strong European influence, but some non-dominant cultures within the United States exhibit Sometime tendencies.

Businesspeople in Sometime cultures do conduct business, but they do it very differently than those in On-time cultures. A businessperson might have a large waiting room outside of his or her office. Several people will be in that waiting room, and they will use the space and time to meet with each other and resolve issues. A great deal of business in On-time cultures is conducted in public rather than in a series of private meetings.

What Are Some Strategies for Improving Intercultural Communication?

Effective intercultural communication often takes considerable time, energy, and commitment. The strategies presented here should provide you with some ways to improve intercultural communication and avoid potential problems. Having some strategies in advance will prepare you for new situations with people from other cultures and will increase your confidence in your ability to communicate effectively with a variety of people.

1. *Conduct a personal self-assessment.* How do your own attitudes toward other cultures influence your communication with them? One of the first steps toward improving your intercultural communication skills is an honest assessment of your own communication style, beliefs, and prejudices.

2. *Practice supportive communication behaviors.* Supportive behaviors, such as empathy, encourage success in intercultural exchanges; defensive behaviors tend to hamper effectiveness.

3. *Develop sensitivity toward diversity.* One healthy communication perspective holds that you can learn something from all people. Diverse populations provide ample opportunity for learning. Take the time to learn about other cultures before a communication situation, but don't forget that you will also learn about others simply by taking a risk and talking to someone who is different from you. Challenge yourself. You may be surprised by what you learn.

sizing things up

Individualism-Collectivism Scale

In this chapter you learned that people from different cultures, and even people from the same culture, can differ across several cultural dimensions. This scale helps you learn how you might compare with others on one such dimension—individualism and collectivism. Read each statement carefully and use the following scale to indicate how well the statement describes you. Place a 1 in on the line in front of the number if the statement does not describe you, a 5 if the statement describes you well, or a 2–4 on the line if those items best describe you in that situation. A guide for interpreting your responses appears in the appendix at the end of the text (p. 348).

1 = Does not describe me at all
2 = Does not describe me very well
3 = Describes me somewhat
4 = Describes me well
5 = Describes me very well

1. I often "do my own thing."
2. The well-being of my co-workers is important to me.
3. One should live one's life independently.
4. If a co-worker got a prize, I would feel proud.
5. I like my privacy.
6. If a relative were in financial difficulty, I would help within my means.
7. I prefer to be direct and forthright when discussing with people.
8. It is important to maintain harmony with my group.
9. I am a unique individual.
10. I like sharing little things with my neighbors.
11. What happens to me is my own doing.
12. I feel good when I cooperate with others.
13. When I succeed, it is usually because of my abilities.
14. My happiness depends very much on the happiness of those around me.
15. I enjoy being unique and different from others in many ways.
16. To me, pleasure is spending time with others.

Source: Sengilis, T. M., Trandis, H. C., Bhawuk, P. S., & Geifand, M. J. (1995). Horizontal and vertical dimensions of individualism and collectivism: A theoretical and measurement refinement. *Cross-Cultural Research, 29,* 240–275. Reprinted by permission.

■ Freedom of expression and a diversity of perspectives are fundamental to a civil society.

4. *Avoid stereotypes.* Cultural generalizations go only so far; avoid making assumptions about another's culture, and get to know individuals for themselves.

5. *Avoid ethnocentrism.* You may know your own culture the best, but that familiarity does not make your culture superior to all others. You will learn more about the strengths and weaknesses of your own culture by learning more about other cultures.

6. *Develop code sensitivity.* **Code sensitivity** refers to the ability to use the verbal and nonverbal language appropriate to the cultural norms of the individual with whom you are communicating. The more you know about another's culture, the better you will be at adapting.

7. *Seek shared codes.* A key ingredient in establishing shared codes is being open-minded about differences while you determine which communication style to adopt during intercultural communication.

8. *Use and encourage descriptive feedback.* Effective feedback encourages adaptation and is crucial in intercultural communication. Both participants should be willing to accept feedback and exhibit supportive behaviors. Feedback should be immediate, honest, specific, and clear.

9. *Open communication channels.* Intercultural communication can be frustrating. One important strategy to follow during such interactions is to be patient as you seek mutual understanding.

10. *Manage conflicting beliefs and practices.* Think ahead about how you might handle minor and major differences, from everyday behavior to seriously different practices, such as punishments (beheading, stoning), realities (starvation, extreme poverty), and beliefs (male superiority, female subjugation).

code sensitivity
The ability to use the verbal and nonverbal language appropriate to the cultural norms of the individual with whom you are communicating.

Of course, the most effective strategy for improving your intercultural communication competence is practice. Fortunately, the increasing diversity of our own culture means that intercultural communication practice can take place with the people at the corner market, at your place of employment, or even with the student sitting next to you in class. To learn from these many instances of intercultural communication, you must learn to be reflexive. **Reflexivity** means being self-aware and learning from interactions with the intent of improving future interactions. That is, you are able to assess the interaction, identify what went well in the conversation and what could have been done better, and then learn from those observations. Through reflexivity not only will you improve your intercultural communication skills but you will also become a more effective communicator in nearly every situation.

reflexivity
Being self-aware and learning from interactions with the intent of improving future interactions.

keeping it real

Getting Involved with Other Cultures

This chapter began with Linda Vasquez explaining her heritage and wishing that others would not stereotype her as someone she is not. Doubtless you or some of your friends on campus feel the same way. To avoid further marginalizing anyone who is not from the dominant culture or is from a different cultural background than yourself, make a point of contacting someone from another culture in your classes, at your school, or in your community. Here are some questions to get you started:

1. Please tell me how people in your culture meet friends, strangers, or business partners.
2. What do people in your culture do to establish trust in someone with whom they plan to have future dealings?
3. What religion, celebrations, and holidays does your culture recognize?
4. How is language in your culture different from English in the United States?
5. How does the dominant culture in your country differ from that in the United States?

Chapter Review & Study Guide

Summary

In this chapter you learned the following:

1. The study of intercultural communication is important because we are increasingly exposed to people of other cultures. We also are curious about and have an economic need to relate to others.

2. Non-dominant cultures communicate with the dominant culture in dealing with different goals. The three goals of non-dominant groups with the dominant culture are separation, accommodation, and assimilation.

3. Ethnocentrism, stereotyping, and prejudice result in communication problems in intercultural interactions.

4. You can strive to improve your own communication competence by
   - Conducting a personal self-assessment
   - Practicing supportive communication behaviors
   - Developing sensitivity toward diversity

- ■ Avoiding stereotypes
- ■ Avoiding ethnocentrism
- ■ Developing code sensitivity
- ■ Seeking shared codes

- ■ Using descriptive feedback
- ■ Opening communication channels
- ■ Managing conflicting beliefs and practices
- ■ Practicing reflexivity

Key Terms

Accommodation goal
Assimilation goal
Code sensitivity
Collectivist cultures
Cultural relativism
Culture
Dominant culture

Ethnocentrism
Individualistic cultures
Intercultural communication
Non-dominant culture
On-time
Prejudice
Reflexivity

Separation goal
Sometime
Stereotype
Uncertainty-accepting cultures
Uncertainty-rejecting cultures

Study Questions

connect
For further review, go to the LearnSmart study module for this chapter.

1. Which of the following statements is *not* true?

   a. The convergence of technologies has created global connectedness.
   b. Communication with people from other cultures is becoming increasingly uncommon.
   c. The influx of foreign-born immigrants, aliens, and refugees has changed the face of America.
   d. Intercultural communication is vital because we are increasingly exposed to people from other cultures.

2. How does the dominant culture differ from a non-dominant culture?

   a. The non-dominant culture is always smaller in number.
   b. The non-dominant culture has the power and authority
   c. The dominant culture makes the rules.
   d. The dominant culture is always larger in number.

3. When marginalized groups try to fit in with the dominant group, they are attempting to achieve

   a. accommodation.
   b. separation.
   c. distinction.
   d. assimilation.

4. When people bring prejudices of their culture to intercultural interactions, they are being

   a. ethnocentric.
   b. stereotypic.
   c. accommodating.
   d. collectivist.

5. When people stereotype, they

   a. judge another person's culture by its own context.
   b. make a generalization about a group of people that oversimplifies their culture.
   c. believe their own culture is superior to other cultures.
   d. avoid making degrading comments with relation to sexual objectification.

6. Cultures that are more concerned with individuality, competition, and private property are which type of culture?

   a. collectivist
   b. relativistic
   c. individualistic
   d. assimilated

7. An example of a non-dominant culture that does not try to fit into the dominant culture in the United States is

   a. the Amish.
   b. women.
   c. Protestants.
   d. the U.S. Army.

8. When you have a negative attitude about other people just because they are who they are, you are demonstrating

   a. prejudice.
   b. ignorance.
   c. ethnocentrism.
   d. stereotyping.

9. Those who schedule their days, are early for appointments, and plan for the future are probably members of a(n)
   a. On-time culture.
   b. Sometime culture.
   c. uncertainty-accepting culture.
   d. collectivist culture.

10. If you are trying to improve your intercultural communication, you should do which of the following?
   a. Be ethnocentric.
   b. Avoid shared codes.
   c. Close communication channels.
   d. Conduct a personal self-assessment.

Answers:

1. (b); 2. (c); 3. (d); 4. (a); 5. (b); 6. (c); 7. (a); 8. (a); 9. (a); 10. (d)

Critical Thinking

1. Many people belong to one or more non-dominant cultures that exist within the dominant culture. For example, you are a woman, you are Jewish, you are gay, or you are African American, or perhaps all of these at the same time. How in your experience does the non-dominant culture with which you are most familiar relate to the dominant culture, especially in the way they communicate with each other—or not?

2. What are the dominant and non-dominant cultures where you live? By what means does the dominant culture in your area reinforce its rules for living? How does it communicate its rules to all others?

small-group communication

When you have read and thought about this chapter, you will be able to:

1. Define and explain the essential characteristics of small groups.

2. Explain how culture develops in small groups.

3. Describe how effective leadership is accomplished in small groups.

4. Enact a process for group problem solving and decision making.

5. Discuss two examples of how technology can be used to facilitate small-group communication.

6. Utilize skills necessary for effective and ethical group communication.

7. Recognize strategies for ethically managing group conflict.

Small groups permeate nearly all facets of our lives. Our families, our jobs, our courses, and our friends are all invigorated and driven by small groups of people. In this chapter we address several issues related to small-group communication. After discussing generally what small-group communication is, we turn to theories explaining concepts such as leadership, group culture, and small-group decision making. The chapter concludes by discussing several processes related to small-group effectiveness: cohesiveness, the use of technology, and skills used by ethical group communicators.

Candice is a student who works part-time in a hive. She is not a busy bee, although her friends might think that at times. Rather, Candice is like millions of workers who work in a new way of organizing, called a hive. Hives are large projects where multiple people work on individual elements and then move on to the next element until the project is completed. Hives are entirely online, so hive projects are typically digital, or online, projects. If you have ever used open source software, played a video game, or even read Wikipedia you have benefited from the result of a hive project.

Hives are created to harness the power of groups. The idea behind a hive is that multiple people, working interdependently, can accomplish more than the same number of people working independently. By staying in constant communication, checking on what needs to be done next and providing feedback to others on their work, hives can accomplish mind-boggling results in a short amount of time. Hives are an increasingly popular way of organizing groups to accomplish tasks, particularly as more and more groups are separated by location. As you conduct work for school and your job, the likelihood that you will complete projects with someone hundreds or thousands of miles away is high; you will be working in a hive.

Not everyone thinks hives are a good thing. A pioneer of virtual reality, Jaron Lanier, noted in an interview with *Popular Science* that hive working is just a modern form of groupthink.[1] He worries that the use of hives to drive projects will reduce creativity and harm artful expression. Lanier believes it is still important for individuals to challenge norms and popular ways of doing things.

Technology is changing the way we communicate and act in small groups. Although many of us still work in face-to-face groups, technology makes it likely, if not certain, that we will work in groups that are conducted entirely through the Web. Despite the advances of such technology, many of the skills required for face-to-face groups are still necessary. A hive can fall into groupthink just as easily as a face-to-face group. Understanding effective group communication skills can help you regardless of whether your group is face-to-face or a virtual hive.

What do you think about the pros and cons of working in hives—and of using technology as a basis for group communication? Do you consider yourself an effective communicator when it comes to working in groups—even if the situation is something informal, such as a group of friends trying to decide on a weekend plan? At the end of the chapter, we'll take another look at Candice's situation and how she might promote effective group communication and avoid groupthink.

Groups are all around us; they are inescapable and they can accomplish extraordinary things. We might even go so far as to say that groups are partly what make humans so . . . human. This chapter looks at the nature of groups—how communication works within groups, how leaders use their skills, and how group members can effectively and ethically contribute to solving problems.

Why Should You Learn About Small Groups?

Small groups are the basic building blocks of our society. Families, work teams, support groups, religious circles, and study groups are all examples of the groups on which our society is built. In organizations, the higher up you go, the more time you will spend working in groups. Membership in small groups is both common and important. In fact, most types of jobs increasingly rely on team-based work, and an increasing number require working in teams that meet over the Web rather than face to face.[2] Of course, not all teamwork happens smoothly. For example, recent reports refer to the "black holes of the workday"[3] in response to polls showing that 75% of workers say that time spent in meetings could be more productive. That's why learning about group communication skills is important—you will have to work in groups, so why not do it well?

Small groups are important for five reasons. First, working in groups is an aspect of nearly every human activity. William Schutz, a psychologist who studied group interaction, said that humans have needs for inclusion, affection, and control.[4] The need for **inclusion**—the state of being involved with others—suggests that we need to belong to, or be included in, groups with others. As humans, we derive much of our identity, our beliefs about who we are, from the groups to which we belong. Starting with our immediate families and including such important groups as our church, mosque, or synagogue; interest groups; work teams; and social groups—all these help us define who we are. The need for **affection**—the emotion of caring for others and/or being cared for—means that we humans need to love and be loved, to know that we are important to others who value us as unique human beings. Finally, we have a need for **control**—the ability to influence our environment. We are better able to exercise such control if we work together

social media make it matter

Classifying Your Facebook Groups

Facebook is not just a way to stay connected with friends; the service is also a powerful way to join together in groups. Review your own Facebook memberships. How many pages representing groups have you joined or liked? For many of us, that number could be fairly high. After counting your groups, classify them according to Schultz's category of human needs. Do you tend to follow Facebook groups that meet your need for inclusion, affection, or control? Do you have each of these needs represented among your Facebook groups? Do you tend to interact differently in a group meeting one need than you do in a group meeting another?

inclusion
The state of being involved with others; a human need.

affection
The emotion of caring for others and/or being cared for.

control
The ability to influence our environment.

■ Teamwork skills are highly sought after in the workplace.

in groups. One person cannot build a school, bridge, or new business. We need others to meet our needs.

Second, groups are everywhere. You will not be able to escape working in them. Think about all the groups to which you currently belong, including informal groups such as study groups or your "lunch bunch." Average students might belong to as many as 10 groups; if you work, that number will expand. If you are active in a church or other community groups, the number will grow even higher. Your presence in groups will not end upon graduation. Nearly every job will require some degree of group communication to accomplish tasks.

Because group work is expected to increase in the future, particularly in business and industry, knowing how groups function and having the ability to operate effectively in them will be highly valued skills. A survey of college graduates showed that oral communication, problem-solving skills, and the ability to motivate and manage others were three of the top four skills taught in college classes that were essential for workplace success—the fourth was written communication.[5] A *Wall Street Journal* poll conducted in December 2007 found that teamwork, leadership, and critical thinking/problem solving, all skills we practice in small groups, were in the top five skills that were more important now than they were five years ago in the workplace.[6]

Third, being an effective group or team member cannot be left to chance. As helpful as groups can be to any organization, they often fail because group leaders have not thought through exactly what they want the groups to accomplish or because group members have not been trained in how to behave appropriately as part of a team.[7] Effective group participation cannot be taken for granted. Group members need training to understand the dynamics of small-group interaction.

Finally, groups can be an important way for Americans to participate in the democratic process. By talking in groups, we can become more confident in articulating our own beliefs, which, in turn, may lead us to be more vocal about our beliefs in a variety of contexts.[8] During the 2008 presidential election, small groups played a key role in increasing voter turnout. At Illinois State University, a small group of communication instructors created assignments in their public-speaking classes designed to get students more involved in politics. Those efforts led to a campus "issues fair," at which small groups of students presented information

cultural note

Groups Help Us Maintain Culture

If you travel 10 minutes northeast of Hermann Park in central Houston, you will find yourself in the middle of the greater Third Ward. Houston's Third Ward is distinctive for many reasons: that area is the home of Texas Southern University, it is one of the original political subdivisions of Houston, and it is just adjacent to downtown Houston and the world-renowned Texas Medical Center campus. The Third Ward has also been the home for much of Houston's African American community. As an article in the *Houston Business Journal* points out, the Third Ward has been threatened with losing its historic identity because of gentrification, or the influx of higher-income development within lower-income areas. Lower-income residents who can no longer afford rent or who pay property taxes mainly feel the effects of gentrification—those residents often become displaced and the historical roots of the area are literally ripped apart.

Small groups of residents in Houston's Third Ward are doing their part to combat the negative effects of gentrification. A group of artists created Project Row Houses (www.projectrowhouses.org) in 1993 as a way to use art to build community. Today, Project Row Houses embraces the philosophy that communities created through art can revitalize inner-city neighborhoods like the Third Ward. Recently, artists Ashley Hunt and Bree Edwards spearheaded a Row House project called "communograph," which uses art to create representations of community life. Through the communograph initiative artists can help community members and other interested individuals understand the culture of the Third Ward through art. Both the Row House project as a whole and the commungraph initiative in particular started with small groups of people working together to effect positive change in their community.

Sources: Bradford, N. (2007, July 22). Houston's Third Ward battles an identity crisis. *Houston Business Journal* (www.bizjournals.com/houston/stories/2007/07/23/focus1).html?page=all. Community, creative arts come together with 'communograph.' (2011, September 19). *The Cypress Times* (www.thecypresstimes.com/article/News/Local_News/COMMUNITY_CREATIVE_ARTS_COME_TOGETHER_WITH_COMMUNOGRAPH/50755).

■ Group art projects can help create community identity.

about local, state, and national issues by setting up tables and booths on their campus quad. These students helped raise awareness of how political issues were relevant to other college students. The same teachers organized small groups of students to receive training from the county board of elections to register new voters. Those efforts not only significantly increased student-voter turnout but also persuaded the county board of elections to expand early voting locations to the campus. Once again, small groups allow us to accomplish extraordinary things.

What Is Small-Group Communication?

Small-group communication is the interaction among three to nine people who are working together to achieve an interdependent goal.[9] This definition implies several things:

■ Groups must be small enough that members are mutually aware that the group is a collective entity. Groups typically contain between three and nine people but may be larger if members perceive the group as an entity. Research does show that groups of three or four people are more productive than are larger groups of five or more people.[10] So, if given a choice, working with a smaller group may produce better results.

■ The substance that creates and holds the group together is the interaction between members.

■ Group members are interdependent—they cannot achieve their goals without the help of other group members. If you watch reality TV shows, such as *Survivor*, you have seen examples of how groups of people must work as interdependent units to achieve success. Business consulting firms are now teaching the importance of interdependence by doing the same thing with corporate work teams. Corporations are charged $75,000 to have team members locked up in a house to develop interdependent teamwork skills.[11]

Based on this definition, *communication* is the essential process within a small group. Communication creates a group, shapes each group in unique ways, and allows the group to function. As with other forms of human communication, small-group communication involves sending verbal and nonverbal signals that are perceived, interpreted, and responded to by other people.

small-group communication
Interaction among three to nine people working together to achieve an interdependent goal.

Group members pay attention to each other and coordinate their behavior in order to accomplish the group's assignment. In fact, group communication is like any other form of communication; however, the greater number of people makes communication even more challenging.

The Types and Functions of Small Groups

Think for a moment about the different groups to which you belong. You may regularly study with other students from your accounting class, you may belong to a club on campus, you may be assigned to participate in a student government group, and you likely have a group of friends with whom you socialize. What are the key differences between these groups? In answering that question, you might think about differences that point to the type of group or the function that the group serves in your life. For instance, there are two types of groups:

- **Assigned groups** occur when individuals are appointed to be members of the group. A student union advisory board is an example of an assigned group.
- **Emergent groups** occur when a group of individuals decide to form a cohesive group out of personal need or desire, but they are not appointed to be part of the group. A group of friends who meet at college are an emergent group.

We can also classify groups according to the function they serve:

- **Task-oriented groups** are formed for the purpose of completing tasks, such as solving a problem or making a decision. A group of students studying for an exam are taking part in a task-oriented group.
- **Relationship-oriented groups** are usually long-term and exist to meet our needs for inclusion and affection. Your family is an example of a relationship-oriented group.

Classifying groups according to whether they are task-oriented, relationship-oriented, assigned, or emergent risks oversimplifying how groups actually work in your life. Because

assigned groups
Groups that evolve out of a hierarchy whereby individuals are assigned membership to the group.

emergent groups
Groups resulting from environmental conditions leading to the formation of a cohesive group of individuals.

task-oriented groups
Also called secondary groups; groups formed for the purpose of completing tasks, such as solving problems or making decisions.

relationship-oriented groups
Also called primary groups; groups that are usually long-term and exist to meet our needs for inclusion and affection.

■ A family is an example of a relationship-oriented group.

people form groups, and because groups can grow and change through communication, lines between these types and functions can easily blur. Members of relationship-oriented groups, such as families, engage in work, make decisions, and must cooperate to complete tasks. Members of task-oriented groups forge strong personal bonds and provide each other with affection and recognition. In fact, some of the best task-oriented groups are those that benefit from strong relational bonds, so members feel appreciated and valued. If positive relationships are established among group members, an assigned group can start to look and feel like an emergent group. As we interact with members of that group, a relationship-oriented social group may emerge. Just as our personal relationships can go through several turning points, our group membership is also constantly in flux.

Establishing Culture in Small Groups

When small groups are created, they immediately begin developing a unique group culture. Some group cultures are pleasant, whereas others are aggressive, hostile, and demeaning. In this section you will learn how group culture develops as a result of group norms, role structures enacted by group members, group cohesiveness, and diversity.

THE DEVELOPMENT OF GROUP NORMS

The first time group members communicate, they begin to establish the **norms**—informal rules for interaction created and sustained through communication—that will eventually guide the members' behaviors. Norms for group behavior tell us implicitly, and sometimes explicitly, how we are to act and behave with others in the group. At first, the full range of human behavior is available to members. For example, they may greet each other formally ("Ms.," "Dr.," "Professor," and so on), or they may speak informally and use first names. The initial pattern of behavior tends to set the tone for subsequent meetings and to establish the general norms that members will follow. The norms of any group tend to mirror the norms of broader cultures in which the group exists. Such norms are also created and altered through communication between group members. As the group interacts, and as leaders extort authority,

norms
Informal rules for group interaction created and sustained through communication.

■ Both positive and negative norms can develop in groups. Ongoing conflict is an example of a negative norm.

the norms of the group can be modified to help the group function more effectively. Of course, sometimes bad norms also develop, which can negatively affect the group's outcomes.

Most norms are not established directly. For example, if Ali comes late to a meeting and no one seems bothered, other members may get the message that coming to meetings on time is unnecessary. By saying nothing to Ali, the group, without consciously thinking about or formally "deciding," has begun to establish a norm that members need not be on time.

Norms often develop rapidly, without members consciously realizing what is occurring. For example, repeated behaviors, such as members always sitting in the same seats, show how easily norms can emerge through communication. Groups naturally use feedback to enforce norms. If a group member continually arrives late to meetings, a group member or leader might say, "It's about time you got here," to indicate that a norm has been violated.

Members should pay attention to group norms to ensure that they are appropriate to the group task. As teachers we often observe students working in groups. As we walk around the classroom, groups seem to notice we are standing near them and quickly stop talking about the band playing at a local club and turn to the topic we asked them to discuss. As we walk away, discussion soon returns to music and fun. Such norms for playfulness, although important for relationship development, may begin to distract the group from assigned tasks. We certainly do not advocate having no "fun time" in groups. Talking about things such as music and sports is fun. Nevertheless, a norm that emphasizes all "fun time" and no "work time" can prevent the group from reaching its goal.

THE DEVELOPMENT OF ROLES FOR GROUP MEMBERS

role
A consistent pattern of interaction or behavior exhibited over time.

Every group member enacts a unique **role,** which is a consistent pattern of interaction or behavior exhibited over time. In movies, characters enact roles to drive the story; in small groups, members enact roles to drive the interaction of the group. Whereas actors learn their roles from scripts, group members create their roles spontaneously during interactions with others and while drawing on their unique skills and attitudes. Just as an actor plays different roles in different scripts, individuals enact many diverse roles in the numerous groups to which they belong.

The Types of Group Roles

formal role
Also called a positional role; an assigned role based on an individual's position or title within a group.

Two major types of group roles are formal and informal. A **formal role** (sometimes called a *positional role*) is an assigned role based on an individual's position or title within a group. You may have a job where you are assigned to bring certain types of information to group meetings. Your job duty could even state that your role is to keep track of finances, or to record agenda items for future meetings. As a result of your formal role, other group members might expect you to behave in certain ways: they might expect you to be organized and have the ability to locate information quickly and without warning. Formal roles bring expectations and your job is to understand and meet those expectations.

informal role
Also called a behavioral role; a role that is developed spontaneously within a group.

An **informal role** (sometimes called a *behavioral role*) is a role that develops naturally, or spontaneously, within a group. The role of each group member is worked out through interactions with the rest of the group and changes to meet emerging needs of the group. Informal roles strongly reflect members' personality characteristics, habits, and typical ways of interacting within a group. If you are the type of person who likes to talk in front of others, you might take on the role of a facilitator. On the other hand, if you are less talkative you might be a person who takes on behind-the-scene roles, such as conducting research or creating documents for the group. Informal roles allow you to play to your strengths; of course, to develop informal roles you may need to talk to other group members about your preferences and abilities.

Behaviors That Define Roles

Roles enacted by group members create a set of behaviors that help the group achieve its objectives. An effective group is like a jigsaw puzzle; each group member performs a slightly different role, but each set of behaviors is coordinated to work with the others, so that a complete picture is formed.

One way of understanding the various types of behaviors performed by group members is to classify them as task, maintenance, or self-centered behaviors. **Task functions** are behaviors that are directly relevant to the group's purpose and that affect the group's productivity; their purpose is to focus group members productively on their assignment. **Maintenance functions** are behaviors that focus on the interpersonal relationships among group members; they are aimed at supporting cooperative and harmonious relationships. Both task and maintenance functions are considered essential to effective group communication. On the other hand, **self-centered functions** are behaviors that serve the needs of the individual at the expense of the group. The person performing a self-centered behavior implies, "I don't care what the group needs or wants. *I* want . . ." He or she uses self-centered functions to manipulate other members for selfish goals that compete with group goals. Examples of statements that support task, maintenance, and self-centered functions are shown in table 8.1. The list is not exhaustive, however; many more functions could be added.

task functions
Behaviors that are directly relevant to the group's task and that affect the group's productivity.

maintenance functions
Behaviors that focus on the interpersonal relationships among group members.

self-centered functions
Behaviors that serve the needs of the individual at the expense of the group.

Table 8.1 Examples of Task, Maintenance, and Self-Centered Statements

Task Functions and Statements

Initiating and orienting	"Let's make a list of what we still need to do."
Information giving	"Last year, the committee spent $150 on publicity."
Information seeking	"John, how many campus muggings were reported last year?"
Opinion giving	"I don't think the cost of parking stickers is the worst parking problem students have."
Clarifying	"Martina, are you saying that you couldn't support a proposal that increased student fees?"
Extending	"Another thing that Toby's proposal would let us do is . . ."
Evaluating	"One problem I see with Cindy's idea is . . ."
Summarizing	"So we've decided that we'll add two sections to the report, and Terrell and Candy will write them."
Coordinating	"If Carol interviews the mayor by Monday, then Jim and I can prepare a response by Tuesday's meeting."
Consensus testing	"We seem to be agreed that we prefer the second option."
Recording	"I think we decided at our last meeting. Let me check the minutes."

Maintenance (Relationship-Oriented) Functions and Statements

Establishing norms	"It doesn't help to call each other names. Let's stick to the issues."
Gatekeeping	"Pat, you look like you want to say something about the proposal."
Supporting	"I think Tara's point is well made, and we should look at it more closely."
Harmonizing	"Jared and Sally, I think there are areas where you are in agreement, and I would like to suggest a compromise that might work for you both."
Tension relieving	"We're getting tired and cranky. Let's take a 10-minute break."
Dramatizing	"That reminds me of a story about what happened last year when . . ."
Showing solidarity	"We've really done good work here!" or "We're all in this together."

Self-Centered Functions and Statements

Withdrawing	"Do whatever you want; I don't care" or not speaking at all.
Blocking	"I don't care if we've already voted; I want to discuss it again!"
Status and recognition seeking	"I have a lot more expertise than the rest of you, and I think we should do it the way I know works."

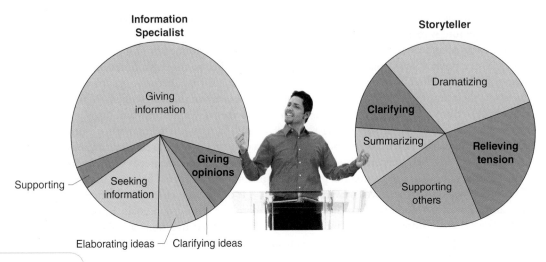

Figure 8.1

Behavioral functions combine to create roles.

Source: Galanes, G. J., & Brilhart, J. K. (1993). Communicating in groups: Applications and skills. Madison, WI: Brown & Benchmark. Copyright © 1993. Times Mirror Higher Education Group, Inc. All rights reserved. Reprinted by permission.

Behaviors are the building blocks for roles. These behavioral functions combine to create a member's informal role, which is a comprehensive, general picture of how a particular member typically acts in a group. An example of how individual functions combine to create a role is shown in figure 8.1. As you can see, information-giving and opinion-giving behaviors primarily characterize the information specialist role. The storyteller role comprises several behaviors, including dramatizing, relieving tension, supporting, summarizing, and clarifying. Numerous other informal roles can be created through combinations of behaviors.

GROUP COHESIVENESS

group climate
The emotional tone or atmosphere members create within the group.

Another important element that helps shape a group's culture is the **group climate,** which is the emotional tone or atmosphere members create within the group. For example, you have probably attended a group meeting where the tension silenced everyone. That atmosphere of tension describes the group's climate. Three factors that contribute heavily to group climate are trust, cohesiveness, and supportiveness.

■ *Trust* means that members believe they can rely on each other. Two types of trust relevant to group work are task trust and interpersonal trust. Task trust develops when you have confidence that others will get their jobs done in support of the group's goals. Interpersonal trust emerges when you perceive that others are working in support of the group rather than trying to achieve personal gain or to accomplish hidden agendas.

■ *Supportiveness* refers to an atmosphere of openness where members care about each other and create cohesiveness. Examples of both supportive and defensive statements are found in table 8.2.

■ *Cohesiveness* is the attachment members feel toward each other and the group. Highly cohesive groups are more open, handle disagreement more effectively, and typically perform better than less cohesive groups.[12]

groupthink
An unintended outcome of cohesion in which the desire for cohesion and agreement takes precedence over critical analysis and discussion.

Although cohesiveness is generally desirable for groups, dangers arise from too much cohesion. **Groupthink** happens when the desire for cohesion and agreement takes precedence over critical analysis and discussion. According to sociologist Irving Janis, groupthink can destroy effective decision making. Several historical decision-making blunders have been attributed to groupthink, including the escalation of the Vietnam conflict, the

Table 8.2 Examples of Defensive and Supportive Statements

Behavior	Description	Sample Statement
Defensive Behaviors and Statements		
Evaluation	Judging another person	"That's a completely ridiculous idea."
Control	Dominating or insisting on your own way	"I've decided what we need to do."
Manipulating	Trying to verbally push compliance	"Don't you think you should try it my way?"
Neutrality	Not caring about how others feel	"It doesn't matter to me what you decide."
Superiority	Pulling rank, maximizing status differences	"As group leader, I think we should . . ."
Certainty	Being a "know-it-all"	"You guys are completely off base. I know exactly how to handle this."
Supportive Behaviors and Statements		
Description	Describing your own feelings without making those of others wrong	"I prefer the first option because . . ."
Problem orientation	Searching for the best solution without predetermining what that should be	"We want to produce the best results, and that may mean some extra time from all of us."
Spontaneity	Reacting honestly and openly	"Wow, that sounds like a great idea!"
Empathy	Showing you care about the other members	"Jan, originally you were skeptical. How comfortable will you be if the group favors that option?"
Equality	Minimizing status differences by treating members as equals	"I don't have all the answers. What do the rest of you think?"
Provisionalism	Expressing opinions tentatively and being open to others' suggestions	"Maybe we should try a different approach . . ."

space shuttle *Challenger* disaster, and potentially the *Columbia* shuttle disaster over Texas.[13] Although groupthink may be difficult to detect when you are in a group, researchers have identified the following observable signs of groupthink:

- An illusion of invulnerability by the group
- An unquestioned belief in the morality of the group
- Collective efforts by group members to rationalize faulty decisions
- Stereotypic views of enemy leaders as evil, weak, or ineffective
- Self-censorship of alternative viewpoints
- A shared illusion that all group members think the same thing
- Direct pressure on group members expressing divergent opinions
- The emergence of "mind guards" to screen the group from information contradictory to the prevailing opinion

Although Janis's original description of groupthink suggests that these characteristics lead to groupthink, and consequently result in bad decisions, recent studies suggest that Janis's groupthink characteristics actually occur after the group has already made a poor decision.[14] Once groups make decisions, group members try to create and reinforce a

■ Group members must make counter-viewpoints known to help the group avoid groupthink.

consensus in support of the decision, even in the face of evidence that the decision is a poor one. The desire for consensus then leads to all of the groupthink characteristics identified by Janis.

Groupthink is possible in nearly every group. To prevent groupthink from occurring, groups should seek all pertinent information, carefully assess the credibility of information relevant to the decision at hand, assign members to present counterarguments, and maintain a commitment to finding the best possible outcome as supported by the available evidence.

THE EFFECT OF DIVERSITY ON GROUP CULTURE

group culture
The socially negotiated system of rules that guide group behavior.

In chapter 7 you learned about the general concept of culture. Although we typically think of culture as belonging to very large groups of people, small groups also develop cultures. **Group culture** is the socially negotiated system of rules that guide group behavior. Group culture differs from national and ethnic cultures in that group cultures are relatively unstable and short-term phenomena. Group cultures are constantly in flux and they disappear when the group dissolves. National and ethnic cultures change slowly and are relatively persistent. If you compare two groups from your own life, you can easily understand the concept of group culture. Your group of friends has implicit rules for behavior—inside jokes, slang, norms for touching, and shared objectives. Your group likely has a culture different from that of an assigned group of students you work with in one of your classes. Classroom groups are typically more formal, less cohesive, and more task-oriented. The two groups reflect different cultures that have emerged.

The culture of a group can be influenced by many things. The norms and behaviors of group members can influence culture; so, too, can the diversity among group members. **Within-group diversity** is the presence of observable and/or implicit differences between group members. We observe within-group diversity when group members differ based on visible characteristics. For example, to visually distinguish between males and females or between members of certain ethnic groups is easy. Group diversity can be implicit

within-group diversity
The presence of observable and/or implicit differences among group members.

Table 8.3 Observable and Implicit Within-Group Diversity

	Observable	Implicit
Definition	Within-group diversity based on physical characteristics that can be seen	Within-group diversity based on individuals' worldviews, perspectives, and other personality characteristics
Example	Ethnicity, sex	Religious orientation, educational background

when members of a group have differing values, attitudes, and perspectives—personal characteristics that cannot be seen. Table 8.3 shows common examples of observable and implicit within-group diversity.

Differences between group members can have an impact on how they interact with one another and how effectively the group functions. To illustrate the effects of group diversity on group members' behaviors, here are several research findings on differences between how men and women interact in groups:

- In online discussion groups and other forms of computer-mediated communication, women tend to use more exclamation points as markers of friendliness—thus emphasizing the relational aspects of group communication.[15]
- Female speakers tend to prefer standard (more formal) speech forms, whereas male speakers tend to prefer vernacular (less formal) speech forms.[16]
- Although men are typically more influential in standard communication contexts, this difference diminishes in groups, especially when more than one woman is present. In such situations the influence of women is roughly equal to that of men.[17]
- Recent research has observed no differences in perceived leadership ability regardless of whether the group is primarily task- or relationship-oriented; previous research had shown that women were better leaders in relationship-oriented groups.[18]

In addition to gender differences, cultural differences can also influence group dynamics. For instance, it is likely that work groups and even classroom groups will have at least one member for whom English is a second language (ESL). You might assume that group members who speak English with different levels of proficiency can diminish the cohesiveness of the group. That assumption would be incorrect, however. Research shows that having various primary languages represented in a group does not impede group cohesiveness as long as members continue to have frequent interactions.[19]

In such situations, all group members should make sure that ESL members are fully included. Strategies for helping non-native speakers feel included are (1) providing written information in advance of discussions, (2) asking someone in the group to take notes that can be copied and distributed to all group members, (3) viewing difference as a strength of the group, and (4) matching tasks to members' abilities. Particularly with the last suggestion, finding out the strengths of all group members is important. Second-language speakers often do not speak as often, but this does not mean that they do not have highly developed skills in other areas, such as computers, artwork, record keeping, and so on.

If you are a second-language speaker who is part of a group with mostly native speakers, you must practice being assertive. You should ask questions to clarify the activities of the group or points made during discussion. You should also let group members know about skills you have that could be useful to the group. Finally, try to recognize that in most situations group discussions are as much about relationship building as task accomplishment. Taking time to get to know other members of your group will not only help all of you build confidence in each other but can lead to meaningful friendships outside of class or the workplace.

The Role of Leadership in Small Groups

For most groups to work effectively, some structure is necessary. Noted group communication scholar Gloria Galanes observed that group leaders must attend to four issues: (1) identifying the task of the group; (2) creating cohesiveness among the group members; (3) monitoring and adapting the behaviors of the group members as needed to accomplish tasks; and (4) keeping the group focused on the task at hand.[20]

WHAT IS LEADERSHIP?

leadership
A process of using communication to influence the behaviors and attitudes of others to meet group goals.

designated leader
Someone who has been appointed or elected to a leadership position.

emergent leader
Someone who becomes an informal leader by exerting influence toward the achievement of a group's goal but does not hold the formal position or role of leader.

power
Interpersonal influence that forms the basis for group leadership.

Hackman and Johnson define **leadership** as a process of using communication to influence the behaviors and attitudes of others to meet group goals.[21] A leader is a person who influences the behavior and attitudes of others through communication. In small groups, two types of leader are designated and emergent. A **designated leader** is someone who has been appointed or elected to a leadership position (such as a chair, team leader, coordinator, or facilitator). An **emergent leader** is someone who becomes an informal leader by exerting influence toward the achievement of a group's goal but does not hold the formal position or role of leader. Groups benefit from having a designated leader because designated leaders add stability and organization to the group's activities. An emergent leader can be any group member who helps the group meet its goals. Groups work best when all members contribute skills and leadership behaviors on behalf of the group.

How do leaders, designated or emergent, gain their ability to influence others? Wilmot and Hocker suggest that group leaders may gain interpersonal influence over groups through the use of **power,** which is the interpersonal influence that forms the basis for small-group leadership.[22] According to Wilmot and Hocker's perspective, group leaders likely use one of three types of power:

- *Distributive power*, whereby the leader exerts influence over others
- *Integrative power*, which highlights interdependence with another person or persons to achieve mutually agreed-upon goals
- *Designated power*, which reflects the importance of relationships between people; marriages, families, and groups often hold such power for us

Whereas Wilmot and Hocker describe how power influences us, a classic study by French and Raven describes different ways in which group members enact power:

- *Reward power*—the ability to give followers what they want and need
- *Punishment power*—the ability to withhold from followers what they want and need; an extreme form of punishment power is *coercion*, in which compliance is forced through hostile acts
- *Referent power*—power based on others' admiration and respect; charisma is an extreme form of referent power that inspires strong loyalty and devotion from others
- *Expert power*—when the other members value a person's knowledge or expertise
- *Legitimate power*—power given to a person because of a title, position, or role[23]

Table 8.4 Tensions Present for Group Leaders

Tension	Description
Leader-centered vs. group-centered	Does the leader maintain complete control over the group, or are aspects of group control given to members of the group?
Listening vs. talking	Does the group leader spend more time talking, to set an agenda for group action, or listening, to build trust and cohesiveness?
Task vs. nontask emphasis	Does the group focus primarily on task-related behaviors or primarily on nontask behaviors? One focus could get the job done quicker, the other could build cohesiveness.
Process vs. outcome focus	Does the group focus only on outcomes, or does it also focus on getting tasks done "the right way"?

Source: Based on Galanes, G. (2009). Dialectical tensions of small group leadership. *Communication Studies, 60,* 409–425.

Understanding how to use power to influence small groups is not easy. Galanes describes the process of leadership as a balancing act, where leaders must learn to manage various tensions, identified in table 8.4.[24] Group leaders must understand how to use power in ways that balance several of these tensions in an effort to push the group to achieve its goals while building and maintaining a positive culture.

WAYS OF ENACTING LEADERSHIP

Since Aristotle's time, people have been interested in what makes a good leader. Is leadership a skill you are born with? Can you learn to be a leader? In this section you will learn about three ways of thinking about effective leadership: leadership as style, leadership as communication competence, and leadership as planning. Although they are presented as separate perspectives, effective leaders learn to embrace key elements from each simultaneously.

Leadership Styles

Style approaches to studying leadership focus on the patterns of behavior that leaders exhibit in groups. Considerable research has examined three major styles of designated leader: democratic, laissez-faire, and autocratic. **Democratic leaders** encourage members to participate in group decisions, even major ones: "What suggestions do you have for solving our problem?" **Laissez-faire leaders** take almost no initiative in structuring a group discussion; they are nonleaders whose typical response is "I don't care; whatever you want to do is fine with me." **Autocratic leaders** maintain strict control over their group, including making assignments and giving orders: "Here's how we'll solve the problem. First, you will . . ." Autocratic leaders ask fewer questions but answer more than democratic leaders; they make more attempts to coerce and fewer attempts to get others to participate.[25]

Groups vary in the amount of structure and control their members want and need, but research findings about style have been consistent.[26] Most people in the United States prefer democratic groups and are more satisfied in democratically rather than autocratically led groups.

The style approaches imply a single leadership style good for all situations. However, most scholars believe that the style should match the needs of the situation. For example, if you are in a group working on a class project and the deadline is tomorrow, a democratic leadership style might be ineffective, because it takes longer to make decisions.

democratic leaders
Leaders who encourage members to participate in group decisions.

laissez-faire leaders
Leaders who take almost no initiative in structuring a group discussion.

autocratic leaders
Leaders who maintain strict control over their group.

■ Democratic groups allow group members to take part in decision making.

The Communication Competencies of Leaders

Communication scholars who adopt the communicative competencies approach have tried to focus on the communicative behaviors of leaders as they exercise interpersonal influence to accomplish group goals. They ask such questions as "What do effective leaders do?" The Communication Competency Model of Group Leadership, developed by Barge and Hirokawa,[27] is one of the most comprehensive models to address this question. This model assumes that leaders help a group achieve its goals through communication skills (competencies). Two competencies include the task and interpersonal, or relationship, distinctions discussed earlier. Leaders must be flexible to draw from a personal repertoire of such competencies. Some of the most important leader competencies are described briefly here:

- Effective leaders are able to clearly and appropriately communicate ideas to the group without dominating the conversation.
- Effective leaders communicate a clear grasp of the task facing the group.
- Effective leaders are skilled at facilitating discussion.
- Effective leaders encourage open dialogue and do not force their own ideas on the group.
- Effective leaders place group needs over personal concerns.
- Effective leaders display respect for others during interaction.
- Effective leaders share in the successes and failures of the group.

The Planning Skills of Leaders

In addition to exhibiting an appropriate style and being a competent communicator, effective leaders must learn to plan. Although planning cannot prevent all problems from occurring, some up-front work can increase the likelihood of successful outcomes. Here are some tips for planning effective meetings:

1. *Know the task at hand.* Later in the chapter you will learn about the group problem-solving model. Effective leaders should understand the problem facing the group and take care to communicate that task to group members.

2. *Know the people.* As you will learn, individual group members have different skills, motivations, frames of reference, and knowledge bases. Understanding how to draw on group members' strengths and manage interpersonal dynamics is a key role of the group leader.

3. *Collect information.* The group leader should attempt to become knowledgeable on all issues facing the group. If you are knowledgeable, you will know when discussions are off track.

4. *Distribute leadership.* In certain situations leadership should be distributed among all group members. The designated leader may need to delegate responsibility, especially

GROUP AGENDA

DATE

I. *Approval of minutes from previous meeting(s).* The group facilitator should determine if there are any changes to the minutes and have group members vote to approve the minutes.

II. *Announcements.* Members of the group should make announcements relevant to the group but not necessarily tied to group business. For example, a group member might read a thank-you note from a person the group helped or might provide personal announcements that may be of interest to group members. Such announcements should be brief.

III. *Reports.* Individuals assigned to collect information or carry out tasks should report on their progress. If a report results in an action item—that is, something the group should discuss and vote on—the report should be included under new business. Reports in this segment of the meeting should be informative, but they do not necessarily require action at this time.

IV. *New business.* Items in this part of the agenda can include important discussions and/or action items. Discussions may or may not result in a vote, but action items should be voted on by the group.

V. *Old business.* Occasionally, action items and discussion from previous meetings may not be complete. In such cases those items should be listed under old business and approached in the same way as new business, with appropriate discussion and voting as necessary.

Figure 8.2

Standard group agenda template.

when smaller tasks need to be assigned to individual group members. Distributed leadership, whereby all members share in leadership responsibilities, can result in highly productive group outcomes.[28]

5. *Organize the discussion.* Although some types of group discussions may not need much organization—a short class discussion assigned by your teacher, for instance—most discussions need more structure. The group leader should plan an agenda for the discussion. The agenda should be adapted to the task at hand; however, a general template for the agenda is provided in figure 8.2. As you can see, the typical agenda requires group members to agree on minutes from the past meeting to clear up any confusion or disagreement, make announcements, hear reports, consider new business, and reconsider old business as necessary.

Problem Solving and Decision Making

A primary task facing many groups is solving problems: student clubs need to raise money, church groups need to plan activities, and social groups must find fun things to do. Group members must be both creative and critical to arrive at the best solutions to these problems. Groups are usually (but not always) better problem solvers than individuals, because several people can provide more information than one person. Groups can bring greater resources to bear on a problem, can collectively have a broader perspective, and can more easily spot flaws in each other's reasoning. However, trade-offs occur. Group problem solving takes longer, and sometimes personality, procedural, or social problems make working as a team difficult for members. Group problem solving is usually more effective when the process is systematic and organized, because a group that does not have an

FACT

How has the divorce rate changed in the past 15 years?

How many Hispanic students graduate from high school each year?

What percentage of college students graduate in four years?

How often, on average, does a person speak each day?

What occupations earn the highest annual incomes?

VALUE

Why should people seek higher education?

How should Americans treat international students?

Does our legal system provide "justice for all"?

How should young people be educated about AIDS?

What is the value of standardized tests for college admission?

POLICY

What courses should students be required to take?

Should the state's drunk driving laws be changed?

What are the arguments for and against mandatory retirement?

Should the United States intervene in foreign disputes for humanitarian reasons?

What advantages should government provide for businesses willing to develop in high-risk areas of a city?

Figure 8.3

Examples of questions of fact, value, and policy.

overall plan for decision making is more likely to make a poor decision.[29] In this section you will learn techniques for making group problem-solving efforts more systematic and organized.

EFFECTIVE GROUP PROBLEM SOLVING

When groups fail by making poor decisions, which can happen because of laziness, poor research or discussion, or even groupthink, they likely have not followed a coordinated process for analyzing and discussing the problem and its solutions. An effective problem-solving process starts with an appropriate discussion question, includes an explicit discussion of the criteria the group will use to assess potential solutions, and follows a systematic problem-solving procedure.

Wording the Discussion Question

Problem-solving groups typically handle three basic types of discussion questions. Questions of *fact* deal with whether something is true or can be verified. Questions of *value* ask whether something is good or bad, better or worse. Cultural and individual values and beliefs are central to questions of value. Questions of *policy* ask what action should be taken. The key word *should* is either stated or implied in questions of policy. Examples of each type of question are presented in figure 8.3.

"I think Ms. Brown is **a good lawyer** because she is *very credible*. She *knows the law* and always *comes up with novel arguments* that her opposing lawyers can't counter."

"Our solution for the parking problem has to be **effective**. I mean, it has to *reduce parking complaints, eliminate the amount of driving around looking for a space that happens now, and not cost the university any money*."

"I think **weapons** should be made illegal. I mean, *guns* are really dangerous in the wrong hands, and you can't tell me that people need *semiautomatic assault rifles* to hunt with."

Figure 8.4

Making abstract concepts more concrete.

Regardless of the type of discussion question guiding a problem-solving group, the leader must state the question appropriately. Remember, a key task of effective leaders is to help focus the group on what is being discussed. First, the language and terminology should be concrete rather than abstract. If ambiguous terms such as *effective, good,* or *fair* are used, providing examples helps each group member have as close to the same meaning as possible. Figure 8.4 gives examples of how abstract terms can be made more concrete. Second, a well-stated discussion question helps group members know when the solution has been achieved. For example, a task force charged with "completing a report by May 15 on why membership has dropped from 100 to 50 members" knows exactly what to do by what deadline. Finally, a group should start its problem solving with a problem question rather than a solution question. Problem questions focus on what is wrong and imply that many solutions are possible for resolving the problem. Problem questions do not bias a group toward one particular solution. Solution questions, on the other hand, slant the group's discussion toward one particular option. They may inadvertently cause a group to ignore creative or unusual options because they blind members to some alternatives. Examples of problem and solution questions appear in figure 8.5.

Discussing Criteria

Criteria are the standards by which a group must judge potential solutions. For example, a solution's likely effectiveness ("Will it work?"), acceptability ("Will people vote for our proposal?"), and cost ("Does this option keep us within the budget?") are common criteria. Group members should discuss and agree on criteria before adopting a solution. Because criteria are based on the values of group members, two members, each using rational tools of decision making, can arrive at different conclusions. The more similar group members are in age, gender, ethnicity, background, attitudes, values, and beliefs, the more easily they can agree on criteria.

criteria
The standards by which a group must judge potential solutions.

Figure 8.5

Problem questions versus solution questions.

PROBLEM QUESTIONS		SOLUTION QUESTIONS
How can we reduce complaints about parking on campus?	SPEED LIMIT 25	How can we increase the number of parking spaces in the campus lots?
What can we do to increase attendance at our club's activities?		How can we improve publicity for our club's activities?
How can we make Ginny Avenue safer to cross?		How can we get the city council to reduce the speed limit on Ginny Avenue?

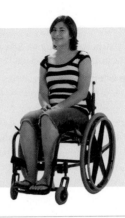

ABSOLUTE CRITERIA

(*Must* be met)

- Must not cost more than $2 million
- Must be wheelchair accessible
- Must include flexible space that can be arranged in different ways

IMPORTANT CRITERIA

(*Should* be met)

- Should be centrally located
- Should have stage space for concerts
- Should be attractive to all campus constituencies, including traditional and nontraditional students, faculty, and staff

Figure 8.6

Absolute criteria versus important criteria for a new student union.

Two kinds of criteria are common. Absolute criteria are those that *must* be met; the group has no leeway. Important criteria are those that *should* be met, but the group has some flexibility. Group members should give the highest priority to criteria that must be met. Ideas that do not meet absolute criteria should be rejected, and the rest should be ranked on how well they meet important criteria. Examples of absolute and important criteria are presented in figure 8.6.

Identifying Alternatives

One of the most important jobs a leader has is to encourage group creativity. One technique that can promote innovation and creative thought among groups is brainstorming.[30] Brainstorming is most effective when group members are free to identify multiple ideas, they are asked to defer any judgment (positive or negative) until all ideas have been identified, and the ideas are succinct. Critical evaluation kills creativity, so the main rule of brainstorming is "no evaluation," at least during the brainstorming process. Evaluation of the ideas takes place *after* the group has exhausted its options.

As a leader, you must carefully guide the brainstorming phase of group discussions. You should start with a specified time period in which brainstorming will occur. Before starting dialogue, providing group members with a few minutes to consider the question before responding can help them start individual brainstorming. As ideas are presented to the group, they should be recorded and displayed for all to see; so doing can generate additional ideas. The initial time period for brainstorming can be modified based on the discussion. If ideas start to become repetitive, you may need to stop sooner; if ideas are still unique and interesting, you may need to slightly extend the time. In research this is called "looking for saturation." When all the new ideas have been tapped out (saturated), that is a good time to stop.

Evaluating Alternatives

After group members have adequately brainstormed alternatives, the final task is to evaluate the alternatives. At this stage in the discussion, the criteria the group has identified are used to judge the efficacy of each idea generated through brainstorming. Before proceeding to this step, it may be useful to determine whether various ideas can be organized together in some way. Solutions failing to meet absolute criteria are quickly eliminated. Once the nonviable alternatives are eliminated, group members must evaluate each alternative based on the remaining important criteria. Eventually, the group must determine which alternative best meets the set of important criteria they identified.

OTHER WORK TO ACCOMPLISH IN GROUPS

Although this section has highlighted the role of problem solving in small groups, other important types of work are also accomplished in group settings. In fact, groups serve multiple functions, sometimes simultaneously. In addition to helping us perform task functions, such as solving problems, groups also allow us to do the following:

1. *Make decisions.* Many groups exist to make decisions that are unrelated to specific problems. For example, student groups on your campus make daily decisions, such as planning events, launching community outreach projects, and maintaining facilities. These decisions do not necessarily solve problems; rather, they sustain the day-to-day functions of the groups.

2. *Effect change.* Some groups want to influence society but do not have the power to make decisions. You might belong to a community association or the student government organization on your campus. Those groups attempt to influence change even though they may not have the power to make final decisions on that change.

3. *Negotiate conflict.* Groups are often created to resolve conflict. In Los Angeles, small groups were used to bring Latino American and Armenian American high school students together to resolve racial tensions. In fact, the National Communication Association in partnership with the Southern Poverty Law Center has used this strategy across the nation to promote intercultural understanding and to help resolve racial conflict.

4. *Foster creativity.* Groups help us achieve a level of creativity not possible when working alone. The idea that "two heads are better than one" is magnified in groups. People working together to identify creative ideas will likely be more successful than one person working alone.

5. *Maintain ties between stakeholders.* A final function for small groups is to bring together stakeholders. **Stakeholders** are groups of people who have an interest in the actions of an organization. For example, most schools have parent–teacher organizations. The principal of a school might bring together selected teachers and parents to discuss issues facing the school, so that open lines of communication between the stakeholders (parents, teachers, and administrators) can be maintained. Various organizations, including businesses, government agencies, and nonprofit organizations, use groups to establish and maintain communication among multiple groups of stakeholders.

> **stakeholders**
> Groups of people who have an interest in the actions of an organization.

As you can see, groups exist for many reasons. Although the heart of group activity may indeed be problem solving, not all groups exist solely for that purpose.

Technology and Group Communication Processes

Throughout this book you have learned how technology impacts various forms of human communication, and group communication is no different. Groups of all types use technology to find and analyze information, to facilitate interaction among group members, and even to aid in the decision-making process.

One form of group communication technology is a **group decision support system,** or **GDSS.** A GDSS system uses networked computers, so that group members can anonymously communicate with one another through text messages, and it allows anonymous voting to help make decisions. If you have ever taken a class in which "clickers," or student response systems, are used, you have seen GDSS technology in action. Clickers allow teachers to ask students practice quiz questions and have a summary of anonymous responses displayed for the class. More advanced GDSS systems (and, in fact, more advanced student

> **group decision support system (GDSS)**
> An interactive network of computers with specialized software, allowing users to generate solutions for unstructured problems.

■ Computers can be used to facilitate group communication.

response systems) simply add the element of anonymous texting. Research shows that GDSS technology has the potential to increase interactions because they allow anonymity for group members, can increase the efficiency of decision making, and can reduce the potential that groupthink will influence outcomes.[31]

As World Wide Web technology has advanced, many other tools have become available to help support the work of groups. Consider how the following free resources can help groups work more efficiently:

■ Facebook. Besides helping group members stay connected as friends, Facebook allows you to create a group page for any group to which you belong. On the group page you can post information, links to other resources, agendas, and other information that may help group members stay prepared. You can also create events to alert group members to upcoming meetings.

■ Dropbox. Dropbox is a free file-sharing service that allows you to create shared folders, so that group members can all store, have access to, and edit group documents, such as word processing files, presentation files, and other documents.

content curation
The collection and storage of documents and other multimedia from the Web, covering a specified topic.

■ Evernote. This free resource can be used for **content curation,** the *collection and storage of information from across the Web.* Your group might locate several webpages, videos, and other resources and use Evernote to maintain a research file in shared notebooks. Evernote is also a powerful note-taking tool, so you can use the service to record and publish notes from meetings.

■ Google Documents. Google provides a free version of office programs used for word processing, spreadsheets, and presentations. You can create, collect, and analyze online forms using Google Docs. All files can be shared and edited by other members of your group.

These resources show several options available on the Web that can be used to facilitate the work of groups. Of course, how you use the Web for group work is limited only by your imagination. A variety of services and social media sites can be readily adapted to support the work of your group.

Of course, not all group technology automatically improves group communication. As communication researcher Paul Turman points out, groups communicating entirely through technology may find that group norms and basic structures for how the group operates are more difficult to create in computer-mediated environments.[32] He cautions that computer-mediated groups must take more time to explicitly talk about how the group will function and about various norms for communication among group members.

How Should You Communicate in Small Groups?

Each member of a group must take personal responsibility to help support the functions of the group. How can you best do that? The ability to speak fluently and with polish is not essential, but the ability to speak clearly is. Other members of the group will understand your views more easily if you follow this advice:

1. *Relate your statements to preceding remarks.* Public speakers do not always have the opportunity to respond to remarks by others, but small-group members do. Your

statement should not appear irrelevant. Clarify the relevance of your remark to the topic under discussion by linking your remark to the preceding remark:

- Briefly note the previous speaker's point that you want to address—for example, "I want to piggyback on Bill's comment by noting that we can meet our goal by . . ."

- State your point clearly and concisely.

- Summarize how your point adds to the comments made by others—for example, "So, I agree with Bill. We need to fundraise, but we can't get so caught up in raising money that we forget about our goal of volunteering."

skill builder

Harnessing Technology for Your Group

Digital tools to support the work of a group are a valuable resource that can help you with any group to which you belong. Go to google.com/docs and explore the various ways in which you can create word processing, spreadsheet, and presentation files. Using this chapter as a guide, create a three-slide presentation explaining what you feel are the three most important of the group communication skills you read about in this chapter. After creating the presentation, share the file with your teacher or at least one other student in your class.

2. *Use conventional word arrangements.* When you speak, you should use clear, common language, so that people can understand you. Consider this comment: "I unequivocally recognize the meaningful contribution made by my colleague." Although the language might impress some, a simple "I agree" would work just as well. Here are some ways to improve your verbal clarity while in group discussions:

- After connecting your idea to the discussion or previous speaker, state your point and then provide one piece of supporting information or additional explanation.

- Explain to group members how you perceive the importance of what you are saying. Not all comments are critical; some are just ideas. Letting others know how important you think something is may influence how they react and respond.

- When done, ask if anyone needs you to clarify your point.

3. *Speak concisely.* The point here is simple: don't be long-winded. The main advantage of small groups is their ability to approach a problem interactively. If you monopolize the discussion, that advantage may be diminished or lost completely. To learn to speak concisely, try the following:

- Write down your idea before speaking. Those who are wordy during group discussions often spend much of their time trying to figure out what they want to say.

- Try to talk for no more than one minute at a time. Of course, this time limit is arbitrary; however, one minute should be enough time to get an idea out for consideration, and you can always answer questions to clarify as needed.

4. *State one point at a time.* Sometimes this rule is violated appropriately, such as when a group member is presenting a report to the group. However, during give-and-take discussion, stating only one idea promotes efficiency and responsiveness. To ensure this practice, try the following strategies:

- As a group, appoint a process observer to be in charge of keeping the group discussion moving along and preventing any member from bringing up more than one idea at a time. After using the process observer a few times, these behaviors become second nature.

- If you have several ideas that vary in importance, provide some of the less important points to group members in written form for later reflection. Save discussion time for the most important ideas.

Being an Ethical Group Member

The unique nature of small groups requires attention to special ethical concerns regarding the treatment of speech, people, and information. First, as noted in the NCA Credo of Ethics, discussed earlier in the book, the field of communication strongly supports the value of free speech. Many secondary groups are formed because several heads perform better than one, but that advantage will not be realized if group members are unwilling or afraid to speak freely in the group. An important ethical principle for small groups is that group members should be willing to share their unique perspectives. But they should also refrain from saying or doing things that prevent others from speaking freely. Members who are trustworthy and supportive are behaving ethically.

Second, group members must be honest and truthful. In a small group they should not intentionally deceive one another or manufacture information or evidence to persuade other members to adopt their point of view.

Third, group members must be thorough and unbiased when they evaluate information. Groups are used to make any number of decisions, both large and small. Such decisions will be only as good as the information on which they are based and the reasoning the members use to assess the information. Group members must consider *all* relevant information in an open-minded, unbiased way by using the best critical thinking skills they can; otherwise, tragedies can result.

Fourth, group members must behave with integrity. That is, they must be willing to place the good of the group ahead of their own goals. Some individuals cannot be team players because they are unable or unwilling to merge their personal agendas with those of the group. Groups are better off without such individuals. If you make a commitment to join a group, you should be the kind of team member who will

sizing things up

Collective Self-Esteem Scale

We are all members of different social groups or social categories. For example, you belong to a university, and as a student you may belong to one or more university groups as well as several social groups. We all belong to groups for different reasons. Read each of the following statements carefully and respond using the following scale:

1 = Strongly disagree
2 = Disagree
3 = Neither agree nor disagree
4 = Agree
5 = Strongly agree

1. I am a worthy member of the social groups I belong to.
2. The social groups I belong to are an important reflection of who I am.
3. I often feel I'm a useless member of my social groups.
4. Most people consider my social groups, on the average, to be more ineffective than other social groups.
5. In general, I'm glad to be a member of the social groups I belong to.
6. I feel good about the social groups I belong to.
7. Overall, my social groups are considered good by others.
8. I feel I don't have much to offer to the social groups I belong to.
9. In general, others respect the social groups that I am a member of.
10. The social groups I belong to are unimportant to my sense of what kind of person I am.
11. Overall, my group membership has very little to do with how I feel about myself.
12. In general, others think that the social groups I am a member of are unworthy.
13. Overall, I often feel that the social groups of which I am a member are not worthwhile.
14. I am a cooperative participant in the social groups I belong to.
15. In general, belonging to my social groups is an important part of my self-image.
16. I often regret that I belong to the social groups I do.

There are no right or wrong answers to these questions. A guide for evaluating your responses appears in the appendix at the end of the text (p. 348).

Source: Luthanen, R., & Croker, J. (1992). A collective self-esteem scale: Self-evaluation of one's social identity. *Personality and Social Psychology Bulletin, 18*, 302–318. © 1992. Reprinted by permission of SAGE Publications.

benefit rather than harm the group. If you cannot in good conscience give a group your support, you should leave the group rather than pretend to support the group while sabotaging it.

Finally, group members must learn to manage **group conflict,** which is an expressed struggle between two or more members of a group.[33] Although some conflict can actually help groups make better decisions because ideas are debated and tested more vigorously, too much conflict may result in decreased group cohesiveness and can cause the group to cease functioning. To manage conflict, group members must be ethical in the way they approach disagreement and be willing to listen to and compromise with others. Ethical disagreement happens when you express your disagreement openly, disagree with ideas rather than people, base your disagreement on evidence and reasoning, and react to disagreement positively rather than defensively.[34]

group conflict
An expressed struggle between two or more members of a group.

keeping it real

Creatively Combating Groupthink

Let's return to the story of Candice and her hive work, described at the start of the chapter. Candice is a creative person and likes working with others over the Web to accomplish creative outcomes for projects. She recognizes, though, that the groups to which she belongs can sometimes start to become stale in terms of creative energy. As a result, Candice does some extra work to help drive new ways of thinking about things. For each of her groups she creates a Google Docs shared folder. In that folder she writes, and encourages others to do the same, ideas about how she would perhaps do a project (or specific aspects of a project) differently if she were working alone. In so doing, she invites others to explore alternate ways of accomplishing the outcome. Sometimes her ideas gain traction, other times not so much.

Candice's approach is important for several reasons. On a basic level she is combating groupthink because she is taking care to make counter-ideas known. But she is also establishing a norm for openness in her group. By being willing to have her own ideas be considered, others will be more likely to do the same. This norm could be essential to the full and open exchange of ideas in the group. Finally, Candice is being a good leader. She is inviting others to think more creatively, but she is not attempting to push her ideas on the group. Even though Candice works in a hive, she can still use basic principles of effective group communication to improve the outcomes of her group.

Chapter Review & Study Guide

Summary

In this chapter, you learned the following:

1. Small-group communication is the interaction of a small group of people working together to achieve a common goal. Small groups can be classified as task-related, relationship-related, assigned, or emergent. Many groups can blur boundaries among these types of groups.

- Task groups are formed to accomplish something, such as solving a problem.
- Relationship groups are formed to meet our needs for inclusion and affection.

- Assigned groups occur because individuals are appointed to the group by someone else.
- Emergent groups occur naturally as individuals meet and decide to become interdependent.

2. Groups form unique cultures as members interact with one another.

- From the first time group members talk, they start to develop norms for how the group will interact. As those norms develop, individual group members begin to take on certain roles in the group.
- Strong group cultures can lead to greater cohesiveness, which can more strongly tie group members together. Groups must take care that cohesiveness does not lead to groupthink.
- Diversity among group members can influence, both positively and negatively, the culture of a group.

3. Leadership is the process of using communication to influence the behaviors and attitudes of people to meet group goals. Various theories discuss how leadership affects small-group communication.

- The most effective leaders are able to adapt their leadership skills to the needs of the group. All members of the group can share leadership responsibilities.
- Leaders must learn to manage various tensions within a group, such as the tension between task and relational goals.

4. Group decision making has four steps:

- Wording the discussion question
- Discussing criteria for evaluating potential solutions
- Brainstorming alternatives
- Evaluating alternatives

5. Small-group communication can utilize technology to help facilitate communication and decision making.

- Group decision support systems use special software to facilitate brainstorming and decision making. Group members are able to anonymously present ideas to other members and are able to anonymously rate and vote for specific alternatives.
- A variety of free Web services and tools can be used to facilitate group communication and group work.

6. To effectively communicate in small groups, you must use clear language and make concise comments that are related to the comments of other group members. You should try to keep your comments limited to one issue at a time.

7. Ethical behaviors in group contexts include allowing others to speak without fear, being honest and truthful, carefully evaluating alternatives, acting with integrity, and managing conflict ethically.

Key Terms

Affection
Assigned groups
Autocratic leaders
Content curation
Control
Criteria
Democratic leaders
Designated leader
Emergent groups
Emergent leader
Formal role

Group climate
Group conflict
Group culture
Group decision support system
  (GDSS)
Groupthink
Inclusion
Informal role
Laissez-faire leaders
Leadership
Maintenance functions

Norms
Power
Relationship-oriented groups
Role
Self-centered functions
Small-group communication
Stakeholders
Task functions
Task-oriented groups
Within-group diversity

Study Questions

1. "Groups meet needs," "groups are everywhere," and "working effectively in groups requires training" are statements that explain
   a. types of small groups.
   b. reasons for studying small-group communication.
   c. ways of interacting in small groups.
   d. methods of studying small-group communication.

2. What is true of small groups?
   a. They are comprised of three to nine people.
   b. Members are interdependent.
   c. Group members work toward a common goal.
   d. All of the above are correct.

connect
For further review, go to the LearnSmart study module for this chapter.

3. A type of online group that focuses on interdependent work among group members is called a
   a. web.
   b. hive.
   c. net.
   d. cluster.

4. A process of using communication to influence the behaviors and attitudes of others to meet group goals and to benefit the group is
   a. groupthink.
   b. inclusion.
   c. leadership.
   d. role.

5. According to French and Raven, referent power is
   a. power based on others' admiration and respect.
   b. the ability to give followers what they want and need.
   c. when other members value a person's knowledge or expertise.
   d. the ability to withhold from followers what they want and need.

6. Informal rules for group interaction, the emotional tone created within a group, and group member roles are comprised in
   a. leadership skills.
   b. brainstorming techniques.
   c. maintenance functions.
   d. a group's culture.

7. Creating a discussion question, evaluating prospective solutions, and brainstorming and evaluating alternatives are steps in
   a. group conflict.
   b. group diversity.
   c. group decision making.
   d. groupthink.

8. Which of the following statements is true?
   a. Groups exist solely for problem solving.
   b. Effective leaders do not adapt their leadership skills to the needs of the group.
   c. Technology can be utilized to help facilitate communication within small groups.
   d. Groupthink is a helpful and effective method of decision making.

9. When communicating with other group members, you should
   a. use technical language, so that you appear more credible.
   b. state numerous points at a time.
   c. be long-winded.
   d. relate your remarks to previous statements.

10. To manage group conflict ethically, members must
    a. be willing to listen to and compromise with others.
    b. base their disagreements on feeling and intuition.
    c. disagree with people rather than ideas.
    d. defend their ideas and refuse to listen to others' ideas.

Answers:

1. (b); 2. (d); 3. (b); 4. (c); 5. (a); 6. (d); 7. (c); 8. (c); 9. (d); 10. (a)

Critical Thinking

1. Think of the groups to which you belong. Do they mesh with the text's definition of a small group? What are the groups' functions? What type of leader does each group have? What group norms are you expected to abide by?

2. When in the presence of a group, note the members' functions and related statements. Under which subcategory do the statements fall (refer to figures 8.1 and 8.3)?

workplace communication

When you have read and thought about this chapter, you will be able to:

1. Explain various dimensions of workplace communication, including different types of organizations and communication networks within organizations.

2. Create an effective résumé and cover letter.

3. Take steps to effectively prepare for employment interviews ranging from creating a self-inventory and personal network to planning for postinterview negotiations.

4. Enact four communication skills needed in the workplace: workplace communication competence, cross-cultural understanding, conflict management, and customer service skills.

5. Recognize and practice ethical workplace communication behaviors.

The very fabric of our social, cultural, and economic worlds is intertwined with various organizations, including schools, clubs, places of worship, and the workplace. Our ability to communicate effectively and ethically within these various organizations determines, in large part, our opportunities for personal, social, and economic advancement. In this chapter you will learn about various skills related to workplace communication.

Rex is known as "Superman" among his friends, because he works hard at everything, from coursework to sports to his job. After consulting with his campus career services office about how to apply for internships prior to his final year of classes, Rex sent out 13 applications and landed a spot with a small business logistics company specializing in shipping.

Rex's first week on the job was a nightmare. Everyone at the company was older than he, and it seemed like they spoke a different language. The jargon they used to describe the computer system, the different types of shipments, and invoicing details was endless. The saving grace for Rex was his supervisor, Carlos Peres. At the end of the first week, Carlos asked Rex whether he wanted to meet after work to talk about the job. During that conversation, Carlos explained that learning the various aspects of the job is hard at first but gets easier with time and repetition. Rex listened carefully and, in his superman way, plowed ahead with the job.

By the end of his internship, Rex had mastered the job. He even worked with Carlos to create documents that future interns could use to aid their transition into their role. He kept copies of the documents to reference when applying for management jobs after graduation. Rex's time at the firm helped him appreciate the complexity of work life while giving him valuable work experience.

Have you ever been in a situation like Rex's? Or like Carlos, who needed to help his intern, who was struggling with the tasks of a new job? What communication strategies would you recommend for Rex and Carlos to help Rex succeed in his internship? At the end of the chapter, we'll take another look at Rex's situation.

Effective workplace communication translates into results. And communication in the workplace includes more than learning how to be pleasant with customers, clients, and co-workers. As individuals with our own values and moral stances, we bring to the workplace certain assumptions and expectations. Learning how to adapt to the dynamics of any organization can be difficult, but it is not impossible. In this chapter you will learn about communication in the workplace—how it works and what skills are needed to make the transition into a new organization and to manage conflict successfully and ethically.

organizations
Social collectives, or groups of people, in which activities are coordinated to achieve both individual and collective goals.

organizational communication
the ways in which groups of people both maintain structure and order through their symbolic interactions and allow individual actors the freedom to accomplish their goals.

What Is Workplace Communication?

Each of us belongs to several different **organizations,** which are social collectives, or groups of people, in which activities are coordinated to achieve both individual and collective goals. According to a 2011 Associated Press/Viacom Survey, nearly two-thirds of college students work at least part-time to help pay for their education.[1] You may belong to a church, student clubs, and community service organizations, and, of course, we are all members of local, state, and national government organizations. Being a competent communicator within organizations requires some understanding of how organizational communication works. We define **organizational communication** as the ways in which groups of people both maintain structure and order through their symbolic interactions and allow individual actors the freedom to accomplish their goals. Organizational communication is what ties the various stakeholders of an organization together. In this section you will learn about organizational communication as it flows through communications networks in various types of organizations.

TYPES OF ORGANIZATIONS

Talcott Parsons classified organizations into four primary types: economic, political, integration, and pattern maintenance.[2] Although some organizations might overlap these categories, we usually can classify organizations according to their primary functions in society.

Organizations with an **economic orientation** tend to manufacture products and/or offer services for consumers. Small businesses, which according to the United States Small Business Administration account for 99.7% of all U.S. employer firms and employ about half of private sector employees, are examples of organizations with an economic orientation.[3] Of course, large corporations, banks, and media organizations also have economic orientations.

Organizations with a **political orientation** generate and distribute power and control within society. Elected local, state, and federal officials and police and military forces are political organizations. Of course, there are Democrats and Republicans who form organizations with political orientations, but did you know there are over 40 third-party political organizations in the United States?[4] Political organizations must adhere to rules established in formal documents, such as the U.S. Constitution, while they attempt to influence the ideology of the electorate. You have witnessed the attempts of the Tea Party and the Occupy Wall Street movement to use the media and social networks to promote particular positions on issues.

Organizations with an **integration orientation** help mediate and resolve discord among members of society. Our court system, public interest groups, and conflict management centers are all examples of integration-oriented organizations. One unique characteristic of communication within integrative organizations is the necessity for impartiality. A judge, for example, must not be biased in the way he or she talks to criminal defendants, and public interest groups must demonstrate that their objective benefits all of society, not just a few individuals.

Organizations with a **pattern-maintenance orientation** promote cultural and educational regularity and development within society. Organizations that teach individuals how to participate effectively in society, including families, schools, and religious groups, promote pattern maintenance. Communication within organizations focused on pattern maintenance emphasizes social support. Your family or your church, for instance, provides you with personal and spiritual support. Even schools support individuals by helping them learn.

COMMUNICATION NETWORKS

Competent workplace communicators understand that the workplace comprises multiple communication networks. **Communication networks** are patterns of relationships through which information flows in an organization. Stohl describes communication networks as capturing "the tapestry

economic orientation
Organizations that manufacture products and/or offer services for consumers.

political orientation
Organizations that generate and distribute power and control within society.

integration orientation
Organizations that help mediate and resolve discord among members of society.

pattern-maintenance orientation
Organizations that promote cultural and educational regularity and development within society.

communication networks
Patterns of relationships through which information flows in an organization.

■ Schools are pattern-maintenance organizations because they teach people how to effectively participate in society.

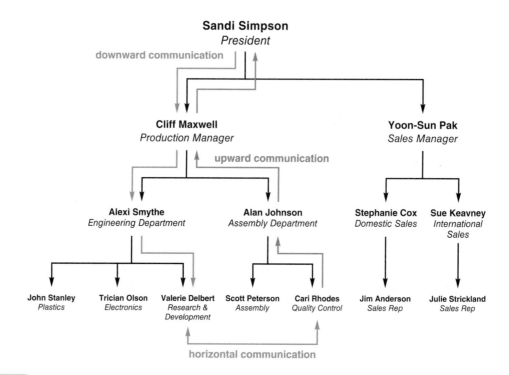

formal communication
Messages that follow prescribed channels of communication throughout the organization.

downward communication
Messages flowing from superiors to subordinates.

upward communication
Messages flowing from subordinates to superiors.

horizontal communication
Messages between members of an organization with equal power.

informal communication
Any interaction that does not generally follow the formal structure of the organization but emerges out of natural social interaction among organization members.

of *relationships*—the complex web of *affiliations* among individuals and organizations as they are woven through the collaborative threads of communication."[5] Communication networks can take many forms, depending on the complexity of the organization. However, we typically classify these networks as broadly formal or informal in nature.

Formal communication consists of messages that follow prescribed channels of communication throughout the organization. The most common way of depicting formal communication networks is with organizational charts like the one in figure 9.1. Organizational charts provide clear guidelines as to who is responsible for a given task and which employees are responsible for others' performance. When communicating occurs in formal networks, information typically flows in three ways:

■ **Downward communication** occurs whenever superiors initiate messages to subordinates. Ideally, downward communication should include such things as job instructions, job rationale, policy and procedures, performance feedback, and motivational appeals.

■ **Upward communication** occurs when messages flow from subordinates to superiors. Obviously, effective decision making depends on timely, accurate, and complete information traveling upward from subordinates.

■ **Horizontal communication** flows between people who are at the same level of the organizational hierarchy. It influences organizational success by allowing members to coordinate tasks, solve problems, share information, and resolve conflict.

Informal communication is any interaction that does not follow the formal structure of the organization but emerges out of social interactions among organization members.

Whereas formal communication consists of messages the organization recognizes as official, informal messages do not follow official lines. Informal communication allows networks to emerge within the organization that do not follow the formal structures of upward and downward communication.[6] For example, co-workers who work from home might use private e-mail accounts, Facebook, or other noncompany mechanisms to have informal discussions about other employees, their boss, or other issues about their jobs.[7] These informal networks, sometimes referred to as "grapevine communication," are typically very accurate, with between 80% and 90% of the information being correct.[8] An understanding of formal and informal networks within organizations is critical as you join and try to fit in to a new organization.

Communication networks can also extend beyond organizations. **Organizational communities** are established when *several organizations—similar businesses, clubs, or community-service organizations—have overlapping interests and become networked together to provide mutual support and resources.*[9] For example, a group of organic farms in your area might act together to make connections with local restaurants and grocery stores to sell their goods. If the farmers and the restaurants form networks to coordinate menus with seasonal local foods, or "30-mile meals," those networks can evolve as the organizational community grows. Organizational networks create connections that can translate into innovation and evolution.

organizational communities Groups of similar businesses or clubs that have common interests and become networked together to provide mutual support and resources.

Preparing for the Job Market

According to the Bureau of Labor Statistics, 12 of the 20 fastest-growing occupations through 2018 will require an Associate degree or higher; virtually none of the 20 fastest-*declining* occupations require anything other than on-the-job training.[10] The implication is clear: your qualifications matter when you are looking for a job. Of course, you must determine effective ways to market your credentials during the job search. Although approaches to personal marketing will vary from profession to profession, this section discusses general principles behind strategies that you might use.

CONDUCTING A SELF-INVENTORY

What do you really know about yourself? When was the last time you took inventory of your assets and liabilities as a potential employee? Could you express these qualities intelligently? Answers to these questions are essential when you are preparing for your job search. You may want to consult with teachers, friends, family members, and professional acquaintances. However, in the end you will need to accumulate information from all these sources to determine how to best articulate your strengths. Consider tallying the following (not an exclusive list):

- Your work and educational experiences
- Your motivations and goals
- Your strengths and weaknesses
- Your likes and dislikes
- Your skills
- Your roles in campus extracurricular activities
- Your professional experience, if any (including co-op programs and internships)
- Your interests and hobbies
- Your talents, aptitudes, and achievements
- What is important to you in a position and an organization

■ Volunteering is a great way to make connections and expand your personal network.

personal network
A web of contacts and relationships to help you gain job leads and make referrals.

Be thorough in your analysis, so that you will be able to define and describe the benefits you can bring to an organization. Ideally, you should then be able to summarize what you know about yourself in a single, detailed answer to the most commonly asked first question in an employment interview: "Tell me about yourself."

CREATING A PERSONAL NETWORK

Many people assume that the key to landing a good job is having a good résumé. Though partly true, this conventional wisdom is also incomplete: the key to finding a great job is getting your résumé into the hands of the right people, and that requires having a great personal network. A **personal network** is an intricate web of contacts and relationships designed to benefit the participants—including identifying leads and giving referrals.[11] People in your network, including family, friends, people you have met at social functions, and people with whom you have worked and studied, can assist you in identifying job leads and introducing you to others who can become a part of your network.

Because many college students have not yet had significant work experience, developing a network is critical to postcollege employment. Here are strategies you can use to develop your network:

1. *Create an inventory of your network.* Using your phone list, e-mail list, set of Facebook friends, and other sources, inventory the people in your social network who could assist you in your job search. Talk with those who have significant work experience to make them aware that you are in the job market.

2. *Contact the career services office on your campus.* Most campuses offer several job fairs throughout the academic year or provide other networking opportunities. Taking advantage of these face-to-face meeting opportunities can be a very productive use of your time.

3. *Contact and join student chapters of professional organizations on your campus.* In communication, for instance, students often join clubs such as the National Communication Association, the Association for Women in Communication, the Public Relations Society of America, or the Society for Professional Journalists. Campus chapters of these organizations provide very useful networking opportunities for members.

4. *Consider an internship.* If you are early in your academic career, an internship can provide valuable networking opportunities. Most colleges and universities offer options for students to earn course credit for internships—you should talk with your academic adviser about such options on your campus.

5. *Volunteer.* Simply taking the time to volunteer in your community can open many doors. Besides giving you the satisfaction that comes from helping others, your hard work and dedication will be noticed by others. Volunteering for a community organization will allow you to get to know many different types of people in your community, thus expanding your network.

SEARCHING FOR A JOB

After you have reflected on your career interests and abilities, you can embark on the exciting, and sometimes frustrating, journey of a job search. With millions of potential employers, how can you possibly begin the process of narrowing your focus? In addition to the traditional methods of meeting with your career-services center on campus, reading job advertisements, contacting your personal network, and attending career and job fairs, you can use a variety of online tools.

One key to successful online searching is to use regional job sites that allow you to focus your efforts by geographic location. The U.S. Bureau of Labor Statistics maintains an employment information database for each state at www.bls.gov/oco /oco20024.htm. Using this resource, you can find links to state employment statistics bureaus, as well as job and employment projections broken down by state. Such information can help you identify potentially good leads in areas where you want to live. Likewise, the Riley Guide, at www .rileyguide.com, provides links to several domestic and international job databases. Using those databases coupled with statistical information, you will have a data-driven starting point for finding potential jobs. Newspaper websites and other sites such as www.localhelpwanted.net can also help you target your search to specific cities and careers.

U.S. adults born between 1957 and 1964 (the youngest group of baby boomers) held an average of 11 jobs from age 18 to 44, more than half of them before they were 27, according to the Bureau of Labor Statistics National Longitudinal Survey of Youth.[12] This trend has changed very little in subsequent generations; people still hold several different types of jobs. If you have held previous jobs, one search strategy is to identify similar or related career fields, which you can do on the My Skills My Future website (www.myskillsmyfuture.org). For example, when entering "professor" into the current job field, we learned that "curating" is a growing and related field where a professor's skills could be useful.

There are thousands of online websites designed to help you search for jobs. Some are free. Before using any online source, particularly one that costs money, consult with professors, individuals from your career-services office, and professionals in the field. You should not waste time or money joining a site that has little relevance to your field(s) of interest.

social media make it matter

Using LinkedIn to Market Yourself

Joining professional discussion boards and posting your résumé online will make you visible in online groups related to your profession. LinkedIn is a highly popular social networking site for professionals. With an estimated 120 million members worldwide, it allows professionals to display their credentials and network with people who have similar interests and are in similar professions. Using a social networking site such as LinkedIn can help you develop wide networks for your job search. Of course, this opportunity is a double-edged sword. Many human resource professionals use LinkedIn, Facebook, and other social networking sites to find out information about the personal lives of job applicants, so, as always, be choosy about the information you post about yourself.

Sources: LinkedIn. (2011, October 24). About us (http://press.linkedin.com/about). Roberts, S. J., & Roach, T. (2009). Social networking web sites and human resource personnel: Suggestions for job searches. *Business Communication Quarterly, 72,* 110–114.

PREPARING COVER LETTERS

A **cover letter** is a short letter to an interviewer persuasively introducing you and your credentials in relationship to the job description, and it typically accompanies your résumé. Cover letters help ensure that your résumé is read and let you target your appeal

cover letter
A short letter introducing you and your résumé to an interviewer.

for a particular job. Like any persuasive document, a cover letter has four main sections or paragraphs designed to achieve the following: (1) attention, (2) interest, (3) desire, and (4) action.[13]

After headings that contain your address and the interviewer's address, your cover letter should gain the *attention* of the reader. At this point you should specify the position for which you are applying, indicate how you heard about it, and provide a general overview of your qualifications. In the second paragraph you need to arouse the reader's *interest* and demonstrate your desire for the job. At this point you want to describe your major experiences and strengths as they relate to the job. If possible, mention one or two accomplishments that illustrate your proficiency and effectiveness. The main idea is to create interest and show how your skills and qualifications can be of value to the organization. You can refer the reader to the enclosed résumé for more detail on your qualifications and experience. In the third paragraph you need to suggest action. Restate your *desire* to learn more about the organization and to have a face-to-face meeting, which is the *action* you are hoping for. Finally, express your appreciation for the reader's time and/or consideration.

A cover letter is an opportunity to demonstrate your writing skills. Take care with respect to grammar, spelling, and other mechanics that could turn off a potential employer. You would be surprised at how easily a perfectly credible applicant is dismissed simply because of correctable errors. If you opt to send e-mail queries to potential employers, remember that the e-mail is, in fact, a cover letter, too. Make it persuasive and include your résumé as an attachment. Tim O'Brien, a manager of a public relations firm, points out that, if you receive a reply to your e-mail inquiry, you should carefully follow the directions about what to do next.

PREPARING RÉSUMÉS AND OTHER CREDENTIALS

Although human resource professionals use a variety of employment screening tools to screen job applicants, ranging from surveys to background checks, the professional résumé remains the foundational source of information.[14] A good résumé is your starting point in any job search, and it is likely to be critical to securing an interview and an eventual offer of employment. To create a successful résumé, you must consider style, content, and format.

Style

Style refers to the way you use language and grammar to construct your written materials. It can range from very informal to very formal in tone. A sample résumé is shown in figure 9.2. Notice it uses several stylistic approaches that are uncommon in other forms of writing.

First, complete sentences and the pronoun "I" are unnecessary in résumés. Descriptive clauses are sufficient as long as they are understandable. Many experts recommend beginning descriptive clauses with action verbs, such as *planned, supervised,* and *conducted.*[15] These words catch employers' attention because they are concrete and indicate what you have done. Some commonly used action verbs are listed in table 9.1. Should you use past- or present-tense verbs? The tense depends on whether you are currently performing the particular job duties. Use present-tense verbs for present employment and activities, and use past-tense verbs for past jobs.

Whenever possible, you should quantify information to illustrate the scope of your accomplishments. Here are some examples:

Managed a $30,000 budget for Lambda Chi Alpha

Supervised 10 customer service representatives

Increased sales by 200%

SAMANTHA BRADSHAW
14 35th St South, Omaha, NE 68048
701-236-8769
bradshaws@umd.edu

OBJECTIVE
To obtain a position in Web design providing quality service to non-profit organizations.

EXPERIENCE
Web Designer Ignus, Inc (Omaha, NE)   2010–Present
- Plan and create websites.
- Scan, resize, and optimize all graphics.
- Attend sales meetings with clients and sales representatives.
- Suggest changes for sites of prospective clients.

Office Assistant Butler Machinery Company (Omaha, NE)   2009–2010
- Updated and maintained the machine inventory on company website.
- Performed miscellaneous office duties, including typing, faxing, and mailing.
- Implemented training course for 20 new employees.

Senior Sales Representative Kinko's (Omaha, NE)   2007–2009
- Packaged and shipped materials for customers.
- Facilitated monetary transactions.
- Assisted customers with document creation.
- Managed 12 long-term business accounts.

EDUCATION
Creighton University (Omaha, NE)   2005–2009
- B.A., Business Administration and Computer Science.
- Graduated Summa Cum Laude.
- GPA 3.85.

SKILLS
Proficient in HTML Language, Microsoft Access, Adobe Photoshop, Microsoft Outlook, Fireworks, PhotoEditor, Internet Explorer, C++ Language, Microsoft Excel, PowerPoint, Word, Dreamweaver, and GoldMine Mktg.

Figure 9.2

Sample chronological résumé.

Employers look for accomplishments like these because they are concrete, measurable, and significant.

Be consistent. Whenever you make stylistic decisions, adhere to them. If you use bullets to present your job duties, use bullets throughout your résumé. If you put periods at the end of your bulleted descriptions, make sure you do so consistently. If you indent one job title five spaces and underline, make sure all your job titles are indented five spaces and underlined.

Be concise. Remember that you do not have to put everything in a résumé. In fact, view your résumé as an appetizer. You can tell about the main course in the interview. Unless you have more than seven years of work experience, most experts agree that your résumé should not be longer than one page.[16]

Table 9.1 Action Verbs for Résumés

Accomplished	Formulated	Ordered	Succeeded
Adapted	Generated	Participated	Supervised
Administered	Handled	Performed	Supplied
Analyzed	Headed	Persuaded	Supported
Balanced	Identified	Prepared	Tabulated
Disbursed	Managed	Revised	Uploaded
Examined	Modified	Searched	Verified
Executed	Notified	Selected	Volunteered
Explained	Obtained	Sponsored	Won
Filed	Offered	Streamlined	Wrote

Be neat. Given that employers have very limited time to spend reading your résumé, the overall impression it creates is important. Employers judge you and your capabilities based in part on the physical appearance of your résumé. Hiring managers will have a hard time ignoring poor proofreading and sloppiness, and your chances of securing an interview will significantly decrease.

Content

The content of résumés for college students typically includes contact information as well as your objectives, education, experience, skills, and campus activities or community involvement. Without contact information the rest of your résumé is useless. On every résumé you send out, you must include complete information about how to reach you, including your e-mail address.

objective statement
An articulation of your goals.

An **objective statement,** or an articulation of your goals, is usually the first information on the résumé, just below your contact information. Objective statements are important because they allow you to tailor your credentials and goals to the needs of a particular organization and job description.[17] In addition to describing your personal goals, you should consider what the organization needs or what types of issues it faces when you are writing your objective statement. The following are examples of objective statements:

- To apply programming skills in an environment with short deadlines and demanding customers.
- To achieve consistent improvement in sales profitability of units under my supervision.

Employers also want to see your educational credentials. Your credentials show that you had the intellect to go to college, the determination to complete high school, and the capability of learning new things and finishing complex projects. In summarizing your education, you should include degrees awarded, completion dates (or anticipated completion dates), schools attended, majors and minors, and honors or scholarships. Employers always look at your education, but the further along you are in your career, the smaller the role it plays on your résumé. Instead, experience becomes more important.

With few exceptions, employers will focus much of their attention on your past jobs, whether you are a freshly minted college graduate or an experienced individual changing jobs or careers. Employers look at the types of jobs you have held, as well as your job tenure, job duties, and accomplishments. When describing your work experience, make sure you include a job title, the name of the organization, the dates of employment, and a description of your major responsibilities and achievements. Remember to use action verbs (see table 9.1) and to quantify accomplishments whenever possible.

When adapting your résumé to a particular job, include key words and phrases from the actual job description. In larger organizations, electronic databases are used to search through hundreds of résumés to find perfect matches between jobs and people—much as what happens when you use Google to search for a webpage.[18] As a result, if your résumé contains more key terms from the job advertisement, the chance that an actual person will review it is increased.

Most résumés also include a skills section highlighting abilities, ranging from the ability to use specialized computer applications to fluency in multiple languages. The skills section of your résumé should be tailored to the job description of the position for which you are applying.

Many college students end their résumé with a list of their campus activities and/or community involvement. Don't stop there. Rather, indicate your level of involvement, including participation on committees and leadership positions. Involvement in campus and community organizations is important because, in the mind of many employers, it translates to workplace citizenship.

Format

Now that you are familiar with stylistic and content choices, you need to consider how to organize the information on your résumé. College students typically rely on chronological, functional, and/or online formats.

The **chronological résumé,** which organizes your credentials over time, is what most people envision when they think of a résumé. A résumé based on time has long been the standard and, despite technological advances allowing for electronic résumés, continues to be the most widely accepted format.[19] The core concept of the chronological résumé is accomplishments over time. To refer to a résumé as "reverse chronological" is actually more accurate, because in describing your work experience (and education), you begin with your present or most recent job and continue back to past jobs. Figure 9.2 is an example of a chronological résumé.

chronological résumé
A document that organizes your credentials over time.

Whereas the chronological format organizes your experience based on when you acquired it, the **functional résumé** organizes your experience by type of function performed. If you have held a variety of jobs (such as teaching, sales, and advertising), the functional résumé allows you to group them by the skills you developed and the duties you performed. Graduating college students will use a functional résumé to group "professional experience" separately from "other work experience," which may include jobs that do not directly relate to your career goal but nonetheless illustrate your work ethic.

functional résumé
A document that organizes your credentials by type of function performed.

Alternatives to Traditional Résumés

A preference for electronic résumés is increasing in most businesses, regardless of their size or type of industry. Research reported in *Business Communication Quarterly* showed that 71% of the companies surveyed preferred standard résumés following the chronological or functional format.[20] The majority, 41%, preferred that résumés be submitted as e-mail attachments, followed closely by 34% preferring they be uploaded to a website. A small minority of very large companies preferred that applicants enter segments of information into text fields on a corporate website. Clearly, you need to be flexible in conveying your qualifications. Electronic résumés are certainly becoming the norm; however, paying attention to style and wording is still important. A poorly constructed résumé will damage your credibility, whether in paper or electronic format.

Portfolios

A variety of technical fields, including technical writing, web design, graphic arts, and even public relations, may require development of a professional portfolio as you enter the job market. A professional portfolio provides examples of your knowledge, skills, and abilities to perform specific field-related tasks.[21] Because the format and design of portfolios will vary by field, your best source of information for how to create yours will be your professors and mentors. However, if you are in a creative field, or any field where you create products that can be shown to others, you should plan early to build your portfolio.

A good rule of thumb is to save everything, and to make notes to yourself indicating what skill you mastered or perfected on each project that you save. Later, when you are applying for an internship or a job, your mentor can assist you in compiling the materials into an acceptable portfolio. Having a portfolio can be valuable for any type of profession—keeping papers and other projects from all your courses could come in handy as you attempt to illustrate the broad repertoire of skills, particularly communication skills, you accumulated in college.

Preparing for the Interview

Although preparing for and conducting a job search is nearly a job unto itself, preparing for a job interview requires careful research and focus. To assume the interview is the easy part would be a mistake. Like any formal communication situation—including speeches and presentations—job interviews start with careful planning and practice. In this section you will learn various strategies for guiding that preparation.

job description
A document that defines a job in terms of its content and scope.

GATHER INFORMATION

Your initial step in preparing for a job interview is carefully researching the company. Although you may not have much time for this step, knowing about the company and the position for which you applied is critical to successfully answering questions during the interview. Your research efforts can be focused around three general goals:

■ Study the job description carefully, so that you can learn the exact skills needed to succeed.

1. *Understand the job.* A **job description** defines the position in terms of its content and scope. Although the format can vary, job descriptions may include information on job duties and responsibilities; the knowledge, skills, and abilities necessary to accomplish the duties; working conditions; relationships with co-workers, supervisors, and external stakeholders; and the extent of supervision required. To obtain a copy of the job description, contact the company's human resources department or the person managing the job search process. Besides providing you with information about the job expectations, the job description also serves as the legal cornerstone of interview questions and job-hiring practices. If you have sufficient time, you can use your professional/social network to try to solicit others' perspectives on the type of job for which you applied.

2. *Understand the company.* Job applicants and interviewees lose all credibility when they cannot demonstrate even superficial knowledge of the organization to which they are applying. Taking time to carefully research the company will showcase your initiative, help you be more conversant, and prepare you to ask better questions. Besides using obvious sources of information, such as the company's website,

check your library for specialized resources, such as the LexisNexis Company Insight database or the BusinessWeek Company Insight Center, to find information about the company's finances, executive officers, and other pertinent facts. Of course, small businesses may not be indexed in such databases. A local library or chamber of commerce may have information about these.

3. *Understand the field.* To present yourself as a mature candidate for employment for any job, you will want to illustrate knowledge of your chosen field by demonstrating awareness of new trends, market forces, and other matters. Keep current on all aspects of your field, because employers will view you more positively if you are conversant with these issues. Professional trade magazines are helpful for this type of research. Of course, by virtue of your major you should be keeping up with this type of information well before a job interview.

Remember that the primary purpose of an interview is to analyze the knowledge, skills, and abilities of a particular applicant in relationship to the required and desired skills in the job description. Taking time to learn about these issues will help you advocate for a close fit between your qualifications and those specified by the employer.

GENERAL INTERVIEWING STRATEGIES

During the interview you must present yourself as a potential asset to the organization. Doing so requires using verbal and nonverbal communication; specifically, you want to (1) create a good first impression, (2) speak with clarity, and (3) demonstrate interest.

Just as your written credentials should reflect a professional and competent image, so should you. One of the most obvious ways to create a good first impression is to dress appropriately. The general rule is to match the style of dress of the interviewer. For professional positions, conservative dress is typically appropriate (dark suits, white shirts or blouses, standard ties for men, dark socks or neutral hose, dark shoes). Be sure to wear clothes that fit and are comfortable but not too casual. Be modest in your use of jewelry and cologne. Of course, you need to arrive on time and learn to take cues from the interviewer on how to act, while trying to present yourself in an honest, positive way.

The way you use grammar can deeply influence the impressions others form about you in professional settings, such as job interviews.[22] Even if you have to pause before responding, organize your answer and avoid slurring your words, using potentially offensive language, or using grammatically incorrect sentences. Many applicants do not convey clear messages because their sentences include vocalized pauses ("uh," "um"), verbal fillers ("you know"), and repetitive phrases ("things like that"). By practicing beforehand

skill **builder**

Practicing Interview Questions

Practice answering these typical job interview questions with a partner:

1. Why would you like to work for us?
2. What do you know about our products or services?
3. How have your previous work positions prepared you for this position?
4. What do you think your previous supervisors would cite as your strengths? Weaknesses?
5. Describe a typical strategy that you would use in a customer service call.
6. What criteria do you use when assigning work to others?
7. How do you follow up on work assigned to others?
8. Which aspect of your education has prepared you most for this position?
9. Which course did you like most in college?
10. If you had your education to do over again, what would you do differently, and why?
11. Why did you choose _____ as your major?
12. What do you think is the greatest challenge facing this field today?
13. Which area of this field do you think will expand the most in the next few years?

■ Be prepared to both answer and ask questions effectively during your interviews.

and thinking quickly on your feet, you should be able to speak with clarity and precision. In sum, the employment interview is a context in which to practice the skills you have been learning about and developing in this course.

To be interpersonally effective in interviews, you must also demonstrate interest. One of the most important and meaningful ways to do so is by maintaining strong eye contact with the interviewer.[23] Although you may be tempted to focus on responding to questions as the central interviewing skill, listening can also improve your responses. Use body language to show interest. Smile, nod, and give nonverbal feedback to the interviewer. Although you want to remain engaged, being confident and somewhat relaxed is ideal. Be sure to thank the interviewer for his or her time and consideration of you as a candidate.

ANSWERING QUESTIONS EFFECTIVELY AND ETHICALLY

Answering questions effectively is critical for interviewees. Research has shown that various strategies are associated with successfully answering questions.[24] Four key guidelines emerge from that body of research: (1) offer relevant answers, (2) substantiate your claims with evidence, (3) provide accurate answers, and (4) be positive.

Your answers should be relevant to the question asked and to the job description. As an interviewee you should never evade questions; rather, you should respond to them thoroughly and directly. In discussing your skills and abilities, try to relate them to the specific position for which you are interviewing. Whenever possible, specify how and why you think you are well suited to the job. By so doing, you demonstrate your knowledge of the position and illustrate the transferability of your knowledge and skills to the job at hand.

Whatever claims you make about your experience, always provide support. Some interviewees give terse, underdeveloped responses, forcing the interviewer to probe endlessly. Presenting claims without evidence can sound self-serving. If you offer evidence

Table 9.2 Answering Questions Effectively

Ineffective	Effective
Question: "Describe your best attribute as an employee."	
"I'm really organized."	"I take time to ensure that materials and documents are put away before leaving my desk. This promotes security and allows me to stay organized."
Question: "Have you ever coded HTML?"	
"I think that I had to do something with HTML when working on my Facebook page."	"I have not actually coded HTML, but I am comfortable working on webpages that use plain text content management systems like you find on social media sites."
Question: "Have you experienced conflict in the workplace?"	
"Yes! One of my previous bosses was always mad at everyone and it was always horrible to go to work!"	"There can always be conflict over issues, but I try hard to focus on my job duties and stay out of preventable conflict."

for your assertions, the objective facts and supporting examples will confirm your strengths.

All employers are searching for honest employees, so always provide accurate information. If an employer finds out you have misrepresented yourself during the interview by exaggerating or lying, everything you do and say will become suspect. Successful interviews feature candid conversation. If you are asked a question you cannot answer, simply say so and do not act embarrassed. An interviewer will have more respect for an interviewee who admits to ignorance than for one who tries to fake an answer.

Being accurate does not mean confessing to every self-doubt or shortcoming. In fact, be as positive as possible during interviews, because in a sense you are "selling" yourself to the employer. To volunteer some limitations or claim personal responsibility for past events is fine, especially in the context of challenges you have met or problems you have encountered. However, avoid being overly critical of others and yourself. You can highlight your strengths and downplay your weaknesses, but always be honest.

Table 9.2 provides examples illustrating these suggestions. Notice how the effective answers demonstrate honesty while presenting the best case possible for your attributes as an employee.

ASKING QUESTIONS EFFECTIVELY AND ETHICALLY

Any potential employer will recognize that you have questions about the job and/or organizational environment. After answering the interviewer's questions, you should be prepared to ask questions. This gives you the insight you need to decide if you want this particular job, shows your interest in the job, and demonstrates communication skills.

Recognize that your questions make indirect statements about your priorities, ambitions, and level of commitment. Consequently, avoid overreliance on questions that focus on financial issues such as salary, vacation time, and benefits. Devise questions that elicit information about the company and/or job that you were unable to obtain through your research. Arrange questions so that the most important ones come first, because you may not get a chance to ask all of your prepared questions. Although your questions will need to be tailored to the organization, here are general types of questions relevant in most interview situations:

"Do you assign mentors to help new employees fit in to the culture of the company while learning their new job roles?"

"What is the average length of time that an employee works for the company?"

"What percentage of entry-level employees stay with the company and get promoted?"

"Does the company offer financial support for continuing education?"

PREPARING FOR ILLEGAL QUESTIONS

Legally, employers must approach the hiring process with reference to the laws that govern employment. These laws, known as equal employment opportunity (EEO) laws, are written and enacted by Congress and individual state legislatures. Although a variety of laws can exist at the state level, the pertinent federal statutes are

- *Title VII of the Civil Rights Act.* This law prevents employment discrimination based on race, color, sex, religion, or national origin.
- *Equal Pay Act.* This act, passed in 1963, prevents unequal pay for men and women for equal work.
- *Pregnancy Discrimination Act.* This law makes it illegal to discriminate, either through hiring or promotion, based on pregnancy or related medical issues.
- *Age Discrimination Act.* According to this law, employers cannot refuse to hire applicants who are 40 years of age or older because of age alone.
- *The Americans with Disabilities Act.* This act prevents discrimination against qualified applicants because of a disability and requires employers to make reasonable accommodations to help them apply and perform work.[25]

The purpose of such laws is to ensure that individuals are selected for employment without bias.

To comply with these laws, employers should (1) describe the qualities and skills needed for the position they hope to fill, (2) construct questions that relate to those attributes, and (3) ask the same questions of all candidates for the position. These questions are known as "bona fide occupational qualification (BFOQ) questions." BFOQ questions should be about skills, training, education, work experience, physical attributes, and personality traits. With rare exceptions, questions should not be about age, gender, race, religion, physical appearance, disabilities, ethnic group, or citizenship.

Even with carefully planned BFOQ questions, employers will occasionally pose questions to interviewees that are intentionally or unintentionally illegal. For example, an employer might ask, "Are you married?" or "How old are your children?" when, in fact, he or she should really ask, "Is there anything that would prevent you from being able to travel frequently?" Often, illegal questions are unintentionally asked by untrained interviewers who are trying to be polite. In any circumstance you must carefully consider how to respond to the illegal question(s), using one or more of these strategies:

1. *Weigh the severity of the violation against your desire for the job.* If you really want the job and the violation was minor, you may opt to provide a short answer or tactfully try to rephrase the question to avoid being forced to provide irrelevant information.

2. *Ask for clarification.* If you suspect that the illegal question is actually attempting to reference a BFOQ for the job, you can clarify what skills, knowledge, or attitudes the interviewer is attempting to assess.

3. *Be assertive.* You can tell the interviewer that the question is not related to the attributes specified in the job description or that the question, as phrased, asks for information you do not have to provide. A less aggressive option is to politely decline to answer the question as phrased.

4. *Report the violation.* If the interviewer continues to ask illegal questions or is otherwise offensive, you might consider reporting the violation to a superior and/or to the federal Equal Employment Opportunity Commission (www.eeoc.gov) or a similar state agency.

THE POSTINTERVIEW STAGE

Most interviews end with some plan for future action on the part of both the interviewee and the interviewer. The interviewer will typically explain the criteria for selection as well as a time frame for the decision. As an interviewee, make certain you carry out appropriate responsibilities, including writing to reconfirm your interest in the position and thanking the interviewer for his or her time. Be prepared to deal with various interview outcomes.

A letter of appreciation is appropriate after an interview and should be sent within one or two days following the interview. If a company has been corresponding with you using e-mail, then you should send an e-mail thank-you letter. If you are still interested in the position, express that interest in the letter. If you are not interested, a letter is still appropriate for withdrawing your candidacy.

After the employment interview you may receive a job offer. Making a final decision about accepting a job involves careful consideration of multiple pieces of information. Here are tips for conducting negotiations with your potential employer and making a final decision:

1. *Wait for the appropriate time.* The interview is not the ideal place to discuss salary expectations and other points of negotiation. In the interview you have little bargaining power. Once the company makes an offer, you are *in demand* and have a better chance of negotiating various items.

2. *Know what you want in advance.* Once you have been offered the job, you should immediately be prepared to begin the negotiation process. Conduct research to determine common salary ranges for your type of position. Online salary databases, such as www.salary.com, provide national and regional salary profiles for different types of jobs. Depending on the type of position, you may also be able to negotiate moving expenses, the start date, continuing education funding, and other types of benefits.

3. *Understand the implications of taking the job.* If the job requires moving, you may want to investigate the living expenses of the new community. Try using Sperling's Cost of Living Calculator, at www.bestplaces.net/col, to compare where you live now with the place you will live if you accept the job.

4. *Get it in writing.* Be aware that a job offer and your acceptance of it are legally binding documents. Take care to ensure that all negotiated items are included in the offer letter, and do not write an acceptance letter until you have a correct offer letter in hand.

5. *Be tactful in your response.* Regardless of whether you are accepting or declining the job offer, your official response should be professional. If you accept the position, your acceptance letter should thank the interviewer and formally state that you are accepting the position as described in the offer letter. If you decline the offer, you should state your reason(s) for not accepting the offer, explicitly decline the offer, and end on a pleasant note.

What Communication Skills Will You Need on the Job?

Previous sections of this chapter provided you with general information about organizations and taught you the skills necessary for obtaining a job. This section emphasizes skills relevant to your role as an employee or organizational member. We begin by identifying several behaviors representing competent workplace communication and then discuss specific skills, such as conflict management and customer service effectiveness.

COMPETENT WORKPLACE COMMUNICATION

Previous chapters stressed the importance of verbal and nonverbal communication, perception, and listening. Clearly, the ability to perceive accurately, use verbal and nonverbal symbols with precision, and listen carefully are skills that benefit workplace communicators. Let us consider four specific behaviors that are important in the workplace: immediacy, supportiveness, strategic ambiguity, and interaction management.

IMMEDIACY

immediacy
Communication behaviors intended to create perceptions of psychological closeness with others.

When people engage in communication behaviors intended to create perceptions of psychological closeness with others, they are enacting **immediacy.** Immediacy can be both verbal and nonverbal. Smiling, reducing physical distance, and using animated gestures and facial expressions are all examples of nonverbally immediate behaviors, whereas calling people by their first names, using "we" language, and telling stories are examples of verbal immediacy behaviors. Using immediacy has been shown to have positive effects in the workplace. For instance, it can improve the relationship between supervisors and subordinates[26] and encourage people to engage in higher levels of self-disclosure.[27] In sales situations, higher levels of self-disclosure can be helpful, because they create more rapport between the salesperson and the customer, and the salesperson can learn valuable information that gives a product or service more value for that customer.

supportive communication
Listening with empathy, acknowledging others' feelings, and engaging in dialogue to help others maintain a sense of personal control.

■ Professional touch, such as a handshake, can help establish immediacy between people.

Supportiveness

People engage in **supportive communication** when they listen with empathy, acknowledge the feelings of others, and engage in dialogue to help others maintain a sense of personal control. Of course, supportive communication is an important skill in any context, including workplace settings. Research reviewed by Hopkins suggests that supportive supervisor communication is one of the most significant factors influencing employee morale.[28] To enhance your supportive communication skills, consider the following strategies adapted from Albrecht and Bach's discussion of supportive communication:

1. *Listen without judging.* Being judgmental while listening to a co-worker's explanation of a problem can cause you to lose your focus on what he or she is really saying.

2. *Validate feelings.* Even if you disagree with something your co-workers say, validating their perceptions and feelings is an important step in building a trusting relationship.

3. *Provide both informational and relational messages.* Supportive communication involves both helping and healing messages. Providing a metaphorical "shoulder to cry on" is equally as important as providing suggestions and advice.

4. *Be confidential.* When co-workers share feelings and personal reflections with you, maintaining their trust and confidence is essential. Telling others or gossiping about the issue will destroy your credibility as a trustworthy co-worker.[29]

Strategic Ambiguity

When learning to be competent communicators, we often assume that being competent always means being clear. Eisenberg disagrees with this assumption and points out that clarity is essential for competent communication only when clear communication is the objective of the communicator.[30] Professional and workplace communication often features the use of **strategic ambiguity**—the purposeful use of symbols to allow multiple interpretations of messages. You have probably witnessed instances of strategic ambiguity on your college campus. At the beginning of each year, various student organizations undertake recruitment drives to gain new members. When presenting their organization, whether a student club or a Greek organization, members are often strategically ambiguous about some aspect of it. After all, recruiting would be difficult if we knew there were really only a few members or there were significant political infighting in the club. When you enter the workforce, you will encounter new examples of strategic ambiguity. During orientation, for example, you might learn about your new company's mission statement. Such mission statements are often strategically ambiguous, so that all stakeholders (employees, managers, owners, and so on) can find relevant meaning in them. Of course, competent communicators must not only be skillful in recognizing the use of strategic ambiguity but also be able to use it themselves when necessary.

strategic ambiguity
The purposeful use of symbols to allow multiple interpretations of messages.

Interaction Management

Workplace communication is somewhat different from other types of communication situations because conversations tend to flow between the technical jargon associated with the workplace and other topics brought up to relieve stress and pass time. Thus, computer technicians might talk about megabytes and megapixels one minute and speculate about who will be voted off *Survivor* the next. Competent workplace communicators engage in **interaction management** to establish a smooth pattern of interaction that allows a clear flow between topics and ideas. Using pauses, changing pitch, carefully listening to the topics being discussed, and responding appropriately are skills related to interaction management.

interaction management
Establishing a smooth pattern of interaction that allows a clear flow between topics and ideas.

Being an effective communicator with co-workers and clients requires carefully observing how they prefer to talk. Recognizing that one co-worker always talks about technical matters related to the job, whereas another always likes to chit-chat about family, is important; adapting your conversational style to the different styles of these individuals will help you fit in more easily. If you aspire to managerial positions in your company, the ability to communicate well with various individuals is critical.

CROSS-CULTURAL SKILLS

The changing nature of the U.S. workplace makes it increasingly a cross-cultural setting. If you speak English as a second language, emphasize these skills initially to aid your transition to the workplace. Because you have both a new language and a new set of technical terms to learn in your workplace, questions are the most effective strategy for avoiding misunderstanding. Ask more of them to clarify instructions or expectations, and

■ Cross-cultural skills are necessary in today's global economy.

pay careful attention to your co-workers. By observing them and asking questions if necessary, you can learn not only important vocabulary but also skills for interacting with customers or clients. Finally, keeping a journal of your daily activities is a good idea. The first few days and weeks may seem overwhelming, but you will learn a great deal. Keeping a journal can help you retain vocabulary, directions, and other important pieces of information more easily.

If you are a native speaker who works with a second-language speaker, you will also have to adapt your communication behaviors. You can help ease your co-worker's transition through some relatively easy steps. First, provide important directions, policies, and procedures in writing. Second-language speakers often find written information easier to process because the pace of spoken language can be challenging. Second, take time to explain. You can help your co-worker(s) learn vocabulary and interaction skills more quickly if you take a few moments to explain how and why you communicate the way you do. Finally, be patient. Becoming impatient and frustrated will introduce new problems and make the situation worse for everyone. Patience makes the transition easier and will likely prevent problems from recurring.

CONFLICT MANAGEMENT SKILLS

Communicating in organizations is not an easy task. In fact, a pervasive part of organizational life is conflict—both destructive and productive. Destructive conflict can destroy work relationships, whereas productive conflict can create a needed impetus for organizational change and development. Workplace conflict can occur because of mundane issues, such as one person playing a radio too loudly in her cubicle, or serious issues, such as office politics pitting one faction of employees against another. Indeed, conflict management skills are not just desirable but necessary for effective workplace communication.

People often view conflict negatively because they associate it with anger. However, conflict occurs anytime two or more people have goals they perceive to be incompatible. When one employee wants to work late to finish a joint project and another wants to go home to be with his or her family, conflict can occur. In short, workplace conflict is a fact of life—the rule rather than the exception.

You can use a variety of techniques to manage conflict productively. Wilmot and Hocker suggest several approaches:

collaborative style
Thoughtful negotiation and reasoned compromise.

- *Avoidance.* With the avoidance style, you deny the existence of conflict. Although avoidance can provide you with time to think through a situation, continued avoidance allows conflict to simmer and flare up with more intensity.

- *Competition.* With the competition style, you view conflict as a battle and advance your own interests over those of others. Although the competition style can be necessary when quick decisions must be made or when you are strongly committed to a position, it can also be highly detrimental to your relationships with your co-workers.

- *Compromise.* With a compromise style, you are willing to negotiate away some of your position as long as the other party in the conflict is willing to do the same. Compromise can be an effective strategy because it is a win–win proposition for both parties, but when used too often, it can become a sophisticated form of conflict avoidance.

- *Accommodation.* With the accommodation style, you set aside your views and accept those of others. Accommodation can maintain harmony in relationships, but it is problematic in many situations, because tacit acceptance of others' views can stifle creative dialogue and decision making.

- *Collaboration.* A **collaborative style** relies on thoughtful negotiation and reasoned compromise whereby both parties agree that the negotiated outcome is the best possible alternative under the circumstances. Although collaboration takes more time and effort to enact, it typically results in the best possible outcome for all parties.[31]

sizing things up

Conflict in the Workplace

Workplace contexts create potential for conflict because they force us to accomplish important task outcomes while managing relationships with others. The way we manage conflict can influence how effective we are as organizational communicators. Below you will find several statements; for each one, indicate how well the statement describes you by using the following scale:

1 = Does not describe me at all
2 = Does not describe me very well
3 = Describes me somewhat
4 = Describes me well
5 = Describes me very well

1. When working on problems, I try to win arguments to support my opinion.
2. When communicating at work, I generally let others have their way.
3. If I sense a conflict brewing, I would rather find a way to leave.
4. When in a conflict with a co-worker, I work to find common ground to resolve the conflict.
5. When I disagree with someone, I am willing to give up some of my own position as long as others are willing to do the same.
6. I am quick to give up on my opinion when I sense conflict coming.
7. I am generally willing to meet others halfway to resolve conflict.
8. When in a conflict, my interests are most important.
9. I generally avoid conflict in the workplace.
10. When involved in a conflict, talking things through is the best way to find a solution.
11. I generally resolve conflict by compromising with the other person.
12. I often try to find ways to delay having to face a conflict situation.
13. When in a conflict, having dialogue can often resolve the situation.
14. I tend to give up on my views to resolve conflicts with others.
15. When in a conflict, I approach the other person ready for battle.

There are no right or wrong answers to these questions. A guide for interpreting your responses appears in the appendix at the end of the text (p. 348).

CUSTOMER SERVICE SKILLS

We often hear that we now live in a "service economy," in which U.S. companies increasingly make money by providing services rather than goods. In this kind of business environment, one of the most important forms of external communication occurs in providing service to organizational customers. Bitner, Booms, and Tetreault define the **customer service encounter** as "the moment of interaction between the customer and the firm."[32] During this moment the organizational representative provides professional assistance in exchange for the customer's money or attention.

Customer service means different things to different people. For some it means being friendly, shaking hands warmly, and initiating pleasant conversations with clients. For others, customer service means processing customers efficiently and quickly. Still others view it as listening intently to identify individual needs and providing sufficient information and/or support to meet those needs. All these perspectives are legitimate; however, the *customer* is the ultimate judge of whether customer service interactions are satisfying.

Regardless of how employees understand the concept of customer service, most providers have the goal of influencing their customers' behaviors. An extensive body of research covers communication techniques for gaining compliance. In her book *Communicating with Customers: Service Approaches, Ethics, and Impact*, W. Z. Ford reviews compliance-gaining strategies used by customer service representatives. Her work is summarized in table 9.3.

A wide range of occupations require interactions between employees and clients or customers. In many of these, the provision of service often involves some degree of emotional content.[33] Nurses interact with dying patients in a hospice, ministers counsel troubled parishioners, and social workers help physically abused women. Emotional communication also characterizes other, less obvious occupations. Flight attendants must appear happy and attentive during flights,[34] and bill collectors must remain stern and avoid any trace of sympathy in interactions.[35]

Arlie Hochschild was the first scholar to deal with this phenomenon, in her book *The Managed Heart*.[36] She uses the term **emotional labor** to refer to jobs in which employees are expected to display certain feelings in order to satisfy organizational role

---

customer service encounter
The moment of interaction between the customer and the firm.

emotional labor
Jobs in which employees are expected to display certain feelings in order to satisfy organizational role expectations.

Table 9.3 Compliance-Gaining Strategies Used By Customer Service Representatives

Promise: Promising a reward for compliance (e.g., "If you purchase this car, I'll give you tickets to a football game.")

Threat: Threatening to punish for noncompliance (e.g., "If you don't buy the car before the end of the week, I cannot guarantee the 1 percent interest rate.")

Pre-giving: Rewarding the customer before requesting compliance (e.g., "I will give you $50 just for test-driving this new car.")

Moral appeal: Implying that it is immoral not to comply (e.g., "Since you have small children, you should be looking at our crossover utility model with more safety features.")

Liking: Being friendly and helpful to get the customer in a good frame of mind to ensure compliance (e.g., "Good afternoon; my, how you look nice today. How can I help you?")

Source: Adapted from Ford, W. Z. (1998). *Communicating with customers: Service approaches, ethics, and impact.* Cresskill, NJ: Hampton Press. Used by permission of Hampton Press, Inc.

expectations. Research has indicated that, although emotional labor may be fiscally rewarding for the organization and the client, it can be dangerous for the service provider and can lead to negative consequences, such as burnout, job dissatisfaction, and turnover.[37]

What Ethical Dimensions Are Found in the Workplace?

In this section we are concerned with the ethical dimensions of workplace communication. In particular, we focus on aggressive communication, honesty, and sexual harassment.

AGGRESSIVE COMMUNICATION

Verbal aggressiveness is communication that attacks the self-concepts of other people in order to inflict psychological pain.[38] It is on the rise in organizational settings, though sometimes unrecognized by management. A recent summary of literature on workplace aggression identified the following types:

- *Abusive supervision* occurs when a supervisor engages in sustained behaviors via hostile verbal and nonverbal messages but does not rise to the level of physical aggression.
- *Bullying* occurs when one person is subjected to ridicule, offensive statements, teasing, social isolation, or other abuse by one or more individuals over an extended period of time.
- *Incivility* is frequent rude behavior that may or may not have the intent of being harmful. Uncivil people may or may not know they are being rude.
- *Social undermining* is action meant to socially isolate another person from a larger group. Whereas incivility can occur unwittingly, social undermining is intentional and often planned.[39]

◼ Any problems with workplace aggression should be reported to a trusted manager or a representative of human resources or the appropriate union.

The psychological pain produced by verbal aggression and other aggressive behaviors includes embarrassment, feelings of inadequacy, humiliation, hopelessness, despair, and depression. If you feel you are the victim of workplace aggression, consult a human resources manager, a union representative, or a trusted manager for advice.

HONESTY

High-profile events during the recent economic crisis have underscored the importance of honesty in organizational communication. Specifically, financial institutions were blamed for not being honest when extending risky mortgages to individuals who went on to purchase homes they could not afford. The Occupy Wall Street movement formed in 2011 largely in reaction to the widely perceived dishonesty of financial institutions. Yet other controversies questioned the ethics of corporate executives who took huge bonuses even after their companies had to accept government bailout money in order to survive. Clearly, a widespread lack of honesty and ethics played a large role in eroding consumer confidence during the crisis.

Honesty in communication is not relevant just to top executives, however. Is it appropriate for you to misrepresent information to your supervisor to make your performance appear better? Is it ethical to integrate key words into your résumé so electronic search engines will highlight them, even if you do not truly possess the requisite skills for that job? Amare and Manning observe that individuals at all levels of organizations have a personal responsibility to act with integrity and to be honest.[40] Even deciding with whom you should be honest is important. If you know a fellow employee is underperforming, should you confront your peer first or go straight to your supervisor?

Honesty is at the heart of personal ethics and must begin with open communication and trust. The fears that drive people to dishonest behaviors at work can often be countered by establishing open communication with co-workers.

SEXUAL HARASSMENT

Sexual harassment includes a set of behaviors that constitute workplace aggression. Unfortunately, instances of sexual harassment litter the news. You may recall problems faced by Herman Cain, who sought the Republican nomination for president, after several accusations of sexual harassment against him were discussed in the media. Indeed, sexual harassment has been a problem in the workplace for decades.

What is sexual harassment? The Equal Employment Opportunity Commission (EEOC) defines **sexual harassment** as

> unwelcome sexual advances, requests for sexual favors, and other verbal or physical conduct of a sexual nature if (1) submission to the conduct is made a condition of employment, (2) submission to or rejection of the conduct is made the basis for an employment decision, or (3) the conduct seriously affects an employee's work performance or creates an intimidating, hostile, or offensive working environment.

sexual harassment
Unwelcome, unsolicited, repeated behavior of a sexual nature.

quid pro quo sexual harassment
A situation in which an employee is offered a reward or is threatened with punishment based on his or her participation in a sexual activity.

hostile work environment sexual harassment
Conditions in the workplace that are sexually offensive, intimidating, or hostile and that affect an individual's ability to perform his or her job.

Simply put, sexual harassment is unwelcome, unsolicited, repeated behavior of a sexual nature.

The EEOC definition outlines two different, although sometimes overlapping, types of sexual harassment. The first type, **quid pro quo sexual harassment,** occurs when an employee is offered a reward or is threatened with punishment based on his or her participation in a sexual activity. For example, a supervisor might tell her employee, "I'll give you Friday off if you meet me at my place tonight." The second type is **hostile work environment sexual harassment,** or conditions in the workplace that are sexually offensive, intimidating, or hostile and that affect an individual's ability to perform his or her job. For example, if two males talk explicitly about the physical features of a female colleague in her presence, sexual harassment has occurred.

A major obstacle to ending sexual harassment is the tendency of victims to avoid confronting the harasser. Most instances of sexual harassment are neither exposed nor reported. Instead, the victim usually avoids the situation by taking time off, transferring to another area, or changing jobs. The perpetrator is usually someone in the organization with authority and status—with power over the victim—and the victim feels exposure or confrontation will backfire.

Clearly, the EEOC's definition indicates that a wide range of communication behaviors can constitute sexual harassment, although many men and women see only serious offenses (for example, career benefits in exchange for sexual favors) as harassment. However, although harassment is judged by its effects on the victim, not on the intentions of the harasser, a person need not suffer severe psychological or work outcomes to be a victim. The courts use the "reasonable person rule" to determine whether a reasonable person would find the behavior in question offensive. One limitation of this rule, however, is evidence that men and women view sexual harassment differently.[41] In particular, sexual overtures that women typically view as insulting are viewed by men, in general, as flattering.

Sexual harassment is a serious and pervasive communication problem in modern organizational life, with both the victims and the perpetrators (and even falsely accused perpetrators) suffering personal and professional anguish. Note that, even though in a majority of cases women are victims, the EEOC guidelines apply equally to men.

keeping it real

Listening and Responding in the Workplace

At the beginning of this chapter you read a short story about Rex, the intern struggling with the duties of a new job. Although the story ended with Rex succeeding in his job, what strategies did Carlos, Rex's supervisor, likely use?

1. *Listening.* Through daily interaction, Carlos could have noticed that Rex was struggling. Although perhaps Rex did not say that there were problems, his nonverbal behaviors and unsure statements could have clued Carlos in to the fact that Rex was not mastering the terminology and other aspects of the job.

2. *Opening communication.* Carlos was the supervisor and had the ability to engage in downward communication with Rex—"This is how you will do your job." By talking with Rex in a less formal setting after work, Carlos was able to get Rex to engage in upward communication to describe the areas that were most challenging.

3. *Being immediate.* Through less formal conversation, Carlos was likely able to build rapport with Rex, so that there was trust. Rex likely became less apprehensive about his job and more motivated to succeed as a result.

Being a supervisor can be difficult. However, competent communication approaches by Carlos helped Rex succeed, and likely resulted in more effective training practices for the company. Effective workplace communication translates into results.

Chapter Review & Study Guide

Summary

In this chapter, you learned the following:

1. Workplace communication takes place within the context of an organization.

   - Organizations are generally classified as having one of four primary functions in society: economic production, political participation, integration, and pattern maintenance.

   - Communication within organizations follows networks. These networks provide for formal communication flow, including upward communication, downward communication, and horizontal communication. Networks also allow informal, or "grapevine," communication.

2. Written credentials for employment interviews include a cover letter and résumé.

   - A cover letter, whether in written form or attached to e-mail, should persuasively establish your qualifications in relation to the job description.

   - The résumé should be concise and stylistically reflect your personality in a professional way.

   - Your résumé should highlight your work qualifications and experiences.

   - Certain professions may require a professional portfolio to illustrate your mastery of key skills.

3. Effective strategies for preparing for a job interview include creating a self-inventory, creating networks, searching for a job, investigating the interviewer, being prepared to ask and answer questions, and conducting postinterview negotiations.

4. Four communication skills will help you succeed in the workplace.

   - Communication competence in the workplace involves using immediacy, supportive communication, strategic ambiguity, and interaction management.

   - Conflict management approaches include avoidance, competition, compromise, accommodation, and collaboration. Each approach may have utility in specific situations; however, the collaborative approach works best in most situations.

- Cross-cultural understanding requires that you act with sensitivity toward those who are different, including those who do not speak your language well.

- Customer service interaction skills include using compliance-gaining strategies with customers while engaging in emotional labor.

5. Unethical workplace communication includes aggressive communication and sexual harassment.

- Workplace aggression occurs when individuals intentionally or unintentionally use verbal or nonverbal aggressive behaviors toward others.

- Sexual harassment is the abuse of power involving either quid pro quo harassment or a hostile work environment.

Key Terms

Chronological résumé
Collaborative style
Communication networks
Cover letter
Customer service encounter
Downward communication
Economic orientation
Emotional labor
Formal communication
Functional résumé

Horizontal communication
Hostile work environment sexual
    harassment
Immediacy
Informal communication
Integration orientation
Interaction management
Job description
Objective statement
Organizational communication

Organizational communities
Organizations
Pattern-maintenance orientation
Personal network
Political orientation
Quid pro quo sexual harassment
Sexual harassment
Strategic ambiguity
Supportive communication
Upward communication

Study Questions

1. An organization with this orientation generates and distributes power and control within society.
   a. economic
   b. pattern-maintenance
   c. political
   d. integration

2. Information flows in an organization through patterns of relationships known as
   a. communication networks.
   b. organizational communication.
   c. objective statements.
   d. pattern-maintenance.

3. When information is transferred formally between a worker and his or her boss, which type of communication takes place?
   a. horizontal
   b. political
   c. societal
   d. upward

4. Which of the following is a true statement regarding written credentials?
   a. The objective statement is usually the last bit of information on the résumé.
   b. The cover letter is a document that organizes credentials by type of function performed.
   c. An effective résumé contains good style, content, and format.
   d. The only way to organize your résumé is chronologically.

5. When preparing for and taking part in an interview, you should
   a. dress a bit more casually than you expect the interviewer to dress.
   b. ignore the job description, because the interviewer will tell you about the job's duties.
   c. avoid using strong eye contact.
   d. ask and answer questions effectively and ethically.

6. By smiling, gesturing, and using facial expressions in the workplace to create perceptions of psychological closeness with others, you are enacting
   a. immediacy.
   b. management.
   c. ambiguity.
   d. preparation.

7. Which technique of conflict management is used to maintain relationship harmony but to stifle creative dialogue and decision making?
   a. compromise
   b. accommodation
   c. avoidance
   d. collaboration

connect For further review, go to the LearnSmart study module for this chapter.

8. Customer service representatives may use which of the following compliance-gaining strategies, in which the representative implies that it is immoral not to comply?

    a. promises
    b. threats
    c. pre-giving
    d. moral appeals

9. Conflict in the workplace can be

    a. destructive.
    b. productive.
    c. neither a nor b.
    d. both a and b.

10. If your boss tells you that you can leave work early on Fridays if you go on a date with him or her, he or she is utilizing a type of sexual harassment called

    a. quid pro quo sexual harassment.
    b. hostile work environment sexual harassment.
    c. emotional labor.
    d. nothing; it is not sexual harassment.

Answers:

1. (c); 2. (a); 3. (d); 4. (c); 5. (d); 6. (a); 7. (b); 8. (d); 9. (d); 10. (a)

Critical Thinking

1. Search online for sample résumés. Based on the text, identify what the creator did correctly and what he or she could improve upon. Focus on the résumé's style, content, and format.

2. Think about some of your past jobs. In the workplace did people display immediacy, supportiveness, strategic ambiguity, or interaction management? What did they do to demonstrate these behaviors? What conflict management skills did your supervisors use? Were they successful?

topic selection
and audience analysis

When you have read and thought about this chapter, you will be able to:

1. Select a topic appropriate for you and your audience.

2. Practice narrowing a topic to save time and energy and increase its relevance to the audience.

3. Analyze your audience through observation, inference, research, and questionnaires.

4. Adapt your topic, yourself, your language, and your purpose for an audience.

How do you choose what to speak about? Many speakers get stuck on this first step in creating a speech and spend way too much time trying to decide on a topic. They have too many choices and cannot settle on just one. So this chapter will help you to more quickly determine what topics are important to you and to your audience, how to more rapidly narrow the focus so you do not waste time by exploring too many avenues, and how to accurately analyze the audience to make sure they will care about what you have to say. Your ability to effectively inform or persuade an audience rests on your skill in selecting an appropriate topic and in adapting that topic to the particular audience. Once you have mastered these skills for your classroom audience, you can apply them at work and in the community.

Stephen Bonsi, an international student from West Africa, was truly surprised when he did not earn a higher grade on his persuasive speech, but his story reveals the importance of topic selection and audience analysis.

Stephen did some things right. He loved politics and economics, so he had a vital topic. He was engaged in some protests over wealth inequality, so he had interest and commitment. He knew much about economics, so his speech was loaded with details about "waves of regulations," "financial time bombs," and "huge mortgage derivatives." He pitted Wall Street against Main Street and waxed eloquent about the pitfalls of joblessness. Moreover, his persuasive purpose was an action goal of urging his audience to join the protest movement against the top 1% in wealth. But Stephen had trouble with topic selection and audience analysis.

His audience, about 20 students from nearly as many different programs, knew practically nothing about economics, cared little about politics, and were the opposite of activist. They had more immediate things to worry about: paying for school, keeping a job, caring for kids, and paying for food and lodging. More importantly, Stephen's speech went way over their heads. He knew so much about economics and politics that little of what he said was actually understood. A speech that would have been a hit in a room full of political activists who knew more about economics was a failure in this particular classroom.

Have you ever had a similar experience? What could Stephen have done to choose a more appropriate topic and adapt it to his audience? What would you suggest? At the end of the chapter, we'll take another look at Stephen's situation.

You can skillfully avoid being a failure with your presentation just by learning in this chapter about the basics of topic selection and audience analysis, two concepts that are bonded in any successful presentation. In this chapter you will learn some quick and effective ways to arrive at a topic without wasting time and effort. You will also learn in this chapter how to size up your audience so you successfully inform and persuade them.

How to Select a Topic Appropriate for You and Your Audience

Finding a topic that is right for you and for your audience can be a challenge. Some speakers spend far too little time finding a suitable topic and end up speaking on something that audience members cannot connect with; others spend too long searching for topics, get forced into making a last-minute decision, and sacrifice valuable preparation time. Although you should devote adequate attention to thoughtful topic selection, this step should require only a small amount of your speech preparation time. This section explores some strategies for making an efficient and effective choice, beginning with two ways to quickly generate a list of ideas.

USE BRAINSTORMING

brainstorming
A creative procedure for thinking of as many topics as you can in a limited time.

Brainstorming consists of thinking of as many topics as you can in a limited time so you can select one that will be appropriate for you and your audience. Individual brainstorming (brainstorming by yourself as opposed to in a group) can be an effective way to find a topic for your public speech, reports, and term papers. Selecting a topic from a list of many that you've generated through brainstorming can be much easier than trying to think of just one perfect idea.

You'll find individual brainstorming to be relatively quick and easy. First, give yourself a limited time—say, five minutes—and without trying to think of titles or even complete thoughts, write down as many potential topics as you can. When your time is up, you should have a rough list of possible ideas or topics for your speech. Repeat this step if you want an even larger list.

Second, select the *three* items from your list that are the most appealing to you as topics for your speech. Third, from those three topics choose the *one* you think would be most appealing to both you and your audience. An alternate strategy, which we look at next, is to target your own interests as possible topics.

SURVEY YOUR INTERESTS

Public speaking starts with the self—with what you know, have experienced, or are willing to learn. Self-analysis can help you uncover the areas in which you are qualified to speak.

To survey your interests, consider the following:

- What you like best and least at work, about family life, about your community, and about our government, politics, and policies
- What causes take up your time and energy: your religion, your political party, and your position on important current issues
- What particular issues bother you personally that you want to bring to the attention of others: discrimination, environmental concerns, and healthcare, for example

How do you select from among the topics that emerge through your brainstorming or a survey of your interests? First consider what you know and how you feel about the topic.

ASSESS YOUR KNOWLEDGE OF THE TOPIC

Once you have established that your topic is interesting to you and to your audience, you need to determine what you and your audience know about the subject. You are in the best position if you know more about the topic than does your audience. You can also add to what you know by talking to others, reading, and visiting websites on the subject. Let's say you really think that something a politician said was far from true, yet your hear classmates saying the same untrue statement. You can check up on the truth or accuracy of a politician's speech by going to a fact-check website like the ones in table 10.1.

commitment
A measure of how much time and effort you put into a cause; your passion and concern about the topic.

skill builder

Using the Internet to Increase Your Knowledge of the Topic

You can find information about any topic by using Google or another search engine and appropriate key words. Table 10.1 lists examples of a few sources on just two topic areas—health and politics. Choose two or three sites that look interesting to you, go to those sites, and see if you can find and write down in your notebook one surprising fact that you learn from each of the sites. Your reason for doing this exercise all on your own is to demonstrate your skill in finding information and determining which information is worth telling others.

EVALUATE YOUR COMMITMENT TO THE TOPIC

Even a topic about which you're well informed is not a good choice for a presentation unless you feel some commitment to it. **Commitment** is a measure of how much

Table 10.1 Internet Sources for Health and Politics

Health

www.cnn.com/HEALTH/   Information on diet, fitness, and parenting; special feature: video clips

www.webmd.com/   Health and medical news and information

www.healthfinder.gov/   Health and human services from the U.S. government; special feature: leads to online publications

http://dir.yahoo.com/Health/   Human health, diseases, medicine, sexual health, fitness, and nutrition

Politics

www.factcheck.org/   A website sponsored by the Annenberg Public Policy Center to check on the accuracy of political statements in ads, debates, and speeches

www.cnn.com/POLITICS/   Cable News Network's political section, a middle-of-the-road, national perspective

www.nytimes.com/pages/politics/index.html   News, opinions, and multimedia about political campaigns and elections from an East Coast, liberal perspective

www.latimes.com/news/politics/   Political news and information on elected officials and candidates with an emphasis on West Coast and national government

www.politico.com/   A widely respected website on politics from D.C.; go to POLITICO (@politico) for Twitter

time and effort you put into a cause. For example, you know many children are waiting to be adopted; you deeply want more people to be concerned about heart disease and cancer because your relatives died from these diseases; or you want less government interference in our personal lives. You spend time and effort on what you care about, so those causes can guide you to select an ideal topic for you and your audience.

Be aware, however, that commitment to a topic may not be enough to overcome poor preparation. One of us, along with a colleague, conducted a study exploring whether commitment to a topic is related to speech performance and found it was not—the strongest predictor of speech performance is actually the work put into preparation.[1] Although you may need to be committed to a topic to put in adequate preparation for a speech, commitment may not be enough to help you deliver an effective presentation.

CONSIDER THE AGE OF THE TOPIC AND OF THE AUDIENCE

Topics, like people, live, change, and die—some have long and varied lives, whereas others pass on quickly. You will want to consider the age and development of your subject matter, as well as the age and development of your audience. Some topics have endured for decades, if not centuries:

- How much should government be allowed to intervene in our lives?
- Should the United States use military force to promote democracy?
- What can and should we do for the poor and marginalized in our society?
- What can and should we do about the privileged and overrewarded in our society?
- Should concern for the environment limit our exploration for oil?

Even very young people have probably heard plenty about many long-standing issues, although more mature audiences, including returning college students, are likely to have more sophisticated ideas about them. Younger audiences may have less hardened positions, however. What all this means is that groups of different ages can be treated differently. You will also want to treat mature topics in new ways, not just rehash what the audience has heard repeatedly in the past. The effective presenter takes into account both the age of the issue and the age of the audience and skillfully adapts the topic to the particular audience for maximum effect.

In fact, here are some suggestions that can keep you on track to success because violating these three suggestions has resulted in poor evaluations for students who ignore them.

social media
make it matter

Using Blogs in Topic Research

To find specific information and some unique sources for your topic, take a close look at blog sites. You can find them by going to a blog directory, such as www.blogtopsites.com. Select a particular area—for instance, "environment"—and you will usually find hundreds of blog sites that reveal specific information about topics such as "living green."

Take care to evaluate the information you find in blogs—some blogs are more reliable than others and better at revealing the source of material presented as fact. And as always, remember to reveal in your speech where you found your information.

1. Stick to vital topics; do not select a trivial topic. You might find fascinating the making of a leather belt, but the topic is neither vital nor necessarily of interest to a general audience.

2. Beware of overused topics—unless you have a novel approach. Gun control and abortion are important topics, but unless you have something new to offer, your teacher and your audience may be bored by hearing more on the topic.

3. Do not demonstrate with visual resources that are banned on campus, such as firearms, illegal drugs, and alcohol.

We turn next from commitment and avoidable topics to determining your audience's interest in a topic.

DETERMINE YOUR TOPIC'S IMPORTANCE TO YOUR AUDIENCE

Once you have selected a possible topic, evaluate whether it is important to your audience. First, you have the advantage of hearing every speech your classmates deliver, so their topic selections give you a good idea of what they think are important subjects. Second, you are in a college context where important issues arise about student rights and the costs of tuition, books, food, and lodging; and often guest speakers come on campus to address issues of interest to college students. Third, your college exists in a community where issues occur between town and gown: noise ordinances, parking restrictions, housing and zoning regulations, slumlords, and overpriced housing. Fourth, you can be among the few who actually know about the larger context to national and international issues that can affect students whether they know it or not. So you can be among the first to warn them of issues such as recessions, employment trends, interest rates, and new legislation that will affect them now or in the near future. The importance of a topic, then, can be as close to home as another student's speech or as far as financial failure in a distant land, as long as you can relate that topic by demonstrating its importance to your audience.

■ Effective speakers know their subject.

TOPIC SELECTION FOR ESL SPEAKERS

Topic selection can be even more challenging for students who speak English as a second language, because different cultures may have quite different norms about what may be discussed in public, about the appropriate use and meaning of silence or long pauses, and about the desirability of looking at your audience when you speak. In this section we provide various suggestions for non-native speakers to keep in mind when selecting a topic.

1. *Draw on personal experience.* Because U.S. culture values individuality, people's unique personal experiences are often viewed as important layers of an explanation or argument, and U.S. speakers are usually quite comfortable about revealing personal experiences to an audience. You may or may not be as comfortable talking about yourself, but while you should also use other types of support to document your speech, selecting a topic with which you have personal experience, and therefore credibility, is often wise.

2. *Review many sample topics.* To get a sense of what types of topics other students are likely to select, review as many sample topics as possible, using this textbook, resources from your library, and an Internet search for "speech topics." You can then adapt your own topic ideas to be consistent with these samples in scope, focus, and viewpoint if necessary.

3. *Consult with your instructor.* Your instructor is your most valuable resource for topic selection. The best approach is to brainstorm three to five topic ideas and meet with your instructor to discuss the advantages and disadvantages of each. You should also talk to your instructor about how to appropriately narrow your chosen topic.

4. *Remember that smaller is better.* If reading material quickly is difficult for you, you might benefit from selecting topics that are narrower in focus. Narrower topics are easier to research and probably easier to organize. Better to talk about only the ecology of the Amazon River than to try to discuss the environment of all of Brazil.

Practice Narrowing Your Topic

Even after thinking about their topic's importance and their own knowledge and commitment, beginning presenters often select a topic that is too large for their time limit. Animal cruelty, buying a car, and overcoming an addiction may meet the requirements of importance, knowledge, and commitment, but they are too broad. They will produce hundreds of sources on the Internet, giving you much more information than you can manage. If you take the time to carefully narrow a topic *before* you begin your search for additional information, you can save much time and even more frustration. Figure 10.1 shows concept mapping, one way to narrow your topic.

Another way to narrow a topic is to take a broad and even abstract category, such as music, and list as many smaller topics as you can that are at least loosely related to it:

- The development of country/western music
- The influence of Les Paul's guitar on rock and blues
- Rap artists
- Music therapy
- Indie's influence on niche music
- Elementary music education
- The history of the electric guitar
- Hip-hop artists as role models

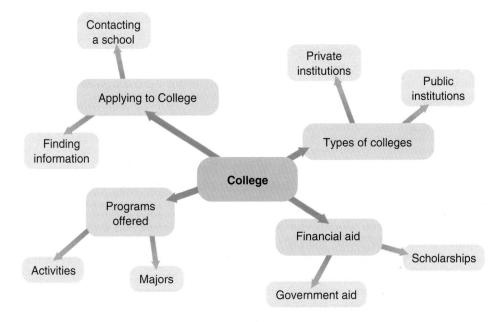

A student can narrow a speech topic down by using an approach called *concept mapping*. Starting with the general topic of college, she is able to visually identify four subtopics: applying to college, types of colleges, programs offered, and financial aid. Each subtopic is further broken down into more specific areas. Visually mapping the topic-narrowing step in this way can help you see important dimensions of a particular topic area as well as connections between several dimensions of the topic.

> **Figure 10.1**
>
> Selecting and narrowing a topic.

Extend your list of more specific and concrete topics until you have a large number from which to choose.

How will you know when your topic is narrow enough? Consider (1) the amount of information available about it, (2) the amount of information you can convey within the time limits for the speech, and (3) whether you can discuss the topic in enough depth to keep audience members interested.

Still another approach is to look at the examples of successful topics in table 10.2. These topics are called "successful" because they have currency, they are related to some issues of national importance, and they are relatively easy to link to listeners' interests. For example, the topic "Ditch Your Bank" is a national issue that can easily affect people in your audience. When federal legislation lowered bank profits by limiting how much

Table 10.2 Possible Presentation Topics

Ditch Your Bank	Successful Job Hunting
Foodborne Illnesses	Keeping Drugs Out of Sports
Pawn with Care	Beware of Paycheck Loans
Why Tuition Keeps Rising	Costs of Insurance

banks can charge merchants for customers who use debit cards, the banks struck back by trying and sometimes failing to impose other fees, such as a fee for having a checking account.[2] People responded so negatively that some of the biggest U.S. banks had to back off their decision and rescind the new fees.[3] But other fees for not using your account, for using a teller, for requesting a canceled check, or for using an ATM remain. So, the "Ditch Your Bank" topic is current and relates directly to anyone who uses a bank. The other topics on the list are similarly related to current concerns and linked to audience interests.

Analyze Your Audience with Observation, Inference, Research, and Questionnaires

audience analysis
The collection and interpretation of audience information obtained by observation, inferences, research, and questionnaires.

Audience analysis is the collection and interpretation of audience characteristics through observation, inference, research, and questionnaires. Why should you analyze your audience? Especially, why should you analyze an audience of classmates?

Suppose you are giving a speech arguing that a state should not take away an individual's right to belong to a union. To give an effective presentation you should know not only state law (some states prohibit unions by denying workers the right to strike) but also how most of the individuals in your audience feel about unionization. If they agree with your view, you will probably take a different persuasive approach than if they disagree. If you plan to inform audience members about the use of performance-enhancing drugs in sports, you will want to know whether any of them have played organized sports, because this activity might have given them personal experience of such drugs, which will influence their attitudes about your information. In both cases you must use audience analysis to learn about your audience members' beliefs and backgrounds; such information will be invaluable as you select, focus, and narrow your topic.

Audience analysis for public speaking is similar to target marketing in advertising and public relations. The process can be as simple as "eyeballing" a group to estimate age, sex, and race or as complicated as polling a group of people to discover their feelings on your topic. The insights you gain about the people to whom you speak will ensure that your speech is as effective as possible.

Next we examine three methods of analyzing an audience. They are based on your observations of the audience, your inferences, and your questions and their answers.

skill builder

Sizing Up Your Audience

Some people are much better than others at sizing up an audience. Check out your own skill at analyzing an audience by inferring audience characteristics. For example, what is the approximate range in age, what cultures are represented, how many wear attire or symbols that indicate their religion, how many wear athletic jackets and letters, do any have the names of fraternities or sororities on their clothing, and do any wear uniforms that indicate armed forces or the kind of work they do? Perhaps your instructor will allow you to check the accuracy of your inferences if classmates are willing to reveal some of this information.

METHOD 1: OBSERVATION

Effective public speakers must engage in active observation, using their senses of sight, hearing, smell, and touch to build information about their audience. An effective lawyer observes jurors' verbal and nonverbal behavior and decides which arguments, evidence, and witnesses are influencing them. Activists and fundraisers have usually spent years watching others and learning which approaches, arguments, and evidence are most likely to be accepted by an audience.

You can learn to observe your class. For every speech you give, you might listen to 20 or 25 given by others, each of which gives you a unique opportunity to discover your classmates' responses. Do they respond well to speakers who come on strong or to speakers who talk to them as equals? Do they like speeches about work, leisure, or ambition? Do they respond well to numbers and statistics, stories and examples, graphs and posters, or PowerPoint and Prezi? Even though your classroom audience may not have gathered just to hear you, you have an advantage over most public speakers: after all, how many of them have had the opportunity to hear every one of their listeners give a speech? Your classmates' responses to a variety of speakers, topics, and visual resources will give you a rich base of information about this audience, which you can use to your advantage when it is your turn to speak.

social media
make it matter

Adapting to Your Social Media Audience

New media and cutting-edge technology have already made you an expert of sorts in audience analysis. You have a Facebook profile that attracts people you like, who become your friends. You have a cell phone so smart that its GPS always knows where you are, and its instant messaging feature allows for quick words among friends, colleagues, and relatives. Even a blog is a site for creating messages to attract an audience. You are already sizing up others to become part of your "audience"—or not.

You can use new media and new technology to sharpen your skill in audience analysis by considering how Facebook and blogs invite you to present both yourself and your message to an audience. You might be a party animal on Facebook or a political junkie on a blog, but just as in public speaking, you are adapting yourself and your message for others.

METHOD 2: INFERENCE

To draw an **inference** is to make a tentative generalization based on some evidence. We infer from a man's wedding band that he is married, and from the children tugging at his sleeve that he is a father. We infer that the woman holding his arm is his wife. We are basing these inferences on thin data, but they are probably (though not infallibly) correct. The more evidence on which an inference is based, the more likely it is to be accurate.

inference
A tentative generalization based on some evidence.

You can base inferences on the observed characteristics of your audience, on demographic information, and on information obtained from questionnaires (discussed later in this section). An **indirect inference** is one we draw by observation. You might, for example, find that most of the students at a particular college hold part-time jobs (an observation). You might further infer that the school is expensive, that financial aid is limited, or that the cost of area housing is high. You might also infer, from your limited information, that most of the students in this school value their education, are exceptionally well motivated, or believe in saving money.

indirect inference
A tentative generalization based on observation.

A **direct inference** is based on deliberately gathered data. You could, for example, ask either orally or in writing how many students in the class have part- or full-time jobs; how many are married, have families, and/or have grown children; how many plan to become wealthy; whether they were raised in an urban or a rural setting; and how many have strong religious ties. The answers to these questions provide valuable information about your audience. If you plan to deliver a presentation encouraging your audience to join the armed forces, your teacher will likely allow you to ask your classroom full of listeners how many of them have been deployed, have close relatives in the military, or plan to serve in the armed forces someday. Their answers to a simple question or two will certainly give you a head start on informing or persuading them.

direct inference
A tentative generalization based on deliberately gathered data.

METHOD 3: RESEARCH ON YOUR AUDIENCE

When speaking outside the classroom, you can improve your chances of success by carefully researching your audience. That research can include inside informants, others who belong to the group, and an organization's website. Often the best inside informant is the person who invited you to speak to a group. Because you are a successful athlete, a high school asks you to speak at its annual athletic awards banquet. You will want to know from the person who invited you who is going to be in the audience (athletes only, or their parents and friends as well?), where the presentation is going to occur (in a crowded gym, a hotel banquet room?), how long you are expected to speak, and what they would like you to talk about. Similarly if you are asked to speak to a service club, such as Rotary, Kiwanis, or the Lions, you need to ask similar questions.

In addition, you will want to research the organization. Rotary International, for example, is very proud of its efforts to eradicate polio worldwide, Kiwanis is committed to changing the world one child and one community at a time, and the Lions are dedicated to solving vision problems here and around the globe. All three serve others, so your speech about any theme related to helping others is welcome at their meetings. Fortunately, the Internet has made your task of researching your audience much easier because most business, social, and religious groups have websites that detail their purpose. You can adapt your message to their mission.

When speaking in the classroom, the Internet offers considerable information about the characteristics of the first-year class; attitudes, beliefs, and practices of beginning college students; and even the way students spend their time. Many universities provide a deep study of their students that goes beyond surface information, such as the ratio of males to females and the number of international students. For example, Stephens Point University in Wisconsin analyzes its entering class to come up with such interesting details as the fact that a much larger percentage of female students use social networking than do males, but substantially more males play computer games. At many schools, the registrar includes detailed information on the university's website about how many students work, students' scores on standardized entrance tests, the highest education level achieved by their families, and much more. The Internet can be a source of information to help you know your classroom audience.

METHOD 4: THE QUESTIONNAIRE

A more formal way to collect data on which you can base inferences is to ask your audience to fill out a **questionnaire** consisting of written questions developed to obtain demographic and attitudinal information.

questionnaire
A set of written questions developed to obtain demographic and attitudinal information.

Finding Demographic Characteristics

An important step in the process of speech preparation is discovering the audience's demographic characteristics. The term *demographics* means "the characteristics of the people." **Demographic analysis** is the collection and interpretation of data about the characteristics of people: name, age, sex, hometown, year in school, race, major subject, religion, and organizational affiliations. By describing the audience in detail, demographic information can reveal to public speakers the extent to which they will have to adapt themselves and their topics to their listeners.

demographic analysis
The collection and interpretation of data about the characteristics of people.

Seasoned public speakers usually rely heavily on demographic information. Politicians send advance staff ahead to find out how many blue-collar workers, faithful party members, elderly people, union members, and hecklers they are likely to encounter. They consult opinion polls, population studies, and reliable persons in the area to discover the nature of a prospective audience. Conducting a demographic analysis of your class can serve a similar purpose—analysis will help you design a speech better adapted to your audience.

The groups to which your audience members belong, for instance, can signal support for or hostility toward your topic. How can you learn about these groups? Bumper stickers you observe on students' cars can signal your audience's attitudes about gun control, abortion, and political parties. In the classroom, jackets or shirts with slogans, Christian crosses, a Star of David, a Muslim hijab, sorority or fraternity letters, ethnic dress, a VFW or American Legion or Rotary pin, a Harley-Davidson jacket, telltale tattoos—many signs such as these indicate memberships that may also reflect attitudes about topics.

Levi wanted to deliver a persuasive speech on joining a fraternity, so he asked before class one day how many students in the class belonged to a sorority or fraternity. Nobody did. He knew from the outset that he had no support in the audience, but he also knew that he had selected a topic that required persuasion to change the audience's mind about joining fraternities and sororities. He started his speech by addressing some issues that people do not like about Greek organizations: hazing, drinking, and cost. He did not manage to get anyone to join a Greek house as a result of his persuasive effort, but his arguments did make his audience review and possibly revise their thinking about the value of Greek organizations when they found out what a high percentage of business leaders were in such organizations when they were in college. Levi just asked one question of his audience before class; you can do the same or develop a very brief questionnaire. You can gather and summarize demographic information from questions similar to the following:

_____1. I am
    a. a first-year student
    b. a sophomore
    c. a junior
    d. a senior

_____2. I am
    a. 17–21 years old
    b. 22–35 years old
    c. 36–45 years old
    d. over 45

_____3. I am
    a. single
    b. married
    c. divorced or separated
    d. widowed

_____4. I have
    a. no children
    b. one child
    c. two children
    d. more than two children

The audience members do not have to identify themselves by name to provide this information. Keeping the questionnaires anonymous encourages honest answers and does not reduce the value of the information.

Finding Attitudes, Beliefs, and Values

You can also use questionnaires to discern audience attitudes, beliefs, and values on an issue before giving the speech. An **attitude** is a predisposition to respond favorably or unfavorably to a person, an object, an idea, or an event. Attitudes are regarded as quite stable and often difficult to change. You can assess the attitudes of audience members through questionnaires, by careful observation, or even by asking the right questions. If your audience shares many attitudes, beliefs, and values, your audience analysis may be easy. For example, a speech about safe sex would be heard in some colleges with as much excitement as a speech on snails; however, at other colleges even guest speakers are not allowed on campus to talk about that subject.[4] Attitudes toward politics, sexual preference, religion, drugs, and even work vary in

attitude
A predisposition to respond favorably or unfavorably to a person, an object, an idea, or an event.

different geographic areas and cultures. Regardless of the purpose of your speech, the attitudes of audience members will make a difference in the appropriateness of your topic and the way you present it. For this reason effective public speakers learn as much as possible about audience attitudes before they speak. Some examples of attitudes follow:

Antigovernment	Pro-business	Pro-conservation
Anti–gun control	Pro-green	Pro-technology
Antipollution	Pro-choice	Pro-diversity
Anti-immigration	Pro-life	Antirefugee
Pro–animal rights	Antitax	Pro–free trade

belief
A conviction; often thought to be more enduring than an attitude and less enduring than a value.

A **belief** is a conviction. Beliefs are usually considered more enduring than attitudes, but our attitudes often spring from our beliefs. Your belief in healthy eating habits may lead to a negative attitude toward overeating and obesity and a positive attitude toward balanced meals and nutrition. Your audience's beliefs make a difference in how they respond to your speech. They may believe in upward mobility through higher education, in higher pay through hard work, or in social welfare. On the other hand, they may not believe in any of these ideas. Beliefs are like anchors to which our attitudes are attached. To discover the beliefs of an audience, you need to ask questions and to observe carefully. Some examples of beliefs follow:

Hard work pays off.	Good people will go to heaven.
Taxes are too high.	Work comes before play.
Anyone can get rich.	Government should be small.
Education pays.	Wickedness will be punished.

Knowing your audience's beliefs about your topic can be a valuable aid in informing and persuading them.

value
A deeply rooted belief that governs our attitude about something.

A **value** is a deeply rooted belief that governs our attitude about something. Both beliefs and attitudes can be traced to a value we hold. Learned from childhood through the family, religion, school, and many other sources, values are often so much a foundation for the rest of what we believe and know that we do not question them. Sometimes we remain unaware of our primary values until they clash. For example, a person might have an unquestioned belief that every individual has the right to be and do whatever he or she wishes—basic values of individuality and freedom—until it comes to sexuality. Table 10.3 shows one method for ranking values.

Table 10.3 Ranking Values

Rank five of the following values in their order of importance to you. If you can persuade some of your classmates, or the entire class, to do this as well, you will have information that will help you prepare your speech.

_____ Wisdom	_____ Wealth	_____ Fame
_____ A World at Peace	_____ Security	_____ Health
_____ Freedom	_____ Fulfillment	_____ Love
_____ Equality	_____ Education	_____ Faith

How does your ranking compare with those of your classmates? What other values might help you with your speech?

You can collect attitudinal information in at least three ways. One way is to ask questions that place audience members in identifiable groups, as these questions do:

_____ 5. I am
    a. active in organizations
    b. not active in organizations

_____ 6. I see myself as
    a. conservative
    b. liberal
    c. independent

_____ 7. I see myself as
    a. strongly religious
    b. moderately religious
    c. not religious

A second method of gaining attitudinal information is to ask people to rank values, such as hard work, higher education, high pay, and security, using a scale like table 10.3. People's ranking of their values can provide additional information about their attitudes and beliefs.

The third method of collecting data about people's attitudes is to list word concepts that reveal attitudes and then ask respondents to assess their attitudes toward these specific issues, such as by using an attitudinal scale like the one in figure 10.2. The reactions to these and similar words or phrases can provide information that will help you approach your audience successfully. For example, if most persons in your audience are neutral to mildly favorable toward taxing tobacco, then your speech advocating higher tobacco taxes could be designed to move their attitudes from mildly favorable to strongly favorable. If the responses are negative, then you may have to work just to move your audience closer to a mildly unfavorable attitude or toward neutrality. Check out your own attitudes toward some word concepts in figure 10.2.

cultural note

Seek Human Values

Some colleges have such diverse audiences that audience analysis seems impossible. Even different parts of the United States exhibit differences. People who live in the southern region of the United States have a reputation for being more passive, slower to get to the point, and more suggestive than demanding. Although challenging, an audience with a rich mix of races, religions, and languages invites the speaker to find topics that we relate to as human beings. All peoples of the world seek safety, security, food, shelter, and loving families.

Figure 10.2

Sample attitudinal scale. Compile data that indicate the attitudes within your class on one of these topics. What does this information tell you about how to approach your audience about this topic?

For each word or phrase, indicate your attitude toward it by selecting the appropriate radio button.

	Strongly favor	Mildly favor	Neutral	Mildly disfavor	Strongly disfavor
Government bailouts of business	◯	◯	◯	◯	◯
Unions' right to collective bargaining	◯	◯	◯	◯	◯
Immigration policies	◯	◯	◯	◯	◯
Employer-sponsored childcare	◯	◯	◯	◯	◯
Military spending	◯	◯	◯	◯	◯
Medical marijuana	◯	◯	◯	◯	◯

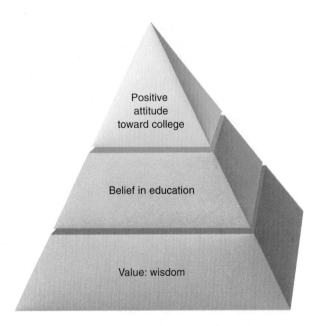

Figure 10.3

Relationships among attitudes, beliefs, and values.

The values your audience members hold and the order in which they rank them can provide important clues about their attitudes and beliefs. A speaker who addresses an audience without knowing its members' values is taking a risk that can be avoided through careful audience analysis. The relationships among attitudes, beliefs, and values are illustrated in figure 10.3.

sizing things up

Evaluating Topics

Brainstorming and eventually selecting an effective speech topic begins with a thorough self-assessment of your own interests and knowledge. Below you will find several topics followed by pairs of opposing adjectives arranged on a scale, or continuum. Check the space on the continuum that best represents your opinion of each topic's appropriateness as a subject for you to speak about. The space closest to "interesting," for example, represents "extremely interesting," and the space in the middle of each pair stands for "neutral." This exercise has no right or wrong answers, but if your teacher approves, you can compare your answers with those of others in your class. You might learn something about your captive audience's attitudes in the process. For additional information, refer to the guide for interpreting your responses that appears in the appendix at the end of the text (p. 348).

1. Politics

Interesting (__) (__) (__) (__) (__) Uninteresting

Good   (__) (__) (__) (__) (__) Bad
Confident   (__) (__) (__) (__) (__) Not Confident
Relevant   (__) (__) (__) (__) (__) Irrelevant

2. The Environment

Interesting (__) (__) (__) (__) (__) Uninteresting
Good   (__) (__) (__) (__) (__) Bad
Confident   (__) (__) (__) (__) (__) Not Confident
Relevant   (__) (__) (__) (__) (__) Irrelevant

3. The Economy

Interesting (__) (__) (__) (__) (__) Uninteresting
Good   (__) (__) (__) (__) (__) Bad
Confident   (__) (__) (__) (__) (__) Not Confident
Relevant   (__) (__) (__) (__) (__) Irrelevant

4. Education

Interesting (__) (__) (__) (__) (__) Uninteresting
Good   (__) (__) (__) (__) (__) Bad

Adapt to the Audience

Audience analysis yields information about your listeners that enables you to adapt yourself and your message to that audience. A speech is not imposed on a collection of listeners; a message is negotiated between a speaker and an audience and is designed to inform, entertain, inspire, teach, or persuade that audience. This negotiation is based on your analysis of your audience.

ADAPTING YOURSELF

In public speaking you also have to adjust to information about the audience. Just as a college senior preparing for a job interview adapts to an interviewer in dress, manner, and language, a public speaker prepares for an audience by adapting to its expectations. How you look, how you behave, and what you say should be carefully tailored to your audience.

ADAPTING YOUR LANGUAGE

The language you use in your speech, as well as your gestures, movements, and even facial expressions, should be adapted to your audience. Does your audience analysis indicate that your language should be conversational, formal, cynical, or technical? Does it suggest that your listeners like numbers and statistics? Do your observations indicate that you should pace the stage or remain behind the lectern? Should you avoid taboo words in your speech, lest you alienate your group, or will the audience respond positively to controversial language?

ADAPTING YOUR TOPIC

Public speakers should be permitted to speak on nearly any topic; after all, the First Amendment provides some protection for free speech. But practical considerations may lead you to avoid certain topics, which will typically be unique to specific situations and contexts. For instance, you would almost certainly never speak about how to create biological weapons or commit financial fraud.

Of course, the right to speak on nearly any topic brings with it a responsibility to adapt the way you approach your subject, given the audience to which you are speaking. Using

Confident (_) (_) (_) (_) (_) Not Confident   Relevant (_) (_) (_) (_) (_) Irrelevant
Relevant (_) (_) (_) (_) (_) Irrelevant

8. Religion

5. Health

Interesting (_) (_) (_) (_) (_) Uninteresting   Interesting (_) (_) (_) (_) (_) Uninteresting
Good (_) (_) (_) (_) (_) Bad   Good (_) (_) (_) (_) (_) Bad
Confident (_) (_) (_) (_) (_) Not Confident   Confident (_) (_) (_) (_) (_) Not Confident
Relevant (_) (_) (_) (_) (_) Irrelevant   Relevant (_) (_) (_) (_) (_) Irrelevant

6. Technology

9. Interpersonal conflict

Interesting (_) (_) (_) (_) (_) Uninteresting   Interesting (_) (_) (_) (_) (_) Uninteresting
Good (_) (_) (_) (_) (_) Bad   Good (_) (_) (_) (_) (_) Bad
Confident (_) (_) (_) (_) (_) Not Confident   Confident (_) (_) (_) (_) (_) Not Confident
Relevant (_) (_) (_) (_) (_) Irrelevant   Relevant (_) (_) (_) (_) (_) Irrelevant

7. Diversity

10. Poverty

Interesting (_) (_) (_) (_) (_) Uninteresting   Interesting (_) (_) (_) (_) (_) Uninteresting
Good (_) (_) (_) (_) (_) Bad   Good (_) (_) (_) (_) (_) Bad
Confident (_) (_) (_) (_) (_) Not Confident   Confident (_) (_) (_) (_) (_) Not Confident
Relevant (_) (_) (_) (_) (_) Irrelevant

■ The public speaker must consider different opinions among audience members that reflect different values.

audience analysis, you must figure out how to best approach your topic to meet your audience's needs. You may adjust your language, visual resources, supporting evidence, or even the points you make during the presentation. For example, suppose you want to speak in favor of physician-assisted suicide, and your audience analysis indicates that the majority of your listeners are opposed to it. You need not conclude that the topic is inappropriate. You may, however, adapt to the members of your audience by starting with a position closer to theirs. Your initial step might be to make audience members feel less comfortable about their present position, so that they are more prepared to hear your views.

ADAPTING YOUR PURPOSE AND GOAL

You should also adapt the purpose of your speech to your audience. Teachers often ask students to state the purpose of a speech—what do you want your audience to know, understand, or do? At first you might think your purpose should be to persuade your audience to save money by buying their clothing at outlet stores. But you discover through your audience analysis that most of your classmates already buy clothing at the outlet stores. So, you adapt your purpose. You change your purpose to an informative speech that reveals which outlet stores sell quality merchandise instead of overstocked items from their retail stores.[5]

immediate purpose
A highly specific statement using "should be able to" plus an action verb to reveal the purpose from the audience's point of view.

long-range goal
The larger goal or end you have in mind for your presentation.

The **immediate purpose** of your speech is what you want listeners to take away with them. It is linked to a larger goal, the end purpose you have in mind, or your **long-range goal**. Some examples will illustrate the difference. First are examples for an informative speech:

Immediate purpose: After listening to this speech, the audience should be able to identify three properties of the most advanced televisions available today.

Long-range goal: To increase the number of people who will chose wisely the next time they replace or purchase a television set.

Here are examples for a persuasive speech:

Immediate purpose: After listening to my speech, the audience should be able to describe the low nutritional value of two popular junk foods.[6]

Long-range goal: To dissuade listeners from eating junk food.

As these examples show, an immediate purpose has four essential features. First, it is highly specific. Second, it includes the phrase *should be able to.* Third, it uses an action verb, such as *state, identify, report, name, list, describe, explain, show,* or *reveal.* Fourth, it is stated from the viewpoint of the audience. You are writing the purpose as what you as the speaker intend to accomplish with this audience through this particular message. Your immediate purpose moves audience members toward a long-range goal.

In this section on adapting to your audience you learned that you do not have to change yourself or your position on an issue, but you can present yourself and your arguments in ways that are more likely to result in success. You learned that even the words you choose are strategic; that is, you select your words with care, so that they convince and persuade rather than offend. You can shape your topic without giving up your integrity by providing information where needed and by persuading without risking a hostile audience response. Finally, you aim for some immediate effects that are possible in a brief presentation, knowing that you have a long-range goal in mind as well.

In this chapter you have learned that topic selection and audience analysis are bonded together because whatever topic you speak about becomes a message whose successful transmission depends on how well you adapt to the audience. You find appropriate vital topics to talk about by considering both what you know and what the audience needs to know. You learned four methods of audience analysis and the various ways to adapt your presentation for an audience.

These skills of knowing what to talk about and how to talk about it are valuable well beyond the public speaking classroom. These skills are the basics for people who are successful at sales, management, and leadership.

keeping it real

Does Your Topic Fit Your Audience?

This chapter began with Stephen Bonsi delivering a high-level speech on economics to an indifferent audience. His speech would have been more successful if he had simplified his topic and explained complex concepts. Stephen was correct when he selected a vital topic, but he needed to adapt his topic to his particular audience. He could have used very simple economics to demonstrate how the wealthy have gained, how the middle class has diminished, and how the poor have grown in number. Instead, he mistakenly gave a sophisticated and jargon-prone presentation to a room full of novices who barely understood the topic.

To check the appropriateness of your own topic for your audience, answer the following questions.

■ Is the topic you selected a vital topic?

■ Is the topic you selected one in which you can arouse audience interest?

■ Do you know more about the topic than most people in your audience?

■ Can you translate what you know for people who do not know about the topic?

■ Can you figure out where the audience stands now on your topic?

■ Can you determine how much more to inform them about the topic?

■ Can you determine how much change to ask in the audience on this topic?

The answers to these questions about the link between your topic and your audience can lead you to a successful presentation.

Chapter Review & Study Guide

Summary

In this chapter, you learned the following:

1. Select a topic appropriate for you and your audience.
   - Try brainstorming and surveying your interests.
   - Assess your knowledge and commitment to the topic.
   - Evaluate your commitment to the topic.
   - Consider the age of the topic and audience.
   - Determine the topic's importance to you and your audience.
   - Recognize the special challenges of ESL in topic selection.

2. Practice narrowing a topic to save time and energy and to increase relevance to the audience.

3. Employ observation, inference, research, and questionnaires to analyze your audience.
   - Observe your audience for demographic and membership cues.
   - Draw direct and indirect inferences about your audience.
   - Research your audience with inside informants and the Internet.
   - Use a questionnaire to assess attitudes, beliefs, and values.

4. Recognize how to adapt your topic, yourself, your language, and your purpose and goal in public speaking.
   - Any topic can be adapted to a particular audience.
   - Without compromising yourself, you can adapt yourself to an audience.
   - Your language choices must be adapted to the specific audience.
   - Your purpose depends heavily on what you can accomplish with a particular audience.
   - Your long-range goal also depends on where the audience stands on an issue.

Key Terms

Attitude
Audience analysis
Belief
Brainstorming
Commitment

Demographic analysis
Direct inference
Immediate purpose
Indirect inference
Inference

Long-range goal
Questionnaire
Value

Study Questions

1. What is one basic strategy to keep in mind when selecting a topic for presentation?
   a. Take a lot of time in choosing a topic.
   b. Begin with a subject you already know.
   c. Select a topic you know nothing about.
   d. Choose a topic that does not affect you personally.

2. After choosing a topic, what should you do?
   a. Evaluate the importance of your topic.
   b. Determine how much you and your audience know about the topic.
   c. Evaluate your commitment to the topic.
   d. All the above are correct.

3. Why is narrowing your topic important?
   a. to save time and effort
   b. to reduce the depth of the topic
   c. to reduce your bias about the topic
   d. to increase the length of your speech

4. When you investigate the audience's demographics, interests, and concerns, you are
   a. brainstorming.
   b. surveying your interests.
   c. analyzing the audience.
   d. creating a captive audience.

5. Which level of audience analysis includes collecting data about the characteristics of people?
   a. audience type
   b. audience interest in the topic
   c. audience's attitudes, beliefs, and values
   d. demographic analysis

connect
For further review, go to the LearnSmart study module for this chapter.

6. A deeply rooted belief that affects how we act toward an idea or a concept is a(n)

   a. attitude.   c. value.
   b. mood.   d. thought.

7. A method of audience analysis that draws tentative generalizations based on some evidence is

   a. observation.   c. a questionnaire.
   b. inference.   d. a survey.

8. If you ask people to rank concepts in order of importance or you ask them questions that place individuals into identifiable groups, you are

   a. conducting a questionnaire.   c. narrowing
   b. brainstorming.   d. inferring.

9. Which method of analysis requires using your senses to interpret information about the audience?

   a. involvement
   b. value
   c. judgment
   d. observation

10. Which is *not* true of immediate purposes?

   a. They are highly specific.
   b. They include the phrase "should be able to."
   c. They use an action verb.
   d. They are stated from the viewpoint of the speaker.

Answers:

1. (b); 2. (d); 3. (a); 4. (c); 5. (d); 6. (c); 7. (b); 8. (a); 9. (d); 10. (d)

Critical Thinking

1. Choose a broad topic, and then narrow it by creating your own concept map (see figure 10.2). At what point do the topics become too specific to be discussed in depth? Which are still too broad for a brief presentation? Choose a few that are just right.

2. You are a white person asked to give a speech to a service club about race relations in the workplace. You expected an all-white audience, but on your arrival you see that at least half the audience consists of people of color. Using the chapter's last section on adaptation, write down how, if at all, you might adapt yourself, your topic, and your purpose to this unexpected reality. Would your answers be different if you were a person of color facing this audience?

being credible
and using evidence

When you have read and thought about this chapter, you will be able to:

1. Define source credibility and explain why source credibility is important.

2. Identify four dimensions of source credibility.

3. Effectively use personal experience, library resources, the Internet, and other people to gather evidence for your speeches.

4. Correctly use both internal and verbal citations to attribute the sources of ideas and evidence.

5. Recognize eight different forms of supporting material that you can use in your speech.

6. Use ethical principles to present an honest and accurate image of yourself and the evidence you use.

Effective public presentations are an artfully drafted combination of you, your ideas, and the ideas and opinions of others. How you present yourself, your ideas, and your evidence will determine how much trust the audience places in the points you make. In this chapter you will learn about source credibility and the ways that you can increase your credibility by using strong evidence.

Abbey was pretty excited to be in college. Her first speech assignment was quickly approaching, and she assumed it would be easy to start working on the outline the day before and get it done with little trouble. When she started looking for information about her topic, the use of Ritalin and other "focus drugs" for academic success, however, Abbey quickly became overwhelmed. To the most obvious key word, "Ritalin," Google returned approximately 21 million results. One of the first results was highlighted, so Abbey clicked on it. The site was labeled an official site and provided significant amounts of information about how Ritalin can help students more easily focus their attention while studying. Armed with the information, and glad that she didn't have to look through all 21 million sites, Abbey embarked on her speech outline.

The next day during class, Abbey gave her speech and felt good about her work. She hit the seven-minute time limit, was able to use quotations and statistics from the source she found, and managed to look up for most of the speech. At the end, the teacher asked whether there were questions. One student asked Abbey how she felt about the fact that there are side effects for some children and that many doctors now feel that the drug is overprescribed. Abbey had not read about that information and was unable to respond effectively. Rather than ending her speech with confidence, she felt pretty mad that a fellow student had caught her off-guard.

What could Abbey have done differently to research her topic more effectively? Was the late start on her speech her only problem? What strategies could have improved her research process, boosted her credibility, and improved the effectiveness of her speech? At the end of the chapter, we'll take another look at Abbey's situation and consider how she might have better planned her speech.

Abbey is like many students who prepare a speech. She assumed that the research process would go quickly, and when engaging in that process she used shortcuts to make her assumption come true. Unfortunately, those shortcuts caught up with her. What could have been an interesting speech ended very flat because it became clear that she did not carefully research her topic. In the end, her credibility as a speaker was weak. In this chapter you will learn about ways to avoid similar problems in your speeches.

What Is Source Credibility and Why Is It Important?

The most important resource you have for convincing an audience is yourself. Audiences do not want to hear from someone they do not trust or respect. They will not listen to or retain information from someone who has not earned the right to talk about that subject. Finding ways to convince your audience that you are trustworthy and qualified is among the most important objectives for any speaker.

As you begin thinking about how you can convince audience members of your credibility, consider the following questions you need to specifically address during your presentation:

- What are your motives for speaking on this topic?
- Why are you qualified to speak on this topic?

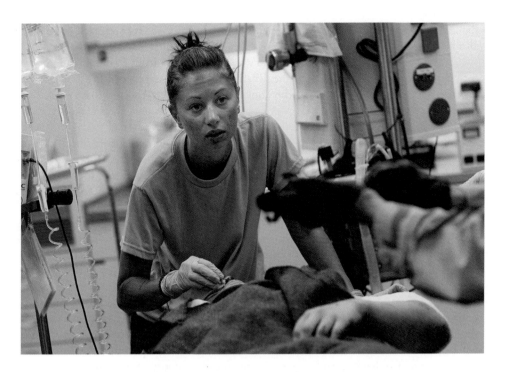

College students can use their personal experiences to establish credibility. For instance, a soldier who served as a medic could establish strong credibility to speak on medical issues.

- What work have you done to ensure that your information is correct?
- In what ways will the audience benefit from your information?
- Why did you choose to present the information in the way that you did?
- What are you *not* telling the audience, and does omitting that information create an unbalanced or biased perspective?

These questions are not a checklist you should run through as you speak. Effective speakers find ways to address these questions more subtly, through the natural course of their presentation. The results add up to the kind of credibility that means audience members are more likely to trust and respect what the speaker has to say.

Credibility is a challenging issue for beginning speakers. Whereas highly experienced speakers typically have a lifetime of experience from which to establish credibility, most college students lack significant expertise on many topics. Fortunately, students can establish credibility through their sincerity and goodwill, resources available to anyone. And credibility is essential. If you have it, the audience will listen and likely remember much of what you say; speakers who lack or fail to establish credibility during their presentation have little chance of having any impact other than boredom.

More than 2,300 years ago Aristotle noted that a speaker's "character may almost be called the most effective means of persuasion he possesses." That's still true today. Scholars have consistently documented the importance of credibility and generally conclude that *who* says something determines *who* will listen.

In the public speaking classroom you are the source of the message. You need to be concerned about your **source credibility**—the audience's perception of your effectiveness as a speaker. You may feel that you do not have the same credibility as a high public official, a great authority on a topic, or an expert in a narrow field. Nonetheless, you can be a very credible source to your classmates, colleagues, or friends. Source credibility is not something a speaker possesses, like a suit of clothes. Instead, the audience determines credibility. Credibility is like many other subjective perceptions—just as each person might have a

source credibility
The audience's perception of your effectiveness as a speaker.

slightly different impression of whether a new song by Lady Gaga is good, each person may also have a slightly different perception of a speaker's credibility.

The audience's perception of a speaker's credibility arises from a combination of factors, including the speaker, the topic, the situation, and the message. Focusing for a moment on the speaker, have you served in the armed forces overseas? You may have earned the right to speak on national defense, the price of being in the National Guard, and the inside story of war. Did you grow up in another country? You may have earned the right to speak on that country's culture, food, or customs. Your qualifications influence the audience's perceptions about your credibility.

How do you establish your qualifications? Students often state that they have done research on the topic—usually a heavy dose of the first three to five hits on Google. Do you think that makes them credible? Probably not. Rather than relying on "I did research," a sincere statement about why you are interested in a particular topic might be convincing for a group of peers in a college classroom. The same approach may not suffice if you are giving the same speech to a group of community activists or business professionals. What it takes to be credible depends on the audience you are addressing, so you'll want to anticipate what each audience will expect.

A final factor influencing your credibility is your message. It should be obvious that a poorly conceived message will lack credibility. Besides relying on research, therefore, you should also focus on relevance. Messages that are connected to the lives of your audience will be perceived as more credible than messages they see as unimportant or disconnected.[1] Stated simply, if audience members perceive the topic as important, they are more likely to perceive you as important and therefore credible.

Dimensions of Credibility

What do audience members perceive that signals speaker credibility? If individuals in the audience base credibility on judgments, what is the basis for those judgments? On what will your classmates be rating you when they judge your credibility? According to research, four of the most important dimensions of credibility are competence, trustworthiness, dynamism, and common ground. Three of these relate to you, the speaker.

COMPETENCE

competence
The degree to which the speaker is perceived as skilled, reliable, experienced, qualified, authoritative, and informed; an aspect of credibility.

The first aspect of credibility is **competence**—the degree to which a speaker is perceived as skilled, qualified, experienced, authoritative, reliable, and informed. A speaker does not have to live up to all these adjectives; any one of them, or a few, might make the speaker credible. A machinist who displays her metalwork in a speech about junk sculpture as art is as credible as a biblical scholar demonstrating his ability to interpret scripture. They have different bases for their competence, but both can demonstrate expertise in their areas of specialization.

Words, skillful use of technology, and an air of authority convey your own competence as a speaker. What can you build into your speech that will help the audience perceive your competence? What experience have you had that is related to the subject? What training or knowledge do you have? How can you suggest to your audience that you have earned the right to speak about the subject? The most obvious way is to tell the audience of your expertise, but a creative speaker can think of dozens of ways to hint and suggest competence without being explicit and without seeming arrogant.

There are several things you can do to improve your competence as a speaker. First, you should become familiar enough with your information and speech that you do not have to rely on extensive notes. Constantly referring to notes for every point can lead audience members to perceive that you really do not understand the information. Second, focus on translating ideas. If you are able to take relatively complex ideas and make them understandable for audience members by using metaphors, vivid descriptions, visual aids, and other resources, you will appear more competent. Third, make yourself comfortable with the speaking situation. If you plan to use technology, make sure that you know how to use the computer, the software, and other resources. Finally, audience members will perceive you as more competent if you deliver the speech well. In chapter 13 you will learn specific ways to practice and improve your delivery.

TRUSTWORTHINESS

The second aspect of credibility is **trustworthiness**—the degree to which a speaker is perceived as honest, fair, sincere, friendly, honorable, and kind. These perceptions are also earned. We judge people's honesty by their past behaviors and whether we perceive them to have goodwill toward their listeners. In a study exploring perceived credibility of the 2008 presidential candidates, communication researcher Jason Teven found that goodwill was the strongest predictor of perceived credibility among the leading candidates in the primary elections.[2] So, too, your classmates will judge your trustworthiness based on how you represent your past behaviors and establish goodwill.

You may have to reveal to your audience why you are trustworthy. Have you held jobs that demanded honesty and responsibility? Have you been a cashier, a bank teller, or a supervisor? Have you given up anything to demonstrate you are sincere? The person who pays his or her own way through college ordinarily has to be very sincere about education. Being respectful of others' points of view can be a sign of fairness. What can you say or do that signals trustworthiness?

Trustworthiness and goodwill are difficult to establish in a short speech. After all, the trust we give to others typically develops after we have known them for some time. During a speech, both what you say and how you say it can affect audience members' perceptions of your trustworthiness. First, you should take care to present fair and balanced information. Using reliable sources and presenting other viewpoints can show audience members that the conclusions you draw are accurate. Talking with a confident tone and maintaining eye contact are also important tools in building trust at the beginning of your speech.

DYNAMISM

The third aspect of credibility is **dynamism**—the extent to which an audience perceives the speaker as bold, active, energetic, strong, empathic, and assertive. Audiences value behavior described by these adjectives. Perhaps when we consider their opposites—timid, tired, and meek—we can see why dynamism is attractive. People who exude energy and show the passion of their convictions impress others. Watch television evangelists and note how they look and sound. You can learn to be dynamic. Evidence indicates that the audience's perception of your dynamism will enhance your credibility.

Dynamism is exhibited mainly by voice, movement, facial expressions, and gestures. A person who speaks forcefully and rapidly and with considerable vocal variety; a speaker who moves toward the audience, back behind the lectern, and over to the visual aid; and a speaker who uses facial expressions and gestures to make a point are all exhibiting dynamism. What can you do with your voice, movement, facial expressions, and gestures to show the audience you are a dynamic speaker?

trustworthiness
The degree to which the speaker is perceived as honest, fair, sincere, honorable, friendly, and kind; an aspect of credibility.

dynamism
The extent to which the speaker is perceived as bold, active, energetic, strong, empathic, and assertive; an aspect of credibility.

■ Steve Jobs is credited with Apple's recent success, partly because of the dynamic ways in which he introduced products such as the iPod, iPhone, and iPad to the world.

skill builder

Establishing Common Ground with Classmates

Practice creating common ground by making a list of experiences that you and your classmates have likely shared. Like the example Sue Coleman gave, your shared experience could be realized in the future. After identifying several possible shared experiences, analyze how you could use one of them to establish common ground that will build your credibility with the other students in your class. How do you think the same approach could be used in speaking situations outside your classroom?

common ground
The degree to which the speaker's values, beliefs, attitudes, and interests are shared with the audience; an aspect of credibility.

■ What actions did the Occupy Wall Street protesters engage in that helped or hurt their credibility?

COMMON GROUND

Common ground occurs when you and your audience share an understanding of the world, either in broad terms or in relationship to specific issues.[3] Common ground comes about in two ways. First, you and your audience might share common ground prior to your speech. If you have significant commonality—you are similar in age, you have the same general education level, or you have similar socioeconomic backgrounds—you are likely to have much in common. Common ground is also created through the act of communicating. As you begin to speak, you express a certain way of looking at the world or a particular topic. Do you take a stance on whether there is too much national debt? Do you assume people value health over personal freedom? As you present information, you begin staking claims for particular ways of thinking about issues. In so doing, you will establish greater common ground with some audience members and reduce it with others.

Making a connection with your audience can mean simply establishing a shared trajectory—showing that we are all doing something together. In a March 2011 speech at an awards ceremony for young scientists, Mary Sue Coleman established common ground in this way:

> *America has long been recognized as a global leader in science and technology. But we know . . . that our nation is slipping in how we prepare and nurture the talent of tomorrow. Your hard work shows us what is possible . . . Your ideas and theories are going to lead our country to new cures, solutions and technologies. That is why I am so happy to be here tonight: to congratulate you, encourage you, and provide a little advice about being a scientist in a country that absolutely must place more value on discovery, innovation and the creation of new knowledge.*

Speaking as a scientist, Coleman was able to create common ground with her audience by pointing to a shared objective—to elevate the training of future scientists. Coleman's approach recognized that she and her audience, who were not yet in college, let alone college presidents, would share a perspective at some future time when the students matured into scientists like her. Her approach established common ground in the present by pointing to where her audience would eventually be. Other approaches to building common ground can include pointing to past shared experiences or present shared circumstances.

WAYS TO CAPITALIZE ON CREDIBILITY

Credibility is influenced by topics, messages, audiences, and circumstances. You may hold the speaker in high regard before the speech, but during the speech your perception of him or her may diminish, and then after the speech you may think better of the speaker again because you decide the message has merit. Here are practical approaches for improving your credibility during your presentation:

■ Speeches with higher-quality arguments convey more credibility on the speaker.[4] Be sure to carefully research your topic and use sound reasoning.

- Sometimes a **sleeper effect** occurs when source and message get separated in the listener's mind over time: a low-credibility speaker's message can gain influence, whereas a high-credibility speaker's message can diminish long after a particular message.[5] Crafting a clear and persuasive message can help capitalize on the possibility of a positive sleeper effect.

- Self-disclosure can increase credibility, even through mechanisms such as Facebook;[6] however, inappropriate self-disclosure can harm it. Use self-disclosure appropriate to the topic and don't overrely on it.

- Speakers who appear younger may be perceived as less credible than those who appear older.[7] Dress professionally when speaking to help increase your perceived age.

- Presenting a message that favors one side of an issue often looks like bias to listeners, resulting in lower perceived credibility.[8] Present a balanced representation of issues, even if you personally take a stand on one side.

- People who are perceived to use referent and expert power (see chapter 8) are seen as more competent, trustworthy, and likable.[9] Build rapport with your audience, and stress your personal knowledge of and careful research on the topic.

- Speaking with fluency can increase perceptions of credibility, including competence, character, and caring.[10] Take care to speak at a moderate place, enunciate your words, and practice your delivery.

- Your use of evidence, coupled with the audience's perception of the topic's importance and your competence as a speaker, interact to influence your credibility. Reinard and Myers found that, although the use of any type of evidence increases your credibility, those effects are even greater when the audience perceives the topic to be important and you to be competent.[11]

- When someone else introduces you to your audience, the timing and content of the introduction are important to your credibility. Mike Allen and colleagues found that, if you do not have automatic credibility based on your qualifications, it may be best to delay letting the audience know your qualifications until after you have spoken.[12]

Where Should You Look for Information?

Although audience members look at several factors to determine your credibility, you have control over only some of them. For instance, you can practice your delivery to avoid mispronunciations, you can work to improve your gestures, and you can take care to create a well-organized speech. In addition, you can improve your own credibility by borrowing on the credibility of others. In this section you will learn how to conduct research and gather supporting material from personal experience, other people, written and visual resources, and the Internet. We also show how to evaluate those sources and use them effectively in your speeches.

PERSONAL EXPERIENCE

The first place you should look for materials for the content of your speech is within yourself. Your **personal experience**—your own life as a source of information—is something about which you can speak with considerable authority. One student had been a "headhunter," a person who finds employees for employers willing to pay a premium for specific kinds of workers. This student gave a speech from his personal experience concerning what employers particularly value in employees. Another student had a brother who was autistic. In her informative speech she explained what autism is and how autistic children can grow up to be self-reliant and successful. Your special causes, jobs, and family can provide you

sleeper effect
A change of audience opinion caused by the separation of the message content from its source over a period of time.

personal experience
Your own life as a source of information.

sizing things up

Research Attitudes Scale

You have a variety of sources in which you can locate evidence and information. Read each statement below and respond using the following scale. There are no right or wrong answers to these questions. A guide for interpreting your responses appears in the appendix at the end of the text (p. 348).

1 = Strongly disagree
2 = Disagree
3 = Neither agree nor disagree
4 = Agree
5 = Strongly agree

1. I feel confident when using the Internet to find good information.
2. I like to use journals to find good articles on a topic.
3. I find it easy to locate good books on a given topic.
4. I have confidence in using reference materials to find good research on topics.
5. I find it easy to locate good popular press articles on topics.
6. I like to look for good books when researching a topic.
7. I find it easy to locate good journal articles on topics.
8. I like to use good reference materials when researching.
9. The Internet is easy to use when looking for good information.
10. I am confident in my abilities to find good popular press articles on topics.
11. I am confident in my ability to find good books on a topic.
12. It is easy to use the reference section in the library to find good information.
13. I like to search for good popular press articles on topics.
14. I like to use the Internet to search for good information.
15. I am confident in my ability to locate good journal articles on a topic.

with firsthand information to use in your speech.

However, you should ask yourself some critical questions about your personal experience before you use it in your speech. Some experiences may be too personal or too intimate to share with strangers or even classmates. Others may be interesting but irrelevant to the topic of your speech. You can evaluate your personal experience as evidence, or as data on which proof may be based, by asking yourself the following questions:

1. Was my experience typical?

2. Was my experience so typical that it will bore an audience?

3. Was my experience so atypical that it was a chance occurrence?

4. Was my experience so personal and revealing that the audience may feel uncomfortable?

5. Was my experience one that this audience will appreciate or from which this audience can learn a lesson?

6. Does my experience really constitute proof or evidence of anything?

Also consider the ethics of using your personal experience in a speech. Will your message harm others? Is the experience your own or someone else's? Experience that is not firsthand is probably questionable, because information about others' experiences often becomes distorted as the message is passed from one person to another. Unless the experience is your own, you may find yourself passing along a falsehood.

PEOPLE RESOURCES

Speakers often overlook the most obvious sources of information—the people around them. The easiest way to secure information from other people is to ask them in an informational interview.

How do you find the right people? Your instructor might have some suggestions about whom to approach. Good and accessible sources of information are professors and administrators who are available on campus. They can be contacted during office hours or by appointment. Government officials, too, have an obligation to be responsive to your questions. Even big business and industrial concerns have public relations offices that can help you with information. Your objective is to find someone, or a few people, who can provide you with the best information in the limited time you have to prepare your speech.

An interview can be an important and impressive source of information for your speech—if you conduct it properly. After you have carefully selected the person or persons you wish to interview, follow these suggestions:

1. *On first contact with your interviewee or the interviewee's assistant, be honest about your purpose.* For example, you might say, "I want to interview Dr. Schwartz for 10 minutes about the plans for student aid for next year, so that I can share that information with the 20 students in my public speaking class." Notice that this request helpfully tells the person how much time the interview will take.

2. *Prepare specific questions for the interview.* Think ahead about exactly what kind of information you will need to satisfy yourself and your audience. Conducting at least some research before the interview is often advisable—you will be able to ask better questions. Keep your list of questions short enough to fit the time limit you have suggested to the interviewee.

3. *Be respectful toward the person you interview.* Remember, the person you interview is doing you a favor. You do not need to question aggressively like a talk show host. Instead, dress appropriately for the person's status, ask your questions politely, and thank your interviewee for granting you an interview.

4. *Tell the interviewee you are going to take notes so you can use the information in your speech.* If you are going to record the interview, you need to ask the interviewee's permission. Be prepared to take notes in case the interviewee does not wish to be recorded. Even if you record the interview, it's a good idea to take notes as a backup in case something happens to the recording.

5. *When you quote the interviewee or paraphrase his or her ideas in your speech, use oral footnotes to indicate where you got the information.* Here's an example: "According to Dr. Fred Schwartz, the director of financial aid, the amount of student financial aid for next year will be slightly less than it was this year."

Sometimes the person you interview will be a good resource for additional information. For example, one student interviewed the director of disability services on campus for her informative speech about learning disabilities. The director not only answered her questions but also gave her an extensive packet of information about the topic. Of course, even with an expert, you should use other types of resources, so that differing opinions and alternate explanations can be identified.

WRITTEN AND VISUAL RESOURCES FROM THE LIBRARY

Modern libraries, such as the ones found at most colleges and universities, are portals to digital information. So, rather than helping you find a particular book or article, a **reference librarian**—someone specifically trained to help you locate sources of information—is far more likely to teach you how to use your school's particular library system and one or more of the available electronic databases.

reference librarian
A librarian specifically trained to help you find sources of information.

Here are some practical principles of library research that you can adapt to your unique situation:

1. *Start at the center and work your way out.* The reference desk is the practical "center" of your library. To find anything, you will start with a search of some type; the reference desk is there to help you conduct that search, so start by asking for help there. In addition to starting at the center of the library, you should begin by searching at the center of your topic. Following the principle that topics will be narrowed as you conduct research, start by researching the broad and typical elements of your topic. As you gain more information, you will be able to narrow your search to more specific (and possibly off-center) aspects of your topic.

Table 11.1   Types of Sources

Source	Uses
Fictional books	Some plots or characters can be used to illustrate points you are making in your speech.
Nonfiction books	Nonfiction books include historical, political, social, and scientific studies. Research reported in books tends to be very detailed but can also be somewhat out of date.
Academic journal articles	Most academic journal articles undergo careful editorial review, which can help ensure high-quality information. Academic articles tend to report the results of very specific studies.
Government documents	The federal government produces publications ranging from compilations of congressional testimony to the results of million-dollar scientific studies. Many university libraries have a separate department for government documents.
Trade journal articles	Trade journals are targeted toward professionals in a particular profession or discipline. Trade journals tend to be practical but based on solid research.
Reference books	Your library reference department will have a number of reference books ranging from dictionaries and biographies to atlases. Depending on your speech topic, such sources can be very useful.
Encyclopedias	Encyclopedias are excellent places to start researching topics about which you know absolutely nothing. Encyclopedia entries provide short, easy-to-read explanations but tend to be dated and too general.
Magazine articles	Magazine articles provide timely information and tend to provide more in-depth coverage. The disadvantage of magazine articles is that they are typically written by journalists with little or no expertise on the topics they write about.
Newspaper articles	Newspaper articles are among the timeliest sources of print information. Although they are up to date, they are written by journalists who may have little or no expertise on the topics they write about. They also tend to provide few details.
Web pages	Web pages are hard to describe because they come in so many variations. Later you will learn about how to locate effective websites. For now, understand that, although websites provide easy access to current information, the quality of information on the Web must always be verified.

2. *Understand that not all sources are equal.* Modern libraries offer access to many different types of sources, ranging from books and academic journals to newspapers and trade magazines. Each will provide you with different types of information, and each will likely be indexed in a different database. Table 11.1 identifies several different types of sources and suggests how you might use them as evidence. A key principle when conducting good research is that source variety is important—finding and using a variety of types of sources from this list is wise.

3. *Know your databases!* Some university libraries can provide access to over 500 electronic databases. With so many options, figuring out which databases to use can seem daunting. Following the principle that you should start at the center, generalized databases such as Academic Search Premier and Lexis-Nexis are excellent places to begin. The library computer catalog will also help you locate books and other resources in your library. Once you have located initial information, you may wish to consult more specific and specialized databases. For example, if you are doing a presentation about a medical topic, you may wish to consult MEDLINE. And if you are doing a persuasive speech, you may wish to consult the Opposing Viewpoints Resource Center to find "pro" and "con" articles on topics ranging from adoption to welfare reform. Remember that the reference librarian is trained to help you select and use the right databases for your topic.

■ Google can be a good starting point for research, but relying only on that resource can limit the types of information that you locate. Using multiple search portals is a better strategy.

4. *Recognize that good research requires reading, thinking, and doing more research.* Many students assume their research task is over with one quick Google search or a quick trip to the library. Although the "one trip fits all" approach is appealing, it does not work well. Once you have obtained initial research on your topic, the best thing you can do is to spend time reading those sources, revising your outline, and conducting more research to fill in gaps and find more specific information. Good research takes time, but the end result is outstanding evidence that is sure to impress.

INTERNET RESOURCES

The Internet has quickly been integrated into nearly every aspect of our lives, appearing on our cell phones, televisions, and even upscale refrigerators. We have access to more information than ever, but not all of it is useful, and filtering through the garbage can be overwhelming.

Good Web searches start with a plan, and we provide a general strategy here. Depending on the nature of your topic and your specific assignment, you might need to perform additional steps.

1. *Use both search engines and other portals.* A **search engine** is a webpage designed to help you search for information; Google is the prime example. Although search engines will locate thousands of sites that contain the word or phrase you are searching for, they also return hundreds of irrelevant websites. An alternative approach is to use a more specialized search engine. For instance, for some topics Google Scholar might be much better than the standard Google search engine. In addition, there are thousands of other types of information portals on the Web. The government has a portal for locating

search engine
A program on the Internet that allows users to search for information.

Table 11.2 Tools for Narrowing Your Web Search

Type	Description	Example
Exact Word Searching	By default, browsers return any webpage containing the word you asked it to search for. For example, if you want to search for the informal speech abbreviation *inform*, the search engine would return sites with the words *informative, information, informal, informing,* and so forth. To prevent this problem, type your search term enclosed in double quotations marks.	*"inform"*
Exact Phrase Searching	If you are looking for a phrase, put the phrase in quotation marks. For example, simply typing in *public speaking* would return all sites that contain the two words anywhere on the site. Placing the phrase in quote marks will return only sites using the phrase.	*"public speaking"*
Excluding Terms	Sometimes you may want to search for a word or phrase, but because it is used in multiple contexts you need to exclude some types of pages. Suppose you wanted to search for the word *apple* with the intention of finding out about the fruit, not the company. One way of accomplishing that search is to type in *apple* followed by words you want to exclude, preceded by minus signs.	*Apple -computer -iPhone -Ipad*
Using Wildcards	For example, suppose you wanted to search for state laws pertaining to voter registration. You could search for each state separately (i.e., State of Alaska voter registration laws) or you could combine the wildcard with quotation marks to search for all states simultaneously, while keeping your search narrowed to documents containing the exact phrase you are interested in.	*"State of * voter registration laws"*

Source: Adapted from Google (www.google.com/support/websearch/?hl=en).

statistics (www.fedstats.com); both YouTube and Ted (www.ted.com) provide portals for finding video; iTunes is a portal for finding podcasts; Visual.ly (www.visual.ly) is a portal for interesting information graphics. Using a variety of search engines and other portals can diversify your research base and help you find better information.

2. *Refine your search.* Many students assume one search will be sufficient. As you discover more information, try using different combinations of search terms. Sometimes adding a few words or rearranging words can make an important change in what your search engine returns. Also, try using more advanced techniques, such as Boolean operators, to narrow searches. Table 11.2 provides recommendations on how to more effectively narrow your searches. Searching for information is easy; being smart about your searches is more challenging. Your objective should be to narrow the search until you have separated the junk from the gold.

3. *Evaluate carefully all sources of information found on the Internet,* especially when you use sources outside your university's Web domain. Later in the chapter we focus specifically on this issue, but it cannot be stated too many times. The critical skills in research are both locating *and* evaluating sources of information. Perhaps you are picky about your clothes or your food. You should be equally picky about the information you consume and, in this case, serve to others.

Keep in mind that people have different motives for creating webpages. Some websites are intended to be informative, others are intended to persuade, and still others are out to make money. Some are designed to conceal their true motive: a website might look informative but actually tell only part of a story to lure you into making an uninformed decision. One way to understand the motive of websites is to pay attention to the server extension. Figure 11.1 explains the parts of a Web address and the characteristics of Web addresses with different server extensions. No single type of Web address—based on the

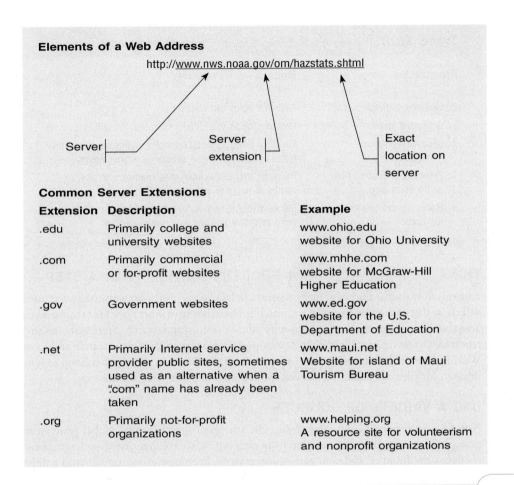

Elements of a Web Address

http://www.nws.noaa.gov/om/hazstats.shtml

Server

Server
extension

Exact
location on
server

Common Server Extensions

Extension	Description	Example
.edu	Primarily college and university websites	www.ohio.edu website for Ohio University
.com	Primarily commercial or for-profit websites	www.mhhe.com website for McGraw-Hill Higher Education
.gov	Government websites	www.ed.gov website for the U.S. Department of Education
.net	Primarily Internet service provider public sites, sometimes used as an alternative when a ".com" name has already been taken	www.maui.net Website for island of Maui Tourism Bureau
.org	Primarily not-for-profit organizations	www.helping.org A resource site for volunteerism and nonprofit organizations

Figure 11.1
Breaking down Web addresses.

server extension—is necessarily better than another. However, you can make initial judgments about the credibility of a site by looking at the extension. Remember that ".com" sites are trying to make money, ".gov" sites are maintained by the government and are typically oriented toward public service, and ".edu" sites are associated with universities. Although only a start, this information can help you sift through certain types of sites that have the potential to present misleading or even deceptive information.

Planning a Research Strategy

Students at all levels generally understand that research is important. Few recognize that research is the foundation for everything else you do in your speech. Table 11.3 analyzes how a good research plan can help nearly every aspect of the speechmaking process, even delivery. This section explains approaches you should embrace and those you should avoid when planning your research strategy.

REFINE YOUR TOPIC, AND THEN REFINE IT SOME MORE

Poor research strategies often result from poorly worded thesis statements or vague ideas for topics. Take time to think carefully about what your topic is, and how others might think of it. After collecting some initial research, do you have information that might help you narrow your topic further? Finding ways to reduce the amount of information you need to review and evaluate will speed up your workflow and help you find higher-quality sources.

Table 11.3 Research and the Speech Preparation Process

Preparation Step	Benefit of Research
1. Selecting a topic	Research helps you discover and narrow topics.
2. Organizing ideas	Research helps you identify main and subordinate points.
3. Researching support materials	Research provides facts, examples, definitions, and other forms of support to give substance to your points.
4. Preparing an introduction and a conclusion	Research may reveal interesting examples, stories, or quotes to begin or end the speech.
5. Practicing and delivering the speech	Because your speech is well researched, you will feel more confident and will seem more credible.

THINK OF RESEARCH AS A PROCESS RATHER THAN A STEP

Experts rarely assume they have many answers. In fact, many professors who conduct research will claim that at the conclusion of a research project they have more questions than answers. You should embrace the same philosophy when conducting research. Start early, research repeatedly while integrating ideas into your presentation, then do more research, and so on. Waiting until the last minute to start your research, viewing it as just another hoop to jump through for your assignment, locks you into an outcome of ineffective research.

USE A VARIETY OF SOURCES

heuristics
Mental shortcuts used to make decisions—for instance, evaluating sources.

Not all sources tell you the same thing. On any given speech topic—global poverty, for example—you can obtain information from each type of source: personal experience, library resources, the Internet, and even personal interviews. Each type of source will yield a different type of information. Personal experience might tell you how poverty is felt in our own lives, either directly or indirectly; magazine and newspaper articles might give general background about regions where poverty is most rampant; scientific journals might provide detailed statistics showing how poverty is linked to disease, famine, and even conflict; and webpages might describe groups committed to reducing poverty and its effects.

■ Start your research early and use more than one source. Research is a process, not a step.

When devising your research plan, be committed to locating a variety of types of sources. Using only Google will skew your research base to certain types of information while excluding others. Likewise, finding one really good book on poverty and relying only on that resource will limit the details you can integrate into your presentation. Using table 11.1 as a guide, try to locate one of each type of source on your topic. Does this seem like a lot of work? Maybe, but given the importance of research to your success in this class and well into the future, the effort will pay off.

EVALUATE SOURCES CAREFULLY

Merely finding sources does not ensure that you have effectively researched your speech. Regardless of what type of source you have found, apply critical criteria to evaluate its quality. Table 11.4 describes several **heuristics,** or *mental shortcuts,* that people use when evaluating sources. Using these is definitely better than simply selecting the first five sources from a Google search. For instance, a poorly constructed site or sloppy article could be indicative of sloppy work overall, so the aesthetic appeal heuristic, though weak, could be useful. However, these shortcuts can lead to faulty conclusions about the quality of any given source and should not be used alone.

Table 11.4 Heuristics Used by College Students to Evaluate Research

Heuristic	Description
1. Reputation	Trusting a source because it has a recognizable name or brand; for example, you might trust CNN because it is a large media organization
2. Endorsements	Believing information because others say it is believable; for example, you might trust a source because reader comments attached to a story are positive
3. Consistency	Trusting one source because it says something similar to what other sources say; for example, you might believe one website because another website says the same thing
4. Expectancy violation	Mistrusting a source because it says something contrary to what you thought or contrary to what other sources say
5. Persuasive intent	Mistrusting a source because it makes an obvious attempt to be persuasive
6. Aesthetic appeal	Trusting a source because it is well designed and visually appealing

Source: Items 1–5 are adapted from Metzger, M. J., Flanagan, A. J., & Medders, R. B. (2010). Social and heuristic approaches to credibility evaluation online. *Journal of Communication, 60,* 413–439.

Rather than shortcuts, therefore, try these more robust criteria for evaluating sources of all types:

1. *Is the supporting material clear?* Does the source present information in a clear and simple manner? Sources that lack clarity could indicate a lack of true understanding on the part of the creator.

2. *Is the supporting material verifiable?* Whereas the consistency heuristic simply suggests that sources are OK if they all say the same thing, verifiability means that you can confirm the source's facts and details. In journalism this process is called independent verification, meaning you can confirm details independently from the source you are using.

3. *Is the source of the supporting material competent?* For each source you should be able to determine qualifications. If your source is a person, what expertise does the person have in the topic? If your source is an organization, what connection does the organization have to the issue? For instance, would you trust a statement on a small business website supporting conceal and carry laws? Your answer might depend on the type of small business and its connection to the issue.

4. *Is the source objective?* All sources—even news reports—have some sort of bias. The National Rifle Association has a bias against gun control; Greenpeace has a bias in favor of environmental protections; TV news programs have a bias toward vivid visual imagery. What biases do your sources have, and how might those biases affect the way the source frames information?

5. *Is the supporting material relevant?* Loading your speech with irrelevant sources might make it *seem* well researched; however, critical listeners will see through this tactic. Include only sources that directly address the key points you want to make.

6. *Is the supporting material current?* Knowledge changes on a daily basis. What we thought was true about the war on drugs, the Internet, health, and the economy a few years ago is now irrelevant. Use older sources sparingly and attempt to find up-to-date information.[13]

These criteria are not yes or no questions. Sources will meet some criteria well and fail others. Your job as speaker is to weigh the benefits and drawbacks of each source and determine whether to include it in your speech. Indeed, you have an ethical responsibility to carefully evaluate your sources.

social media
make it matter

The Evils (or Not) of Wikipedia

The National Communication Association is the largest scholarly organization in the field of communication. One of the services it offers members is a listserv called CRT-NET (Communication Research and Theory Network). Recently, several communication professors engaged in an ongoing discussion on the listserv about the use of Wikipedia as a source in student speeches. Some argued that Wikipedia is largely unregulated and nothing more than an encyclopedia with little editorial oversight. (Encyclopedias have been discouraged as a resource for college students' speeches for decades.) Others argued that Wikipedia reflects a type of source unique to the Internet—a user-created dialogue in which information is generated and edited by a community. If communication scholars believe that knowledge is socially constructed, what better form of evidence could exist than a socially created database of knowledge on nearly every imaginable topic? How do you feel about Wikipedia? Under what circumstances could your credibility be harmed by using this type of source? In the end, your answers to these questions will likely be determined by the faith you place in the "social" part of social media.

How Should You Cite Sources of Information Correctly?

All the work you put into conducting great research will be lost if you do not find ways to explain well the sources that you used. When reading or watching the news, how often have you heard reports from anonymous sources? It turns out that the use of anonymous sources lowers both the credibility and the believability of news stories.[14] The same holds true for speeches. If you do not identify your sources and show why they are credible, you can damage your own credibility.

You will provide references for your sources both on your outline and during your presentation. **Bibliographic references** are complete citations that appear in the "references" or "works cited" section of your speech outline (or term paper). Your outline should also contain **internal references,** which are brief notations of which bibliographic refer-

bibliographic references
Complete citations that appear in the "references" or "works cited" section of your speech outline.

internal references
Brief notations indicating a bibliographic reference that contains the details you are using in your speech.

ence contains the details you are using in your speech. Internal and bibliographic references help readers understand what sources you used to find specific details, such as statistics, quotations, and examples. Ask your instructor whether you should use a particular format for references. The next chapter explains how you should prepare a bibliography for your outline using common style guidelines.

In addition to citing sources in your outline, you must provide verbal citations during your presentation. **Verbal citations** tell listeners who the source is, how recent the information is, and what the source's qualifications are. The examples in table 11.5 illustrate how to orally cite different types of sources.

Table 11.5 Examples of Verbal Citations

Type of Source	Example
Magazine article	"According to an article by Hannah Beech in the April 13, 2009, edition of *Time* magazine, scores of people have been injured during antigovernment protests in Bangkok, Thailand."
Research study	"Erika Kirby, a communication researcher, found in a 2006 study that businesses are starting to take on more family-like roles that blur the separation between family life and work life."
Webpage	"According to a statement on the American Red Cross website, which I visited on April 13, 2009, that organization had to battle three simultaneous disasters—tornados, wildfires, and floods—during the week of April 9th."
Graphic or picture	"As you can see in this picture, taken from the ESPN website yesterday, fans ridiculed players for what they tweeted prior to their game."

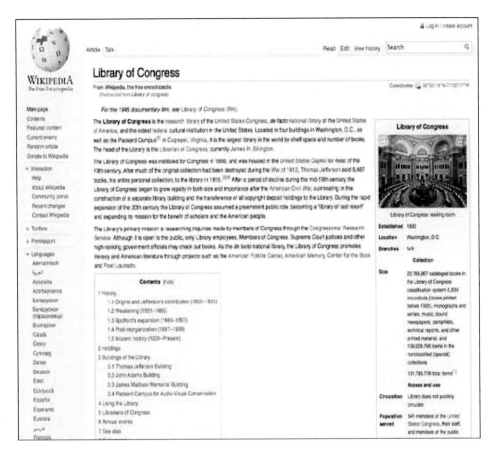

■ The decision to use some Web resources, such as Wikipedia, is controversial. The appropriateness of these sites is determined by your speaking situation, for which your professor's opinion is important.

Students often have the most difficulty citing webpages. Remember that the Web address is only that—an address. Although you should list it in the references or works cited page of your outline, giving the address during your presentation is seldom necessary unless you want your audience to visit that website.

verbal citations
Oral explanations of who the source is, how recent the information is, and what the source's qualifications are.

Turning Sources into Support

Now that you know where to look for information, the next step is pulling key facts, quotations, stories, and other details out of those sources to use in your presentation. Such details are called **supporting material,** which are details you can use to substantiate your arguments and to clarify your ideas. In this section you will learn about examples, narratives, surveys, testimonial evidence, numbers and statistics, analogies, explanations, and definitions.

supporting material
Information you can use to substantiate your arguments and to clarify your position.

EXAMPLES

Examples—specific instances used to illustrate your point—are among the most common supporting materials found in speeches. Sometimes a single example helps convince an audience; other times a relatively large number of examples may be necessary to achieve your purpose. For instance, you could support the argument that a university gives admission priority to out-of-state students by showing the difference between the numbers of in-state and out-of-state students who are accepted in relationship to the number of

examples
Specific instances used to illustrate your point.

skill **builder**

Verbally Citing Sources

Making verbal citations is one of the most important skills you will learn in this course, and it will benefit you for years to come. Start by drafting possible ways to state your sources in written form. For each source you plan to use in your presentation, write down statements similar to those in table 11.5 that you could use when identifying your sources. You should not read aloud from these drafts during your presentation, but planning the wording ahead of time will help you state the information more effectively. When writing your drafts, take care to emphasize the credentials, expertise, and timeliness of the sources.

students who applied in each group. Likewise, in a persuasive speech designed to motivate everyone to vote, you could present cases in which a few more votes would have meant a major change in election results.

You should be careful when using examples. Sometimes an example is so unusual that an audience will not accept the story as evidence or proof of anything. For instance, would you find information obtained from Hawaii a good example for illustrating the price of consumable goods? Probably not, because Hawaii is geographically isolated and requires many of its consumable goods to be transported to the islands. A good example must be plausible, typical, and related to the main point of the speech.

Two types of examples are factual and hypothetical: a *hypothetical* example is fictional but realistic, whereas a *factual* example is based on real circumstances. Either type can be brief or extended. The following is a brief factual example:

> Several online memorial sites on Facebook illustrate how social networking sites have started to serve a larger role than simply helping people connect.

Here is an extended hypothetical example:

> An example of a good excuse for a student missing class is that he or she has a serious auto accident on the way to class, ends up in the hospital, and has a signed medical statement from a physician to prove hospitalization for a week. A poor excuse for a student missing class is that the student, knowing beforehand when the final examination will be held, schedules a flight home for the day before the exam and wants an "excused absence."

The brief factual example is *verifiable,* meaning it can be supported by a source that the audience can check. The extended hypothetical example is not verifiable and is actually a composite of excuses.

NARRATIVES

narratives
Stories to illustrate an important point.

Whereas examples are primarily intended to present factual information, **narratives**—stories to illustrate an important point—focus more on telling a human story. Think about the difference between hearing that Michael J. Fox has Parkinson's disease (an example) and hearing a detailed story about how his acting career has been affected by the disease—narratives provide richer detail and dimension to people's lives.

Narratives are important parts of speeches. Major elections like 2012 turn on the power of narrative—the ability of a particular candidate to describe a vision that a majority of the electorate can buy into with their vote. Think how your speech would be improved if, rather than simply describing the 2011 flooding in Thailand, you interviewed and told a story about a fellow college student who is from Thailand and witnessed the disaster firsthand. When using narratives in your speech, take care to focus on the human element, to be truthful in telling the story, and to help the audience understand what can be learned from the story. Because they tend to draw us into human dramas, narratives can sometimes cause audience members to lose sight of potential implications and outcomes.

SURVEYS

Another source of supporting material commonly used in speeches is **surveys,** studies in which we ask a sample of the population a limited number of questions to discover public opinions on issues. Surveys are found most often in magazines or journals and are usually seen as more credible than an example or one person's experience, because they synthesize the experience of hundreds or thousands of people. One person's experience with alcohol can have an impact on an audience, but a survey indicating that one-third of all U.S. adults abstain, one-third drink occasionally, and one-third drink regularly provides better support for an argument. As when dealing with personal experience, you should ask some important questions about the evidence found in surveys:

1. *How reliable is the source?* A report in a professional journal of sociology, psychology, or communication is likely to be more thorough and more valid than one found in a local newspaper.

2. *How broad was the sample used in the survey?* Did the survey include the entire nation, the region, the state, the city, the campus, or the class? Larger samples allow the survey to be more precise in representing a broader viewpoint. In political and other polls you have heard mention of a "margin of error." Larger sample sizes reduce the margin of error, which can boost confidence in the accuracy of a poll's results.

3. *Who was included in the survey?* Did everyone in the sample have an equally good chance of being selected, or were volunteers asked to respond to the questions? If people are randomly selected to be in a survey, the results are less likely to be biased by a particular viewpoint. If you conducted a poll only through Facebook, responses to questions could be very different from those in a paper-and-pencil survey conducted at a shopping mall. Although those approaches to sampling are used all the time, they do risk biasing results in a certain way, because certain types of people had greater opportunity to participate than did others.

4. *How representative was the survey sample?* For example, *Playboy*'s readers may not be typical of the population in your state.

5. *Who performed the survey?* Was the survey firm nationally recognized, such as Lou Harris or Gallup, or did the local newspaper perform the survey? Did professionals such as professors, researchers, or management consultants administer the survey?

6. *Why was the survey done?* Was the survey performed for any self-serving purpose—for example, to attract more readers—or did the government conduct the study to help establish policy or legislation?

TESTIMONIAL EVIDENCE

Testimonial evidence, a third kind of supporting material, consists of written or oral statements of others' experience used by a speaker to substantiate or clarify a point. One assumption behind testimonial evidence is that you are not alone in your beliefs, ideas, and arguments: other people also support them. Another assumption is that the statements of others should help the audience accept your point of view because those other people may have additional credibility that can transfer to your argument. The three kinds of testimonial evidence you can use in your speeches are lay, expert, and celebrity.

  Lay testimony is statements made by an ordinary person that substantiate or support what you say. In advertising, this kind of testimony shows ordinary people using or buying products and stating the fine qualities of those products. In a speech, lay testimony might be the words of your relatives, neighbors, or colleagues concerning an issue. Such testimony

■ Telling narratives can bring issues to life by introducing characters and emotions into your speech.

surveys
Studies in which a limited number of questions are answered by a sample of the population to discover opinions on issues.

testimonial evidence
Written or oral statements of others' experience used by a speaker to substantiate or clarify a point.

lay testimony
Statements made by an ordinary person that substantiate or support what you say.

shows the audience that you and other ordinary people support the idea. Other examples of lay testimony are proclamations of faith by fundamentalist Christians at a church gathering and statements about the wonderful qualities of their college by alumni at a recruiting session.

Expert testimony is statements made by someone who has special knowledge or expertise about an issue or idea. In your speech you might quote a mechanic about problems with an automobile, an interior decorator about the aesthetic qualities of fabrics, or a political pundit about the elections. The idea is to demonstrate that people with specialized experience or education support the positions you advocate in your speech.

Celebrity testimony is statements made by a public figure who is known to the audience. Celebrity testimony occurs in advertising when someone famous endorses a particular product. In your speech you might point out that a famous politician, a syndicated columnist, or a well-known entertainer endorses the position you advocate.

Although testimonial evidence may encourage your audience to adopt your ideas, you need to use such evidence with caution. An idea may have little credence even though many laypeople believe in it; an expert may be quoted on topics well outside his or her area of expertise; and a celebrity usually is paid for endorsing a product. To protect yourself and your audience, ask yourself the following questions before using testimonial evidence in your speeches:

1. Is the person you quote an expert whose opinions or conclusions are worthier than most other people's opinions?

2. Are you quoting someone's statements about his or her own area of expertise?

3. Is the person's statement based on extensive personal experience, professional study or research, or another form of firsthand proof?

4. Will your audience find the statement more believable because you got the quotation from this outside source?

NUMBERS AND STATISTICS

A fourth kind of evidence useful for clarification or substantiation is numbers and statistics. Because numbers are sometimes easier to understand and digest when they appear in print, the public speaker often has to simplify, explain, and translate their meaning in a spoken presentation. For example, instead of saying "There were 323,462 high school graduates," say "There were more than 300,000 graduates." Other ways to simplify a number like 323,462 include writing the number on a chalkboard or poster and using a comparison, such as "Three hundred thousand high school graduates are equivalent to the entire population of Lancaster."

Statistics—numbers that summarize numerical information or compare quantities—are also difficult for audiences to interpret. For example, an audience will have difficulty interpreting a statement such as "Honda sales increased 47%." Instead, you could round off the figure to "nearly 50%," or you could reveal the actual dollar value of Honda care sales this year and last year. You can also help the audience interpret the significance with a comparison such as "That is the biggest increase in sales experienced by any domestic or imported car dealer in our city this year."

You can greatly increase your effectiveness as a speaker if you illustrate your numbers by using visual resources, such as pie charts, line graphs, and bar graphs. Both say and show your figures. Try using visual imagery—for example, "That amount of money is greater than all the money in all our local banks" or "That many discarded tires would cover our city 6 feet deep in a single year."

ANALOGIES

Another kind of supporting material used in public speeches is analogies. An **analogy** is a comparison of things that are otherwise dissimilar. For instance, one government official said that trying to find Osama bin Laden in Afghanistan was like trying to find one particular

expert testimony
Statements made by someone who has special knowledge or expertise about an issue or idea.

celebrity testimony
Statements made by a public figure who is known to the audience.

statistics
Numbers that summarize numerical information or compare quantities.

analogy
A comparison of things in some respects, especially in position or function, that are otherwise dissimilar.

rabbit in the state of West Virginia. Similarly, analogies can be used to show that ancient Roman society is analogous to U.S. society and that a law applied in one state will work the same way in another.

An analogy also provides clarification, but it is not proof, because the comparison inevitably breaks down. Therefore, a speaker who argues that U.S. society will fail just as Roman society did can carry the comparison only so far because the form of government and the institutions in the two societies are quite different. Likewise, you can question the rabbit-in-West-Virginia analogy by pointing out the vast differences between the two things being compared. Nonetheless, analogies can be quite useful as a way to illustrate or clarify.

EXPLANATIONS

Explanations are another important means of clarification and persuasion that you will often find in written and visual sources and in interviews. An **explanation** clarifies what something is or how it works. A discussion

of psychology would offer explanations and answers, as well as their relationship to the field—for example, "How does Freud explain our motivations?" "What is *catharsis,* and how is it related to aggression?" or "What do *id, ego,* and *superego* mean?"

A good explanation usually simplifies a concept or an idea by explaining the idea from the audience's point of view. If you have ever watched Sanjay Gupta from CNN or other medical correspondents, you've seen them attempt to explain highly technical medical procedures in ways that lay audiences can understand. Likewise, legal reporters covering the Penn State or Syracuse sex-abuse scandals must use explanations to simplify detailed legal issues. Explanations are the lifeblood of great journalism; they are also critical for great speeches.

DEFINITIONS

Some of the most contentious arguments in our society center on **definitions,** or determinations of meaning through description, simplification, examples, analysis, comparison, explanation, or illustration. Experts and ordinary citizens have argued for years about definitions. For instance, when does art become pornography? Is withdrawal of life-support systems euthanasia or mercy? The way you define a concept can make a considerable difference.

Definitions in a public speech enlighten the audience by revealing what a term means. Sometimes you can use definitions that appear in standard reference works, such as dictionaries and encyclopedias, but simply trying to explain the word in language the audience will understand is often more effective. For example, suppose you use the term *subcutaneous hematoma* in your speech. *Subcutaneous hematoma* is jargon used by physicians to explain a blotch on your flesh, but you could explain the term in this way: "*Subcutaneous* means 'under the skin,' and *hematoma* means 'swelled with blood,' so the words mean 'blood swelling under the skin,' or what most of us call a 'bruise.'"

Ethical Principles to Follow for Credibility and Research

As you have learned, credibility is a perceptual variable that is not based on external, objective measures of competence, trustworthiness, dynamism, and common ground. However, you retain an ethical obligation to project an honest image of yourself to your

■ Using graphs and tables can help you present statistics and numbers more effectively. You will learn more about how to do this in chapter 13.

explanation
A clarification of what something is or how it works.

definitions
determinations of meaning through description, simplification, examples, analysis, comparison, explanation, or illustration.

audience. The well-known adage that you can fool all the people some of the time may be accurate, but an ethical communicator avoids fooling anyone.

ETHICS AND SOURCE CREDIBILITY

To determine whether you are behaving ethically, answer the following questions:

1. *Are your speech's immediate purpose and long-range goal sound?* Are you providing information or recommending change that would be determined worthy by current standards? Attempting to sell a substandard product or to encourage people to injure others would clearly not be sound; persuading people to accept new, more useful ideas and to be kinder to each other would be sound.

2. *Does your end justify your means?* This time-honored notion suggests that communicators can have ethical ends but may use unethical means of bringing the audience to a particular conclusion. You want listeners to join the armed forces, but should you use scare tactics to achieve your goal?

3. *Are you being honest with your audience?* Are you well informed about the subject instead of being a poseur who only pretends to know? Are you using good evidence and reasoning to convince your audience? Are your passions about the subject sincere?

Your credibility does lie in the audience's perception of you, but you also have an ethical obligation to be the sort of person you project yourself to be. In addition, you must consider the influence of your message on the audience. Persuasive speeches, particularly, may lead to far-reaching changes in others' behaviors. Are the changes you are recommending consistent with standard ethical and moral guidelines? Have you thoroughly studied your topic, so that you are convinced of the accuracy of the information you are presenting? Are you presenting the entire picture? Are you using valid and true arguments? In short, are you treating the listeners in the way you wish to be treated when someone else is speaking and you are the listener? The Golden Rule applies to the communication situation.

THE ETHICAL USE OF SUPPORTING MATERIAL

Throughout this book we have emphasized various ethical requirements for communication that stem from the NCA Credo on Ethics (see the inside front cover of the book). And at various points in this chapter, we have pointed out ethical obligations faced by speakers when searching for and using supporting materials. Recall that the first point in the NCA Credo on Ethics states that accuracy and honesty are essential for ethical communication. In this final section we summarize the ethical obligations faced by speakers when working with supporting materials:

- *Speakers have an ethical obligation to find the best possible sources of information.* The Internet and full-text databases certainly provide us with easier research options; however, these tools do not necessarily improve the quality of our research. Nor are the best sources of information always available online or in full-text form. When you speak, your audience depends on you to present the best and most accurate information possible. As a result, many communication instructors emphasize the importance of using *high-quality* sources of information during a presentation. That's why selecting a variety of sources, including print, Internet, and possibly even interviews, can help improve the overall quality of your presentation.

plagiarism
The intentional use of information from another source without crediting the source.

- *Speakers have an ethical obligation to cite their sources of information.* Of course, one reason to cite sources of information is to avoid **plagiarism,** which is the intentional use of information from another source without crediting the source. All universities have specific codes of conduct that identify sanctions levied against those who are caught plagiarizing. Although we see relatively few cases of full plagiarism, we often see students mistakenly commit **incremental plagiarism,** which is the intentional or unintentional use of information from one or more sources without fully divulging how much information is directly quoted. We commonly see students use large chunks of information from webpages and other sources—many times this information is directly copied and pasted from the website. Failing to clearly identify what is directly quoted, even accidentally, is a form of plagiarism. Moreover, your instructor will likely evaluate your speech more favorably if you interpret the meaning of short quotations for the audience rather than over-relying on very large quotations.

- *Speakers have an ethical obligation to fairly and accurately represent sources.* How often have you heard politicians and other public figures complain that the media take their comments "out of context"? To avoid unfair and inaccurate representations of sources, whether they are newspaper articles, webpages, books, or even interviews, you must ensure that you fully understand the points being made by the source. Remember, for example, that two-sided arguments are often used to present a point. A **two-sided argument** is one in which a source advocating one position presents an argument from the opposite viewpoint and then goes on to refute that viewpoint. To take an excerpt from a source in which the opposing argument is being presented for refutation and implying that the source was advocating the opposing argument is unethical. As a speaker you are free to disagree with points made by the sources you consult; however, you may not misrepresent them.

Locating, understanding, and incorporating supporting material is one of the most important tasks you will undertake as a presenter of information and argument. As illustrated by table 11.3, research affects every step in the process of preparing and delivering a presentation. Taking care to effectively and ethically use your information will make you a better speaker and will garner the respect of your peers and teachers.

incremental plagiarism
The intentional or unintentional use of information from one or more sources without fully divulging how much information is directly quoted.

two-sided argument
A source advocating one position presents an argument from the opposite viewpoint and then goes on to refute that argument.

keeping it real

Planning for Good Research

At the beginning of this chapter you learned about Abbey, who thought her speech was going well only to discover that poor research had left her with an embarrassing inability to respond to a critical question. Abbey's poor research led to a credibility problem. How could Abbey have prepared more effectively?

1. Don't rely on Google. Abbey only used Google, rather than relying on multiple databases and portals. This approach limited the types of sources she considered for her presentation. An effective research plan would have emphasized source variety.

2. Don't rely on heuristics for evaluating your sources. Abbey relied on one primary source for her speech about Ritalin, the highlighted result on Google labeled the "official" site. This shortcut led her to think she had found a good source, when, in fact, the webpage was entirely designed to sell Ritalin to consumers. A more effective research plan would consider criteria such as bias and motive before selecting a site.

3. Don't wait. Abbey started her research the evening before her presentation. Although Abbey is certainly not alone in this approach, her failure to devote enough time to her speech showed in her results. Effective research and planning for a speech takes several days, so plan for that.

Chapter Review & Study Guide

Summary

In this chapter, you learned the following:

1. Source credibility is the audience's perception of your effectiveness as a speaker.

   - Source credibility stems from audience members' perceptions of the speaker, topic, message, and situation.

   - Source credibility is important because it helps the audience understand "why you are telling us about this topic in this manner."

2. Source credibility is created from the audience's perceptions of four dimensions of credibility.

   - Competence is the speaker's qualifications to speak on a topic.

   - Trustworthiness is the perceived dependability and ethics of the speaker.

   - Dynamism is the extent to which the speaker appears confident and comfortable to the audience. A lack of dynamism can make the speaker appear less competent and less trustworthy.

   - Common ground exists when there is perceived shared understanding between the speaker and the audience. The shared understanding or experience can happen in the past, present, or future.

3. Evidence for your speeches and other discussions come from various types of sources.

   - Your personal experience can add to your credibility and clarify your personal knowledge; however, personal experience should be carefully evaluated before use.

   - When using other persons as sources, you should carefully plan interview questions to make your use of testimony more valid.

   - Library materials come in a variety of forms. Various types of databases can help you find information, and a reference librarian is specifically trained to help you select and use appropriate databases.

   - The Internet provides quick access to a variety of information, but that information must be carefully verified for accuracy.

4. Use citations to document your use of evidence, both in your outline and in your speech.

   - Internal citations are used in the body of your outline or paper to indicate where you are using information from one of your sources.

   - Bibliographic citations appear in the references section of your outline or paper and typically follow some sort of prescribed format style.

   - Verbal citations are presented orally during your speech and typically emphasize the qualifications, credibility, and timeliness of your source.

5. When looking for evidence, eight types of supporting material are typically used: examples, narratives, surveys, testimonials, numbers and statistics, analogies, explanations, and definitions.

6. Speakers are obligated to follow ethical principles for establishing credibility and using evidence.

   - You have an obligation to be true to yourself and have worthy purposes and goals. You should employ ethical means to achieve ethical ends.

   - You have an obligation to use accurate information and to cite the sources of such information.

Key Terms

Analogy
Bibliographic references
Celebrity testimony
Common ground
Competence
Definitions
Dynamism
Examples
Expert testimony
Explanation

Heuristics
Incremental plagiarism
Internal references
Lay testimony
Narratives
Personal experience
Plagiarism
Reference librarian
Search engine

Sleeper effect
Source credibility
Statistics
Supporting material
Surveys
Testimonial evidence
Trustworthiness
Two-sided argument
Verbal citations

Study Questions

connect
For further review, go to the LearnSmart study module for this chapter.

1. Which of the following statements regarding source credibility is *not* true?

   a. Source credibility is the audience's perception of the effectiveness of a speaker.
   b. Source credibility depends on the speaker, the subject discussed, the situation, and the audience.
   c. Source credibility is something a speaker possesses.
   d. The audience determines credibility.

2. Which aspect of source credibility is the degree to which a speaker is perceived as honest, friendly, and honorable?

   a. competence
   b. trustworthiness
   c. dynamism
   d. common ground

3. If a person speaks with vocal variety, moves toward the audience, or uses facial expressions and gestures, he or she is exhibiting which aspect of credibility?

   a. competence
   b. trustworthiness
   c. dynamism
   d. common ground

4. Which of the following results in higher credibility?

   a. disorganized speeches
   b. people perceived as low in status
   c. fumbling over words
   d. effective delivery skills

5. Which of the following cannot be effectively utilized when gathering evidence for your speeches?

   a. personal experience
   b. library resources
   c. the Internet
   d. a friend's speech

6. Which type of source undergoes blind peer review to ensure high-quality information and contains specified studies?

   a. nonfiction books
   b. academic journal articles
   c. government documents
   d. trade journal articles

7. Brief notations in your outline that indicate a reference used in your speech are called _____ references, whereas _____ references are complete citations that appear in the "references" section of the speech outline.

   a. internal, bibliographic
   b. verbal, internal
   c. bibliographic, external
   d. external, verbal

8. When evaluating sources, you should ensure that the supporting material

   a. contains jargon and technical explanations.
   b. includes relevant and irrelevant information.
   c. contains bias and is subjective.
   d. is verifiable.

9. Which type of supporting material includes written or oral statements of others' experiences?

   a. examples
   b. testimonial evidence
   c. numbers and statistics
   d. definitions

10. Information used to substantiate arguments and clarify a speaker's position is called

    a. competence.
    b. the sleeper effect.
    c. supporting material.
    d. dynamism.

Answers:

1. (c); 2. (b); 3. (c); 4. (d); 5. (d); 6. (b); 7. (a); 8. (d); 9. (b); 10. (c)

Critical Thinking

1. What topics do you feel most credible speaking about in your class? Why?

2. When watching the news or reading a newspaper, note whether the newscasters or writers cite their sources. Do they appear less credible if they do not mention where the information originated? Give examples.

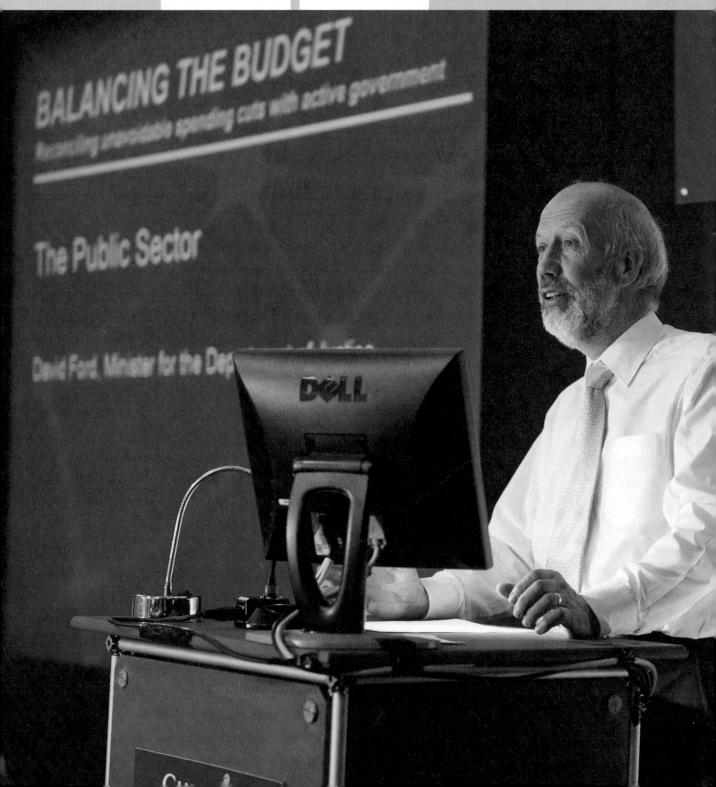

organizing your presentation

When you have read and thought about this chapter, you will be able to:

1. Present an effective introduction that captures the interest of your audience in your topic, the purpose of the speech, and the development of the talk.

2. Write an effective outline for a presentation.

3. Describe the most frequently used patterns of organization in public presentations.

4. Use transitions and signposts that link ideas and indicate direction to the audience.

5. Present an effective conclusion.

6. Compile a list of references, or sources, to accompany your complete outline.

In this chapter you will learn how to organize your presentation. You will examine the three main parts of a speech: introduction, body, and conclusion; you will learn the functions of each part and how to effectively organize the content. Understanding the parts of a speech, the functions of each part, and ways to organize the entire message is essential to becoming a successful presenter.

Alan Perrault wanted to give a speech on geocaching, the GPS treasure-hunting game, which was a favorite personal activity. He was not sure whether his classmates knew about the game, so he began to informally talk about this activity before and after class. He learned that a couple of people had geocached in their hometowns, one had geocached near the campus, but most did not know what the term meant. From these interactions, Alan began to think about how he could structure his talk.

What would you suggest to Alan about the organization of his speech? Where should he start, and what information should he include? At the end of the chapter, we'll take another look at Alan's situation and how he decides to organize his speech.

How you organize a speech sends signals to audience members. Your speech will be more likely to accomplish its goals if you can gain and hold your audience's attention, make clear and smooth transitions between major sections, and end with a clear statement of what you want your audience to take away from your presentation. This chapter will teach you about organization by discussing the key elements of a speech—the introduction, body, and conclusion—as well as how to outline your speech effectively.

Creating the Introduction

introduction
The first part of your presentation, where you fulfill the five functions of an introduction.

The **introduction,** the first part of your presentation, lets audiences assess you as a speaker. During your first few sentences, and certainly in the first few minutes of your speech, audience members decide whether to listen to you. They also decide whether your topic is important enough to hear. In those crucial early minutes, you can capture your audience's attention and keep their focus, or you can lose their attention—perhaps for the remainder of the presentation.

The five functions of an introduction are to gain the audience's attention, to arouse interest, to state the purpose or thesis of your speech, to establish your qualifications, and to briefly forecast for listeners the organization of your speech and the way you will develop your ideas. You do not need to fulfill the functions in this order. Gaining audience attention often comes at the beginning, but maintaining attention is an important function throughout the speech. Forecasting the speech's organization often comes toward the end of an introduction, but it does not have to be last. Let us systematically explore the five functions and some examples of each.

GAINING AND MAINTAINING AUDIENCE ATTENTION

The first function of an introduction is to gain and maintain attention by involving your audience in your topic. Here are some suggestions:

1. *Bring to the presentation the object or person about which you are going to speak.* A student speaking on health foods brings a tray full of health foods, which he shares with the audience after the speech; a student speaking on weight lifting brings her 250-pound friend to demonstrate the moves during the speech.

2. *Invite your audience to participate.* Ask questions and invite audience members to raise their hands and answer. Or have the audience stand up and perform the exercise you are teaching them.

Ministers often invite the congregation to participate actively in the service.

3. *Let your clothing relate to your presentation.* A nurse talking about the dangers of acute hepatitis wears a nurse's uniform; a construction worker dons a hard hat.

4. *Exercise your audience's imagination.* Have the audience members close their eyes and imagine they are poised on a ski slope, standing before a judge on a driving-while-intoxicated charge, or slipping into a cool Minnesota lake on a hot and humid day. Preston Gilderhus, a student in industrial engineering and management, presented a talk on the importance of bees. He began, "Imagine the world without apples, oranges, strawberries, or carrots. None of these foods would exist without bees."

5. *Start with sight or sound.* A student who gave a powerful presentation on motorcycle safety showed six slides as he talked about the importance of wearing a helmet while riding. Only one item appeared in color on each slide: a crushed or battered helmet that had been worn by someone who lived through a motorcycle accident. His words spoke of safety; the battered helmets reinforced the message.

6. *Arouse audience curiosity.* Five hundred white people gathered to hear a presentation on diversity. The speaker was a Chinese man dressed in traditional Chinese attire. He started his presentation by saying nothing; he just slowly scanned his audience. The audience, accustomed to speakers who start by speaking, was mystified by his quiet demeanor but exceedingly attentive. Then the speaker said, "Do you know how it feels to stand in front of a group this large and to see no one who looks like you?"

7. *Role-play.* A student invites an audience member to pretend to be a choking victim. The speaker then "saves" the victim by using the maneuver she is teaching the audience.

8. *Show a very short video.* A football player speaking on violence in that sport shows a short video of punt returns. He points out which players were deliberately trying to maim their opponents with face guards—as they have been taught to do.

9. *Present a brief quotation or have the audience read something you have provided.* One enterprising student handed every class member an official-looking letter right before

his speech. Each letter was a personalized court summons for a moving violation detected by a police-owned spy camera at a busy intersection.

10. *State striking facts or statistics.* Emily Knilans, a first-year human development and family science student, introduced her speech on the importance of drinking water thus: "The human brain weighs about 3 pounds, about 2.4 of those pounds are water, and water contributes to all mental functions."

11. *Self-disclose.* Tell audience members something about yourself—related to the topic—that they would not otherwise know: "I took hard drugs for six years"; "I was an Eagle scout"; "I earn over $50,000 a year—legally."

12. *Tell a story, a narration.* A student told this story: the little boy asked his grandfather whether he was a hero, because the boy had heard that his grandpa fought in Vietnam when he was a young man. "No," said the grandfather, "I was not a hero, but I was in an entire battalion of heroes."

These suggestions for gaining and maintaining audience attention certainly are not the only possibilities available to you, but they have all been used successfully by other students. Your introduction should not simply imitate what you read in this book; instead, think of ideas of your own that will work best for you and your audience.

Some words of caution about gaining and maintaining attention: no matter what method you use, avoid being overly dramatic. A student who pretended to cut himself and shot fake blood all over the front of the room got his teacher and his audience so upset that they could not listen to his presentation.

Always make sure your attention-getting strategy is related to your topic. Some speakers think every public speech must start with a joke, but this is a big mistake if you are not good at telling jokes or your audience is not interested in hearing them. Topically relevant jokes may be acceptable, but they are still just one of hundreds of ways a speaker can gain attention. Another overused device is writing something such as "S-E-X" on the chalkboard and then announcing your speech has nothing to do with sex—you just wanted to get the audience's attention. Your attention-getting strategy here has nothing to do with the topic. Finally, be wary of guests, animals, and PowerPoint, because all three can eliminate you from the speaking situation. They can all be effective to gain audience attention, but they must not become center stage while you and your message become background music.

AROUSING AUDIENCE INTEREST

The second function of an introduction is to arouse audience interest in the subject matter. The best way is to show clearly how the topic is related to the audience. A highly skilled speaker can adapt almost any topic to a given audience. Do you want to talk about collecting coins? Thousands of coins pass through each person's hands every year. Can you tell your audience how to spot a rare one? If you can arouse the audience's interest in currency, you will find it easier to encourage them to listen to your speech about the rare coins you have collected. Similarly, speeches about your life as a parent of four, a camp counselor, or the manager of a business can be linked to audience interests. The following good example relates the topic to the audience; these words are quoted from a student speech on drinking and driving:

> Do you know what the leading cause of death is for people who attend this college? Some of you might think it is a disease that causes the most deaths—cancer, heart attacks, or AIDS. No, the leading cause of death among students at this college is car accidents. Not just ordinary car accidents, but accidents in which the driver has been drinking.

One of the four main purposes of a speech introduction is to arouse audience interest by showing how the topic relates to them.

The speaker related her topic to the audience by linking a national problem to her own college. She prepared the audience to receive more information and ideas about this common problem.

STATING THE PURPOSE OR THESIS

The third function of an introduction is to state the purpose or thesis of your speech. Why? Because informative speeches invite learning, and learning is more likely to occur if you reveal to the audience what you want them to know. Consider the difficulty of listening to a history professor who spends 50 minutes telling you every detail and date related to the Crusades. Observe how much more easily you can listen to a professor who begins the lecture by stating what you are supposed to learn: "I want you to understand why the Crusades began, who the main participants were, and when the Crusades occurred."

Here are four examples of statements of purpose or thesis:

Thesis statement for a demonstration speech: "This afternoon I am going to demonstrate how you can mix three common household products to make your own antiseptic and reduce germs in your home."

Thesis statement for an informative speech: "Today I ask you to remember at least three of the five methods I will recommend to avoid identity theft."

Thesis statement for a persuasive speech: "After you hear me today, you will be eager to join our movement to change the grading system at this college."

Thesis statement for an inspirational or motivational speech: "Our banquet tonight is to remind us of the sacrifice our soldiers made on our behalf."

In public speaking, as in education, audience members are more likely to learn and understand if you make your expectations clear. You can accomplish that goal by stating your purpose in the introduction. Sometimes in a persuasive speech you may wish to delay revealing your purpose until you have set the stage for audience acceptance. Under most circumstances, though—and especially in informative speeches—you should reveal your purpose or thesis in your introduction.

Alan Perrault fulfilled the five functions of the introduction.

Sample Introduction That Fulfills the Five Functions

Introduction

I. *Attention getter:* Today, 1.54 million active geocaches exist around the globe.

II. *Listener relevance:* Geocaching is fun and it will allow you to visit new and interesting places. It is suitable for anyone, and the over 5 million geocachers worldwide include families with little kids all the way through older retirees.

III. *Speaker credibility:* I have been geocaching since I was 15 years old and I have nearly 200 finds to my name.

IV. *Thesis:* I am going to talk to you about the game of geocaching.

V. *Preview:* I will explain to you what geocaching is, how it works, and how you can get involved with it.

ESTABLISHING YOUR QUALIFICATIONS

The fourth function of an introduction is to describe any special qualifications you have to enhance your credibility. You can talk about your experience, your research, the experts you interviewed, and your own education and training in the subject. Although you should be wary about self-praise, you need not be reserved in stating why you can speak about the topic with authority. Here is an example of establishing credibility through self-disclosure:

> You can probably tell from my fingernails that my day job is repairing automobiles, a job I have held at the same dealership for over 12 years. I have repaired thousands of cars. That is why I want to tell you today why you and your insurance company have to pay such high prices for repair.

For more information about establishing source credibility, return to chapter 11 on this subject.

FORECASTING DEVELOPMENT AND ORGANIZATION

The fifth function of an introduction is to forecast the organization and development of the presentation. The forecast provides a preview of the main points you plan to cover. Audience members feel more comfortable when they know what to expect. You can help by revealing your plan for the speech. Are you going to discuss a problem and its solution? Are you going to make three main arguments with supporting materials? Let your audience know what you plan to do early in your speech. Emily Knilans, the student who was quoted earlier, stated, "I will discuss what water does for our bodies and the differences between drinking bottled water and drinking tap water." Another student asserted, "Today

I plan to present three good reasons why race should be a factor in college admissions."

The Body

Most speakers begin composing their presentations with the body rather than the introduction, because they need to know the content of the presentation to write an effective introduction.

The **body** of a presentation is the largest portion of the presentation, in which you place your arguments and ideas, your evidence and examples, your proofs and illustrations, and your stories and testimonials. Since you usually do not have time to state in a presentation everything you know about a subject, you need to decide what information to include in the body and what to exclude. Because the material you will use may not all be of equal importance, you need to decide placement—first, last, or in the middle. Generally, the most important information should be placed first or last. Audiences remember information in these positions more easily than they recall information in the middle of the body. Selecting, prioritizing, and organizing are three skills that you will use in developing the body of your speech.

Just as the introduction of a speech has certain functions to fulfill, so does the body. These are its main functions:

1. Increase what an audience knows about a topic (informative presentation)

2. Change an audience's attitudes or actions about a topic (persuasive presentation)

3. Present a limited number of arguments, stories, and/or ideas

4. Provide support for your arguments and/or ideas

5. Indicate the sources of your information, arguments, and supporting materials

You already know something about organization. Every sentence you utter is organized. The words are arranged according to rules of syntax for the English language. Even

sizing things up

Clarity Behaviors Inventory

The first step in understanding how to sound organized when presenting information is to learn how others do this. As college students, you have the opportunity to watch teachers present information nearly every day. Below are 12 statements describing things a teacher might do. Select a teacher from another class, and think of that teacher when responding to the statements. Or consider another student who has already presented in your class. Use the following scale to respond:

1 = Strongly disagree
2 = Disagree
3 = Neither agree nor disagree
4 = Agree
5 = Strongly agree

_____ 1. The speaker verbally stresses important issues presented in the presentation.

_____ 2. Written examples of topics covered in the presentation are provided in the form of handouts or visual materials (PowerPoint, dry-erase board, or chalkboard).

_____ 3. The organization of the talk is given to me in written form, either on paper or as part of a visual aid, such as an overhead or the chalkboard.

_____ 4. The speaker tells us what definitions, explanations, or conclusions are important to make note of.

_____ 5. The speaker explains how we are supposed to see relationships between topics covered in the presentation.

_____ 6. The speaker provides us with written descriptions of the most important things in the presentation.

_____ 7. The speaker explains when he or she is presenting something that is important for us to know.

_____ 8. The speaker provides us with written or visual definitions, explanations, or conclusions of topics covered in the presentation.

_____ 9. The speaker verbally identifies examples that illustrate concepts we are supposed to learn from the talk.

_____ 10. Written explanations of how ideas in the presentation fit together are presented on the chalkboard, on the overhead, on PowerPoint, or in handouts.

_____ 11. The speaker explains when he or she is providing an important definition of a concept.

This exercise can measure both oral and written clarity. A guide for interpreting your responses appears in the appendix at the end of the text (p. 348).

Source: Adapted from Titsworth, S., Novak, D., Hunt, S., & Meyer, K. (2004). The effects of teacher clarity on affective and cognitive learning: A causal model of clear teaching behaviors. International Communication Association, May, New Orleans, LA. Used by permission of the author.

body
The largest part of the presentation, which contains the arguments, evidence, and main content.

skill builder

Crafting an Effective Introduction: Things to Avoid

Here are some tips for strengthening your introduction by avoiding some common mistakes. Once you've drafted your introduction, check it against this list.

- Do not start talking until you are up in front and settled. Starting your speech on the way up to the lectern is bad form.

- Do not say negative things about you or your abilities: "I'm not used to public speaking," "I've never done this before," "I couldn't be more nervous than I am right now." You are supposed to build your credibility in the introduction, not give an audience more doubts about your ability.

- Do not let your nonverbal unease overcome your message. Crossing your legs, refusing to look at the audience, jingling the change in your pocket, repeatedly pushing your hair off your face—all of these signal to the audience your lack of confidence. So act confident even if you are not.

- Do not say negative things about your message: "I didn't have much time to prepare this speech," "I couldn't find much information on my topic," or "I really don't know much about this issue." Do the best you can to convey your message, but do not tell the audience to disregard your message.

when you are in conversation, you organize your speech. The first statement you make is often more general than that which follows. For instance, you might say, "I don't like DeMato for Congress," after which you might say why you don't like DeMato. You probably don't start by stating a specific fact, such as DeMato's voting record, her position on healthcare, or the issue that her love life has been reported on the gossip pages. Likewise, when we compose a speech, we tend to limit what we say, prioritize our points, and back them as necessary with support—all organized according to principles we have either subconsciously learned (such as the rules of syntax) or consciously studied (such as the rules of organization).

THE PRINCIPLES OF OUTLINING

An **outline** is a written plan that uses symbols, margins, and content to reveal the order, importance, and substance of your speech. An outline shows the sequence of your arguments or main points, indicates their relative importance, and states the content of your arguments, main points, and subpoints. The outline is a simplified, abstract version of your speech.

Why should you learn how to outline? Here are three good reasons:

outline
A written plan that uses symbols, margins, and content to reveal the order, importance, and substance of a presentation.

- Outlining is a skill that can be used to develop written compositions, to write notes in class, and to compose speeches.

- Outlining reinforces important skills, such as determining what is most important, what arguments and evidence will work best with this audience, and roughly how much time and effort will go into each part of your presentation.

- Outlining encourages you to speak conversationally, because you do not have every word in front of you.

You will find that learning how to outline can provide you with a useful tool in your classes and at work. Outlining is versatile and easy to learn as long as you keep six principles in mind:

- *Principle 1: Link outline to purpose.* All the items of information in your outline should be directly related to your purpose and long-range goal. The immediate purpose, you will recall, is what you expect to achieve *on the day of your presentation*. You might want the audience to be able to distinguish between a row house and a townhouse, to rent a particular DVD, or to talk with others about a topic. All these purposes can be achieved shortly after the audience hears about the idea. Remember that the long-range goal is what you expect to achieve by your message *in the days, months, or years ahead*. You may be talking about a candidate two months before the election, but you want your audience to vote a certain way at that future date. You may want to push people to be more tolerant toward persons of your race, gender, sexual preference, or religion, but tolerance is more likely to develop over time than instantly—so your goal is long-range.

■ *Principle 2: Your outline is an abstract of the message you will deliver.* As a simplification, the outline should be less than every word you will speak but should include all important points and supporting materials. Some instructors say an outline should be about one-third the length of the actual presentation, if the message were in manuscript form. However, you should ask what your instructor expects, because some instructors like to see a very complete outline, whereas others prefer a brief outline. Nonetheless, even a complete outline is not a manuscript but an abstract of the talk you intend to deliver, a plan that includes the important arguments or information you intend to present.

■ *Principle 3: Each outline part is a single idea.* That is, the outline should consist of single units of information, usually in the form of complete sentences that express a single idea:

■ Creating an outline will help you structure your speech in the most effective way possible.

I. Government regulation of handguns should be implemented to reduce the number of murders in this country.

    A. Half the murders in the United States are committed by criminals using handguns.

    B. Half the handgun deaths in the United States are caused by relatives, friends, or acquaintances of the victim.

■ *Principle 4: Your outline symbols signal importance.* In the portion of a sample outline that follows, the **main points,** or most important points, are indicated by Roman numerals, such as I, II, III, IV, and V. The number of main points in a 5- to 10-minute message, or even a longer presentation, should be limited to the number you can reasonably cover, explain, or prove in the time permitted. Most 5-minute messages have from one to three main points. Even hour-long presentations must have a limited number of main points, because most audiences are unable to remember more than seven main points.

main points
The most important points in a presentation; indicated by Roman numerals in an outline.

    Subpoints, less important points supporting the main points, are indicated by capital letters, such as A, B, C, D, and E. Ordinarily, two subpoints under a main point are regarded as the minimum if any subpoints are to be presented. Like main points, subpoints should be limited in number; otherwise, the audience may lose sight of your main points. A good guideline is to present two or three of your best pieces of supporting material in support of each main point.

subpoints
The points in a presentation that support the main points; indicated by capital letters in an outline.

■ *Principle 5: Your outline margins signal importance.* The margins of your outline are coordinated with the symbols assigned to the outline items, so the main points all have the same left margin, the subpoints all have a slightly larger left margin, and sub-subpoints have a still larger one. The larger the margin on the left, the less important the item is to your purpose Amber Rasche presented a speech on why we need embryonic stem cell research. A portion of her outline is presented on the following page to illustrate the relationship of main points and subpoints in the outline.

■ *Principle 6: Use parallel form.* **Parallel form** relies on the consistent use of complete sentences, clauses, phrases, or words, but not a mixture of these. Hacker and Sommers, in their text on writing, explain, "Readers expect items in a series to appear in parallel grammatical form."[1] So do listeners. Most teachers prefer an outline consisting entirely of complete sentences, because such an outline reveals the speaker's message more completely. The outline on stem cell research is composed entirely of complete sentences; the form is parallel because no dependent clauses, phrases, or single words appear.

parallel form
The consistent use of complete sentences, clauses, phrases, or words in an outline.

THE ROUGH DRAFT

Before you begin composing your outline, you can save time and energy by (1) selecting a topic that is appropriate for you, your audience, your purpose, and the situation; (2) finding arguments, examples, illustrations, quotations, stories, and other supporting materials from your experience, from written and visual resources, and from other people; and (3) narrowing your topic, so that you can select the best materials from a large supply of available items (see chapters 10 and 11).

Once you have gathered materials consistent with your purpose, you can begin by developing a **rough draft** of your outline—a preliminary organization of the outline. The most efficient way to develop a rough draft is to choose a limited number of main points important for your purpose and your audience.

Next, you should see what materials you have from your experience, from written and visual resources, and from other people to support these main ideas, including facts, statistics, testimony, and examples. What arguments, illustrations, and supporting materials will be most likely to have an impact on the audience? Sometimes speakers get so involved in a topic that they select mainly those items that interest them. In public speaking you should select the items likely to have the maximum impact on the audience, not on you.

Composing an outline for a speech is a process. Even professional speechwriters may have to make important changes to their first draft. Some of the questions you need to consider as you revise your rough draft follow:

1. Are your main points consistent with your purpose?
2. Do your subpoints and sub-subpoints relate to your main points?

rough draft
The preliminary organization of the outline of a presentation.

Sample Partial Outline Illustrating the Principles of Outlining

Principle 1: Outline links all major points to purpose.

Principle 2: Outline simplifies and reduces presentation to series of related sentences.

Principle 3: Each item in outline is one sentence.

Principle 4: Symbols (I, II, and A, B, etc.) indicate main and subordinate ideas.

Principle 5: Margins (far left for main points and indented for subordinate points) indicate importance.

Principle 6: Each item is in parallel form.

II. In the search for a cure, James Thomson in 1998 was the first biologist to isolate human embryonic stem cells.

    A. The goal of this research is to use stem cells to replace cells that have failed in the human body.

    B. Congress passed a bill in October 1998 prohibiting experimentation with embryonic stem cells except under very limited circumstances.

    C. Congress banned funding for any experimentation that would harm embryos.

III. People favoring stem cell research demonstrate that the prohibition is unnecessarily keeping us from medical advances.

    A. Experts estimate that 400,000 embryos already exist in fertility clinics.

    B. Most of the existing embryos are discarded if they are not donated to science.

3. Are the items in your outline the best possible ones for this audience, for this topic, for you, for the purpose, and for the occasion?

4. Does your outline follow the principles of outlining?

Even after you have rewritten your rough draft, you would be wise to have another person—perhaps a classmate—examine your outline and provide an opinion about its content and correctness.

The sample outline for a speech on blogging is an example of what a rough draft of a speech looks like.

Blogging
by Daniel Kalis

Introduction

My immediate purpose is to help my audience understand the origins, present practice, and future of blogging.

I. What is blogging and what is its importance now and in the future?

   A. What is blogging?

   B. Why is it important?

II. History

   A. Origin

      1. When?

      2. Who?

   B. Original uses

III. Present

   A. Reasons for popularity

   B. Complications

III. Future

   A. Trends

   B. Genres

IV. Conclusion: Blogging is growing exponentially because of its many possibilities.

Rough draft can have sentences, phrases, or just a word or two to indicate your overall plan for presentation.

Rough draft should be easy to change as you decide what to keep and what to discard based on what you can find about topic.

Rough draft is an early plan containing cues about what you want to say.

A rough draft of a speech does not necessarily follow parallel form, nor is it as complete as the sentence outline, which often develops out of the rough draft. Mostly, the rough draft provides an overview so that you can see how the parts of the speech—the main points and subpoints—fit together. When you are ready to finalize your outline, you have several options. However, the sentence outline is preferred by many communication instructors.

THE SENTENCE OUTLINE

sentence outline
An outline consisting entirely of complete sentences.

The sentence outline does not have all the words that will occur in the delivered speech, but it does provide a complete guide to the content. A **sentence outline** consists entirely of complete sentences. It shows in sentence form your order of presentation; what kinds of arguments, supporting material, and evidence you plan to use; and where you plan to place them. A look at your outline indicates strengths and weaknesses. You might note, for instance, that you have insufficient information about one main point or a surplus of information on another.

In addition to the sentence outline itself, you may want to make notes on the functions being served by each part of your outline. For example, where are you trying to gain and maintain attention? Where are you trying to back up a major argument with supporting materials, such as statistics, testimony, or specific instances?

A sentence outline consists of complete sentences. It shows the order of the presentation as well as the arguments and supporting material you intend to use.

Why All College Students Should Eat Breakfast
by Michael Burns

Introduction

I. Many people choose to sleep 30 minutes longer every day rather than take the time to eat breakfast.

    A. How many of you ate breakfast this morning? Your cup of coffee does not count. (*show of hands*)

    B. College students who eat breakfast perform better in classes and are healthier.

    C. Eating breakfast should be a part of all college students' daily schedules.

Body

II. There are many reasons eating breakfast is beneficial.

    A. Breakfast is a great way to jumpstart your metabolism and your day.

    B. Students who eat breakfast are healthier than students who don't eat breakfast.

        1. WebMD reports that people who eat breakfast are less overweight than people who don't eat breakfast.

A sentence outline, along with side notes indicating functions, is a blueprint for your speech. The sentence outline can strengthen your speech performance by helping you present evidence or supporting materials that will make sense to audience members and will help you inform or persuade them.

The sample sentence outline below is based on a student's speech. The immediate purpose of the presentation was to explain the reasons students should eat breakfast. The action goal of the speech was to persuade classmates to get in the habit of eating breakfast every day. Notice that every entry in the outline is a sentence.

cultural note

Different Cultures Use Different Organizational Patterns

The dominant culture in North America embraces linear organizational patterns that move from a distinct beginning to a middle and end, that tend to state early and boldly who the speaker is and what the main point is, and that are rather detailed in structure with main points, subpoints, and even sub-subpoints. Do not assume that other cultures are the same. For example, in some Pacific Rim cultures, speakers start their presentations by suggesting they are inadequate rather than building up their credibility in an introduction. By doing so, they are showing deference to the audience and demonstrating respect. Some Native American groups fill their messages with colorful imagery, metaphors, and illustrative stories instead of generating arguments and evidence. African Americans, among other groups, hit on a recurring refrain with a pattern of organization that keeps circling back to a main point with many related narratives between each repetition. When addressing people from cultures different from your own, you should be aware of how they like to organize their messages. You might intersperse your organizational pattern with some elements of your audience's preferred organizational patterns.

    2. The Florida Department of Citrus claims that people who eat a breakfast that includes a glass of orange juice have a stronger immune system, but this might not be an impartial source.

  C. Students who eat breakfast also perform better in school.

    1. Mayo Clinic doctors have reported that people who eat breakfast regularly have more energy and are able to focus longer on tasks.

    2. The American Dietetic Association claims that students who eat breakfast are more likely to have better concentration and problem-solving skills than students who don't eat breakfast.

Conclusion

  III. As college students, we need to eat breakfast daily.

    A. Eating breakfast every day will make us healthier.

    B. Eating breakfast every day will improve our performance in classes.

    C. Eating breakfast should be just as an important to our daily schedules as taking a shower.

THE KEY-WORD OUTLINE

Using a manuscript for your entire speech may invite you to become too dependent on the manuscript. Too much attention to notes reduces your eye contact and minimizes your attention to audience responses. Nonetheless, you can become very proficient at reading from a manuscript on which you have highlighted the important words, phrases, and quotations. A complete sentence outline may be superior to a manuscript in that it forces you to extemporize, to maintain eye contact, and to respond to audience feedback. Key words and phrases can also be underlined or highlighted on a sentence outline. An alternative method is simply to use a **key-word outline,** an outline consisting of important words or phrases to remind you of the content of the speech.

A key-word outline shrinks the ideas in a speech considerably more than does a sentence outline. It ordinarily consists of important words and phrases, but it can also include statistics or quotations that are long or difficult to remember. The sample key-word outline came from a student's speech about the youth vote. Notice how the key-word format reduces the content to the bare essentials.

key-word outline
An outline consisting of important words or phrases to remind you of the content of the presentation.

A key word outline consists of important words or phrases to help remind the speaker of the content of the speech. It may also include key statistics and quotations.

The Youth Vote
by Amanda Peterson

Introduction

   I.   Politicians ignore youth vote

      A. Mostly 18- to 24-year-olds don't vote

      B. Statistics on voting

      C. Forecast of the reasons

Body

   II. Youth apathetic to politics

      A. Sports & beer more interesting

      B. Don't know who represents them

   III. Politics unappealing

      A. Partisanship

      B. Political scandals

Conclusion

   IV. What solution?

      A. More focus on youth

      B. More attention on campus

ORGANIZATIONAL PATTERNS

You can outline the body of a presentation using a number of **organizational patterns,** arrangements of the contents of the message. Exactly which pattern of organization is most appropriate for your presentation depends in part on your purpose and on the nature of your material. For instance, if your purpose is to present a solution to a problem, your purpose lends itself well to the problem/solution organizational pattern. If your material focuses on events that occurred over time, then it might be most easily outlined within a time-sequence pattern.

In this section we will examine four organizational patterns, prototypes from which a skilled presenter can construct many others. Keep in mind that a number of organizational patterns may appear in the same message: an overall problem/solution organization may have within it a time-sequence pattern that explains the history of the problem.

The Time-Sequence Pattern

The **time-sequence pattern** is a method of organization in which the presenter explains a sequence of events in chronological order. Most frequently seen in informative presentations, this pattern can serve in presentations that consider the past, present, and future of an idea, an issue, a plan, or a project. It is most useful for such topics as

How the Salvation Army Began	The Future of International Space Exploration
The Naming of a Team	The Development of Drugs for Treating HIV

Any topic that requires attention to events, incidents, or steps that take place over time is appropriate for this pattern of organization. Following is a brief outline of a composition organized in a time-sequence pattern:

skill builder

Tips for Using Note Cards

A key-word outline fits easily on 3-by-5-inch or 4-by-6-inch note cards or on 8½-by-11-inch paper. If you choose note cards, the following suggestions may be useful:

1. Write instructions to yourself on your note cards. For instance, if you are supposed to write the title of your speech and your name on the chalkboard before your presentation begins, then you can write that instruction on the top of your first card.
2. Write on one side of the cards only. To use more cards with your key-word outline on one side only is better than to write front and back, which is more likely to result in confusion.
3. Number your note cards on the top, so that they will be unlikely to get out of order. If you drop them, you can quickly reassemble them.
4. Write out items that might be difficult to remember. Extended quotations, difficult names, unfamiliar terms, and statistics are items you may want to include on your note cards to reduce the chances of error.
5. Practice delivering your presentation at least two times using your note cards. Effective delivery may be difficult to achieve if you have to fumble with unfamiliar cards.
6. Write clearly and legibly.

organizational patterns
Arrangements of the contents of a presentation.

time-sequence pattern
A method of organization in which the presenter explains a sequence of events in chronological order.

social media make it matter

Online Brainstorming

One social networking site that might be useful as you are planning and organizing your speech is wallwisher, which allows you to collaborate with other students and your teacher by posting your thoughts on a common topic using electronic sticky notes on a shared "wall." You can type up to 160 characters per note as you think about alternative ways to introduce your presentation, to conclude your presentation, and even to organize it. You can also brainstorm outside class and at your convenience, testing ideas with others in a safe environment. To get started with wallwisher, go to www.wallwisher.com/. After you register and log in, you are ready to share ideas and receive valuable feedback.

How Ford Drove the Auto Industry
by Jared Fougner

Purpose: I plan to highlight the history of the Ford Motor Company in the United States from its beginnings to today, so my audience will be informed about this important background in a truly American industry.

Introduction

> *Relates source credibility.*
>
> *Announces topic.*
>
> *Relates topic to audience.*
>
> *Reveals purpose.*

I. I've been interested in the automobile industry for many years, but until the recent financial troubles I never thought much about the vital role that the first mass-production automobile company, Ford, had in our industrial base.

> *Shows organization.*

   A. Automobiles play a vital role in all our lives.

   B. Automobiles are important to the economy.

   C. The Ford Motor Company illustrates the dynamic nature of the automobile market.

Body

> *Forecasts chronological order.*

II. Henry Ford started the Industrial Revolution in this country with the mass production of autos and his company continued to be a key player in the auto industry in its early, middle, and later years.

> *Introduces part I: early years.*

   A. In the early years Ford experimented, developed mass production, and created cars ahead of their time.

> *Offers two examples.*

     1. Henry Ford ran the first experimental car, the Quadricycle, down Detroit streets in 1896.

     2. Dr. Ernst Pfennig of Chicago purchased the first Ford vehicle in 1903.

> *Introduces part II: middle years.*

   B. In the middle years Ford produced some of the nation's best-selling vehicles.

> *Offers two examples.*

     1. Ford released the F-series pickup trucks in 1948 that even today outnumber all competitors.

     2. Ford launched the Taurus, another top seller, in 1986.

> *Introduces part III: modern times.*

   C. In modern times Ford innovated and competed in an ever-tightening market.

> *Offers three examples.*

     1. In 2000 Ford innovated with a Taurus Flex Fuel Vehicle.

     2. In 2005 Ford innovated with the Escape Hybrid.

     3. Today, Ford offers electric and hybrid automobiles, and the new EcoBoost engine which combines V8 power with V6 efficiency.

Conclusion

III. Ford Motor Company was an industry pioneer that evolved over the years and contributed mightily to our daily life.

   A. Now you know that Henry Ford started the Industrial Revolution in this country with the mass production of autos.

   B. With the advent of mass-produced cars came a need for an extensive system of hard-surface roads, highways, and interstates that changed the face of the United States.

   C. I hope that my look backward at one U.S. industry gives you new appreciation of Ford's contribution to our society.

(Jared Fougner, a communication major, worked in retail sales before returning to school to complete his undergraduate education.)

> Summarizes topic.
>
> Signals ending with review.
>
> Offers example of effect.
>
> Fulfills purpose.

The Cause/Effect Pattern

In using a **cause/effect pattern,** the presenter first explains the causes of an event, a problem, or an issue and then discusses its consequences, results, or effects. The presentation may be cause–effect, effect–cause, or even effect–effect. A presentation on inflation that uses the cause/effect pattern might review the causes of inflation, such as low productivity, and then review the effects of inflation, such as high unemployment and interest rates. The cause/effect pattern is often used in informative presentations that seek to explain an issue. This pattern differs from the problem/solution pattern in that the cause/effect pattern does not necessarily reveal what to do about a problem; instead, the organization allows for full explanation of an issue. The outline for a speech on the effects of smoking is an example of the cause/effect pattern.

> **cause/effect pattern**
> A method of organization in which the presenter first explains the causes of an event, a problem, or an issue and then discusses its consequences, results, or effects.

Confessions of a Smoker
by Linzey Crockett

Purpose: This speech by a confessed smoker notes the effects of smoking on the health of the smoker, an effect that includes early death.

Introduction

I. I'm a guy from South Chicago who has smoked at least 10 or more cigarettes a day for the past 15 years, a habit that will greatly increase my chances of getting lung cancer.

   A. Smoking cigarettes is an addiction that is exceedingly difficult to beat.

> Relates source credibility.
>
> Gains attention.
>
> Uses cause/effect argument.
>
> Offers fact.

CONTINUED

Gives personal testimony.	B. I've been in denial for years about how smoking is damaging my lungs.
Provides purpose.	C. Today I will talk with you about the effects of smoking on the human body because I want you to know how lucky you are if you don't smoke and how threatened you are if you do.
Relates topic to audience.	

Body

Provides main argument on causes.	II. Smoking has physiological effects on heart and blood.
	A. Smoking increases the heart rate.
Offers supporting facts.	B. Smoking increases blood pressure but slows the blood flow by constricting arteries and veins.
Relates serious effects.	C. Smoking increases your chances of both heart attack and stroke.
States second argument.	III. Carbon monoxide increases while oxygen depletes when you smoke.
	A. When you inhale a cigarette, carbon monoxide immediately flows throughout the body to make the heart and lungs work harder.
Offers supporting facts.	B. Oxygen has difficulty reaching the extremities.
States third argument.	IV. As the cigarette burns close to your mouth the dangerous toxins concentrate in the cigarette butt.
	A. Tobacco tar is a known carcinogen, a cancer-producing agent.
Offers supporting facts.	B. Nicotine from tobacco can increase cholesterol levels, which corrode the arterial system.

Conclusion

Provides cause/effect argument.	V. Smoking cigarettes can and will lead to pulmonary problems like lung cancer and emphysema, diseases that lead to an early death.
	A. Smoking affects heart rate and blood pressure, which makes the smoker vulnerable to heart attack and stroke.
Summarizes argument.	B. Toxins like tobacco tar and nicotine increase cholesterol and contribute to cardiovascular disease, a result of smoking and major cause of premature death.
Reviews facts.	
Restates purpose.	C. I hope you now know considerably more about the physiological effects of smoking and why the habit is dangerous.

(This African American male in his late thirties is now in graduate school.)

The cause/effect pattern of organization is common in fields as varied as medicine (tobacco causes cancer), economics (when a recession ends, corporate profits rise, the economy improves, and inflation increases), and education (people with a college education nearly double their annual earnings).

The Problem/Solution Pattern

The third pattern of organization, used most often in persuasive presentations, is the **problem/solution pattern,** in which the presenter describes a problem and proposes a solution. A message based on this pattern can be divided into two distinct parts, with an optional third part in which the presenter meets any anticipated objections to the proposed solution.

The problem/solution pattern can contain other patterns. For example, you might discuss the problem in time-sequence order, and you might discuss the solution using a topical-sequence pattern. Some examples of problem/solution topics follow:

Reducing Fat in Your Diet   Helping the Homeless

A New Way to Stop Smoking   Eliminating Nuclear Waste

Each example implies both a problem and a solution.

The problem/solution pattern of organization requires careful audience analysis, because you have to decide how much time and effort to spend on each portion of the speech. Is the audience already familiar with the problem? If so, you might be able to discuss the problem briefly, with a few reminders to the audience of the problem's seriousness or importance. On the other hand, the problem may be so complex that you cannot cover both the problem and the solution in a single presentation. In that case you may have found a topic that requires both a problem presentation and a solution presentation. The outline for the speech on "Routine Body Shrinking" illustrates the organizational pattern of a problem/solution speech.

problem/solution pattern
A method of organization in which the presenter describes a problem and proposes a solution to that problem.

Routine Body Shrinking
by Greg Heller

Purpose: This presentation will persuade the audience to start a steady and well-planned exercise routine with positive, beneficial, and healthy results.

Introduction

I.   For years I was a fat guy, but since 2005 I have lost 130 pounds (the equivalent of another person) by simply starting and maintaining an exercise routine.

    A. My personal experience will help you see the benefits of a well-planned routine to lose weight.

Relates topic to speaker. Source credibility.

Gains attention.

Relates topic to audience.

Announces topic.

Reveals organization.

CONTINUED

Announces purpose.

B. My personal experience will reveal the effects of an exercise routine and the real benefits, so you can have the same kind of success without much stress.

Body

States first argument.

II. Over the last decade many high-quality studies have proven the benefits of exercise.

Offers two points to support claim.

   A. Regular exercise increases stamina, agility, coordination, and balance.

   B. Physical activity promotes a healthier lifestyle.

States second argument.

III. What did a well-planned workout regimen do for me?

Offers three points to support claim.

   A. I lost weight and gained a normal metabolism.

   B. I could run long distances and remain alert all day.

   C. I felt much better about myself and how I looked.

Conclusion

Summary/review.

IV. Launching and sustaining a well-structured exercise routine yields benefits uncovered in studies and demonstrated in my own life.

Offers ethos: personal proof.

   A. No longer obese, my new body is evidence of the effects of a structured workout routine.

States action purpose.

   B. Now that you know the benefits, have heard about the studies, and see me in the flesh (actually a lot less flesh), you should consider an exercise routine for a healthier self.

(Greg Heller was a communication major and ROTC student and is now serving in the army.)

The Topical-Sequence Pattern

topical-sequence pattern
A method of organization that emphasizes the major reasons an audience should accept a point of view by addressing the advantages, disadvantages, qualities, and types of a person, place, or thing.

The **topical-sequence pattern,** used in both informative and persuasive presentations, emphasizes the major reasons the audience should accept a point of view by addressing the advantages, disadvantages, qualities, and types of a person, place, or thing. This pattern can be used to explain to audience members why you want them to adopt a certain point of view. It is appropriate when you have three to five points to make, such as three reasons people should buy used cars, four of the main benefits of studying speech, or five characteristics of a good football player. The topical-sequence pattern of organization is among the most versatile. The topic-sequence pattern can be seen in the outline for a speech informing the audience about global warming.

Global Warming: What Can You Do?

by Emily Holt

Purpose: This speech informs by exploring the negative effects of global warming and persuades the audience to take steps to avoid even more damage to the Earth.

Introduction

I. Always interested in the natural world and the out-of-doors with Mother Nature, I study global warming and passionately spread the word on how to reduce the harmful effects.

> *Relates speaker to topic.*

   A. The impact of global warming on the environment and on human life affect us all.

> *Relates topic to audience.*

   B. "Global warming" refers to the warm blanket of carbon dioxide that now envelopes the earth with more CO_2 than in the past 650,000 years.

> *Defines key term.*

   C. I hope that by the end of this presentation you will understand the magnitude of the problem and feel confident that you can make a positive difference in helping planet Earth.

> *Forecasts organization. States purpose.*

Body

II. As a direct consequence of human activity the average global temperature rises, causing glacial melting, Arctic ice shrinkage, and rising sea levels.

> *Provides first argument & overview.*

   A. Since 1980, glacial melting has increased rapidly, threatening the existence of global glaciers.

> *Includes facts to support argument.*

   B. Since the end of the nineteenth century (the 1800s) the total surface area of glaciers has decreased by 50%.

   C. Rising ocean levels—an estimated 6 feet over the next 100 years (or sooner)—will be catastrophic to coastal regions and waterways where most humans live.

> *Uses prediction to support argument.*

III. You can make smart choices in your daily life, choices that will affect your contribution to reducing global warming.

> *Provides second main argument.*

   A. One smart choice is to buy at a farmers' market to avoid shipping costs and to obtain fresher food.

> *Offers three choices.*

CONTINUED

Provides possible actions.

Relates intended outcomes.

Provides summary/review and intended result.

B. Another smart choice is to buy a fuel-efficient car, because such vehicles leave a smaller carbon footprint.

C. Unplug unused electronics, because they drain energy unnecessarily.

Conclusion

IV. We have looked at the issue of global warming, explored some evidence of global warming's existence, and looked at some ways that you as an individual or as a family can decrease CO_2 and help reduce global warming.

(Emily Holt received her undergraduate degree in environmental and conservation science.)

TRANSITIONS AND SIGNPOSTS

So far, we have examined organization in its broadest sense. To look at the presentation as a problem/solution or cause/effect pattern is like looking at a house's first floor and basement. We also need to look more closely at the design of the presentation by examining the elements that connect the parts of a speech—transitions and signposts.

A **transition** is a bridge between sections of a message that helps a presenter move smoothly from one idea to another. Transitions also relax the audience momentarily. A typical transition is a brief flashback and a brief forecast that tell your audience when you are moving from one main point to another.

The most important transitions are between the introduction and the body, between the main points of the body, and between the body and the conclusion of the presentation. Other transitions can appear between the main heading and main points, between main points and subpoints, between subpoints and sub-subpoints, between examples, and between visual aids and the point being illustrated. They can review, preview, or even be an internal summary, but they always explain the relationship between one idea and another. Transitions are the mortar between the building blocks of the speech. Without them cracks appear, and the structure is less solid. Table 12.1 gives examples of transitions.

Signposts are ways in which a presenter signals to an audience where the presentation is going. Signposts, as the name implies, are like road signs that tell a driver there is a curve, bump, or rough road ahead; they are a warning, a sign that the presenter is making a move. Whereas transitions are often a sentence or two, signposts can be as brief as a few words. Transitions review, state a relationship, and forecast; signposts merely point.

You'll want to avoid using signposts that are too blatant: "This is my introduction," "Here is my third main point," or "This is my conclusion." More experienced presenters choose more subtle but equally clear means of signposting: "Let me begin by showing you . . . ," "A third reason for avoiding the sun is . . . ," or "The best inference you can draw from what I have told you is . . ." Table 12.2 gives examples of signposts.

Transitions and signposts help presenters map a message for the audience. Transitions explain the relationships in the message by reflecting backward and forward. Signposts point more briefly to what the presenter is going to do at the moment. Both transitions and signposts help bind the message into a unified whole.

transition
A bridge between sections of a presentation that helps the presenter move smoothly from one idea to another.

signposts
Ways in which a presenter signals to an audience where the presentation is going.

Table 12.1 Examples of Transitions

Transition from one main point to another: "Now that we have seen why computers are coming down in cost, let us look next at why software is so expensive."

Transition from a main point to a visual aid: "I have explained that higher education is becoming more and more expensive. This bar graph will show exactly how expensive it has become over the past five years."

Transition that includes a review, an internal summary, and a preview: "You have heard that suntanning ages the skin, and I have shown you pictures of a Buddhist monk and a nighttime bartender who hardly ever exposed themselves to direct sunlight. Now I want to show you a picture of a 35-year-old woman who spent most of her life working in direct sunlight."

Table 12.2 Examples of Signposts

"First, I will illustrate . . ."

"Look at this bar graph . . ."

"See what you think of this evidence . . ."

"A second idea is . . ."

"Another reason for . . ."

"Finally, we will . . ."

The Conclusion

Like the introduction, the **conclusion** fulfills specific functions. These four functions need not occur in the order shown here, but they are all normally fulfilled in the last minutes of a presentation:

1. Forewarn the audience that you are about to finish.
2. Remind the audience of your central idea and the main points of your presentation.
3. Specify what the audience should think or do in response to your speech.
4. End the speech in a manner that makes audience members want to think and do as you recommend.

Let us examine these functions of a conclusion in greater detail.

The first function, the **brakelight function,** warns the audience that the end of the presentation is near. Can you tell when a song is about to end? Do you know when someone in a conversation is about to complete a story? Can you tell in a TV drama when the narrative is drawing to a close? The answer to these questions is usually yes, because you get verbal and nonverbal signals that songs, stories, and dramas are about to end.

How do you use the brakelight function in a presentation? One student signaled the end of her speech by stating that her time was up: "Five minutes is hardly time to consider all the complications of this issue . . ." Another said, "Thus men have the potential for much greater role flexibility than our society encourages . . ." The word *thus,* like *therefore,* signals the conclusion of a logical argument and indicates that the argument is drawing to a close.

You can fulfill the second function of a conclusion—reminding the audience of your central idea or the main points in your message—by restating the main points,

conclusion
The part that finishes the presentation by fulfilling the four functions of an ending.

brakelight function
A forewarning to the audience that the end of the presentation is near.

An effective way to conclude a speech is with an inspirational statement.

summarizing them briefly, or selecting the most important point for special treatment. Elizabeth Nnoko ended her persuasive speech on legalizing drug purchases from Canada by briefly summarizing her message:

> We have discussed the rising cost of prescription drugs, the problem with Medicare, myth and reality concerning importation of prescription drugs, and solutions that can be implemented to solve this issue.

The third function of a conclusion is to specify what you expect audience members to do as a result of your presentation. Do you want the audience to simply remember a few of your important points? Then tell them one last time the points you think are worth remembering. Do you want the audience to write down the argument they found most convincing, sign a petition, or talk to their friends? If so, state what you would regard as an appropriate response to your presentation. One student's presentation on unions concluded with the slogan "Buy the union label," specifying what she expected of the audience.

The fourth function of a conclusion is to provide a "clincher," a memorable statement that encourages listeners to think and do as you recommend. You can conclude with a rhetorical question: "Knowing what you know now, will you feel safe riding with a driver who has had a few drinks?"; an interesting statement: "When you are making the choice between bottled and tap, just remember this, there is no such a thing as 'new' water; the water we drink today is the same water the dinosaurs drank, so whatever you choose, you'll be choosing well"; a quotation: "As John F. Kennedy said, 'Forgive your enemies, but never forget their names'"; a literary passage: "We conclude with the words of Ralph Waldo Emerson, who said, 'It is one light which beams out a thousand stars; it is one soul which animates all men'"; or an action: a tennis player demonstrates proper form for serving the ball.

Some cautions about conclusions: in ending a presentation, as in initiating one, you need to avoid being overly dramatic. Do not behave in a way that will offend members of your audience, create high tension, or frighten listeners. A better idea is to conclude your presentation with an inspirational statement, words that make audience members glad they spent the time and energy listening to you. One student delivered a single line at the end of his talk on using seat belts: "It is not who is right in a traffic accident that really counts," he said, "it is who is left." That conclusion was clever and memorable, it provided a brief summary, and it was an intelligent and safe way to end a presentation.

Following are two sample conclusions that fulfill the four functions described in this section. The first is from Danelle Hopkins, a political science major, from

skill **builder**

Crafting an Effective Conclusion: Things to Avoid

Once you've drafted your conclusion, check it against this list of things to avoid in a speech conclusion.

- Do not just end abruptly with no forewarning.
- Remind the audience of your main points but do not provide a detailed replay of everything you did in the speech.
- Do not say negative things about your own presentation: "Well, I guess that didn't go so well," "Probably I should have done more research," or "I sure blew that assignment."
- Do not let your own nonverbal communication signal a poor presentation by letting your voice trail off at the end, by dropping your arms and looking defeated, or by walking off to your seat as you finish.

Sample Conclusions That Fulfill the Four Functions

Sample Conclusion 1

I. From what I have told you about No Child Left Behind, it is obvious that the program needs to be reformed.

II. I told you about the problems associated with No Child Left Behind, informed you about a proposed reform to the program, and let you know how you can help.

III. Please contact your congressional representatives—I have provided you with their e-mail addresses and their phone numbers.

IV. If nothing is done about No Child Left Behind, it might be that no children will be left behind. But the real problem is that no child might get ahead.

Sample Conclusion 2

I. *Brake light function:* I do not want to overwhelm you with too many details about geocaching.

II. *Summary:* Today I told you about the sport of geocaching. I explained to you what geocaching is, how it works, and how you can get involved.

III. *Specific audience action:* I hope that this information might inspire you to learn more about this sport.

IV. *Clincher:* If current trends continue, we will likely see the 2,000,000th active geocache by the end of 2012. (*put up graph showing cache numbers and trend line*)

Danelle Hopkins fulfilled the four functions of a conclusion.

Uses brakelight function: warns that ending is near.

Reminds audience of main points: summary.

Specifies what the audience should do.

Ends by recommending an action.

Alan Perrault fulfilled the four functions of a conclusion.

her speech about No Child Left Behind legislation. The second is from Alan Perrault, from his speech about geocaching that was described at the beginning of the chapter.

The References

When you have completed your outline, you may be asked to provide a list of **references,** or the sources you used in your presentation. The main idea behind a reference list is to inform others of what sources you used for your speech and to enable them to check those sources for themselves. Each entry in your references should be written according to a uniform style. Several accepted style manuals can answer your questions about the correct format: *The*

references
A list of sources used in a presentation.

Publication Manual of the American Psychological Association (APA), *The MLA Handbook*, and *The Chicago Manual of Style*. Since some teachers prefer MLA and others prefer APA, you should ask your instructor's preference. You can learn more about APA style at www.apastyle.org and more about MLA style at www.mla.org/style. Because it is so efficient to find examples of the two styles on the Internet, we do not provide the correct forms for these sources here.

An example of a reference list on the importance of water, used in a speech by Emily Knilans, is provided below. Note that Emily used the APA style manual and that she included many online sources.

References

Baskind, C. (2010, March 15). *5 reasons not to drink bottled water.* Retrieved September 27, 2011 from the Mother Nature Network website http://www.mnn.com/food/healthy-eating/stories/5-reasons-not-to-drink-bottled-water

Brain Statistics Galore. (2011). *Fun facts about the brain.* Retrieved October 13, 2011 from the Brain Health and Puzzles website http://www.brainhealthandpuzzles.com/fun_facts_about_the_brain.html

Culligan Water Company. (2011). *Common water problems.* Retrieved September 27, 2011 from the Culligan website http://northernplainsculligan.com/at-home-or-work/common-water-problems

Drinking Water Research Foundation. (2011). *Water and your health.* Retrieved September 26, 2011 from the Drinking Water Research Foundation website http://www.thefactsaboutwater.org/health/

Education Database Online. (2011). *The facts about bottled water.* Retrieved September 26, 2011 from the Education Database Online website http://www.onlineeducation.net/bottled_water

Environmental Protection Agency (EPA). (2009, December). *Water on tap: What you need to know.* Retrieved September 27, 2011 from the EPA, office of water website http://www.epa.gov/ogwdw/wot/pdfs/book_waterontap_full.pdf

Environmental Protection Agency (EPA). (2010, October 12). *Is bottled water safer than tap water?* Retrieved September 26, 2011 from the Environmental Protection Agency website http://safewater.supportportal.com/link/portal/23002/23015/Article/18873/Is-bottled-water-safer-than-tap-water

Friday, L. (2011, March 24). *Bottled vs. tap: Which tastes better?* Retrieved September 27, 2011 from the BU Today website http://www.bu.edu/today/2011/bottled-vs-tap-which-tastes-better/

Howard, B. (2003, December 9). *Despite the hype, bottled water is neither cleaner nor greener than tap water.* Retrieved September 27, 2011 from the Common Dreams website http://www.commondreams.org/headlines03/1209-10.htm

Klessig, L. (2004). *Bottled water industry.* Retrieved September 27, 2011 from the Water is life website http://academic.evergreen.edu/g/grossmaz/klessill/

Mayo Clinic Staff. (2011). *Water: How much should you drink every day?* Retrieved September 27, 2011 from the Mayo Clinic website http://www.mayoclinic.com/health/water/NU00283

Stossel, J. (2005, May 6). *Is bottled water better than tap?* Retrieved September 27, 2011 from the ABC website http://abcnews.go.com/2020/Health/story?id=728070&page=1

The facts about the global drinking water crisis. (2010). Retrieved September 27, 2011 from the Blue Planet Network website http://blueplanetnetwork.org/water/facts

keeping it real

Organizing the Body of the Speech

As Alan Perrault studied this chapter and thought about his audience's knowledge of geocaching, he decided to organize his speech around the topics of what geocaching was, what a person needed to geocache, and finally, how to get involved in geocaching.

I.   What is a geocache?

  A. The basic geocache is a container with a log book and items to trade, known as "swag," that is hidden somewhere.

  B. Cache sizes can range from micro, the size of a music earbud, to large, which is typically an ammo box or ice cream bucket. (*show geocache pictures*)

  C. The larger caches will usually have items that you can trade. With these the general rule is to trade items of equal monetary value.

  D. The log book contains a listing of every person who has found the cache. When you find a cache, you sign and date the log.

  E. The log book is usually a small notebook in larger caches and a strip of paper in micro caches.

Transition: Now that you know what a geocache is, how do you find one?

II. How do you find a geocache?

  A. There are only two things you need to find a geocache.

   1. You need a free account at geocaching.com.

   2. You also need a GPS.

   3. If you have a smartphone, you may be able to use that with a geocaching or GPS app, instead of an actual GPS.

  B. When you sign up for a geocaching.com account, you will choose a geocaching nickname. This is what you will use to sign a cache's log.

  C. Once you are signed up, do a search for your city or zip code to locate a nearby cache.

   1. On each cache's page, there are attributes for the cache's terrain and difficulty.

   2. It usually works best if your first cache has low ratings for both these.

Transition: There is a whole world of caches available for you to find. Here is a quick overview.

III. Where can you find geocaches?

  A. Geocaches can be found all around the world (*map slide*), there are ~140 caches hidden within 5 miles of the campus. (Groundspeak, 2011). (*Fargo-Moorhead slide*)

  B. Coordinates for every active geocache can be found on geocaching.com.

  C. Many caches are hidden to bring attention to a place of interest.

  D. (*Pictures of some locations I've found caches*)

Can you think of another way that Alan could have organized his talk? Using the material you discovered in this chapter, how might you organize an informative or a persuasive speech?

Chapter Review & Study Guide

Summary

In this chapter, you learned the following:

1. An effective introduction fulfills five functions, which can occur in any order:

   ■ It gains and maintains audience attention.

   ■ It arouses audience interest in the topic.

   ■ It states the purpose of the presentation.

   ■ It describes the presenter's qualifications.

   ■ It forecasts the organization and development of the presentation.

2. An effective outline for a presentation follows six principles:

   ■ It relates the information presented to the immediate purpose and long-range goal.

   ■ It is an abstract of the message you will deliver.

   ■ It expresses ideas in single units of information.

   ■ It indicates the importance of items with rank-ordered symbols.

   ■ It provides margins that indicate the importance of each entry visually.

   ■ It states entries in parallel form (such as complete sentences, as in this list).

3. The most frequently used patterns of organization in public presentations are

   ■ Time-sequence pattern, or chronology, with items presented serially over time.

   ■ Cause/effect pattern, which posits a cause that results in some effect.

   ■ Problem/solution pattern, which poses a problem followed by a suggested solution.

   ■ Topical-sequence pattern, with items listed as a limited number of qualities or characteristics.

4. Transitions and signposts link ideas and indicate direction to the audience.

5. An effective conclusion fulfills certain functions:

   ■ It forewarns listeners that the presentation is about to end.

   ■ It reminds the audience of the central idea and main points of your presentation.

   ■ It specifies what you expect from the audience as a result of the presentation.

   ■ It ends the presentation in a manner that encourages the audience to think and act as you recommend.

6. Often a list of references, or sources, accompanies the complete outline.

Key Terms

Body	Organizational patterns	Signposts
Brakelight function	Outline	Subpoints
Cause/effect pattern	Parallel form	Time-sequence pattern
Conclusion	Problem/solution pattern	Topical-sequence pattern
Introduction	References	Transition
Key-word outline	Rough draft	
Main points	Sentence outline	

Study Questions

1. Which function of the introduction shows how the topic is related to the audience?

   a. gaining and maintaining audience attention
   b. arousing audience interest
   c. stating the purpose or thesis
   d. establishing speaker qualifications

2. Stating your purpose in the introduction

   a. is necessary because informative speeches do not invite learning, and this is your only opportunity to explain.
   b. is unnecessary, because the audience will learn of the purpose in the body of the speech.
   c. is not appropriate, because you will lose an element of surprise in the body of the speech.
   d. is important, because audience members are more likely to learn and understand if your expectations are clear.

3. When developing the body of a speech, you must

   a. select, prioritize, and organize.
   b. write your introduction first.
   c. use as much information as possible.
   d. utilize sources but not cite them.

4. Which of the following statements is *not* true with regard to outlining?

   a. It uses symbols, margins, and content to reveal the order, importance, and substance of a presentation.
   b. All items of information in your outline do not need to be directly related to the speech's purpose and long-range goal.
   c. It encourages a conversational speaking tone, because not every word is in front of you.
   d. Items should appear in parallel form.

5. Which type of outline consists mostly of important words or phrases but not complex information?

   a. main point
   b. sentence
   c. key-word
   d. cause/effect pattern

6. If you were giving a speech about the parking problem at your university with possible means to resolve it, which organizational pattern would be best?

   a. time-sequence
   b. cause/effect
   c. problem/solution
   d. topical-sequence

7. When a presenter explains a progression of events in chronological order, he or she is most likely using which organizational pattern?

   a. time-sequence
   b. cause/effect
   c. problem/solution
   d. topical-sequence

8. Which of the following help speakers move from one idea to another by reviewing, stating a relationship, and forecasting?

   a. transitions
   b. signposts
   c. subpoints
   d. goals

9. Reminding the audience of the speech's central idea and main points, specifying what is expected of audience members, and ending soundly are functions of the

   a. introduction.
   b. transitions.
   c. brakelight.
   d. conclusion.

10. A reference list is

   a. a list of the sources that you might have considered to use in your presentation.
   b. ideas that you do not want to forget as you are preparing your presentation.
   c. a list of sources organized as books, articles, interviews, and other sources.
   d. sources that you actually used in your presentation.

Answers:
1. (b); 2. (d); 3. (a); 4. (b); 5. (c); 6. (c); 7. (a); 8. (a); 9. (d); 10. (d)

Critical Thinking

1. Using the suggestions from the text, how would you begin your speech in order to gain the audience's attention if your speech topic was movies? Your university? Problems of the world, such as war, famine, or poverty? Why did you choose these methods?

2. What happens on morning talk shows when the hosts wish to change subjects? Do they transition smoothly or simply announce the next topic? As a listener, which do you prefer?

delivery
and visual resources

When you have read and thought about this chapter, you will be able to:

1. Explain four methods of delivery.

2. Name and explain each of the vocal and nonverbal aspects of delivery.

3. Describe methods for managing your communication apprehension.

4. Understand when and why you should use visual resources in your speech.

5. Apply design principles to improve the way you make visuals for presentations.

Many presentations with good content never reach the listener because of poor delivery skills. This chapter explores the delivery of your presentation and the various visual aids you may use. You will discover four modes of delivery and the various vocal and bodily aspects of delivery. Attention in a public presentation is supposed to be on you, not on your visuals, but you will learn in this chapter that you can use Internet resources, such as YouTube, Google photos, and PowerPoint graphics, to make your presentation attractive to the eye and the ear.

Devon would admit it to anyone who asked: giving speeches made him nervous. Although he was a star athlete in high school and gave many pre-game pep talks to teammates, giving a speech in front of his class was a different game altogether. His dread made it easy to stop working on his speech once his preliminary outline had been approved by his teacher.

The day before he was to give his final speech, Devon thought about how to use visual aids, since part of his grade depended on using some sort of visual resource. He sat down with his computer and started making slides in Keynote. It dawned on him that the slides could have enough points on them that he could easily remember what he intended to say just by looking at them. His nervousness dropped a few notches as he busily prepared detailed slides for each of his points.

As Devon presented his speech, he felt better about things. His slides were right behind him, and all he needed to do to remember what he wanted to say was glance at the computer running the projector. As his speech progressed, he noticed that more and more audience members stopped looking at him or his slides and instead looked down at their cell phones or scanned their own notes before speaking. He thought that was pretty rude, but he thought there wasn't much he could do about it.

Why do you think Devon's audience was bored? What would you suggest he do differently with regard to his visual aids? At the end of the chapter, we'll take another look at Devon's situation and consider how he might have better held his audience's attention.

Devon is like most of us; he has some nerves before speaking. So he used what seemed to him to be a perfectly reasonable solution: the slides he created for his audience would also help him remember what he wanted to say. Unfortunately, Devon's strategy backfired. Although he may have felt more confident, constantly looking down at a computer to reference his talking points made his verbal and nonverbal delivery ineffective. Coupled with that was his use of multiple slides filled with words—the same words he was saying. The audience couldn't help but be bored. This chapter helps you avoid some of these mistakes by discussing delivery, communication apprehension, and tips for using visual resources effectively.

What Is Delivery?

delivery
The presentation of a speech using your voice and body to communicate your message.

Delivery is the presentation of a speech using your voice and body to communicate your message. People have contradictory ideas about the importance of speech delivery. Some people think, "It's not what you say but how you say it that really counts." According to others, "What you say is more important than how you say it." Actually, what you say *and* how you say it are both important.

A solid message chosen to accomplish specific goals with your audience, coupled with a delivery style demonstrating energy and passion, should be your objective for every speech.[1] Just as you cannot ignore the need to prepare your speech well in advance, you also cannot ignore the need to practice your delivery. Delivery is like other learned behaviors, such as playing basketball, sewing, or cooking: a lack of practice will show. In this section you will learn about the methods of delivering a presentation; the next section will teach you the building blocks of effective delivery.

In most public speaking situations there are four general methods of delivery—extemporaneous, impromptu, manuscript, and memorized. These methods vary in the amount of preparation required and in their degree of spontaneity. Although they are all possible choices, students of public speaking are least likely to use the manuscript and memorized methods. They may be asked to try the impromptu method at times, but most speech assignments require the extemporaneous method.

THE EXTEMPORANEOUS METHOD

A presentation delivered in the **extemporaneous method** is carefully prepared and practiced, but the presenter delivers the message conversationally without heavy dependence on notes. This method places equal importance on the message and the audience, with the speaker focused not on notes but on the ideas being expressed. Considerable eye contact, freedom of movement and gesture, the language and voice of conversation, and the use of an outline or key words to keep the speaker from reading or paying undue attention to the written script characterize this method.

The word *extemporaneous* literally means "on the spur of the moment" in Latin; however, as practiced in the classroom, this method of delivery only *appears* to be spontaneous. In fact, the processes of planning your speech and creating your outline require you to invest considerable effort before you actually deliver your presentation. Although you are not reading a manuscript—and should not read your outline—you'll plan a fair amount of detail well before the speaking situation. By using your speaking outline as a guide, you will be able to seem spontaneous while sticking carefully to your talking points.

You have seen this method of delivery in the classroom, in some professors' lectures, sometimes in the pulpit, often in political and legal addresses, and usually in speeches by athletes, businesspeople, and community leaders who are experienced speakers. In each of these cases the speaker typically has planned several talking points but avoids reading those points to the audience, favoring instead a more natural appearance. This method is the one you will learn best in the classroom and the one that has the most utility outside the classroom.

THE IMPROMPTU METHOD

In the **impromptu method** you deliver a presentation without notes, plans, or formal preparation and with spontaneity and conversational language. The word *impromptu* has Latin and French roots and means "in readiness."

You use the impromptu method when you answer a question in class, when you introduce yourself in a meeting, and when you give people directions on the street. At a celebration or an informal gathering you may be asked to say a few remarks to welcome people or to express thanks. When executives or other visitors tour your workplace, you may be asked to talk about what you do. All these situations require your impromptu speaking skills, because you have no time to prepare but must still provide clear and relevant comments.

Ordinarily, this method of delivery does not allow for practice and planning beforehand. The impromptu method encourages you to "think on your feet" without research, preparation, or practice. Although you cannot practice your actual speech, you can (and should) practice speaking on various topics without specific preparation.

extemporaneous method
A carefully prepared and researched presentation delivered in a conversational style.

impromptu method
Delivery of a presentation without notes, plans, or formal preparation; characterized by spontaneity and conversational language.

■ Experienced speakers, such as Chelsea Clinton, learn to make clear points and use support without being tied to a manuscript or relying on memorization. This is called extemporaneous delivery.

THE MANUSCRIPT METHOD

manuscript method
Delivery of a presentation from a script of the entire speech.

memorized method
Delivering a presentation that has been committed to memory.

As the name implies, in the **manuscript method** you deliver your presentation from a script of the entire speech. The advantage is that you know exactly what to say. The disadvantages are that the written message invites you to pay more attention to the script than to the audience, discourages eye contact, and prevents response to audience feedback.

Professors, clergy, and politicians—especially those who are likely to be quoted—sometimes use this method of delivery, but students are rarely asked to, except when reading an essay, a poem, or a short story to the class. Some students essentially turn extemporaneous speeches into manuscript speeches by reading their outline, notes, or even presentation slides to the audience. Avoid this! Reading from a manuscript, whether it is prepared as a word-for-word script or a set of presentation slides, is difficult to do well. Your classmates, and particularly your teacher, will know that you are reading, not speaking, and your credibility will be diminished.

sizing things up

Perceived Nonverbal Immediacy Behaviors Scale

One way to learn about your delivery is to think carefully about how others deliver presentations. As a college student you get to observe presentations nearly every day when you watch teachers lecture. Below you will find statements describing how your teacher uses various nonverbal delivery techniques. Select the teacher from the class immediately before your communication class, and with that teacher in mind, answer the following questions using this scale. There are no right or wrong answers, just answer each question as honestly as you can. A guide for interpreting your responses appears in the appendix at the end of the text (p. 348).

0 = Never
1 = Rarely
2 = Occasionally
3 = Often
4 = Very often

1. The teacher gestures while talking to the class.
2. The teacher uses a dull/monotone voice while talking to the class.
3. The teacher looks at the class while talking.
4. The teacher smiles at the class while talking.
5. The teacher has a very tense body position while talking to the class.
6. The teacher moves around the classroom while teaching.
7. The teacher looks at the board, visual materials, or notes while teaching.
8. The teacher has a very relaxed body position while talking to the class.
9. The teacher smiles at individual students in the class.
10. The teacher uses a variety of vocal expressions while talking to the class.

Source: McCroskey, J., Sallinen, A., Fayer, J., Richmond, V., & Barraclough, R. (1996). Nonverbal immediacy and cognitive learning: A cross-cultural investigation. *Communication Education, 45,* 200–211. Reprinted by permission of the publisher (Taylor & Francis Ltd, http://www.tandf.co.uk/journals).

THE MEMORIZED METHOD

A presentation delivered in the **memorized method** is committed to memory. This method requires considerable practice and allows ample eye contact, movement, and gestures. However, it also discourages the speaker from responding to feedback, from adapting to the audience during the speech, and from choosing words that might be appropriate at the moment. In other words, memorization removes spontaneity and increases the danger of forgetting. You have experienced this method if you ever acted in a play and memorized your part. Politicians, athletes, and businesspeople who repeatedly speak to the same kind of audience about the same subjects often end up memorizing their speeches. Even professors, when they teach a class for the third time in a week, may memorize the lesson for the day.

Like the manuscript method, the memorization method is extremely difficult to pull off well. If you practice your speech several times, you will begin to memorize certain parts through repetition. However, your goal should be extreme familiarity rather than absolute memorization. Such familiarity will give you confidence but will help you avoid potential problems associated with rigid memorization.

The method you choose should be appropriate for the message, the audience, and the occasion. Students use the extemporaneous method most often in learning public speaking, because that approach teaches good preparation, adaptation to the audience, and focus on the message. Learning to use the extemporaneous method effectively is critical to your success as a speaker, because it is the most common approach used both in the classroom and in professional situations outside the classroom.[2]

What Behaviors Influence Your Delivery?

Effective delivery is a learned behavior. Accomplished musicians must practice daily to achieve success; the same is required for excellent delivery. Fortunately, we all get chances to practice every day. Our conversations with others teach us everything we need to know to be great deliverers of speeches. Think for a moment about how you behave when you talk with others. You naturally use gestures; you naturally vary your vocal pitch, volume, and inflections; and you naturally maintain eye contact. You work hard at improving your verbal and nonverbal delivery skills, starting as an infant and continuing throughout your life. So why is it that some people struggle as public speakers?

Giving presentations is different from casual conversation. You become the center of attention; hundreds of eyes may be focusing just on you. That fact alone can cause us to forget what we have learned over the course of our lifetime. We look for safety blankets in the form of lecterns to hold onto and notes to read, and we fall back on rapid delivery to get the whole thing done. These problems are not limited to the classroom. John Takash, president of the Chicago-based Victory Consulting Firm, identified five common delivery problems in business presentations: (1) using non-words, (2) failing to pause and let audience members think, (3) failing to maintain eye contact, (4) speaking with a lack of confidence and volume, and (5) standing on one spot.[3] All these are problems with verbal and nonverbal delivery. The key to effective delivery is training yourself not to wrap yourself in safety blankets, and you achieve that through practice.

Before learning about ways to practice effectively, let's first discuss vocal and nonverbal aspects of delivery.

THE VOCAL ASPECTS OF DELIVERY

Just as different musicians can make the same notes sound quite different, public speakers can say the same words in different ways to get the audience to respond in various ways. The way you say words creates emotion. The seven vocal aspects of presentation are pitch, rate, pauses, volume, enunciation, fluency, and vocal variety. As we'll see next, your objective with these aspects of vocal delivery should be to naturally vary your voice and not talk in a monotone.[4] Using vocal variance will help you sound more passionate and convincing during your presentation.

Pitch

Pitch is the highness or lowness of a speaker's voice—the voice's upward and downward movement, the melody produced by the voice. Pitch is what makes the difference between the "ohhh" you utter when you earn a poor grade in a class and the "ohhh" you utter when you see something or someone really attractive. The pitch of your voice can make you sound either lively or listless. As a speaker you learn to avoid the two extremes: the lack of change in pitch that results in a monotone and repeated changes in pitch that result in a singsong delivery. The best public speakers use the full range of their normal pitch.

One technique for learning to strategically use pitch is to think about how you use bold, italics, and different style fonts when you write. There are certain words in a written document that you may want to *emphasize*. When speaking, you may want to do the same

pitch
The highness or lowness of the speaker's voice.

thing. When talking about the national debt, for instance, you may want to emphasize the "T" in "trillion" to highlight the unimaginable scope of the issue. Obviously your voice does not have buttons like a word processor to make that happen. When emphasizing the word vocally, you might naturally raise your pitch an octave or so to make it stand out—the vocal equivalent of bold and italics.

Rate

How fast should you speak when delivering a public presentation? Instructors often caution students to "slow down," because talking fast is a sign of anxiety or nervousness. At the same time, talking too slowly can bore the listener, because we think much faster than people typically talk. What is the best way for you to deliver your speech?

Rate is the speed of delivery, or how fast you say your words. The normal rate for U.S. speakers is between 125 and 190 words per minute, but many variations occur. You need to remember that your rate of delivery depends on you—how fast you normally speak—and on the situation—few people talk fast at a funeral. Rate also depends on the audience and the subject matter. Audience members unfamiliar with the topic material may have a hard time following rapid delivery—the situation and topic may necessitate a slower approach.

Your rate of delivery can be strategically used to build drama during your presentation. Think about a great action sequence in a movie. Typically, the background music has a more upbeat tempo to emphasize the action. So, too, in a speech, your rate of delivery can be used to build excitement. Talking slowly at a pep rally may curb spirit, but fast delivery can get fans pumped up. Varying your rate of delivery can help you set certain moods as your speech develops.

Pauses

A third vocal characteristic of speech delivery is the **pause**—an absence of vocal sound used for dramatic effect, transition, or emphasis. Presentations are often a steady stream of words without silences, yet pauses can be used for dramatic effect and to get an audience to consider content. The speaker may begin a speech with rhetorical questions: "Have you had a cigarette today? Have you had two or three? Ten or eleven? Do you know what your habit is costing you in a year? A decade? A lifetime?" After each rhetorical question a pause allows audience members to answer the question mentally.

Pauses invite the audience to think, which is a silent but important form of engagement. When using pauses, make sure they are long enough to have this desired effect but not so long that they become uncomfortable. Use your instincts while speaking and remember that the pause will feel longer to you as the speaker than it does to the audience.

On the other hand, **vocalized pauses** are breaks in fluency that negatively affect an audience's perception of the speaker's competence and dynamism. The "ahhhs" and "mmhhs" of the beginning speaker are disturbing and distracting. Unfortunately, even some experienced speakers have the habit of filling silences with vocalized pauses.

rate
The speed at which a speech is delivered, normally between 125 and 190 words per minute.

pause
The absence of vocal sound used for dramatic effect, transition, or emphasis.

vocalized pauses
Breaks in fluency that negatively affect an audience's perception of the speaker's competence and dynamism.

skill **builder**

Diagnosing Problems with Vocalized Pauses

After creating your outline and visual materials, you should practice your speech out loud. Once you have practiced several times and feel comfortable with the material, record your speech using your cell phone, your computer, or some other device. When playing back the recording, note the total time and make a tally mark each time you say any type of vocalized pause. How many did you have? Did you notice a pattern that might explain why you inserted them? Were they in places where you were transitioning between ideas? Places where you were unsure of the material? Once you identify possible causes, how can you try to work those vocalizations out of your delivery?

Volume

Volume is the relative loudness of your voice. Variations in volume can convey emotion, importance, suspense, and changes in meaning. When speaking more loudly we also tend to speak more quickly and at a higher pitch; when speaking more softly we tend to be lower and slower. Thus, changes in volume often happen in conjunction with changes in tone and rate of delivery. You can use a stage whisper in front of an audience, just as you would whisper a secret to a friend. You can speak loudly and strongly on important points, letting your voice carry your conviction. Volume can also change with the situation. For example, a pep rally may be filled with loud, virtually shouted speeches teeming with enthusiasm, whereas a eulogy may be delivered at a lower, respectful volume. An orchestra never plays so quietly that patrons cannot hear, but the musicians vary their volume. Similarly, a presenter who considers the voice an instrument learns how to speak softly, loudly, and in between to convey meaning.

Enunciation

Enunciation, the fifth vocal aspect of speech delivery, is the pronunciation and articulation of sounds and words. In everyday conversation we are informal, and our friends know how we talk. In speeches, however, you need to think more carefully about how you enunciate the syllables of words. In a large room, better enunciation may be necessary in order for people in the back to fully understand you. You can also overenunciate words to give them emphasis, the verbal equivalent of typing "I am R-E-A-L-L-Y happy!" Enunciation is especially important for words that have similar sounds. How are its two components, pronunciation and articulation, different?

Pronunciation is the act of correctly saying *words*. The difference between saying "Washington" and "Worshintun" is pronunciation. If you have ever watched James Carville, a popular political commentator, speak on television, you'll notice that his Cajun dialect leads to many mispronunciations. He can get by with that because he has credibility through his experiences. If speakers have little established credibility, mispronunciations can doom their chances of building it. The best way to avoid pronunciation errors is to look up unfamiliar words. Most online dictionaries have options for hearing how a word is correctly pronounced via a small audio file.

Articulation—the accurate production of *sounds*—is the second part of enunciation. If you order "dry toast" (without butter) and get "rye toast" or ask for a "missing statement" and get a "mission statement," you are experiencing the results of poor or careless articulation. Among the common articulation problems are the dropping of final consonants and "-ing" sounds ("goin'," "comin'," and "leavin'"), the substitution of "fer" for "for," and the substitution of "ta" for "to." An important objective in public presentations, as in all communication, is to articulate accurately.

Fluency

The sixth vocal characteristic of delivery is **fluency**—the smoothness of the delivery, the flow of the words, and the absence of vocalized pauses. This quality is often more notable by its absence: a fluent speaker will present an effortless flow of words that moves along at a natural pace, which listeners may take for granted as they focus on the message. A nonfluent speaker, on the other hand, will present a speech that sounds choppy and disjointed, and these errors draw attention to themselves.

To achieve fluency, public speakers must be confident about the content of their speeches. If they know what they are going to say and have practiced the words over and over, they will reduce disruptive repetition and vocalized pauses. Speakers must pace, build, and time the various parts of the speech, so that they unite in a coherent and fluent whole.

enunciation
The pronunciation and articulation of sounds and words.

pronunciation
The act of correctly articulating words.

articulation
The production of sounds; a component of enunciation.

fluency
The smoothness of delivery, the flow of words, and the absence of vocalized pauses.

Remember that you will need to stick to the time limits imposed by your teacher or the situation; failing to do so will diminish your credibility and perhaps harm your grade!

Vocal Variety

vocal variety
Vocal quality, intonation patterns, inflections of pitch, and syllabic duration.

The seventh vocal aspect of speech delivery—one that summarizes many of the others—is **vocal variety.** This term refers to voice quality, intonation patterns, inflections of pitch, and how you draw out spoken sounds and syllables. Public presentations encourage vocal variety, because studies show that variety improves effectiveness. One of the founders of the National Communication Association, Charles Woolbert, found in a very early study of public reading that audiences retain more information when there are large variations in rate, force, pitch, and voice quality.[5] Woolbert's research is relevant even today. Having variety in your voice is consistently identified as one of the most important speaking skills, though achieving it can be challenging for inexperienced speakers.

Kathleen Propp, a communication professor at Western Michigan University, pointed out that many students lose their natural vocal variety when speaking because of the natural nervousness they feel.[6] To retrain yourself to maintain effective variety, Propp suggests that you (1) read a children's story aloud at home and take note of how you naturally use vocal variety, (2) practice transferring those behaviors when reading more advanced material, and (3) synthesize those two steps to use vocal variety during your speeches.

NONVERBAL ASPECTS OF PRESENTATION

The importance of delivery has been recognized for thousands of years. In the *Rhetoric ad Herennium,* the great Roman orator Cicero observed, "Delivery is the graceful regulation of voice, countenance, and gesture." Whereas the previous section talked in detail about the voice, this section focuses on how to use your body to effectively convey meaning.

Gestures

gestures
Movements of the head, arms, and hands to illustrate, emphasize, or signal ideas in a presentation.

■ Using gestures helps you speak with conviction.

Gestures are movements of the head, arms, and hands that illustrate, emphasize, or signal ideas in a speech. People rarely worry about gestures in conversation, but when they give a speech in front of an audience, arms and hands seem to be bothersome. The most common mistake inexperienced speakers make is holding onto a lectern, a computer, or notes. Some teachers ban the use of these devices to help students overcome the tendency to rely on them.

What can you do to help yourself gesture naturally when delivering your presentation? The answer is to connect your feelings to your behavior. When speakers really care about a topic, you can see their passion in the way they deliver their message: they are more animated, their face shows a range of emotion, their voice is strong, and their eyes connect with yours. Students speaking on a variety of topics ranging from environmental awareness to business ethics have demonstrated that passion and conviction translate into effective delivery. In addition to focusing on finding a topic about which you are passionate, you should also concentrate on your message. Being self-conscious about your delivery, or trying to focus too much on "perfect" delivery, can actually backfire and cause your delivery to seem unnatural. Some students trained in competitive speaking exhibit unnatural delivery behaviors that cause audience members to become so focused on delivery that they lose the message of the speech. Focusing on your message and your conviction is more important than trying to sound like the next master orator.

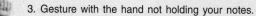

1. Keep your hands out of your pockets and at your sides when not gesturing.
2. Do not lean on the lectern.
3. Gesture with the hand not holding your notes.
4. Make your gestures deliberate—big and broad enough so that they do not look accidental or timid.
5. Keep your gestures meaningful by using them sparingly and only when they reinforce something you are saying.
6. Practice your gestures just as you do the rest of your speech so that you become comfortable with the words and gestures.
7. Make your gestures appear natural and spontaneous.

Figure 13.1

Tips for gesturing effectively.

Source: Gamble, T. K., & Gamble, M. (2005). *Communication works* (8th ed.). New York: McGraw-Hill. © 2005 The McGraw-Hill Companies, Inc. Used by permission.

Another way of learning to make appropriate gestures is to practice a speech in front of friends who are willing to make positive suggestions. Actors spend hours rehearsing lines and gestures, so that they will look spontaneous and unrehearsed on stage. In time, and after many practice sessions, public speakers learn which arm, head, and hand movements seem to help and which seem to hinder their message. Through practice you, too, can learn to gesture naturally, in a way that reinforces, rather than detracts from, your message (see figure 13.1). Constructive criticism is also one of the benefits you can receive from your speech instructor and your classmates, of course.

Facial Expressions

Gestures are powerful, but your face is the most expressive part of your body. **Facial expressions** consist of the nonverbal cues expressed by the speaker's face. Eyebrows rise and fall; eyes twinkle, glare, and cry; lips pout or smile; cheeks can dimple or harden; and a chin can jut out in anger or recede in yielding. Some people's faces are a barometer of their feelings; others' faces seem to maintain the same appearance whether they are happy or sad or in pain. Because you do not ordinarily see your own face when you are speaking, you may not be fully aware of how you appear when you give a speech. In general, speakers are trying to maintain a warm and positive relationship with the audience, and they signal that intent by smiling as they would in conversation with someone they liked. However, the topic, the speaker's intent, the situation, and the audience all help determine the appropriate facial expressions in a public speech. You can discover the appropriateness of your facial expressions by having friends, relatives, or classmates tell you how you look when practicing your speech. You can also observe how your instructors use facial expressions to communicate. Although you can also observe your facial expressions by practicing in front of a mirror, many people find this technique distracting. A better strategy might be to record your speech using a webcam or phone and then watching the video to observe how you use facial expressions during your speech.

facial expressions
Any nonverbal cues expressed by the speaker's face.

Eye Contact

Eye contact refers to the extent to which the speaker looks directly at the audience. Staring down the audience is too much of a good thing, but staring at your notes is poor delivery.

Lack of eye contact is one of the most common problem speakers have when making presentations.[7] It can suggest that you lack knowledge, are unsure of your position, or are

eye contact
The extent to which a speaker looks directly at the audience.

skill builder

Moving Eye Contact Around

Experienced speakers learn how to spread their eye contact around to multiple audience members. One technique for learning to do this is to divide the audience up into different sections—think of the sections as analogous to rooms in a house, or countries on a map. Your objective early in the speech should be to visit each location with your eyes. Some locations may seem more pleasing because people in that room/country might give you better nonverbal responses. Perhaps that's a place you can visit more often as the speech progresses! Using this approach will help you build rapport with your audience. Even when you are visiting other sections with your eyes, audience members will notice that you are trying to connect with the entire room and will react more positively to you and your ideas.

even being deceitful. Appropriate eye contact, on the other hand, creates connections with the audience.

How can you learn to maintain eye contact with your audience? One way is to know your speech so well that you have to glance only occasionally at your notes. A speaker who does not know the speech well is manuscript-bound. Delivering an extemporaneous speech from key words or an outline is a way of encouraging yourself to keep an eye on the audience. One of the purposes of extemporaneous delivery is to enable you to adapt to your audience. That adaptation is not possible unless you are continually observing the audience's behavior to see whether your listeners appear to understand your message.

Movement

bodily movement
What the speaker does with his or her entire body during a presentation.

A fourth physical aspect of delivery is **bodily movement**—what the speaker does with his or her entire body during a presentation. Sometimes the situation limits movement. The presence of a fixed microphone, a lectern, a pulpit, or any other physical feature of the environment may limit your activity. The length of the speech can also make a difference. If your speech is short, movement may be less important. For a speech lasting longer than a few minutes, movement can help keep audience members more engaged.

Good movement is appropriate and purposeful. The "caged lion" who paces back and forth to work off anxiety is moving in a way that distracts; a speaker who stands in one spot creates boredom. You should move for a reason, such as walking a few steps when delivering a transition, thereby literally helping your audience "follow you" to the next idea. Some speakers move toward the audience when expressing points they regard as most important.

Because eye contact is vital, you should always strive to face the audience, even when moving. Speakers who read from slides typically turn their back on the audience. Instead, locate your body, and particularly your face, in ways that allow you to establish rapport with your audience.

social media make it matter

Using Social Media for Feedback

Your network of friends can be important sources of feedback for your presentation. If you recorded a video of your speech and uploaded it to YouTube or Facebook, you could ask your friends to watch and critique your presentation. If you are having particular problems, such as vocalizations or lack of eye contact, your friends will be helpful in pointing those things out. You may even generate discussion about the focus of your speech and obtain quotes or ideas that you can integrate into it. Social media resources give us ways to get feedback from more people than ever before. Who knows, your speech may even go viral!

You can learn through practice and observation. Watch your professors, teaching assistants, and fellow students when they deliver their speeches to determine what works for them. (They may provide positive or negative examples.) Then determine what works best for you when you practice your speech. You can use the form in table 13.1 to evaluate your own and others' nonverbal delivery.

Table 13.1 Evaluation Form for Nonverbal Aspects of Delivery

Use this form to evaluate your own and others' vocal and nonverbal delivery, using this scale:
1 = excellent, 2 = good, 3 = average, 4 = fair, 5 = weak.

Vocal aspects of delivery—the voice

_____ Pitch: upward and downward inflections

_____ Rate: speed of delivery

_____ Pause: appropriate use of silence

_____ Volume: loudness of the voice

_____ Enunciation: articulation and pronunciation

_____ Fluency: smoothness of delivery

_____ Vocal variety: overall effect of all of the above

Bodily aspects of delivery

_____ Gestures: use of arms and hands

_____ Facial expression: use of the face

_____ Eye contact: use of eyes

_____ Movement: use of legs and feet

DELIVERY TIPS FOR NON-NATIVE SPEAKERS

If you are a student who speaks English as a second language, you may be particularly concerned about your delivery. After all, you must simultaneously remember what you want to say and select and correctly pronounce the appropriate words. Here are some suggestions for how to work on delivery issues that may be of unique concern to you:

1. *Recognize that you are not alone.* For most speakers the actual delivery of the speech is what causes the most anxiety. Even native speakers worry that they will forget what they intend to say or that they will say something incorrectly. If you have anxiety about delivery, your classmates will certainly empathize with you.

2. *Give yourself time.* Most of the other suggestions on this list require that you devote some extra time to improving your delivery. This means you may need to begin working on your speeches much earlier than many of your classmates.

3. *Check pronunciation.* On several online pronunciation dictionaries, you can look up words and hear them pronounced. For new and unfamiliar words or words with many syllables, such resources can help you determine and practice correct pronunciation.

4. *Talk with your instructor about reasonable goals.* If you are still working on several pronunciation or grammar issues, you can use your public speaking class as an opportunity to improve. With your instructor's help, identify a short list of items that you can work on over the course of the term. Your practice efforts will be more focused, and your instructor will have a clearer idea of what to concentrate on when giving feedback. If you do not set such objectives beforehand, both you and your instructor may have difficulty concentrating on specific and attainable areas for improvement.

communication apprehension (CA)
An individual's level of fear or anxiety associated with either real or anticipated communication with another person or persons.

skills approach
Reducing fear by systematically improving presenting skills.

5. *Understand that eye contact is important.* Especially if you come from a culture that does not emphasize eye contact, you should recognize that U.S. audiences tend to weight this nonverbal delivery characteristic very heavily. To improve your eye contact, first get more comfortable maintaining eye contact during conversation. As this skill improves during one-on-one interactions, you can then work on better eye contact during speeches.

6. *Practice using audio or video recordings.* By listening to and/or watching yourself, you will be better able to isolate specific ways to improve your delivery. While observing a recording, make a list of two to four things you could do to improve your delivery, and then practice the speech again while focusing on those items.

How Can You Reduce Your Fear of Presenting?

Anxiety is a natural part of speaking. Beginning speakers often feel fear before and during their early presentations. Even experienced speakers are sometimes apprehensive when they face a new audience or a new situation. How, then, do we reduce and control any fear of presenting?

The person who has studied this subject the most, James McCroskey, calls fear of presenting **communication apprehension (CA),** defined as "an individual's level of fear or anxiety associated with either real or anticipated communication with another person or persons."[8] This definition implies a couple of points to note. First, apprehension can stem from any type of communication. Just as some people fear public speaking, others have significant apprehension during interpersonal conversations. Second, apprehension can stem from anticipated interactions with others. In fact, much of the anxiety associated with public speaking stems from *anticipation* rather than from the act of speaking itself.

▣ Communication apprehension is common for inexperienced speakers. Reframing negative thoughts into positive thoughts can boost your confidence.

Communication apprehension is connected to all aspects of our communication with others. Research shows that people who have higher levels of communication apprehension tend to view themselves as lower in communication competence.[9] Of course, this also means that those with higher levels of communication anxiety have the most to gain in improving their communication skills.

In the context of public speaking, apprehension has a more specific name: *public speaking anxiety.* High levels of public speaking anxiety can not only result in shaking knees, dry mouth, and other physical symptoms but can also create a self-fulfilling prophecy. People who are high in public speaking anxiety often spend less time preparing, which creates a series of cascading problems with the speech—everything that can go wrong will go wrong.[10]

Fear of presenting is similar to other fears in life: You cannot overcome it unless you want to. Fortunately, you can reduce fear in many ways, including the following:

■ The **skills approach** reduces fear by systematically improving your presenting skills. In other words, by taking a course in public speaking you can learn through the coaching of your teacher and your fellow students to reduce your anxiety. You will find that repeatedly exposing yourself to something you find threatening—such as standing in front of an audience to give a speech—reduces your fear over time.

Table 13.2 Negative Thoughts Reframed in More Positive Ways

Negative Thinking	Positive Thinking
I'm afraid of public speaking.	I see public speaking as a personal challenge.
I don't want to go up front.	I have the courage to go up front.
I don't want to see all those eyes.	I appreciate the attention I get.
I'm afraid my voice won't work.	I plan to speak with confidence.
They will see I'm afraid.	I'll act confident until I feel confident.
Things will go wrong.	I'll work hard to be prepared and do my best.

Remember that much of our public speaking anxiety occurs in anticipation of the actual speech. We often begin framing negative thoughts about what can happen, and those thoughts build negative momentum, which dramatically increases our anxiety.[11] The **positive thinking approach** reframes those negative thoughts as positive ones. Table 13.2 provides examples. Reframing will show you how you can counteract potential sources of anxiety through preparation and planning for success rather than for failure.

positive thinking approach
Using positive thoughts to bolster speaker confidence.

The **visualization approach** invites you to picture yourself succeeding, as the positive approach does but with the addition of imagery.[12] See yourself striding to the front of the room with confidence; see yourself speaking loud enough for all to hear without a sign of fear; and see yourself moving through the speech with an attentive audience eagerly receiving your message. Athletes often use visualization along with practice to perform better on the field or court. Visualizing the act of shooting a free throw can help improve technique and consistency. The same principle can be effective as you prepare for your speech.

visualization approach
Picturing yourself succeeding.

The **relaxation approach** trains you to associate public speaking with positive thoughts.[13] Although you can do this by yourself, another person, such as a facilitator, usually provides the relaxation commands. The facilitator asks you to relax (actually lying down helps) and to think of a situation in which you are totally unstressed. The facilitator links your relaxed state to a word, such as *calm*. After repeating this process, you start relaxing whenever you hear the word (you have been conditioned). The facilitator then walks you through whatever frightens you ("You are now walking to the front of the room") and says "calm" at the first signs of fright. This approach takes time, but the procedure does work for most people with high anxiety about presenting. See figure 13.2 for a formula for this relaxation technique.

relaxation approach
Combining deep relaxation with fear-inducing thoughts.

The **self-managed approach** means that you reduce your fear of presenting with self-diagnosis and a variety of therapies. In other words, you attempt to uncover your fears and then decide what approach might reduce them. Dwyer points out that many therapies can reduce your fears, but no one therapy works for all people.[14] You might decide that group therapy with a psychologist at the health service center would work best for you. Or you might decide that just taking a public speaking course will help you overcome your fear of presenting.

self-managed approach
Reducing the fear of presenting with self-diagnosis and a variety of therapies.

To practice the relaxation techniques, do the following:

1. Sit in a comfortable chair or lie down in a comfortable place. As much as possible, rid the area of distracting noises. If possible, play relaxing music or a tape with the sounds of nature.

2. Begin with your face and neck, and tense the muscles. Then relax them. Tense again and hold the tensed position for 10 seconds. Relax again.

3. Tense your hands by clenching your fists. Relax. Tense again and hold for 10 seconds. Relax.

4. Tense your arms above your hands and to your shoulders. Relax. Tense again and hold for 10 seconds. Relax.

5. Tense your chest and stomach. Relax. Tense again and hold for 10 seconds. Relax.

6. Tense your feet by pulling the toes under. Relax. Tense again and hold for 10 seconds. Relax.

7. Tense your legs above the feet and up to the hips. Relax. Tense again and hold for 10 seconds. Relax.

8. Tense your entire body and hold for 10 seconds. Relax and breathe slowly.

9. Repeat the word *calm* to yourself. This will help you relate the word to the relaxed feeling you are now experiencing. In the future, when you feel anxious, the word *calm* should help you arrest the apprehension you experience.

Figure **13.2**

Calming normal communication apprehension.

Source: Gamble, T. K., & Gamble, M. (2005). *Communication works* (8th ed.). New York: McGraw-Hill. © 2005 The McGraw-Hill Companies, Inc. Used by permission.

■ Using a model to visually illustrate your descriptions can add interest and clarity to your presentation.

When and Why Use Visual Resources?

Do you learn best when you read something, when you watch something, or when you do something? Certainly, some skills are best learned by doing. Reading about how to insert streaming video into a PowerPoint presentation or watching another person perform the task is no substitute for trying to perform the task yourself. However, not everything lends itself to doing. You cannot "do" economics in the same way you can change a tire. Because so much of public speaking deals with issues and topics that cannot be performed, you must know the most effective methods of communicating in a public presentation. Often this means showing audience members visual representations of what you are speaking about.

Visual resources are any items that can be seen by an audience for the purpose of reinforcing a message, from the way you dress, to words on a dry-erase board, to items you bring in for a demonstration. Setting up a computer to display images or slides is another use of visual resources. A student who wears her police uniform when talking about careers in law enforcement, one who provides a handout with an outline of her speech for the class, and yet another who brings in chemistry equipment are all using visual resources. As you can see, the options are many and diverse, and some work better than others. A handout could distract audience members, whereas chemistry equipment could bring a speech to life. Learning to use visuals effectively is a key skill for speakers.

A classic study, still cited as a definitive justification for using visual aids, shows that using visual supplements for your presentation dramatically improves the chances that audience members will remember what you say.[15] Figure 13.3 shows the benefits of visual aids. More recent research has considered whether visual aids like

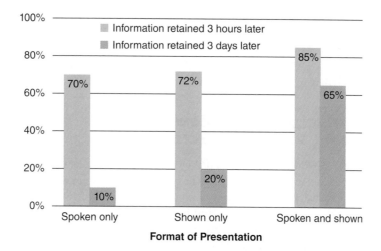

Figure 13.3

Immediate and delayed re-
tention of spoken and
viewed information.

Source: Data from Zayas-Boya,
E. P. (1977–1978). Instructional
media in the total language
picture. *International Journal of
Instructional Media, 5*, 145-150.

PowerPoint slides have the same benefits as those discovered in the earlier study.
When hearing lectures with slides and without slides, students tend to remember
spoken information better when slides are not present, but they remember visual
images like graphs and pictures more easily when these are shown rather than
described (Savoy, Proctor, Salvendy, 2009). The implication is that you need to use
visuals when visual imagery is important; hide them when what you are saying is most
important.

A listing of various types of visual resources and their advantages and disadvantages is
shown in table 13.3. Remember, too, that most instructors have rules governing the use of

visual resources
Any items that can be
seen by an audience for
the purpose of reinforcing
a message.

Table 13.3 Advantages and Disadvantages of Some Typical Visual Aids

Type	Advantages	Disadvantages
Chalkboard/ dry-erase board	Easy to use Allows impromptu reactions from the audience	Requires turning your back to the audience Can be difficult to read
Poster displays	Allow you to plan ahead for content and style Can demonstrate creativity	Can look unprofessional if not done well Can cost money if professionally produced
Handouts	Provide a takeaway for audience members Can provide notes to help audience members with details	Can create distractions Can leave a mess if listeners don't take handouts with them
Models	Provide greater realism Can demonstrate greater detail for explanation	Can be expensive to obtain Can be hard to transport, depending on size
People	Can add realism Can increase audience members' attention	Can be unpredictable
Computers	Allow pre-planning for content and design Can present diverse information	Can be difficult to prepare if you don't have expertise Speaker must be able to react to glitches

visual resources. Few instructors allow live animals, and university policies usually forbid bringing to campus firearms, illegal substances/materials, and anything potentially dangerous to others. A good rule of thumb to follow is to *always* tell your teacher in advance what you plan to use as a visual resource. Prevent problems before they become problems. Remember, too, that you must practice with any visual aid you opt to use.

Design Principles to Follow When Using Visual Resources

Visual resources lose their effectiveness if they are not integrated effectively into your presentation. Because there are so many different types of visual resources, figure 13.4 provides general principles that you should keep in mind, regardless of what you are using.

When using visual aids, be prepared to handle them effectively. If you use a computer to display PowerPoint or a YouTube video, what will you do if the computer crashes? How should you best prepare visual aids, so that they look professional and are not too cluttered? In addition to following the tips in figure 13.4, plan to carefully analyze your approach to using visual aids. If you are relying on technology, have a backup in case the technology fails. Strive for professionalism—homemade posters are old school. Finally, if someone cannot look at your visual aid and in a few seconds be able to explain what he or she sees, you may have included too much information. Your visual points should be clear and concise, just like your verbal points.

slide-deck visuals
A collection of slides, usually created with a computer program, that are displayed during a presentation.

Apple's Keynote and Microsoft's PowerPoint remain the staple visual aids for most public speakers. There is very little difference between these two options. Both employ an approach referred to as **slide-deck visuals,** which help you create, arrange, and display various slides. Following basic visual design principles can dramatically increase the artistic appeal of your slides and help you make your points more effectively.[16] The remainder of this section discusses strategies for using these types of programs effectively.

1. *Use images, not words.* The most common mistake speakers make when designing slides is to approach it as a writing assignment rather than a visual creativity assignment and therefore to create slides filled with words, not pictures or images. Visual aids should be visual, and very few word-based slides are visually appealing.

Figure 13.4

Tips for using visual resources.

1. Do not talk to your visual resources. Keep your eyes on your audience.
2. Display visual resources only when you are using them. Before or after they are discussed, they usually become a needless distraction to the audience.
3. Make sure everyone in the room can see your visual resources. Check the visibility of your visual resources before your speech, during practice. If the classroom is 25 feet deep, have a friend or family member determine if the visual resources can be read from 25 feet away. Above all, make sure you are not standing in front of your visual resources.
4. Leave visual resources in front of the audience long enough for complete assimilation. Few things are more irritating to an audience than to have half-read visual resources whipped away by a speaker.
5. Use a pointer or your inside arm for pointing to visual resources. The pointer keeps you from masking the visual, and using your inside arm helps you to avoid closing off your body from the audience.

■ One of the most ineffective things you can do when using presentation software is talk to your slides rather than to the audience. Keep audience members' attention on you, and point them to the screen at appropriate times.

You should look for ways to decrease your reliance on words and increase your use of graphics. Figure 13.5 shows two options for creating a slide about iPhone apps, one emphasizing words and the other pictures. Notice how the picture-based slide is more visually appealing yet provides the same basic information. If you do want to display words, find ways to integrate text boxes into relevant images—you will see an example of this in the next tip.

2. *Use the rule of thirds.* Photographers learn that interesting photos make strategic use of composition. One element of composing a photograph is to employ the **rule of thirds,** which simply assumes that the shot view can be divided into three imaginary columns and three imaginary rows. Where the lines for these columns and rows intersect are hot zones where focal points can be established. By using the hot zones strategically, you can present information in a much more visually appealing way.

rule of thirds
Using three rows, three columns, and four hot zones at the intersections of those row and column lines to compose a visual image.

Figure 13.5
Using images rather than words on a slide is more effective.

Step 1: Divided slides into thirds **Step 2: Place picture on slides** **Step 3: Add text box**

Figure 13.6

Following the rule of thirds can add visual interest to your slides.

Notice in figure 13.6 how a slide was constructed using the rule of thirds. The first step shows the rows and columns on the slide. Remember that these are imaginary, although you can set PowerPoint and Keynote to show you a similar grid when composing your slides. In the second step you will see how an image was placed on the slide. The person standing in the image is placed near the lower-left hot zone, with the rest of the picture showing a rural river landscape. The final step shows how another element, in this case a text box, can be placed near another hot zone to increase impact. Using the rule of thirds helps make this slide go from being a boring text slide to a visually significant slide. Notice, too, how the person in the slide appears to be looking in the direction of the text box; this helps draw the viewer to the text and, like the person in the picture, become engaged by what the text states.

3. *Minimize rather than maximize details.* It's a natural tendency to include too much information. Notice the difference between the slides in figure 13.7. The slide on the left includes a somewhat visually interesting set of words; the slide on the right makes the emphasis much clearer, and with more impact.

4. *Capitalize on what's available.* Keynote and PowerPoint are more robust when you use them to display a variety of multimedia. For instance, using a free website called www.keepvid.com, you can create a downloadable file of a YouTube video and embed the movie into your Keynote or PowerPoint file to play a short clip. You can even trim the clip down to play exactly what you want. Likewise, you can

Figure 13.7

Cluttering a slide with too much information can diminish its impact.

More is said with less.

More is said with less.

embed MP3 music files or other audio files and have them automatically play when you advance to a new slide. These are only a few of the multimedia options available. Although you should try to utilize these options if they are appropriate for your message, audience, and situation, remember that you need to practice with them. The visual interest they add also increases the complexity of your presentation, which means that more can go wrong.

Alternatives to slide-deck programs are emerging. Prezi (www.prezi.com) offers an entirely different way of creating visuals that can be much more effective for highly visual and creative presentations. Adobe Flash and other multimedia authoring tools can help you create presentation aids that are highly interactive and less linear than slide decks; these tools require significantly more expertise, but they may be useful for speakers who frequently give the same presentation and want more interactive elements.

Whatever approach you decide to use, remember that your primary purpose is to deliver an effective message. The visual resources you employ can be critical in helping or hindering your audience's interest and understanding. The better your visuals are, the more time they will likely take to create, and the more practice you will need. An excellent way to see how visuals enhance messages is to watch any TED (www.ted.com) presentation. Those speakers use a variety of types of visual resources and emphasize many of the principles discussed here. You can also do a Google search for "infographics" to find clever examples of how details, ranging from statistics to historical facts, can be displayed visually.

keeping it real

Controlling Nerves and Delivering Well

At the beginning of this chapter you learned about Devon, who combated his nervousness by overrelying on his slides as notes. His delivery was poor, and his slides were uninteresting. What could Devon have done differently?

1. *Isolate sources of nervousness.* There are a variety of techniques for managing communication apprehension. Devon should start by trying to identify specific things that contribute to his nervousness and take steps to resolve those fears. For instance, if he is afraid of forgetting what he wants to say, practicing with progressively fewer notes may help him grow confident while weaning him away from reading his information.

2. Use delivery to connect with the audience. By reading from the computer, Devon failed to establish rapport and connection with his audience. He should use a variety of verbal and nonverbal delivery behaviors to establish that connection.

3. Make visual resources pop. Devon's slides were boring because they basically provided a transcript of his speech. Although some words on slides might provide clarity and even impact, Devon should have relied on more visual imagery and less text. Reading to the audience is always a mistake; having too much text on a slide is highly ineffective; reading text-heavy slides to an audience is a recipe for speech disaster.

These tips take a bit of time to implement and require several realistic practice sessions. If Devon wants to do his speech the right way, with impact, the additional work is necessary.

Chapter Review & Study Guide

Summary

In this chapter, you learned the following:

1. Delivery is how you use your voice and body to communicate your message to the audience. There are four general methods of delivering a presentation:
   - The extemporaneous method, in which the speech is carefully prepared but appears relatively spontaneous and conversational.
   - The impromptu method, which actually is spontaneous and without specific preparation.
   - The manuscript method, whereby the presenter uses a script throughout delivery.
   - The memorized method, which employs a script committed to memory.

2. There are various vocal and bodily behaviors you can use to improve your delivery.
   - Vocal aspects of delivery include pitch, rate, pauses, volume, enunciation, fluency, and vocal variety.
   - Nonverbal aspects of delivery include gestures, eye contact, facial expressions, and movement.

3. Most speakers experience nervousness before giving a speech. There are five general approaches to managing your communication apprehension related to speaking:
   - The skills approach requires taking steps to improve your competence as a speaker. By improving your skills, you will gain more confidence.
   - Positive thinking can reframe fears into steps you'll use to improve your speaking.

   - The visualization technique lets you mentally picture yourself doing well during a speech.
   - The relaxation technique, usually enacted by a trained facilitator, trains you to associate public speaking with relaxing thoughts.
   - Self-management is when you focus on what your actual fears are and develop techniques for addressing specific fears rather than the general condition.

4. Using visual resources in your presentation can increase interest in your speech and help the audience retain more of what you say. Three days after your speech, audience members typically remember only about 10% of what you said if your speech does not include visuals; if you include visuals they typically remember about 65%.

5. Most speakers create unappealing slides because they do not follow general principles of design when creating PowerPoint or Keynote slide decks. These design principles can help you make clearer and more appealing slides:
   - Use images, not words.
   - Apply the rule of thirds to use various areas of a slide as anchors for people and other objects.
   - Minimize details, so that your slide does not become cluttered.
   - Use multimedia resources to add interactivity, but practice with your materials several times to predict and avoid problems.

Key Terms

Articulation	Gestures	Relaxation approach
Bodily movement	Impromptu method	Rule of thirds
Communication apprehension (CA)	Manuscript method	Self-managed approach
Delivery	Memorized method	Skills approach
Enunciation	Pause	Slide-deck visuals
Extemporaneous method	Pitch	Visual resources
Eye contact	Positive thinking approach	Visualization approach
Facial expressions	Pronunciation	Vocal variety
Fluency	Rate	Vocalized pauses

Study Questions

connect
For further review, go to the LearnSmart study module for this chapter.

1. Which method of delivery encourages you to improvise and speak without previous research or preparation?

   a. extemporaneous
   b. impromptu
   c. manuscript
   d. memorized

2. A disadvantage of a presentation delivered in the memorized method is

   a. the need to create carefully prepared notes.
   b. a lack of practice.
   c. a lack of eye contact.
   d. the removal of spontaneity and the danger of forgetting.

3. "Ummmms" or "aahhhhs" that disrupt a speaker's fluency are termed

   a. vocalized pauses.
   b. enunciation.
   c. articulation.
   d. pitch.

4. _____ is the highness or lowness of a speaker's voice, and _____ is to the smoothness of delivery and flow of words.

   a. Volume; rate
   b. Pitch; fluency
   c. Rate; vocal variety
   d. Pitch; enunciation

5. Gestures are movements of the head, arms, and hands

   a. used to improve source credibility.
   b. that appear rehearsed and out of rhythm.
   c. used to illustrate, emphasize, or signal ideas.
   d. that convey a relationship with the audience.

6. With regard to movement, the speaker should

   a. pace back and forth.
   b. move without purpose.
   c. move backwards when introducing an important point.
   d. avoid turning his or her back to the audience.

7. If you are nervous or anxious about giving your presentation, you may be experiencing

   a. gestures.
   b. communication apprehension.
   c. cognitive modification.
   d. audience adaptation.

8. Why are visual resources used?

   a. Speakers do not need to prepare as much because they can just read their PowerPoint.
   b. They are appropriate for all types of speeches.
   c. People tend to learn and retain more when they both see and listen.
   d. They are fun to watch.

9. When using PowerPoint, you should

   a. use a lot of text on each slide.
   b. move the slides quickly, because the audience will get bored.
   c. vary your slides to keep the presentation interesting.
   d. utilize all color combinations.

10. The rule of thirds divides a slide into how many hot zones?

    a. 1   c. 3
    b. 2   d. 4

Answers:

1. (b); 2. (d); 3. (a); 4. (b); 5. (c); 6. (d); 7. (b); 8. (c); 9. (c); 10. (d)

Critical Thinking

1. The next time you see your favorite late-night television host deliver the monologue, evaluate his or her delivery. Assess both vocal and bodily aspects of delivery.

2. In your classes, from which types of visual resources do you benefit the most? Which ones are not as useful?

informative presentations

When you have read and thought about this chapter, you will be able to:

1. Identify the intent, goal, and appropriate topics for informative presentations.

2. Apply the strategies for informing others.

3. Shape the informative content by selecting the appropriate language and number of main points.

4. Apply the skills for making informative presentations.

The goal of informative presentations is to enhance an audience's knowledge and understanding of a topic. In this chapter you will learn how to choose topics for an informative speech and how to develop behavioral purposes for them. The chapter discusses techniques that will help you effectively present an informational speech to an audience. Effective informative speakers demonstrate certain skills that contribute to their effectiveness, so the chapter covers the skills of defining, describing, explaining, narrating, and demonstrating. Finally, the chapter includes two examples of informative presentations.

Jennifer Williams is 39 years old and married with two children. She worked in a large software company on the East Coast after she graduated from high school and while she attended college part-time. When she had her daughter, who is now 9 years old, Jennifer quit her job and stopped taking classes to be a full-time parent.

She planned on going back to school, but she had a son 4 years after her daughter was born. Jennifer's husband, with a college degree in electrical and computing engineering, recently received a promotion, and the family moved from the greater Washington, D.C., area to Chicago. Their daughter is in the fourth grade and their son is enrolled in kindergarten. Jennifer has decided it is time for her to get her undergraduate degree.

Jennifer feels a little out of place in some of her general education courses. Most of the students are 18 to 20 years old, single, and working part-time. Jennifer's mind is on her husband and children. What should she make for dinner? Who is picking up their son from kindergarten? Can either parent go to their daughter's soccer game? When is she supposed to bring snacks for her son's class?

Jennifer finds her communication class to be especially difficult— not because she is afraid of public speaking but because she does not think she has anything in common with the other students. Should she talk about meal planning, carpooling, or feeling middle-aged in a world of youthful people? She knows about these topics, but she also knows that her classmates would not even feign interest. She is hoping that, as she learns more about the informative process, a relevant topic will occur to her.

What would you suggest as a topic for Jennifer? At the end of this chapter, we'll take another look at Jennifer's situation and how she might solve the problem of choosing a topic relevant to her audience.

Even if you've never given an informative speech in a formal setting, you've probably had a lot of experience informing others about topics that interest you. Do you think your descriptions and explanations are effective and efficient? Do people enjoy learning new information from you? This chapter provides many guidelines for shaping and delivering effective informative presentations.

How Do You Prepare an Informative Presentation?

To prepare an informative speech, ask yourself the following:

1. Why deliver the speech? That is, what are your intent, purpose, and goal for informative speaking?
2. What kinds of topics best lend themselves to informative speaking?
3. What are the immediate behavioral purposes of informative speaking, and how can you tell whether you have fulfilled them?

WHAT IS YOUR GOAL?

The end product of informative speaking is to increase what your listeners know about a topic, to help them learn information that will be useful to them, to clarify complex issues, to demonstrate something useful, to show how things are related in space, or to arouse interest in topics that might initially seem boring or uninteresting but that really are important.

To increase what your listeners know about a topic is one kind of informative speaking that is very much like what you experience in higher education every day, because it is like most teaching. Your professors are trying to increase what you know. The good news is that in your informative presentation you can use strategies you learn from watching professionals in nearly every class. Some examples of topics for such a presentation are

What can we learn from cave drawings?

What is chronic fatigue syndrome?

The possibilities of geothermal power

What are stem cells?

These and countless other topics like them simply add to what your audience knows about a topic.

To help your audience learn information that will be useful to them is another common goal of informative presentations. You take courses that provide useful information, courses such as food and nutrition, exercise physiology, wellness, and intercultural communication. In this kind of informative speaking you can also imitate or adapt strategies that you have seen in the classroom, in your workplace, in workshops, or in seminars in which you have participated. Some examples of topics for such a presentation are

How to keep fit even when you are busy

Easy steps for avoiding the flu

How to avoid home accidents

Chinese customs for greeting and leaving

These and many other topics like them increase what the audience knows and provide a path for those who wish to take it. Unlike the persuasive presentation that presses the audience to act, the informative speech provides useful information the listener can choose to use or not. Think of the difference between commercial and public broadcasting. Commercial stations carry advertisements that end with an action step suggesting or often insisting on a purchase, but public broadcasters are allowed only to name a sponsor without pushing for an action. Similarly, informative presentations give you information on which you *could* act, but the primary purpose is to give you tools, not to insist that you use them.

To clarify complex issues is another goal of informative presentations. The recent financial meltdown is an excellent topic for this kind of presentation. Many complex issues emerge every day: increased violence in parts of the world; economic systems that do not seem to work and that sharply divide the rich and the poor; outbreaks of war; cases of widespread famine; abuse of children, the elderly, women, and men; increased penalization and associated crowding in prisons. We hear about these issues, but most of us do not fully understand their causes or effects. An informative speech can tackle such complex issues and clarify them. Here are some questions this type of presentation might answer:

What is the historic relationship between Israel and the Palestinians?

How does identity theft work?

Should some street drugs become legal in the United States?

What is the relationship between recession and antisocial behaviors?

These topics and many more are spawned by the news as it unfolds daily, weekly, and monthly. All you have to do is select a topic that leaves people scratching their heads and explain to your listeners what the issue can mean to them.

To demonstrate something useful is still another possible goal of an informative presentation. You already know listeners remember better if they not only hear what you say but also do it. That's why a demonstration presentation often has more impact on an audience than one that relies on words and images only. Some possible topics for a demonstration presentation are

> Save a life with the Heimlich maneuver
>
> The correct way to lift weights
>
> How to train for a marathon
>
> How to give yourself a mini-massage

These and other topics lend themselves nicely to showing an audience how something looks or works. In some cases—such as the Heimlich maneuver—you can even have audience members participate to show that they understand your message.

To show how things are related in space is still another possible kind of informative presentation. Much of what engineers, architects, electricians, plumbers, and fashion designers do is to demonstrate how to relate items in space. Here are some examples of this type of informative presentation:

> How to arrange a small residence for multiple purposes
>
> Where are the major islands in the Indian Ocean?
>
> Using electronics in a green residence
>
> Planning a vegetable garden

Finding your way around a foreign city, showing the best-rated restaurants on Yelp.com, explaining the most useful ways to do research online at your college or university library, and locating the main features of a national park all require that you inform your listeners about spatial relationships. Even if they never go to the Indian Ocean, your presentation will show them its relative location in the vast expanse of the ocean.

Finally, *to arouse interest in topics that might at first seem uninteresting or boring* is a legitimate goal of an informative presentation. Teachers often try to arouse your interest in subjects that you might find uninteresting or boring; when they are effective, they use strategies you can also employ. Some examples of topics that might at first blush appear uninteresting but can be lively, given the right treatment, are

> The lessons provided by Shakespeare
>
> The function of the catalytic converter
>
> The most common phobias
>
> The rarest animals in the world

■ The informative speaker must arouse the interest of the audience and show the significance of the topic. In this case, it's how to dress for success.

Remember, the idea is to render possibly unexciting topics more interesting to your listeners, not to select some totally insignificant or unimportant topic, so that you can put lipstick on it, because even after your presentation the topic will remain unimportant. Examples of such unimportant topics include the difference between a bolt and a screw, the presidential record of William Henry Harrison (who died in office 31 days after delivering one of the longest inaugural addresses in history, perhaps a lesson here), and the history of paper clips. You can render an overlooked or unexciting topic more interesting to an audience, but you should not strive to revive topics that deserve to remain buried.

WHAT IS YOUR PURPOSE?

Two important questions for the informative speaker are these:

1. What do you want your audience to know or do as a result of your presentation?

2. How will you know whether you are successful?

Students learn better if they know exactly what the instructor expects them to learn. Similarly, an audience learns more from an informative presentation if the speaker states exactly what they are expected to know or do. The results of your informative presentation will remain unknown, however, unless you make them behavioral; that is, your presentation should result in change you can observe. An instructor discovers whether students learned from a lecture by giving a quiz or having the students answer questions in class. In the same way, the informative speaker seeks to discover whether a message was effectively communicated by seeking overt feedback from the audience. This overt feedback is about the **immediate behavioral purposes** of your presentation—the actions you expect from an audience during and immediately after a presentation.

immediate behavioral purposes
The actions expected from an audience during and immediately after a presentation.

The most common immediate behavioral purposes in an informative presentation encourage listeners to do the following:

1. *Define words, objects, or concepts.* For example, after hearing my presentation my audience members can define the term *foreclosure,* tell what anthropologists mean by an *artifact,* or provide a meaningful definition for the concept of *eminent domain.*

    A statement of purpose for a presentation to define looks like this: My purpose is to have my listeners tell me upon asking that the law allows government to acquire private or commercial property as long as the government pays market rates in a concept called "eminent domain."

2. *Describe objects, persons, or issues.* For example, after hearing my presentation my listeners can describe sedimentary rock formations, reveal the appearance of *contact dermatitis* (a common skin ailment in adults), or describe in a way we can all understand the pros and cons of the bond issue for a new school.

    A statement of purpose for a presentation to describe looks like this: My purpose is to have my listeners correctly explain back to me the main parts of the controversy surrounding the new athletic stadium.

3. *Distinguish between different things.* For example, after hearing my presentation the audience should be able to distinguish between a counterfeit dollar and a real dollar, between a conservative position and a liberal position, or between an ordinary automobile and a luxury automobile.

    A statement of purpose for a presentation to distinguish between different things will look like this: My purpose is to have my audience show me that they can tell the difference between a socialist position on state ownership and a democratic position on state ownership.

4. *Compare and/or contrast items.* For example, after hearing my speech my audience should be able to contrast a real diamond with a cubic zirconia, faux fur and actual animal fur, and Democratic and Republican positions on raising taxes.

    A statement of purpose for a presentation to compare and/or contrast looks like this: Upon completion of my presentation members of the audience will be able to accurately reveal the major differences between Pentecostal churches and the so-called main line Protestant churches.

In each of these behavioral purposes of an informative speech, the audience can be asked to prove they know and understand the speaker's purpose by stating, writing, or demonstrating what they have learned. The speaker can call on a few individuals after the presentation to see whether they can recall what the speech sought to teach, can ask some listeners to write down what they understood the speech topic to be, or ask the audience to prove they understood by inviting them to do what the speech taught: correctly lift heavy objects, use electric paddles to re-start the heart, or use a defensive maneuver during an attack.

How Do You Effectively Present Information to an Audience?

Audience analysis can help you determine how much audience members already know and how much you will have to tell them. Then you have to decide how to generate information hunger, achieve information relevance, use extrinsic motivation, select content, and avoid information overload in your presentation.

CREATING INFORMATION HUNGER

information hunger
The audience's need for the information contained in the presentation.

rhetorical questions
Questions asked for effect, with no answer expected.

An informative presentation is more effective if the presenter can generate **information hunger** in the audience—that is, if the presenter can create a need for information in the audience. Arousal of interest during the speech is related to how much the audience will comprehend. You could use the following **rhetorical questions**—questions asked for effect, with no answer expected—to introduce an informative speech and to arouse audience interest: "Are you aware of the number of abused children in your hometown?" "Can you identify five warning signs of cancer?" or "Do you know how to get the best college education for your money?" Depending on the audience, these rhetorical questions could arouse interest.

Another method is to arouse the audience's curiosity. For example, you might state, "I have discovered a way to add 10 years to my life," "The adoption of the following plan will ensure lower taxes," or "I have a secret for achieving marital success." Giving out a brief quiz on your topic early in the speech arouses audience interest in finding the answers. Unusual clothing is likely to make people wonder why you are so attired, and an object you created will likely inspire the audience to wonder how you made it. Rhetorical questions and arousing curiosity are just a few of the many ways the presenter can generate information hunger.

DEMONSTRATING INFORMATION RELEVANCE

information relevance
The importance, novelty, and usefulness of the information to the audience.

A second factor relating an informative presentation to an audience is **information relevance**—*the importance, novelty, and usefulness of the information to the audience.* When selecting a topic for an informative presentation, carefully consider the relevance of the topic to the particular audience. Skin cancer might be a better topic in the summer when students are sunbathing than in the winter when they are studying for finals. Whereas a presentation on taxes could be dull, a speech on how current tax laws cost audience members more than they cost the rich might be more relevant, and a speech on three ways to reduce personal taxes might be even more relevant. However, if your audience happens to be composed of young people who have never paid taxes, none of the three topics will likely be compelling. Similarly, a speech on raising racehorses, writing a textbook, or living on a pension might be informative but not relevant because of the financial status, occupation, or age of the listeners. Thus, you should exercise some care in selecting a topic that interests your audience.

People expose themselves first to information that supports or fits in with what they already believe or know. Thus, your intended listeners' position on a topic can determine whether they will hear your speech, and then whether they will listen.[1]

REVEALING EXTRINSIC MOTIVATION

extrinsic motivation
A method of making information relevant by providing the audience with reasons outside the presentation itself for listening to the content of the presentation.

A third way to relate an informative presentation to an audience is to use **extrinsic motivation**—reasons outside the presentation itself for listening to its content. An

audience is more likely to listen to and comprehend a presentation if reasons exist outside the
speech itself for concentrating on the content.[2]
A teacher who tells students to listen carefully
because they will be tested at the end of the
hour is using extrinsic motivation. A student
can use extrinsic motivation at the beginning of
a presentation by telling an audience, "Attention
to this speech will alert you to ways you can
increase energy and creativity," or "After hearing
this speech, you will never purchase a poor-
quality used car again."

Extrinsic motivation is related to the concept of information relevance. The audience
member who would ordinarily lack interest in
the topic of fashion might find that topic relevant when it is linked to learning about hot
new fashion trends. The audience member's interest in looking good is an extrinsic
motivation for listening carefully to the presentation.

Mention any external reasons for listening early in the presentation, *before* the message you want the audience to remember. A statement such as "You will need this background material for the report due at the end of this week" provides extrinsic motivation
for the managers who hear it from their employer. Similarly, in an informative presentation, you may be able to command more attention, comprehension, and action from
audience members if they know some reasons outside the presentation itself for attending to your message.

skill builder

Relating the Topic to the Audience

Either by yourself or with a partner, think or talk about
your answer to each of the following:

1. What can you do in your presentation to generate
   information hunger, to make your audience famished
   for more?
2. What can you do to make sure the audience knows
   the importance and usefulness of your topic?
3. What reasons outside the presentation itself (extrinsic motivation) does the audience have for listening
   to you?

DESIGNING INFORMATIVE CONTENT

A fourth way to relate an informative presentation to an audience is to select **informative content**—the main points and subpoints, illustrations, and examples you use to
clarify and inform. The following principles can guide you in selecting your speech
content:

> **informative content**
> The main points and
> subpoints, illustrations,
> and examples used to
> clarify and inform.

- *Audiences tend to remember and comprehend generalizations and main ideas better than
  details and specific facts.* The usual advice to speakers—to limit content to a relatively small
  number of main points and generalizations, say two to five—is well founded. Audiences
  are unlikely to remember a larger number of main points.

- *Relatively simple words and concrete ideas are significantly easier to retain than are more
  complex materials.* Long or unusual words may dazzle an audience into thinking you
  are intellectually gifted or verbally skilled, but they may also reduce audience understanding of the content. Keep the ideas and the words used to express those ideas at
  an appropriate level.

- *Humor can make a dull presentation more interesting to an audience, but humor does not
  seem to increase information retention.* The use of humor also improves the audience's
  perception of the character of the speaker and can increase a speaker's authoritativeness
  when a presentation is dull.

- *Early remarks about how the presentation will meet the audience's needs can create anticipation and increase the chances that the audience will listen and understand.* Whatever topic
  you select, you should tell audience members early in your presentation how the topic is
  related to them. Unless you relate the topic to their needs, they may choose not to listen.

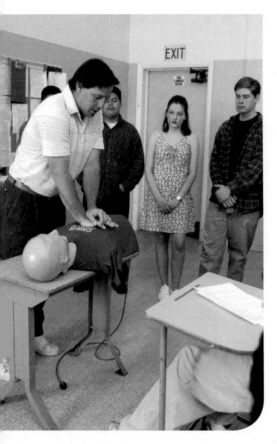

■ Having the audience practice what you preach greatly increases their comprehension.

information overload
Providing much more information than the audience can absorb in amount, complexity, or both.

■ *Calling for overt audience response, or actual behavior, increases comprehension more than repetition does.* An informative presenter can ask for overt responses from audience members by having them perform the task being demonstrated (for example, two people dance after you explain the technique of the waltz); by having them stand, raise hands, or move chairs to indicate affirmative understanding of the speaker's statements (for example, "Raise your hand if you are familiar with local building codes"); or by having them write answers that will indicate understanding of the informative speech (for example, "List three ways to lower your blood pressure"). Having an audience go through an overt motion provides feedback for you and can be rewarding and reinforcing for both you and your listeners.

AVOIDING INFORMATION OVERLOAD

The informative speaker needs to be wary about the amount of information included in a presentation. The danger is creating **information overload**—providing much more information than the audience can absorb in terms of amount, complexity, or both.

Information overload comes in two forms. One is *quantity:* the speaker tells audience members more than they ever wanted to know about a subject, even if they were interested in it. Unfortunately, cramming too much information into the time allowed decreases understanding.

A second form of information overload is *complexity:* the speaker uses language or ideas that are beyond the capacity of the audience to understand. An engineer or a mathematician who unloads detailed formulas on the audience or a philosopher who soars into the ethereal heights of abstract ideas may leave the audience feeling frustrated and more confused than before the speech.

The solution to information overload is to speak on a limited number of main points with only the best supporting materials, and to keep the message at a level the audience can understand.

ORGANIZING CONTENT

In an informative presentation, you can help the audience learn content by following these recommendations on how to organize your presentation:

1. Tell an audience what you are going to tell them (forecast), tell them, and tell them what you told them.
2. Use transitions and signposts to increase understanding.
3. Tell your audience which points are most important.
4. Repeat important points for better understanding.

Audiences can more easily grasp information when they are invited to anticipate and to review the organization and content of your speech. That is why the body of your presentation is bracketed by a preview of what you are going to say and a summary/review of what you said.

When you have completed this section on how to effectively present your material, check your presentation against the checklist in table 14.1.

Skills for Informative Speaking

Highly effective informative speakers demonstrate certain skills that contribute to their effectiveness. One of these skills is *defining;* much of what an informative speaker does is reveal to an audience what certain terms, words, and concepts mean. Another is *describing;* the informative speaker often tells an audience what something looks, sounds, feels, and even smells like. A third skill is *explaining,* or trying to say what something is in words the audience can understand. A fourth skill is *narrating*—an oral interpretation of a story, an event, or a description. A fifth skill is *demonstrating,* or showing an audience how to do something. Let's look at ways you can improve each of these skills.

DEFINING

Far from being dull, definitions often give shape to the issues we debate in our society. For example, when does a collection of cells become a fetus? When does a fetus become a premature infant? Is a soul produced with the meeting of sperm and egg? Can marriage exist between same-sex partners? What is a family? If a baby boomer is someone born between 1946 and 1964, what is someone born in 1985 called?

sizing things up

Using Language Effectively

Much of our communication with others, particularly informative speaking, uses language to express meaning. Not surprisingly, one source of miscommunication is the use of language that others do not understand. Using concepts from chapter 3, take a moment to assess your use of various approaches to improving the clarity of your language. The following statements are things you might say to help others understand you more clearly. Read each question carefully and respond using the following scale:

1 = I never do that.
2 = I sometimes do that.
3 = I regularly do that.
4 = I frequently do that.

1. Use descriptive statements to check your perception.
2. Restate another person's message by repeating back what you thought the person meant.
3. Describe exactly how you think something works, how it happens, or what it consists of.
4. Explain the meaning of important words you use.
5. Specify the time when you made the observation.
6. Identify the uniqueness of objects, events, or people you encounter, so that others can categorize or contextualize them.
7. Use words others do not understand.
8. Talk in abstract terms.
9. Base your messages only on your own perceptions.
10. Make statements that do not provide the situation or timing of your observation.
11. Talk about people, places, and things from a general viewpoint, rather than precisely.
12. Go with your instinct about what you think the other person means.

A guide for interpreting your responses appears in the appendix at the end of the text (p. 348).

Table 14.1 An Informative Presentation Checklist

_____1. Does your audience have some generalizations to remember from your details and specific facts?

_____2. Have you used simple words and concrete ideas to help your audience remember?

_____3. Can you comfortably use humor or wit in your presentation?

_____4. Have you told your listeners early in your presentation how your message will meet their needs?

_____5. Have you determined some way to actively engage the audience in your presentation?

_____6. Have you avoided information overload?

_____7. Have you used transitions, highlighted the most important points, included some repetition, and provided advance organizers?

comparison
Shows the similarity between something well known and something less known.

contrast
Clarifies by showing differences.

synonym
Defines by using a word close or similar in meaning to the one you are trying to define.

antonym
Defines an idea by opposition.

operational definition
Defines by explaining a process.

imagery
Use of words that appeal to the senses, that create pictures in the mind.

metaphor
A figure of speech that likens one thing to another by treating it as if it were that thing.

We can define by using comparison and contrast, synonyms and antonyms, and even operational definitions. A **comparison** shows the similarity between something well known and something less known. A student explained that tying a bow tie (unfamiliar to most) is the same as tying your shoelace (familiar to all), but since we are unaccustomed to tying a shoelace around our neck, the bow tie is challenging. A **contrast** clarifies by showing differences: "He was taller than you, had longer hair, and had sharper features."

A **synonym** defines by using a word similar in meaning to the one you are trying to define. A student speaking about depression used synonyms to help the listeners understand: "A depressed person feels demoralized, purposeless, isolated, and distanced from others." An **antonym** defines an idea by opposition. Hence, a student defined "a good used car" by what it is not: "Not full of dents, not having high mileage, not worn on the seats, not using lots of oil, and not involved in a serious accident."

An **operational definition** defines by explaining a process. An operational definition of a cake is the sequence of actions depicted in a recipe. An operational definition of concrete is the formula-driven sequence of ingredients correctly added over the correct time period.

DESCRIBING

You already know from chapter 3 on language that speakers are better off being concrete than abstract, specific instead of general, and accurate instead of ambiguous. You also know about paraphrasing, indexing, and dating. But effective descriptions have other qualities we have not yet considered, qualities such as **imagery,** a figure of speech that arouses the senses and stimulates your synapses to see, hear, and feel what the words are saying.

Look first at this description of Reggie Watts, who started his career as a singer with bands but ended up being a stand-up comedian. Here is how one writer characterized him:

> He arrives on stage with enormous amber rings dripping like tree sap from his fingers, his Afro a Miracle-Gro spider plant. Sometimes he's painted a pinkie nail pink. He might be wearing a ridiculous sweater.[3]

That's how he looks. Here is how he sounds:

■ Singer-turned-comedian Reggie Watts.

> Then he lays down a track. He starts with the sound of a kick drum, from deep in his throat, recorded into a loop sampler—a small machine often used by guitarists to layer melodies. He adds a snare with a few controlled exhales. A couple of high notes with his tongue against his teeth. And then he starts to sing, in French or gibberish German. Morphing imperceptibly into a cockney slang, he seems to be talking about something from a human-resources manual or a dating disaster . . .[4]

Do these words help you picture in your mind what Reggie Watts looks and sounds like? In two sentences the words tell you that he wears large amber rings, wears his hair in an uncontrolled Afro, colors his pinkie nail pink, and does not care much about his clothing. The actual imagery occurs with words such as "enormous amber rings dripping like tree sap" and "his Afro a Miracle-Gro spider plant." Words can paint pictures in the mind that appeal to the senses.

Another figure of speech appears in the description of Watts' voice. **Metaphor** likens one thing to another by treating it as if it were that thing. The paragraph on how Watts sounds is metaphorical in that the writer describes his voice as if it were an entire band: "sound of a kick drum," "recorded into a loop sampler," "he adds a snare"—all done with voice and throat. You can perform similar magic with your own words if you recognize the potential of speaking with imagery and metaphor.

EXPLAINING

A third skill for the informative presenter is explaining an idea in words the audience can understand. An **explanation** simplifies or clarifies an idea while arousing audience interest.

An important step in explaining is analyzing, deconstructing, or dissecting something to enhance audience understanding. Unless you become skilled at dissecting a concept, your explanation may leave audience members more confused than they were before your presentation. Determine what you can do to make the concept more palatable to the audience. For example, in an article about global warming, a biology professor explained how animals and plants are migrating north or climbing higher—if they can—to survive:

> Wild species don't care who is in the White House. It is very obvious they are desperately trying to move to respond to the changing climate. Some are succeeding. But for the ones that are already at the mountain top or the poles, there is no place for them to go. They are the ones that are going extinct.[5]

explanation
A means of idea development that simplifies or clarifies an idea while arousing audience interest.

NARRATING

A fourth skill for informative speakers is **narrating**—the oral presentation and interpretation of a story, a description, or an event. In a presentation, narration includes the dramatic reading of some lines from a play, a poem, or another piece of literature; the voice-over on a series of slides or a silent film to illustrate a point; and even the reading of such information as a letter, a quotation, or a selection from a newspaper, blog, or magazine. The broadcaster who relays the play-by-play account of a ball game is narrating, and so is the presenter who explains what a weaver is doing in an informative presentation on home crafts.

The person who uses narration in a presentation moves just a little closer to oral interpretation of literature, or even acting, because the narration is highlighted by being more dramatic than the surrounding words. Sections of your presentation that require this kind of special reading also require special practice. If you want a few lines of poetry in your presentation to have the desired impact, you will need to rehearse them.

narrating
The oral presentation and interpretation of a story, a description, or an event; includes dramatic reading of prose or poetry.

DEMONSTRATING

A fifth skill for informative speakers is **demonstrating**—showing the audience what you are explaining. Some topics are communicated best through words; other topics are best communicated by demonstrating. You can talk about self-defense, efficient ways to navigate the online research holdings of your college or university library, the latest men's and women's cologne fragrances, and weight lifting, and you can even read about these subjects. But nothing enhances understanding better than seeing and trying self-defense moves, seeing and trying to navigate the library online research holdings, seeing and smelling the latest colognes on the market, or actually lifting some weights while learning about them.

demonstrating
Showing the audience what you are explaining.

Two Examples of Informative Presentations

So far in this chapter, you have learned how to select a topic for your informative presentation; how to determine behavioral purposes and goals for the informative presentation; how to present information to an audience; how to organize the informative presentation; and how to define, describe, explain, narrate, and demonstrate

skill **builder**

Practicing Explanations

Think of something you have explained to others many times at work or at home—for example, a job skill, a hobby, a course project, or a favorite TV show, film, website, or app. Does your explanation get increasingly efficient with practice? The answer is probably yes. To help prepare for your informative speech, practice some of the explanations from your presentation on others before you address an audience, so that they will be easy to understand.

College Admissions

by Brittany Fondakowski

Links audience to topic.

Relationship between the topic and myself.

Central idea and main points previewed for audience.

Included sources of information throughout

Transitions let audience know what I have talked about and what I am going to talk about.

How many people do you know that don't need financial aid in order to pay for their education? Many of us in this room have some type of financial aid whether it be scholarships, loans or grants. In my search for the right college, scholarships and tuition played a major role. Private universities were more likely to have higher tuition but larger scholarships whereas public universities had lower tuition and smaller scholarships. Due to the current economic situation here in the U.S. many colleges are now looking for students who can pay for their education without the help of financial aid. I am going to talk about why colleges want students who don't need financial aid and the pros and cons of that decision.

First, you should understand that college admissions officers are looking more closely at applicants. Rebecca Ruiz from the *New York Times* recently noted that a survey was taken of 450 college admissions officers. The survey showed that officers are working harder to recruit students who can pay full price for their tuition. Tamar Lewin also from the *New York Times* explained that 22% of the officers surveyed said the financial downturn has led them to pay more attention to those students that don't need financial aid. These students include transfer and out of state students who pay a higher tuition. They are being recruited more often by public universities while private universities and community colleges mainly focus on providing aid for low and middle income students. This is due to the status of the economy; public universities are receiving less money from the government.

Now that we know what is going on with the college admissions process, let's look at the pros and cons. If universities decide to change their criteria for admitting students they are going to lose both socioeconomic and racial diversity. Kate Zernike from the *New York Times* noted that by admitting more wealthy students universities would be offsetting their goals to be socioeconomically diverse because many of the students that need financial aid are usually more racially

the concepts in your presentation. Now let's look at the manuscripts of two actual informative presentations delivered by students. The first student is majoring in pharmaceutical sciences and the second student is majoring in mechanical engineering. Both are honors students in their first year of college.

Notice how the presenters gain and maintain the audience's attention, relate the topic to the speaker and to the audience, and forecast the organization and development diverse than those who don't. Another disadvantage to admitting more students who can pay their own way is that those students aren't always academically elite. Tamar Lewin explained that full pay students who were admitted on average had lower grades and test scores. However, this new admission process also has its advantages. Admitting students of means gives universities more money to allocate to different departments. Kate Zernike noted that most colleges are increasing their financial aid budgets; however, the number of students that need financial aid is increasing also. Therefore, by cutting back on the number of students who need financial aid the amount of financial aid given to other students can be increased.

Section provides both sides of the issue.

We have now seen what the college admissions process is becoming and discussed the pros and cons. As some of us continue our education through graduate school or professional programs we will begin to see just how much family wealth affects college admissions. Universities require financial support but the way they are acquiring it has both advantages and disadvantages. Family wealth plays a bigger part in admissions now than it has in the past.

References

Cohen, J. (2011, September 21). 1 in 4 college admissions officers report outside pressure. Retrieved from http://www.chicagotribune.com/news/education/ct-met-admissions-survey-0921-20110921,0,5507311.story

Lewin, T. (2011, September 21). Universities seeking out students of means. Retrieved from http://www.nytimes.com/2011/09/21/education/21admissions.html?_r=1

Ruiz, R. (2011, September 21). Colleges increasingly look for applicants who can pay full price. Retrieved from http://thechoice.blogs.nytimes.com/2011/09/21/full-price/?ref=education

Zernike, K. (2009, March 30). Paying in full as the ticket into colleges. Retrieved from http://www.nytimes.com/2009/03/31/education/31college.html?pagewanted=all

of the topic. Notice also how the presenters clarify the topic with examples high in audience interest; translate the ideas into language the audience can understand; and define, describe, and explain. The marginal notes will help identify how the presenters fulfilled the important functions of the introduction, body, and conclusion of an informative presentation.

The Pros and Cons of Wind Turbines

Joe Rogers

Attention getter.

Listener relevance.

Introduces topic and establishes credibility.

Previews arguments.

Transition to main point #1.

Audience participation.

Visual aid.

Generalization that can be more easily comprehended than an example using specific dollar values.

Provide an example of an energyless safety system.

Examples of turbines saving money.

Transition between main points.

Energy is being consumed at an alarming rate in today's society. By the year 2050, energy use will more than double. If nothing is done to change our usage habits or create more energy to use, we will run out in the not so distant future. One of the options proposed has been wind turbines. Over the last eight years, I have done some research into wind turbines which are one of the options to supplement our energy needs. The choice to use wind turbines to supplement our energy needs has its pros and cons. Some of the points of comparison include cost, public opinion, and efficiency.

The first point to consider should be the cost of wind turbines. Wind turbines are a large financial investment. Even small wind generators, like the ones installed at Minneapolis-St. Paul International Airport, can cost up to $94,000. Can I get a quick show of hands? Who here has seen a wind turbine before today? (*Respond to the number of hands.*) That $94,000 is the cost for smaller wind generators, not even full sized turbines like the ones typically seen on the roadside or the one seen behind me. (*Show turbine on screen.*) Something to also remember when considering cost is that maintenance fees add up over time. Having work done every couple months to make sure a turbine is running properly can add up to a very large sum over the span of even a few years of owning one turbine let alone multiple turbines.

On the other hand, excluding the obvious wind energy, very little energy input is needed to support a wind turbine. Little to no energy is needed to run safety monitoring systems on turbines. Some may be as simple as a ball attached to a chain where unsafe vibrations cause the ball to fall from its place, causing a braking mechanism to be engaged. Most of the energy produced by the turbine is going directly to the home or business it is supplying. The energy that is produced saves money because it is not being paid for through an electric company that charges high premiums to provide the same energy. As I mentioned before, Minneapolis-St. Paul International Airport has installed wind generators on its fire station roof to harness the area's prevalent Northwest winds. This energy is being used to power the airport's fleet of Cushman electric carts which cost about $200 per year to maintain. That means that each year these generators are in use, $200 per cart is saved and can be put toward other purposes. At St. Olaf College in Northfield, MN, up to a third of the school's energy is provided by wind energy. All the money saved by doing so allows tuition money go to bettering programs and facilities at the school.

Although wind turbines may help keep some money in people's wallets, the public still is not convinced that wind turbines are a great option for alternative energy. Homeowners with wind turbines generally grow to dislike them. Owning a wind turbine may actually decrease property values. Even though turbines can cut energy costs, many people view them as eyesores. Another reason that people find turbines problematic is the noise they create. The nearly constant hum a turbine can produce when in motion can cause nearby neighbors to have trouble sleeping creating an obvious issue between the sleep-deprived and the turbine owner.

Many, however, like the green factor of owning a wind turbine. Since most of America's energy comes from fossil fuels, a domestic clean energy source can cut down both dependence on foreign oil and harmful emissions. Unlike with burning gas or coal, no harmful pollutants are emitted from harnessing wind energy. Just harvesting the fossil fuels can be very dangerous. Wind energy offers little possibility that someone can be injured or have long-term health consequences as occurs with fossil fuels.

While wind turbines may have some environmental benefits, some questions remain as to their efficiency. It would be impossible to harness all of the energy from wind. To do that, the wind would have to be stopped which would mean that the blades of the turbine would not move and no energy would be produced. Friction also causes some of the wind's energy to be lost. The energy that is able to be harnessed must be used almost immediately or transferred to somewhere else to be used or it will be lost. Currently, large amounts of wind energy cannot be stored. These factors contribute to some people's skepticism about wind turbine efficiency.

Transition between main points.

Others disagree. Unlike fossil fuels and nuclear energy sources, wind energy does not produce byproducts that can be harmful to the environment and anyone that encounters these byproducts. In addition, very little wind is needed to start spinning the blades of a wind turbine and wherever there is wind, energy can be produced. Some other energy sources need specific areas to produce energy in the most efficient manner. Wind turbines just need to be in any place that has wind.

Although turbines can almost continually produce energy, the question that people want answered is whether or not turbines can produce enough energy to help keep up with growing energy demands. To truly understand if wind turbines are an acceptable way to help meet energy needs, one must consider the pros and cons of the situation. Points to consider include cost, public opinion, and efficiency. No matter what decision is made, remember that the decision not only affects our futures but the futures of those to come as well.

Transition to conclusion.

Thesis restatement and main point summary.

Clincher.

References

America's most beautiful college campuses. (2011, September 14). Retrieved from http://www.travelandleisure.com/articles/americas-most-beautiful-college-campuses/25

Nocera, D. *The role of new technologies in a sustainable energy economy.* Cambridge, MA: Massachusetts Institute of Technology. (2010, May 25)

The low-down on renewable energy. (n.d.). Retrieved from http://www.dosomething.org/tipsandtools/the-low-down-renewable-energy

keeping it real

Creating an Audience-Appropriate Informative Speech

Jennifer Williams, featured at the beginning of this chapter, realized she had more in common with her younger fellow students than she had at first realized. Jennifer knew a great deal about healthy eating. She also knew that some of the students in her class were regularly snacking on candy bars, potato chips, and soft drinks. She decided she would talk about the difference between a healthy diet and one that was primarily comprised of processed foods high in fat and calories. She recalled that she had not thought very much about what she ate and drank when she was just out of high school, but now as a parent she was much more aware of the need to make good food choices. Jennifer also realized that she could build on the information in her informative speech later in the course when she gave a persuasive speech on the same topic. As you internalize the information in this chapter and as you emulate the best informative speakers you have witnessed, you will be able to teach audience members new information, too.

Chapter Review & Study Guide

Summary

In this chapter, you learned the following:

1. Before you offer an informative presentation, you need to know
   - The intent and goal of informative presentations
   - The kinds of topics that are most appropriate
   - The kinds of immediate behavioral purposes that are appropriate for informative presentations and how to determine if you have fulfilled them
2. The strategies for informing others include
   - Generating information hunger, an audience need for the information
   - Achieving information relevance by relating information to the audience
   - Using extrinsic motivation, reasons outside the presentation itself for understanding the presentation's content
3. Shaping the informative content requires
   - Limiting the number of main points
   - Limiting the number of generalizations
   - Selecting language the audience can understand
   - Using specifics to illustrate an abstract idea
   - Including humor or wit when appropriate
   - Revealing how the information meets audience needs
   - Avoiding information overload
   - Organizing content for greater understanding
4. The skills for informative presentations include
   - Defining meanings for an audience
   - Describing by using specific, concrete language
   - Explaining by clarifying and simplifying complex ideas
   - Narrating by using stories to illustrate your ideas
   - Demonstrating by showing a process or procedure to your audience

Key Terms

Antonym
Comparison
Contrast
Demonstrating
Explanation
Extrinsic motivation

Imagery
Immediate behavioral purposes
Information hunger
Information overload
Information relevance
Informative content

Metaphor
Narrating
Operational definition
Rhetorical questions
Synonym

Study Questions

1. The goal of informative presentations is to
   a. induce change in the audience.
   b. discourage the audience from taking action.
   c. increase an audience's knowledge or understanding of a topic.
   d. identify a problem and determine a solution.

2. How do you make an informational topic interesting to the audience?
   a. Relate your own experiences with the subject.
   b. Avoid telling stories of your own experiences with the subject.
   c. Maintain the gaps in your listeners' knowledge of your subject.
   d. Arousing interest is not important.

3. Which is *not* an appropriate topic for an informative presentation?
   a. CPR techniques
   b. animals and their positive effects on the elderly
   c. wedding traditions
   d. everyone should donate blood

4. If audiences are able to describe information or define words related to your topic during and after a presentation, you have successfully accomplished your
   a. demonstration.
   b. immediate behavioral purposes.
   c. imagery.
   d. information overload.

5. The first step in planning your presentation should be
   a. asking a few people questions after the presentation is complete.
   b. teaching or informing your audience.
   c. determining what objectives you want your audience to meet.
   d. surveying the audience.

6. Asking rhetorical questions and arousing curiosity are two ways a speaker can create
   a. behavioral purposes.
   b. topics for informative speeches.
   c. persuasive messages.
   d. information hunger.

7. When presenting information to an audience, a topic's importance, novelty, and usefulness is a key factor known as
   a. information relevance.
   b. information hunger.
   c. informative content.
   d. information overload.

8. Which of the following is *not* a guideline to follow when choosing the content of your presentation?
   a. Use relatively simple words, because they are easier to understand.
   b. Tell the audience early in your presentation how the topic is related to them, so that they will choose to listen.
   c. Develop as many main ideas and use as many details as possible to make the presentation interesting.
   d. Ask for overt responses from audience members to increase comprehension.

9. When organizing the content of your presentation, you should
   a. keep the topic a mystery until the body of the speech.
   b. use transitions to increase understanding.
   c. let the audience decide which points are the most important.
   d. avoid repeating important points, so that the audience isn't bored.

10. _____ simplify or clarify ideas while stimulating audience attention, and _____ is when you show the audience what you are explaining.
    a. Explanations; demonstrating
    b. Definitions; narrating
    c. Descriptions; demonstrating
    d. Narrations; defining

Answers:
1. (c); 2. (a); 3. (d); 4. (b); 5. (c); 6. (d); 7. (a); 8. (c); 9. (b); 10. (a)

Critical Thinking

1. Think of stories you and your friends tell each other. How do they or you effectively create information hunger at the beginning of the story? Why are these methods successful?

2. Find a manuscript of an important speech (such as Martin Luther King Jr.'s "I Have a Dream" or Ronald Reagan's "Challenger" speech). On the manuscript, identify the important presentation functions being fulfilled. Did the speaker use transitions? Gain attention? Describe, explain, or define?

persuasive presentations

When you have read and thought about this chapter, you will be able to:

1. Describe a persuasive presentation.

2. Identify your immediate purpose and long-range goal.

3. Introduce your persuasive presentation.

4. Use arguments effectively.

5. Identify three forms of proof.

6. Organize your persuasive message using the Monroe Motivated Sequence.

7. Apply ethical considerations to your presentation.

8. Prepare a detailed outline of a persuasive presentation.

9. Resist persuasive efforts by others.

Few students think they will ever give a persuasive speech, but they admit they are likely to be asked to introduce new products, convince others to use new methods, and talk with fellow workers about complying with policies and procedures. All these efforts are simply variations on making a persuasive presentation.

ésar Ordez was 28 when he went to college. Impressed that he would pursue a college degree, his employer—an automobile dealer—promoted him to service manager to handle customers as they came to the dealership for auto repairs. César never expected to use at work the persuasive presentation material he was learning in his communication class, but he discovered that, in his new role as service manager, persuasion was his main job.

Often customers were incorrect about what was causing the problem with their car, so he had to persuade them that the squeaking noise in their motor was caused by a slipping serpentine belt. He had to convince them they were not being overcharged for a replacement water pump, that they really should change their oil more frequently, and that they should come in sooner once the brakes begin to squeal. César soon realized that effective persuasion was going to be an important contributor to his success on the job.

How many times have you acted as a persuasive speaker? Have you ever thought about all the different ways you might have to use persuasion in your job—and in many other situations in everyday life? At the end of the chapter, we'll think more about César's situation and other times you might be called on to persuade others.

The vast majority of jobs require that you persuade other people. The big challenge is to learn how to use this potent force in ways that are not harmful to others. That is why this chapter is dedicated to helping you learn just what persuasion is and how it functions. You will learn the purposes and goals of persuasion, as well as strategies that persuaders use to gain change in other people. Because some scoundrels try to change other people in unfair and deceptive ways, the chapter provides some ethical guidelines. At the end of the chapter we tell you some ways to resist persuasion, so that unethical people cannot take advantage of you. You will be armed with knowledge about what persuasion is, how it works, some strategies that can be used ethically, and ways to resist persuasion.

What Is a Persuasive Presentation?

Most people misunderstand how persuasion works. For instance, some people think it is the skillful manipulation of images to get people to do something they would not otherwise do. Actually, forcing people to unwillingly think or behave as you wish is not persuasion but **coercion.** Likewise, tricking people or using fraudulent means to gain compliance is not persuasion but **manipulation.** Both coercion and manipulation override a person's ability to choose, to make a decision based on sound information and ideas. Thus, neither resembles persuasion as portrayed in this text.

You will be expected to deliver at least one persuasive presentation in your class, and perhaps many in your lifetime. A **persuasive presentation** is a message strategically designed to induce change in the audience in some way consistent with your purpose. Here are some examples of persuasive topics:

New Rules Needed for Drug Use Among Athletes

How to Succeed as a Single Mom

coercion
The act of forcing people to think or behave as you wish; not a form of persuasion.

manipulation
The act of tricking people or using fraudulent means to gain compliance; not a form of persuasion.

persuasive presentation
A message designed to strategically induce change in an audience.

Managing Difficult People in the Workplace

Why Our Legislature Must Lower Tuition

You can generate possible topics by using brainstorming or concept mapping, as described in chapter 10. Then make sure your topic relates to you (source credibility) and your audience (audience analysis), as well as being a topic of importance.

WHAT IS YOUR IMMEDIATE PURPOSE?

Your presentation should have an **immediate purpose**—a statement of what you intend it to accomplish. Given that a single presentation to a captive audience is unlikely to produce dramatic results, you need to be realistic about anticipated results. So you might state: "My immediate purpose is to have my listeners write down the e-mail addresses of legislators, so they can communicate with them about lowering our tuition."

immediate purpose
A statement of what you intend to accomplish in this particular presentation.

WHAT IS YOUR LONG-RANGE GOAL?

You may also have a **long-range goal**—a statement of purposes that could be achieved with continuing efforts to persuade. You know, for instance, that your one-shot persuasive effort to alert your listeners to steroids and designer drugs used by athletes is not going to produce a lot of action. But you also know that, the more your audience hears about this issue from many sources, the more likely something will be done about it. You may be just one drop in a pond, but if enough raindrops fall, the pond itself will change. Your long-range goal could be stated like this: "My long-range goal is to encourage my listeners to learn more about this issue over time, so eventually new rules will keep performance-enhancing drugs out of the sports arena."

long-range goal
A statement of purposes that could be achieved with continuing attempts to persuade.

Introducing Your Persuasive Presentation

The introduction for your persuasive presentation has many similarities to other introductions. It seeks to gain and maintain attention (see chapter 12), relate the topic to the speaker (see chapter 11), and forecast the organization and development of the presentation. Where a persuasive introduction differs is in revealing the purpose of the presentation.

REVEALING THE PURPOSE OF THE PRESENTATION

In an informative presentation you state clearly at the outset what you want to accomplish and tell the audience what you want them to learn. In a persuasive presentation, however, your listeners may reject your intention to change their thinking or behavior unless you prepare the way, so you need to analyze the audience to determine when and how you should reveal your immediate purpose.

If you are not asking for much of a change, you may reveal your purpose in the introduction of the speech, or your introducer may even reveal the purpose for you. But if it will require some preparation before your audience is likely to accept your immediate purpose, then you should provide your reasons first and reveal your action step toward the end of the presentation. If you ask your listeners for too much change, you are likely to get a **boomerang effect**—that is, the audience will like you and your message less after the presentation than they did before. To avoid this effect, analyze your audience and decide when you should reveal your purpose. (In chapter 10 you learned how to analyze an audience using everything from demographic analysis to surveys.)

boomerang effect
The audience likes you and your message less after your presentation than they did before.

WHAT PURPOSES ARE PERSUASIVE?

Most persuasive presentations in the classroom have one of two immediate purposes: persuading the audience to do something new or persuading the audience to stop doing something they presently do. These two immediate goals are called adoption and discontinuance.

adoption
The listeners start a new behavior as a result of the persuasive presentation.

Adoption means listeners start a new behavior as a result of the persuasive presentation—for example, they start exercising, start eating healthy foods, or go on a diet.[1] The persuader has some proof of effectiveness if people in the audience state on a post-presentation questionnaire that they are going to take up some new behavior. Suppose a regional sales manager presents new and higher goals for the local sales representatives, and sales increase by 25% over the next three months. This increase is proof that the persuasive effort by the regional sales manager had the desired effect.

discontinuance
A persuasive purpose rooted in convincing listeners to stop some current behavior.

Discontinuance is a persuasive purpose rooted in convincing listeners to stop some current behavior—for example, to quit your gang, stop taking so much sick leave, or desist from drinking so much caffeine.[2] Despite decades of messages discouraging them from eating too much, from exercising too little, and from smoking at all, U.S. adults are the fattest people on earth, exercise way too little, and continue to die in large numbers from obesity and smoking-related diseases. Discontinuance and adoption are challenging persuasive purposes well worth your efforts in a presentation. They can change your listeners' lives in very positive ways.

WHY SHOULD YOU TRY TO PERSUADE?

After reading that years of public service campaigns have failed to change U.S. consumers' eating, exercise, and smoking habits, you might wonder why anyone should expect you to be successful in a classroom presentation. The key factor is that face-to-face persuasive efforts are more effective than public service campaigns for at least two reasons.

One reason is that face-to-face communication is one of the most effective modes of communication. Consider the difference between a public service announcement on TV discouraging bulimia and a classroom presentation on the same subject by a classmate who confesses to bulimia and reveals the awful, life-threatening effects of the disease. Which mode—a TV spot or the person herself—would have the most influence on you? Although you can see almost any entertainer on video, thousands of people show up for concerts because they want to see the entertainer in the flesh. The live concert has more soul than a video can provide. The same is true of classroom speeches: actually experiencing someone's message in person and in real time is a more powerful persuader than is a mediated message.

captive audience
A group consisting of people who did not gather to hear about your particular topic.

voluntary audience
A group that came to hear you, in particular, talk about your topic.

A second reason a face-to-face presentation is more effective is that the classroom has a **captive audience** consisting of people who did not gather to hear about your particular topic. In other words, your classmates are not a **voluntary audience** that came to hear you, in particular, talk about your topic. Voluntary audiences listen to a speaker because they already care about the topic and often are in agreement with the speaker. In the classroom you are going to persuade some people in your audience who never would have gone to a speech about this topic, but as a member of the classroom audience they learn about a topic from you, and your persuasive speech changes their thinking or their behavior. A speaker in your class gives a presentation to persuade you that producers of meat products are cruel to animals. Perhaps you never knew or cared about how the chicken gets to the table. Probably you never would have gone to a speech about the topic. But because you were in class and you listened , you may have been convinced that calling a chicken "free range" because the producers left the hen house door open is a bit of a stretch.[3]

How Do You Persuade?

To persuade others in school, at home, or at work, you must employ strategies chosen to work best on your listeners. The strategies described in this section will work only if you have correctly determined that your audience will respond positively to them. Here again, audience analysis is the key to effectiveness.

USING ARGUMENT TO PERSUADE: FACT, POLICY, AND VALUE

social media make it matter

Micro-Persuading with Twitter

Sure, you can use your Twitter account to follow your friends, experts, favorite celebrities, and breaking news, but while you study this chapter on persuasion notice how often your exceedingly brief text messages are persuasive in intent. That is, you ask others to meet you somewhere, go someplace, look at something, and so on. Interestingly, many a tweet is a bare-bones textual attempt to persuade others without fanfare. Tweeting is **micro-persuasion,** or attempting to change others with as few words or symbols as possible.

Listeners who know or like logic respond positively to arguments with evidence that constitutes proof. Lawyers and debaters are well versed in logical argument, and many educated people respond positively to this approach. An **argument** consists of a proposition that asserts some course of action. Ordinarily, the proposition concerns a question of fact, policy, or value. An example of a **proposition of fact**—an assertion that can be proved or disproved to be consistent with reality—is "College student indebtedness is the highest in history."[4] To demonstrate the accuracy of this fact, you can cite Mark Whitehouse's article in the *Wall Street Journal* that had the headline "Number of the week: Class of 2011 most indebted ever." Or you could cite any number of authoritative sources on this subject, because college student loan debt now exceeds credit card debt.[5]

An example of a **proposition of policy**—a proposal of a new rule—is President Obama's student loan forgiveness program: "Under the terms of this program, anyone who makes his monthly payments for twenty years after leaving college is eligible to have his/her remaining balance forgiven . . . Individuals who spend ten years in public service positions become eligible to have their loans forgiven at that point rather than having to wait the full twenty years. This means that their debt is forgiven in half the time and their debt reduced significantly sooner."[6]

An example of a **proposition of value**—a statement of what we should embrace as more important to our culture—is "We must put security above First Amendment freedoms." To demonstrate the merit of this proposition, you would provide evidence that airline searches, wiretapping, and profiling are more important than our right to protection against unreasonable searches, our expectation of privacy, and our right not to be singled out for negative treatment because of race or ethnicity. Why? Because those violations of rights keep us safe, and we want security more than we want freedoms.

WHAT IS THE DIFFERENCE BETWEEN EVIDENCE AND PROOF?

As anyone knows who watches *Law and Order* or any of the *CSI* spinoffs, evidence is what forensic scientists produce to convict felons. They bring out DNA tests, fingerprints, weapons, fiber samples, rape kits, and bloodstains as evidence that a perp committed a specific crime. In argumentation you are more likely to use other kinds of evidence, such as examples, surveys, testimonials, and numbers and statistics, as we saw in chapter 11. The question is, "Is your evidence proof to your listeners?"

micro-persuasion
An exceedingly brief text message designed to persuade, as in a tweet.

argument
A proposition that asserts some course of action.

proposition of fact
An assertion that can be proved or disproved as consistent with reality.

proposition of policy
A proposal of a new rule.

proposition of value
A statement of what we should embrace as more important to our culture.

■ Collecting evidence: a scene from the television show *CSI*.

proof
Evidence that the receiver believes.

tests of evidence
Questions that can be used to test the validity of evidence.

Proof is evidence the receiver believes. In other words, you can listen to evidence without believing it, and if you do not believe it, you are not going to accept the presenter's argument. Suppose a presenter is arguing that you should accept her policy proposition that "the United States should abolish the death penalty." Her evidence is that the Bible says, "Thou shalt not kill," an idea that is elevated in importance because it is a commandment Moses brought down from the mountaintop on a tablet of stone. A person who believes that the Bible is without error and that we should obey every word will accept the commandment as proof. A person who does not accept the Bible as an authority or who sees contradictions in it like the various offenses for which individuals can be stoned to death might not accept the commandment as proof. In other words, many things can constitute evidence, but only those items the audience accepts constitute proof.

HOW CAN YOU TEST EVIDENCE?

Your evidence must meet the **tests of evidence**—questions you can use to test the validity of the evidence in your presentations or in those of others:

1. *Is the evidence consistent with other known facts?* For instance, is the statement accurate that the top 20% of U.S. taxpayers own 85% of the country's wealth, leaving only 15% for the remaining 80%?[7] Many sources specify how wealth in the United States is increasingly concentrated in the hands of a few, while the bulk of the population has gained little and lost much in the last decade. Just Google "wealth top 1%" for a number of links about wealth inequity. This statement is consistent with known facts about income and wealth.

2. *Would another observer draw the same conclusions?* Perhaps we could find two witnesses who agree they saw someone trip and fall, but getting people to interpret facts the same way is actually a tricky business. Most experts agree that global warming is occurring, but broad disagreements occur about its extent and cause. When other observers agree with your inferences and you can cite them, your persuasive argument is strengthened.

3. *Does the evidence come from unbiased sources?* The information about wealth in item 1 came from G. William Domhoff, a research professor of psychology and sociology at the University of California, Santa Cruz. Professors are more often perceived as unbiased than are politicians and business leaders. But everyone has biases, so you should seek sources of information that are as free of conflicts of interest as you can.

4. *Is the source of the information qualified by education and/or experience to make a statement about the issue?* Professor Domhoff admits that he got much of his information about wealth from Edward Wolff, senior researcher and professor of economics at New York University. Wolff earned his bachelor's degree from Harvard and his Ph.D. from Yale. He has written half a dozen authoritative books about the economy and wealth, and he and Domhoff are both experts on economic issues. But if the information you are seeking is about how undocumented people feel, the story of José Antonia Vargas, an undocumented Filipino youth,

can be your best source.[8] Remember that sources can be qualified by education and/or by experience.

5. *If the evidence is based on personal experience, how typical is that personal experience?* Personal experience that is typical, generalizable, realistic, and relevant can be good evidence. If many people have been treated badly by the nearby bookstore, then your own bad experience there is usable evidence about its quality. If you are one of the very rare ones to have a bad experience, then your story is not usable evidence.

6. *If statistics are used as evidence, are they from a reliable source; comparable with other known information; and current, applicable, and interpreted so the audience can understand them?* Let's say you are going to explain tuition increases at your school over the last five years. Admissions, the registrar, and the business office all are reliable sources. You can help your audience understand the percentages of change, average increases, and amounts of increase by comparing your school's figures with those of other schools like yours. Use statistics carefully. To demonstrate how misleading they can be, a "whopping" 8% tuition increase is only $200 on a tuition bill of $2,500.

7. *If studies and surveys are used, are they authoritative, valid, reliable, objective, and generalizable?* Many studies, surveys, and even Internet evaluations of products are sponsored by the very companies that benefit from the research. The easiest way to check objectivity is to see who authorized the study. If it was performed by an independent source, such as a university, an independent laboratory, or a professional survey company, such as JD Power (www.jdpower.com) or Gallup Poll (www.gallup.com), it is more likely to be valid and trustworthy.

8. *Are the speaker's inferences appropriate to the data presented?* One instance or even a few does not allow for a generalization. If many students have been falsely accused of illegally downloading music, then you could support a generalization for that claim.

9. *Is important counterevidence overlooked?* Often, in our haste to make a positive case, we ignore or omit counterevidence. Try to get a right-wing Republican to admit that anything in Obama's health plan is worthwhile, or a left-wing Democrat to admit that taxes and spending must be reined in. Recognize that most complex issues include some aspects that are worthy and some that are not.

10. *What is the presenter's credibility on the topic?* Has the speaker earned the right to speak on the topic through research, interviews, experience, and a thorough examination of the issue? Tell the audience about your experience with the topic, even if it is the time and effort

cultural **note**

Norms for Persuasion

How we prepare and react to persuasive messages can vary from one culture to the next. For example, if you are from a high-context culture, you may prefer to be less direct when communicating. If you are from a highly individualistic culture, you may prefer to advance your own opinion without taking other viewpoints into consideration. When preparing your persuasive speech, you will likely need to blend some of the persuasive norms of your culture with the persuasive norms of U.S. culture.

This chapter explains many of those Anglo-American norms. If you opt to use norms from your culture, you may need to provide some explanation for what you are doing. For example, African cultures tend to rely on stories to teach lessons or principles. If you use an extended story during your speech, you may need to be somewhat direct and tell audience members what they should learn from the story. While you should not abandon the norms for persuasion you are familiar with, your persuasive messages may need additional explanation to be adapted to the expectations of your classmates.

you invested to research it. A soldier can speak with authority about healthcare for veterans, a mother or father can speak of the trials of finding decent childcare, and factory workers can address safety and sanitation issues in the workplace. The soldier, the parent, and the worker have source credibility concerning their experience.

Evidence that meets these 10 tests has met the requirements of good evidence.

Forms of Proof

To persuade an audience you need to know some methods of doing so. In this section you will learn about some methods of persuasion that began in ancient Greece and have been refined for centuries. Aristotle in his *Rhetoric* wrote about three modes of proof: *ethos, pathos,* and *logos. **Ethos*** referred to the reputation, authority, and integrity of the speaker; ***pathos*** referred to the use of emotional means of persuasion; and ***logos*** referred to persuasion by using logical argument. If you happen to be a visual learner, you may want to take six minutes to see a video on this subject at www.youtube.com/watch?v=tAsxyffBqm0.

ethos
Called "source credibility" today, the audience's perception of your effectiveness as a communicator.

pathos
The use of emotional "proofs" in an argument.

logos
The use of logical reasoning in an argument.

inductive argument
A logical structure that provides enough specific instances for the listener to make an inferential leap to a generalization that summarizes the individual instances.

THE FIRST FORM OF PROOF: LOGOS, OR LOGICAL PROOF

First we take a close look at logical proof.

What Is the Structure of Argument?

Inductive argument provides enough specific instances for the listener to make an inferential leap to a generalization that summarizes the individual instances. For example, you might try to demonstrate that "low taxes are bad for our economy." Your specific instances might include the following:

Schools that are underfunded

Federal programs that are underfunded

Roads and highways that are neither repaired nor maintained

Social programs for the poor that are unfunded

Tuition that goes up because government support goes down

This series of individual instances can lead to an "inferential leap" to a generalization that low taxes are bad for our economy.

Another logical structure is **deductive argument,** which uses a general proposition applied to a specific instance to draw a conclusion. For example, from the major premise (generalization) "All drunk drivers are dangerous," you can move to the minor premise "Joann drives while drunk" to conclude that "Joann is dangerous." This logical structure is called a **syllogism;** it contains a major premise (a generalization) applied to a particular instance (a minor premise) that leads to a conclusion.

deductive argument
A logical structure that uses a general proposition applied to a specific instance to draw a conclusion.

syllogism
A logical structure that contains a major premise (a generalization) applied to a particular instance (a minor premise) that leads to a conclusion.

rebuttal
Arguing against someone else's position on an issue.

How Can You Rebut Arguments?

In class, at home, and in the workplace, others may rebut your arguments. A **rebuttal** is an argument against someone else's position on an issue. If someone in your class gives a presentation with which you profoundly disagree, you may deliver a passionate persuasive presentation opposing that person's position on the issue. There are several ways to rebut arguments.

The weak points in any inductive argument are the clarity of the proposition, the quality of the individual instances, and the place where the inferential leap occurs. In the argument about local taxes, you could argue that it needs to state more clearly to what taxes the proposition refers. Does it refer to all taxes? To local or state taxes? To federal taxes only? The proposition is unclear. On the quality of the individual instances, does the presenter have any evidence that tuition goes up because taxes go down? Finally, how many instances do you have to have before you make the inferential leap?

How many individual instances are needed to persuade people that violent crime is on the rise? The answer is that nobody really knows. All we know is that at some point you can quit providing individual instances, because most of the audience agrees and the remainder never will. That is why you can always question the point at which the inferential leap occurred.

Likewise, you can always rebut deductive arguments by questioning the major premise, the application of the minor premise, and the meaning of the conclusion. Are all drunk drivers dangerous? Perhaps the answer depends on how the state defines "drunk." Some states set a blood alcohol level of .08, some say .10, and others have some other limit. Apparently, we cannot even agree on what percentage constitutes "drunkenness." Also, do we know Joann's alcohol level? She may or may not be drunk, depending on the standard.

The point is that you can critically analyze both inductive and deductive arguments.

THE SECOND FORM OF PROOF: ETHOS, OR SOURCE CREDIBILITY

Chapter 11 focused on source credibility, so our discussion here will be brief. The fact is that you can persuade some listeners because you have earned the right to speak. You have competence, trustworthiness, and dynamism, or you share common ground. Your personal power or expertise, or your charisma or personality, can gain compliance. Popular preachers build mega-churches with thousands of worshipers who thrive on the minister's message. They are persuaded not just by proofs from the Bible but by the personal authority of the preacher. They believe him because of who he is. The pope and some politicians, entertainers, and community leaders have such credibility. In jury trials the lawyer who is most liked by the jury often wins regardless of the evidence, because the jury believes the lawyer they like. But even in the classroom some presenters have more source credibility than others. For example, third-year students have more credibility than first-year students. The lesson here is that who and what you are can help you persuade others.

THE THIRD FORM OF PROOF: PATHOS, OR EMOTIONAL PROOF

You may not be dazzled by a string of statistics that show how many people slide into bankruptcy each year, but you might get tears in your eyes about a local person—very much like yourself—who was so consumed by credit card debt that she and her family had to declare publicly that they would never be able to pay their debts.

Narrative—the telling of a story—is a powerful persuader. The world's holy books, such as the Koran and the Bible, and the teachings of Buddha are practically devoid of statistics but are full of stories and parables. We tell our children stories that teach them life lessons. In jury trials the person who wins often has the best story that accounts for

cultural **note**

What Do Different Groups Find Convincing?

U.S. businesspeople are known around the word for their bluntness, for diving for the bottom line swiftly, and for thinking their way is the only way. The dominant U.S. culture values argument, evidence, and proof as the way to convince someone to change his or her mind or behavior. In most of Asia, Africa, and the Middle East, however, establishing trust by building a relationship comes before serious decision making. Native Americans tend to use stories to make their point instead of argument and evidence. Many Asian and Pacific Rim people want to have tea and talk before serious business can occur. Form and social harmony trump triumph and gain. U.S. and European adults have little difficulty saying "no" to someone trying to persuade them, but many Asian, Mexican, Central American, and South American cultures have difficulty saying "no" without "losing face." Hence, a U.S. speaker from the dominant culture may think he or she has convinced the person from Costa Rica, whose silence might indicate merely politeness and saving face. Korean students are much less likely to negotiate with a teacher over grades than are U.S. students, and U.S. women sometimes adopt a feminist alternative to traditional persuasion in which the goal is not to vanquish the opponent but to achieve understanding through "invitational rhetoric." Persuasion works differently from culture to culture and even among marginalized groups in the United States.

Sources: Martin, J., & Nakayama, T. (2011). *Experiencing intercultural communication* (4th ed.). New York: McGraw-Hill. Foss, S. K., & Griffin, C. L. (1995). Beyond persuasion: A proposal for an invitational rhetoric. *Communication Monographs, 62,* 2–19. Yook, E., & Albert, R. (1998). Perceptions of the appropriateness of negotiation in educational settings: A cross-cultural comparison among Koreans and Americans. *Communication Education, 47,* 18–29.

fear appeal
Eliciting fear to change behavior.

all the known facts in the case. You, too, can harness the power of the narrative by telling stories that support your proposition. A student whose persuasive purpose was to get Harley drivers to wear protective helmets had a simple strategy: he told three stories about motorcycle operators who wore helmets and lived. At the beginning of each story, he showed a single slide of that person's badly dented helmet. The visual image of the banged-up helmets and the stories of the three survivors made an indelible impression.

Although logical and emotional appeals are often seen as diametrically opposed concepts, most of our behavior and beliefs are based on a mixture of emotional and rational factors. A speaker may persuade an audience to accept his or her immediate behavioral purposes for emotional, rather than logical, reasons. A story about one person's bad experience with the campus bookstore may inspire many audience members to take their business to another store. The experience may have been a one-in-a-thousand situation, or as much the customer's fault as the manager's. Such is the power of our emotions that they can persuade us to defy the law, fight another nation, or ignore the evidence.

The **fear appeal** is one of the most common appeals to emotion. Political ads remind us of impending economic collapse, predict that an opponent will tax us to oblivion, and suggest that only one political party can protect us from our enemies. Financial gurus use fear to guide investments (bonds are losers, stocks are winners, or vice versa); businesses use fear to invite sales (prices go up this Wednesday); auto dealers use fear to close a sale (this one is the last of this model for this year at this price). Fear appeals get us to brush our teeth, use deodorant, buy certain clothing, and wear certain perfumes and colognes.

Clearly, fear appeals work in advertising and in everyday life. As a speaker you can use fear appeals in an ethical manner if you do not exaggerate the threat and if you offer means of avoiding the fear. In other words, a presenter who arouses fear in an audience has an ethical obligation to provide reassurance as well. This sentence illustrates fear appeals and reassurances in a single thesis statement: "Not brushing your teeth can lead to gum disease and tooth loss, so listen to my tips on dental hygiene." A presentation that combines fear with reassurance results in greater shifts of opinion, and the audience holds the presenter in higher regard.[9]

Other examples of emotional appeals are testimonials at funerals about the virtues of the deceased, appeals to loyalty and dedication at retirement ceremonies, appeals to patriotism in times of crisis, and appeals to justice in times of legal strife.

PERSUASION THROUGH VISUALIZATION

A company will typically spend up to $3 million for a 30-second spot during the Super Bowl, one of television's most-watched events, and all told advertisers pay for 48 minutes of advertising during that annual game. They would not spend that much money if advertising did not work.[10] However, those 30-second spots do not make an argument with evidence, tell an emotional story, or even dazzle you with source credibility. Instead, they use **persuasive imagery** to persuade by means of amusing, rapid-fire scenes of youthful drinkers having fun, beautiful vehicles spinning down mountain roads without guard rails, and mountains of junk food being washed down with gallons of soft drinks. Words are not important; the emphasis is on beguiling the eye.

persuasive imagery
The advertiser's method of persuading an audience with fast-paced and dazzling visualization of products.

You can use imagery in your persuasive presentations, with either PowerPoint or more advanced software, such as Prezi, and you can imitate some advertising techniques by studying impressive videos on YouTube. "Inspiring videos," for example has short videos about many topics, including technology. You should check with your teacher about using YouTube video clips in your presentations, because teachers are wary about too much YouTube in a presentation that is supposed to be yours. As long as you do not allow the YouTube video to dominate your presentation, you can make it more visual and more exciting for your audience.

We turn next to ways to organize your persuasive presentation effectively.

Organizing Your Persuasive Message: The Monroe Motivated Sequence

You already know that you may not want to announce your immediate purpose at the outset of a persuasive message because you may need to build toward acceptance at the end. Here we consider some macro-organizational features: how you build, construct, or design your presentation to achieve your persuasive purpose.

In chapter 12 you learned that some organizational patterns are used more often in persuasive presentations: cause/effect, problem/solution, and topical-sequence. The topical-sequence pattern is especially useful in arguing the advantages and disadvantages of some course of action.

This next pattern of organization is not another topic sequence. Instead, this pattern is a series of moves designed to persuade. Developed by University of Iowa professor Alan Monroe, the **Monroe Motivated Sequence** has been used successfully for four decades and is popular for having five easy-to-follow steps:

Monroe Motivated Sequence
A problem-solving format that encourages an audience to become concerned about an issue; especially appropriate for a persuasive presentation.

- *Step 1: Attention.* You gain and maintain audience attention, and you determine a way to focus it on the content of your presentation.

- *Step 2: Need.* Once you have the audience's attention, you show audience members how the speech is relevant to them. You arouse a need for the change you suggest in your persuasive presentation.

- *Step 3: Satisfaction.* Your speech either presents the information the audience needs or suggests a solution to their needs. You satisfy the audience by meeting their needs with your plan.

- *Step 4: Visualization.* You reinforce your idea in the audience's minds by getting them to *see* how your information or ideas will help them.

- *Step 5: Action.* Once the audience has visualized your idea, you plead for action. The audience might remember your main points in an informative presentation and state them to others, or the audience may go out and do what you ask in a persuasive presentation.[11]

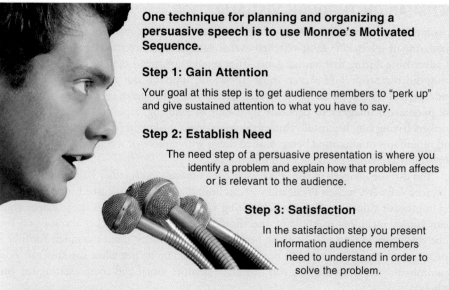

One technique for planning and organizing a persuasive speech is to use Monroe's Motivated Sequence.

Step 1: Gain Attention

Your goal at this step is to get audience members to "perk up" and give sustained attention to what you have to say.

Step 2: Establish Need

The need step of a persuasive presentation is where you identify a problem and explain how that problem affects or is relevant to the audience.

Step 3: Satisfaction

In the satisfaction step you present information audience members need to understand in order to solve the problem.

Step 4: Visualization

Your goal is to reinforce the solution in the audience's mind by getting audience members to see how they can take part in a solution that will benefit them and others.

Step 5: Call to Action

Often found in the conclusion, the call to action asks the audience members to take specific, concrete steps.

Figure 15.1

Monroe's Motivated Sequence.

The Monroe Motivated Sequence is an appropriate organizational pattern for persuasive presentations, especially when the audience is reluctant to change or to accept a proposed action. See an illustration of the sequence in figure 15.1.

Ethical Considerations

Ethics are a set of principles of right conduct. Many of our standards for ethical behavior are codified into law. We do not slander or libel someone who is an ordinary citizen. We do not start a panic that can endanger the lives of others. And we do not advocate the overthrow of our government.

Many other principles of ethics are not matters of law, but violations of these unwritten rules do have consequences. No law exists against pointing out acne sufferers in the audience during your speech on dermatology or having your audience unknowingly eat cooked hamster meat, but audience members may find your methods so distasteful that they reject you and your persuasive message.

Here are some generally accepted ethical standards that govern the preparation and delivery of a persuasive presentation.

1. *Accurately cite sources.* When you are preparing and delivering your speech, you should be very careful to gather and state your information accurately. Specifically,

you should reveal from whom you received information. Making up quotations, attributing an idea to someone who never made the statement, omitting important qualifiers, quoting out of context, and distorting information are all examples of ethical violations.

2. *Respect sources of information.* Show respect for your sources, especially people you interview, by demonstrating their credibility as completely as possible. These people are willing to share information with you, so it behooves you to treat them and their information with respect, in person and in your presentation.

3. *Respect your audience.* Persuasion is a process that works most effectively with mutual respect between presenter and receiver. Attempts to trick the audience into believing something, lying, distorting the views of your opposition, and exaggerating claims for your own position are all ethically questionable acts. A presenter should speak truthfully and accurately; the best persuasive presenters can accurately portray the opposing arguments and still win with their own arguments and evidence. Audiences can be very hostile toward a person who has tricked them or who has lied, distorted, or exaggerated information simply to meet an immediate behavioral purpose or an ultimate goal.

4. *Respect your opponent.* Persuasive presentations invite rebuttal. Nearly always, someone in or outside your audience thinks your ideas or positions are wrong. A good rule of thumb is to respect your opponent, not only because he or she may be right but also because an effective persuasive presenter can take the best the opposition has to offer and still convince the audience he or she should be believed. Do not indulge in name-calling or in bringing up past behaviors that are irrelevant to the issue. You should attack the other person's evidence, sources, or logic—not the person. Few issues about which people persuade are ever settled, and you may find in time that your opponent's position is better in many respects than your own.

■ Professional persuaders tempt you to part with your money for their product.

sizing things up

Need for Cognition

The way we construct and respond to persuasive messages depends, in part, on the way we process information. One of the personality characteristics that govern information processing is our need for cognition, or our tendency to put significant effort into thinking about things such as arguments and ideas. Below are 10 statements that describe how you might like to process information. Read each question carefully and respond using the following scale:

1 = Strongly disagree
2 = Disagree
3 = Neither agree nor disagree
4 = Agree
5 = Strongly agree

1. I prefer complex to simple problems.
2. Thinking is not my idea of fun.
3. I would rather do something that requires little thought than something that is sure to challenge my thinking abilities.
4. I find satisfaction in thinking hard for a long time.
5. I only think as hard as I have to.
6. I try to avoid situations where there is a good chance I will have to think hard about something.
7. I really enjoy a task that involves coming up with new solutions to problems.
8. I enjoy thinking abstractly.
9. I prefer a task that is intellectual, difficult, and important to one that is somewhat important but does not require much thought.
10. I enjoy solving puzzles.

This exercise has no right or wrong answers; instead, your responses provide insight into your own ways of thinking. A guide for interpreting your responses appears in the appendix at the end of the text (p. 348).

Source: Perse, E. (1992, Winter). Predicting attention to local television news: Need for cognition and motives for viewing. *Communication Reports, 5,* 40–49. Copyrighted by the Western States Communication Association. Used by permission of the publisher.

You may get the impression from these four ethical guidelines that every persuasive speaker must be part angel. Not quite. The ethical rules for persuasive speaking allow for critical analysis of arguments and ideas, for profound differences of opinion, for the weighing of evidence and supporting materials, and for the swaying of the audience to your point of view. All these strategies simply work best if you accurately cite your sources and respect them, your audience, and your opponent.

Figure 15.2 gives additional tips for organizing your arguments.

An Outline of a Persuasive Presentation

We turn now to an outline for an annotated persuasive presentation that illustrates many of the concepts introduced in the chapter. This outline was written by a student majoring in broadcasting and a guitarist who played at the Montreaux Jazz Festival. He composed this presentation to persuade the audience to change their behavior. Read it carefully for its strengths and its weaknesses. What methods does the presenter use to influence listeners? Do the arguments and evidence meet the tests discussed in this chapter? What could the presenter have done differently that would have made the message more appealing to you?

Figure 15.2

Tips for organizing your arguments.

Below is some final advice on what kinds of arguments are most persuasive and where you should consider placing them for maximum effectiveness.

1. Place your best argument first for a "primacy effect," meaning early items are remembered over middle items (Primacy, 2011).

2. Place your best argument last for a "recency effect," meaning last items are remembered over items in the middle (Recency, 2011).

3. Middle items in a series are less remembered than those presented first or last, so avoid placing your best argument in the easily overlooked or forgotten middle.

Change Your Dial to NPR
by Stephen Anderson

How many times have you heard the phrase, "don't change that dial" before your favorite radio station plays five straight minutes of commercials?

Attention getter

That's what I figured. Not very many people enjoy listening to hokey ads telling you to "come on down to your local car dealer" or to start taking diet pills while waiting for their intended programming. NPR, that's National Public Radio, is on twenty-four hours a day and doesn't play one single commercial.

Listener relevance

I have been an avid listener of NPR's fine programming for the last four years.

Speaker credibility

NPR's wide variety of talk, news, and music programs is delightfully enlightening.

Thesis

By listening to NPR, you can hear the latest and greatest in news and entertainment without ever sitting through a pesky commercial.

Preview

I. So how can NPR survive without commercials?

    A. NPR is commercial-free because of federal grants and "underwriting spots," which are brief announcements given by an NPR announcer identifying organizations that have sponsored a certain program (NPR, 2011).

    B. In this world of pop-up ads and product placement, NPR is a haven of commercial-free entertainment and news.

So if NPR has no commercials, just what *is* on NPR? you may ask.

Transition

II. NPR is dedicated to providing the most relevant, trusted, and consumed news in the United States.

    A. Other news sources, such as Fox, CBS, and MSNBC news stations have been stained by claims of bias, while NPR remains one of seemingly few radio news outlets to be truly balanced in its journalism (Dvorkin, 2002).

    B. NPR's news programs and talk programs offer something for everyone: *All Things Considered and Morning Edition,* two of the highest-rated radio programs on the airwaves today, are broadcast through NPR.

But why listen to boring talk radio when you can listen to the same songs over and over again on your local Top 40 station?

Transition

III. NPR invests a huge portion of programming time playing music of all genres.

    A. NPR's *World Café* shines a light on up-and-coming acts, as well as established artists. Artists such as Adele, the Black Keys, and

CONTINUED

Coldplay have given interviews and even live, in-studio concerts on the program (*About World Café*, 2011).

B. For those looking to relax and decompress while driving, NPR's classical and jazz programs offer soothing background music.

In a way, NPR is a bit like *Sesame Street*. You enjoy every minute of it, and when you're done, you walk away with a bit more than you had at the start.

NPR delivers the finest talk, news, and music on the airwaves today—all without commercial interruption.

So the next time you are commanded not to "change that dial," disobey. Reward yourself by tuning in to NPR. You may never change your dial again.

Thesis restatement

Main point summary

Clincher

REFERENCES

About world café (2011). Retrieved from http://xpn.org/xpn-programs/world-cafe/about-cafe

Dvorkin, J. (2002, November 26). *How do you know NPR is unbiased?* Retrieved from http://www.npr.org/yourturn/ombudsman/2002/021126.html

NPR underwriting credit guidelines. (2011). Retrieved from http://www.npr.org/blogs/ombudsman/NPR Underwriting Credit Guidelines.pdf

How to Resist Persuasion

Listed here are some measures you can take to resist persuasion, not only in public presentations but also on the telephone, in advertising, and when dealing with salespeople:

1. *Remember, the best resistance is avoidance.* You do not have to watch or read advertising, go into stores where you do not intend to buy, listen to telemarketers, or watch infomercials.

2. *Be skeptical about all messages.* Persuaders who are seeking easy prey look for the uneducated, the desperate, the angry, the very young, the very old, and the unsuspecting. They avoid people who are educated, articulate, cautious, and careful. You should use your knowledge of argumentation, evidence, and proof to analyze claims.

3. *Check claims with other, unbiased sources.* A good rule is to verify any persuasive claims with at least two other sources of information. A politician tells you that lower taxes will be good for you. What do the editorials, the political commentators, and the opposition say about that plan? Consumer magazines, especially those

that take no advertising, are less likely to be biased, as are news sources that embrace objectivity.

4. *Check out the credibility of the source.* Be suspicious if a salesperson will not reveal the phone numbers of satisfied customers, if a business is new or changes location often, or if a speaker has a questionable reputation for truth or reliability. Customers, institutions, and satisfied audiences will vouch for credible sources. The Internet offers ratings of products, businesses, and professionals, but beware because some rating services are sponsored by the vendors being evaluated. In other words, some ranking and rating services are bogus; they are just another attempt to trick you.

5. *Be cautious about accepting a persuasive appeal.* Most states have laws that allow even a signed contract to be rejected by the customer in the first 24 to 48 hours—in case you have second thoughts. Accepting claims on impulse is a dangerous practice that you can avoid by never making an important decision in the context of a sales pitch. Have you ever heard of a businessperson who refused to take the money the next day?

6. *Question the ethical basis of proposed actions.* Angry people are easy to turn to violence, desperate people willingly consider desperate measures, and frustrated people can easily become an unruly mob. Ask yourself whether the proposed action is self-serving, pits one group against another, or will be good for you when viewed in retrospect.

7. *Use your knowledge and experience to analyze persuasive claims.* A claim that sounds too good to be true probably is. If you have a gut feeling that a claim seems wrong, find out why. Use all you know about logic, evidence, and proof to see whether the persuader is drawing a sound conclusion or making an inferential leap that is justified by the evidence. Finally, assume all evidence is open to scrutiny.

8. *Use your own values as a check against fraudulent claims.* If someone is trying to get you to do something that runs counter to what you learned in your religion, in your home, in the law, or from your friends, be wary. Sales always enrich the seller but not always the buyer. You can choose to sacrifice, but you should not sacrifice unwittingly. Your values are good protection against those who would cheat you. Ask yourself, "What would my parents, my friends, my neighbors, my professor, or my religious leaders think of this decision?"

■ Learn to be wary about good deals. Use your brain to protect yourself.

9. *Check what persuaders say against what they do.* Judge persuaders more by what they do than by what they say. Talk may not be cheap, but words cost less than deeds, and the proof of what a person says is his or her behavior. We learn to trust people who do what they say; we learn to distrust those who say one thing and do another.

10. *Use your freedom of expression and freedom of choice as protection against unethical persuaders.* In the United States you can hear competing ideas, and the choice to accept or reject them is yours. You can educate yourself about issues and ideas by reading, watching, and listening. Education and learning are powerful protection against persuaders who would take advantage of you. Use your freedoms to help defend yourself.

Now that you know 10 suggestions for resisting persuasion, you can practice the strategies for keeping others from manipulating your mind and picking your pocket.

keeping it real

Using Persuasion in Everyday Life

This chapter opened with César Ordez discovering that his new job required him to use persuasion more than he ever expected. How would you apply the information in this chapter to these situations?

1. You have to give a speech to the local Rotary International Club about your school.

2. You are supposed to find an argument in favor of lowering the age for drinking alcohol.

3. You are supposed to find support material for the argument that global warming is occurring.

4. You are advising César Ordez on how to sell extra services to customers who arrive for routine maintenance on their vehicles.

5. You want to avoid spending any money over the next three months. How do you resist persuaders who want to encourage you to spend?

Chapter Review & Study Guide

Summary

1. A persuasive presentation is a message strategically designed to induce change in an audience.

2. Modest changes you can accomplish in a brief presentation represent your immediate purpose, whereas major changes your presentation may contribute to in the future make up your long-range goal.

3. Instead of immediately revealing your purpose in the introduction, as you do in most informative presentations, you may have to delay stating your immediate purpose until you have prepared the way with persuasive strategies.

4. An effective argument consists of a statement of fact, policy, or value backed by supporting material that meets the tests of evidence.

5. You can use *ethos* (source credibility), *pathos* (emotional argument), or *logos* (logical argument) as persuasive strategies in your presentations.

6. The Monroe Motivated Sequence is an appropriate organizational pattern for persuasive presentations, especially when the audience is reluctant to change or to accept a proposed action. It consists of five steps: attention, need, satisfaction, visualization, and action.

7. High ethical standards require you to cite sources accurately, respect your audience, and even respect your opponents.

8. The chapter's annotated, detailed outline of a successful persuasive presentation by a student provides a model you can follow in preparing your own presentation.

9. There are many ways to resist persuasion, the most important of which is to avoid placing yourself in a position to be persuaded.

Key Terms

Adoption	Immediate purpose	Persuasive presentation
Argument	Inductive argument	Proof
Boomerang effect	*Logos*	Proposition of fact
Captive audience	Long-range goal	Proposition of policy
Coercion	Manipulation	Proposition of value
Deductive argument	Micro-persuasion	Rebuttal
Discontinuance	Monroe Motivated Sequence	Syllogism
Ethos	*Pathos*	Tests of evidence
Fear appeal	Persuasive imagery	Voluntary audience

Study Questions

For further review, go to the LearnSmart study module for this chapter.

1. The intention of a persuasive presentation is to
   a. inform listeners of a certain topic.
   b. change listeners' minds or behavior.
   c. explain a concept.
   d. describe an important issue.

2. If an audience likes you and your message less after the presentation than they did before, what term correctly describes what has taken place?
   a. source credibility reversal
   b. believability impasse
   c. boomerang effect
   d. continuance cessation

3. When a presenter attempts to convince listeners to stop a current behavior, what has taken place?
   a. discontinuance
   b. adoption
   c. continuance
   d. deterrence

4. If your evidence meets the tests of evidence, it will do all the following *except*
   a. come from unbiased sources.
   b. be consistent with other well-known facts.
   c. overlook counterevidence.
   d. consist of authoritative, valid, and reliable surveys.

5. When resisting persuasion from salespeople and advertisers, you should do all the following *except*
   a. avoid using your own values as a check against fraudulent claims.
   b. listen to all messages while thinking critically.
   c. question the credibility of all sources.
   d. evaluate the ethical basis of proposed actions.

6. Which type of argument uses a series of individual instances that lead to a generalization?
   a. deductive
   b. inductive
   c. rebuttal
   d. syllogism

7. You can rebut a deductive argument by questioning the
   a. major premise.
   b. clarity of the proposition.
   c. quality of individual instances.
   d. place where the inferential leap occurs.

8. Which of the following statements regarding argument organization is true?
   a. Place your best argument in the middle.
   b. Present one side of an issue to reduce the effects of contrary arguments.
   c. Present one side of an issue when you are seeking immediate, temporary change of opinion.
   d. Familiar arguments have more effect than novel arguments.

9. In the Monroe Motivated Sequence, the visualization step includes
   a. gaining and maintaining audience attention.
   b. presenting information or a solution to audience needs.
   c. asking the audience to take specific steps.
   d. demonstrating how the solution will benefit the audience.

10. Which is *not* an ethical standard to follow when preparing and delivering a persuasive presentation?
   a. Accurately cite sources when the words are not your own.
   b. Respect sources of information by revealing their credibility.
   c. Speak truthfully and accurately out of respect for your audience.
   d. Attack the other person's character instead of his or her evidence, sources, or logic.

Answers:
1. (b); 2. (c); 3. (a); 4. (c); 5. (a); 6. (b); 7. (a); 8. (c); 9. (d); 10. (d)

Critical Thinking

1. Especially when listening to national-level politicians speak, see whether you can determine the truth and accuracy of what they say. Then Google one of the fact-checking services, such as Annenberg's Factcheck.org, to see what a politically neutral organization finds accurate about speeches, advertisements, and campaign claims. Were you able to detect any of the inaccuracies that emerge in presentations by politicians in all parties?

2. Take one often-repeated charge, such ase "the federal government is too big" or "CEOs are paid too much" and see what evidence you can find to back that claim. Next look at each piece of evidence that you found and decide whether that evidence will be perceived as believable and to whom.

Appendix

Sizing Things Up Scoring and Interpretation

Throughout *Human Communication* you have noticed a feature called Sizing Things Up. In communication and other fields, researchers use surveys like these to collect and summarize people's opinions about a variety of issues. When averaged together, those opinions can serve as evidence for theorizing about best practices in communication or other disciplines. For this class, you can use these surveys to self-assess your perspectives, opinions, or skills related to a variety of communication topics. This appendix provides instructions for how to score and interpret each of the Sizing Thing Up boxes found in the chapters.

CHAPTER 1: COMMUNICATION SKILLS IN CONTEXT

This chapter introduces the concept of communication competence (CC). The survey you completed measures your competence. Each question in the survey asks you to indicate how effectively you can communicate within a particular context of communication (e.g., friendships or computer-mediated communication); some questions also target specific purposes for communicating (e.g., resolving conflict). You can use this scale either as a global Communication Competence Scale, in which case you should average together your answers for all questions to achieve an overall score, or as a way of analyzing particular communication contexts or processes. This latter approach would involve analyzing your responses to each statement. If your overall average or response to any individual question is below 3, you may be lower in self-perceived communication competence. A score near 3 is average and a score higher than 3 suggests that you perceive yourself higher in communication competence.

CHAPTER 2: SELF-ESTEEM SCALE

Self-esteem is a central component of the discussion of self-perception in chapter 2. The Rosenberg Self-Esteem Scale is one of the most popular scales designed to measure your general positive or negative self-assessment. After completing and scoring this scale, talk with your teacher about self-esteem and how your communication behaviors are related to this self-perception.

Scoring of the Rosenberg Self-Esteem Scale is very straightforward. Items 2, 5, 6, 8, and 9 should be reverse-coded. This means that, if you answered with a 4 or 5 to one of those statements, your score should be reversed to be a 1 (if the original answer was 5) or a 2 (if the original answer was 4). Reverse-coding will account for the fact that some questions are positively worded, whereas others are negatively worded. After reverse-coding, sum all items; values should range from 4 to 40, with higher values indicating more positive assessments of self-esteem.

CHAPTER 3: ROLE CATEGORY QUESTIONNAIRE

In chapter 3 you learned about the ways in which language might influence how you perceive the world around you. One way that language might do that is through implicit categories and hierarchies found in language systems. For instance, you might comment that a dog is "cute" and "friendly." Those terms indicate that you place the dog into certain categories and perhaps even rank the dog into some sort of hierarchy. The role category questionnaire (RCQ) provides one mechanism through which you can identify such hierarchies in how you use language.

The traditional method of scoring the RCQ involves circling and then counting each separate construct used to identify the "liked" person and the "disliked" person. A construct is any adjective or other description that you use to describe the people you analyze. All constructs should be counted, even duplicates, although you should not count descriptions of physical appearance. The total value represents a differentiation score; higher scores represent higher levels of cognitive complexity.

To further explore the hierarchical nature of language, think about the following questions:

1. Are the number of constructs you identified for "liked" and "disliked" people generally the same or different? Why?

2. In comparing your scores with others in your class, or even friends you ask to complete the RCQ, are there differences between male and female students in their number of constructs? Are there differences between you and students with other characteristics such as those who are older, younger, or from different ethnic backgrounds?

3. Do differentiation scores differ depending on whether the person being described is male or female?

You may develop other ways of analyzing results. For instance, you may observe that there are clusters (i.e., hierarchies) of constructs that people use to describe others.

CHAPTER 4: BERKELEY NONVERBAL EXPRESSIVENESS QUESTIONNAIRE

Simple observation suggests that some people are just more nonverbally expressive than others. Whereas one person may remain stiff and deadpan, another may appear to be landing planes based on the nature of how they naturally gesture. The nonverbal expressiveness questionnaire assesses the extent to which a person "leaks" implicit meanings (especially emotional) through their nonverbal behaviors. Although this scale is typically used to assess expressiveness, you will notice that expressivity is enacted, based on these statements, through nonverbal cues.

The expressivity scale taps three dimensions of nonverbal/emotional expressivity. To achieve a score for each dimension, simply average the values for each item after reverse-coding the items with the "(R)" next to the item number; higher values indicate higher levels for that dimension. To reverse-code items indicted below, take your original responses and make a 1 become a 7, a 2 become a 6, or a 3 become a 5. If you answered initially with a 7, 6, or 2, do the opposite. After reverse-coding your answers, average all questions related to each of the three dimensions.

■ *Negative expressivity.* The extent to which others observe you feeling negative emotions, such as nervousness, fear, and anger. The following items are included in this dimension: 9(R), 13, 16, 3(R), 5, and 8(R).

■ *Positive expressivity.* The extent to which others can observe you experiencing positive emotions, such as happiness and joy. The following items should be averaged for this dimension: 6, 1, 4, and 10.

■ *Impulse strength.* The extent to which you can control, diminish, or manage your emotional expression. Items for this dimension are 15, 11, 14, 7, 2, and 12.

You can also average all questions to obtain an overall expressiveness value. Higher overall scores indicate, regardless of positive or negative emotions, how expressive you are.

CHAPTER 5: BARRIERS TO LISTENING

Multiple barriers to effective listening confront us on a daily basis. Table 5.1 in chapter 5 lists several of the most common barriers. The barriers to listening survey created to accompany this chapter helps you determine the type of barrier that may pose the greatest difficulty for you in most situations. You will note that the 9 items on the barriers scale closely align with barriers listed in table 5.1.

The Listening Barriers Scale can be assessed question-by-question to determine which barrier or group of barriers is most challenging for you. You can also average all questions to obtain an overall value indicating the extent to which barriers listed in table 5.1 potentially impede effective listening. If you want to orient responses so that higher values always represent better listening behaviors, reverse-code responses for the following statements: 1, 3, 4, 5, 6, 7, 8, and 9. To do this an initial response of 1 should be converted to be a 5 and a response of 2 should become a 4; do the opposite if your initial response was a 4 or 5.

CHAPTER 6: INTERPERSONAL MOTIVES

You might have various motives for entering into interpersonal relationships with others. Although the list of motives could be very specific, you learned about inclusion, affection, and control in this chapter. The interpersonal motives questionnaire created for this chapter helps students assess whether one or more of those motives are more dominant in explaining why they enter into relationships.

You responded to three questions for each of the three motives. To calculate scores for each motive, sum or average responses as follows:

- *Inclusion.* This motive suggests that we enter into interpersonal relationships to feel part of a group or to be included with others: items 3, 4, and 9.
- *Affection.* Affective motivation stems from our need to share emotion and support with others: items 2, 5, and 8.
- *Control.* To have more instrumental control over our lives and our surroundings, a motivation to control may cause us to enter into relationships: items 1, 6, and 7.

This scale is not designed to generate an overall score; you should calculate scores for each dimension separately. For a variation on this scale, change the target from multiple relationships to a particular relationship, such as the selection of your roommate, your best friend, and so on. When analyzing response patterns, your motives could be multidimensional with high scores for each dimension, or you could emphasize or de-emphasize one or more motives.

CHAPTER 7: INDIVIDUALISM–COLLECTIVISM SCALE

The individualism–collectivism scale by Sengilis, Trandis, Bhawuk, and Geifand is commonly used to assess individual differences in collectivist or individualist orientations. Although individualism and collectivism are sometimes viewed as mutually exclusive, they actually represent two distinct orientations; as a consequence, individuals may be high in one or the other, high in both, low in both, and so on.

Scores on both the individualism and collectivism dimensions can range from 8 to 40. For either dimension, scores of 8–22 represent low levels, 23–30 moderate, and 31–40 high. To derive scores for the two dimensions, add values for the following questions:

■ *Individualism:* questions 1, 3, 5, 7, 9, 11, 13, and 15
■ *Collectivism:* questions 2, 4, 6, 8, 10, 12, 14, and 16

CHAPTER 8: CONFLICT IN THE WORKPLACE

People have different natural orientations toward how conflict should be resolved. Although most people adapt to the circumstances in which they find themselves to select approaches to conflict resolution, predispositions might make some options more likely than others. The conflict in the workplace scale assesses your predispositions toward five approaches for managing conflict.

You should sum/average responses to determine scores for each one of the five dimensions:

■ *Avoidance:* attempting to deny the existence of conflict; items 3, 9, and 12
■ *Competition:* viewing conflict as a battle; items 1, 8, and 15
■ *Compromise:* being willing to negotiate away some things if others will as well; items 5, 7, and 11
■ *Accommodation:* setting aside your views and accepting the views of another; items 2, 6, and 14
■ *Collaboration:* using dialogue to reach a mutually beneficial solution; items 4, 10, and 13

As worded, this scale can be used to assess a general predisposition toward conflict resolution. You can adapt the scale by tying it to various scenarios of conflict to determine if approaches toward conflict resolution differ from situation to situation or because of the source of conflict, and so on. For example, you could complete the scale once when thinking about conflict with your roommate and again when thinking about conflict with your parents or another family member.

CHAPTER 9: COLLECTIVE SELF-ESTEEM SCALE

All of us belong to groups for different reasons, and many of those reasons stem from the feelings we get from belonging to those groups. The Collective Self-Esteem (CSE) scale assesses your perceptions about the self-esteem "boost" you get from being part of various groups.

The CSE scale assesses the following dimensions, which should be calculated separately:

■ *Membership:* assesses the extent to which you feel good or worthy of membership in a particular group; items 1, 3, 6, and 14
■ *Private:* assesses your personal assessment of the groups to which you belonged; items 5, 6, 13 and 16
■ *Public:* assesses perceptions of others' assessments of the groups to which one belonged; items 4, 7, 9, and 12
■ *Identity:* assesses the importance of group membership in your self-concept; items 2, 10, 11, and 13

As written in the text, the CSE scale can be used for more general assessments. The scale has been adapted to target membership in a university community, fan communities of sports groups, particular racial/cultural groups, and the like.

CHAPTER 10: TOPIC EVALUATION

Personal inventories are typically qualitative in nature; that is, you write down topics for which you are interested or knowledgeable. The scale created for chapter 10 provides a quantitative way of assessing interest in 10 broad topic areas. Results of this survey can be used in two ways. First, you may select a topic area in which you score very high and use that as a guide for generating speech topics. Second, if you average responses from your classmates you can use this information as a simple audience-analysis survey.

To score this survey, notice that each topic has a four-item semantic-differential scale. Rather than writing/circling numbers, simply check a space to indicate how strongly a particular adjective represents you views toward the general topic. From left to right on each semantic-differential item, score responses as a 5, 4, 3, 2, or 1 based on which space you checked. Thus, higher values will indicate more positive perceptions toward that topic. Sum scores for the four items under each topic area to achieve a total score between 4 and 20. Values closer to 20 indicate more positive perceptions toward that topic.

CHAPTER 11: RESEARCH ATTITUDES SCALE

Effective speakers use a variety of types of supporting materials and research in their speeches. The scale created for this chapter helps you assess your strengths and weaknesses in using various types of research resources. After completing and scoring the scale, you can use the results as a diagnostic tool to determine strategies for which you may need additional assistance from your teacher or a reference librarian.

The Research Attitudes Scale assesses your comfort and ability in using five different types of research resources: the Internet (items 1, 9, and 14), journals (items 2, 7, and 15), books (items 3, 6, and 11), reference materials (items 4, 8, and 12), and popular press sources (items 5, 10, and 13). You should sum responses to questions for each resource to find specific scores. Sums of 3 to 6 indicate areas needing greater attention or assistance.

CHAPTER 12: CLARITY BEHAVIORS INVENTORY

Chapter 12 helps you learn how to organize presentations. A significant body of literature in communication and education addresses the issue of "clarity" in academic settings. Although nearly all of this research approaches clarity from the perspective of the teacher—how to present clear lessons to students—this research is directly translatable to other types of speaking situations. The Clarity Behaviors Inventory (CBI) was developed by one of the authors and his colleagues to assess students' perceptions of teachers' clarity. You can use this survey to analyze the clarity of one of your other teachers (e.g., the teacher in the class you attend just before your communication class). You should *not* identify the name or identity of the teacher you are rating. As you compare your teacher's score with those from your classmates, discuss some of the things those teachers do that likely results in differences in scores. How can you learn from this to influence how you deliver your speeches?

The CBI is used to assess teachers' clarity in both written and oral form. Calculate scores for both dimensions of clarity by averaging responses to the following items:

- *Written clarity:* items 2, 3, 6, 8, 10, and 12
- *Verbal clarity:* items 1, 4, 5, 7, 9, and 11

In both cases, higher values indicate higher levels of clarity. You can also average all items on the survey to obtain an overall assessment of clarity. An average score of 1 or 2 indicates low clarity and an average of 4 or 5 indicates high clarity.

CHAPTER 13: PERCEIVED NONVERBAL IMMEDIACY BEHAVIORS SCALE

Although speech delivery addresses a broad array of behaviors, instructional communication researchers have successfully used the concept of nonverbal immediacy to analyze the presentation styles of teachers and have found that higher levels of immediacy are positively associated with students' positive feelings toward learning as well as perceived cognitive learning in classes. You can use the Perceived Nonverbal Immediacy Behaviors (PNIB) Scale to analyze a teacher from another of your classes (e.g., the teacher of the class you attend immediately prior to your communication class). You should not identify the teacher you rate. You can compare your teacher's score with those from your classmates and discuss what likely contributes to differences in scores.

To score the PNIB Scale, you should reverse-code items 2 and 5 (i.e., a 0 becomes a 4, a 1 becomes a 3, etc.). After reverse-coding those items, average all responses from the survey. Higher values indicate higher levels of immediacy. An average of 1 or less indicates low immediacy, whereas an average of 3 or more indicates high immediacy.

CHAPTER 14: EFFECTIVE USE OF LANGUAGE SCALE

Informative speeches require effective language use to help audience members learn new information. The scale created for chapter 14 draws on concepts from chapter 3 to emphasize the importance of language during informative speaking.

The 12-item scale allows you to assess how well you implement the following strategies to improve you language use:

- *Perception checking:* items 1 and 9
- *Paraphrasing:* items 2 and 12
- *Using operational definitions:* items 3 and 8
- *Using definitions:* items 4 and 7
- *Dating:* items 5 and 10
- *Indexing:* items 6 and 11

The second item in each category (items 9, 12, 8, 7, 10, and 11) should be reverse-coded before calculating scores. Using scores for each language strategy, you can self-assess areas in which your language use could be improved.

CHAPTER 15: NEED FOR COGNITION SCALE

A key objective in chapter 15 is to help you think strategically about strategies for persuading others. In persuasion literature a number of research studies have explored personality characteristics that influence how people react to persuasive messages. A person's need for cognition addresses the extent to which he or she wants to think about information. Those who have a greater need for cognition will react differently to persuasive messages than those who have a lower need for cognition. By using this survey, you can determine your personal need for cognition when being persuaded.

To score the Need for Cognition Scale, you should first reverse-code items 2, 3, 5, and 6. Then average responses for all items; higher values indicate a greater need for cognition. Although reliable national norms for this scale have not been identified, an average above the midpoint of 3 would certainly indicate a higher need for cognition, whereas values below the midpoint would indicate a lower need for cognition. As you compare your score with those of your classmates, is your need for cognition higher or lower?

Glossary

A

accommodation goal The marginalized group manages to keep its identity while striving for positive relationships with the dominant culture.

active listening Involved listening with a purpose.

active perception Perception in which your mind selects, organizes, and interprets that which you sense.

adaptors Nonverbal movements that you might perform fully in private but only partially in public.

adoption The listeners start a new behavior as a result of the persuasive presentation.

affect displays Nonverbal movements of the face and body used to show emotion.

affection The emotion of caring for others and/or being cared for.

ageist language Language that describes and denigrates people on the basis of their age.

aggressiveness The assertion of one's rights at the expense of others and care about one's own needs but no one else's.

analogy A comparison of some respects, especially position and function, of things that are otherwise dissimilar.

antonym Defines an idea by opposition.

argument A proposition that asserts some course of action.

argumentativeness The quality or state of being argumentative; synonymous with contentiousness or combativeness.

articulation The production of sounds; a component of enunciation.

artifacts Ornaments or adornments you display that hold communicative potential.

assigned groups Groups that evolve out of a hierarchy whereby individuals are assigned membership to the group.

assimilation goal The marginalized group attempts to fit in with the dominant group.

attitude A predisposition to respond favorably or unfavorably to a person, an object, an idea, or an event.

attractiveness A concept that includes physical attractiveness, how desirable a

person is to work with, and how much "social value" the person has for others.

audience analysis The collection and interpretation of audience information obtained by observation, inference, research, or questionnaires.

autocratic leaders Leaders who maintain strict control over their group.

automatic attention The instinctive focus we give to stimuli signaling a change in our surroundings, stimuli that we deem important, or stimuli that we perceive to signal danger.

B

bargaining The process in which two or more parties attempt to reach an agreement on what each should give and receive in a transaction between them.

behavioral flexibility The ability to alter behavior to adapt to new situations and to relate in new ways when necessary.

belief A conviction; often thought to be more enduring than an attitude and less enduring than a value.

bibliographic references Complete citations that appear in the "references" or "works cited" section of your speech outline.

bodily movement What the speaker does with his or her entire body during a presentation.

body The largest part of a presentation, which contains the arguments, evidence, and main content.

boomerang effect The audience likes you and your message less after your presentation than they did before.

brainstorming A creative procedure for thinking of as many topics as you can in a limited time.

brakelight function A forewarning to the audience that the end of the presentation is near.

C

captive audience An audience that has not chosen to hear a particular speaker or speech.

cause/effect pattern A method of organization in which the presenter first explains the causes of an event, a problem, or an issue and then discusses its consequences, results, or effects.

celebrity testimony Statements made by a public figure who is known to the audience.

channel The means by which a message moves from the source to the receiver of a message.

chronemics Also called temporal communication; the way people organize and use time and the messages that are created because of their organization and use of it.

chronological résumé A document that organizes your credentials over time.

cliché An expression that has lost originality and force through overuse.

closure The tendency to fill in missing information in order to complete an otherwise incomplete figure or statement.

code A systematic arrangement of symbols used to create meanings in the mind of another person or persons.

code sensitivity The ability to use the verbal and nonverbal language appropriate to the cultural norms of the individual with whom you are communicating.

coercion The act of forcing people to think or behave as you wish; not a form of persuasion.

collaborative style Thoughtful negotiation and reasoned compromise.

collectivist cultures Cultures that value the group over the individual.

commitment A measure of how much time and effort you put into a cause; your passion and concern about the topic.

common ground The degree to which the speaker's values, beliefs, attitudes, and interests are shared with the audience; an aspect of credibility.

communication The process of using messages to generate meaning.

communication apprehension (CA) An individual's level of fear or anxiety associated with either real or anticipated communication with another person or persons.

communication competence The ability to effectively exchange meaning through a common system of symbols, signs, or behavior.

communication networks Patterns of relationships through which information flows in an organization.

comparison Shows the similarity between something well known and something less known.

competence The degree to which the speaker is perceived as skilled, reliable, experienced, qualified, authoritative, and informed; an aspect of credibility.

complementarity The idea that we sometimes bond with people whose strengths are our weaknesses.

complementary relationships Relationships in which each person supplies something the other person or persons lack.

complementing Nonverbal and verbal codes add meaning to each other and expand the meaning of either message alone.

compliance-gaining Those attempts made by a source of messages to influence a target "to perform some desired behavior that the target otherwise might not perform."

compliance-resisting The refusal of targets of influence messages to comply with requests.

conclusion The part that finishes the presentation by fulfilling the four functions of an ending.

concrete language Words and statements that are specific rather than abstract or vague.

connotative meaning An individualized or personalized meaning of a word, which may be emotionally laden.

content curation The collection and storage of information from across the World Wide Web.

context A set of circumstances or a situation.

contradicting Verbal and nonverbal messages conflict.

contradictions In dialectic theory, the idea that each person in a relationship might have two opposing desires for maintaining the relationship.

contrast Clarifies by showing differences.

control The ability to influence our environment.

cover letter A short letter introducing you and your résumé to an interviewer.

criteria The standards by which a group must judge potential solutions.

critical listening Listening that challenges the speaker's message by evaluating its accuracy, meaningfulness, and utility.

critical thinking Analyzing the speaker, the situation, and the speaker's ideas to make critical judgments about the message being presented.

cultural relativism The belief that another culture should be judged by its own context rather than measured against your culture.

culture The socially transmitted behavior patterns, beliefs, attitudes, and values of a particular period, class, community, or population.

customer service encounter The moment of interaction between the customer and the firm.

D

dating Specifying when you made an observation, since everything changes over time.

deceptive communication The practice of deliberately making somebody believe things that are not true.

decode The process of assigning meaning to others' words in order to translate them into thoughts of your own.

decoding The process of assigning meaning to the idea or thought in a code.

deductive argument A logical structure that uses a general proposition applied to a specific instance to draw a conclusion.

defensiveness Occurs when a person feels attacked.

definitions Determinations of meaning through description, simplification,

examples, analysis, comparison, explanation, or illustration.

delivery The presentation of a speech using your voice and body to communicate your message.

democratic leaders Leaders who encourage members to participate in group decisions.

demographic analysis The collection and interpretation of data about the characteristics of people.

demonstrating Showing the audience what you are explaining.

denotative meaning The agreed-upon meaning or dictionary meaning of a word.

descriptiveness The practice of describing observed behavior or phenomena instead of offering personal reactions or judgments.

designated leader Someone who has been appointed or elected to a leadership position.

dialectic The tension that exists between two conflicting or interacting forces, elements, or ideas.

dialogue The act of taking part in a conversation, discussion, or negotiation.

direct inference A tentative generalization based on deliberately gathered data.

discontinuance A persuasive purpose rooted in convincing listeners to stop some current behavior.

dominant culture Determined by who has the power and influence in a group; in the United States the dominant culture is white, male, able-bodied, straight, married, and employed.

downward communication Messages flowing from superiors to subordinates.

dyadic communication Two-person communication.

dynamism The extent to which the speaker is perceived as bold, active, energetic, strong, empathic, and assertive; an aspect of credibility.

E

economic orientation Organizations that manufacture products and/or offer services for consumers.

emblems Nonverbal movements that substitute for words and phrases.

emergent groups Groups resulting from environmental conditions leading to the formation of a cohesive group of individuals.

emergent leader Someone who becomes an informal leader by exerting influence toward achievement of a group's goal but does not hold the formal position or role of leader.

emotional labor Jobs in which employees are expected to display certain feelings in order to satisfy organizational role expectations.

empathic listening Listening with a purpose and attempting to understand the other person.

emphasizing The use of nonverbal cues to strengthen verbal messages.

encode The process of translating your thoughts into words.

encoding The process of translating an idea or thought into a code.

enunciation The pronunciation and articulation of sounds and words.

ethics A set of moral principles or values.

ethnocentrism The belief that your own group or culture is superior to other groups or cultures.

ethos Now called "source credibility," this concept refers to the source's character as a means of persuasion.

euphemism A more polite, pleasant expression used instead of a socially unacceptable form.

examples Specific instances used to illustrate your point.

expert testimony Statements made by someone who has special knowledge or expertise about an issue or idea.

explanation A clarification of what something is or how it works.

extemporaneous method A carefully prepared and researched presentation delivered in a conversational style.

extrinsic motivation A method of making information relevant by providing the audience with reasons outside the presentation itself for listening to the content of the presentation.

eye contact The extent to which a speaker looks directly at the audience.

F

facial expressions Any nonverbal cues expressed by the speaker's face.

fear appeal Eliciting fear to change behavior.

feedback The receiver's verbal and non-verbal response to the source's message.

figure The focal point of your attention.

first impression An initial opinion about people upon meeting them.

first-person observation An observation based on something that you personally have sensed.

fluency The smoothness of delivery, the flow of words, and the absence of vocalized pauses.

formal communication Messages that follow prescribed channels of communication throughout an organization.

formal role Also called positional role; an assigned role based on an individual's position or title within a group.

frozen evaluation An assessment of a concept that does not change over time.

functional résumé A document that organizes your credentials by type of function performed.

G

gestures Movements of the head, arms, and hands to illustrate, emphasize, or signal ideas in a presentation.

ground The background against which your focused attention occurs.

group climate The emotional tone or atmosphere members create within the group.

group conflict An expressed struggle between two or more members of a group.

group culture The socially negotiated system of rules that guide group behavior.

group decision support system (GDSS) An interactive network of computers with specialized software, allowing users to generate solutions for unstructured problems.

groupthink An unintended outcome of cohesion in which the desire for cohesion and agreement takes precedence over critical analysis and discussion.

H

hearing The act of receiving sound.

heterosexist language Language that implies that everyone is heterosexual.

heuristics Mental shortcuts used to perform analytic tasks like evaluating sources and/or research.

horizontal communication Messages between members of an organization with equal power.

hostile work environment sexual harassment Conditions in the workplace that are sexually offensive, intimidating, or hostile and that affect an individual's ability to perform his or her job.

hurtful messages Messages that create emotional pain or upset.

I

identity management The control (or lack of control) of the communication of information through a performance.

illustrators Nonverbal movements that accompany or reinforce verbal messages.

imagery The use of words that appeal to the senses, that create pictures in the mind.

immediacy Communication behaviors intended to create perceptions of psychological closeness with others.

immediate behavioral purposes The actions expected from an audience during and immediately after a presentation.

immediate purpose A statement of what you intend to accomplish in this particular presentation.

impromptu method Delivery of a presentation without notes, plans, or formal preparation; characterized by spontaneity and conversational language.

inclusion The state of being involved with others; a human need.

incremental plagiarism The intentional or unintentional use of information from one or more sources without fully divulging how much information is directly quoted.

indexing Identifying the uniqueness of objects, events, and people.

indirect inference One we draw by observation.

individualistic cultures Cultures that value individual freedom, choice, uniqueness, and independence.

inductive argument A logical structure that provides enough specific instances for the listener to make an inferential leap to a generalization that summarizes the individual instances.

inference A tentative generalization based on some evidence.

inflection The variety or changes in pitch.

informal communication Any interaction that does not generally follow the formal structure of the organization but emerges out of natural social interaction among organization members.

informal role Also called a behavioral role; a role that is developed spontaneously within a group.

information hunger The audience's need for the information contained in the presentation.

information literacy The ability to recognize when information is needed and to locate, evaluate, and effectively use the information needed.

information overload Providing much more information than the audience can absorb in amount, complexity, or both.

information relevance The importance, novelty, and usefulness of the information to the audience.

informative content The main points and subpoints, illustrations, and examples used to clarify and inform.

integration orientation Organizations that help mediate and resolve discord among members of society.

interaction management Establishing a smooth pattern of interaction that allows a clear flow between topics and ideas.

intercultural communication The exchange of information between individuals who are unalike culturally.

internal references Brief notations indicating a bibliographic reference that contains the details you are using in your speech.

interpersonal communication The process of using messages to generate meaning between at least two people in a situation that allows mutual opportunities for both speaking and listening.

interpersonal relationships Associations between at least two people who are interdependent, who use some consistent patterns of interaction, and who have interacted for an extended period of time.

interpretive perception Perception that involves a blend of internal states and external stimuli.

intrapersonal communication The process of using messages to generate meaning within the self.

introduction The opening words of the speech where you fulfill five functions.

J

jargon The technical language developed by a professional group.

job description A document that defines a job in terms of its content and scope.

K

key-word outline An outline consisting of important words or phrases to remind you of the content of the presentation.

kinesics The study of bodily movements, including posture, gestures, and facial expressions.

L

laissez-faire leaders Leaders who take almost no initiative in structuring a group discussion.

language A collection of symbols, letters, or words with arbitrary meanings that are governed by rules and used to communicate.

lay testimony Statements made by an ordinary person that substantiate or support what you say.

leadership A process of using communication to influence the behaviors and attitudes of others to meet group goals.

lecture cues Verbal or nonverbal signals that stress points or indicate transitions between ideas during a lecture.

lecture listening The ability to listen to, mentally process, and recall lecture information.

listening The active process of receiving, constructing meaning from, and responding to spoken and/or nonverbal messages. It involves the ability to retain information, as well as to react empathically and/or appreciatively to spoken and/or nonverbal messages.

listening for enjoyment Situations involving relaxing, fun, or emotionally stimulating information.

logos The use of logical reasoning in an argument.

long-range goal What you expect to achieve by your message in the days, months, or years ahead.

long-term memory Our permanent storage place for information, including but not limited to past experiences; language; values; knowledge; images of people; memories of sights, sounds, and smells; and even fantasies.

M

main points The most important points in a presentation; indicated by Roman numerals in an outline.

maintenance functions Behaviors that focus on the interpersonal relationships among group members.

manipulation Tricking people or using fraudulent means to gain compliance.

manuscript method Delivery of a presentation from a script of the entire speech.

mass communication The process of using messages to generate meanings in a mediated system, between a source and a large number of unseen receivers.

meaning The understanding of the message.

media convergence The way that broadcasting, publishing, and digital communication are congregating.

memorized method Delivering a presentation that has been committed to memory.

message The verbal or nonverbal form of the idea, thought, or feeling that one person (the source) wishes to communicate to another person or group of people (the receivers).

metaphor A figure of speech that likens one thing to another by treating it as if it were that thing.

micro-persuading An exceedingly brief text message designed to persuade, as in a tweet.

Monroe Motivated Sequence A problem-solving format that encourages an audience to become concerned about an issue; especially appropriate for a persuasive presentation.

N

narrating The oral presentation and interpretation of a story, a description, or an event; includes dramatic reading of prose or poetry.

narratives Stories to illustrate an important point.

noise Any interference in the encoding and decoding processes that reduces message clarity.

non-dominant culture This term includes people of color, women, gays/lesbians/ bisexuals, people with disabilities, the lower/ working class, the unemployed, the underemployed, the bankrupt, the young, and the elderly.

nonverbal codes Codes of communication consisting of symbols that are not words, including nonword vocalizations.

nonverbal communication The process of using wordless messages to generate meaning.

nonword sounds "Mmh," "huh," "ahh," and the like as well as pauses or the absence of sound for effect in speaking.

norms Informal rules for group interaction created and sustained through communication.

O

objectics Also called object language; the study of the human use of clothing and other artifacts as nonverbal codes.

objective statement An articulation of your goals.

On-time The time schedule that compart-mentalizes time to meet personal needs, separates task and social dimensions, and points to the future.

operational definition A definition that identifies something by revealing how it works, how it is made, or what it consists of.

organization The grouping of stimuli into meaningful units or wholes.

organizational communication The ways in which groups of people both maintain structure and order through their symbolic interactions and allow individual actors the freedom to accomplish their goals.

organizational communities Groups of similar businesses or clubs that have common interests and become networked together to provide mutual support and resources.

organizational patterns Arrangements of the contents of a presentation.

organizations Social collectives, or groups of people, in which activities are coordinated to achieve both individual and collective goals.

out-group A group of people excluded from another group with higher status; a group marginalized by the dominant culture.

outline A written plan that uses symbols, margins, and content to reveal the order, importance, and substance of a presentation.

P

paralinguistic features The nonword sounds and nonword characteristics of language, such as pitch, volume, rate, and quality.

parallel form The consistent use of complete sentences, clauses, phrases, or words in an outline.

paraphrasing Restating another person's message by rephrasing the content or intent of the message.

pathos The use of emotional "proofs" in an argument.

pattern-maintenance orientation Organizations that promote cultural and educational regularity and development within society.

pause The absence of vocal sound used for dramatic effect, transition, or emphasis.

perception The process of becoming aware of objects and events from the senses.

perceptual checking A process of describing, interpreting, and verifying that helps us understand another person and his or her message more accurately.

perceptual constancy The idea that your past experiences lead you to see the world in a way that is difficult to change; your initial perceptions persist.

personal experience Your own life as a source of information.

personal idioms Unique forms of expression and language understood only by individual couples.

personal inventory An analysis of your own reading, viewing, and listening habits and behavior to discover topics of personal interest.

personal network A web of contacts and relationships that can assist you in identifying job leads and by giving job referrals.

persuasive imagery The advertiser's method of persuading an audience with fast-paced and dazzling visualization of products.

persuasive presentation A message designed to strategically induce change in an audience.

phatic communication Communication that is used to establish a mood of sociability rather than to communicate information or ideas.

pitch The highness or lowness of the speaker's voice.

plagiarism The use of information from another source without crediting the source.

political orientation Organizations that generate and distribute power and control within society.

positive thinking approach Using positive thoughts to bolster speaker confidence.

power Interpersonal influence that forms the basis for group leadership.

pragmatics The study of language as it is used in a social context, including its effect on the communicators.

prejudice A negative attitude toward a group of people just because they are who they are.

problem/solution pattern A method of organization in which the presenter describes a problem and proposes a solution to that problem.

process An activity, an exchange, or a set of behaviors that occurs over time.

profanity Language that is disrespectful of things sacred.

pronunciation The act of correctly articulating words.

proof Evidence that the receiver believes.

proposition of fact An assertion that can be proved or disproved as consistent with reality.

proposition of policy A proposal of a new rule.

proposition of value A statement of what we should embrace as more important to our culture.

proxemics The study of the human use of space and distance.

proximity The principle that objects physically close to each other will be perceived as a unit or whole. Also, the location, distance or range between persons and things.

public communication The process of using messages to generate meanings in a situation in which a single source transmits a message to a number of receivers.

Q

quality The unique resonance of your voice such as huskiness, nasality, raspiness, or whininess.

questionnaire A set of written questions developed to obtain demographic and attitudinal information.

quid pro quo sexual harassment A situation in which an employee is offered a reward or is threatened with punishment based on his or her participation in a sexual activity.

R

racist language Language that insults a group because of its skin color or ethnicity.

rate The pace of your speech.

rebuttal Arguing against someone else's position on an issue.

receiver A message target.

reference librarian A librarian specifically trained to help you find sources of information.

references A list of sources used in a presentation.

reflexivity Being self-aware and learning from interactions with the intent of improving future interactions.

regionalisms Words and phrases specific to a particular region or part of the country.

regulating Using nonverbal codes to monitor and control interactions with others.

regulators Nonverbal movements that control the flow or pace of communication.

relational deterioration In Knapp's model, the process by which relationships disintegrate.

relational development In Knapp's model, the process by which relationships grow.

relational maintenance In Knapp's model, the process of keeping a relationship together.

relationship-oriented groups Also called primary groups; groups that are usually long-term and exist to meet our needs for inclusion and affection.

relaxation approach Combining deep relaxation with fear-inducing thoughts.

repeating Sending the same message both verbally and nonverbally.

responsiveness The idea that we tend to select our friends and loved ones from people who demonstrate positive interest in us.

rhetorical questions Questions asked for effect, with no answer expected.

rituals Formalized patterns of actions or words followed regularly.

role The part an individual plays in a group; an individual's function or expected behavior.

rough draft The preliminary organization of the outline of a presentation.

rule of thirds Using three rows, three columns, and four hot zones at the intersections of those row and column lines to compose a visual image.

S

Sapir-Whorf hypothesis A theory that our perception of reality is determined by our thought processes, our thought processes are limited by our language, and therefore that language shapes our reality.

schema Organizational "filing systems" for thoughts held in long-term memory.

search engine A program on the Internet that allows users to search for information.

second-person observation A report of what another person observed.

selective attention The tendency, when you expose yourself to information and ideas, to focus on certain cues and ignore others.

selective exposure The tendency to expose yourself to information that reinforces, rather than contradicts, your beliefs or opinions.

selective perception The tendency to see, hear, and believe only what you want to see, hear, and believe.

selective retention The tendency to remember better the things that reinforce your beliefs than those that oppose them.

self-centered functions Behaviors that serve the needs of the individual at the expense of the group.

self-disclosure The process of making intentional revelations about yourself that others would be unlikely to know and that generally constitute private, sensitive, or confidential information.

self-managed approach Reducing the fear of presenting with self-diagnosis and a variety of therapies.

semantics The study of the way humans use language to evoke meaning in others.

sentence outline An outline consisting entirely of complete sentences.

separation goal The marginalized group relates as exclusively as possible with its own group and as little as possible with the dominant group.

sexist language Language that excludes individuals on the basis of gender.

sexual harassment Unwelcome, unsolicited, repeated behavior of a sexual nature.

short-term memory A temporary storage place for information.

signposts Ways in which a presenter signals to an audience where the presentation is going.

silence The lack of sound.

similarity The idea that our friends and loved ones are usually people who like or dislike the same things we do. Also, the principle that elements are grouped together because they share attributes, such as size, color, or shape.

skills approach Reducing fear by systematically improving presenting skills.

slang A specialized language of a group of people who share a common interest or belong to a similar culture.

sleeper effect A change of audience opinion caused by the separation of the message content from its source over a period of time.

slide-deck visuals A collection of slides, usually created with a computer program, that are displayed during a presentation.

small-group communication The process of using messages to generate meaning in a small group of people. Also, interaction among three to nine people working together to achieve an interdependent goal.

Sometime The time schedule that views time as "contextually based and relationally oriented."

source A message initiator.

source credibility The extent to which the speaker is perceived as competent to make the claims he or she is making. Also the audience's perception of your effectiveness as a speaker.

stakeholders Groups of people who have an interest in the actions of an organization.

statistics Numbers that summarize numerical information or compare quantities.

stereotype A generalization about some group of people that oversimplifies their culture.

strategic ambiguity The purposeful use of symbols to allow multiple interpretations of messages.

subjective perception Your uniquely constructed meaning attributed to sensed stimuli.

subpoints The points in a presentation that support the main points; indicated by capital letters in an outline.

substituting Using nonverbal codes instead of verbal codes.

supporting material Information you can use to substantiate your arguments and to clarify your position.

supportive communication Listening with empathy, acknowledging others' feelings, and engaging in dialogue to help others maintain a sense of personal control.

surveys Studies in which a limited number of questions are answered by a sample of the population to discover opinions on issues.

syllogism A logical structure that contains a major premise (a generalization) applied to a particular instance (a minor premise) that leads to a conclusion.

symbolic interactionism The process in which the self develops through the messages and feedback received from others.

symmetrical relationships Relationships in which participants mirror each other or are highly similar.

synonym Defines by using a word close or similar in meaning to the one you are trying to define.

syntax The way in which words are arranged to form phrases and sentences.

T

tactile communication The use of touch in communication.

task functions Behaviors that are directly relevant to the group's task and that affect the group's productivity.

task-oriented groups Also called secondary groups; groups formed for the purpose of completing tasks, such as solving problems or making decisions.

technological convergence The way that technological systems are changing to perform similar tasks.

testimonial evidence Written or oral statements of others' experience used by a speaker to substantiate or clarify a point.

tests of evidence Questions that can be used to test the validity of evidence.

time-sequence pattern A method of organization in which the presenter explains a sequence of events in chronological order.

topical-sequence pattern A method of organization that emphasizes the major reasons an audience should accept a point of view by addressing the advantages, disadvantages, qualities, and types of a person, place, or thing.

transition A bridge between sections of a presentation that helps the presenter move smoothly from one idea to another.

trustworthiness The degree to which the speaker is perceived as honest, fair, sincere, honorable, friendly, and kind; an aspect of credibility.

two-sided argument A source advocating one position presents an argument from the opposite viewpoint and then goes on to refute that argument.

U

uncertainty-accepting cultures Cultures that tolerate ambiguity, uncertainty, and diversity.

uncertainty-rejecting cultures Cultures that have difficulty with ambiguity, uncertainty, and diversity.

upward communication Messages flowing from subordinates to superiors.

V

value A deeply rooted belief that governs our attitude about something.

verbal citations Oral explanations of who the source is, how recent the information is, and what the source's qualifications are.

verbal codes Symbols and their grammatical arrangement, such as languages.

visual resources Any items that can be seen by an audience for the purpose of reinforcing a message.

visualization approach Picturing yourself succeeding.

vocal cues All of the oral aspects of sound except words themselves.

vocal variety Vocal quality, intonation patterns, inflections of pitch, and syllabic duration.

vocalized pauses Breaks in fluency that negatively affect an audience's perception of the speaker's competence and dynamism.

volume The loudness or softness of one's voice.

voluntary audience A collection of people who choose to listen to a particular speaker or speech.

W

within-group diversity The presence of observable and/or implicit differences among group members.

working memory The part of our consciousness that interprets and assigns meaning to stimuli we pay attention to.

References

Chapter 1

1. Petraglia, Joseph. (2009). The importance of being authentic: Persuasion, narration, and dialogue in health communication and education. *Health Communication, 24,* 176–185. Robertson-Malt, Suzi, & Chapman, Ysanne. (2008). Finding the right direction: The importance of open communication in a governance model of nurse management. *Contemporary Nurse: A Journal for the Australian Nursing Profession, 29,* 60–66.

2. Griffin, Em. (2012). *A first look at communication theory* (8th ed.). New York: McGraw-Hill.

3. Morreale, S. P., Osborn, M. M., & Pearson, J. C. (2000). Why communication is important. *Journal of the Association for Communication Administration, 29,* 1–25. (p. 4)

4. Ford, W. S. Z., & Wolvin, A. D. (1993). The differential impact of a basic communication course on perceived communication competencies in class, work, and social contexts. *Communication Education, 42,* 215–233.

5. Rubin, R. B., Perse, E. M., & Barbato, C. A. (1988). Conceptualization and measurement of interpersonal communication motives. *Human Communication Research, 14,* 602–628.

6. Egeci, I., & Gencoz, T. (2006). Factors associated with relationship satisfaction: Importance of communication skills. *Contemporary Family Therapy: An International Journal, 28,* 383–391.

7. Ireland, J. L., Sanders, M. R., & Markie-Dodds, C. (2003). The impact of parent training on marital functioning: A comparison of two group versions of the triple-p positive parenting program for parents of children with early-onset conduct problems. *Behavioural and Cognitive Psychotherapy, 31,* 127–142.

8. Dutta-Bergman, M. J. (2005). The relation between health-orientation, provider-patient communication, and satisfaction: An individual-difference approach. *Health Communication, 18,* 291–303.

9. Manne, S. L., Ostroff, J. S., Norton, T. R., Fox, K., Goldstein, L., & Grana, G. (2006). Cancer-related relationship communication in couples coping with early stage breast cancer. *Psycho-Oncology, 15,* 234–247.

10. Allen, M., Berkowitz, S., Hunt, S., & Louden, A. (1999). A meta-analysis of the impact of forensics and communication education on critical thinking. *Communication Education, 48,* 18–30.

11. Metallinos, N. (1992, September–October). *Cognitive factors in the study of visual image recognition standards.* Paper presented to the Annual Conference of the International Visual Literacy Association, Pittsburgh. (ERIC Document Reproduction Service No. ED 352936.)

12. Blumer, J. G. (1983). Communication and democracy: The crisis beyond and the ferment within. *Journal of Communication, 33,* 166–173. (p. 166)

13. Hart, R. P. (1993). Why communication? Why education? Toward a politics of teaching. *Communication Education, 42,* 97–105. (p. 102)

14. Ibid., 101.

15. Bardwell, C. B. (1997). Standing out in the crowd. *Black Collegian, 28,* 71–79. Peterson, M. S. (1997). Personnel interviewers' perceptions of the importance and adequacy of applicants' communication skills. *Communication Education, 46,* 287–291.

16. Messmer, M. (1997, August). Career strategies for accounting graduates. *Management Accounting,* 4–10. Nisberg, J. N. (1996). Communication: What we hear, what we say vs. what they hear, what they say. *The National Public Accountant, 41,* 34–38. Ridley, A. J. (1996). A profession for the twenty-first century. *Internal Auditor, 53,* 20–25.

17. Coopersmith, J. (2006). The dog that did not bark during the night. *Technology and Culture, 47,* 623–637. Glen, P. (2006, October 2). How indispensable should you be? *Computerworld, 40*(40): 50.

18. Bubela, T. (2006). Science communication in transition: Genomics hype, public engagement, education and commercialization pressures. *Clinical Genetics, 70,* 445–450.

19. Harper, B. (2006, August 25). Communication is crucial. *Farmer's Weekly, 145*(8): 2.

20. Lavin Colky, D., & Young, W. H. (2006). Mentoring in the virtual organization: Keys to building successful schools and businesses. *Mentoring and Tutoring: Partnership in Learning, 14,* 433–447.

21. Petraglia, The importance of being authentic. Robertson-Malt & Chapman, Finding the right direction.

22. Bekiaris, Maria. (2010, February). First, how to get that job. *Money, 120,* 30. Peterson, Personnel interviewers' perceptions of the importance and adequacy of applicants' communication skills.

23. Curtis, D. B., Winsor, J. L., & Stephens, R. D. (1989). National preferences in business and communication education. *Communication Education, 38,* 6–14.

24. Bekiaris, First, how to get that job. Bubela, Science communication in transition. Coopersmith, The dog that did not bark during the night. Glen, How indispensable should you be? Harper, Communication is crucial. Lavin, Colky, & Young, Mentoring in the virtual organization. Nichols, L., & Webb, C. (2006). What makes a good midwife: An integrative review of methodologically diverse research. *Journal of Advanced Nursing, 56,* 414–429. Winsor, J. L., Curtis, D. B., & Stephens, R. D. (1997). National preferences in business and communication education: A survey update. *Journal of the Association of Communication Administration, 3,* 170–179.

25. Pearson, J. C., Sorenson, R. L., & Nelson, P. E. (1981). How students and alumni perceive the basic course. *Communication Education, 30,* 296–299.

26. Dauphinais, W. (1997). Forging the path to power. *Security Management, 41,* 21–23.

27. Argenti, P. A., & Forman, J. (1998). Should business schools teach Aristotle? *Strategy & Business* (www.strategy-business.com/briefs/98312).

28. Edwards, N., Peterson, W. E., & Davies, B. L. (2006, October). Evaluation of

a multiple component intervention to support the implementation of a "therapeutic relationships" best practice guideline on nurses' communication skills. *Patient Education and Counseling, 63*(1/2): 3–11. Mlynek, A. (2006, September 11). Say goodbye to shy. *Canadian Business, 79*(18): 125–128. Nichols, M. (2006, September 15). Listen up for better sales. *Business Week Online,* 12.

29. Nichols, Listen up for better sales.
30. Cano, C. P., & Cano, P. Q. (2006). Human resources management and its impact on innovation performance in companies. *International Journal of Technology Management, 35,* 11–27. Houssami, N., & Sainsbury, R. (2006). Breast cancer: Multidisciplinary care and clinical outcomes. *European Journal of Cancer, 42,* 2480–2491. Miller, J. F. (2006). Opportunities and obstacles for good work in nursing. *Nursing Ethics, 13,* 471–487.
31. Johnson, L. M., & Johnson, V. E. (1995, January/February). Help wanted—accountant: What the classifieds say about employer expectations. *Journal of Education for Business, 70*(3): 130–134.
32. Bates, J. (2004, December 15). Unaccustomed as I am . . . *Nursing Standard, 19*(14–16): 25.
33. Gray, F., Emerson, L., & MacKay, B. (2005). Meeting the demands of the workplace: Science students and written skills. *Journal of Science Education and Technology, 14*(4): 425–435.
34. Berlo, D. (1960). *The process of communication.* New York: Holt, Rinehart & Winston.
35. Lee, W. S. (1998). In the names of Chinese women. *Quarterly Journal of Speech, 84,* 283–302.
36. Rogers, C. (1951). *Client-centered therapy.* Boston: Houghton Mifflin, 483.
37. Shotter, J. (2000). Inside dialogical realities: From an abstract-systematic to a participatory-wholistic understanding of communication. *Southern Communication Journal, 65,* 119–132. (p. 119)

38. Mead, G. H. (1967). *Mind, self, and society from the standpoint of a social behaviorist.* Charles W. Morris (ed.). Chicago: University of Chicago Press.
39. Hamilton, K. (1998, November 2). A very ugly gym suit. *Newsweek,* 52.
40. Thompson, Blair, & Mazer, Joseph P. (2009). College student ratings of student academic support: frequency, importance, and modes of communication. *Communication Education, 58,* 433–458.
41. Czubaroff, J. (2000). Dialogical rhetoric: An application of Martin Buber's philosophy of dialogue. *Quarterly Journal of Speech, 86,* 168–189.
42. Poole, M. Scott, & Hollingshead, Andrea B. (2005). *Theories of small groups: Interdisciplinary perspectives.* Thousand Oaks, CA: Sage.
43. Bekiaris, First, how to get that job.

Chapter 2

1. Wright, R. (1994, July–August). That never really happened. *The Humanist,* 30–31.
2. Nelson, B. (2011, Fall). Brief Paper One in Communication 114, Introduction to Human Communication, North Dakota State University.
3. Gilligan, M. (2011, Fall). Brief Paper One in Communication 114, Introduction to Human Communication, North Dakota State University.
4. Restak, R. (1984). *The brain.* New York: Bantam Books.
5. Lutz. C. (2011, Fall). Brief Paper One in Communication 114, Introduction to Human Communication, North Dakota State University.
6. Bedsaul, J. (2011, Fall). Brief Paper One in Communication 114, Introduction to Human Communication, North Dakota State University.
7. Wilson, J., & Wilson, S. (Eds.). (1998). *Mass media/mass culture.* New York: McGraw-Hill.
8. Ibid.
9. Curtin, E. (2005). Instructional styles used by regular classroom teachers while teaching recently mainstreamed ESL students: Six urban middle school teachers share their experiences and

perceptions. *Multicultural Education, 12*(4): 36–42.
10. Wilson & Wilson, *Mass media/mass culture.*
11. Mentalblog.com. (2004). (http://mentalblog.com/2004/12/cdnudt-blveiee-that.html).
12. Leary, M. (2002). The self as a source of relational difficulties. *Self and Identity, 1,* 137–142.
13. Hendrix, K. G. (2002). "Did being black introduce bias into your study?" Attempting to mute the race-related research of black scholars. *Howard Journal of Communication, 13,* 153–171.
14. Hughes, P. C., & Baldwin, J. R. (2002). Communication and stereotypical impressions. *Howard Journal of Communication, 13,* 113–128. (p. 113)
15. Sterling, M. (2006). Do you make your first impression your best impression? (http://entrepreneurs.about.com/cs/marketing/a/uc051603a.htm).
16. Ibid.
17. Ambady, N., & Skowronski, J. (Eds.). (2008). *First impressions.* New York: Guilford Press.
18. Levine, S. (2006, March 20–26). Culturally sensitive medicine: Doctors learn to adapt to immigrant patients' ethnic and religious customs. *Washington Post National Weekly Edition, 23*(22): 31.
19. Seta, C. E., Schmidt, S., & Bookhout, C. M. (2006). Social identity orientation and social role attributions: Explaining behavior through the lens of self. *Self and Identity, 5,* 355–364.
20. Oyserman, D., Bybee, D., & Terry, K. (2006). Possible selves and academic outcomes: How and when possible selves impel action. *Journal of Personality and Social Psychology, 91,* 188–204.
21. Nelson, T. E., & Garst, J. (2005). Values-based political messages and persuasion: Relationships among speaker, recipient, and evoked values. *Political Psychology, 26,* 489–515.
22. Shedletsky, L. J. (1989). The mind at work. In L. J. Shedletsky (Ed.), *Meaning and mind: An intrapersonal approach to human communication.* ERIC and the Speech Communication Association.

23. Mead, G. H. (1934). *Mind, self, and society*. Chicago: University of Chicago Press.
24. Schutz, W. (1982). *Here comes everyone* (2nd ed.). New York: Irvington, p. 1.
25. O'Connor, J. T. (1998, May 25). A view from Mount Ritter: Two weeks in the Sierras changed my attitude toward life and what it takes to succeed. From *Newsweek*, May 25, 1998, p. 17. © 1998 Newsweek, Inc. All rights reserved. Reprinted by permission.
26. Goffman, E. (1959). *The presentation of self in everyday life*. New York: Doubleday Anchor. Goffman, E. (1974). *Frame analysis: An essay on the organization of experience*. New York: Harper & Row. Goffman, E. (1981). *Forms of talk*. Oxford: Basil Blackwell.
27. Chovil, N. (1991). Social determinants of facial displays. *Journal of Nonverbal Behavior, 15,* 141–154.
28. Wiggins, J. A., Wiggins, B. B., & Vander Zanden, J. (1993). *Social psychology* (4th ed.). New York: McGraw-Hill.

Chapter 3

1. Schilling-Estes, N. (2002). American English social dialect variation and gender. *Journal of English Linguistics, 30,* 122–137.
2. Whorf, B. L. (1956). Science and linguistics. In J. B. Carroll (Ed.), *Language, thought and reality* (pp. 207–219). Cambridge, MA: MIT Press.
3. Bakhurst, D., & Shanker, S. G. (Eds.). (2001). *Jerome Bruner: Language, culture, and self.* Kent, UK: W. B. Saunders. Cragan, J. F., & Shields, D. C. (Eds.). (1995). *Symbolic theories in applied communication research: Bormann, Burke and Fisher.* Cresskill, NJ: Hampton Press. Wood, J. T. (1997). *Communication theories in action.* Belmont, CA: Wadsworth.
4. Samovar, L. A., & Porter, R. E. (2000). *Intercultural communication: A reader* (9th ed.). Belmont, CA: Wadsworth. Whorf, Science and linguistics.
5. Waquet, F., & Howe, J. (2001). *Latin: A symbol's empire.* New York: Verso Books.

6. Bruess, C. J. S., & Pearson, J. C. (1993). "Sweet pea" and "pussy cat": An examination of idiom use and marital satisfaction over the life cycle. *Journal of Social and Personal Relationships, 10,* 609–615.
7. Hayakawa, S. I. (1978). *Language in thought and action.* Orlando, FL: Harcourt Brace Jovanovich.
8. Bond, K. (2011). Most annoying grammar mistakes in English (www3.tellus.net/linguisticissues/commonerrorsinenglish.html).
9. ManyThings.org. (2011). (www.ManyThings.org).
10. Rothwell, J. D. (1982). *Telling it like it isn't: Language misuse and malpractice/what we can do about it.* Englewood Cliffs, NJ: Prentice-Hall, 93.
11. Nordquist, R. (2011). Regionalisms (http://grammar.about.com/od/rslg/regionalismterm.htm).
12. Ibid.
13. Hecht, M. L. (Ed.). (1998). *Communicating prejudice.* Thousand Oaks, CA: Sage. Taylor, A., & Hardman, M. J. (Eds.). (1998). *Hearing muted voices.* Cresskill, NJ: Hampton Press.
14. Famous gay, lesbian, and bi-sexual people. (2011). (http://knowledgerush.com/kr/encyclopedia/famous_gay_lesbian_and_bisexual_people.)
15. Gay, lesbian celebrities. (2011). (http://lisal.com/list/gay_lesbian_celebrities.)
16. When words get old: Ageist language. (2008, September 9). *NewsBlaze* (http://newsblaze.com/story/2008090913190200009.wi/topstory.html).
17. Nuessel, F., & Stewart, A. V. (1999). Research summary: Patronizing names and forms of address used with older adults. *Names, 47,* 401–409.
18. Korzybski, A. (1994). *Science and sanity.* Forest Hills, NY: Institute of General Semantics.

Chapter 4

1. Lapakko, D. (1997). Three cheers for language: A closer examination of a widely cited study of nonverbal communication. *Communication Education, 46,* 63–67.

2. Grahe, J. E., & Bernieri, F. J. (1999). The importance of nonverbal cues in judging rapport. *Journal of Nonverbal Behavior, 23,* 253–269. Vedantam, S. (2006, October 2–8). A mirror on reality: Research shows that neurons in the brain help us understand social cues. *Washington Post National Weekly Edition, 23*(50): 35.
3. Nikolaus, Jackob, Roessing, Thomas, & Petersen, Thomas. (2011). The effects of verbal and nonverbal elements in persuasive communication: Findings from two multi-method experiments. *Communications: The European Journal of Communication Research, 36,* 245–271.
4. Horgan, T., & Smith, J. (2006). Interpersonal reasons for interpersonal perceptions: Gender-incongruent purpose goals and nonverbal judgment accuracy. *Journal of Nonverbal Behavior, 30,* 127–140.
5. Motley, M. T., & Camden, C. T. (1988). Facial expression of emotion: A comparison of posed expressions versus spontaneous expressions in an interpersonal communication setting. *Western Journal of Speech Communication, 52,* 1–22.
6. Mehrabian, A. (1971). *Silent messages.* Belmont, CA: Wadsworth.
7. Teven, Jason J. (2010). The effects of supervisor nonverbal immediacy and power use on employees' ratings of credibility and affect for the supervisor. *Human Communication, 13,* 69–85.
8. Bower, B. (2002, July 6). The eyes have it. *Science News, 162*(1): 4.
9. Ekman, P. (1997). Should we call it expression or communication? *Innovations in Social Science Research, 10,* 333–344. Ekman, P. (1999). Basic emotions. In T. Dalgleish & T. Power (Eds.), *The handbook of cognition and emotion* (pp. 45–60). Sussex, UK: John Wiley. Ekman, P. (1999). Facial expressions. In T. Dalgleish & T. Power (Eds.), *The handbook of cognition and emotion* (pp. 301–320). Sussex, UK: John Wiley.
10. Yang, Ping. (2011). Nonverbal aspects of turn taking in Mandarin

Chinese interaction. *Chinese Language and Discourse, 2,* 99–130.

11. Ekman, P., & Friesen, W. V. (1967). Head and body cues in the judgment of emotion: A reformulation. *Perceptual and Motor Skills, 24,* 711–724.

12. Krumhuber, E., Manstead, A., Cosker, D., Marshall, D., & Rosin, P. (2009). The effects of dynamic attributes of smiles in human and synthetic faces: A simulated job interview setting. *Journal of Nonverbal Behavior, 33,* 1–15.

13. LoBue, V. (2009). More than just another face in the crowd: Superior detection of threatening facial expressions in children and adults. *Developmental Science, 12,* 305–313.

14. Seiter, John S., Weger, Harry, Jensen, Andrea, & Kinzer, Harold J. (2010). The role of background behavior in televised debates: Does displaying nonverbal agreement and/or disagreement benefit either debater? *Journal of Social Psychology, 150,* 278–300.

15. McCarthy, R., Blackwell, A., DeLahunta, S., Wing, A., Hollands, K., Barnard, P., Nimmo-Smith, I., & Marcel, A. (2006). Bodies meet minds: Choreography and cognition. *Leonardo, 39,* 475–477.

16. Cash, T. F. (1980, July 7). If you think beautiful people hold all the cards, you're right, says a researcher. *People Weekly, 14,* 74–79. Kowner, R. (1996, June). Facial asymmetry and attractiveness judgment in developmental perspective. *Journal of Experimental Psychology, 22,* 662–675.

17. Brody, J. E. (1994, March 21). Notions of beauty transcend culture, new study suggests. *New York Times,* A14.

18. Rhode, Deborah L. (2010). *The beauty bias: The injustice of appearance in life and law.* Oxford: Oxford University Press.

19. Jaeger, Mads Meier. (2011). "A thing of beauty is a joy forever": Returns to physical attractiveness over the life course. *Social Forces, 89,* 983–1003.

20. Cash, If you think beautiful people hold all the cards, you're right, says a researcher.

21. Knapp, M. L., & Hall, J. A. (2010). *Nonverbal communication in human interaction* (7th ed.). Boston: Wadsworth.

22. Swami, V., Furnham, A., & Joshi, K. (2008). The influence of skin tone, hair length, and hair colour on ratings of women's physical attractiveness, health and fertility. *Scandinavian Journal of Psychology, 49,* 429–437.

23. Knapp & Hall, *Nonverbal communication in human interaction.*

24. Eastwick, P. W., & Finkel, E. J. (2008). Sex differences in mate preferences revisited: Do people know what they initially desire in a romantic partner? *Journal of Personality and Social Psychology, 94,* 245–264.

25. Lee, L., Loewenstein, G., Ariely, D., Hong, J., & Young, J. (2008). If I'm not hot, are you hot or not? Physical attractiveness evaluations and dating preferences as a function of one's own attractiveness. *Psychological Science, 19,* 669–677.

26. Carmalt, J. H., Cawley, J., Joyner, K., & Sobal, J. (2008). Body weight and matching with a physically attractive romantic partner. *Journal of Marriage and Family, 70,* 1287–1296.

27. Widgery, R. N. (1974). Sex of receiver and physical attractiveness of source as determinants of initial credibility perception. *Western Speech, 38,* 13–17.

28. Davies, A. P. C., Goetz, A. T., & Shackelford, T. K. (2008). Exploiting the beauty in the eye of the beholder: The use of physical attractiveness as a persuasive tactic. *Personality and Individual Differences, 45,* 302–306.

29. Haas, A., & Gregory, S. (2005). The impact of physical attractiveness on women's social status and interactional power. *Sociological Forum, 20,* 449–471.

30. Hall, E. T. (1966). *The hidden dimension.* New York: Doubleday.

31. Werner, C. M. (1987). Home interiors: A time and place for interpersonal relationships. *Environment and Behavior, 19,* 169–179.

32. Hall, *The hidden dimension.*

33. Burgoon, J. K. (1978). A communication model of personal space violations: Explication and an initial test. *Human Communication Research, 4,* 129–142.

34. See, for example, McMurtray, J. W. (2000). Exploring that other space. *Ad Astra, 12*(1): 38–39; and Terneus, S. K., & Malone, Y. (2004). Proxemics and kinesics of adolescents in dual-gender groups. *Guidance and Counseling, 19,* 118–123.

35. Bailenson, J. N., Blascovich, J., Beall, A. C., & Loomis, J. M. (2001). Equilibrium theory revisited: Mutual gaze and personal space in virtual environments. *Presence: Teleperators and Virtual Environments, 10,* 583–598.

36. Ro'sing, I. (2003). The gender of space. *Philosophy and Geography, 6,* 189–211.

37. Argyle, M., & Dean, J. (1965). Eye-contact, distance, and affiliation. *Sociometry, 28,* 289–304.

38. Leventhal, G., & Matturro, M. (1980). Differential effects of spatial crowding and sex on behavior. *Perceptual and Motor Skills, 51,* 111–119.

39. Sommer, R. (1962). The distance for comfortable conversation: A further study. *Sociometry, 25,* 111–116.

40. Burgoon, Judee K., & Hubbard, Amy Ebesu. (2004). Cross-cultural and intercultural applications of expectancy violations theory and interaction adaptation theory. In William B. Gudykunst (Ed.), *Theorizing about intercultural communication* (pp. 149–171). Thousand Oaks, CA: Sage.

41. Hall, E. T. (1963). Proxemics: The study of man's spatial relations and boundaries. In I. Galdston (Ed.), *Man's image in medicine and anthropology* (pp. 422–445). New York: International Universities Press. (p. 422)

42. Bruneau, T. J. (2007). Time, change, and sociocultural communication: A chronemic perspective. *Sign Systems Studies, 35,* 89–117.

43. Ballard, D. I., & Seibold, D. R. (2006). The experience of time at work: Relationship to communication load, job satisfaction, and interdepartmental communication. *Communication Studies, 57,* 317–340.

44. Cecchini, Marco, Baroni, Eleonora, Di Vito, Cinzia, & Lai, Carlo. (2011). Smiling in newborns during communicative wake and active sleep. *Infant Behavior & Development, 34,* 417–423.

45. Schutz, W. C. (1971). *Here comes everybody.* New York: Harper & Row, 16.

46. Hertenstein, M. J. (2002). Touch: Its communicative functions in infancy. *Human Development, 45,* 70–94. Loots, G., & Devise, I. (2003). The use of visual-tactile communication strategies by deaf and hearing fathers and mothers of deaf infants. *Journal of Deaf Studies and Deaf Education, 8,* 31–43.

47. Aguinis, H., Simonsen, M. M., & Pierce, C. A. (1998). Effects of nonverbal behavior on perceptions of power bases. *Journal of Social Psychology, 138*(4): 455–475.

48. Siegel, B. S. (1990). *Peace, love and healing: Bodymind communication and the path to self-healing: An exploration.* New York: Harper Perennial, 134.

49. Molinuevo, Beatriz, Escorihuela, Rosa M., Fernandez-Teruel, Albert, Tobena, Adolf, & Torrubia, Raphael. (2011). How we train undergraduate medical students in decoding patients' nonverbal clues. *Medical Teacher, 33,* 804–807.

50. Ishikawa, Hirono, Hashimoto, Hideki, Kinoshita, Makoto, & Yano, Eiji. (2010). Can nonverbal skills be taught? *Medical Teacher, 32,* 860–863.

51. Lee, J. W., & Guerrero, L. K. (2001). Types of touch in cross-sex relationships between coworkers: Perceptions of relational and emotional messages, inappropriateness, and sexual harassment. *Journal of Applied Communication Research, 29,* 197–220.

52. Fisher, J. D., Rytting, M., & Heslin, R. (1976). Hands touching hands: Affective and evaluative effects of interpersonal touch. *Sociometry, 3,* 416–421.

53. Goldberg, S., & Lewis, M. (1969). Play behavior in the year-old infant: Early sex differences. *Child Development, 40,* 21–31.

54. Ibid.

55. Jourard, S., & Rubin, J. E. (1968). Self-disclosure and touching: A study of two modes of interpersonal encounter and their inter-relation. *Journal of Humanistic Psychology, 8,* 39–48.

56. Jourard, S. M. (1966). An exploratory study of body accessibility. *British Journal of Social and Clinical Psychology, 5,* 221–231.

57. Henley, N. (1973–1974). Power, sex, and nonverbal communication. *Berkeley Journal of Sociology, 18,* 10–11.

58. Ibid.

59. McDaniel, E., & Andersen, P. A. (1998). International patterns of interpersonal tactile communication: A field study. *Journal of Nonverbal Behavior, 22,* 59–76.

60. Jourard, S. M. (1968). *Disclosing man to himself.* Princeton, NJ: Van Nostrand.

61. Kane, M. N. (2006). Research note: Sexual misconduct, non-sexual touch, and dual relationships: Risks for priests in light of the code of pastoral conduct. *Review of Religious Research, 48,* 105–110. Lee & Guerrero, Types of touch in cross-sex relationships between coworkers. Strozier, A. L., Krizek, C., & Sale, K. (2003). Touch: Its use in psychotherapy. *Journal of Social Work Practice, 17,* 49–62.

62. Vaish, A., & Striano, T. (2004). Is visual reference necessary? Contributions of facial versus vocal cues in 12-month-olds' social referencing behavior. *Developmental Science, 7,* 261–269.

63. Kramer, E. (1963). The judgment of personal characteristics and emotions from nonverbal properties of speech. *Psychological Bulletin, 60,* 408–420.

64. Laukka, P., Juslin, P. N., & Bresin, R. (2005). A dimensional approach to vocal expression of emotion. *Cognition and Emotion 19,* 633–653. Planalp, S. (1996). Varieties of cues to emotion in naturally occurring situations. *Cognition and Emotion, 10,* 137–154.

65. Kramer, The judgment of personal characteristics and emotions from nonverbal properties of speech.

66. Bateson, G., Jackson, D. D., Haley, J., & Weakland, J. H. (1956). Toward a theory of schizophrenia. *Behavioral Science, 1,* 251–264.

67. Bryant, G. A., & Tree, J. E. F. (2005). Is there an ironic tone of voice? *Language and Speech, 48,* 257–277.

68. Hardman, P. (1971, September). Every human being is a separate language. *Salt Lake Tribune.*

69. Olson, L. C. (1997). On the margins of rhetoric: Audre Lorde transforming silence into language and action. *Quarterly Journal of Speech, 83,* 49–70.

70. Frith, K. T., Hong, C., & Ping Shaw, K. T. (2004). Race and beauty: A comparison of Asian and Western models in women's magazine advertisements. *Sex Roles, 50*(1/2): 53–61.

71. Fisher, S. (1975). Body decoration and camouflage. In L. M. Gurel & M. S. Beeson (Eds.), *Dimensions of dress and adornment: A book of readings.* Dubuque, IA: Kendall/Hunt.

72. Boswell, R. (2006). Say what you like: Dress, identity, and heritage in Zanzibar. *International Journal of Heritage Studies, 12,* 440–457.

73. Laurie, Alison. (2000). *The language of clothes.* New York: Holt.

74. Taylor, L. C., & Compton, N. H. (1968). Personality correlates of dress conformity. *Journal of Home Economics, 60,* 653–656.

75. Henricks, S. H., Kelley, E. A., & Eicher, J. B. (1968). Senior girls' appearance and social acceptance. *Journal of Home Economics, 60,* 167–172.

76. Douty, H. I. (1963). Influence of clothing on perception of persons. *Journal of Home Economics, 55,* 197–202.

77. Williams, M. C., & Eicher, J. B. (1966). Teenagers' appearance and social acceptance. *Journal of Home Economics, 58,* 457–461.

78. Panja, Ayan. (2004, January 3). The death of the white coat? *British Medical Journal, 328*(7430): 57.

79. Dress, religion, identity. (2010). *Material Religion, 6,* 371. Laurie, *The language of clothes.*

80. Triggs, Charlotte, West, Kay, & Aradillas, Elaine. (2011, September 26). *People,* 160–168.

81. Wohlrab, Silke, Fink, Bernhard, Kappeler, Peter M., & Brewer, Gayle. (2009). Differences in personality attributions toward tattooed and nontattooed virtual human characters. *Journal of Individual Differences, 30*(1): 1–5.

82. Rosenthal, R., Hall, J. A., Matteg, M. R. D., Rogers, P. L., & Archer, D. (1979). *Sensitivity to nonverbal communication: The PONS Test.* Baltimore: Johns Hopkins University Press.

83. Wei, Fang-Yi Flora, & Wang, Y. Ken. (2010). Students' silent messages: Can teacher verbal and nonverbal immediacy moderate student use of text messaging in class? *Communication Education, 59,* 475–496.

Chapter 5

1. Janusic, L. A., & Wolvin, A. D. (2009). 24 hours in a day: A listening update to the time studies. *International Journal of Listening, 23,* 104–120.

2. Ledbetter, A., & Schrodt, P. (2008). Family communication patterns and cognitive processing: Conversation and conformity orientations as predictors of informational reception apprehension. *Communication Studies, 59,* 388–401. (p. 397)

3. Haigh, G. (2006, September 22). Listen, don't just consult. *Times Educational Supplement,* 35.

4. Nichols, M. (2006, September 15). Listen up for better sales. *Business Week Online,* 12.

5. Nett, W. (2011, September 23). Best Buy chairman says listening skills critical to thriving business. *Lubbock Avalanche Journal Online* (http://lubbockonline.com).

6. Heussner, M. (2011, September 26). Listening to digital chatter by audience, not keywords: TrendingTarget aims to spot trending topics by consumer group. *AdWeek Online* (www.adweek.com/news/technology/listening-digital-chatter-audience-not-keywords-135217).

7. Lenckus, D. (2005, November 28). Physician apologies, listening skills found to reduce medical malpractice claims. *Business Insurance,* 4.

8. Dewey, J. (1947). *The public and its problems.* Athens, OH: Swallow Press.

9. Tamesue, T., Tetsuro, S., & Itoh, K. (2009). Prediction method for listening score and psychological impression taking into account hearing loss due to factors such as aging. *Applied Acoustics, 70,* 426–431.

10. An ILA definition of listening. (1995). *Listening Post, 53,* 1.

11. Barker, L. L. (1971). *Listening behavior.* Englewood Cliffs, NJ: Prentice-Hall.

12. Wood, J. T. (2002). *Communication in our lives* (3rd ed.). Belmont, CA: Wadsworth.

13. A dose of music may ease the pain. (2000, December). *Current Health, 27,* 2.

14. Janusik, L. (2005). Conversational listening span: A proposed measure of conversational listening. *International Journal of Listening, 19,* 12–28.

15. Hoffman, W., Friese, M., Schmeichel, B. J., & Baddeley, A. D. (2011). Working memory and self-regulation. In R. F. Baumeister [& K. D. Vohs (Eds.), *Handbook of self-regulation: Research, theory and practice* (pp. 204–225). New York: Guilford Press.

16. Davidson, K. (2011). *Now you see it: How the brain science of attention will transform the way we live, work, and learn.* New York: Viking.

17. Briscoe, J., & Rankin, P. M. (2009). Exploration of a "double jeopardy" hypothesis within working memory profiles for children with specific language impairment. *International Journal of Language & Communication Disorders, 44,* 236–250.

18. Miller, G. A. (1994). The magical number seven, plus or minus two: Some limits on our capacity for processing information. *Psychology Review, 101,* 343–352.

19. Gilbert, M. B. (1988). Listening in school: I know you can hear me—but are you listening? *Journal of the International Listening Association, 2,* 121–132.

20. Salopek, J. (1999, September). Is anyone listening? Listening skills in the corporate setting. *Training & Development, 53,* 58–59.

21. Stansfield, S. (2008, December 16). Noise as a public health problem. *ASHA Leader,* 5–6.

22. Skenazy, L. (2009, February 9). Smartphone apps great for marketing, bad for social skills. *Advertising Age,* np.

23. Thompson, W. F., Schellenberg, E. G., & Letnic, A. K. (2011, May 20). Fast and loud background music disrupts reading comprehension. *Psychology of Music* (doi:10.1177/0305735611400173).

24. Wicken, C. D., & McCarley, J. S. (2007). *Applied attention theory.* Boca Raton, FL: CRC Press.

25. Burbles, N. C., & Rice, S. (2010). On pretend listening. *Teachers College Record, 112,* 2875.

26. Tannen, D. (2001). *You just don't understand: Women and men in conversation.* New York: HarperCollins.

27. Toulmin, S. E. (1958). *The uses of argument.* New York: Cambridge University Press.

28. Berman, J. M. (2005, November). Industry output and employment projections to 2014. *Monthly Labor Review,* 45–69.

29. Gunn, B. (2001, February). Listening as feeling. *Strategic Finance, 82,* 12–15. Copyright 2001 by Institute of Management Accountants. Reproduced with permission of Institute of Management Accountants in the format Textbook via Copyright Clearance Center.

30. Anderson, T. H., & Armbruster, B. B. (1986). *The value of taking notes* (Reading Education Report No. 374). Champaign: University of Illinois at Urbana-Champaign, Center for the Study of Reading.

31. Armbruster, B. B. (2000). Taking notes from lectures. In R. Flippo & D. Caverly (Eds.), *Handbook of college reading and study strategy research* (pp. 175–199). Mahwah, NJ: Lawrence Erlbaum.

32. Vinson, L., & Johnson, C. (1990). The relationship between the use of hesitations and/or hedges and lecture

listening: The role of perceived importance and a mediating variable. *Journal of the International Listening Association, 4,* 116–127. (p. 116)

33. Gilbert, Listening in school.

34. O'Hair, M., O'Hair, D., & Wooden, S. (1988). Enhancement of listening skills as a prerequisite to improved study skills. *Journal of the International Listening Association, 2,* 113–120.

35. Titsworth, B. S., & Kiewra, K. (1998, April). *By the numbers: The effects of organizational lecture cues on notetaking and achievement.* Paper presented at the American Educational Research Association Convention, San Diego.

36. Ibid.

37. Centers for Disease Control and Prevention. (2010, July 16). Television and video viewing time among children aged 2 years—Oregon, 2006–2007. *Morbidity and Mortality Weekly Report, 59,* 837–841.

38. American Library Association. (2001). *Report of the Presidential Committee on Information Literacy* (www.ala.org/acrl/nili/ilit1st.html).

39. International Telecommunications Union. (2011). *The world in 2011: ICT facts and figures* (www.itu.int/ITU-D/ict/facts/2011/index.html).

40. Nielsen Company. (2011). State of the media: The social media report Q3 2011 (http://blog.nielsen.com/nielsenwire/social/).

41. Vandergrift, L. (2006). Second language listening: Listening ability or language proficiency? *Modern Language Journal, 90,* 6–18.

42. Cross, J. (2009). Effects of listening strategy instruction on news videotext comprehension. *Language Teaching Research, 13,* 151–176.

43. Rehling, L. (2004). Improving teamwork through awareness of conversational styles. *Business Communication Quarterly, 67,* 475–482.

Chapter 6

1. Miller, G. R., & Steinberg, M. (1975). *Between people: A new analysis of interpersonal communication.* Chicago: Science Research Associates.

2. Crawford, L. (1996). Everyday Tao: Conversation and contemplation. *Communication Studies, 47,* 25–34. (p. 25)

3. Julien, D., Chartrand, E., Simard, M. C., Bouthillier, D., & Begin, J. (2003). Conflict, social support, and relationship quality: An observational study of heterosexual, gay male, and lesbian couples' communication. *Journal of Family Psychology, 17,* 419–428.

4. Schutz, W. (1976). *The interpersonal underworld.* Palo Alto, CA: Science and Behavior Books.

5. Spitzberg, B. H., & Cupach, W. R. (2007). *The dark side of interpersonal communication* (2nd ed.). Mahwah, NJ: Lawrence Erlbaum.

6. Pearce, W. B., & Sharp, S. M. (1973). Self-disclosing communication. *Journal of Communication, 23,* 409–425.

7. Jourard, S. M. (1964). *The transparent self: Self-disclosure and well-being.* New York: Van Nostrand Reinhold.

8. Hastings, S. O. (2000). Self-disclosure and identity management by bereaved parents. *Communication Studies, 51,* 352–371.

9. LePoire, B. A., Haynes, J., Driscoll, J., Driver, B. N., Wheelis, T. F., Hyde, M. K., Prochaska, M., & Ramos, L. (1997). Attachment as a function of parental and partner approach–avoidance tendencies. *Human Communication Research, 23,* 413–441.

10. Dindia, K., Fitzpatrick, M. A., & Kenny, D. A. (1997). Self-disclosure in spouse and stranger interaction. *Human Communication Research, 23,* 388–412.

11. Darling, N., Cumsille, P., Caldwell, L. L., & Dowdy, B. (2006). Predictors of adolescents' disclosure to parents and perceived parental knowledge: Between- and within-person differences. *Journal of Youth and Adolescence, 35,* 659–670. Smetana, J. G., Metzger, A., Gettman, D. C., & Campione-Barr, N. (2006). Disclosure and secrecy in adolescent–parent relationships. *Child Development, 77,* 201–217.

12. Tam, T., Hewstone, M., Harwood, J., Voci, A., & Kenworthy, J. (2006). Intergroup contact and grandparent–grandchild communication: The effects of self-disclosure on implicit and explicit biases against older people. *Group Processes and Intergroup Relations, 9,* 413–429.

13. Afifi, W. A., & Guerrero, L. K. (1998). Some things are better left unsaid II: Topic avoidance in friendships. *Communication Quarterly, 46,* 231–249. (p. 231)

14. Roloff, M. E., & Johnson, D. I. (2001). Reintroducing taboo topics: Antecedents and consequences of putting topics back on the table. *Communication Studies, 52,* 37–50.

15. Lucchetti, A. E. (1999). Deception in disclosing one's sexual history: Safe-sex avoidance or ignorance? *Communication Quarterly, 47,* 300–314.

16. Wang, S. H.-Y., & Chang, H.-C. (1999). Chinese professionals' perceptions of interpersonal communication in corporate America: A multidimensional scaling analysis. *Howard Journal of Communications, 10,* 297–315.

17. Kim, M.-S., & Bresnahan, M. (1994). A process model of request tactic evaluation. *Discourse Processes, 18,* 317–344.

18. Sherman, A. M., Lansford, J. E., & Volling, B. L. (2006). Sibling relationships and best friendships in young adulthood: Warmth, conflict, and well-being. *Personal Relationships, 13,* 151–165.

19. Rawlins, W. (1992). *Friendship matters: Communication, dialectics, and the life course.* New York: Aldine de Gruyter.

20. Radmacher, K., & Azmitia, M. (2006). Are there gendered pathways to intimacy in early adolescents' and emerging adults' friendships? *Journal of Adolescent Research, 21,* 415–448.

21. Pahl, R., & Pevalin, D. J. (2005). Between family and friends: A longitudinal study of friendship choice. *British Journal of Sociology, 56,* 433–450.

22. Rawlins, *Friendship matters.*

23. Way, N., & Greene, M. L. (2006). Trajectories of perceived friendship quality during adolescence: The patterns

and contextual predictors. *Journal of Research on Adolescence, 16,* 293–320.

24. Saferstein, J. A., Neimeyer, G. J., & Hagans, C. L. (2005). Attachment as a predictor of friendship qualities in college youth. *Social Behavior and Personality, 33,* 767–775.

25. Rawlins, *Friendship matters.*

26. Ibid.

27. Guerrero, L. K., & Chavez, A. M. (2005). Relational maintenance in cross-sex friendships characterized by different types of romantic intent: An exploratory study. *Western Journal of Communication, 69,* 339–358.

28. Neary Dunleavy, K., & Booth-Butterfield, M. (2008). Chilling effects and binge drinking in platonic and romantic relationships. *Human Communication, 11,* 39–51.

29. French, D. C., Bae, A., Pidada, S., & Okhwa, L. (2006). Friendships of Indonesian, South Korean, and U.S. college students. *Personal Relationships, 13,* 69–81.

30. Mesch, G., & Talmud, I. (2006). The quality of online and offline relationships: The role of multiplexity and duration of social relationships. *Information Society, 22,* 137–148.

31. www.facebook.com.

32. Smith, C. (2011, May 2). Osama Bin Laden's death leaked via Twitter. *The Huffington Post* (www.huffingtonpost.com).

33. Gaudin, S. (2011, October 5). Twitter, Facebook flooded with reaction to Jobs' death. *Computerworld* (www.computerworld.com).

34. Ross, C., Orr, E. S., Sisic, M., Arseneault, J. M., Simmering, M. G., & Orr, R. R. (2009). Personality and motivations associated with Facebook use. *Computers in Human Behavior, 25,* 578–586.

35. Puentes, J., Knox, D., & Zusman, M. E. (2008). Participants in "friends with benefits" relationships. *College Student Journal, 42,* 176–180.

36. McGinty, K., Knox, D., & Zusman, M. E. (2007). Friends with benefits: Women want "friends," men want "benefits." *College Student Journal, 41,* 1128–1131.

37. Bisson, M. A., & Levine, T. R. (2009). Negotiating a friends with benefits relationship. *Archives of Sexual Behavior, 38,* 66–73.

38. Ronesi, L. M. (2003). Enhancing postsecondary intergroup relations at the university through student-run ESL instruction. *Journal of Language, Identity, and Education, 2,* 191–210.

39. Miller, G. R. (1976). *Explorations in interpersonal communication.* Beverly Hills, CA: Sage.

40. La France, B. H. (2010). Predicting sexual satisfaction in interpersonal relationships. *Southern Communication Journal, 75,* 195–214.

41. La France, B. H. (2010). What verbal and nonverbal communication cues lead to sex?: An analysis of the traditional sexual script. *Communication Quarterly, 58,* 297–318.

42. Wilmot, W. W. (1995). *Relational communication.* New York: McGraw-Hill.

43. Baxter, L. (1993). The social side of personal relationships: A dialectical perspective. In S. Duck (Ed.), *Understanding relationship processes: Vol. 3. Social context and relationships* (pp. 139–165). Newbury Park, CA: Sage. Baxter, L., & Montgomery, B. (1996). *Relating: Dialogues and dialects.* New York: Guilford Press. Dindia, K., & Baxter, L. A. (1987). Strategies for maintaining and repairing marital relationships. *Journal of Social and Personal Relationships, 4,* 143–158.

44. Chory, R. M., & Banfield, S. (2009). Media dependence and relational maintenance in interpersonal relationships. *Communication Reports, 22,* 41–53.

45. Johnson, A. J., Haigh, M. M., Becker, J. A. H., Craig, E. A., & Wigley, S. (2008). College students' use of relational management strategies in email in long-distance and geographically close relationships. *Journal of Computer-Mediated Communication, 13,* 381–404.

46. Friedman, H. S., Riggio, J. R. E., & Casella, D. F. (1988). Nonverbal skill, personal charisma, and initial attraction. *Personality and Social Psychology Bulletin, 14,* 203–211.

47. Sias, P. M., & Cahill, D. J. (1998). From coworkers to friends: The development of peer friendships in the workplace. *Western Journal of Communication, 62,* 273–299.

48. McCroskey, J. C., & McCain, T. A. (1974). The measurement of interpersonal attraction. *Speech Monographs, 41,* 267–276.

49. Pearson, J. C., & Spitzberg, B. H. (1990). *Interpersonal communication: Concepts, components, and contexts.* Dubuque, IA: Wm. C. Brown.

50. Hetsroni, A., & Bloch, L.-R. (1999). Choosing the right mate when everyone is watching: Cultural and sex differences in television dating games. *Communication Quarterly, 47,* 315–332.

51. Rick, S. I., Small, D. A., & Finkel, E. J. (2011). Fatal (fiscal) attraction: Spendthrifts and tightwads in marriage. *Journal of Marketing Research, 48,* 228–237.

52. Perse, E. M., & Rubin, R. B. (1989). Attribution in social and parasocial relationships. *Communication Research, 16,* 59–77.

53. Berger, C. R., & Kellermann, K. (1989). Personal opacity and social information gathering. *Communication Research, 16,* 314–351.

54. Davis, M. H., & Oathout, H. A. (1987). Maintenance of satisfaction in romantic relationships: Empathy and relational competence. *Journal of Personality and Social Psychology, 53,* 397–498.

55. Ragsdale, J. D. (1996). Gender, satisfaction level, and the use of relational maintenance strategies in marriage. *Communication Monographs, 63,* 354–369.

56. Collier, M. J. (1996). Communication competence problematics in ethnic friendships. *Communication Monographs, 63,* 314–336. (p. *i*)

57. Harwood, J., McKee, J., & Lin, M.-C. (2000). Younger and older adults' schematic representations of intergenerational communication. *Communication Monographs, 67,* 20–41.

58. Guerrero, L. K. (1996). Attachment-style differences in intimacy and involvement: A test of the four-category model. *Communication Monographs, 63,* 269–292.

59. Pearson, J. C. (1996). Forty-forever years? Primary relationships and senior citizens. In N. Vanzetti & S. Duck (Eds.), *A lifetime of relationships* (pp. 383–405). Pacific Grove, CA: Brooks/Cole.

60. Sillars, A., Shellen, W., McIntosh, A., & Pomegranate, M. (1997). Relational characteristics of language: Elaboration and differentiation in marital conversations. *Western Journal of Communication, 61,* 403–422.

61. Vangelisti, A. L., & Crumley, L. P. (1998). Reactions to messages that hurt: The influence of relational contexts. *Communication Monographs, 65,* 173–196.

62. Duck, S., & Pond, K. (1989). Friends, Romans, countrymen, lend me your retrospections: Rhetoric and reality in personal relationships. In C. Hendrick (Ed.), *Close relationships* (pp. 17–38). Newbury Park, CA: Sage.

63. Vangelisti & Crumley, Reactions to messages that hurt.

64. di Battista, P. (1997). Deceivers' responses to challenges of their truthfulness: Difference between familiar lies and unfamiliar lies. *Communication Quarterly, 45,* 319–334.

65. Martin, M. M., & Anderson, C. M. (1997). Aggressive communication traits: How similar are young adults and their parents in argumentativeness, assertiveness, and verbal aggressiveness? *Western Journal of Communication, 61,* 299–314.

66. Semic, B. A., & Canary, D. J. (1997). Trait argumentativeness, verbal aggressiveness, and minimally rational argument: An observational analysis of friendship discussions. *Communication Quarterly, 45,* 355–378.

67. Schullery, N. M., & Schullery, S. E. (2003). Relationship of argumentativeness to age and higher education. *Western Journal of Communication, 67,* 207–224.

68. Martin & Anderson, Aggressive communication traits.

69. Gibb, J. R. (1991). *Trust: A new vision of human relationships for business, education, family, and personal living* (2nd ed). North Hollywood, CA: Newcastle.

70. Floyd, K. (1997). Affectionate communication in nonromantic relationships: Influences of communicator, relational, and contextual factors. *Western Journal of Communication, 61,* 279–298. Floyd, K. (1997). Communicating affection in dyadic relationships: An assessment of behavior and expectancies. *Communication Quarterly, 45,* 68–80. Floyd, K., & Morman, M. T. (1998). The measurement of affectionate communication. *Communication Quarterly, 46,* 144–162. Floyd, K., & Morman, M. T. (2000). Reacting to the verbal expression of affection in same-sex interaction. *Southern Communication Journal, 65,* 287–299.

71. Floyd, K., & Burgoon, J. K. (1999). Reacting to nonverbal expressions of liking: A test of interaction adaptation theory. *Communication Monographs, 66,* 219–239.

72. LePoire, B. A., & Yoshimura, S. M. (1999). The effects of expectancies and actual communication on nonverbal adaptation and communication outcomes: A test of interaction adaptation theory. *Communication Monographs, 66,* 1–30.

73. Caplan, S. E., & Samter, W. (1999). The role of facework in younger and older adults' evaluations of social support messages. *Communication Quarterly, 47,* 245–264.

74. MacGeorge, E. L. (2001). Support providers' interaction goals: The influence of attributions and emotions. *Communication Monographs, 68,* 72–97.

75. Clark, R. A., Pierce, K. F., Hsu, K., Toosley, A., & Williams, L. (1998). The impact of alternative approaches to comforting, closeness of relationship, and gender on multiple measures of effectiveness. *Communication Studies, 49,* 224–239.

76. Wilson, S. R. (1998). Introduction to the special issue on seeking and resisting compliance: The vitality of compliance-gaining research. *Communication Studies, 49,* 273–275. (p. 273)

77. Marshall, L. J., & Levy, V. M., Jr. (1998). The development of children's perceptions of obstacles in compliance-gaining interactions. *Communication Studies, 49,* 342–357.

78. Saeki, M., & O'Keefe, B. (1994). Refusals and rejections: Designing messages to serve multiple goals. *Human Communication Research, 21,* 67–102.

79. Ifert, D. E., & Roloff, M. E. (1997). Overcoming expressed obstacles to compliance: The role of sensitivity to the expressions of others and ability to modify self-presentation. *Communication Quarterly, 45,* 55–67.

80. Betcher, W. (1987). *Intimate play: Creating romance in everyday life.* New York: Viking Press.

81. Bruess, C. J. S., & Pearson, J. C. (1993). "Sweet Pea" and "Pussy Cat"? An examination of idiom use and marital satisfaction over the life cycle. *Journal of Social and Personal Relationships, 10,* 609–615.

82. Bruess, C. J. S., & Pearson, J. C. (1997). Interpersonal rituals in marriage and adult friendship. *Communication Monographs, 64,* 25–46.

83. Deusch, M., & Kraus, R. M. (1962). Studies of interpersonal bargaining. *Journal of Conflict Resolution, 6,* 52.

84. Thibaut, J. W., & Kelley, H. H. (1959). *The social psychology of groups.* New York: John Wiley, 37.

85. Sheehy, G. (1976). *Passages: Predictable crises of adult life.* New York: Dutton.

86. A to Z of world: Top ten tips for good interpersonal communication skills (www.blogspot.com/2009/08/top-ten-tips-for-good-interpersonal-communication-skills).

Chapter 7

1. Martin, J. N., & Nakayama, T. K. (2011). *Experiencing intercultural communication: An introduction.* New York: McGraw-Hill.

2. *Women in Congress.* (2011). http://womenincongress.house.gov/historical-data/representatives-senators-by-congress.html?congress=112.
3. *Women CEOs in Fortune 500 companies.* http://money.cnn.com/magazines/fortune/fortune500/2011/womenceos/.
4. *Women in the military.* (2011). http://usmilitary.about.com/od/womeninthemilitary/Women_in_the_United_States_Military.html.
5. Kramarae, C. (1981). *Women and men speaking.* Rowley, MA: Newbury House.
6. Orbe, M. P. (1996). Laying the foundation for co-cultural communication theory: An inductive approach to studying "nondominant" communication strategies and the factors that influence them. *Communication Studies, 47,* 157–176.
7. Folb, E. (1994). Who's got the room at the top? Issues of dominance and nondominance in intracultural communication. In L. A. Samovar & R. E. Porter (Eds.), *Intercultural communication: A reader* (pp. 119–127). Belmont, CA: Wadsworth.
8. Dodd, C. H. (1998). *Dynamics of intercultural communication* (5th ed.). New York: McGraw-Hill.
9. Rogers, E. M., & Steinfatt, T. M. (1999). *Intercultural communication.* Prospect Heights, IL: Waveland Press.
10. Bruno, R. L. (1999). "Beating" the tribal drum: Rejecting disability stereotypes and preventing self-discrimination. *Disability and Society, 14,* 855–857. (p. 855)
11. Allport, G. W. (1954/1958). *The nature of prejudice.* Cambridge, MA: Addison-Wesley/Garden City, NY: Doubleday.
12. Henderson-King, E., & Nisbett, R. E. (1996). Anti-black prejudice as a function of exposure to the negative behavior of a single black person. *Journal of Personality and Social Psychology, 71,* 654–664.
13. Garcia, A. L., Miller, D. A., Smith, E. R., & Mackie, D. M. (2006). Thanks for the compliment? Emotional reactions to group-level versus individual-level compliments and insults. *Group Processes and Intergroup Relations, 9,* 307–324.
14. Czopp, A. M., Monteith, M. J., & Mark, A. Y. (2006). Standing up for a change: Reducing bias through interpersonal confrontation. *Journal of Personality and Social Psychology, 90,* 784–803.
15. Richeson, J., & Shelton, J. N. (2005). Brief report: Thin slices of racial bias. *Journal of Nonverbal Behavior, 29,* 75–86.
16. Swim, J. K., Hyers, L. L., Cohen, L. L., & Ferguson, M. J. (2001). Everyday sexism: Evidence for its incidence, nature, and psychological impact from three daily diary studies. *Journal of Social Issues, 57,* 31–53.
17. Hofstede, G. (1980). *Culture's consequences: International differences in work-related values.* Newbury Park, CA: Sage.
18. Ibid.
19. Coleman, D. (1998, December 22). The group and self: New focus on a cultural rift. *The New York Times,* 40.
20. Hofstede, *Culture's consequences.*
21. Ibid.
22. Samovar, L. A., Porter, R. E., & Stefani, L. A. (1998). *Communication between cultures* (3rd ed.). Belmont, CA: Wadsworth.
23. Lee, G.-L., & Manning, M. L. (2001). Treat Asian parents and families right. *Education Digest, 67,* 39–45.
24. Ting-Toomey, S. (1997). Managing intercultural conflicts effectively. In L. A. Samovar & R. E. Porter (Eds.), *Intercultural communication: A reader* (8th ed., pp. 392–404). Belmont, CA: Wadsworth.
25. Ibid., 395.

Chapter 8

1. Frenkel, K. A. (2010, February, 16). The wisdom of the hive: Is the Web a threat to creativity and cultural values? One cyber pioneer thinks so. *Scientific American* (www.scientificamerican.com/article.cfm?id=jaron-lanier-gadget).
2. Terris, D. (2011, October 14). Teaching virtual teamwork. *Inside Higher Education* (www.insidehighered.com/views/2011/10/14/essay_calls_for_more_of_an_emphasis_on_teaching_virtual_teamwork).
3. Herring, H. B. (2006, June 18). Endless meetings: The black hole of the workday. *The New York Times,* 2.
4. Schutz, W. C. (1958). *FIRO: A three-dimensional theory of interpersonal behavior.* New York: Rinehart.
5. Zekeri, A. A. (2004). College curriculum competencies and skills former students found essential to their careers. *College Student Journal, 38,* 412–423.
6. Miller, S. (2008, August). Skills critical for a changing workforce. *HR Magazine, 53,* 24.
7. Vengel, A. (2006). Lead your team to victory: The dos and don'ts of effective group influence. *Contract Management, 46,* 69–70.
8. Zorn, T. E., Roper, J., Broadfoot, K., & Weaver, C. K. (2006). Focus groups as sites of influential interaction: Building communicative self-efficacy and effecting attitudinal change in discussing controversial topics. *Journal of Applied Communication Research, 34,* 115–140.
9. Galanes, G. J., & Adams, K. H. (2009). *Effective group discussion.* New York: McGraw-Hill.
10. Whelan, S. A. (2009). Group size, group development, and group productivity. *Small Group Research, 40,* 247–262.
11. Jana, R. (2009, March 23). Real life imitates real world. *BusinessWeek,* 42.
12. Barker, D. B. (1991, February). The behavioral analysis of interpersonal intimacy in group development. *Small Group Research, 22,* 76–91. Kelly, L., & Duran, R. L. (1985). Interaction and performance in small groups: A descriptive report. *International Journal of Small Group Research, 1,* 182–192.
13. Ferraris, C. (2004). Investigating NASA's intergroup decision-making: Groupthink and intergroup social dynamics. International Communication Association Convention, May 2004, New Orleans, LA.
14. Henningsen, D. D., Henningsen, M. L., Eden, J., & Cruz, M. G. (2006). Examining the symptoms of groupthink

and retrospective sense making. *Small Group Research, 37,* 36–64.

15. Waseleski, C. (2006). Gender and the use of exclamation points in computer-mediated communication: An analysis of exclamation points posted to two electronic discussion lists. *Journal of Computer Mediated Communication, 11,* 1012–1024.

16. Ladegaard, H. J., & Dorthe, B. (2003). Gender differences in your children's speech: The acquisition of sociolinguistic competence. *International Journal of Applied Linguistics, 13,* 222–233.

17. Carli, L. L. (2001). Gender and social influence. *Journal of Social Issues, 57,* 725–742.

18. Won, H. L. (2006). Links between personalities and leadership perception in problem-solving groups. *Social Science Journal, 43,* 659–672.

19. Lauring, J., & Selmer, J. (2010). Multicultural organizations: Common language and group cohesiveness. *International Journal of Cross Cultural Management, 10,* 267–284.

20. Galanes, G. (2003). In their own words: An exploratory study of bona fide group leaders. *Small Group Research, 34,* 741–770.

21. Hackman, M. Z., & Johnson, C. E. (2003). *Leadership: A communication perspective* (4th ed.). Prospect Heights, IL: Waveland Press.

22. Wilmot, W. W., & Hocker, J. L. (2007). *Interpersonal conflict* (7th ed.). New York: McGraw-Hill.

23. French, J. R. P., & Raven, B. (1981). The bases of social power. In D. Cartwright & A. Zander (Eds.), *Group dynamics: Research and theory* (3rd ed.). New York: McGraw-Hill.

24. Galanes, G. (2009). Dialectical tensions of small group leadership. *Communication Studies, 60,* 409–425.

25. Foels, R., Driskell, J. E., Mullen, B., & Salas, E. (2000). The effects of democratic leadership on group member satisfaction. *Small Group Research, 31,* 676–702.

26. See Brown, M. E., & Trevino, L. K. (2006). Socialized charismatic leadership, values congruence, and deviance

in work groups. *Journal of Applied Psychology, 91,* 954–962.

27. Barge, J. K., & Hirokawa, R. Y. (1989). Toward a communication competency model of group leadership. *Small Group Behavior, 20,* 167–189.

28. Ibid.

29. Gouran, D. S., & Hirokawa, R. Y. (1986). Counteractive functions of communication in effective group decision-making. In R. Y. Hirokawa & M. S. Poole (Eds.), *Communication and group decision-making.* Beverly Hills, CA: Sage.

30. Blomstrom, S., Boster, F. J., Levine, K. J., Butler, E. M., & Levine, S. L. (2008).The effect of training on brainstorming. *Journal of the Communication, Speech, & Theatre Association of North Dakota, 21,* 41–50.

31. Craig, R. (2004). Benefits and drawbacks of anonymous online communication: Legal challenges and communicative recommendations. *Free Speech Yearbook, 41,* 127–141.

32. Turman, P. (2005). Norm development, decision-making, and structuration in CMC group interaction. *Communication Teacher, 19,* 121–125.

33. Galanes & Adams, *Effective group discussion.* Wilmot & Hocker, *Interpersonal conflict.*

34. Galanes & Adams, *Effective group discussion.*

Chapter 9

1. Cass, C. (2011, April 21). Poll: College students get hard lessons in finance. *USA Today* (www.usatoday.com/money/perfi/college/2011-04-23-college-students-money-poll.htm).

2. Parsons, T. (1963). *Structure and process in modern societies.* New York: Free Press.

3. United States Small Business Administration. (2011, October 22). How important are small businesses to the U.S. economy? (www.sba.gov/advocacy/7495/8420).

4. Election Countdown. (2011, October 24). *Political parties* (www.electioncountdown.us/parties.htm).

5. Stohl, C. (1995). *Organizational communication: Connectedness in action.* Thousand Oaks, CA: Sage. (p. 18)

6. Susskind, A. M., Schwartz, D. F., Richards, W. D., & Johnson, J. D., (2005). Evolution and diffusion of the Michigan State University tradition of organizational communication network research. *Communication Studies, 56,* 397–418.

7. Fay, M. J., & Kline, S. L. (2011). Co-worker relationships and informal communication in high-intensity telecommuting. *Journal of Applied Communication Research, 39,* 144–163.

8. Caudron, S. (1998). They hear it through the grapevine. *Workforce, 77,* 25–27.

9. Monge, P., Heiss, B., & Margolin, D. (2008). Communication network evolution in organizational communities. *Communication Theory, 18,* 449–477.

10. Bureau of Labor Statistics. (2011, October 21). *Occupational outlook handbook (2010–2011 ed.)* (www.bls.gov/oco/).

11. See Boase, J. (2008). Personal networks and the personal communication system. *Information, Communication & Society, 11,* 490–508.

12. Bureau of Labor Statistics. (2011, June 6). *National Longitudinal Survey of Youth* (www.bls.gov/nls/nlsy79.htm).

13. Krizan, A., Merrier, P., & Jones, C. (2002). *Business communication* (5th ed.). Cincinnati: South-Western.

14. Wright, E. W., Domagalski, T. A., & Collins, R. (2011). Improving employee selection with a revised resume format. *Business Communication Quarterly, 74,* 272–286.

15. Henricks, M. (2000). *Kinko's guide to the winning résumé.* United States of America: Kinko's.

16. Ibid.

17. Bennett, S. (2005). *The elements of résumé style: Essential rules and eye-opening advice for writing résumés and cover letters that work.* New York: AMACOM.

18. Amare, N., & Manning, A. (2009). Writing for the robot: How employer search tools have influenced resume rhetoric and ethics. *Business Communication Quarterly, 72,* 35–60.

19. Henricks, *Kinko's guide to the winning résumé*.
20. Schullery, N. M., Ickes, L., & Schullery, S. E. (2009). Employer preferences for résumés and cover letters. *Business Communication Quarterly, 72,* 163–176.
21. Belicove, M. E. (2011, March). The master of your domain. *Entrepreneur, 39,* 58.
22. Lipovsky, C. (2006). Candidates' negotiation of their expertise in job interviews. *Journal of Pragmatics, 38,* 1147–1174.
23. Young, M. J., Behnke, R. R., & Mann, Y. M. (2004). Anxiety patterns in employment interviews. *Communication Reports, 17,* 49–57.
24. See, for example, Tey, C., Ang, S., & Van Dyne, L. (2006). Personality, biographical characteristics, and job interview success: A longitudinal study of the mediating effects of interviewing self-efficacy and the moderating effects of internal locus of causality. *Journal of Applied Psychology, 91,* 446–454.
25. Lawsuit free hiring: The 5 laws you need to know & 4 steps you need to take. (2010, January). *HR Specialist: Employment Law, 40,* 4.
26. Teven, J. J., McCroskey, J. C., & Richmond, V. P. (2006). Communication correlates of perceived Machiavellianism of supervisors: Communication orientations and outcomes. *Communication Quarterly, 54,* 127–142.
27. Lee, D. & LaRose, R. (2011). The impact of personalized social cues of immediacy on consumers' information disclosure: A social cognitive approach. *CyberPsychology, Behavior, & Social Networking, 14,* 337–343.
28. Hopkins, K. M. (2001). Manager intervention with troubled supervisors: Help and support at the top. *Management Communication Quarterly, 15,* 83–99.
29. Albrecht, T. L., & Bach, B. W. (1997). *Communication in complex organizations: A relational approach.* New York: Harcourt Brace.
30. Eisenberg, E. M. (1984). Ambiguity as strategy in organizational communication. *Communication Monographs, 51,* 227–242.
31. Wilmot, W. W., & Hocker, J. L. (2005). *Interpersonal conflict* (7th ed.). New York: McGraw-Hill.
32. Bitner, M. J., Booms, B. H., & Tetreault, M. S. (1990). The service encounter: Diagnosing favorable and unfavorable incidents. *Journal of Marketing, 54,* 71–84. (p. 71)
33. Waldron, V. R. (1994). Once more, with feeling: Reconsidering the role of emotion in work. In S. A. Deetz (Ed.), *Communication yearbook* (Vol. 17, pp. 388–416). Thousand Oaks, CA: Sage.
34. Murphy, A. (2001). The flight attendant dilemma: An analysis of communication and sensemaking during in-flight emergencies. *Journal of Applied Communication Research, 29,* 30–53.
35. Rafeili, A., & Sutton, R. I. (1990). Busy stores and demanding customers: How do they affect the display of positive emotion? *Academy of Management Journal, 33,* 623–637.
36. Hochschild, A. (1983). *The managed heart: Commercialization of human feeling.* Berkeley: University of California Press.
37. Tracy, S. (2005). Locking up emotion: Moving beyond dissonance for understanding emotional labor discomfort. *Communication Monographs, 72,* 261–283.
38. Infante, D., Riddle, B., Horvath, G., & Tumlin, S. (1992). Verbal aggressiveness: Messages and reasons. *Communication Quarterly, 40,* 116–126.
39. Herschovis, M. S. (2011). "Incivility, social undermining, bullying . . oh my!": A call to reconcile constructs within workplace aggression research. *Journal of Organizational Behavior, 32,* 499–519.
40. Amare & Manning, Writing for the robot.
41. Solomon, D., & Williams, A. (1997). Perceptions of social-sexual communication at work: The effects of message, situation, and observer characteristics on judgments of sexual harassment. *Journal of Applied Communication Research, 25,* 196–216.

Chapter 10

1. Mazer, J., & Titsworth, S. (2008). *Testing a common public speaking claim: An examination of students' ego-involvement with speech topics in the basic communication course.* National Communication Association Convention, San Diego, CA.
2. Bernard, T. S., & Protess, B. (2011, September 29). Banks to make customers pay fee for using debit cards. *New York Times.*
3. Bernard, T. S. (2011, November 1). In retreat, Bank of America cancels debit card fee. *New York Times.*
4. Dhanagom, C. (2011, September 26). Catholic college cancels pro-abortion speaker (www.lifesitenews.com).
5. Sizing up bargains and quality at outlets vs. retail shops. (2011, November 17). (http://news.consumerreports.org/money/).
6. Kelley. (2011, July 1). 2011 news: *Consumer Reports* releases first fast food survey; shockingly, big chains don't fare well (junkfoodbetter.com).

Chapter 11

1. Heikkilä, H., Kunelius, R., & Ahva, L. (2010, August). From credibility to relevance. *Journalism Practice, 4,* 274–284.
2. Teven, J. (2008). An examination of perceived credibility of the 2008 presidential candidates: Relationships with believability, likeability, and deceptiveness. *Human Communication, 11,* 391–407.
3. Kecskes, I., & Zhang, F. (2009). Activating, seeking, and creating common ground. A socio-cognitive approach. *Pragmatics & Cognition, 17,* 331–355.
4. Hosman, L. A., & Siltanen, S. A. (2011). Hedges, tag questions, message processing, and persuasion. *Journal of Language & Social Psychology, 30,* 341–349.
5. Kleinnijenhuis, J., van Hoof, A. J., & Oegema, D. (2006). Negative news and the sleeper effect of distrust. *Harvard International Journal of Press/Politics, 11,* 86–104.

6. Mazer, J. P., Murphy, R. E., & Simonds, C. J. (2009). The effects of teacher self-disclosure via Facebook on teacher credibility. *Learning, Media & Technology, 34,* 175–183.

7. Masip, J. (2003). Facial appearance and judgments of credibility: The effects of facial babyishness and age on statement credibility. *Genetic, Social & General Psychology Monographs, 129*(3): 269–311.

8. Fico, F., Richardson, J. D., & Edwards, S. M. (2004). Influence of story and structure on perceived story bias and news organization credibility. *Mass Communication & Society, 7,* 301–318.

9. Teven, J. J. (2010). The effects of supervisor nonverbal immediacy and power use on employees' ratings of credibility and affect for the supervisor. *Human Communication, 13,* 69–85.

10. Myers, S. A., & Bryant, L. E. (2004). College students' perceptions of how instructors convey credibility. *Qualitative Research Reports in Communication, 5,* 22–27.

11. Reinard, J., & Meyers, K. (2005, May). *Comparisons of models of persuasive effects of types of evidence introductions.* Paper presented at the International Communication Association Convention, New York.

12. Allen, M. (2002). Effect of timing of communicator identification and level of source credibility on attitude. *Communication Research Reports, 19,* 46–55.

13. Bourhis, J., Adams, C., Titsworth, S., & Harter, L. (2008). *A style manual for communication studies* (3rd ed.). New York: McGraw-Hill.

14. Sternadori, M. M., & Thorson, E. (2009). Anonymous sources harm credibility of all stories. *Newspaper Research Journal, 30,* 54–66.

Chapter 12

1. Hacker, D., & Sommers, N. (2011). *A writer's reference* (7th ed.). Boston: Bedford Books of St. Martin's Press, 63.

Chapter 13

1. Daniels, J. (2005). The art of making persuasive presentations. *Employment Relations Today, 31,* 39–49.

2. Dwyer, S. (2001). Selling an idea: Extemporaneous speaking in sales education. *Journal of Personal Selling & Sales Management, 21,* 313–321.

3. Takash, J. (2011, September). FACING YOUR FEARS. *Smart Business Chicago, 8,* 6.

4. Roark, R. M. (2006). Frequency and voice: Perspectives in the time domain. *Journal of Voice, 20,* 325–354.

5. Woolbert, C. (1920). The effects of various modes of public reading. *Journal of Applied Psychology, 4,* 162–185.

6. Propp, K. (2007, November). Bye-bye monotone: Enhancing vocal variety and expressiveness in public speaking. Presented at the National Communication Association Convention, Chicago, IL.

7. Hanke, S. (2011). Can you hear me now? Top tips to make sure your communication isn't breaking up. *Communication Briefings, 30,* 5–6.

8. McCroskey, J. C. (1997). Oral communication apprehension: A summary of recent theory and research. *Human Communication Research, 4,* 78–96. (p. 78)

9. Teven, J. J., Richmond, V. P., McCroskey, J. C., & McCroskey, L. L. (2010). Updating relationships between communication traits and communication competence. *Communication Research Reports, 27,* 263–270.

10. Bodie, G. D. (2010). A racing heart, rattling knees, and ruminative thoughts: Defining, explaining, and treating public speaking anxiety. *Communication Education, 59,* 70–105.

11. Vassilopoulos, S. H. (2005). Anticipatory processing plays a role in maintaining social anxiety. *Anxiety, Stress & Coping, 18,* 321–332.

12. Ayres, J. (2005). Performance visualization and behavioral disruption: A clarification. *Communication Reports, 18,* 55-63.

13. Friedrich, G., & Goss, B. (1984). Systematic desensitization. In J. A. Daly & J. C. McCroskey (Eds.), *Avoiding communication: Shyness, reticence, and communication apprehension* (pp. 173–188). Beverly Hills, CA: Sage.

14. Dwyer, K. K. (2000). The multidimensional model: Teaching students to self-manage high communication apprehension by self-selecting treatments. *Communication Education, 49,* 72–81.

15. Zayas-Boya, E. P. (1977–1978). Instructional media in the total language picture. *International Journal of Instructional Media, 5,* 145–150.

16. Duarte, N. (2010). *Resonate: Present visual stories that transform audiences.* Hoboken, NJ: John Wiley & Sons. Reynolds, G. (2009). *Presentation Zen: Simple ideas on presentation design and delivery.* Berkeley, CA: New Riders.

Chapter 14

1. Wheeless, L. R. (1974). The effects of attitude, credibility, and homophily on selective exposure to information. *Speech Monographs, 41,* 329–338.

2. Petrie, C. R., Jr., & Carrel, S. D. (1976). The relationship of motivation, listening, capability, initial information, and verbal organizational ability to lecture comprehension and retention. *Speech Monographs, 43,* 187–194.

3. Tourtelot, N. (2008, December). Lunatic. *Esquire 150*(6): 167.

4. Ibid.

5. Harden, B., & Eilperin, J. (2006, December 4–10). Wild species and ski resorts are on the move. *Washington Post Weekly Edition,* 19.

Chapter 15

1. Fotheringham, W. (1966). *Perspectives on persuasion.* Boston: Allyn & Bacon.

2. Ibid.

3. United Poultry Concerns. (2011). (www.upc-online.org/freerange. html).

4. Whitehouse, M. (2011, May 9). Number of the week: Class of 2011 most indebted ever." *Wall Street Journal*

(http://finance.yahoo.com/news/class-2011-most-indebted-ever-070000924.html).

5. Collins, A. (2009). *The student loan scam: The most oppressive debt in U.S. history—and how we can fight back.* New York: Beacon Press.

6. Understanding Obama's student loan forgiveness program. (2011). (obomastudentloanforgiveness.com).

7. Domhoff, G. W. (2011). Who rules America (http://sociology.uscs.edu/whorulesamerica/power/wealth.html).

8. Vargas, J. A. (2011, June 22). My life as an undocumented immigrant. *New York Times Magazine. NP.*

9. Perloff, R. M. (2010). *The dynamics of persuasion: Communication and attitudes in the 21st century* (4th ed.). New York: Routledge.

10. Super Bowl ad spending reached $1.6 billion over the past 10 years. (2011, January 18). (www.hollywoodreporter.com/news/superbowl).

11. Ehninger, D. (1970). Argument as method: Its nature, its limitations, and its uses. *Speech Monographs, 37,* 101–110.

Credits

Text

Back inside cover: NCA Credo for Ethical Communication, National Communication Association, Washington, DC. Used by permission of National Communication Association.

Chapter 2 Page 28: definition of *perception* from Microsoft Encarta Dictionary. © Bloomsbury Publishing PLC, London. **29:** definition of *role* from Microsoft Encarta Dictionary. © Bloomsbury Publishing PLC, London. **37:** definitions of *stereotyping, prejudice,* and *out-group* from Microsoft Encarta Dictionary. © Bloomsbury Publishing PLC, London. **41:** quotation from O'Connor, J.T. "A View from Mount Ritter: Two weeks in the Sierras changed by attitude toward life and what it takes to succeed." From *Newsweek,* May 25, 1998, Page 17. www.newsweek.com © 1998 Newsweek/ Daily Beast Company LLC. All rights reserved. Used by permission and protected by the copyright Laws of the United States. The printing, copying, redistribution, or retransmission of the material without express written permission is prohibited.

Chapter 3 Page 53: definition of *slang* from Microsoft Encarta Dictionary. © Bloomsbury Publishing PLC, London. **54:** definition of *euphemism* from Microsoft Encarta Dictionary. © Bloomsbury Publishing PLC, London. **55:** definition of *jargon* from Microsoft Encarta Dictionary. © Bloomsbury Publishing PLC, London.

Chapter 4 Page 81: Berkeley Nonverbal Expressiveness Questionnaire, Copyright © 1997 by the American Psychological Association. Reproduced with permission. Gross, J.J., & John, O.P. (1997). "Revealing feelings: Facets of emotional expressivity in self-reports, peer ratings, and behavior." *Journal of Personality and Social Psychology,* Vol. 72, No. 2, pp. 435–448.

Chapter 5 Page 102: quotation from Bob Gunn, "Listening as feeling," *Strategic Finance, 82,* 12–15, February 2001. Copyright 2001 by Institute of Management Accountants. Reproduced with permission of Institute of Management Accountants via Copyright Clearance Center.

Chapter 6 Page 117: Figure 6.1 from Joseph Luft, *Group Processes: An Introduction to Group Dynamics.* NY: Mayfield Publishing Company. Copyright 1984, 1970, and 1969 by Joseph Luft. © The McGraw-Hill Companies, Inc. Used by permission. **132:** quotation from C.J.S. Bruess and J. Pearson (1997) "Interpersonal rituals in marriage and adult friendship." *Communication Monographs,* 64, 25–46, March 1, 1997. Reprinted by permission of the publisher (Taylor & Francis Ltd., http://www.tandf.co.uk/journals).

Chapter 7 Page 146: quotation from R.L. Bruno (1999) "Beating" the tribal drum: Rejecting disability stereotypes and preventing self-discrimination. *Disability and Society,* 14(6), 855–857, Nov. 1, 1999. Reprinted by permission of the publisher (Taylor & Francis Ltd., http://www.tandf.co.uk/journals). **148:** Table 7.1 from Carley Dodd (1998) *Dynamics of Intercultural Communication* 4e. © 1998 The McGraw-Hill Companies, Inc. Used by permission. **151:** Individualism-Collectivism Scale from Singelis, T.M., Triandis, H.C., Bhawuk, P.S., & Gelfand, M.J. (1995). "Horizontal and vertical dimensions of individualism and collectivism: A theoretical and measurement refinement." *Cross-Cultural Research,* 29, 240–275. Reprinted by permission.

Chapter 8 Page 180: Collective Self-Esteem Scale from Luhtanen, R. & Crocker, J. (1992). "A collective self-esteem scale: Self-evaluation of one's social identity." *Personality and Social Psychology Bulletin,* 18, 302–318. © 1992. Reprinted by permission of SAGE Publications. **166:** Figure 8.1 from Gloria J. Galanes and John K. Brilhart, *Communicating in Groups* 2e. Copyright © 1993. Times Mirror Higher Education Group, Inc. All rights reserved. Reprinted by permission.

Chapter 9 Page 206: Table 9.2 from W.Z. Ford, *Communicating with customers: Service approaches, ethics, and impact.* Cresskill, NJ: Hampton Press, 1998. Used by permission of Hampton Press Inc.

Chapter 11 Page 247: Table 11.4 from Metzger, M.J., Flanagin, A.J., and Medders, R.B. (2010). "Social and heuristic approaches to credibility evaluation online." *Journal of Communication,* 60(3), 413–439. © 2010. Used by permission. **248:** Wikipedia search page on the Library of Congress, http://en.wikipedia.org/wiki/Library_of_Congress. Photo of Library of Congress reading room: Library of Congress, Prints & Photographs Division, photograph by Carol M. Highsmith, reproduction number LC-USZ62-123456.

Chapter 12 Page 265: Clarity Behaviors Inventory from Titsworth, S., Novak, D., Hunt, S. & Meyer, K. (2004). "The effects of teacher clarity on affective and cognitive learning: a causal model of clear teaching behaviors." International Communication Association, May, New Orleans, LA. Used by permission of the author.

Chapter 13 Page 292: Perceived Nonverbal Immediacy Behaviors Scale from J. McCroskey, A. Sallinen, J. Fayer, V. Richmond, & R. Barraclough (1996). "Nonverbal immediacy and cognitive learning: A cross-cultural investigation." *Communication Education,* 45, 200–211, July 1, 1996. Reprinted by permission of the publisher (Taylor & Francis Ltd., http://www.tandf.co.uk/journals). **297:** Figure 13.1 from Teri Kwal Gamble and Michael Gamble, *Communication Works* 8e. © 2005 The McGraw-Hill Companies, Inc. Used by permission. **302:** Figure 13.2 from Teri Kwal Gamble and Michael Gamble, *Communication Works* 8e. © 2005 The McGraw-Hill Companies, Inc. Used by permission.

Chapter 14 Page 320: quotation from "The YouTube

Star Who's Crazy in a Funny Way" by Nicole Tourtelot, *Esquire,* December 2, 2008. Used by permission of the author.

Chapter 15 Page 342: Need for Cognition from Perse, E. (1992). "Predicting attention to local television news: Need for cognition and motives for viewing." *Communication Reports,* Vol. 5, No. 1, pp. 40–49. Copyrighted by the Western States Communication Association. Used by permission of the publisher.

Photos

Chapter 1 Opener: © Fuse/Getty Images RF; page 4: © McGraw-Hill Companies; p. 5: © Jordan Siemens/Getty Images; p. 7: © Hill Street Studios/Getty Images RF; p. 10: © OJO Images/Getty Images RF; p. 14: © Design Pics/Kristy-Anne Glubish RF; p. 17: © John Lund/Drew Kelly/Sam Diephuis/Blend Images LLC RF; p. 21: © Burke/Triolo/Brand X Pictures/Jupiterimages RF.

Chapter 2 Opener: © Frank Gaglione/Getty Images RF; p. 28: © Comstock Images/Alamy RF; p. 30: © Aliza Averbach/Photo Researchers; p. 31: © Ingram Publishing/SuperStock RF; p. 38: © Laurence Mouton/Getty Images RF; p. 42: © Matthius Engelien/Alamy RF.

Chapter 3 Opener: © Harry Sieplinga/HMS Images/Getty Images; p. 48: © C Squared Studios/Getty Images RF; p. 51: © Izabela Habur/istockphoto RF; p. 54: © Fancy/Alamy RF; p. 55: © David M. Grossman/The Image Works; p. 59: © PhotoAlto RF.

Chapter 4 Opener: © Fancy Photography/Veer RF; p. 66: © CMCD/Getty Images RF; p. 69: © Sigrid Olsson/PhotoAlto/Corbis RF; p. 72: © WireImage/Getty Images; p. 75: © AP Photo/Shawn Baldwin; p. 79: © Medioimages/Photodisc/Getty Images RF.

Chapter 5 Opener: © Bob Daemmrich/The Image Works; p. 88: © Comstock/JupiterImages RF; p. 89: © Mike Kemp/Rubberball/Getty Images RF; p. 90: © Mark Newton/Taxi/GettyImages; p. 91: © Ingram Publishing RF; p. 93: © Tampa Bay Times/Octavio Jones/The Image Works; p. 95: © Westend61/Getty Images RF; p. 100: © Eric Audras/Getty Images RF; p. 101: © Andersen Ross/Getty Images RF; p. 105: © Onoky/Getty Images RF.

Chapter 6 Opener: © Ariel Skelley/Getty Images RF; p. 112: © The McGraw-Hill Companies, Inc./Ken Karp photographer; p. 115: © Floresco Productions/Corbis RF; p. 117: © Design Pics/Kristy-Anne Glubish RF; p. 121: © James Woodson/Getty Images RF; p. 125: © Corbis RF; p. 127: © Design Pics/Don Hammond RF; p. 133: © Peter Cade/Getty Images.

Chapter 7 Opener: © James Marshall/The Image Works; p. 140: © Photographer's Choice/Getty Images RF; p. 144: © Getty Images; p. 146: © Brand X Pictures/PunchStock RF; p. 152: © Francis Dean/Dean Pictures/The Image Works.

Chapter 8 Opener: © SuperStock RF; p. 158: © Science Photo Library/Getty Images RF; p. 159: © Rubberball/Getty Images RF; p. 161:

© Jeff Greenberg/Alamy; p. 162: © Hill Street Studios/Crystal Cartier/Getty Images RF; p. 163: © Juice Images/Getty Images RF; p. 166: © PictureNet/Corbis RF; p. 168: © ColorBlind Images/Blend Images LLC RF; p. 172: © Hybrid Images/Getty Images RF; p. 174 (top): © Brand X Pictures/PunchStock RF; p. 174 (middle): © Comstock/Jupiterimages RF; p. 174 (bottom): © Siede Preis/Getty Images RF; p. 175 (top): © Andersen Ross/Getty Images RF; p. 175 (bottom): © Photodisc/Punchstock RF; p. 176: © Thinkstock/Jupiterimages RF; p. 178: © Ariel Skelley/Getty Images RF.

Chapter 9 Opener: © ImagesBazaar/Getty Images; p. 186: © Ingram Publishing/SuperStock RF; p. 187: © Jonathan Kirn/Getty Images; p. 190: © Ariel Skelley/Blend Images/Corbis RF; p. 196: © John Birdsall/The Image Works; p. 198: © MBI/Alamy RF; p. 202: © DCA Productions/Taxi/Getty Images; p. 204: © Andersen Ross/Blend Images LLC RF; p. 207: © Olix Wirtinger/Corbis RF.

Chapter 10 Opener: © Hill Street Studios/Getty Images RF; p. 214: © Getty Images RF; p. 217: © Syracuse Newspapers/The Image Works; p. 228: © AP Photo/Seth Perlman.

Chapter 11 Opener: © PhotoAlto/Sigrid Olsson/Getty Images RF; p. 235: © Chris Hondros/Getty Images; p. 237: © Getty Images; p. 238: © David Grossman/Alamy; p. 246: © Image Source/Getty Images RF; p. 251: © Peter Hvizdak/

The Image Works; p. 253: © Getty Images; p. 257: © Comstock/PunchStock RF.

Chapter 12 Opener: © Roger Bradley/Alamy; p. 260: © Brand X Pictures/PunchStock RF; p. 261: © Ed Kashi/Corbis; p. 263: © Jeff Greenberg/The Image Works; p. 267: © Ingram Publishing RF; p. 284: © The Star-Ledger/Tim Farrell/The Image Works.

Chapter 13 Opener: © Monty Rakusen/Getty Images RF; p. 290: © Stockbyte/Punchstock RF; p. 291: © Getty Images; p. 296: © Marty Heitner/The Image Works ; p. 297: © photosindia/Getty Images RF; p. 300: © Fotosearch/Getty Images RF; p. 302 (top): © Raymond Patrick/Getty Images; p. 302 (bottom): © The Star-Ledger/Ed Murray/The Image Works; p. 304: © Jose Luis Pelaez Inc/Blend Images LLC RF; p. 305: © Helen King/Corbis.

Chapter 14 Opener: © Hill Street Studios/Blend Images/Corbis; p. 312: © Comstock/PunchStock RF; p. 314: © Jeff Greenberg/The Image Works; p. 318: © Michael Newman/Photo Edit; p. 320: © Noah Kalina.

Chapter 15 Opener: © Monika Graff/The Image Works; p. 330: © Ryan McVay/Getty Images RF; p. 334: Robert Voets/© CBS Courtesy Everett Collection; p. 340: © Image Source/Getty Images RF; p. 341: © David M. Grossman/The Image Works; p. 342: © Comstock Images/SuperStock RF; p. 345: © Laura Dwight/Photo Edit.

Index